TRAINERS

JUMPS STATISTICS 2012-2013

Edited by Mark Brown

Published in 2013 by Raceform Ltd
Compton, Newbury, Berkshire RG20 6NL

A catalogue record of this book is available from the British Library.

ISBN 978-1-908216-92-2

Printed and bound by CPI Group (UK) Ltd, Croydon, CR0 4YY

CONTENTS

WINNING BRITISH TRAINERS   5

LEADING TRAINERS BY MONTH   186

LEADING TRAINERS BY COURSE   198

LEADING PRIZEMONEY WINNERS   220

WINNING TRAINERS

Jumps statistics for the 2012-2013 season for winning British-based trainers. Trainers with less than ten winners are shown with abbreviated statistics.

Winning horses preceded by an asterisk joined the stable during the course of the season; an asterisk following the horse's name denotes a switch to another trainer during the season. Names may be abbreviated due to the pressure of space.

N W ALEXANDER

KINNESTON, PERTH & KINROSS

	No. of Hrs	Races Run	1st	2nd	3rd	Unpl	Per cent	£1 Level Stake
NH Flat	7	11	3	0	2	6	27.3	+10.00
Hurdles	30	118	13	13	10	82	11.0	-28.55
Chases	17	57	12	9	4	32	21.1	+22.95
Totals	41	186	28	22	16	120	15.1	+4.40
11-12	23	88	9	7	11	61	10.2	+6.75
10-11	17	56	4	3	7	42	7.1	-32.00

Chases	1-5	20.0	+12.00	Chases	9-43	20.9	+11.25
Sell/Claim	1-2	50.0	+3.00	Sell/Claim	0-0	0.0	0.00

RACE CLASS

	W-R	Per cent	£1 Level Stake
Class 1	0-1	0.0	-1.00
Class 2	0-3	0.0	-3.00
Class 3	3-31	9.7	+1.50
Class 4	12-84	14.3	-17.85
Class 5	10-53	18.9	+11.75
Class 6	3-14	21.4	+13.00

FIRST TIME OUT

	W-R	Per cent	£1 Level Stake
Bumpers	1-7	14.3	-3.00
Hurdles	3-22	13.6	+8.00
Chases	1-12	8.3	-5.50
Totals	5-41	12.2	-0.50

BY MONTH

NH Flat	W-R	Per cent	£1 Level Stake	Hurdles	W-R	Per cent	£1 Level Stake
May	0-1	0.0	-1.00	May	0-12	0.0	-12.00
June	0-0	0.0	0.00	June	1-2	50.0	+15.00
July	0-0	0.0	0.00	July	0-2	0.0	-2.00
August	0-0	0.0	0.00	August	0-2	0.0	-2.00
September	0-0	0.0	0.00	September	0-5	0.0	-5.00
October	0-0	0.0	0.00	October	1-14	7.1	-9.00
November	0-2	0.0	-2.00	November	4-15	26.7	+9.25
December	1-2	50.0	+2.00	December	1-11	9.1	-9.80
January	0-2	0.0	-2.00	January	1-12	8.3	-4.00
February	1-2	50.0	+4.00	February	2-11	18.2	-5.00
March	0-1	0.0	-1.00	March	2-12	16.7	+3.00
April	1-1	100.0	+10.00	April	1-20	5.0	-7.00

Chases	W-R	Per cent	£1 Level Stake	Totals	W-R	Per cent	£1 Level Stake
May	1-7	14.3	-0.50	May	1-20	5.0	-13.50
June	0-2	0.0	-2.00	June	1-4	25.0	+13.00
July	0-2	0.0	-2.00	July	0-4	0.0	-4.00
August	0-3	0.0	-3.00	August	0-5	0.0	-5.00
September	1-1	100.0	+10.00	September	1-6	16.7	+5.00
October	2-6	33.3	+2.00	October	3-20	15.0	-7.00
November	2-6	33.3	+1.20	November	6-23	26.1	+8.45
December	2-7	28.6	+7.50	December	4-20	20.0	-0.30
January	1-5	20.0	-1.25	January	2-19	10.5	-7.25
February	1-6	16.7	-0.50	February	4-19	21.1	-1.50
March	1-7	14.3	-0.50	March	3-20	15.0	+1.50
April	1-5	20.0	+12.00	April	3-26	11.5	+15.00

JOCKEYS

	W-R	Per cent	£1 Level Stake
Lucy Alexander	21-128	16.4	+16.70
Wilson Renwick	2-5	40.0	+5.00
Mr Kit Alexander	2-24	8.3	-2.00
Joe Colliver	1-1	100.0	+4.00
Brian Harding	1-3	33.3	-0.80
Peter Buchanan	1-13	7.7	-6.50

COURSE RECORD

	Total W-R	Non-Hndcps Hurdles	Chases	Hndcps Hurdles	Chases	NH Flat	Per cent	£1 Level Stake
Newcastle	5-23	2-9	0-0	2-9	1-4	0-1	21.7	-0.25
Hexham	4-16	1-5	2-4	0-6	1-1	0-0	25.0	+11.20
Musselbgh	4-20	1-3	0-0	1-10	2-5	0-2	20.0	+10.00
Ayr	4-24	0-1	0-1	2-10	1-5	1-5	16.7	+1.75
Kelso	4-32	1-10	0-5	1-10	2-7	0-0	12.5	-14.30
Perth	4-40	1-9	0-1	1-18	1-10	1-2	10.0	+12.00
Carlisle	3-16	0-4	0-1	0-3	2-7	1-1	18.8	-1.00

DISTANCE

Hurdles	W-R	Per cent	£1 Level Stake	Chases	W-R	Per cent	£1 Level Stake
2m-2m3f	2-45	4.4	-39.30	2m-2m3f	0-10	0.0	-10.00
2m4f-2m7f	9-49	18.4	+18.75	2m4f-2m7f	6-21	28.6	+12.75
3m+	2-24	8.3	-8.00	3m+	6-26	23.1	+20.20

WINNING HORSES

Horse	Races Run	1st	2nd	3rd	£
Isla Pearl Fisher	5	2	1	0	14296
*Makhzoon	10	2	0	1	7183
*Rossini's Dancer	9	1	2	1	5198
Tipsy Dara	8	3	0	0	11126
Little Glenshee	8	3	3	1	3899
Papamoa	8	2	2	1	6963
Bertie Milan	5	1	1	0	3769
Or De Grugy	5	2	2	0	5653
Daasij	5	2	0	0	5848
Buffalo Ballet	3	1	0	0	3249
*Standintheband	5	2	0	0	5003
Goldtrek	9	1	1	1	2599
Caught In The Act	3	1	0	0	2144
Frankie's Promise	4	2	0	1	3696
Northern Acres	6	2	1	0	3899
*Ocarina	2	1	0	1	1497
Total winning prize-money					**£86022**
Favourites	4-10		40.0%		-2.10

TYPE OF RACE

Non-Handicaps	W-R	Per cent	£1 Level Stake	Handicaps	W-R	Per cent	£1 Level Stake
Nov Hrdls	2-26	7.7	-23.30	Nov Hrdls	0-14	0.0	-14.00
Hrdls	3-17	17.6	+7.25	Hrdls	7-59	11.9	-1.50
Nov Chs	1-7	14.3	-4.80	Nov Chs	1-2	50.0	+4.50

WILLIAM AMOS

BROADHAUGH, SCOTTISH BORDERS

	No. of Hrs	Races Run	1st	2nd	3rd	Unpl	Per cent	£1 Level Stake
NH Flat	0	0	0	0	0	0	0.0	0.00
Hurdles	13	31	1	1	1	28	3.2	-24.50
Chases	10	30	2	3	3	22	6.7	-16.25
Totals	20	61	3	4	4	50	4.9	-40.75
11-12	27	85	5	11	9	60	5.9	-56.79
10-11	23	79	5	8	5	61	6.3	-51.13

JOCKEYS

	W-R	Per cent	£1 Level Stake
Henry Brooke	1-4	25.0	+6.00
Alexander Voy	1-10	10.0	-3.50
Brian Harding	1-30	3.3	-26.25

COURSE RECORD

	Total W-R	Non-Hndcps Hurdles	Chases	Hndcps Hurdles	Chases	NH Flat	Per cent	£1 Level Stake
Carlisle	2-11	0-3	0-0	0-0	2-8	0-0	18.2	+2.75
Hexham	1-8	1-2	0-0	0-3	0-3	0-0	12.5	-1.50

WINNING HORSES

Horse	Races Run	1st	2nd	3rd	£
Oil Burner	6	2	0	1	5588
Julia Too	4	1	0	0	3249
Total winning prize-money					£8837
Favourites	0-3		0.0%		-3.00

MICHAEL APPLEBY

DANETHORPE, NOTTS

	No. of Hrs	Races Run	1st	2nd	3rd	Unpl	Per cent	£1 Level Stake
NH Flat	5	10	1	0	0	9	10.0	+31.00
Hurdles	14	37	2	7	2	26	5.4	-21.75
Chases	1	1	0	0	0	1	0.0	-1.00
Totals	19	48	3	7	2	36	6.3	+8.25
11-12	18	55	7	1	5	42	12.7	+55.50
10-11	8	20	0	1	0	19	0.0	-20.00

JOCKEYS

	W-R	Per cent	£1 Level Stake
Ryan Mahon	3-36	8.3	+20.25

COURSE RECORD

	Total W-R	Non-Hndcps Hurdles	Chases	Hndcps Hurdles	Chases	NH Flat	Per cent	£1 Level Stake
Leicester	1-2	1-1	0-0	0-1	0-0	0-0	50.0	+0.25
Uttoxeter	1-2	0-1	0-0	0-0	0-0	1-1	50.0	+39.00
Stratford	1-5	1-3	0-0	0-1	0-1	0-0	20.0	+8.00

WINNING HORSES

Horse	Races Run	1st	2nd	3rd	£
*Reaction	3	2	0	0	4094
Squire Trelawney	4	1	0	0	1365
Total winning prize-money					£5459
Favourites	0-0		0.0%		0.00

DAVID ARBUTHNOT

BEARE GREEN, SURREY

	No. of Hrs	Races Run	1st	2nd	3rd	Unpl	Per cent	£1 Level Stake
NH Flat	3	6	0	0	0	6	0.0	-6.00
Hurdles	12	34	4	3	2	25	11.8	+2.50
Chases	6	24	2	4	5	13	8.3	-17.50
Totals	17	64	6	7	7	44	9.4	-21.00
11-12	15	51	6	6	7	32	11.8	-22.84
10-11	19	66	19	5	6	36	28.8	+38.45

JOCKEYS

	W-R	Per cent	£1 Level Stake
Daryl Jacob	3-14	21.4	+1.50
Tom Cannon	3-36	8.3	-8.50

COURSE RECORD

	Total W-R	Non-Hndcps Hurdles	Chases	Hndcps Hurdles	Chases	NH Flat	Per cent	£1 Level Stake
Cheltenham	1-2	0-0	0-0	1-2	0-0	0-0	50.0	+11.00
Huntingdon	1-3	0-0	0-0	1-1	0-2	0-0	33.3	+2.50
Lingfield	1-4	0-0	0-1	0-0	1-3	0-0	25.0	-0.50
Wincanton	1-4	0-0	0-1	0-1	1-2	0-0	25.0	-1.00
Plumpton	1-5	0-2	0-1	1-1	0-0	0-1	20.0	+2.00
Stratford	1-6	1-2	0-0	0-2	0-1	0-1	16.7	+5.00

WINNING HORSES

Horse	Races Run	1st	2nd	3rd	£
Shuil Royale	6	1	1	0	6389
Starluck	6	1	0	0	6256
Preuty Boy	7	1	1	1	3970
Rocky Elsom	7	2	0	0	6671
Urcalin	3	1	0	0	3249
Total winning prize-money					£26535
Favourites	1-5		20.0%		-2.00

PETER ATKINSON

YAFFORTH, N YORKS

	No. of Hrs	Races Run	1st	2nd	3rd	Unpl	Per cent	£1 Level Stake
NH Flat	1	1	0	0	0	1	0.0	-1.00
Hurdles	2	10	2	0	1	7	20.0	+8.50

Chases	0	0	0	0	0	0	0.0	0.00
Totals	**2**	**11**	**2**	**0**	**1**	**8**	**18.2**	**+7.50**
11-12	*3*	*10*	*1*	*1*	*0*	*8*	*10.0*	*+1.00*
10-11	*5*	*23*	*2*	*1*	*0*	*20*	*8.7*	*+27.00*

JOCKEYS

	W-R	Per cent	£1 Level Stake
Harry Challoner	1-2	50.0	+6.50
Henry Brooke	1-3	33.3	+7.00

COURSE RECORD

	Total W-R	Non-Hndcps Hurdles	Chases	Hndcps Hurdles	Chases	NH Flat	Per cent	£1 Level Stake
Sedgefield	2-4	0-0	0-0	2-4	0-0	0-0	50.0	+14.50

WINNING HORSES

Horse	Races Run	1st	2nd	3rd	£
Sparkling Hand	4	1	0	0	3119
Croco Bay	7	1	0	1	3119
Total winning prize-money					**£6238**
Favourites	0-0		0.0%		0.00

KIM BAILEY

ANDOVERSFORD, GLOUCS

	No. of Hrs	Races Run	1st	2nd	3rd	Unpl	Per cent	£1 Level Stake
NH Flat	14	25	7	2	4	12	28.0	+52.80
Hurdles	40	124	9	13	23	79	7.3	-84.25
Chases	27	92	11	17	10	54	12.0	-26.79
Totals	**68**	**241**	**27**	**32**	**37**	**145**	**11.2**	**-58.24**
11-12	*58*	*210*	*32*	*29*	*26*	*123*	*15.2*	*+18.38*
10-11	*52*	*196*	*36*	*16*	*29*	*115*	*18.4*	*+26.19*

BY MONTH

NH Flat	W-R	Per cent	£1 Level Stake	Hurdles	W-R	Per cent	£1 Level Stake
May	2-6	33.3	+4.30	May	1-17	5.9	-15.00
June	0-1	0.0	-1.00	June	1-6	16.7	-3.13
July	0-0	0.0	0.00	July	1-8	12.5	0.00
August	0-0	0.0	0.00	August	2-5	40.0	+3.00
September	0-0	0.0	0.00	September	0-2	0.0	-2.00
October	0-1	0.0	-1.00	October	1-21	4.8	-17.50
November	1-2	50.0	+8.00	November	1-18	5.6	-13.50
December	0-2	0.0	-2.00	December	1-11	9.1	-8.13
January	1-2	50.0	+3.00	January	0-6	0.0	-6.00
February	2-3	66.7	+40.00	February	0-5	0.0	-5.00
March	1-2	50.0	+7.50	March	1-11	9.1	-3.00
April	0-6	0.0	-6.00	April	0-14	0.0	-14.00

Chases	W-R	Per cent	£1 Level Stake	Totals	W-R	Per cent	£1 Level Stake
May	1-10	10.0	0.00	May	4-33	12.1	-10.70
June	0-7	0.0	-7.00	June	1-14	7.1	-11.13
July	0-4	0.0	-4.00	July	1-12	8.3	-4.00
August	0-2	0.0	-2.00	August	2-7	28.6	+1.00
September	0-2	0.0	-2.00	September	0-4	0.0	-4.00
October	2-10	20.0	-1.25	October	3-32	9.4	-19.75
November	5-13	38.5	+23.38	November	7-33	21.2	+17.88
December	1-13	7.7	-8.67	December	2-26	7.7	-18.80
January	0-4	0.0	-4.00	January	1-12	8.3	-7.00
February	1-6	16.7	-3.75	February	3-14	21.4	+31.25
March	0-14	0.0	-14.00	March	2-27	7.4	-9.50
April	1-7	14.3	-3.50	April	1-27	3.7	-23.50

DISTANCE

Hurdles	W-R	Per cent	£1 Level Stake	Chases	W-R	Per cent	£1 Level Stake
2m-2m3f	4-64	6.3	-46.63	2m-2m3f	2-14	14.3	-6.50
2m4f-2m7f	3-44	6.8	-28.00	2m4f-2m7f	1-37	2.7	-34.63
3m+	2-16	12.5	-9.63	3m+	8-41	19.5	+14.33

TYPE OF RACE

Non-Handicaps	W-R	Per cent	£1 Level Stake	Handicaps	W-R	Per cent	£1 Level Stake
Nov Hrdls	3-27	11.1	-17.75	Nov Hrdls	2-18	11.1	-11.50
Hrdls	2-27	7.4	-11.00	Hrdls	1-49	2.0	-44.50
Nov Chs	3-22	13.6	-9.92	Nov Chs	1-5	20.0	+4.00
Chases	1-5	20.0	-2.75	Chases	6-60	10.0	-18.13
Sell/Claim	1-3	33.3	+0.50	Sell/Claim	0-0	0.0	0.00

RACE CLASS / FIRST TIME OUT

Race Class	W-R	Per cent	£1 Level Stake	First Time Out	W-R	Per cent	£1 Level Stake
Class 1	2-18	11.1	-4.50	Bumpers	3-14	21.4	+2.80
Class 2	1-7	14.3	-4.75	Hurdles	3-32	9.4	-17.50
Class 3	2-33	6.1	-6.00	Chases	1-22	4.5	-18.25
Class 4	9-119	7.6	-76.17				
Class 5	8-48	16.7	+14.88	Totals	7-68	10.3	-32.95
Class 6	5-16	31.3	+18.30				

JOCKEYS

	W-R	Per cent	£1 Level Stake
Nick Scholfield	12-66	18.2	+13.58
Jason Maguire	5-68	7.4	-53.83
Ed Cookson	4-43	9.3	+15.50
Charles Greene	2-30	6.7	-23.50
Sam Thomas	1-1	100.0	+2.50
Mr M J McIntyre	1-2	50.0	+6.50
A P McCoy	1-4	25.0	+4.00
Timmy Murphy	1-10	10.0	-6.00

COURSE RECORD

	Total W-R	Non-Hndcps Hurdles	Chases	Hndcps Hurdles	Chases	NH Flat	Per cent	£1 Level Stake
Southwell	4-8	1-2	0-0	1-3	2-3	0-0	50.0	+13.50
Exeter	4-11	0-2	2-2	1-3	1-4	0-0	36.4	+1.00
Huntingdon	3-9	2-3	0-0	0-2	0-3	1-1	33.3	+11.50
Ascot	2-5	0-0	0-0	0-2	2-3	0-0	40.0	+21.00

	Total W-R	Non-Hndcps Hurdles	Chases	Hndcps Hurdles	Chases	NH Flat	Per cent	£1 Level Stake
Kempton	2-11	0-2	0-0	0-3	1-5	1-1	18.2	+28.00
Uttoxeter	2-33	1-14	0-2	0-8	0-6	1-3	6.1	-23.20
Folkestone	1-1	0-0	0-0	0-0	0-0	1-1	100.0	+9.00
Doncaster	1-3	1-2	0-0	0-1	0-0	0-0	33.3	-0.13
Fakenham	1-4	0-0	1-1	0-1	0-0	0-2	25.0	+0.33
Sandown	1-6	0-0	0-1	0-2	0-1	1-2	16.7	+3.50
Ffos Las	1-6	0-0	0-1	0-1	0-3	1-1	16.7	-1.00
Bangor	1-10	0-2	0-1	0-1	0-4	1-2	10.0	-1.50
Worcester	1-11	1-1	0-4	0-2	0-2	0-2	9.1	-8.13
Newbury	1-12	0-3	1-1	0-3	0-5	0-0	8.3	-8.00
Towcester	1-13	0-3	0-0	0-4	1-4	0-2	7.7	-10.63
Mrket Rsn	1-15	0-1	0-2	1-6	0-6	0-0	6.7	-10.50

WINNING HORSES

Horse	Races Run	1st	2nd	3rd	£
Molly's A Diva	4	3	0	0	17966
Harry Topper	4	3	0	0	30143
The Rainbow Hunter	7	2	0	1	12512
Lord Tomnoddy	5	1	1	2	6977
Savant Bleu	7	1	2	1	4094
Basoda	8	1	1	1	3899
Dance Tempo	4	2	1	1	5848
Sparville	5	1	1	1	3769
Midnight Oscar	3	1	0	1	3249
*Hefner	2	1	0	0	3119
South Stack	10	2	2	4	4549
Smokey George	5	1	0	0	2274
Lion On The Prowl	4	1	1	1	2144
Viking Ridge	4	1	0	1	2144
Set In Her Ways	1	1	0	0	2079
Such A Legend	2	1	0	0	1949
Mrs Peachey	6	1	1	1	1848
Bishophill Jack	6	1	0	0	1819
Supreme Present	4	1	0	1	1754
Agent Fedora	3	1	0	0	1437
Total winning prize-money					£113573
Favourites	7-28	25.0%			-7.70

MRS T L BAILEY

HUNGERFORD, BERKS

	No. of Hrs	Races Run	1st	2nd	3rd	Unpl	Per cent	£1 Level Stake
NH Flat	0	0	0	0	0	0	0.0	0.00
Hurdles	0	0	0	0	0	0	0.0	0.00
Chases	1	3	1	0	0	2	33.3	+8.00
Totals	1	3	1	0	0	2	33.3	+8.00
11-12	1	2	1	0	0	1	50.0	+7.00
10-11	1	3	0	0	3	0	0.0	-3.00

JOCKEYS

	W-R	Per cent	£1 Level Stake
Mr Dominic Sutton	1-1	100.0	+10.00

COURSE RECORD

	Total W-R	Non-Hndcps Hurdles	Chases	Hndcps Hurdles	Chases	NH Flat	Per cent	£1 Level Stake
Newbury	1-1	0-0	1-1	0-0	0-0	0-0	100.0	+10.00

WINNING HORSES

Horse	Races Run	1st	2nd	3rd	£
Offshore Account	3	1	0	0	988
Total winning prize-money					£988
Favourites	0-0	0.0%			0.00

CAROLINE BAILEY

BRIXWORTH, NORTHANTS

	No. of Hrs	Races Run	1st	2nd	3rd	Unpl	Per cent	£1 Level Stake
NH Flat	2	4	0	0	0	4	0.0	-4.00
Hurdles	10	29	3	3	4	19	10.3	+5.75
Chases	12	53	10	3	11	29	18.9	-9.75
Totals	22	86	13	6	15	52	15.1	-8.00
11-12	27	108	18	12	10	68	16.7	+3.95
10-11	29	121	6	16	22	77	5.0	-84.50

BY MONTH

NH Flat	W-R	Per cent	£1 Level Stake	Hurdles	W-R	Per cent	£1 Level Stake
May	0-1	0.0	-1.00	May	0-2	0.0	-2.00
June	0-1	0.0	-1.00	June	0-0	0.0	0.00
July	0-0	0.0	0.00	July	0-4	0.0	-4.00
August	0-0	0.0	0.00	August	1-1	100.0	+4.00
September	0-0	0.0	0.00	September	1-1	100.0	+2.75
October	0-0	0.0	0.00	October	0-0	0.0	-5.00
November	0-0	0.0	0.00	November	0-1	0.0	-1.00
December	0-2	0.0	-2.00	December	1-4	25.0	+22.00
January	0-0	0.0	0.00	January	0-1	0.0	-1.00
February	0-0	0.0	0.00	February	0-4	0.0	-4.00
March	0-0	0.0	0.00	March	0-3	0.0	-3.00
April	0-0	0.0	0.00	April	0-3	0.0	-3.00

Chases	W-R	Per cent	£1 Level Stake	Totals	W-R	Per cent	£1 Level Stake
May	0-5	0.0	-5.00	May	0-8	0.0	-8.00
June	0-1	0.0	-1.00	June	0-2	0.0	-2.00
July	0-1	0.0	-1.00	July	0-5	0.0	-5.00
August	0-2	0.0	-2.00	August	1-3	33.3	+2.00
September	0-0	0.0	0.00	September	1-1	100.0	+2.75
October	1-4	25.0	-0.25	October	1-9	11.1	-5.25
November	1-5	20.0	-2.00	November	1-6	16.7	-3.00
December	1-7	14.3	-2.50	December	2-13	15.4	+17.50
January	0-5	0.0	-5.00	January	0-6	0.0	-6.00
February	1-9	11.1	-2.00	February	1-13	7.7	-6.00
March	5-9	55.6	+12.88	March	5-12	41.7	+9.88
April	1-5	20.0	-1.88	April	1-8	12.5	-4.88

| Total winning prize-money | | | £79795 |
| Favourites | 5-14 | 35.7% | 0.00 |

DISTANCE

Hurdles	W-R	Per cent	£1 Level Stake	Chases	W-R	Per cent	£1 Level Stake
2m-2m3f	0-14	0.0	-14.00	2m-2m3f	1-11	9.1	-6.50
2m4f-2m7f	3-15	20.0	+19.75	2m4f-2m7f	8-29	27.6	+2.75
3m+	0-0	0.0	0.00	3m+	1-13	7.7	-6.00

TYPE OF RACE

Non-Handicaps	W-R	Per cent	£1 Level Stake	Handicaps	W-R	Per cent	£1 Level Stake
Nov Hrdls	2-19	10.5	+10.75	Nov Hrdls	0-0	0.0	0.00
Hrdls	1-5	20.0	0.00	Hrdls	0-5	0.0	-5.00
Nov Chs	0-3	0.0	-3.00	Nov Chs	1-3	33.3	+1.50
Chases	0-0	0.0	0.00	Chases	9-47	19.1	-8.25
Sell/Claim	0-0	0.0	0.00	Sell/Claim	0-0	0.0	0.00

RACE CLASS

	W-R	Per cent	£1 Level Stake	FIRST TIME OUT	W-R	Per cent	£1 Level Stake
Class 1	0-0	0.0	0.00	Bumpers	0-2	0.0	-2.00
Class 2	1-1	100.0	+6.00	Hurdles	1-9	11.1	+17.00
Class 3	2-21	9.5	-16.00	Chases	1-11	9.1	-7.25
Class 4	9-53	17.0	+8.00				
Class 5	1-7	14.3	-2.00	Totals	2-22	9.1	+7.75
Class 6	0-4	0.0	-4.00				

JOCKEYS

	W-R	Per cent	£1 Level Stake
Andrew Thornton	10-60	16.7	-16.75
Robert Thornton	2-6	33.3	+2.75
Adam Pogson	1-5	20.0	+21.00

COURSE RECORD

	Total W-R	Non-Hndcps Hurdles	Chases	Hndcps Hurdles	Chases	NH Flat	Per cent	£1 Level Stake
Wetherby	3-10	1-1	0-0	0-2	2-6	0-1	30.0	+26.13
Haydock	2-2	0-0	0-0	0-0	2-2	0-0	100.0	+8.75
Uttoxeter	2-8	0-3	0-0	0-0	2-4	0-1	25.0	-2.13
Sedgefield	1-3	1-2	0-0	0-0	0-1	0-0	33.3	+0.75
Warwick	1-3	0-1	0-1	0-0	1-1	0-0	33.3	-0.63
Bangor	1-7	1-4	0-0	0-0	0-3	0-0	14.3	-2.00
Huntingdon	1-7	0-2	0-1	0-1	1-3	0-0	14.3	0.00
Southwell	1-9	0-4	0-0	0-0	1-5	0-0	11.1	-6.38
Leicester	1-10	0-2	0-1	0-0	1-7	0-0	10.0	-5.50

WINNING HORSES

Horse	Races Run	1st	2nd	3rd	£
Noble Legend	7	4	1	1	46070
Denali Highway	4	3	0	0	13451
Galway Jack	6	2	1	1	8309
Dermatologiste	3	1	0	0	3769
Malapie	2	1	0	0	2924
Quinsman	8	2	2	1	5272

| Total winning prize-money | | | £79795 |
| Favourites | 5-14 | 35.7% | 0.00 |

EMMA BAKER

NAUNTON, GLOUCS

	No. of Hrs	Races Run	1st	2nd	3rd	Unpl	Per cent	£1 Level Stake
NH Flat	2	7	0	0	1	6	0.0	-7.00
Hurdles	6	22	1	2	2	17	4.5	+4.00
Chases	2	11	1	1	2	7	9.1	-6.00
Totals	8	40	2	3	5	30	5.0	-9.00
11-12	6	24	1	1	2	20	4.2	-11.00
10-11	7	19	1	2	2	14	5.3	-8.00

JOCKEYS

	W-R	Per cent	£1 Level Stake
James Banks	2-24	8.3	+7.00

COURSE RECORD

	Total W-R	Non-Hndcps Hurdles	Chases	Hndcps Hurdles	Chases	NH Flat	Per cent	£1 Level Stake
Bangor	1-1	0-0	0-0	1-1	0-0	0-0	100.0	+25.00
Taunton	1-4	0-0	0-0	0-2	1-1	0-1	25.0	+1.00

WINNING HORSES

Horse	Races Run	1st	2nd	3rd	£
Midnight Charmer	9	1	1	2	3422
Petrarchick	6	1	0	0	1689
Total winning prize-money				£5111
Favourites	0-0	0.0%		0.00

GEORGE BAKER

MANTON, WILTS

	No. of Hrs	Races Run	1st	2nd	3rd	Unpl	Per cent	£1 Level Stake
NH Flat	4	6	1	1	0	4	16.7	-1.50
Hurdles	6	10	1	0	1	8	10.0	+1.00
Chases	3	9	1	4	0	4	11.1	-6.50
Totals	11	25	3	5	1	16	12.0	-7.00
11-12	18	53	4	8	7	34	7.5	-29.10
10-11	28	86	7	12	15	52	8.1	-20.88

JOCKEYS

	W-R	Per cent	£1 Level Stake
Trevor Whelan	2-13	15.4	+0.50
Conor O'Farrell	1-1	100.0	+3.50

COURSE RECORD

	Total W-R	Non-Hndcps Hurdles	Chases	Hndcps Hurdles	Chases	NH Flat	Per cent	£1 Level Stake
Lingfield	1-1	0-0	0-0	0-0	1-1	0-0	100.0	+1.50
Huntingdon	1-2	0-0	0-0	1-2	0-0	0-0	50.0	+9.00
Worcester	1-3	0-0	0-0	0-1	0-1	1-1	33.3	+1.50

WINNING HORSES

Horse	Races Run	1st	2nd	3rd	£
Double Dash	6	1	4	0	3970
Belle De Fontenay	4	1	0	1	2534
I'm Fraam Govan	2	1	0	0	1437
Total winning prize-money					**£7941**
Favourites	1-4		25.0%		-1.50

ANDREW BALDING

KINGSCLERE, HANTS

	No. of Hrs	Races Run	1st	2nd	3rd	Unpl	Per cent	£1 Level Stake
NH Flat	0	0	0	0	0	0	0.0	0.00
Hurdles	1	4	1	0	0	3	25.0	+5.00
Chases	0	0	0	0	0	0	0.0	0.00
Totals	1	4	1	0	0	3	25.0	+5.00
11-12	2	2	1	0	0	1	50.0	+1.00
10-11	3	6	0	0	0	6	0.0	-6.00

JOCKEYS

	W-R	Per cent	£1 Level Stake
Paddy Brennan	1-2	50.0	+7.00

COURSE RECORD

	Total W-R	Non-Hndcps Hurdles	Chases	Hndcps Hurdles	Chases	NH Flat	Per cent	£1 Level Stake
Newbury	1-1	1-1	0-0	0-0	0-0	0-0	100.0	+8.00

WINNING HORSES

Horse	Races Run	1st	2nd	3rd	£
Chiberta King	4	1	0	0	3899
Total winning prize-money					**£3899**
Favourites	0-744		0.0%		-744.00

R BARBER

BEAMINSTER, DORSET

	No. of Hrs	Races Run	1st	2nd	3rd	Unpl	Per cent	£1 Level Stake
NH Flat	0	0	0	0	0	0	0.0	0.00
Hurdles	0	0	0	0	0	0	0.0	0.00
Chases	3	4	1	0	0	3	25.0	-2.43
Totals	3	4	1	0	0	3	25.0	-2.43
11-12	3	5	2	2	0	1	40.0	+1.25
10-11	3	7	1	2	2	2	14.3	-5.09

JOCKEYS

	W-R	Per cent	£1 Level Stake
Mr J Barber	1-2	50.0	-0.43

COURSE RECORD

	Total W-R	Non-Hndcps Hurdles	Chases	Hndcps Hurdles	Chases	NH Flat	Per cent	£1 Level Stake
Newbury	1-1	0-0	1-1	0-0	0-0	0-0	100.0	+0.57

WINNING HORSES

Horse	Races Run	1st	2nd	3rd	£
Chapoturgeon	2	1	0	0	988
Total winning prize-money					**£988**
Favourites	1-2		50.0%		-0.43

M BARBER

NARBERTH, PEMBROKESHIRE

	No. of Hrs	Races Run	1st	2nd	3rd	Unpl	Per cent	£1 Level Stake
NH Flat	0	0	0	0	0	0	0.0	0.00
Hurdles	0	0	0	0	0	0	0.0	0.00
Chases	1	1	1	0	0	0	100.0	+25.00
Totals	1	1	1	0	0	0	100.0	+25.00

JOCKEYS

	W-R	Per cent	£1 Level Stake
Mr Matthew Barber	1-1	100.0	+25.00

COURSE RECORD

	Total W-R	Non-Hndcps Hurdles	Chases	Hndcps Hurdles	Chases	NH Flat	Per cent	£1 Level Stake
Chepstow	1-1	0-0	1-1	0-0	0-0	0-0	100.0	+25.00

WINNING HORSES

Horse	Races Run	1st	2nd	3rd	£
*Hawkeye Native	1	1	0	0	2184
Total winning prize-money					**£2184**
Favourites	0-0		0.0%		0.00

MAURICE BARNES

FARLAM, CUMBRIA

	No. of Hrs	Races Run	1st	2nd	3rd	Unpl	Per cent	£1 Level Stake
NH Flat	6	9	0	1	1	7	0.0	-9.00
Hurdles	17	92	8	9	15	60	8.7	+41.75

Chases	7	17	2	1	2	12	11.8	+22.00
Totals	**24**	**118**	**10**	**11**	**18**	**79**	**8.5**	**+54.75**
11-12	*35*	*155*	*11*	*11*	*14*	*119*	*7.1*	*-45.26*
10-11	*35*	*155*	*15*	*7*	*20*	*113*	*9.7*	*-15.58*

BY MONTH

NH Flat	W-R	Per cent	£1 Level Stake		Hurdles	W-R	Per cent	£1 Level Stake
May	0-1	0.0	-1.00		May	1-19	5.3	-8.00
June	0-0	0.0	0.00		June	0-5	0.0	-5.00
July	0-0	0.0	0.00		July	0-1	0.0	-1.00
August	0-0	0.0	0.00		August	0-6	0.0	-6.00
September	0-0	0.0	0.00		September	1-5	20.0	+21.00
October	0-1	0.0	-1.00		October	2-19	10.5	+51.00
November	0-0	0.0	0.00		November	2-5	40.0	+5.00
December	0-1	0.0	-1.00		December	0-2	0.0	-2.00
January	0-1	0.0	-1.00		January	1-4	25.0	-0.25
February	0-0	0.0	0.00		February	1-8	12.5	+5.00
March	0-2	0.0	-2.00		March	0-8	0.0	-8.00
April	0-3	0.0	-3.00		April	0-10	0.0	-10.00

Chases	W-R	Per cent	£1 Level Stake		Totals	W-R	Per cent	£1 Level Stake
May	1-1	100.0	+12.00		May	2-21	9.5	+3.00
June	0-1	0.0	-1.00		June	0-6	0.0	-6.00
July	0-0	0.0	0.00		July	0-1	0.0	-1.00
August	0-1	0.0	-1.00		August	0-7	0.0	-7.00
September	0-0	0.0	0.00		September	1-5	20.0	+21.00
October	0-1	0.0	-1.00		October	2-21	9.5	+49.00
November	0-2	0.0	-2.00		November	2-7	28.6	+3.00
December	0-0	0.0	0.00		December	0-3	0.0	-3.00
January	0-2	0.0	-2.00		January	1-7	14.3	-3.25
February	0-1	0.0	-1.00		February	1-9	11.1	+4.00
March	1-2	50.0	+24.00		March	1-12	8.3	+14.00
April	0-6	0.0	-6.00		April	0-19	0.0	-19.00

DISTANCE

Hurdles	W-R	Per cent	£1 Level Stake		Chases	W-R	Per cent	£1 Level Stake
2m-2m3f	6-40	15.0	+23.00		2m-2m3f	1-2	50.0	+24.00
2m4f-2m7f	1-33	3.0	-29.25		2m4f-2m7f	0-6	0.0	-6.00
3m+	1-19	5.3	+48.00		3m+	1-9	11.1	+4.00

TYPE OF RACE

Non-Handicaps	W-R	Per cent	£1 Level Stake		Handicaps	W-R	Per cent	£1 Level Stake
Nov Hrdls	4-26	15.4	+75.00		Nov Hrdls	0-5	0.0	-5.00
Hrdls	1-12	8.3	-1.00		Hrdls	3-48	6.3	-26.25
Nov Chs	1-6	16.7	+20.00		Nov Chs	0-2	0.0	-2.00
Chases	0-2	0.0	-2.00		Chases	1-7	14.3	+6.00
Sell/Claim	0-1	0.0	-1.00		Sell/Claim	0-0	0.0	0.00

RACE CLASS / FIRST TIME OUT

	W-R	Per cent	£1 Level Stake			W-R	Per cent	£1 Level Stake
Class 1	0-2	0.0	-2.00		Bumpers	0-6	0.0	-6.00
Class 2	1-7	14.3	+6.00		Hurdles	2-16	12.5	+62.00
Class 3	2-19	10.5	-10.25		Chases	1-2	50.0	+11.00
Class 4	6-66	9.1	+74.00					
Class 5	1-16	6.3	-5.00		Totals	3-24	12.5	+67.00
Class 6	0-8	0.0	-8.00					

JOCKEYS

	W-R	Per cent	£1 Level Stake
Michael McAlister	7-83	8.4	+60.75
Stephen Mulqueen	2-28	7.1	-12.00
Alexander Voy	1-4	25.0	+9.00

COURSE RECORD

	Total W-R	Non-Hndcps Hurdles	Chases	Hndcps Hurdles	Chases	NH Flat	Per cent	£1 Level Stake
Wetherby	4-13	2-5	0-0	1-6	1-1	0-1	30.8	+21.00
Ayr	2-11	0-0	1-1	1-7	0-1	0-2	18.2	+18.75
Carlisle	2-13	1-2	0-2	1-7	0-1	0-1	15.4	+3.00
Perth	1-10	1-4	0-0	0-4	0-1	0-1	10.0	+16.00
Hexham	1-11	1-7	0-0	0-2	0-1	0-1	9.1	+56.00

WINNING HORSES

Horse	Races Run	1st	2nd	3rd	£
Garleton	5	1	1	0	12512
Pas Trop Tard	13	4	1	1	12996
About Thyne	4	1	0	0	4106
Carrigdhoun	4	1	0	1	3899
Overpriced	9	2	2	0	3899
My Idea	11	1	1	4	3119
Total winning prize-money					**£40531**
Favourites	1-2		50.0%		1.00

BRIAN BARR

LONGBURTON, DORSET

	No. of Hrs	Races Run	1st	2nd	3rd	Unpl	Per cent	£1 Level Stake
NH Flat	2	2	0	0	1	1	0.0	-2.00
Hurdles	9	18	1	2	1	14	5.6	-13.50
Chases	1	2	0	0	1	1	0.0	-2.00
Totals	**11**	**22**	**1**	**2**	**3**	**16**	**4.5**	**-17.50**
11-12	*7*	*37*	*1*	*5*	*6*	*25*	*2.7*	*-32.50*

JOCKEYS

	W-R	Per cent	£1 Level Stake
Gavin Sheehan	1-12	8.3	-7.50

COURSE RECORD

	Total W-R	Non-Hndcps Hurdles	Chases	Hndcps Hurdles	Chases	NH Flat	Per cent	£1 Level Stake
Taunton	1-1	0-0	0-0	1-1	0-0	0-0	100.0	+3.50

WINNING HORSES

Horse	Races Run	1st	2nd	3rd	£
*Castlemorris King	5	1	1	0	3080
Total winning prize-money					£3080
Favourites	2-2		100.0%		7.00

CHRIS BEALBY

BARROWBY, LINCS

	No. of Hrs	Races Run	1st	2nd	3rd	Unpl	Per cent	£1 Level Stake
NH Flat	6	7	0	0	0	7	0.0	-7.00
Hurdles	15	32	0	1	4	27	0.0	-32.00
Chases	13	45	5	8	7	25	11.1	-21.88
Totals	29	84	5	9	11	59	6.0	-60.88
11-12	30	105	14	12	15	64	13.3	-16.50
10-11	28	87	6	4	9	68	6.9	-42.75

JOCKEYS

	W-R	Per cent	£1 Level Stake
Tom Messenger	4-70	5.7	-49.75
Mr Matthew Stanley	1-5	20.0	-2.13

COURSE RECORD

	Total W-R	Non-Hndcps Hurdles	Chases	Hndcps Hurdles	Chases	NH Flat	Per cent	£1 Level Stake
Catterick	1-4	0-2	0-0	0-1	1-1	0-0	25.0	+2.50
Southwell	1-11	0-3	0-0	0-2	1-5	0-1	9.1	-7.25
Towcester	1-12	0-3	0-0	0-1	1-6	0-2	8.3	-7.50
Wetherby	1-13	0-3	0-2	0-2	1-6	0-0	7.7	-7.50
Mrket Rsn	1-19	0-2	0-2	0-1	1-13	0-1	5.3	-16.13

WINNING HORSES

Horse	Races Run	1st	2nd	3rd	£
Chac Du Cadran	6	1	2	1	12512
Roi De Garde	9	2	1	2	5068
L'Eldorado	6	1	0	1	3054
Ifonlyalfie	7	1	4	1	3054
Total winning prize-money					£23688
Favourites	2-10		20.0%		-3.38

ALASTAIR BELL

HAWICK, BORDERS

	No. of Hrs	Races Run	1st	2nd	3rd	Unpl	Per cent	£1 Level Stake
NH Flat	0	0	0	0	0	0	0.0	0.00
Hurdles	0	0	0	0	0	0	0.0	0.00
Chases	1	1	1	0	0	0	100.0	+1.38
Totals	1	1	1	0	0	0	100.0	+1.38
10-11	1	1	0	0	0	1	0.0	-1.00

JOCKEYS

	W-R	Per cent	£1 Level Stake
Mr J Hamilton	1-1	100.0	+1.38

COURSE RECORD

	Total W-R	Non-Hndcps Hurdles	Chases	Hndcps Hurdles	Chases	NH Flat	Per cent	£1 Level Stake
Musselbgh	1-1	0-0	1-1	0-0	0-0	0-0	100.0	+1.38

WINNING HORSES

Horse	Races Run	1st	2nd	3rd	£
*Buckstruther	1	1	0	0	1872
Total winning prize-money					£1872
Favourites	1-1		100.0%		1.38

JIM BEST

LEWES, E SUSSEX

	No. of Hrs	Races Run	1st	2nd	3rd	Unpl	Per cent	£1 Level Stake
NH Flat	4	10	0	0	2	8	0.0	-10.00
Hurdles	26	88	7	10	7	64	8.0	-52.63
Chases	3	6	0	1	0	5	0.0	-6.00
Totals	30	104	7	11	9	77	6.7	-68.63
11-12	30	100	15	9	14	62	15.0	-33.05
10-11	38	109	19	8	11	71	17.4	-40.96

JOCKEYS

	W-R	Per cent	£1 Level Stake
Jamie Moore	6-54	11.1	-22.63
A P McCoy	1-8	12.5	-4.00

COURSE RECORD

	Total W-R	Non-Hndcps Hurdles	Chases	Hndcps Hurdles	Chases	NH Flat	Per cent	£1 Level Stake
Hereford	2-5	1-1	0-0	1-4	0-0	0-0	40.0	+3.50
Plumpton	2-13	1-7	0-0	1-5	0-0	0-1	15.4	+0.38
Southwell	1-5	1-2	0-0	0-2	0-1	0-0	20.0	-1.00
Uttoxeter	1-10	1-5	0-0	0-5	0-0	0-0	10.0	-5.00
Worcester	1-12	1-8	0-0	0-3	0-1	0-0	8.3	-7.50

WINNING HORSES

Horse	Races Run	1st	2nd	3rd	£
Ace Fighter Pilot	3	2	0	1	5337
Weybridge Light	5	1	1	1	2144
Wayward Glance	7	2	4	0	3743
Goodwood Starlight	4	1	1	0	2053
*On The Feather	10	1	1	2	2053
Total winning prize-money					£15330
Favourites	2-5		40.0%		1.38

S L BEVAN

BRIDGEND, BRIDGEND

	No. of Hrs	Races Run	1st	2nd	3rd	Unpl	Per cent	£1 Level Stake
NH Flat	0	0	0	0	0	0	0.0	0.00
Hurdles	0	0	0	0	0	0	0.0	0.00
Chases	4	5	1	1	0	3	20.0	+1.00
Totals	4	5	1	1	0	3	20.0	+1.00
11-12	1	1	0	0	1	0	0.0	-1.00

JOCKEYS

	W-R	Per cent	£1 Level Stake
Mr Nick Williams	1-3	33.3	+3.00

COURSE RECORD

	Total W-R	Non-Hndcps Hurdles	Chases	Hndcps Hurdles	Chases	NH Flat	Per cent	£1 Level Stake
Ffos Las	1-2	0-0	1-2	0-0	0-0	0-0	50.0	+4.00

WINNING HORSES

Horse	Races Run	1st	2nd	3rd	£
Bobs Law	2	1	0	0	3743
Total winning prize-money					£3743
Favourites	0-0		0.0%		0.00

GEORGE BEWLEY

BONCHESTER BRIDGE, BORDERS

	No. of Hrs	Races Run	1st	2nd	3rd	Unpl	Per cent	£1 Level Stake
NH Flat	6	11	2	0	3	6	18.2	+1.50
Hurdles	11	37	6	4	5	22	16.2	-0.25
Chases	2	7	0	0	1	6	0.0	-7.00
Totals	14	55	8	4	9	34	14.5	-5.75
11-12	8	36	3	6	8	19	8.3	-30.26
10-11	6	21	2	3	3	13	9.5	+16.25

JOCKEYS

	W-R	Per cent	£1 Level Stake
Jonathon Bewley	8-47	17.0	+2.25

COURSE RECORD

	Total W-R	Non-Hndcps Hurdles	Chases	Hndcps Hurdles	Chases	NH Flat	Per cent	£1 Level Stake
Perth	4-12	0-0	0-1	2-7	0-0	2-4	33.3	+8.75
Kelso	3-15	1-6	0-0	2-6	0-2	0-1	20.0	+4.50
Hexham	1-1	1-1	0-0	0-0	0-0	0-0	100.0	+8.00

WINNING HORSES

Horse	Races Run	1st	2nd	3rd	£
South Leinster	4	1	1	0	4549
*Hunters Belt	7	2	0	2	7148
Teerie Express	4	1	0	0	3422
Inoogoo	9	1	2	1	3249
Our Joey	8	3	0	2	7355
Total winning prize-money					£25723
Favourites	2-7		28.6%		1.25

ROBERT BEWLEY

JEDBURGH, BORDERS

	No. of Hrs	Races Run	1st	2nd	3rd	Unpl	Per cent	£1 Level Stake
NH Flat	1	1	0	0	0	1	0.0	-1.00
Hurdles	2	4	0	1	0	3	0.0	-4.00
Chases	2	4	1	0	1	2	25.0	+2.00
Totals	3	9	1	1	1	6	11.1	-3.00
11-12	3	8	3	1	1	3	37.5	+5.06
10-11	2	2	0	0	0	2	0.0	-2.00

JOCKEYS

	W-R	Per cent	£1 Level Stake
Henry Brooke	1-1	100.0	+5.00

COURSE RECORD

	Total W-R	Non-Hndcps Hurdles	Chases	Hndcps Hurdles	Chases	NH Flat	Per cent	£1 Level Stake
Carlisle	1-2	0-0	1-1	0-1	0-0	0-0	50.0	+4.00

WINNING HORSES

Horse	Races Run	1st	2nd	3rd	£
Bury Parade	2	1	0	0	3054
Total winning prize-money					£3054
Favourites	0-0		0.0%		0.00

KEVIN BISHOP

SPAXTON, SOMERSET

	No. of Hrs	Races Run	1st	2nd	3rd	Unpl	Per cent	£1 Level Stake
NH Flat	1	1	0	0	0	1	0.0	-1.00
Hurdles	23	70	11	8	7	44	15.7	+46.92
Chases	8	16	4	0	1	11	25.0	+20.50
Totals	24	87	15	8	8	56	17.2	+66.42
11-12	17	67	2	2	7	56	3.0	-52.00
10-11	21	67	2	2	3	60	3.0	-40.00

	W-R	Per cent	+£			
Class 5	4-29	13.8	+8.00	Totals	2-24	8.3	-8.00
Class 6	0-1	0.0	-1.00			

BY MONTH

NH Flat	W-R	Per cent	£1 Level Stake	Hurdles	W-R	Per cent	£1 Level Stake
May	0-1	0.0	-1.00	May	0-8	0.0	-8.00
June	0-0	0.0	0.00	June	0-1	0.0	-1.00
July	0-0	0.0	0.00	July	0-0	0.0	0.00
August	0-0	0.0	0.00	August	0-2	0.0	-2.00
September	0-0	0.0	0.00	September	0-2	0.0	-2.00
October	0-0	0.0	0.00	October	1-3	33.3	+23.00
November	0-0	0.0	0.00	November	3-7	42.9	+8.25
December	0-0	0.0	0.00	December	3-15	20.0	+9.17
January	0-0	0.0	0.00	January	0-4	0.0	-4.00
February	0-0	0.0	0.00	February	2-12	16.7	+1.50
March	0-0	0.0	0.00	March	0-6	0.0	-6.00
April	0-0	0.0	0.00	April	2-10	20.0	+28.00

Chases	W-R	Per cent	£1 Level Stake	Totals	W-R	Per cent	£1 Level Stake
May	0-0	0.0	0.00	May	0-9	0.0	-9.00
June	0-1	0.0	-1.00	June	0-2	0.0	-2.00
July	0-0	0.0	0.00	July	0-0	0.0	0.00
August	0-0	0.0	0.00	August	0-2	0.0	-2.00
September	0-0	0.0	0.00	September	0-2	0.0	-2.00
October	0-0	0.0	0.00	October	1-3	33.3	+23.00
November	0-1	0.0	-1.00	November	3-8	37.5	+7.25
December	2-2	100.0	+21.50	December	5-17	29.4	+30.67
January	0-2	0.0	-2.00	January	0-6	0.0	-6.00
February	0-0	0.0	0.00	February	2-12	16.7	+1.50
March	1-6	16.7	+2.50	March	1-12	8.3	-3.50
April	1-4	25.0	+0.50	April	3-14	21.4	+28.50

DISTANCE

Hurdles	W-R	Per cent	£1 Level Stake	Chases	W-R	Per cent	£1 Level Stake
2m-2m3f	3-38	7.9	-2.25	2m-2m3f	0-2	0.0	-2.00
2m4f-2m7f	4-16	25.0	+27.67	2m4f-2m7f	0-6	0.0	-6.00
3m+	4-16	25.0	+21.50	3m+	4-8	50.0	+28.50

TYPE OF RACE

Non-Handicaps	W-R	Per cent	£1 Level Stake	Handicaps	W-R	Per cent	£1 Level Stake
Nov Hrdls	0-10	0.0	-10.00	Nov Hrdls	0-8	0.0	-8.00
Hrdls	0-7	0.0	-7.00	Hrdls	11-45	24.4	+71.92
Nov Chs	0-3	0.0	-3.00	Nov Chs	0-0	0.0	0.00
Chases	0-0	0.0	0.00	Chases	4-13	30.8	+23.50
Sell/Claim	0-0	0.0	0.00	Sell/Claim	0-0	0.0	0.00

RACE CLASS / FIRST TIME OUT

RACE CLASS	W-R	Per cent	£1 Level Stake	FIRST TIME OUT	W-R	Per cent	£1 Level Stake
Class 1	2-3	66.7	+10.50	Bumpers	0-1	0.0	-1.00
Class 2	0-4	0.0	-4.00	Hurdles	2-21	9.5	-5.00
Class 3	1-8	12.5	+7.00	Chases	0-2	0.0	-2.00
Class 4	8-42	19.0	+45.92				

JOCKEYS

	W-R	Per cent	£1 Level Stake
James Best	6-25	24.0	+17.42
Brendan Powell	4-7	57.1	+42.00
Hadden Frost	2-12	16.7	+1.50
Mr J Park	2-24	8.3	+20.00
Daryl Jacob	1-1	100.0	+3.50

COURSE RECORD

	Total W-R	Non-Hndcps Hurdles	Non-Hndcps Chases	Hndcps Hurdles	Hndcps Chases	NH Flat	Per cent	£1 Level Stake
Fontwell	4-9	0-1	0-0	1-1	3-7	0-0	44.4	+24.67
Taunton	3-16	0-1	0-0	3-14	0-1	0-0	18.8	+0.75
Aintree	2-3	0-0	0-0	1-2	1-1	0-0	66.7	+10.50
Towcester	1-3	0-0	0-0	1-3	0-0	0-0	33.3	+3.50
Uttoxeter	1-3	0-1	0-0	1-2	0-0	0-0	33.3	+2.50
Hereford	1-6	0-0	0-0	1-6	0-0	0-0	16.7	+1.50
Chepstow	1-7	0-2	0-0	1-4	0-1	0-0	14.3	+8.00
Exeter	1-8	0-5	0-1	1-2	0-0	0-0	12.5	+21.00
Wincanton	1-10	0-3	0-0	1-7	0-0	0-0	10.0	+16.00

WINNING HORSES

Horse	Races Run	1st	2nd	3rd	£
*Battle Group	2	2	0	0	62645
Fred The Shred	6	1	1	0	5848
Wild Ground	7	3	0	0	7497
Queens Grove	7	4	0	0	12384
Bathwick Brave	8	1	2	1	3249
Tara Tavey	5	1	0	0	3249
Tarabela	2	2	0	0	4687
Cruise In Style	6	1	1	0	2599
Total winning prize-money					**£102158**
Favourites	4-7		57.1%		5.42

ALAN BLACKMORE

LITTLE BERKHAMSTED, HERTS

	No. of Hrs	Races Run	1st	2nd	3rd	Unpl	Per cent	£1 Level Stake
NH Flat	1	1	0	0	0	1	0.0	-1.00
Hurdles	2	15	1	2	1	11	6.7	-2.00
Chases	1	3	0	0	0	3	0.0	-3.00
Totals	3	19	1	2	1	15	5.3	-6.00
11-12	3	18	1	0	1	16	5.6	-9.00
10-11	3	11	1	1	4	5	9.1	-1.00

JOCKEYS

	W-R	Per cent	£1 Level Stake
Marc Goldstein	1-4	25.0	+9.00

COURSE RECORD

	Total W-R	Non-Hndcps Hurdles	Non-Hndcps Chases	Hndcps Hurdles	Chases	NH Flat	Per cent	£1 Level Stake
Fontwell	1-4	0-0	0-0	1-3	0-0	0-1	25.0	+9.00

WINNING HORSES

Horse	Races Run	1st	2nd	3rd	£
Occasionally Yours	9	1	2	1	3119
Total winning prize-money					£3119
Favourites	0-2		0.0%		-2.00

MICHAEL BLAKE

TROWBRIDGE, WILTS

	No. of Hrs	Races Run	1st	2nd	3rd	Unpl	Per cent	£1 Level Stake
NH Flat	1	1	0	0	0	1	0.0	-1.00
Hurdles	17	66	8	5	8	45	12.1	-12.75
Chases	4	27	4	3	5	15	14.8	-11.12
Totals	21	94	12	8	13	61	12.8	-24.87
11-12	19	91	6	16	13	56	6.6	-54.88
10-11	19	105	11	14	13	67	10.5	-42.38

BY MONTH

NH Flat	W-R	Per cent	£1 Level Stake	Hurdles	W-R	Per cent	£1 Level Stake
May	0-0	0.0	0.00	May	1-4	25.0	+1.50
June	0-0	0.0	0.00	June	1-5	20.0	-1.75
July	0-0	0.0	0.00	July	0-2	0.0	-2.00
August	0-0	0.0	0.00	August	0-1	0.0	-1.00
September	0-0	0.0	0.00	September	0-1	0.0	-1.00
October	0-0	0.0	0.00	October	2-5	40.0	+13.25
November	0-0	0.0	0.00	November	2-9	22.2	+3.25
December	0-0	0.0	0.00	December	1-11	9.1	0.00
January	0-0	0.0	0.00	January	0-3	0.0	-3.00
February	0-0	0.0	0.00	February	0-6	0.0	-6.00
March	0-0	0.0	0.00	March	1-9	11.1	-6.00
April	0-1	0.0	-1.00	April	0-10	0.0	-10.00

Chases	W-R	Per cent	£1 Level Stake	Totals	W-R	Per cent	£1 Level Stake
May	0-1	0.0	-1.00	May	1-5	20.0	+0.50
June	1-2	50.0	+2.33	June	2-7	28.6	+0.58
July	0-1	0.0	-1.00	July	0-3	0.0	-3.00
August	0-1	0.0	-1.00	August	0-2	0.0	-2.00
September	1-1	100.0	+5.00	September	1-2	50.0	+4.00
October	0-2	0.0	-2.00	October	2-7	28.6	+11.25
November	0-5	0.0	-5.00	November	2-14	14.3	-1.75
December	0-4	0.0	-4.00	December	1-15	6.7	-4.00
January	0-1	0.0	-1.00	January	0-4	0.0	-4.00
February	0-1	0.0	-1.00	February	0-7	0.0	-7.00
March	1-4	25.0	-2.20	March	2-13	15.4	-8.20
April	1-4	25.0	-0.25	April	1-15	6.7	-11.25

DISTANCE

Hurdles	W-R	Per cent	£1 Level Stake	Chases	W-R	Per cent	£1 Level Stake
2m-2m3f	5-36	13.9	+2.00	2m-2m3f	0-2	0.0	-2.00
2m4f-2m7f	3-25	12.0	-9.75	2m4f-2m7f	2-12	16.7	-2.25
3m+	0-5	0.0	-5.00	3m+	2-13	15.4	-6.87

TYPE OF RACE

Non-Handicaps	W-R	Per cent	£1 Level Stake	Handicaps	W-R	Per cent	£1 Level Stake
Nov Hrdls	0-4	0.0	-4.00	Nov Hrdls	2-6	33.3	+2.50
Hrdls	0-6	0.0	-6.00	Hrdls	5-47	10.6	-5.50
Nov Chs	0-4	0.0	-4.00	Nov Chs	0-3	0.0	-3.00
Chases	0-0	0.0	0.00	Chases	4-20	20.0	-4.12
Sell/Claim	0-1	0.0	-1.00	Sell/Claim	1-2	50.0	+1.25

RACE CLASS

	W-R	Per cent	£1 Level Stake
Class 1	0-1	0.0	-1.00
Class 2	0-1	0.0	-1.00
Class 3	1-16	6.3	-12.75
Class 4	4-44	9.1	-8.50
Class 5	7-31	22.6	-0.62
Class 6	0-1	0.0	-1.00

FIRST TIME OUT

	W-R	Per cent	£1 Level Stake
Bumpers	0-1	0.0	-1.00
Hurdles	4-17	23.5	+6.00
Chases	1-3	33.3	+1.33
Totals	5-21	23.8	+6.33

JOCKEYS

	W-R	Per cent	£1 Level Stake
Tom Cannon	5-31	16.1	-6.50
Micheal Nolan	3-17	17.6	-7.12
Tom Scudamore	2-6	33.3	+12.25
Nick Scholfield	2-18	11.1	-1.50

COURSE RECORD

	Total W-R	Non-Hndcps Hurdles	Non-Hndcps Chases	Hndcps Hurdles	Chases	NH Flat	Per cent	£1 Level Stake
Ludlow	2-3	0-0	0-0	2-2	0-1	0-0	66.7	+17.50
Fontwell	2-4	0-1	0-0	1-2	1-1	0-0	50.0	+5.25
Ffos Las	2-14	0-0	0-0	0-7	2-7	0-0	14.3	-8.45
Sandown	1-2	0-0	0-0	1-2	0-0	0-0	50.0	+7.00
Wetherby	1-2	0-0	0-0	1-2	0-0	0-0	50.0	+1.25
Worcester	1-2	0-0	0-0	1-2	0-0	0-0	50.0	+1.25
Plumpton	1-3	0-0	0-0	1-2	0-1	0-0	33.3	+8.00
Nton Abbot	1-6	0-2	0-0	0-2	1-2	0-0	16.7	-1.67
Uttoxeter	1-13	0-3	0-0	1-9	0-1	0-0	7.7	-10.00

WINNING HORSES

Horse	Races Run	1st	2nd	3rd	£
Sporting Boy	7	3	0	0	11372
Lamps	4	1	0	3	3249
Torrential Raine	7	1	0	0	2599
Sadler's Star	8	1	1	2	2469
Pacha D'Oudairies	9	1	1	2	2395

Royal Chatelier	9	2	1	1	4289
Bathwick Junior	4	1	1	1	2053
Sovereign Spirit	4	1	0	0	1779
Sahrati	6	1	1	1	1689
Total winning prize-money					£31894
Favourites	4-9		44.4%		3.05

MARTIN BOSLEY
CHALFONT ST GILES, BUCKS

	No. of Hrs	Races Run	1st	2nd	3rd	Unpl	Per cent	£1 Level Stake
NH Flat	3	5	0	0	1	4	0.0	-5.00
Hurdles	11	30	2	0	2	26	6.7	-9.00
Chases	1	6	2	0	1	3	33.3	+6.33
Totals	13	41	4	0	4	33	9.8	-7.67
11-12	13	42	2	3	2	35	4.8	-9.50
10-11	10	24	1	0	4	19	4.2	-1.00

JOCKEYS

	W-R	Per cent	£1 Level Stake
Miss Rachel King	2-3	66.7	+18.00
Sam Twiston-Davies	1-1	100.0	+3.33
Wayne Hutchinson	1-6	16.7	+2.00

COURSE RECORD

	Total W-R	Non-Hndcps Hurdles	Chases	Hndcps Hurdles	Chases	NH Flat	Per cent	£1 Level Stake
Ludlow	4-7	0-0	0-0	2-4	2-3	0-0	57.1	+26.33

WINNING HORSES

Horse	Races Run	1st	2nd	3rd	£
*Topthorn	6	2	0	1	9747
*Drussell	5	2	0	0	6863
Total winning prize-money					£16610
Favourites	1-59		1.7%		-55.00

PETER BOWEN
LITTLE NEWCASTLE, PEMBROKES

	No. of Hrs	Races Run	1st	2nd	3rd	Unpl	Per cent	£1 Level Stake
NH Flat	20	45	7	10	6	22	15.6	-1.75
Hurdles	43	149	15	22	17	95	10.1	-76.72
Chases	41	170	27	21	19	103	15.9	-11.38
Totals	83	364	49	53	42	220	13.5	-89.85
11-12	85	409	52	46	37	274	12.7	-111.50
10-11	71	384	59	61	40	224	15.4	+8.82

BY MONTH

NH Flat	W-R	Per cent	£1 Level Stake	Hurdles	W-R	Per cent	£1 Level Stake
May	1-5	20.0	+6.00	May	3-19	15.8	-3.50
June	1-5	20.0	-3.50	June	4-16	25.0	-0.55
July	1-6	16.7	-2.25	July	2-15	13.3	-7.50
August	1-4	25.0	+1.50	August	2-15	13.3	-5.67
September	1-5	20.0	-1.00	September	0-12	0.0	-12.00
October	0-5	0.0	-5.00	October	1-14	7.1	-3.00
November	0-1	0.0	-1.00	November	0-12	0.0	-12.00
December	0-0	0.0	0.00	December	0-7	0.0	-7.00
January	0-2	0.0	-2.00	January	0-7	0.0	-7.00
February	0-2	0.0	-2.00	February	0-12	0.0	-12.00
March	0-5	0.0	-5.00	March	1-9	11.1	-5.00
April	2-5	40.0	+12.50	April	2-11	18.2	-1.50

Chases	W-R	Per cent	£1 Level Stake	Totals	W-R	Per cent	£1 Level Stake
May	5-17	29.4	+15.00	May	9-41	22.0	+17.50
June	5-17	29.4	+1.00	June	10-38	26.3	-3.05
July	4-22	18.2	+3.88	July	7-43	16.3	-5.87
August	4-18	22.2	+5.00	August	7-37	18.9	+0.83
September	4-18	22.2	+4.50	September	5-35	14.3	-8.50
October	1-20	5.0	-13.00	October	2-39	5.1	-21.00
November	2-14	14.3	+8.00	November	2-27	7.4	-5.00
December	0-11	0.0	-11.00	December	0-18	0.0	-18.00
January	0-9	0.0	-9.00	January	0-18	0.0	-18.00
February	0-5	0.0	-5.00	February	0-19	0.0	-19.00
March	0-9	0.0	-9.00	March	1-23	4.3	-19.00
April	2-10	20.0	-1.75	April	6-26	23.1	+9.25

DISTANCE

Hurdles	W-R	Per cent	£1 Level Stake	Chases	W-R	Per cent	£1 Level Stake
2m-2m3f	7-31	22.6	-1.05	2m-2m3f	3-28	10.7	-11.00
2m4f-2m7f	3-70	4.3	-49.50	2m4f-2m7f	11-68	16.2	-10.63
3m+	5-48	10.4	-26.17	3m+	13-74	17.6	+10.25

TYPE OF RACE

Non-Handicaps	W-R	Per cent	£1 Level Stake	Handicaps	W-R	Per cent	£1 Level Stake
Nov Hrdls	2-23	8.7	-8.75	Nov Hrdls	0-10	0.0	-10.00
Hrdls	3-21	14.3	-13.05	Hrdls	10-94	10.6	-43.92
Nov Chs	4-26	15.4	-2.50	Nov Chs	2-10	20.0	+2.50
Chases	0-1	0.0	-1.00	Chases	21-133	15.8	-10.38
Sell/Claim	0-2	0.0	-2.00	Sell/Claim	0-0	0.0	0.00

RACE CLASS

	W-R	Per cent	£1 Level Stake
Class 1	1-20	5.0	-14.50
Class 2	3-28	10.7	-12.50
Class 3	13-67	19.4	+16.08
Class 4	23-152	15.1	-31.42
Class 5	4-57	7.0	-33.25
Class 6	5-40	12.5	-14.25

FIRST TIME OUT

	W-R	Per cent	£1 Level Stake
Bumpers	2-20	10.0	+2.00
Hurdles	2-32	6.3	-20.00
Chases	7-31	22.6	+8.50
Totals	11-83	13.3	-9.50

JOCKEYS

	W-R	Per cent	£1 Level Stake
Tom O'Brien	17-84	20.2	+6.83

Jamie Moore	14-129	10.9	-36.50
Donal Devereux	10-92	10.9	-37.50
Denis O'Regan	4-18	22.2	-2.42
Dougie Costello	2-11	18.2	+1.00
Adam Wedge	1-1	100.0	+5.00
Dave Crosse	1-3	33.3	-0.25

COURSE RECORD

	Total W-R	Non-Hndcps Hurdles	Chases	Hndcps Hurdles	Chases	NH Flat	Per cent	£1 Level Stake
Ffos Las	8-71	1-17	3-8	2-16	2-21	0-9	11.3	-39.25
Southwell	7-17	1-2	0-1	2-7	4-6	0-1	41.2	+26.25
Mrket Rsn	5-21	0-0	0-1	1-8	4-10	0-2	23.8	+5.38
Fakenham	4-10	1-1	1-3	1-2	1-4	0-0	40.0	+12.75
Aintree	4-30	1-3	0-0	0-9	1-15	2-3	13.3	-9.80
Perth	3-10	0-1	0-2	1-2	2-5	0-0	30.0	+6.00
Stratford	3-14	0-0	0-1	0-1	1-5	2-7	21.4	-1.75
Nton Abbot	3-24	0-2	0-1	2-8	1-9	0-4	12.5	-9.67
Plumpton	2-7	0-0	0-0	0-3	2-4	0-0	28.6	+5.00
Carlisle	1-2	0-0	0-0	0-0	1-1	0-1	50.0	+10.00
Newbury	1-2	0-1	0-0	0-0	1-1	0-0	50.0	+8.00
Ayr	1-3	0-0	0-0	0-2	0-0	1-1	33.3	+3.50
Haydock	1-5	0-0	0-0	0-0	1-5	0-0	20.0	+2.00
Cartmel	1-7	0-0	0-2	0-2	1-3	0-0	14.3	-3.00
Hereford	1-8	0-1	0-0	0-4	1-3	0-0	12.5	-5.25
Cheltenham	1-9	0-1	0-0	1-5	0-3	0-0	11.1	-3.50
Worcester	1-14	0-3	0-1	0-2	0-5	1-3	7.1	-8.50
Chepstow	1-16	1-3	0-1	0-4	0-7	0-1	6.3	-5.00
Ludlow	1-18	0-2	0-3	0-6	0-5	1-2	5.6	-7.00

WINNING HORSES

Horse	Races Run	1st	2nd	3rd	£
Mumbles Head	8	3	0	2	29449
Kian's Delight	8	3	2	0	21488
Buachaill Alainn	7	2	2	1	17091
Rio Gael	7	1	0	0	12512
Harouet	7	2	0	0	11696
*Big Time Billy	4	2	1	0	14964
Lamboro Lad	4	1	1	0	7148
*Ballybough Gorta	8	5	2	0	22948
Sizing Santiago	8	2	1	2	6882
Al Co	4	2	1	0	9378
Miss Kalifa	8	1	0	2	5991
*Dineur	6	1	1	2	5198
Regal Diamond	2	1	0	0	5198
Prankster	4	2	0	0	7083
Sansili	4	1	1	0	4549
No Panic	5	1	0	0	3899
Forever My Friend	12	1	0	2	3899
Taffy Thomas	6	2	0	1	6303
Strumble Head	6	2	1	0	6444
Awaywiththegreys	8	2	0	2	6498
Sun Tzu	4	1	1	0	3119
Pension Plan	7	1	2	0	3119
With Grace	7	1	2	0	3119
Cardigan Island	3	1	0	0	3054

Land Of Vic	1	1	0	0	2599
Amazing Valour	8	1	0	3	2339
Royal Scoundrel	6	1	3	1	1949
Vinnie My Boy	7	2	0	1	3574
Azure Fly	4	2	1	0	3379
Henri Parry Morgan	4	1	1	0	1437
Total winning prize-money					£236306
Favourites	11-38		28.9%		-4.34

SUE BRADBURNE

CUNNOQUHIE, FIFE

	No. of Hrs	Races Run	1st	2nd	3rd	Unpl	Per cent	£1 Level Stake
NH Flat	0	0	0	0	0	0	0.0	0.00
Hurdles	1	1	0	0	1	0	0.0	-1.00
Chases	1	1	1	0	0	0	100.0	+2.25
Totals	2	2	1	0	1	0	50.0	+1.25
11-12	12	55	3	5	10	37	5.5	-26.75
10-11	14	68	3	4	6	55	4.4	-41.00

JOCKEYS

	W-R	Per cent	£1 Level Stake
Peter Buchanan	1-1	100.0	+2.25

COURSE RECORD

	Total W-R	Non-Hndcps Hurdles	Chases	Hndcps Hurdles	Chases	NH Flat	Per cent	£1 Level Stake
Perth	1-2	0-1	0-0	0-0	1-1	0-0	50.0	+1.25

WINNING HORSES

Horse	Races Run	1st	2nd	3rd	£
Rossini's Dancer	1	1	0	0	5848
Total winning prize-money					£5848
Favourites	1-2		50.0%		1.25

MILTON BRADLEY

SEDBURY, GLOUCS

	No. of Hrs	Races Run	1st	2nd	3rd	Unpl	Per cent	£1 Level Stake
NH Flat	0	0	0	0	0	0	0.0	0.00
Hurdles	4	6	0	0	0	6	0.0	-6.00
Chases	3	10	1	1	0	8	10.0	-3.50
Totals	6	16	1	1	0	14	6.3	-9.50
11-12	7	24	1	5	1	17	4.2	-19.50
10-11	7	21	0	0	1	20	0.0	-21.00

JOCKEYS

	W-R	Per cent	£1 Level Stake
Charlie Wallis	1-11	9.1	-4.50

COURSE RECORD

	Total W-R	Non-Hndcps Hurdles	Chases	Hndcps Hurdles	Chases	NH Flat	Per cent	£1 Level Stake
Hereford	1-4	0-2	0-0	0-0	1-2	0-0	25.0	+2.50

WINNING HORSES

Horse	Races Run	1st	2nd	3rd	£
The Grey One	7	1	1	0	2339
Total winning prize-money					£2339
Favourites	0-0		0.0%		0.00

MARK BRADSTOCK

LETCOMBE BASSETT, OXON

	No. of Hrs	Races Run	1st	2nd	3rd	Unpl	Per cent	£1 Level Stake
NH Flat	4	7	0	0	0	7	0.0	-7.00
Hurdles	7	15	5	1	1	8	33.3	+9.10
Chases	1	6	2	0	0	4	33.3	+3.88
Totals	10	28	7	1	1	19	25.0	+5.98
11-12	10	23	3	2	1	17	13.0	+10.00
10-11	13	49	3	7	3	36	6.1	-18.50

JOCKEYS

	W-R	Per cent	£1 Level Stake
Nico de Boinville	4-6	66.7	+10.88
Mattie Batchelor	3-18	16.7	-0.90

COURSE RECORD

	Total W-R	Non-Hndcps Hurdles	Chases	Hndcps Hurdles	Chases	NH Flat	Per cent	£1 Level Stake
Ffos Las	3-3	0-0	0-0	1-1	2-2	0-0	100.0	+10.38
Cheltenham	2-6	2-4	0-0	0-0	0-2	0-0	33.3	+5.10
Chepstow	1-2	0-1	0-0	1-1	0-0	0-0	50.0	+1.50
Uttoxeter	1-4	1-3	0-0	0-0	0-1	0-0	25.0	+2.00

WINNING HORSES

Horse	Races Run	1st	2nd	3rd	£
Carruthers	7	2	0	0	25488
Coneygree	4	3	0	1	31009
Super Villan	3	2	0	0	8512
Total winning prize-money					£65009
Favourites	3-4		75.0%		4.47

OWEN BRENNAN

DERBY, DERBYS

	No. of Hrs	Races Run	1st	2nd	3rd	Unpl	Per cent	£1 Level Stake
NH Flat	4	6	1	0	1	4	16.7	+28.00
Hurdles	5	21	1	5	3	12	4.8	-8.00

Chases	2	7	1	1	0	5	14.3	+60.00
Totals	11	34	3	6	4	21	8.8	+80.00
11-12	12	39	0	1	4	34	0.0	-39.00
10-11	1	2	0	0	0	2	0.0	-2.00

JOCKEYS

	W-R	Per cent	£1 Level Stake
Harry Haynes	1-4	25.0	+63.00
Tommy Phelan	1-8	12.5	+26.00
Gavin Sheehan	1-8	12.5	+5.00

COURSE RECORD

	Total W-R	Non-Hndcps Hurdles	Chases	Hndcps Hurdles	Chases	NH Flat	Per cent	£1 Level Stake
Uttoxeter	2-22	0-8	0-1	1-6	0-3	1-4	9.1	+25.00
Southwell	1-4	0-1	0-0	0-1	1-1	0-1	25.0	+63.00

WINNING HORSES

Horse	Races Run	1st	2nd	3rd	£
Sonic Anthem	4	1	1	0	2395
Killala Quay	2	1	0	0	1754
Amazingreyce	6	1	0	2	1689
Total winning prize-money					£5838
Favourites	0-1		0.0%		-1.00

BARRY BRENNAN

UPPER LAMBOURN, BERKS

	No. of Hrs	Races Run	1st	2nd	3rd	Unpl	Per cent	£1 Level Stake
NH Flat	4	5	0	1	0	4	0.0	-5.00
Hurdles	16	39	6	1	5	27	15.4	-6.38
Chases	7	15	3	3	1	8	20.0	+7.50
Totals	25	59	9	5	6	39	15.3	-3.88
11-12	20	62	7	3	8	44	11.3	-1.92
10-11	22	47	2	4	5	36	4.3	-34.50

JOCKEYS

	W-R	Per cent	£1 Level Stake
Sam Twiston-Davies	3-15	20.0	-0.63
Felix De Giles	2-12	16.7	-2.00
Gavin Sheehan	1-2	50.0	+9.00
Richard Johnson	1-3	33.3	-0.75
Thomas Garner	1-4	25.0	+0.50
Miss Pernilla Hermansson	1-5	20.0	+8.00

COURSE RECORD

	Total W-R	Non-Hndcps Hurdles	Chases	Hndcps Hurdles	Chases	NH Flat	Per cent	£1 Level Stake
Ffos Las	2-4	1-1	0-0	0-0	1-2	0-1	50.0	+5.05
Leicester	1-2	0-0	0-0	1-2	0-0	0-0	50.0	+0.25
Taunton	1-2	0-0	0-0	0-1	1-1	0-0	50.0	+9.00

Warwick	1-2	0-0	0-0	0-1	1-1	0-0	50.0 +2.50
Stratford	1-4	1-3	0-0	0-0	0-1	0-0	25.0 -1.00
Uttoxeter	1-4	1-3	0-0	0-0	0-1	0-0	25.0 +9.00
Ludlow	1-5	1-2	0-0	0-2	0-1	0-0	20.0 +0.50
Towcester	1-5	1-3	0-0	0-0	0-1	0-1	20.0 +1.50

February	2-5	40.0	+7.50	
March	1-5	20.0	-2.80	
April	0-3	0.0	-3.00	

February	2-14	14.3	-1.50
March	2-11	18.2	-5.93
April	0-8	0.0	-8.00

WINNING HORSES

Horse	Races Run	1st	2nd	3rd	£
*Manger Hanagment	6	1	0	0	4094
Bin End	8	2	0	1	5928
*Dunkelly Castle	3	2	1	0	4938
Lucky Vic	4	2	0	0	4744
Bathcounty	7	1	0	3	2274
Clowance House	2	1	0	0	1949
Total winning prize-money					**£23927**
Favourites	**2-3**		**66.7%**		**1.63**

DISTANCE

Hurdles	W-R	Per cent	£1 Level Stake	Chases	W-R	Per cent	£1 Level Stake
2m-2m3f	3-24	12.5	-7.63	2m-2m3f	6-32	18.8	+2.00
2m4f-2m7f	1-11	9.1	-8.25	2m4f-2m7f	1-4	25.0	-1.80
3m+	0-2	0.0	-2.00	3m+	5-21	23.8	+2.40

TYPE OF RACE

Non-Handicaps	W-R	Per cent	£1 Level Stake	Handicaps	W-R	Per cent	£1 Level Stake
Nov Hrdls	1-10	10.0	-7.13	Nov Hrdls	1-6	16.7	+0.50
Hrdls	1-10	10.0	-3.00	Hrdls	1-10	10.0	-7.25
Nov Chs	0-4	0.0	-4.00	Nov Chs	0-6	0.0	-6.00
Chases	0-5	0.0	-5.00	Chases	12-42	28.6	+17.60
Sell/Claim	0-2	0.0	-2.00	Sell/Claim	0-0	0.0	0.00

DAVID BRIDGWATER

ICOMB, GLOUCS

	No. of Hrs	Races Run	1st	2nd	3rd	Unpl	Per cent	£1 Level Stake
NH Flat	4	7	0	0	1	6	0.0	-7.00
Hurdles	10	37	4	4	4	25	10.8	-17.88
Chases	12	57	12	16	8	21	21.1	+2.60
Totals	**26**	**101**	**16**	**20**	**13**	**52**	**15.8**	**-22.28**
11-12	20	70	13	9	2	45	18.6	+24.63
10-11	15	65	7	6	8	44	10.8	-22.17

RACE CLASS

	W-R	Per cent	£1 Level Stake
Class 1	1-7	14.3	-2.00
Class 2	0-2	0.0	-2.00
Class 3	1-16	6.3	-12.00
Class 4	9-48	18.8	-6.77
Class 5	5-24	20.8	+4.50
Class 6	0-4	0.0	-4.00

FIRST TIME OUT

	W-R	Per cent	£1 Level Stake
Bumpers	0-4	0.0	-4.00
Hurdles	0-10	0.0	-10.00
Chases	1-12	8.3	-8.00
Totals	**1-26**	**3.8**	**-22.00**

BY MONTH

NH Flat	W-R	Per cent	£1 Level Stake	Hurdles	W-R	Per cent	£1 Level Stake
May	0-0	0.0	0.00	May	0-0	0.0	0.00
June	0-0	0.0	0.00	June	1-4	25.0	+2.50
July	0-0	0.0	0.00	July	1-3	33.3	-0.25
August	0-0	0.0	0.00	August	0-1	0.0	-1.00
September	0-0	0.0	0.00	September	0-0	0.0	0.00
October	0-0	0.0	0.00	October	1-2	50.0	+5.00
November	0-0	0.0	0.00	November	0-5	0.0	-5.00
December	0-0	0.0	0.00	December	0-2	0.0	-2.00
January	0-2	0.0	-2.00	January	0-5	0.0	-5.00
February	0-3	0.0	-3.00	February	0-6	0.0	-6.00
March	0-2	0.0	-2.00	March	1-4	25.0	-1.13
April	0-0	0.0	0.00	April	0-5	0.0	-5.00

Chases	W-R	Per cent	£1 Level Stake	Totals	W-R	Per cent	£1 Level Stake
May	0-1	0.0	-1.00	May	0-1	0.0	-1.00
June	3-6	50.0	+3.00	June	4-10	40.0	+5.50
July	1-5	20.0	+7.00	July	2-8	25.0	+6.75
August	0-8	0.0	-8.00	August	0-9	0.0	-9.00
September	0-2	0.0	-2.00	September	0-2	0.0	-2.00
October	2-6	33.3	-0.10	October	3-8	37.5	+4.90
November	2-8	25.0	+5.00	November	2-13	15.4	0.00
December	1-5	20.0	0.00	December	1-7	14.3	-2.00
January	0-3	0.0	-3.00	January	0-10	0.0	-10.00

JOCKEYS

	W-R	Per cent	£1 Level Stake
Tommy Phelan	6-50	12.0	-15.00
Tom Scudamore	5-29	17.2	-8.93
Robert Thornton	2-3	66.7	+6.50
Brendan Powell	1-1	100.0	+1.40
Tom Cannon	1-2	50.0	+0.75
Jake Hodson	1-11	9.1	-2.00

COURSE RECORD

	Total W-R	Non-Hndcps Hurdles Chases		Hndcps Hurdles Chases		NH Flat	Per cent	£1 Level Stake
Fontwell	5-10	0-0	0-1	1-2	4-7	0-0	50.0	+7.35
Mrket Rsn	2-4	0-0	0-0	1-1	1-2	0-1	50.0	+4.75
Nton Abbot	2-7	0-0	0-0	0-2	2-5	0-0	28.6	+7.75
Plumpton	2-10	1-5	0-0	0-2	1-3	0-0	20.0	+0.50
Towcester	1-2	0-0	0-1	0-0	1-1	0-0	50.0	+4.50
Wetherby	1-2	0-1	0-0	0-0	1-1	0-0	50.0	+2.00
Ascot	1-4	0-1	0-0	0-0	1-2	0-1	25.0	+1.00
Warwick	1-5	1-1	0-0	0-0	0-2	0-2	20.0	-2.13
Stratford	1-8	0-3	0-0	0-0	1-5	0-0	12.5	+1.00

WINNING HORSES

Horse	Races Run	1st	2nd	3rd	£
Wyck Hill	3	2	0	0	32323
Sawpit Supreme	6	1	3	1	4094
Present To You	10	1	3	3	3899
Speedy Bruere	5	2	0	1	7538
Dont Do Mondays	3	1	0	0	3119
Double Chocolate	7	2	2	1	6108
Escardo	10	2	4	0	4687
Dirty Bertie	4	2	0	1	5068
Blue Hills	6	2	2	1	4735
Regal One	6	1	0	0	2053
Total winning prize-money					**£73624**
Favourites	7-13		53.8%		6.22

CHARLIE BROOKS

SARSDEN, OXON

	No. of Hrs	Races Run	1st	2nd	3rd	Unpl	Per cent	£1 Level Stake
NH Flat	5	8	1	2	0	5	12.5	-1.00
Hurdles	1	1	0	0	0	1	0.0	-1.00
Chases	1	1	0	0	0	1	0.0	-1.00
Totals	7	10	1	2	0	7	10.0	-3.00
11-12	6	13	0	2	2	9	0.0	-13.00

JOCKEYS

	W-R	Per cent	£1 Level Stake
Sam Twiston-Davies	1-3	33.3	+4.00

COURSE RECORD

	Total W-R	Non-Hndcps Hurdles	Chases	Hndcps Hurdles	Chases	NH Flat	Per cent	£1 Level Stake
Ludlow	1-3	0-0	0-0	0-0	0-0	1-3	33.3	+4.00

WINNING HORSES

Horse	Races Run	1st	2nd	3rd	£
Sergeant Thunder	1	1	0	0	2599
Total winning prize-money					**£2599**
Favourites	0-0		0.0%		0.00

ALAN BROWN

YEDINGHAM, N YORKS

	No. of Hrs	Races Run	1st	2nd	3rd	Unpl	Per cent	£1 Level Stake
NH Flat	3	5	0	0	0	5	0.0	-5.00
Hurdles	3	10	0	0	0	10	0.0	-10.00
Chases	2	11	1	0	1	9	9.1	+10.00
Totals	6	26	1	0	1	24	3.8	-5.00

11-12	11	30	4	2	1	23	13.3	-9.50
10-11	6	16	0	1	1	14	0.0	-16.00

JOCKEYS

	W-R	Per cent	£1 Level Stake
Danny Cook	1-17	5.9	+4.00

COURSE RECORD

	Total W-R	Non-Hndcps Hurdles	Chases	Hndcps Hurdles	Chases	NH Flat	Per cent	£1 Level Stake
Mrket Rsn	1-6	0-2	0-0	0-0	1-4	0-0	16.7	+15.00

WINNING HORSES

Horse	Races Run	1st	2nd	3rd	£
O Crotaigh	10	1	0	1	3899
Total winning prize-money					**£3899**
Favourites	0-0		0.0%		0.00

GARY BROWN

LAMBOURN, BERKS

	No. of Hrs	Races Run	1st	2nd	3rd	Unpl	Per cent	£1 Level Stake
NH Flat	1	1	0	0	0	1	0.0	-1.00
Hurdles	10	30	2	1	1	26	6.7	-20.75
Chases	2	7	0	2	1	4	0.0	-7.00
Totals	11	38	2	3	2	31	5.3	-28.75
11-12	10	18	3	2	0	13	16.7	-6.75
10-11	13	42	5	3	3	31	11.9	+15.91

JOCKEYS

	W-R	Per cent	£1 Level Stake
A P McCoy	2-10	20.0	-0.75

COURSE RECORD

	Total W-R	Non-Hndcps Hurdles	Chases	Hndcps Hurdles	Chases	NH Flat	Per cent	£1 Level Stake
Stratford	1-3	1-3	0-0	0-0	0-0	0-0	33.3	-0.75
Nton Abbot	1-4	1-2	0-0	0-2	0-0	0-0	25.0	+3.00

WINNING HORSES

Horse	Races Run	1st	2nd	3rd	£
Hilali	5	2	1	0	9032
Total winning prize-money					**£9032**
Favourites	1-5		20.0%		-2.75

REGINALD BROWN

CROSS ASH, MONMOUTHS

	No. of Hrs	Races Run	1st	2nd	3rd	Unpl	Per cent	£1 Level Stake
NH Flat	0	0	0	0	0	0	0.0	0.00
Hurdles	2	9	1	0	0	8	11.1	-3.50
Chases	1	6	0	1	1	4	0.0	-6.00
Totals	2	15	1	1	1	12	6.7	-9.50
11-12	2	10	0	1	2	7	0.0	-10.00
10-11	2	6	1	0	0	5	16.7	+95.00

JOCKEYS

	W-R	Per cent	£1 Level Stake
Mr P John	1-13	7.7	-7.50

COURSE RECORD

	Total W-R	Non-Hndcps Hurdles	Chases	Hndcps Hurdles	Chases	NH Flat	Per cent	£1 Level Stake
Hereford	1-3	0-0	0-1	1-2	0-0	0-0	33.3	+2.50

WINNING HORSES

Horse	Races Run	1st	2nd	3rd	£
Roses Legend	10	1	1	1	1689
Total winning prize-money					**£1689**
Favourites	**0-0**		**0.0%**		**0.00**

MRS F J BROWNE

KINGSTON LISLE, OXON

	No. of Hrs	Races Run	1st	2nd	3rd	Unpl	Per cent	£1 Level Stake
NH Flat	0	0	0	0	0	0	0.0	0.00
Hurdles	0	0	0	0	0	0	0.0	0.00
Chases	1	3	2	0	0	1	66.7	+1.30
Totals	1	3	2	0	0	1	66.7	+1.30

JOCKEYS

	W-R	Per cent	£1 Level Stake
Mr S Clements	2-3	66.7	+1.30

COURSE RECORD

	Total W-R	Non-Hndcps Hurdles	Chases	Hndcps Hurdles	Chases	NH Flat	Per cent	£1 Level Stake
Sandown	1-1	0-0	1-1	0-0	0-0	0-0	100.0	+2.00
Warwick	1-1	0-0	1-1	0-0	0-0	0-0	100.0	+0.30

WINNING HORSES

Horse	Races Run	1st	2nd	3rd	£
Bold Addition	3	2	0	0	3120

Total winning prize-money £3120
Favourites 1-1 100.0% 0.30

KATE BUCKETT

UPHAM, HANTS

	No. of Hrs	Races Run	1st	2nd	3rd	Unpl	Per cent	£1 Level Stake
NH Flat	1	1	0	0	0	1	0.0	-1.00
Hurdles	2	14	0	3	2	9	0.0	-14.00
Chases	2	12	3	1	1	7	25.0	-4.13
Totals	5	27	3	4	3	17	11.1	-19.13
11-12	2	9	2	0	1	6	22.2	-1.38
10-11	2	9	1	2	1	5	11.1	+2.00

JOCKEYS

	W-R	Per cent	£1 Level Stake
Miss C Boxall	1-4	25.0	-1.50
Liam Treadwell	1-4	25.0	-1.25
Mark Grant	1-17	5.9	-14.38

COURSE RECORD

	Total W-R	Non-Hndcps Hurdles	Chases	Hndcps Hurdles	Chases	NH Flat	Per cent	£1 Level Stake
Fontwell	2-11	0-4	0-0	0-2	2-5	0-0	18.2	-5.88
Taunton	1-2	0-0	0-0	0-1	1-1	0-0	50.0	+0.75

WINNING HORSES

Horse	Races Run	1st	2nd	3rd	£
Upham Atom	6	1	1	0	12972
*Join The Navy	6	2	0	1	5273
Total winning prize-money					**£18245**
Favourites	**3-4**		**75.0%**		**3.88**

BOB BUCKLER

HENLEY, SOMERSET

	No. of Hrs	Races Run	1st	2nd	3rd	Unpl	Per cent	£1 Level Stake
NH Flat	9	16	1	2	1	12	6.3	-5.00
Hurdles	9	16	1	0	0	15	6.3	+7.00
Chases	12	56	7	5	6	38	12.5	-1.42
Totals	25	88	9	7	7	65	10.2	+0.58
11-12	28	130	14	7	22	87	10.8	-50.17
10-11	31	142	11	13	11	107	7.7	-69.08

JOCKEYS

	W-R	Per cent	£1 Level Stake
Andrew Glassonbury	9-56	16.1	+32.58

COURSE RECORD

	Total W-R	Non-Hndcps Hurdles	Chases	Hndcps Hurdles	Chases	NH Flat	Per cent	£1 Level Stake
Fontwell	2-5	0-0	0-0	0-0	2-4	0-1	40.0	+11.50
Worcester	1-2	0-0	0-0	0-0	1-2	0-0	50.0	+1.25
Plumpton	1-4	0-0	0-1	0-0	1-3	0-0	25.0	+17.00
Ffos Las	1-5	0-0	0-0	1-2	0-2	0-1	20.0	+18.00
Folkestone	1-6	0-0	0-1	0-0	1-4	0-1	16.7	-2.50
Nton Abbot	1-8	0-0	0-0	0-1	1-5	0-2	12.5	-2.00
Wincanton	1-11	0-2	0-0	0-0	1-7	0-2	9.1	-6.67
Exeter	1-14	0-5	0-3	0-0	0-4	1-2	7.1	-3.00

WINNING HORSES

Horse	Races Run	1st	2nd	3rd	£
Mister Matt	8	3	2	0	29286
Sulpius	10	4	1	1	10028
Small Fly	1	1	0	0	2599
Southfield Vic	1	1	0	0	1625
Total winning prize-money					£43538
Favourites	1-5		20.0%		-1.50

DAI BURCHELL

BRIERY HILL, BLAENAU GWENT

	No. of Hrs	Races Run	1st	2nd	3rd	Unpl	Per cent	£1 Level Stake
NH Flat	3	4	0	0	0	4	0.0	-4.00
Hurdles	11	34	3	3	0	28	8.8	-5.00
Chases	4	25	3	1	2	19	12.0	+7.50
Totals	16	63	6	4	2	51	9.5	-1.50
11-12	20	103	6	7	14	76	5.8	-51.00
10-11	22	78	8	7	13	50	10.3	-34.70

JOCKEYS

	W-R	Per cent	£1 Level Stake
Christian Williams	2-11	18.2	+16.00
Mrs Alex Dunn	1-2	50.0	+15.00
Matt Griffiths	1-4	25.0	+1.50
Robert Dunne	1-7	14.3	-2.00
Robert Williams	1-7	14.3	0.00

COURSE RECORD

	Total W-R	Non-Hndcps Hurdles	Chases	Hndcps Hurdles	Chases	NH Flat	Per cent	£1 Level Stake
Towcester	1-2	0-0	0-0	0-1	1-1	0-0	50.0	+3.50
Warwick	1-2	0-0	0-0	0-1	1-1	0-0	50.0	+8.00
Hereford	1-4	0-0	0-0	1-2	0-0	0-2	25.0	+3.00
Uttoxeter	1-9	0-1	0-0	0-3	1-5	0-0	11.1	+8.00
Chepstow	1-10	1-2	0-0	0-5	0-3	0-0	10.0	-5.00
Stratford	1-12	0-7	0-0	1-3	0-2	0-0	8.3	+5.00

WINNING HORSES

Horse	Races Run	1st	2nd	3rd	£
Rebeccas Choice	8	2	1	0	10423
Flying Phoenix	5	1	1	0	3119
Notabotheronme	7	1	0	0	2599
Feeling	5	1	0	0	2144
Acapulco Bay	6	1	0	0	1689
Total winning prize-money					£19974
Favourites	0-1		0.0%		-1.00

MRS K BURKE

MIDDLEHAM MOOR, N YORKS

	No. of Hrs	Races Run	1st	2nd	3rd	Unpl	Per cent	£1 Level Stake
NH Flat	1	2	1	0	0	1	50.0	+2.33
Hurdles	2	3	1	0	0	2	33.3	+0.25
Chases	2	4	0	1	0	3	0.0	-4.00
Totals	5	9	2	1	0	6	22.2	-1.42
11-12	5	16	2	3	4	7	12.5	-8.50
10-11	3	8	2	2	1	3	25.0	+4.50

JOCKEYS

	W-R	Per cent	£1 Level Stake
A P McCoy	1-1	100.0	+2.25
Alexander Voy	1-5	20.0	-0.67

COURSE RECORD

	Total W-R	Non-Hndcps Hurdles	Chases	Hndcps Hurdles	Chases	NH Flat	Per cent	£1 Level Stake
Catterick	1-1	0-0	0-0	0-0	0-0	1-1	100.0	+3.33
Worcester	1-2	1-1	0-0	0-0	0-1	0-0	50.0	+1.25

WINNING HORSES

Horse	Races Run	1st	2nd	3rd	£
Red Jade	1	1	0	0	1779
*Fair Loch	2	1	0	0	1643
Total winning prize-money					£3422
Favourites	0-1		0.0%		-1.00

KEIRAN BURKE

SEABOROUGH, DORSET

	No. of Hrs	Races Run	1st	2nd	3rd	Unpl	Per cent	£1 Level Stake
NH Flat	7	10	1	1	1	7	10.0	+24.00
Hurdles	11	22	0	2	1	19	0.0	-22.00
Chases	6	26	3	3	3	17	11.5	-9.00
Totals	18	58	4	6	5	43	6.9	-7.00
11-12	13	42	10	4	5	23	23.8	+8.82

JOCKEYS

	W-R	Per cent	£1 Level Stake
Gavin Sheehan	2-7	28.6	+7.00
Liam Treadwell	1-3	33.3	+31.00
Nick Scholfield	1-30	3.3	-27.00

COURSE RECORD

	Total W-R	Non-Hndcps Hurdles	Non-Hndcps Chases	Hndcps Hurdles	Hndcps Chases	NH Flat	Per cent	£1 Level Stake
Ludlow	1-1	0-0	0-0	0-0	0-0	1-1	100.0	+33.00
Kempton	1-4	0-0	0-2	0-0	1-2	0-0	25.0	+1.50
Taunton	1-4	0-3	0-0	0-0	1-1	0-0	25.0	-1.00
Wincanton	1-7	0-2	0-0	0-1	1-3	0-1	14.3	+1.50

WINNING HORSES

Horse	Races Run	1st	2nd	3rd	£
Hunt Ball	6	1	1	2	21896
Whispering Jack	9	2	1	1	8447
Big Casino	2	1	1	0	1949
Total winning prize-money					£32292
Favourites	1-4	25.0%			-1.00

BARBARA BUTTERWORTH

BOLTON, CUMBRIA

	No. of Hrs	Races Run	1st	2nd	3rd	Unpl	Per cent	£1 Level Stake
NH Flat	0	0	0	0	0	0	0.0	0.00
Hurdles	4	26	2	1	3	20	7.7	+15.00
Chases	2	7	0	0	1	6	0.0	-7.00
Totals	4	33	2	1	4	26	6.1	+8.00
11-12	4	30	1	2	4	23	3.3	-23.50
10-11	5	21	2	3	5	11	9.5	+0.50

JOCKEYS

	W-R	Per cent	£1 Level Stake
Miss E Butterworth	2-28	7.1	+13.00

COURSE RECORD

	Total W-R	Non-Hndcps Hurdles	Non-Hndcps Chases	Hndcps Hurdles	Hndcps Chases	NH Flat	Per cent	£1 Level Stake
Carlisle	2-6	1-1	0-0	1-4	0-1	0-0	33.3	+35.00

WINNING HORSES

Horse	Races Run	1st	2nd	3rd	£
*Fred Bojangals	12	1	0	3	3249
Knight Valliant	11	1	1	1	2738
Total winning prize-money					£5987
Favourites	0-1	0.0%			-1.00

JENNIE CANDLISH

BASFORD GREEN, STAFFS

	No. of Hrs	Races Run	1st	2nd	3rd	Unpl	Per cent	£1 Level Stake
NH Flat	8	13	2	0	3	8	15.4	-1.00
Hurdles	32	118	8	13	15	82	6.8	-68.67
Chases	12	46	3	7	9	27	6.5	-35.50
Totals	37	177	13	20	27	117	7.3	-105.17
11-12	31	162	18	25	16	103	11.1	-21.75
10-11	27	112	15	14	12	71	13.4	+172.77

BY MONTH

NH Flat	W-R	Per cent	£1 Level Stake	Hurdles	W-R	Per cent	£1 Level Stake
May	2-4	50.0	+8.00	May	0-8	0.0	-8.00
June	0-1	0.0	-1.00	June	0-2	0.0	-2.00
July	0-1	0.0	-1.00	July	0-7	0.0	-7.00
August	0-1	0.0	-1.00	August	0-5	0.0	-5.00
September	0-0	0.0	0.00	September	0-4	0.0	-4.00
October	0-0	0.0	0.00	October	0-8	0.0	-8.00
November	0-1	0.0	-1.00	November	0-12	0.0	-12.00
December	0-1	0.0	-1.00	December	1-23	4.3	-18.00
January	0-0	0.0	0.00	January	0-9	0.0	-9.00
February	0-1	0.0	-1.00	February	0-15	0.0	-15.00
March	0-1	0.0	-1.00	March	6-14	42.9	+15.33
April	0-2	0.0	-2.00	April	1-11	9.1	+4.00

Chases	W-R	Per cent	£1 Level Stake	Totals	W-R	Per cent	£1 Level Stake
May	0-2	0.0	-2.00	May	2-14	14.3	-2.00
June	1-3	33.3	+1.00	June	1-6	16.7	-2.00
July	0-0	0.0	0.00	July	0-8	0.0	-8.00
August	0-1	0.0	-1.00	August	0-7	0.0	-7.00
September	0-3	0.0	-3.00	September	0-7	0.0	-7.00
October	0-2	0.0	-2.00	October	0-10	0.0	-10.00
November	0-3	0.0	-3.00	November	0-16	0.0	-16.00
December	0-7	0.0	-7.00	December	1-31	3.2	-26.00
January	0-4	0.0	-4.00	January	0-13	0.0	-13.00
February	0-8	0.0	-8.00	February	0-24	0.0	-24.00
March	0-5	0.0	-5.00	March	6-20	30.0	+9.33
April	2-8	25.0	-1.50	April	3-21	14.3	+0.50

DISTANCE

Hurdles	W-R	Per cent	£1 Level Stake	Chases	W-R	Per cent	£1 Level Stake
2m-2m3f	4-63	6.3	-47.67	2m-2m3f	2-13	15.4	-5.50
2m4f-2m7f	4-33	12.1	+1.00	2m4f-2m7f	0-22	0.0	-22.00
3m+	0-22	0.0	-22.00	3m+	1-11	9.1	-8.00

TYPE OF RACE

Non-Handicaps	W-R	Per cent	£1 Level Stake	Handicaps	W-R	Per cent	£1 Level Stake
Nov Hrdls	2-29	6.9	-21.50	Nov Hrdls	1-10	10.0	-4.50
Hrdls	1-23	4.3	-14.00	Hrdls	4-56	7.1	-28.67
Nov Chs	2-9	22.2	-1.50	Nov Chs	0-4	0.0	-4.00

Chases	0-0	0.0	0.00	Chases	1-33	3.0	-30.00
Sell/Claim	0-0	0.0	0.00	Sell/Claim	0-0	0.0	0.00

RACE CLASS / FIRST TIME OUT

	W-R	Per cent	£1 Level Stake		W-R	Per cent	£1 Level Stake
Class 1	0-11	0.0	-11.00	Bumpers	2-8	25.0	+4.00
Class 2	1-12	8.3	+3.00	Hurdles	0-23	0.0	-23.00
Class 3	0-17	0.0	-17.00	Chases	1-6	16.7	-2.00
Class 4	9-96	9.4	-56.67				
Class 5	2-30	6.7	-17.00	Totals	3-37	8.1	-21.00
Class 6	1-11	9.1	-6.50				

JOCKEYS

	W-R	Per cent	£1 Level Stake
Sean Quinlan	7-90	7.8	-43.90
Alan O'Keeffe	4-74	5.4	-53.00
Conor Ring	2-5	40.0	-0.27

COURSE RECORD

	Total W-R	Non-Hndcps Hurdles	Chases	Hndcps Hurdles	Chases	NH Flat	Per cent	£1 Level Stake
Mrket Rsn	3-17	0-5	0-0	0-3	1-6	2-3	17.6	-2.00
Cartmel	1-1	0-0	1-1	0-0	0-0	0-0	100.0	+3.00
Newcastle	1-3	0-1	0-0	1-1	0-0	0-1	33.3	-0.90
Huntingdon	1-4	1-1	0-0	0-2	0-1	0-0	25.0	+5.00
Southwell	1-4	0-0	0-1	1-3	0-0	0-0	25.0	+1.50
Towcester	1-5	0-2	0-0	1-2	0-1	0-0	20.0	-3.27
Warwick	1-7	0-2	0-0	1-4	0-0	0-1	14.3	+1.50
Cheltenham	1-8	0-2	0-0	1-5	0-0	0-0	12.5	+7.00
Sedgefield	1-8	1-2	0-1	0-3	0-2	0-0	12.5	-5.50
Wetherby	1-11	1-5	0-0	0-3	0-2	0-1	9.1	-6.00
Uttoxeter	1-16	0-4	1-2	0-6	0-3	0-1	6.3	-12.50

WINNING HORSES

Horse	Races Run	1st	2nd	3rd	£
Party Rock	6	3	0	1	18880
Granville Island	8	1	3	3	4431
Dont Tell Sailor	5	1	0	0	3970
Maoi Chinn Tire	4	1	0	0	3899
Chestertern	5	1	0	0	3899
Bob's World	5	2	1	0	6238
Detour Ahead	8	1	1	3	2599
Yippee Kiyay	2	1	0	0	1949
Wintered Well	2	1	0	1	1365
Wake Your Dreams	5	1	1	1	1365
Total winning prize-money					£48595
Favourites	20-28		71.4%		29.33

GRANT CANN
CULLOMPTON, DEVON

	No. of Hrs	Races Run	1st	2nd	3rd	Unpl	Per cent	£1 Level Stake
NH Flat	3	4	0	1	1	2	0.0	-4.00
Hurdles	4	13	0	3	1	9	0.0	-13.00
Chases	3	15	1	2	3	9	6.7	-12.38
Totals	8	32	1	6	5	20	3.1	-29.38
11-12	9	47	5	3	3	36	10.6	-9.17
10-11	8	27	3	5	2	17	11.1	-12.00

JOCKEYS

	W-R	Per cent	£1 Level Stake
Nick Scholfield	1-12	8.3	-9.38

COURSE RECORD

	Total W-R	Non-Hndcps Hurdles	Chases	Hndcps Hurdles	Chases	NH Flat	Per cent	£1 Level Stake
Towcester	1-7	0-1	1-1	0-0	0-3	0-2	14.3	-4.38

WINNING HORSES

Horse	Races Run	1st	2nd	3rd	£
How's My Friend	7	1	2	3	1819
Total winning prize-money					£1819
Favourites	1-4		25.0%		-1.38

DON CANTILLON
NEWMARKET, SUFFOLK

	No. of Hrs	Races Run	1st	2nd	3rd	Unpl	Per cent	£1 Level Stake
NH Flat	1	1	0	0	0	1	0.0	-1.00
Hurdles	2	4	0	1	2	1	0.0	-4.00
Chases	2	10	5	1	2	2	50.0	+2.45
Totals	4	15	5	2	4	4	33.3	-2.55
11-12	8	17	1	2	3	11	5.9	-15.17
10-11	14	23	4	2	4	13	17.4	-4.33

JOCKEYS

	W-R	Per cent	£1 Level Stake
Peter Carberry	3-6	50.0	+1.82
Paul Moloney	1-3	33.3	-1.00
Leighton Aspell	1-3	33.3	-0.38

COURSE RECORD

	Total W-R	Non-Hndcps Hurdles	Chases	Hndcps Hurdles	Chases	NH Flat	Per cent	£1 Level Stake
Mrket Rsn	2-2	0-0	1-1	0-0	1-1	0-0	100.0	+4.25
Huntingdon	2-3	0-1	1-1	0-0	1-1	0-0	66.7	+1.20
Worcester	1-1	0-0	0-0	0-0	1-1	0-0	100.0	+1.00

	W-R	Per cent	£1 Level Stake		W-R	Per cent	£1 Level Stake
2m4f-2m7f	2-31	6.5	-13.50	2m4f-2m7f	0-5	0.0	-5.00
3m+	0-6	0.0	-6.00	3m+	1-5	20.0	-2.25

WINNING HORSES

Horse	Races Run	1st	2nd	3rd	£
Green To Gold	3	2	0	1	5815
Alpine Breeze	8	3	1	2	6368
Total winning prize-money					**£12183**
Favourites	**4-24**		**16.7%**		**-14.55**

TONY CARROLL

CROPTHORNE, WORCS

	No. of Hrs	Races Run	1st	2nd	3rd	Unpl	Per cent	£1 Level Stake
NH Flat	4	6	0	0	0	6	0.0	-6.00
Hurdles	52	159	15	12	12	120	9.4	-55.72
Chases	8	25	2	3	2	18	8.0	-12.25
Totals	59	190	17	15	14	144	8.9	-73.97
11-12	57	234	23	28	22	161	9.8	-53.25
10-11	53	202	17	13	19	153	8.4	-9.88

BY MONTH

NH Flat	W-R	Per cent	£1 Level Stake	Hurdles	W-R	Per cent	£1 Level Stake
May	0-1	0.0	-1.00	May	2-10	20.0	-4.09
June	0-1	0.0	-1.00	June	4-21	19.0	-10.13
July	0-0	0.0	0.00	July	1-10	10.0	0.00
August	0-0	0.0	0.00	August	0-9	0.0	-9.00
September	0-1	0.0	-1.00	September	0-5	0.0	-5.00
October	0-1	0.0	-1.00	October	1-11	9.1	+15.00
November	0-0	0.0	0.00	November	0-19	0.0	-19.00
December	0-1	0.0	-1.00	December	0-18	0.0	-18.00
January	0-0	0.0	0.00	January	0-5	0.0	-5.00
February	0-1	0.0	-1.00	February	1-12	8.3	+1.00
March	0-0	0.0	0.00	March	6-21	28.6	+16.50
April	0-0	0.0	0.00	April	0-18	0.0	-18.00

Chases	W-R	Per cent	£1 Level Stake	Totals	W-R	Per cent	£1 Level Stake
May	1-1	100.0	+1.75	May	3-12	25.0	-3.34
June	0-2	0.0	-2.00	June	4-24	16.7	-13.13
July	0-1	0.0	-1.00	July	1-11	9.1	-1.00
August	0-0	0.0	0.00	August	0-9	0.0	-9.00
September	0-0	0.0	0.00	September	0-6	0.0	-6.00
October	0-0	0.0	0.00	October	1-12	8.3	+14.00
November	0-3	0.0	-3.00	November	0-22	0.0	-22.00
December	0-9	0.0	-9.00	December	0-28	0.0	-28.00
January	1-6	16.7	+4.00	January	1-11	9.1	-1.00
February	0-2	0.0	-2.00	February	1-15	6.7	-2.00
March	0-1	0.0	-1.00	March	6-22	27.3	+15.50
April	0-0	0.0	0.00	April	0-18	0.0	-18.00

DISTANCE

Hurdles	W-R	Per cent	£1 Level Stake	Chases	W-R	Per cent	£1 Level Stake
2m-2m3f	13-122	10.7	-36.22	2m-2m3f	1-15	6.7	-5.00

TYPE OF RACE

Non-Handicaps	W-R	Per cent	£1 Level Stake	Handicaps	W-R	Per cent	£1 Level Stake
Nov Hrdls	2-8	25.0	+21.75	Nov Hrdls	1-18	5.6	-9.00
Hrdls	0-16	0.0	-16.00	Hrdls	11-104	10.6	-47.47
Nov Chs	0-2	0.0	-2.00	Nov Chs	0-6	0.0	-6.00
Chases	0-3	0.0	-3.00	Chases	2-14	14.3	-1.25
Sell/Claim	1-9	11.1	-1.00	Sell/Claim	0-5	0.0	-5.00

RACE CLASS

	W-R	Per cent	£1 Level Stake
Class 1	0-3	0.0	-3.00
Class 2	0-9	0.0	-9.00
Class 3	1-22	4.5	-19.63
Class 4	10-71	14.1	+6.00
Class 5	6-80	7.5	-43.34
Class 6	0-5	0.0	-5.00

FIRST TIME OUT

	W-R	Per cent	£1 Level Stake
Bumpers	0-4	0.0	-4.00
Hurdles	4-50	8.0	-8.25
Chases	1-5	20.0	-2.25
Totals	5-59	8.5	-14.50

JOCKEYS

	W-R	Per cent	£1 Level Stake
Lee Edwards	9-102	8.8	-61.47
Josh Hamer	7-39	17.9	+31.00
Miss Sally Randell	1-1	100.0	+4.50

COURSE RECORD

	Total W-R	Non-Hndcps Hurdles	Chases	Hndcps Hurdles	Chases	NH Flat	Per cent	£1 Level Stake
Uttoxeter	3-17	0-1	0-0	3-16	0-0	0-0	17.6	+1.91
Towcester	3-24	2-6	0-0	0-9	1-8	0-1	12.5	+15.75
Newbury	2-5	0-1	0-0	2-4	0-0	0-0	40.0	+11.50
Hereford	2-11	0-1	0-0	1-8	1-1	0-1	18.2	-6.15
Aintree	1-2	0-0	0-0	1-2	0-0	0-0	50.0	+0.38
Cartmel	1-3	0-0	0-0	1-2	0-1	0-0	33.3	+2.00
Nton Abbot	1-4	0-0	0-0	1-4	0-0	0-0	25.0	-2.60
Doncaster	1-9	1-1	0-0	0-7	0-1	0-0	11.1	-1.00
Worcester	1-9	0-0	0-0	1-8	0-1	0-0	11.1	+1.00
Sandown	1-13	0-2	0-1	1-10	0-0	0-0	7.7	-7.50
Warwick	1-14	0-3	0-1	1-9	0-0	0-1	7.1	-10.25

WINNING HORSES

Horse	Races Run	1st	2nd	3rd	£
Jolly Roger	7	6	0	0	16531
Arctic Wings	7	1	0	1	3899
Shalambar	2	1	0	0	3899
Le Bacardy	4	1	0	0	3899
*Roseini	7	1	0	1	3899
Dirty Deal	3	1	1	0	3379
Walden Prince	5	1	0	0	3120
Thinger Licht	2	1	0	0	3119
Mujamead	5	1	1	0	2339

Boston Blue	1	1	0	0	1949
Huckleberry	3	1	0	0	1819
Direct Flo	4	1	0	1	1712
Total winning prize-money					**£49564**
Favourites	**6-12**		**50.0%**		**2.53**

BEN CASE

EDGCOTE, NORTHANTS

	No. of Hrs	Races Run	1st	2nd	3rd	Unpl	Per cent	£1 Level Stake
NH Flat	6	14	0	0	4	10	0.0	-14.00
Hurdles	16	49	4	6	9	30	8.2	+4.00
Chases	8	31	6	3	3	19	19.4	+19.00
Totals	**22**	**94**	**10**	**9**	**16**	**59**	**10.6**	**+9.00**
11-12	22	93	6	13	9	65	6.5	-61.54
10-11	20	86	6	10	11	59	7.0	-42.75

BY MONTH

NH Flat	W-R	Per cent	£1 Level Stake	Hurdles	W-R	Per cent	£1 Level Stake
May	0-1	0.0	-1.00	May	0-1	0.0	-1.00
June	0-0	0.0	0.00	June	0-0	0.0	0.00
July	0-0	0.0	0.00	July	0-3	0.0	-3.00
August	0-1	0.0	-1.00	August	0-2	0.0	-2.00
September	0-1	0.0	-1.00	September	0-1	0.0	-1.00
October	0-0	0.0	0.00	October	2-5	40.0	+27.50
November	0-3	0.0	-3.00	November	0-7	0.0	-7.00
December	0-1	0.0	-1.00	December	0-8	0.0	-8.00
January	0-2	0.0	-2.00	January	0-3	0.0	-3.00
February	0-2	0.0	-2.00	February	0-4	0.0	-4.00
March	0-2	0.0	-2.00	March	1-8	12.5	-4.50
April	0-1	0.0	-1.00	April	1-7	14.3	+10.00

Chases	W-R	Per cent	£1 Level Stake	Totals	W-R	Per cent	£1 Level Stake
May	1-4	25.0	+2.00	May	1-6	16.7	0.00
June	1-6	16.7	+2.00	June	1-6	16.7	+2.00
July	0-2	0.0	-2.00	July	0-5	0.0	-5.00
August	0-1	0.0	-1.00	August	0-4	0.0	-4.00
September	0-0	0.0	0.00	September	0-2	0.0	-2.00
October	0-0	0.0	0.00	October	2-5	40.0	+27.50
November	1-2	50.0	+4.00	November	1-12	8.3	-6.00
December	2-5	40.0	+16.00	December	2-14	14.3	+7.00
January	0-3	0.0	-3.00	January	0-8	0.0	-8.00
February	0-3	0.0	-3.00	February	0-9	0.0	-9.00
March	0-3	0.0	-3.00	March	1-13	7.7	-9.50
April	1-2	50.0	+7.00	April	2-10	20.0	+16.00

DISTANCE

Hurdles	W-R	Per cent	£1 Level Stake	Chases	W-R	Per cent	£1 Level Stake
2m-2m3f	0-14	0.0	-14.00	2m-2m3f	0-3	0.0	-3.00
2m4f-2m7f	3-24	12.5	+3.00	2m4f-2m7f	4-14	28.6	+12.00
3m+	1-11	9.1	+15.00	3m+	2-14	14.3	+10.00

TYPE OF RACE

Non-Handicaps	W-R	Per cent	£1 Level Stake	Handicaps	W-R	Per cent	£1 Level Stake
Nov Hrdls	0-9	0.0	-9.00	Nov Hrdls	1-6	16.7	+0.50
Hrdls	1-8	12.5	+9.00	Hrdls	2-23	8.7	+6.50
Nov Chs	1-5	20.0	+1.00	Nov Chs	1-7	14.3	-1.00
Chases	0-1	0.0	-1.00	Chases	4-18	22.2	+20.00
Sell/Claim	0-3	0.0	-3.00	Sell/Claim	0-0	0.0	0.00

RACE CLASS

	W-R	Per cent	£1 Level Stake	FIRST TIME OUT	W-R	Per cent	£1 Level Stake
Class 1	0-4	0.0	-4.00	Bumpers	0-6	0.0	-6.00
Class 2	0-7	0.0	-7.00	Hurdles	2-10	20.0	+13.50
Class 3	3-19	15.8	+12.00	Chases	2-6	33.3	+6.00
Class 4	5-36	13.9	+3.00				
Class 5	2-16	12.5	+18.00	Totals	4-22	18.2	+13.50
Class 6	0-12	0.0	-12.00				

JOCKEYS

	W-R	Per cent	£1 Level Stake
Killian Moore	7-36	19.4	+45.50
Daryl Jacob	3-37	8.1	-15.50

COURSE RECORD

	Total W-R	Non-Hndcps Hurdles	Chases	Hndcps Hurdles	Chases	NH Flat	Per cent	£1 Level Stake
Huntingdon	3-11	1-3	0-1	2-5	0-0	0-2	27.3	+35.50
Towcester	2-10	0-4	1-2	1-2	0-2	0-0	20.0	+2.50
Wincanton	1-2	0-0	0-0	0-1	1-1	0-0	50.0	+4.00
Cheltenham	1-4	0-1	0-0	0-2	1-1	0-0	25.0	+5.00
Doncaster	1-5	0-1	0-0	0-1	1-2	0-1	20.0	+10.00
Mrket Rsn	1-5	0-1	0-0	0-0	1-3	0-1	20.0	+1.00
Worcester	1-6	0-1	0-0	0-1	1-2	0-2	16.7	+2.00

WINNING HORSES

Horse	Races Run	1st	2nd	3rd	£
Handtheprizeover	5	2	0	0	11372
Top Dancer	8	1	0	2	6256
Phare Isle	9	1	1	1	3249
Thoresby	5	2	0	2	5393
Orangeaday	1	1	0	0	3119
Everdon Brook	7	2	0	0	4266
Brass Tax	5	1	1	1	0
Total winning prize-money					**£33655**
Favourites	**0-4**		**0.0%**		**-4.00**

-NOEL CHANCE

LAMBOURN, BERKS

	No. of Hrs	Races Run	1st	2nd	3rd	Unpl	Per cent	£1 Level Stake
NH Flat	1	3	0	0	1	2	0.0	-3.00
Hurdles	5	12	0	1	0	11	0.0	-12.00
Chases	3	19	1	2	2	14	5.3	-12.00
Totals	7	34	1	3	3	27	2.9	-27.00
11-12	15	38	4	1	3	30	10.5	-2.00
10-11	19	48	1	5	8	34	2.1	-45.00

JOCKEYS

	W-R	Per cent	£1 Level Stake
Nico de Boinville	1-1	100.0	+6.00

COURSE RECORD

	Total W-R	Non-Hndcps Hurdles	Chases	Hndcps Hurdles	Chases	NH Flat	Per cent	£1 Level Stake
Kempton	1-2	0-0	0-0	0-0	1-2	0-0	50.0	+5.00

WINNING HORSES

Horse	Races Run	1st	2nd	3rd	£
Brackloon High	6	1	1	0	11574
Total winning prize-money					£11574
Favourites	0-2		0.0%		-2.00

R B CHANIN

THORVERTON, DEVON

	No. of Hrs	Races Run	1st	2nd	3rd	Unpl	Per cent	£1 Level Stake
NH Flat	0	0	0	0	0	0	0.0	0.00
Hurdles	0	0	0	0	0	0	0.0	0.00
Chases	1	5	3	0	0	2	60.0	+10.91
Totals	1	5	3	0	0	2	60.0	+10.91

JOCKEYS

	W-R	Per cent	£1 Level Stake
Mr M Legg	1-1	100.0	+6.00
Mr I Chanin	1-1	100.0	+6.00
Mr Thomas Chanin	1-2	50.0	-0.09

COURSE RECORD

	Total W-R	Non-Hndcps Hurdles	Chases	Hndcps Hurdles	Chases	NH Flat	Per cent	£1 Level Stake
Chepstow	1-1	0-0	1-1	0-0	0-0	0-0	100.0	+0.91
Exeter	1-1	0-0	1-1	0-0	0-0	0-0	100.0	+6.00
Wincanton	1-1	0-0	1-1	0-0	0-0	0-0	100.0	+6.00

WINNING HORSES

Horse	Races Run	1st	2nd	3rd	£
Kirkleigh	5	3	0	0	3795
Total winning prize-money					£3795
Favourites	1-2		50.0%		-0.09

MICK CHANNON

WEST ILSLEY, BERKS

	No. of Hrs	Races Run	1st	2nd	3rd	Unpl	Per cent	£1 Level Stake
NH Flat	2	4	1	1	0	2	25.0	-0.88
Hurdles	15	46	5	8	6	27	10.9	-16.00
Chases	6	27	4	4	4	15	14.8	+1.41
Totals	21	77	10	13	10	44	13.0	-15.47
11-12	3	16	2	1	0	13	12.5	-2.50
10-11	1	3	0	1	1	1	0.0	-3.00

BY MONTH

NH Flat	W-R	Per cent	£1 Level Stake	Hurdles	W-R	Per cent	£1 Level Stake
May	1-1	100.0	+2.13	May	0-0	0.0	0.00
June	0-0	0.0	0.00	June	1-5	20.0	+4.00
July	0-0	0.0	0.00	July	1-5	20.0	-1.00
August	0-0	0.0	0.00	August	0-1	0.0	-1.00
September	0-0	0.0	0.00	September	1-7	14.3	-2.00
October	0-0	0.0	0.00	October	1-3	33.3	+6.00
November	0-1	0.0	-1.00	November	0-5	0.0	-5.00
December	0-0	0.0	0.00	December	0-4	0.0	-4.00
January	0-0	0.0	0.00	January	0-3	0.0	-3.00
February	0-0	0.0	0.00	February	0-8	0.0	-8.00
March	0-1	0.0	-1.00	March	1-3	33.3	0.00
April	0-1	0.0	-1.00	April	0-2	0.0	-2.00

Chases	W-R	Per cent	£1 Level Stake	Totals	W-R	Per cent	£1 Level Stake
May	0-0	0.0	0.00	May	1-1	100.0	+2.13
June	0-0	0.0	0.00	June	1-5	20.0	+4.00
July	0-0	0.0	0.00	July	1-5	20.0	-1.00
August	0-0	0.0	0.00	August	0-1	0.0	-1.00
September	0-0	0.0	0.00	September	1-7	14.3	-2.00
October	1-1	100.0	+14.00	October	2-4	50.0	+20.00
November	1-6	16.7	-3.50	November	1-12	8.3	-9.50
December	0-6	0.0	-6.00	December	0-10	0.0	-10.00
January	1-3	33.3	+6.00	January	1-6	16.7	+3.00
February	1-4	25.0	-2.09	February	1-12	8.3	-10.09
March	0-4	0.0	-4.00	March	1-8	12.5	-5.00
April	0-3	0.0	-3.00	April	0-6	0.0	-6.00

DISTANCE

Hurdles	W-R	Per cent	£1 Level Stake	Chases	W-R	Per cent	£1 Level Stake
2m-2m3f	5-36	13.9	-6.00	2m-2m3f	0-3	0.0	-3.00
2m4f-2m7f	0-10	0.0	-10.00	2m4f-2m7f	1-12	8.3	+3.00

TYPE OF RACE

Non-Handicaps	W-R	Per cent	£1 Level Stake	Handicaps	W-R	Per cent	£1 Level Stake
Nov Hrdls	1-10	10.0	-7.00	Nov Hrdls	0-5	0.0	-5.00
Hrdls	4-27	14.8	0.00	Hrdls	0-4	0.0	-4.00
Nov Chs	2-5	40.0	+11.91	Nov Chs	0-8	0.0	-8.00
Chases	0-4	0.0	-4.00	Chases	2-10	20.0	+1.50
Sell/Claim	0-0	0.0	0.00	Sell/Claim	0-0	0.0	0.00

RACE CLASS

	W-R	Per cent	£1 Level Stake
Class 1	0-12	0.0	-12.00
Class 2	0-1	0.0	-1.00
Class 3	1-16	6.3	-7.00
Class 4	8-45	17.8	+4.41
Class 5	0-1	0.0	-1.00
Class 6	1-2	50.0	+1.13

FIRST TIME OUT

	W-R	Per cent	£1 Level Stake
Bumpers	1-2	50.0	+1.13
Hurdles	1-14	7.1	-5.00
Chases	2-5	40.0	+12.50
Totals	4-21	19.0	+8.63

JOCKEYS

	W-R	Per cent	£1 Level Stake
Will Kennedy	5-28	17.9	+2.13
Dominic Elsworth	4-22	18.2	+7.50
Conor O'Farrell	1-17	5.9	-15.09

COURSE RECORD

	Total W-R	Non-Hndcps Hurdles	Chases	Hndcps Hurdles	Chases	NH Flat	Per cent	£1 Level Stake
Fakenham	2-4	1-3	1-1	0-0	0-0	0-0	50.0	+6.91
Bangor	1-1	0-0	1-1	0-0	0-0	0-0	100.0	+14.00
Uttoxeter	1-3	1-3	0-0	0-0	0-0	0-0	33.3	+6.00
Kempton	1-4	0-3	0-0	0-0	1-1	0-0	25.0	-1.50
Sandown	1-4	1-3	0-0	0-1	0-0	0-0	25.0	-1.00
Stratford	1-4	1-3	0-0	0-1	0-0	0-0	25.0	+1.00
Wincanton	1-4	0-1	0-0	0-1	0-1	1-1	25.0	-0.88
Newbury	1-5	0-0	0-0	0-1	1-4	0-0	20.0	+4.00
Mrket Rsn	1-10	1-7	0-0	0-2	0-1	0-0	10.0	-6.00

WINNING HORSES

Horse	Races Run	1st	2nd	3rd	£
Loch Ba	5	2	1	0	9747
*Ballypatrick	6	1	1	1	4549
Ctappers	5	1	1	1	3899
Viva Steve	4	1	2	0	3899
Spanish Fork	10	1	1	1	3249
Balbriggan	6	1	2	1	3217
Foster's Road	8	2	0	2	5458
Sgt Reckless	3	1	0	0	1430
Total winning prize-money					£35448
Favourites	2-5		40.0%		-0.59

MICHAEL CHAPMAN

MARKET RASEN, LINCS

	No. of Hrs	Races Run	1st	2nd	3rd	Unpl	Per cent	£1 Level Stake
NH Flat	1	1	0	0	0	1	0.0	-1.00
Hurdles	9	47	0	1	9	37	0.0	-47.00
Chases	6	52	4	2	9	37	7.7	-19.25
Totals	12	100	4	3	18	75	4.0	-67.25
11-12	17	120	4	6	8	102	3.3	+27.00
10-11	19	104	4	12	12	76	3.8	-75.50

JOCKEYS

	W-R	Per cent	£1 Level Stake
Gerard Galligan	2-42	4.8	-22.50
Sam Twiston-Davies	1-1	100.0	+1.25
Miss Alice Mills	1-33	3.0	-22.00

COURSE RECORD

	Total W-R	Non-Hndcps Hurdles	Chases	Hndcps Hurdles	Chases	NH Flat	Per cent	£1 Level Stake
Cartmel	2-14	0-0	0-1	0-6	2-7	0-0	14.3	-0.75
Leicester	1-5	0-0	0-1	0-0	1-4	0-0	20.0	+5.00
Fakenham	1-13	0-0	0-1	0-5	1-7	0-0	7.7	-3.50

WINNING HORSES

Horse	Races Run	1st	2nd	3rd	£
Epee Celeste	17	2	0	3	16895
Peak Seasons	16	2	1	3	4549
Total winning prize-money					£21444
Favourites	1-1		100.0%		1.25

GEORGE CHARLTON

STOCKSFIELD, NORTHUMBERLAND

	No. of Hrs	Races Run	1st	2nd	3rd	Unpl	Per cent	£1 Level Stake
NH Flat	7	10	0	1	0	9	0.0	-10.00
Hurdles	8	18	0	0	2	16	0.0	-18.00
Chases	8	29	1	4	4	20	3.4	-25.50
Totals	21	57	1	5	6	45	1.8	-53.50
11-12	27	117	1	14	12	90	0.9	-112.50
10-11	28	128	8	13	12	95	6.3	-69.27

JOCKEYS

	W-R	Per cent	£1 Level Stake
Lucy Alexander	1-19	5.3	-15.50

COURSE RECORD

	Total W-R	Non-Hndcps Hurdles	Chases	Hndcps Hurdles	Chases	NH Flat	Per cent	£1 Level Stake
Kelso	1-12	0-5	0-0	0-1	1-6	0-0	8.3	-8.50

WINNING HORSES

Horse	Races Run	1st	2nd	3rd	£
Knockara Beau	8	1	0	1	7148
Total winning prize-money					**£7148**
Favourites	0-3		0.0%		**-3.00**

MRS ALISON CHRISTMAS

SILKSTONE, S YORKS

	No. of Hrs	Races Run	1st	2nd	3rd	Unpl	Per cent	£1 Level Stake
NH Flat	0	0	0	0	0	0	0.0	0.00
Hurdles	0	0	0	0	0	0	0.0	0.00
Chases	1	2	1	0	0	1	50.0	+8.00
Totals	1	2	1	0	0	1	50.0	+8.00
10-11	2	2	0	0	0	2	0.0	-2.00

JOCKEYS

	W-R	Per cent	£1 Level Stake
Mr G Brewer	1-2	50.0	+8.00

COURSE RECORD

	Total W-R	Non-Hndcps Hurdles	Chases	Hndcps Hurdles	Chases	NH Flat	Per cent	£1 Level Stake
Sedgefield	1-1	0-0	1-1	0-0	0-0	0-0	100.0	+9.00

WINNING HORSES

Horse	Races Run	1st	2nd	3rd	£
Palos Conti	2	1	0	0	936
Total winning prize-money					**£936**
Favourites	0-1		0.0%		**-1.00**

JANE CLARK

KELSO, BORDERS

	No. of Hrs	Races Run	1st	2nd	3rd	Unpl	Per cent	£1 Level Stake
NH Flat	0	0	0	0	0	0	0.0	0.00
Hurdles	1	1	0	0	0	1	0.0	-1.00
Chases	1	2	1	0	1	0	50.0	+2.00
Totals	1	3	1	0	1	1	33.3	+1.00
11-12	2	3	1	1	0	1	33.3	+9.00
10-11	2	4	0	1	0	3	0.0	-4.00

JOCKEYS

	W-R	Per cent	£1 Level Stake
Denis O'Regan	1-1	100.0	+3.00

COURSE RECORD

	Total W-R	Non-Hndcps Hurdles	Chases	Hndcps Hurdles	Chases	NH Flat	Per cent	£1 Level Stake
Perth	1-1	0-0	0-0	0-0	1-1	0-0	100.0	+3.00

WINNING HORSES

Horse	Races Run	1st	2nd	3rd	£
Fiddlers Reel	3	1	0	1	7148
Total winning prize-money					**£7148**
Favourites	1-1		100.0%		**3.00**

STUART COLTHERD

SELKIRK, BORDERS

	No. of Hrs	Races Run	1st	2nd	3rd	Unpl	Per cent	£1 Level Stake
NH Flat	2	3	0	0	0	3	0.0	-3.00
Hurdles	13	34	3	5	0	26	8.8	-9.00
Chases	9	36	2	7	5	22	5.6	+68.25
Totals	18	73	5	12	5	51	6.8	+56.25
11-12	15	72	8	4	5	55	11.1	+78.00
10-11	10	44	5	1	4	34	11.4	-3.00

JOCKEYS

	W-R	Per cent	£1 Level Stake
Gary Rutherford	3-33	9.1	-8.00
Mr J Hamilton	2-5	40.0	+99.25

COURSE RECORD

	Total W-R	Non-Hndcps Hurdles	Chases	Hndcps Hurdles	Chases	NH Flat	Per cent	£1 Level Stake
Kelso	2-13	0-4	1-4	1-2	0-3	0-0	15.4	-3.75
Fakenham	1-2	0-0	0-0	1-1	0-1	0-0	50.0	+7.00
Catterick	1-3	0-0	0-0	1-1	0-2	0-0	33.3	+7.00
Aintree	1-4	0-0	1-2	0-2	0-0	0-0	25.0	+97.00

WINNING HORSES

Horse	Races Run	1st	2nd	3rd	£
Tartan Snow	7	2	3	0	25232
Talkin Sence	5	1	2	0	4549
Royal Curtsy	8	1	0	2	3249
Aye Well	3	1	1	0	2534
Total winning prize-money					**£35564**
Favourites	0-2		0.0%		**-2.00**

SUSAN CORBETT

OTTERBURN, NORTHUMBERLAND

	No. of Hrs	Races Run	1st	2nd	3rd	Unpl	Per cent	£1 Level Stake
NH Flat	3	7	0	0	0	7	0.0	-7.00
Hurdles	6	23	1	0	1	21	4.3	+18.00

	No. of Hrs	Races Run	1st	2nd	3rd	Unpl	Per cent	£1 Level Stake
Chases	3	14	1	0	2	11	7.1	-3.00
Totals	10	44	2	0	3	39	4.5	+8.00
11-12	6	23	1	3	3	16	4.3	-16.00

JOCKEYS

	W-R	Per cent	£1 Level Stake
Stephen Mulqueen	1-10	10.0	+31.00
Gary Rutherford	1-12	8.3	-1.00

COURSE RECORD

	Total W-R	Non-Hndcps Hurdles	Non-Hndcps Chases	Hndcps Hurdles	Hndcps Chases	NH Flat	Per cent	£1 Level Stake
Carlisle	1-1	0-0	0-0	1-1	0-0	0-0	100.0	+40.00
Newcastle	1-6	0-1	0-0	0-2	1-2	0-1	16.7	+5.00

WINNING HORSES

Horse	Races Run	1st	2nd	3rd	£
Definite Appeal	4	1	0	1	3444
Dun To Perfection	8	1	0	1	2144
Total winning prize-money					£5588
Favourites	0-0		0.0%		0.00

LIAM CORCORAN

LOVINGTON, SOMERSET

	No. of Hrs	Races Run	1st	2nd	3rd	Unpl	Per cent	£1 Level Stake
NH Flat	3	4	0	0	0	4	0.0	-4.00
Hurdles	16	33	1	0	1	31	3.0	-16.00
Chases	5	15	0	0	2	13	0.0	-15.00
Totals	19	52	1	0	3	48	1.9	-35.00
11-12	21	60	2	4	5	49	3.3	-46.50
10-11	24	74	6	4	4	60	8.1	-16.00

JOCKEYS

	W-R	Per cent	£1 Level Stake
Noel Fehily	1-3	33.3	+14.00

COURSE RECORD

	Total W-R	Non-Hndcps Hurdles	Non-Hndcps Chases	Hndcps Hurdles	Hndcps Chases	NH Flat	Per cent	£1 Level Stake
Fontwell	1-12	0-1	0-1	1-5	0-4	0-1	8.3	+5.00

WINNING HORSES

Horse	Races Run	1st	2nd	3rd	£
Murcar	3	1	0	0	2534
Total winning prize-money					£2534
Favourites	0-0		0.0%		0.00

JOHN CORNWALL

LONG CLAWSON, LEICS

	No. of Hrs	Races Run	1st	2nd	3rd	Unpl	Per cent	£1 Level Stake
NH Flat	0	0	0	0	0	0	0.0	0.00
Hurdles	6	7	0	0	0	7	0.0	-7.00
Chases	9	52	4	5	9	34	7.7	-16.00
Totals	10	59	4	5	9	41	6.8	-23.00
11-12	9	60	3	3	4	50	5.0	-46.25
10-11	10	73	6	3	7	57	8.2	-24.50

JOCKEYS

	W-R	Per cent	£1 Level Stake
Joe Cornwall	4-59	6.8	-23.00

COURSE RECORD

	Total W-R	Non-Hndcps Hurdles	Non-Hndcps Chases	Hndcps Hurdles	Hndcps Chases	NH Flat	Per cent	£1 Level Stake
Fakenham	3-12	0-0	0-3	0-0	3-9	0-0	25.0	+14.00
Worcester	1-4	0-0	0-0	0-1	1-3	0-0	25.0	+6.00

WINNING HORSES

Horse	Races Run	1st	2nd	3rd	£
That's The Deal	14	2	2	3	11047
Phoenix Des Mottes	7	1	0	0	3249
Mad Professor	12	1	0	5	2014
Total winning prize-money					£16310
Favourites	0-2		0.0%		-2.00

MRS T CORRIGAN

SCARBOROUGH, N YORKS

	No. of Hrs	Races Run	1st	2nd	3rd	Unpl	Per cent	£1 Level Stake
NH Flat	0	0	0	0	0	0	0.0	0.00
Hurdles	0	0	0	0	0	0	0.0	0.00
Chases	1	5	1	1	0	3	20.0	+46.00
Totals	1	5	1	1	0	3	20.0	+46.00
11-12	1	1	0	0	1	0	0.0	-1.00

JOCKEYS

	W-R	Per cent	£1 Level Stake
Miss H Bethell	1-5	20.0	+46.00

COURSE RECORD

	Total W-R	Non-Hndcps Hurdles	Non-Hndcps Chases	Hndcps Hurdles	Hndcps Chases	NH Flat	Per cent	£1 Level Stake
Catterick	1-1	0-0	1-1	0-0	0-0	0-0	100.0	+50.00

WINNING HORSES

Horse	Races Run	1st	2nd	3rd	£
Killary Bay	5	1	1	0	1248
Total winning prize-money					£1248
Favourites	0-0		0.0%		0.00

MRS C A COWARD

DALBY, NORTH YORKS

	No. of Hrs	Races Run	1st	2nd	3rd	Unpl	Per cent	£1 Level Stake
NH Flat	0	0	0	0	0	0	0.0	0.00
Hurdles	0	0	0	0	0	0	0.0	0.00
Chases	5	6	1	0	4	1	16.7	+3.00
Totals	5	6	1	0	4	1	16.7	+3.00
11-12	5	10	2	1	1	6	20.0	-0.25
10-11	6	6	0	0	1	5	0.0	-6.00

JOCKEYS

	W-R	Per cent	£1 Level Stake
Miss J Coward	1-5	20.0	+4.00

COURSE RECORD

	Total W-R	Non-Hndcps Hurdles Chases		Hndcps Hurdles Chases		NH Flat	Per cent	£1 Level Stake
Cheltenham	1-2	0-0	1-2	0-0	0-0	0-0	50.0	+7.00

WINNING HORSES

Horse	Races Run	1st	2nd	3rd	£
Amicelli	1	1	0	0	4679
Total winning prize-money					£4679
Favourites	0-0		0.0%		0.00

CLIVE COX

LAMBOURN, BERKS

	No. of Hrs	Races Run	1st	2nd	3rd	Unpl	Per cent	£1 Level Stake
NH Flat	1	2	0	0	0	2	0.0	-2.00
Hurdles	2	3	1	0	0	2	33.3	+1.00
Chases	0	0	0	0	0	0	0.0	0.00
Totals	2	5	1	0	0	4	20.0	-1.00

JOCKEYS

	W-R	Per cent	£1 Level Stake
Dominic Elsworth	1-2	50.0	+2.00

COURSE RECORD

	Total W-R	Non-Hndcps Hurdles Chases		Hndcps Hurdles Chases		NH Flat	Per cent	£1 Level Stake
Newbury	1-2	1-2	0-0	0-0	0-0	0-0	50.0	+2.00

WINNING HORSES

Horse	Races Run	1st	2nd	3rd	£
Poet	2	1	0	0	3899
Total winning prize-money					£3899
Favourites	0-0		0.0%		0.00

TONY COYLE

NORTON, N YORKS

	No. of Hrs	Races Run	1st	2nd	3rd	Unpl	Per cent	£1 Level Stake
NH Flat	7	10	0	3	2	5	0.0	-10.00
Hurdles	9	31	2	4	4	21	6.5	-25.63
Chases	4	23	3	3	4	13	13.0	-6.25
Totals	15	64	5	10	10	39	7.8	-41.88
11-12	10	20	4	2	3	11	20.0	+23.71

JOCKEYS

	W-R	Per cent	£1 Level Stake
Brian Toomey	4-45	8.9	-25.25
Jack Quinlan	1-11	9.1	-8.63

COURSE RECORD

	Total W-R	Non-Hndcps Hurdles Chases		Hndcps Hurdles Chases		NH Flat	Per cent	£1 Level Stake
Sedgefield	1-5	0-0	0-1	0-2	1-2	0-0	20.0	-1.25
Hexham	1-6	0-2	0-0	1-2	0-2	0-0	16.7	-3.63
Carlisle	1-7	0-0	0-0	0-2	1-3	0-2	14.3	+0.50
Wetherby	1-12	0-3	0-1	0-3	1-2	0-3	8.3	-6.50
Mrket Rsn	1-13	1-5	0-1	0-3	0-3	0-1	7.7	-10.00

WINNING HORSES

Horse	Races Run	1st	2nd	3rd	£
River Dragon	5	1	1	0	6498
Billy Cuckoo	15	3	3	2	10072
Lucky Landing	9	1	2	2	3249
Total winning prize-money					£19819
Favourites	3-7		42.9%		2.13

ANDREW CROOK

MIDDLEHAM MOOR, N YORKS

	No. of Hrs	Races Run	1st	2nd	3rd	Unpl	Per cent	£1 Level Stake
NH Flat	6	10	1	0	0	9	10.0	+11.00
Hurdles	14	37	1	1	3	32	2.7	+30.00

Chases	8	31	2	0	3	26	6.5	-1.00
Totals	21	78	4	1	6	67	5.1	+40.00
11-12	26	102	8	10	12	72	7.8	+20.00
10-11	20	83	6	8	10	59	7.2	-37.00

JOCKEYS

	W-R	Per cent	£1 Level Stake
Brian Hughes	1-1	100.0	+18.00
John Winston	1-6	16.7	+61.00
Dougie Costello	1-8	12.5	+3.00
Adam Nicol	1-20	5.0	+1.00

COURSE RECORD

	Total W-R	Non-Hndcps Hurdles	Chases	Hndcps Hurdles	Chases	NH Flat	Per cent	£1 Level Stake
Wetherby	2-9	1-3	0-0	0-1	0-2	1-3	22.2	+79.00
Hexham	1-4	0-1	0-0	0-1	1-2	0-0	25.0	+15.00
Sedgefield	1-21	0-2	0-1	0-8	1-9	0-1	4.8	-10.00

WINNING HORSES

Horse	Races Run	1st	2nd	3rd	£
Jimmie Brown	5	1	0	0	3285
Along Came Rosie	6	1	0	1	3054
Matmata De Tendron	9	1	0	3	2144
Master Red	1	1	0	0	1848
Total winning prize-money					£10331
Favourites	0-1		0.0%		-1.00

MRS EDWARD CROW

SHREWSBURY, SHROPSHIRE

	No. of Hrs	Races Run	1st	2nd	3rd	Unpl	Per cent	£1 Level Stake
NH Flat	0	0	0	0	0	0	0.0	0.00
Hurdles	0	0	0	0	0	0	0.0	0.00
Chases	4	7	1	2	0	4	14.3	-4.25
Totals	4	7	1	2	0	4	14.3	-4.25
11-12	3	8	4	1	0	3	50.0	+1.35
10-11	2	2	0	0	0	2	0.0	-2.00

JOCKEYS

	W-R	Per cent	£1 Level Stake
Mr Tom David	1-7	14.3	-4.25

COURSE RECORD

	Total W-R	Non-Hndcps Hurdles	Chases	Hndcps Hurdles	Chases	NH Flat	Per cent	£1 Level Stake
Mrket Rsn	1-1	0-0	1-1	0-0	0-0	0-0	100.0	+1.75

WINNING HORSES

Horse	Races Run	1st	2nd	3rd	£
Current Exchange	4	1	2	0	936
Total winning prize-money					£936
Favourites	0-0		0.0%		0.00

BARNEY CURLEY

NEWMARKET, SUFFOLK

	No. of Hrs	Races Run	1st	2nd	3rd	Unpl	Per cent	£1 Level Stake
NH Flat	0	0	0	0	0	0	0.0	0.00
Hurdles	4	10	2	1	2	5	20.0	-2.92
Chases	1	1	0	0	0	1	0.0	-1.00
Totals	4	11	2	1	2	6	18.2	-3.92
11-12	4	6	0	0	0	6	0.0	-6.00
10-11	8	24	0	0	1	23	0.0	-24.00

JOCKEYS

	W-R	Per cent	£1 Level Stake
Paul Moloney	2-7	28.6	+0.08

COURSE RECORD

	Total W-R	Non-Hndcps Hurdles	Chases	Hndcps Hurdles	Chases	NH Flat	Per cent	£1 Level Stake
Fakenham	1-2	0-0	0-0	1-2	0-0	0-0	50.0	+2.33
Hereford	1-2	0-0	0-0	1-2	0-0	0-0	50.0	+0.75

WINNING HORSES

Horse	Races Run	1st	2nd	3rd	£
Me Fein	3	1	1	1	2053
Pindar	4	1	0	1	1689
Total winning prize-money					£3742
Favourites	1-3		33.3%		-0.25

SEAN CURRAN

HATFORD, OXON

	No. of Hrs	Races Run	1st	2nd	3rd	Unpl	Per cent	£1 Level Stake
NH Flat	1	1	0	0	0	1	0.0	-1.00
Hurdles	12	43	7	5	7	24	16.3	+26.33
Chases	3	3	0	0	1	2	0.0	-3.00
Totals	13	47	7	5	8	27	14.9	+22.33
10-11	15	31	0	3	2	26	0.0	-31.00

JOCKEYS

	W-R	Per cent	£1 Level Stake
Jason Maguire	3-10	30.0	+15.83
Mikey Hamill	2-6	33.3	+20.00

Daryl Jacob	1-3	33.3	+9.00
Maurice Linehan	1-3	33.3	+2.50

COURSE RECORD

	Total W-R	Non-Hndcps Hurdles	Chases	Hndcps Hurdles	Chases	NH Flat	Per cent	£1 Level Stake
Southwell	3-9	1-2	0-0	2-6	0-1	0-0	33.3	+15.33
Mrket Rsn	1-1	0-0	0-0	1-1	0-0	0-0	100.0	+8.00
Stratford	1-4	0-2	0-0	1-2	0-0	0-0	25.0	+5.00
Fakenham	1-5	0-0	0-1	1-4	0-0	0-0	20.0	+7.00
Worcester	1-7	0-5	0-1	1-1	0-0	0-0	14.3	+8.00

WINNING HORSES

Horse	Races Run	1st	2nd	3rd	£
Chargen	9	1	3	2	3574
Zelos Diktator	6	2	0	0	5302
*Likearollingstone	5	2	0	1	3249
*Sergeant Dick	4	1	0	0	3119
*Natural High	2	1	0	0	2534
Total winning prize-money					£17778
Favourites	1-3		33.3%		-1.17

ROGER CURTIS

LAMBOURN, BERKS

	No. of Hrs	Races Run	1st	2nd	3rd	Unpl	Per cent	£1 Level Stake
NH Flat	2	4	0	0	0	4	0.0	-4.00
Hurdles	10	32	4	3	6	19	12.5	+17.00
Chases	6	16	2	0	4	10	12.5	-4.50
Totals	13	52	6	3	10	33	11.5	+8.50
11-12	15	71	6	5	11	49	8.5	-30.50
10-11	24	97	7	10	10	69	7.2	-54.67

JOCKEYS

	W-R	Per cent	£1 Level Stake
Hadden Frost	4-28	14.3	+13.50
Dave Crosse	1-1	100.0	+5.00
Mr F Tett	1-14	7.1	-1.00

COURSE RECORD

	Total W-R	Non-Hndcps Hurdles	Chases	Hndcps Hurdles	Chases	NH Flat	Per cent	£1 Level Stake
Plumpton	2-16	0-1	0-0	1-10	1-5	0-0	12.5	+2.50
Leicester	1-1	1-1	0-0	0-0	0-0	0-0	100.0	+16.00
Lingfield	1-1	0-0	0-0	0-0	1-1	0-0	100.0	+5.00
Huntingdon	1-5	0-0	0-0	1-4	0-1	0-0	20.0	+8.00
Fontwell	1-6	0-2	0-0	1-3	0-1	0-0	16.7	0.00

WINNING HORSES

Horse	Races Run	1st	2nd	3rd	£
Elegant Olive	6	1	0	3	3249
Bally Gunner	7	1	0	2	3054

Romney Marsh	11	2	3	2	3743
*Maccabees	5	1	0	1	1949
*Ahwaak	1	1	0	0	1916
Total winning prize-money					£13911
Favourites	0-1		0.0%		-1.00

REBECCA CURTIS

NEWPORT, DYFED

	No. of Hrs	Races Run	1st	2nd	3rd	Unpl	Per cent	£1 Level Stake
NH Flat	25	40	8	6	10	16	20.0	-1.07
Hurdles	35	127	35	17	12	63	27.6	+1.72
Chases	9	43	6	10	6	21	14.0	-18.88
Totals	56	210	49	33	28	100	23.3	-18.23
11-12	58	179	39	24	22	94	21.8	-20.86
10-11	41	146	25	20	12	89	17.1	-55.83

BY MONTH

NH Flat	W-R	Per cent	£1 Level Stake	Hurdles	W-R	Per cent	£1 Level Stake
May	1-5	20.0	+0.50	May	5-9	55.6	+7.15
June	1-3	33.3	+1.33	June	1-4	25.0	-2.00
July	0-1	0.0	-1.00	July	0-0	0.0	0.00
August	0-0	0.0	0.00	August	2-3	66.7	-0.71
September	0-2	0.0	-2.00	September	3-5	60.0	+1.77
October	1-4	25.0	-1.75	October	2-16	12.5	-8.50
November	0-5	0.0	-5.00	November	4-18	22.2	-9.51
December	1-2	50.0	+0.63	December	4-16	25.0	+2.08
January	0-3	0.0	-3.00	January	4-12	33.3	+11.50
February	1-4	25.0	+13.00	February	2-16	12.5	-11.00
March	1-4	25.0	-1.90	March	4-12	33.3	+14.88
April	2-7	28.6	-1.88	April	4-16	25.0	-3.93

Chases	W-R	Per cent	£1 Level Stake	Totals	W-R	Per cent	£1 Level Stake
May	0-4	0.0	-4.00	May	6-18	33.3	+3.65
June	1-3	33.3	+0.75	June	3-10	30.0	+0.08
July	0-0	0.0	0.00	July	0-1	0.0	-1.00
August	0-2	0.0	-2.00	August	2-5	40.0	-2.71
September	1-2	50.0	-0.75	September	4-9	44.4	-0.98
October	1-5	20.0	+2.00	October	4-25	16.0	-8.25
November	2-6	33.3	+2.13	November	6-29	20.7	-12.38
December	1-7	14.3	-3.00	December	6-25	24.0	-0.29
January	0-3	0.0	-3.00	January	4-18	22.2	+5.50
February	0-4	0.0	-4.00	February	3-24	12.5	-2.00
March	0-2	0.0	-2.00	March	5-18	27.8	+10.98
April	0-5	0.0	-5.00	April	6-28	21.4	-10.81

DISTANCE

Hurdles	W-R	Per cent	£1 Level Stake	Chases	W-R	Per cent	£1 Level Stake
2m-2m3f	14-47	29.8	+1.04	2m-2m3f	3-13	23.1	+0.75
2m4f-2m7f	14-53	26.4	+5.18	2m4f-2m7f	0-9	0.0	-9.00
3m+	7-27	25.9	-4.50	3m+	3-21	14.3	-10.63

TYPE OF RACE

Non-Handicaps	W-R	Per cent	£1 Level Stake	Handicaps	W-R	Per cent	£1 Level Stake
Nov Hrdls	19-42	45.2	+11.92	Nov Hrdls	0-2	0.0	-2.00
Hrdls	7-27	25.9	-0.25	Hrdls	7-50	14.0	-7.95
Nov Chs	2-11	18.2	-7.13	Nov Chs	0-1	0.0	-1.00
Chases	0-2	0.0	-2.00	Chases	4-29	13.8	-8.75
Sell/Claim	2-6	33.3	0.00	Sell/Claim	0-0	0.0	0.00

RACE CLASS

	W-R	Per cent	£1 Level Stake	FIRST TIME OUT	W-R	Per cent	£1 Level Stake
Class 1	4-25	16.0	-7.25	Bumpers	5-25	20.0	+4.88
Class 2	3-27	11.1	-11.25	Hurdles	9-22	40.9	+8.46
Class 3	9-46	19.6	-3.83	Chases	1-9	11.1	-7.75
Class 4	18-54	33.3	-0.37				
Class 5	8-27	29.6	+2.05	Totals	15-56	26.8	+5.59
Class 6	7-31	22.6	+2.43				

JOCKEYS

	W-R	Per cent	£1 Level Stake
A P McCoy	29-86	33.7	+1.50
Patrick Corbett	14-72	19.4	+7.56
Tom Scudamore	3-14	21.4	+1.50
Dougie Costello	1-2	50.0	+0.63
Aidan Coleman	1-3	33.3	+1.50
Richard Johnson	1-4	25.0	-1.90

COURSE RECORD

	Total W-R	Non-Hndcps Hurdles	Chases	Hndcps Hurdles	Chases	NH Flat	Per cent	£1 Level Stake
Ffos Las	16-54	8-24	0-2	3-13	1-4	4-11	29.6	+15.19
Aintree	5-15	3-4	0-0	0-5	2-4	0-2	33.3	+2.13
Uttoxeter	3-6	3-5	0-0	0-1	0-0	0-0	50.0	+4.50
Ludlow	3-9	1-3	0-1	0-1	0-1	2-3	33.3	+0.95
Newbury	3-13	1-3	0-0	2-5	0-4	0-1	23.1	+9.75
Stratford	3-13	2-3	1-2	0-2	0-1	0-5	23.1	-7.98
Chepstow	3-17	2-7	0-0	0-2	0-3	1-5	17.6	-5.54
Cheltenham	3-22	2-8	0-3	1-7	0-2	0-2	13.6	-8.38
Fontwell	2-5	1-2	1-1	0-1	0-1	0-0	40.0	+0.63
Bangor	2-8	2-2	0-2	0-1	0-1	0-2	25.0	-3.86
Wincanton	2-9	1-2	0-0	1-5	0-1	0-1	22.2	+0.80
Hereford	1-5	1-3	0-0	0-0	0-0	0-2	20.0	-3.90
Worcester	1-5	0-2	0-0	0-0	0-1	1-2	20.0	-0.67
Ascot	1-7	0-1	0-0	0-3	1-2	0-1	14.3	-1.50
Taunton	1-8	1-4	0-0	0-2	0-0	0-2	12.5	-6.33

WINNING HORSES

Horse	Races Run	1st	2nd	3rd	£
At Fishers Cross	6	6	0	0	171703
Gus Macrae	9	2	0	2	40987
Meganisi	8	3	2	0	15672
Herons Well	4	1	1	1	5848
Benheir	10	2	4	0	9747
Scoter Fontaine	4	1	0	0	5393
O'Faolains Boy	5	3	0	1	10397
The Romford Pele	7	2	2	0	8447
Stow	5	2	0	0	6628
One Term	7	3	0	1	11047
Peckhamecho	8	1	1	3	3899
Bob Ford	4	2	0	2	5412
High Storm	4	2	0	0	4938
Vegas Cash	4	4	0	0	3249
Boyfromnowhere	5	2	1	0	3249
The Bear Trap	5	1	1	0	3119
Bally Rone	5	2	1	1	3119
Monte Cavallo	6	1	1	0	2738
Rendl Beach	4	1	0	1	2534
The Jugopolist	8	1	2	1	2144
In The Post	5	1	0	0	1949
Monkey Kingdom	5	2	1	0	3509
Mister W K	2	1	0	0	1848
Salomo	1	1	0	0	1689
Carningli	1	1	0	0	1643
My Lad Percy	4	1	0	1	1437
Total winning prize-money					**£332345**
Favourites	27-56		48.2%		6.32

LUKE DACE

FIVE OAKS, W SUSSEX

	No. of Hrs	Races Run	1st	2nd	3rd	Unpl	Per cent	£1 Level Stake
NH Flat	0	0	0	0	0	0	0.0	0.00
Hurdles	9	24	1	0	0	23	4.2	-13.00
Chases	1	1	0	0	0	1	0.0	-1.00
Totals	9	25	1	0	0	24	4.0	-14.00
11-12	10	30	1	7	3	19	3.3	-26.00
10-11	5	23	2	2	2	17	8.7	-12.63

JOCKEYS

	W-R	Per cent	£1 Level Stake
Jamie Moore	1-8	12.5	+3.00

COURSE RECORD

	Total W-R	Non-Hndcps Hurdles	Chases	Hndcps Hurdles	Chases	NH Flat	Per cent	£1 Level Stake
Haydock	1-2	0-0	0-0	1-2	0-0	0-0	50.0	+9.00

WINNING HORSES

Horse	Races Run	1st	2nd	3rd	£
American Spin	6	1	0	0	15640
Total winning prize-money					**£15640**
Favourites	0-0		0.0%		0.00

HENRY DALY

STANTON LACY, SHROPSHIRE

	No. of Hrs	Races Run	1st	2nd	3rd	Unpl	Per cent	£1 Level Stake
NH Flat	16	24	2	5	5	12	8.3	-11.75
Hurdles	26	74	8	5	9	52	10.8	-26.89
Chases	20	76	10	8	8	50	13.2	-13.04
Totals	50	174	20	18	22	114	11.5	-51.68
11-12	50	186	26	26	31	103	14.0	-9.52
10-11	49	186	8	26	26	126	4.3	-128.75

BY MONTH

NH Flat	W-R	Per cent	£1 Level Stake	Hurdles	W-R	Per cent	£1 Level Stake
May	0-2	0.0	-2.00	May	0-3	0.0	-3.00
June	0-0	0.0	0.00	June	0-0	0.0	0.00
July	0-0	0.0	0.00	July	0-0	0.0	0.00
August	0-0	0.0	0.00	August	0-0	0.0	0.00
September	0-0	0.0	0.00	September	0-0	0.0	0.00
October	0-1	0.0	-1.00	October	0-6	0.0	-6.00
November	1-2	50.0	+7.00	November	0-6	0.0	-6.00
December	0-2	0.0	-2.00	December	1-8	12.5	-1.00
January	0-1	0.0	-1.00	January	2-10	20.0	+7.50
February	1-8	12.5	-4.75	February	1-12	8.3	-7.00
March	0-3	0.0	-3.00	March	1-9	11.1	+1.00
April	0-5	0.0	-5.00	April	3-20	15.0	-12.39

Chases	W-R	Per cent	£1 Level Stake	Totals	W-R	Per cent	£1 Level Stake
May	0-6	0.0	-6.00	May	0-11	0.0	-11.00
June	1-4	25.0	-2.67	June	1-4	25.0	-2.67
July	1-4	25.0	-1.38	July	1-4	25.0	-1.38
August	0-1	0.0	-1.00	August	0-1	0.0	-1.00
September	0-2	0.0	-2.00	September	0-2	0.0	-2.00
October	0-8	0.0	-8.00	October	0-15	0.0	-15.00
November	2-8	25.0	+6.50	November	3-16	18.8	+7.50
December	0-9	0.0	-9.00	December	1-19	5.3	-12.00
January	2-6	33.3	+3.25	January	4-17	23.5	+9.75
February	1-10	10.0	-6.25	February	3-30	10.0	-18.00
March	2-7	28.6	+9.50	March	3-19	15.8	+7.50
April	1-11	9.1	+4.00	April	4-36	11.1	-13.39

DISTANCE

Hurdles	W-R	Per cent	£1 Level Stake	Chases	W-R	Per cent	£1 Level Stake
2m-2m3f	1-30	3.3	-26.50	2m-2m3f	0-14	0.0	-14.00
2m4f-2m7f	7-35	20.0	+8.61	2m4f-2m7f	5-29	17.2	-8.79
3m+	0-9	0.0	-9.00	3m+	5-33	15.2	+9.75

TYPE OF RACE

Non-Handicaps	W-R	Per cent	£1 Level Stake	Handicaps	W-R	Per cent	£1 Level Stake
Nov Hrdls	3-30	10.0	-18.14	Nov Hrdls	1-6	16.7	-1.00
Hrdls	1-17	5.9	-10.50	Hrdls	3-20	15.0	+3.75
Nov Chs	6-20	30.0	+4.96	Nov Chs	1-3	33.3	+3.50

	W-R	Per cent	£1 Level Stake		W-R	Per cent	£1 Level Stake
Chases	0-3	0.0	-3.00	Chases	3-50	6.0	-18.50
Sell/Claim	0-1	0.0	-1.00	Sell/Claim	0-0	0.0	0.00

RACE CLASS

	W-R	Per cent	£1 Level Stake
Class 1	1-11	9.1	+4.00
Class 2	1-14	7.1	-5.50
Class 3	2-40	5.0	-25.50
Class 4	12-74	16.2	-19.43
Class 5	3-20	15.0	+0.75
Class 6	1-15	6.7	-6.00

FIRST TIME OUT

	W-R	Per cent	£1 Level Stake
Bumpers	2-16	12.5	-3.75
Hurdles	0-15	0.0	-15.00
Chases	3-19	15.8	+2.00
Totals	5-50	10.0	-16.75

JOCKEYS

	W-R	Per cent	£1 Level Stake
Jake Greenall	7-67	10.4	-24.88
Richard Johnson	6-39	15.4	-8.89
Andrew Tinkler	4-47	8.5	-13.17
Robert Thornton	3-3	100.0	+13.25

COURSE RECORD

	Total W-R	Non-Hndcps Hurdles	Chases	Hndcps Hurdles	Chases	NH Flat	Per cent	£1 Level Stake
Ludlow	3-28	3-14	0-0	0-3	0-8	0-3	10.7	-13.14
Chepstow	2-4	1-1	1-1	0-0	0-2	0-0	50.0	+3.25
Doncaster	2-7	0-1	0-0	0-1	2-4	0-1	28.6	+8.00
Stratford	2-8	0-1	2-3	0-1	0-2	0-1	25.0	+0.13
Huntingdon	2-9	0-4	0-1	2-2	0-1	0-1	22.2	+12.00
Cartmel	1-1	0-0	1-1	0-0	0-0	0-0	100.0	+0.33
Leicester	1-3	0-1	1-1	0-0	0-1	0-0	33.3	-0.25
Newbury	1-3	0-0	0-0	0-0	1-2	0-1	33.3	+5.00
Ffos Las	1-3	0-0	0-1	1-1	0-0	0-1	33.3	-0.25
Exeter	1-6	0-2	1-2	0-2	0-0	0-0	16.7	+3.00
Mrket Rsn	1-6	0-0	0-1	1-1	0-2	0-2	16.7	-1.00
Sandown	1-7	0-0	0-1	0-1	1-4	0-1	14.3	+8.00
Uttoxeter	1-7	0-0	0-0	0-3	0-3	1-1	14.3	+2.00
Warwick	1-15	0-5	0-2	0-2	0-1	1-5	6.7	-11.75

WINNING HORSES

Horse	Races Run	1st	2nd	3rd	£
Quentin Collonges	4	2	0	0	117915
Grove Pride	5	1	1	1	5558
Safran De Cotte	6	3	0	1	12866
Mickie	8	2	3	0	7798
Toby Belch	1	1	0	0	3861
Arctic Ben	6	1	0	0	3769
Kingsmere	7	2	1	0	6303
Winds And Waves	5	2	0	2	5198
Lord Grantham	5	1	0	1	3249
Upbeat Cobbler	5	1	1	2	3119
Top Totti	3	1	0	1	3119
Heronshaw	3	2	0	0	3964
Vice Et Vertu	2	1	0	0	1949
Total winning prize-money					**£178668**
Favourites	**7-13**		**53.8%**		**4.82**

VICTOR DARTNALL

BRAYFORD, DEVON

	No. of Hrs	Races Run	1st	2nd	3rd	Unpl	Per cent	£1 Level Stake
NH Flat	10	13	2	1	0	10	15.4	+9.50
Hurdles	19	59	10	3	2	44	16.9	+12.41
Chases	15	43	3	5	1	34	7.0	-13.50
Totals	**37**	**115**	**15**	**9**	**3**	**88**	**13.0**	**+8.41**
11-12	43	152	23	25	19	85	15.1	-0.47
10-11	38	148	27	19	14	88	18.2	+19.75

BY MONTH

NH Flat	W-R	Per cent	£1 Level Stake	Hurdles	W-R	Per cent	£1 Level Stake
May	1-3	33.3	+14.00	May	0-6	0.0	-6.00
June	0-0	0.0	0.00	June	0-3	0.0	-3.00
July	0-0	0.0	0.00	July	0-2	0.0	-2.00
August	0-0	0.0	0.00	August	0-0	0.0	0.00
September	0-0	0.0	0.00	September	2-2	100.0	+6.25
October	0-0	0.0	0.00	October	0-6	0.0	-6.00
November	0-0	0.0	0.00	November	1-4	25.0	-0.50
December	0-0	0.0	0.00	December	0-1	0.0	-1.00
January	1-1	100.0	+4.50	January	0-3	0.0	-3.00
February	0-4	0.0	-4.00	February	2-8	25.0	+3.50
March	0-2	0.0	-2.00	March	1-12	8.3	-6.00
April	0-3	0.0	-3.00	April	4-12	33.3	+30.16

Chases	W-R	Per cent	£1 Level Stake	Totals	W-R	Per cent	£1 Level Stake
May	0-1	0.0	-1.00	May	1-10	10.0	+7.00
June	0-1	0.0	-1.00	June	0-4	0.0	-4.00
July	0-1	0.0	-1.00	July	0-3	0.0	-3.00
August	0-0	0.0	0.00	August	0-0	0.0	0.00
September	0-0	0.0	0.00	September	2-2	100.0	+6.25
October	0-7	0.0	-7.00	October	0-13	0.0	-13.00
November	1-4	25.0	+1.50	November	2-8	25.0	+1.00
December	0-2	0.0	-2.00	December	0-3	0.0	-3.00
January	0-7	0.0	-7.00	January	1-11	9.1	-5.50
February	1-7	14.3	+8.00	February	3-19	15.8	+7.50
March	1-8	12.5	+1.00	March	2-22	9.1	-7.00
April	0-5	0.0	-5.00	April	4-20	20.0	+22.16

DISTANCE

Hurdles	W-R	Per cent	£1 Level Stake	Chases	W-R	Per cent	£1 Level Stake
2m-2m3f	2-25	8.0	-14.50	2m-2m3f	0-7	0.0	-7.00
2m4f-2m7f	5-25	20.0	-4.09	2m4f-2m7f	1-11	9.1	-2.00
3m+	3-9	33.3	+31.00	3m+	2-25	8.0	-4.50

TYPE OF RACE

Non-Handicaps	W-R	Per cent	£1 Level Stake	Handicaps	W-R	Per cent	£1 Level Stake
Nov Hrdls	2-17	11.8	-8.09	Nov Hrdls	2-6	33.3	0.00

Hrdls	0-5	0.0	-5.00	Hrdls	6-31	19.4	+25.50
Nov Chs	0-4	0.0	-4.00	Nov Chs	0-4	0.0	-4.00
Chases	1-4	25.0	+5.00	Chases	2-31	6.5	-10.50
Sell/Claim	0-1	0.0	-1.00	Sell/Claim	0-0	0.0	0.00

RACE CLASS

	W-R	Per cent	£1 Level Stake
Class 1	0-5	0.0	-5.00
Class 2	0-5	0.0	-5.00
Class 3	6-31	19.4	+34.00
Class 4	4-48	8.3	-29.34
Class 5	2-12	16.7	-3.75
Class 6	3-14	21.4	+17.50

FIRST TIME OUT

	W-R	Per cent	£1 Level Stake
Bumpers	1-10	10.0	+7.00
Hurdles	2-14	14.3	-5.50
Chases	1-13	7.7	-7.50
Totals	4-37	10.8	-6.00

JOCKEYS

	W-R	Per cent	£1 Level Stake
Jack Doyle	5-30	16.7	+3.16
Andrew Glassonbury	3-26	11.5	+1.50
Harry Derham	2-14	14.3	-8.25
Edmond Linehan	1-1	100.0	+33.00
Mr David Prichard	1-1	100.0	+1.50
Mr Joshua Guerriero	1-6	16.7	+3.00
Ryan Mahon	1-8	12.5	-2.50
Denis O'Regan	1-21	4.8	-15.00

COURSE RECORD

	Total W-R	Non-Hndcps Hurdles	Chases	Hndcps Hurdles	Chases	NH Flat	Per cent	£1 Level Stake
Chepstow	3-12	0-3	0-0	2-4	0-3	1-2	25.0	+1.50
Exeter	3-21	0-6	0-3	1-6	1-1	1-5	14.3	+7.50
Perth	2-4	0-0	0-0	2-2	0-2	0-0	50.0	+2.25
Fontwell	2-8	1-3	0-0	1-3	0-1	0-1	25.0	-0.09
Ascot	1-2	0-0	0-0	1-1	0-1	0-0	50.0	+32.00
Wetherby	1-2	1-1	0-0	0-1	0-0	0-0	50.0	+5.00
Nton Abbot	1-4	0-0	0-0	1-2	0-2	0-0	25.0	-1.75
Sandown	1-4	0-0	0-0	0-2	1-1	0-1	25.0	+11.00
Taunton	1-5	0-0	1-1	0-3	0-1	0-0	20.0	+4.00

WINNING HORSES

Horse	Races Run	1st	2nd	3rd	£
Richard's Sundance	5	2	0	0	13646
Seebright	7	4	1	0	14621
Shammick Boy	6	1	1	0	5718
Regal Presence	6	1	0	0	5630
Pocket Too	2	2	0	0	9874
Tolkeins Tango	5	1	0	0	3249
*Jewellery	5	2	0	0	4198
Nicto De Beauchene	4	1	0	0	1976
Three Old Amigos	3	1	0	0	1430
Total winning prize-money					**£60342**
Favourites	7-15		46.7%		6.41

TRISTAN DAVIDSON

IRTHINGTON, CUMBRIA

	No. of Hrs	Races Run	1st	2nd	3rd	Unpl	Per cent	£1 Level Stake
NH Flat	0	0	0	0	0	0	0.0	0.00
Hurdles	1	3	2	0	1	0	66.7	+9.50
Chases	0	0	0	0	0	0	0.0	0.00
Totals	1	3	2	0	1	0	66.7	+9.50
11-12	1	1	0	1	0	0	0.0	-1.00

JOCKEYS

	W-R	Per cent	£1 Level Stake
Gary Rutherford	2-2	100.0	+10.50

COURSE RECORD

	Total W-R	Non-Hndcps Hurdles	Chases	Hndcps Hurdles	Chases	NH Flat	Per cent	£1 Level Stake
Kelso	1-1	0-0	0-0	1-1	0-0	0-0	100.0	+3.50
Newcastle	1-1	0-0	0-0	1-1	0-0	0-0	100.0	+7.00

WINNING HORSES

Horse	Races Run	1st	2nd	3rd	£
Grey Area	3	2	0	1	5198
Total winning prize-money					**£5198**
Favourites	0-0		0.0%		0.00

PAUL DAVIES

BROMYARD, H'FORDS

	No. of Hrs	Races Run	1st	2nd	3rd	Unpl	Per cent	£1 Level Stake
NH Flat	1	2	0	1	0	1	0.0	-2.00
Hurdles	1	1	1	0	0	0	100.0	+25.00
Chases	2	6	1	0	1	4	16.7	+20.00
Totals	4	9	2	1	1	5	22.2	+43.00
11-12	4	13	0	0	1	12	0.0	-13.00
10-11	4	5	1	1	0	3	20.0	+8.00

JOCKEYS

	W-R	Per cent	£1 Level Stake
Miss Alice Mills	1-1	100.0	+25.00
Peter Carberry	1-6	16.7	+20.00

COURSE RECORD

	Total W-R	Non-Hndcps Hurdles	Chases	Hndcps Hurdles	Chases	NH Flat	Per cent	£1 Level Stake
Warwick	1-2	0-0	0-1	0-0	1-1	0-0	50.0	+24.00
Worcester	1-2	1-1	0-0	0-0	0-0	0-1	50.0	+24.00

WINNING HORSES

Horse	Races Run	1st	2nd	3rd	£
Emma Soda	3	1	0	0	3861
Samtheman	1	1	0	0	1779
Total winning prize-money					**£5640**
Favourites	0-0		0.0%		0.00

SARAH-JAYNE DAVIES

LEOMINSTER, H'FORDS

	No. of Hrs	Races Run	1st	2nd	3rd	Unpl	Per cent	£1 Level Stake
NH Flat	0	0	0	0	0	0	0.0	0.00
Hurdles	6	17	1	3	2	11	5.9	-10.50
Chases	2	6	0	1	0	5	0.0	-6.00
Totals	8	23	1	4	2	16	4.3	-16.50

JOCKEYS

	W-R	Per cent	£1 Level Stake
Mr J Mahot	1-7	14.3	-0.50

COURSE RECORD

	Total W-R	Non-Hndcps Hurdles	Chases	Hndcps Hurdles	Chases	NH Flat	Per cent	£1 Level Stake
Mrket Rsn	1-4	0-0	0-0	1-2	0-2	0-0	25.0	+2.50

WINNING HORSES

Horse	Races Run	1st	2nd	3rd	£
The Society Man	2	1	1	0	1689
Total winning prize-money					**£1689**
Favourites	0-1		0.0%		-1.00

JO DAVIS

EAST GARSTON, BERKS

	No. of Hrs	Races Run	1st	2nd	3rd	Unpl	Per cent	£1 Level Stake
NH Flat	6	12	0	2	0	10	0.0	-12.00
Hurdles	11	32	1	5	1	25	3.1	-28.50
Chases	2	12	3	1	0	8	25.0	-0.50
Totals	16	56	4	8	1	43	7.1	-41.00
11-12	14	45	2	8	4	31	4.4	-9.00
10-11	14	51	5	4	7	35	9.8	-20.25

JOCKEYS

	W-R	Per cent	£1 Level Stake
Paddy Brennan	2-9	22.2	-0.75
Timmy Murphy	2-13	15.4	-6.25

COURSE RECORD

	Total W-R	Non-Hndcps Hurdles	Chases	Hndcps Hurdles	Chases	NH Flat	Per cent	£1 Level Stake
Worcester	2-8	1-5	0-0	0-2	1-1	0-0	25.0	+0.50
Bangor	1-1	0-0	1-1	0-0	0-0	0-0	100.0	+2.25
Stratford	1-4	0-1	0-0	0-0	1-2	0-1	25.0	-0.75

WINNING HORSES

Horse	Races Run	1st	2nd	3rd	£
Passato	6	1	0	0	7820
Nataani	10	3	2	0	9487
Total winning prize-money					£17307
Favourites	1-2		50.0%		1.25

ZOE DAVISON

HAMMERWOOD, E SUSSEX

	No. of Hrs	Races Run	1st	2nd	3rd	Unpl	Per cent	£1 Level Stake
NH Flat	7	9	0	0	0	9	0.0	-9.00
Hurdles	17	55	5	2	4	44	9.1	+0.25
Chases	5	30	1	7	7	15	3.3	-25.00
Totals	24	94	6	9	11	68	6.4	-33.75
11-12	19	70	1	7	7	55	1.4	-55.00
10-11	21	81	5	9	7	59	6.2	-40.75

JOCKEYS

	W-R	Per cent	£1 Level Stake
Gemma Gracey-Davison	6-73	8.2	-12.75

COURSE RECORD

	Total W-R	Non-Hndcps Hurdles	Chases	Hndcps Hurdles	Chases	NH Flat	Per cent	£1 Level Stake
Plumpton	4-30	0-3	0-0	4-19	0-7	0-1	13.3	+19.75
Kempton	1-4	0-2	0-0	0-0	1-1	0-1	25.0	+1.00
Uttoxeter	1-4	0-0	0-0	1-3	0-0	0-1	25.0	+1.50

WINNING HORSES

Horse	Races Run	1st	2nd	3rd	£
Nozic	7	1	3	0	6256
Lindsay's Dream	10	3	0	2	9765
Just Beware	9	1	2	0	2738
John's Gem	5	1	0	1	2053
Total winning prize-money					£20812
Favourites	0-0		0.0%		0.00

C T DAWSON

FERRYHILL, DURHAM

	No. of Hrs	Races Run	1st	2nd	3rd	Unpl	Per cent	£1 Level Stake
NH Flat	0	0	0	0	0	0	0.0	0.00
Hurdles	0	0	0	0	0	0	0.0	0.00
Chases	2	2	1	0	0	1	50.0	+6.00
Totals	2	2	1	0	0	1	50.0	+6.00
11-12	3	4	0	0	1	3	0.0	-4.00
10-11	1	1	0	1	0	0	0.0	-1.00

JOCKEYS

	W-R	Per cent	£1 Level Stake
John Dawson	1-1	100.0	+7.00

COURSE RECORD

	Total W-R	Non-Hndcps Hurdles	Chases	Hndcps Hurdles	Chases	NH Flat	Per cent	£1 Level Stake
Mrket Rsn	1-1	0-0	1-1	0-0	0-0	0-0	100.0	+7.00

WINNING HORSES

Horse	Races Run	1st	2nd	3rd	£
*Kealshore Boy	1	1	0	0	873
Total winning prize-money					£873
Favourites	0-0		0.0%		0.00

MRS J DAWSON

GRAINTHORPE, LINCS

	No. of Hrs	Races Run	1st	2nd	3rd	Unpl	Per cent	£1 Level Stake
NH Flat	0	0	0	0	0	0	0.0	0.00
Hurdles	0	0	0	0	0	0	0.0	0.00
Chases	1	1	1	0	0	0	100.0	+2.00
Totals	1	1	1	0	0	0	100.0	+2.00

JOCKEYS

	W-R	Per cent	£1 Level Stake
Miss C V Hart	1-1	100.0	+2.00

COURSE RECORD

	Total W-R	Non-Hndcps Hurdles	Chases	Hndcps Hurdles	Chases	NH Flat	Per cent	£1 Level Stake
Wetherby	1-1	0-0	1-1	0-0	0-0	0-0	100.0	+2.00

WINNING HORSES

Horse	Races Run	1st	2nd	3rd	£
*Palypso De Creek	1	1	0	0	988
Total winning prize-money					£988
Favourites	1-1		100.0%		2.00

ANTHONY DAY
WOLVEY, LEICS

	No. of Hrs	Races Run	1st	2nd	3rd	Unpl	Per cent	£1 Level Stake
NH Flat	2	5	0	0	0	5	0.0	-5.00
Hurdles	1	2	0	0	0	2	0.0	-2.00
Chases	1	3	1	0	0	2	33.3	+10.00
Totals	3	10	1	0	0	9	10.0	+3.00
11-12	1	8	0	0	0	8	0.0	-8.00

JOCKEYS

	W-R	Per cent	£1 Level Stake
Ollie Garner	1-10	10.0	+3.00

COURSE RECORD

	Total W-R	Non-Hndcps Hurdles	Chases	Hndcps Hurdles	Chases	NH Flat	Per cent	£1 Level Stake
Mrket Rsn	1-3	0-0	0-0	0-0	1-2	0-1	33.3	+10.00

WINNING HORSES

Horse	Races Run	1st	2nd	3rd	£
Ohms Law	5	1	0	0	2599
Total winning prize-money					**£2599**
Favourites	0-0		0.0%		0.00

ROBIN DICKIN
ALCESTER, WARWICKS

	No. of Hrs	Races Run	1st	2nd	3rd	Unpl	Per cent	£1 Level Stake
NH Flat	7	10	2	0	0	8	20.0	+8.00
Hurdles	26	69	7	4	8	50	10.1	-31.93
Chases	11	36	4	1	1	30	11.1	+9.63
Totals	36	115	13	5	9	88	11.3	-14.30
11-12	37	141	11	15	20	95	7.8	-83.25
10-11	37	145	19	17	21	88	13.1	+5.88

BY MONTH

NH Flat	W-R	Per cent	£1 Level Stake	Hurdles	W-R	Per cent	£1 Level Stake
May	0-0	0.0	0.00	May	0-6	0.0	-6.00
June	0-0	0.0	0.00	June	0-3	0.0	-3.00
July	0-0	0.0	0.00	July	0-1	0.0	-1.00
August	0-0	0.0	0.00	August	1-1	100.0	+4.50
September	0-0	0.0	0.00	September	0-0	0.0	0.00
October	1-1	100.0	+4.00	October	2-9	22.2	+3.00
November	0-3	0.0	-3.00	November	2-7	28.6	+9.00
December	0-0	0.0	0.00	December	2-15	13.3	-11.43
January	0-2	0.0	-2.00	January	0-5	0.0	-5.00
February	0-0	0.0	0.00	February	0-5	0.0	-5.00
March	1-2	50.0	+11.00	March	0-10	0.0	-10.00
April	0-2	0.0	-2.00	April	0-7	0.0	-7.00

Chases	W-R	Per cent	£1 Level Stake	Totals	W-R	Per cent	£1 Level Stake
May	0-3	0.0	-3.00	May	0-9	0.0	-9.00
June	0-3	0.0	-3.00	June	0-6	0.0	-6.00
July	0-2	0.0	-2.00	July	0-3	0.0	-3.00
August	1-2	50.0	+13.00	August	2-3	66.7	+17.50
September	0-0	0.0	0.00	September	0-0	0.0	0.00
October	1-2	50.0	+24.00	October	4-12	33.3	+31.00
November	1-3	33.3	-0.63	November	3-13	23.1	+5.37
December	1-6	16.7	-3.75	December	3-21	14.3	-15.18
January	0-4	0.0	-4.00	January	0-11	0.0	-11.00
February	0-2	0.0	-2.00	February	0-7	0.0	-7.00
March	0-1	0.0	-1.00	March	1-13	7.7	0.00
April	0-8	0.0	-8.00	April	0-17	0.0	-17.00

DISTANCE

Hurdles	W-R	Per cent	£1 Level Stake	Chases	W-R	Per cent	£1 Level Stake
2m-2m3f	4-36	11.1	-17.43	2m-2m3f	2-17	11.8	+0.38
2m4f-2m7f	2-18	11.1	-3.50	2m4f-2m7f	1-8	12.5	+18.00
3m+	1-15	6.7	-11.00	3m+	1-11	9.1	-8.75

TYPE OF RACE

Non-Handicaps	W-R	Per cent	£1 Level Stake	Handicaps	W-R	Per cent	£1 Level Stake
Nov Hrdls	2-22	9.1	-17.00	Nov Hrdls	0-8	0.0	-8.00
Hrdls	1-8	12.5	+4.00	Hrdls	4-30	13.3	-9.93
Nov Chs	1-10	10.0	-7.63	Nov Chs	0-4	0.0	-4.00
Chases	1-1	100.0	+1.25	Chases	2-21	9.5	+20.00
Sell/Claim	0-1	0.0	-1.00	Sell/Claim	0-0	0.0	0.00

RACE CLASS

	W-R	Per cent	£1 Level Stake
Class 1	0-7	0.0	-7.00
Class 2	1-5	20.0	-2.75
Class 3	2-8	25.0	+27.00
Class 4	4-58	6.9	-45.13
Class 5	5-31	16.1	+6.57
Class 6	1-6	16.7	+7.00

FIRST TIME OUT

	W-R	Per cent	£1 Level Stake
Bumpers	1-7	14.3	-2.00
Hurdles	1-23	4.3	-20.00
Chases	1-6	16.7	+20.00
Totals	3-36	8.3	-2.00

JOCKEYS

	W-R	Per cent	£1 Level Stake
Charlie Poste	6-55	10.9	-4.63
Ben Poste	3-11	27.3	+7.57
Henry Oliver	3-16	18.8	+0.75
Wayne Kavanagh	1-13	7.7	+2.00

COURSE RECORD

	Total W-R	Non-Hndcps Hurdles	Chases	Hndcps Hurdles	Chases	NH Flat	Per cent	£1 Level Stake
Towcester	3-24	2-9	0-3	1-8	0-4	0-0	12.5	-8.43
Bangor	2-9	0-4	1-1	1-2	0-2	0-0	22.2	-1.13

Ludlow	2-12	0-6	0-0	1-3	0-1	1-2	16.7	-3.00
Newbury	1-2	0-1	1-1	0-0	0-0	0-0	50.0	+0.25
Stratford	1-2	0-0	0-0	0-1	1-1	0-0	50.0	+24.00
Huntingdon	1-3	0-1	0-0	0-1	1-1	0-0	33.3	+12.00
Worcester	1-6	1-1	0-0	0-1	0-4	0-0	16.7	-3.00
Southwell	1-7	0-1	0-0	0-3	0-1	1-2	14.3	+6.00
Chepstow	1-10	0-2	0-1	1-5	0-2	0-0	10.0	-1.00

WINNING HORSES

Horse	Races Run	1st	2nd	3rd	£
Restless Harry	8	1	0	1	10397
Kitegen	8	2	1	1	13377
Sir Du Bearn	3	1	0	0	6963
Thomas Crapper	5	2	0	1	6433
Entertain Me	5	1	0	0	3054
Dancing Daffodil	5	2	0	1	4652
Troyan	2	1	0	0	2274
Guns Of Love	10	1	0	1	1819
Valrene	5	1	1	2	1689
Ballyhooley Boy	2	1	0	0	1560
Total winning prize-money					**£52218**
Favourites	**6-11**		**54.5%**		**4.20**

ROSE DOBBIN

SOUTH HAZELRIGG, NORTHUMBRIA

	No. of Hrs	Races Run	1st	2nd	3rd	Unpl	Per cent	£1 Level Stake
NH Flat	4	10	1	1	2	6	10.0	+5.00
Hurdles	18	66	3	2	6	55	4.5	-42.50
Chases	7	25	4	6	2	13	16.0	+10.25
Totals	**26**	**101**	**8**	**9**	**10**	**74**	**7.9**	**-27.25**
11-12	30	96	4	9	15	68	4.2	-68.50
10-11	33	119	10	15	9	85	8.4	-64.34

JOCKEYS

	W-R	Per cent	£1 Level Stake
Shaun Dobbin	3-15	20.0	+9.50
Wilson Renwick	3-40	7.5	-11.75
Jason Maguire	2-11	18.2	+10.00

COURSE RECORD

	Total W-R	Non-Hndcps Hurdles	Chases	Hndcps Hurdles	Chases	NH Flat	Per cent	£1 Level Stake
Sedgefield	2-13	0-2	0-0	1-6	1-4	0-1	15.4	+10.00
Hexham	1-2	0-0	0-0	0-0	1-1	0-1	50.0	+6.00
Ayr	1-6	0-1	0-1	0-3	1-1	0-0	16.7	+1.00
Carlisle	1-7	0-2	0-1	1-3	0-1	0-0	14.3	-0.50
Musselbgh	1-9	0-3	0-0	0-4	0-0	1-2	11.1	+6.00
Kelso	1-15	0-7	1-2	0-3	0-2	0-1	6.7	-11.75
Wetherby	1-16	0-6	0-1	1-4	0-2	0-3	6.3	-5.00

WINNING HORSES

Horse	Races Run	1st	2nd	3rd	£
Purcell's Bridge	8	2	0	2	9236
Ros Castle	5	1	3	0	3899
Jurisdiction	4	1	1	0	3769
Flying Squad	8	1	0	1	2197
Pyjama Game	9	1	0	1	2144
Spitz	4	1	0	1	1949
Snooker	3	1	0	0	1689
Total winning prize-money					**£24883**
Favourites	**0-6**		**0.0%**		**-6.00**

CHRIS DOWN

MUTTERTON, DEVON

	No. of Hrs	Races Run	1st	2nd	3rd	Unpl	Per cent	£1 Level Stake
NH Flat	7	8	0	0	0	8	0.0	-8.00
Hurdles	19	80	9	6	12	53	11.3	+72.88
Chases	4	5	0	0	1	4	0.0	-5.00
Totals	**25**	**93**	**9**	**6**	**13**	**65**	**9.7**	**+59.88**
11-12	30	74	7	4	2	61	9.5	-18.00
10-11	41	118	4	11	12	91	3.4	-87.00

JOCKEYS

	W-R	Per cent	£1 Level Stake
James Davies	7-62	11.3	+72.38
Giles Hawkins	2-13	15.4	+5.50

COURSE RECORD

	Total W-R	Non-Hndcps Hurdles	Chases	Hndcps Hurdles	Chases	NH Flat	Per cent	£1 Level Stake
Wincanton	2-14	1-2	0-0	1-9	0-0	0-3	14.3	+58.50
Taunton	2-19	0-5	0-0	2-12	0-0	0-2	10.5	-2.00
Exeter	2-20	1-7	0-1	1-10	0-0	0-2	10.0	+8.00
Huntingdon	1-2	0-0	0-0	1-2	0-0	0-0	50.0	+24.00
Nton Abbot	1-7	1-3	0-0	0-2	0-1	0-1	14.3	-4.63
Chepstow	1-9	0-3	0-0	1-6	0-0	0-0	11.1	-2.00

WINNING HORSES

Horse	Races Run	1st	2nd	3rd	£
Billy Dutton	7	2	0	1	8772
Extremely So	7	1	1	1	3764
Kings Flagship	2	1	0	0	3249
Ladies Dancing	6	1	0	1	3119
Loyaute	7	1	1	1	2843
Key To Milan	5	2	0	0	4687
Some Secret	5	1	1	1	1949
Total winning prize-money					**£28383**
Favourites	**1-6**		**16.7%**		**-2.00**

D L DRAKE

PIDDLETRENTHIDE, DORSET

	No. of Hrs	Races Run	1st	2nd	3rd	Unpl	Per cent	£1 Level Stake
NH Flat	0	0	0	0	0	0	0.0	0.00
Hurdles	0	0	0	0	0	0	0.0	0.00
Chases	1	3	1	0	0	2	33.3	+12.00
Totals	**1**	**3**	**1**	**0**	**0**	**2**	**33.3**	**+12.00**

JOCKEYS

	W-R	Per cent	£1 Level Stake
Mr R G Henderson	1-3	33.3	+12.00

COURSE RECORD

	Total W-R	Non-Hndcps Hurdles	Chases	Hndcps Hurdles	Chases	NH Flat	Per cent	£1 Level Stake
Nton Abbot	1-1	0-0	0-0	0-0	1-1	0-0	100.0	+14.00

WINNING HORSES

Horse	Races Run	1st	2nd	3rd	£
Louis Pasteur	3	1	0	0	3431
Total winning prize-money					**£3431**
Favourites	**0-0**		**0.0%**		**0.00**

MISS SALLY DUCKETT

MORETON-IN-MARSH, GLOUCS

	No. of Hrs	Races Run	1st	2nd	3rd	Unpl	Per cent	£1 Level Stake
NH Flat	0	0	0	0	0	0	0.0	0.00
Hurdles	0	0	0	0	0	0	0.0	0.00
Chases	3	11	5	1	1	4	45.5	+0.33
Totals	**3**	**11**	**5**	**1**	**1**	**4**	**45.5**	**+0.33**
11-12	1	1	1	0	0	0	100.0	+0.91
10-11	2	2	0	0	1	1	0.0	-2.00

JOCKEYS

	W-R	Per cent	£1 Level Stake
Mr Nicholas Wakefield	3-5	60.0	+1.23
Mr S Drinkwater	2-4	50.0	+1.10

COURSE RECORD

	Total W-R	Non-Hndcps Hurdles	Chases	Hndcps Hurdles	Chases	NH Flat	Per cent	£1 Level Stake
Bangor	2-2	0-0	2-2	0-0	0-0	0-0	100.0	+2.50
Fontwell	1-1	0-0	1-1	0-0	0-0	0-0	100.0	+1.10
Lingfield	1-1	0-0	1-1	0-0	0-0	0-0	100.0	+2.00
Uttoxeter	1-1	0-0	1-1	0-0	0-0	0-0	100.0	+0.73

WINNING HORSES

Horse	Races Run	1st	2nd	3rd	£
*Radetsky March	4	2	0	0	1248
That's Rhythm	5	3	1	0	3036
Total winning prize-money					**£4284**
Favourites	**4-4**		**100.0%**		**4.33**

IAN DUNCAN

COYLTON, AYRSHIRE

	No. of Hrs	Races Run	1st	2nd	3rd	Unpl	Per cent	£1 Level Stake
NH Flat	2	4	0	0	0	4	0.0	-4.00
Hurdles	2	9	2	3	1	3	22.2	+5.25
Chases	3	8	0	1	0	7	0.0	-8.00
Totals	**7**	**21**	**2**	**4**	**1**	**14**	**9.5**	**-6.75**
11-12	6	26	3	5	3	15	11.5	+8.25
10-11	6	10	0	0	1	9	0.0	-10.00

JOCKEYS

	W-R	Per cent	£1 Level Stake
Graham Watters	2-4	50.0	+10.25

COURSE RECORD

	Total W-R	Non-Hndcps Hurdles	Chases	Hndcps Hurdles	Chases	NH Flat	Per cent	£1 Level Stake
Musselbgh	1-3	0-1	0-1	1-1	0-0	0-0	33.3	+8.00
Perth	1-5	0-0	0-0	1-1	0-2	0-2	20.0	-1.75

WINNING HORSES

Horse	Races Run	1st	2nd	3rd	£
Golden Sparkle	8	2	3	1	7798
Total winning prize-money					**£7798**
Favourites	**1-2**		**50.0%**		**1.25**

ALEXANDRA DUNN

WELLINGTON, SOMERSET

	No. of Hrs	Races Run	1st	2nd	3rd	Unpl	Per cent	£1 Level Stake
NH Flat	0	0	0	0	0	0	0.0	0.00
Hurdles	5	13	2	2	2	7	15.4	+3.00
Chases	3	5	2	0	1	2	40.0	-1.67
Totals	**7**	**18**	**4**	**2**	**3**	**9**	**22.2**	**+1.33**

JOCKEYS

	W-R	Per cent	£1 Level Stake
Mrs Alex Dunn	3-7	42.9	+6.33
Paul Moloney	1-3	33.3	+3.00

COURSE RECORD

	Total W-R	Non-Hndcps Hurdles	Chases	Hndcps Hurdles	Chases	NH Flat	Per cent	£1 Level Stake
Taunton	2-5	1-3	0-0	1-2	0-0	0-0	40.0	+11.00
Wetherby	1-1	0-0	1-1	0-0	0-0	0-0	100.0	+0.67
Southwell	1-2	0-1	1-1	0-0	0-0	0-0	50.0	-0.33

WINNING HORSES

Horse	Races Run	1st	2nd	3rd	£
*Helium	3	1	1	1	4549
Arrayan	4	1	1	0	2738
*Double Mead	2	2	0	0	1976
Total winning prize-money					£9263
Favourites	2-5		40.0%		-1.67

SEAMUS DURACK

BAYDON, WILTS

	No. of Hrs	Races Run	1st	2nd	3rd	Unpl	Per cent	£1 Level Stake
NH Flat	4	7	1	0	1	5	14.3	-4.00
Hurdles	9	28	4	0	3	21	14.3	+6.25
Chases	0	0	0	0	0	0	0.0	0.00
Totals	12	35	5	0	4	26	14.3	+2.25
11-12	10	16	0	0	1	15	0.0	-16.00
10-11	2	4	0	1	0	3	0.0	-4.00

JOCKEYS

	W-R	Per cent	£1 Level Stake
Conor O'Farrell	3-12	25.0	+8.50
Jason Maguire	1-3	33.3	+0.75
Richard Killoran	1-4	25.0	+9.00

COURSE RECORD

	Total W-R	Non-Hndcps Hurdles	Chases	Hndcps Hurdles	Chases	NH Flat	Per cent	£1 Level Stake
Mrket Rsn	1-2	1-2	0-0	0-0	0-0	0-0	50.0	+8.00
Uttoxeter	1-2	0-0	0-0	1-1	0-0	0-1	50.0	+5.50
Worcester	1-3	0-0	0-0	1-2	0-0	0-1	33.3	+10.00
Ffos Las	1-3	1-1	0-0	0-2	0-0	0-0	33.3	+0.75
Wincanton	1-4	0-1	0-0	0-1	0-0	1-2	25.0	-1.00

WINNING HORSES

Horse	Races Run	1st	2nd	3rd	£
Grand Gold	3	2	0	0	12671
On Alert	6	1	0	2	2144
Canadian Diamond	3	1	0	0	1949
Centasia	1	1	0	0	1365
Total winning prize-money					£18129
Favourites	2-5		40.0%		1.75

CLAIRE DYSON

CLEEVE PRIOR, WORCS

	No. of Hrs	Races Run	1st	2nd	3rd	Unpl	Per cent	£1 Level Stake
NH Flat	6	9	0	0	1	8	0.0	-9.00
Hurdles	19	69	9	5	4	51	13.0	+30.63
Chases	10	40	4	4	7	25	10.0	-17.00
Totals	27	118	13	9	12	84	11.0	+4.63
11-12	21	94	3	8	5	78	3.2	-77.00
10-11	29	114	8	9	7	90	7.0	-15.67

BY MONTH

NH Flat	W-R	Per cent	£1 Level Stake	Hurdles	W-R	Per cent	£1 Level Stake
May	0-1	0.0	-1.00	May	0-3	0.0	-3.00
June	0-2	0.0	-2.00	June	0-6	0.0	-6.00
July	0-0	0.0	0.00	July	0-5	0.0	-5.00
August	0-0	0.0	0.00	August	0-5	0.0	-5.00
September	0-0	0.0	0.00	September	0-2	0.0	-2.00
October	0-1	0.0	-1.00	October	3-7	42.9	+57.63
November	0-3	0.0	-3.00	November	1-4	25.0	-2.00
December	0-0	0.0	0.00	December	1-9	11.1	-3.50
January	0-2	0.0	-2.00	January	0-4	0.0	-4.00
February	0-0	0.0	0.00	February	3-12	25.0	+11.50
March	0-0	0.0	0.00	March	0-6	0.0	-6.00
April	0-0	0.0	0.00	April	1-6	16.7	-2.00

Chases	W-R	Per cent	£1 Level Stake	Totals	W-R	Per cent	£1 Level Stake
May	0-2	0.0	-2.00	May	0-6	0.0	-6.00
June	0-5	0.0	-5.00	June	0-13	0.0	-13.00
July	0-1	0.0	-1.00	July	0-6	0.0	-6.00
August	0-2	0.0	-2.00	August	0-7	0.0	-7.00
September	0-0	0.0	0.00	September	0-2	0.0	-2.00
October	0-5	0.0	-5.00	October	3-13	23.1	+51.63
November	2-4	50.0	+8.00	November	3-11	27.3	+3.00
December	0-4	0.0	-4.00	December	1-13	7.7	-7.50
January	0-4	0.0	-4.00	January	0-10	0.0	-10.00
February	1-3	33.3	+3.00	February	4-15	26.7	+14.50
March	1-4	25.0	+1.00	March	1-10	10.0	-5.00
April	0-6	0.0	-6.00	April	1-12	8.3	-8.00

DISTANCE

Hurdles	W-R	Per cent	£1 Level Stake	Chases	W-R	Per cent	£1 Level Stake
2m-2m3f	1-21	4.8	-15.50	2m-2m3f	0-5	0.0	-5.00
2m4f-2m7f	5-30	16.7	+42.13	2m4f-2m7f	3-15	20.0	+3.00
3m+	3-18	16.7	+4.00	3m+	1-20	5.0	-15.00

TYPE OF RACE

Non-Handicaps	W-R	Per cent	£1 Level Stake	Handicaps	W-R	Per cent	£1 Level Stake
Nov Hrdls	1-12	8.3	-8.00	Nov Hrdls	1-14	7.1	-5.00
Hrdls	0-6	0.0	-6.00	Hrdls	6-32	18.8	+49.13

Nov Chs	0-5	0.0	-5.00	Nov Chs	1-4	25.0	+2.00
Chases	0-0	0.0	0.00	Chases	3-31	9.7	-14.00
Sell/Claim	1-4	25.0	+1.50	Sell/Claim	0-1	0.0	-1.00

Totals	8	29	4	3	0	22	13.8	+17.75
11-12	*10*	*30*	*4*	*5*	*2*	*19*	*13.3*	*-9.00*
10-11	*10*	*25*	*3*	*0*	*1*	*21*	*12.0*	*+8.00*

RACE CLASS / FIRST TIME OUT

	W-R	Per cent	£1 Level Stake		W-R	Per cent	£1 Level Stake
Class 1	0-0	0.0	0.00	Bumpers	0-6	0.0	-6.00
Class 2	0-2	0.0	-2.00	Hurdles	1-15	6.7	-6.00
Class 3	0-6	0.0	-6.00	Chases	0-6	0.0	-6.00
Class 4	3-43	7.0	-24.00				
Class 5	10-59	16.9	+44.63	Totals	1-27	3.7	-18.00
Class 6	0-8	0.0	-8.00				

JOCKEYS

	W-R	Per cent	£1 Level Stake
Nick Scholfield	7-33	21.2	+10.63
Gerald Quinn	5-46	10.9	+24.00
Daniel Hiskett	1-4	25.0	+5.00

JOCKEYS

	W-R	Per cent	£1 Level Stake
A P McCoy	2-2	100.0	+8.00
Andrew Thornton	1-8	12.5	-5.25
Gerard Tumelty	1-16	6.3	+18.00

COURSE RECORD

	Total W-R	Non-Hndcps Hurdles	Chases	Hndcps Hurdles	Chases	NH Flat	Per cent	£1 Level Stake
Taunton	2-5	0-1	0-0	0-2	2-2	0-0	40.0	+7.00
Wincanton	2-7	0-2	0-0	2-2	0-3	0-0	28.6	+46.63
Towcester	2-14	0-1	0-0	0-4	2-8	0-1	14.3	-3.00
Folkestone	1-4	0-1	0-2	1-1	0-0	0-0	25.0	+1.50
Chepstow	1-6	0-2	0-0	1-3	0-1	0-0	16.7	+3.00
Doncaster	1-7	0-1	0-0	1-4	0-1	0-1	14.3	+2.00
Ludlow	1-7	1-2	0-0	0-3	0-1	0-1	14.3	-1.50
Stratford	1-7	0-2	0-0	1-4	0-1	0-1	14.3	-5.00
Worcester	1-8	0-0	0-0	1-2	0-4	0-2	12.5	+3.00
Uttoxeter	1-11	1-4	0-0	0-4	0-2	0-1	9.1	-7.00

COURSE RECORD

	Total W-R	Non-Hndcps Hurdles	Chases	Hndcps Hurdles	Chases	NH Flat	Per cent	£1 Level Stake
Fakenham	1-1	0-0	0-0	1-1	0-0	0-0	100.0	+33.00
Worcester	1-1	0-0	1-1	0-0	0-0	0-0	100.0	+1.50
Hereford	1-2	0-0	1-1	0-1	0-0	0-0	50.0	+0.75
Uttoxeter	1-3	0-0	0-0	1-3	0-0	0-0	33.3	+4.50

WINNING HORSES

Horse	Races Run	1st	2nd	3rd	£
Musical Wedge	11	2	1	5	5829
Neltara	6	1	3	0	3639
*Cheat The Cheater	4	1	0	0	3119
*Khazium	3	1	0	1	2599
Boomtown	8	3	0	0	5873
Quayside Court	10	2	3	0	4204
Giveitachance	6	3	0	1	6114
Total winning prize-money					**£31377**
Favourites	2-4		**50.0%**		0.63

WINNING HORSES

Horse	Races Run	1st	2nd	3rd	£
Shilpa	6	1	0	0	4874
Red Not Blue	7	3	0	0	10279
Total winning prize-money					**£15153**
Favourites	2-3		**66.7%**		2.25

SIMON EARLE

TYTHERINGTON, WILTS

	No. of Hrs	Races Run	1st	2nd	3rd	Unpl	Per cent	£1 Level Stake
NH Flat	0	0	0	0	0	0	0.0	0.00
Hurdles	7	23	2	3	0	18	8.7	+18.50
Chases	2	6	2	0	0	4	33.3	-0.75

TIM EASTERBY

GREAT HABTON, N YORKS

	No. of Hrs	Races Run	1st	2nd	3rd	Unpl	Per cent	£1 Level Stake
NH Flat	10	15	2	0	2	11	13.3	+11.00
Hurdles	15	58	10	8	7	33	17.2	-10.63
Chases	6	24	4	2	3	15	16.7	-2.59
Totals	28	97	16	10	12	59	16.5	-2.22
11-12	*21*	*87*	*7*	*12*	*13*	*55*	*8.0*	*-54.44*
10-11	*27*	*94*	*9*	*15*	*14*	*56*	*9.6*	*-42.17*

BY MONTH

NH Flat	W-R	Per cent	£1 Level Stake	Hurdles	W-R	Per cent	£1 Level Stake
May	0-0	0.0	0.00	May	0-6	0.0	-6.00
June	0-0	0.0	0.00	June	0-3	0.0	-3.00
July	0-0	0.0	0.00	July	0-2	0.0	-2.00
August	0-0	0.0	0.00	August	1-1	100.0	+3.33
September	0-0	0.0	0.00	September	0-5	0.0	-5.00
October	0-2	0.0	-2.00	October	0-5	0.0	-5.00
November	1-2	50.0	+15.00	November	3-10	30.0	+14.50
December	0-2	0.0	-2.00	December	1-7	14.3	-4.75
January	0-0	0.0	0.00	January	0-3	0.0	-3.00
February	0-2	0.0	-2.00	February	1-5	20.0	-3.33
March	1-3	33.3	+6.00	March	1-4	25.0	0.00
April	0-4	0.0	-4.00	April	3-7	42.9	+3.63

Chases	W-R	Per cent	£1 Level Stake	Totals	W-R	Per cent	£1 Level Stake
May	1-3	33.3	+3.50	May	1-9	11.1	-2.50

Month	W-R	Per cent	£1 Level Stake	Month	W-R	Per cent	£1 Level Stake
June	0-1	0.0	-1.00	June	0-4	0.0	-4.00
July	0-1	0.0	-1.00	July	0-3	0.0	-3.00
August	0-0	0.0	0.00	August	1-1	100.0	+3.33
September	0-0	0.0	0.00	September	0-5	0.0	-5.00
October	1-2	50.0	+7.00	October	1-9	11.1	0.00
November	0-2	0.0	-2.00	November	4-14	28.6	+27.50
December	0-4	0.0	-4.00	December	1-13	7.7	-10.75
January	1-2	50.0	+2.00	January	1-5	20.0	-1.00
February	1-6	16.7	-4.09	February	2-13	15.4	-9.42
March	0-2	0.0	-2.00	March	2-9	22.2	+4.00
April	0-1	0.0	-1.00	April	3-12	25.0	-1.37

	Total W-R	Non-Hndcps Hurdles	Chases	Hndcps Hurdles	Chases	NH Flat	Per cent	£1 Level Stake
Hexham	1-3	1-2	0-0	0-0	0-0	0-1	33.3	-0.50
Sedgefield	1-13	1-10	0-0	0-1	0-1	0-1	7.7	-10.75

WINNING HORSES

Horse	Races Run	1st	2nd	3rd	£
Trustan Times	4	2	1	1	50758
Zitenka	10	1	0	0	12512
Fourjacks	8	4	1	0	17097
Tiptoeaway	1	1	0	0	5954
Deepsand	5	2	2	0	7798
Mojolika	4	2	1	0	7018
Runswick Royal	2	1	0	0	3899
Favours Brave	5	1	1	1	2534
One For Luck	6	1	0	1	2053
Run Ructions Run	2	1	0	1	1625
Total winning prize-money					**£111248**
Favourites	7-13		53.8%		5.78

DISTANCE

Hurdles	W-R	Per cent	£1 Level Stake	Chases	W-R	Per cent	£1 Level Stake
2m-2m3f	6-42	14.3	-21.38	2m-2m3f	1-6	16.7	+3.00
2m4f-2m7f	3-13	23.1	+2.75	2m4f-2m7f	3-12	25.0	+0.41
3m+	1-3	33.3	+8.00	3m+	0-6	0.0	-6.00

TYPE OF RACE

Non-Handicaps	W-R	Per cent	£1 Level Stake	Handicaps	W-R	Per cent	£1 Level Stake
Nov Hrdls	2-12	16.7	-7.25	Nov Hrdls	3-14	21.4	-3.88
Hrdls	1-20	5.0	-18.33	Hrdls	4-11	36.4	+19.83
Nov Chs	2-3	66.7	+2.91	Nov Chs	0-1	0.0	-1.00
Chases	0-0	0.0	0.00	Chases	2-20	10.0	-4.50
Sell/Claim	0-1	0.0	-1.00	Sell/Claim	0-0	0.0	0.00

RACE CLASS

	W-R	Per cent	£1 Level Stake
Class 1	1-8	12.5	+3.00
Class 2	1-9	11.1	-2.50
Class 3	4-12	33.3	+14.41
Class 4	7-41	17.1	-4.04
Class 5	2-13	15.4	-8.08
Class 6	1-14	7.1	-5.00

FIRST TIME OUT

	W-R	Per cent	£1 Level Stake
Bumpers	2-10	20.0	+16.00
Hurdles	1-13	7.7	-2.00
Chases	2-5	40.0	+10.50
Totals	5-28	17.9	+24.50

JOCKEYS

	W-R	Per cent	£1 Level Stake
Brian Harding	6-10	60.0	+14.03
Dougie Costello	5-25	20.0	+7.08
A P McCoy	2-5	40.0	+3.17
Wilson Renwick	2-5	40.0	+21.00
Lucy Alexander	1-12	8.3	-7.50

COURSE RECORD

	Total W-R	Non-Hndcps Hurdles	Chases	Hndcps Hurdles	Chases	NH Flat	Per cent	£1 Level Stake
Wetherby	4-25	0-5	1-2	2-5	1-9	0-4	16.0	+2.25
Carlisle	3-6	0-0	0-0	2-3	0-1	1-2	50.0	+9.88
Mrket Rsn	3-17	0-3	1-1	1-8	1-3	0-2	17.6	-4.26
Haydock	2-7	0-4	0-0	1-1	0-1	1-1	28.6	+21.00
Ayr	1-1	1-1	0-0	0-0	0-0	0-0	100.0	+0.67
Perth	1-2	0-0	0-0	1-1	0-1	0-0	50.0	+2.50

MICHAEL EASTERBY

SHERIFF HUTTON, N YORKS

	No. of Hrs	Races Run	1st	2nd	3rd	Unpl	Per cent	£1 Level Stake
NH Flat	6	7	1	0	1	5	14.3	+10.00
Hurdles	20	53	4	5	2	42	7.5	-27.50
Chases	8	32	4	5	5	18	12.5	+0.50
Totals	29	92	9	10	8	65	9.8	-17.00
11-12	32	97	8	5	17	67	8.2	-49.50
10-11	35	99	8	14	10	67	8.1	-42.90

JOCKEYS

	W-R	Per cent	£1 Level Stake
Jake Greenall	7-78	9.0	-10.50
Richard Johnson	1-1	100.0	+3.50
Wilson Renwick	1-2	50.0	+1.00

COURSE RECORD

	Total W-R	Non-Hndcps Hurdles	Chases	Hndcps Hurdles	Chases	NH Flat	Per cent	£1 Level Stake
Catterick	2-9	0-1	0-2	1-3	0-1	1-2	22.2	+14.00
Mrket Rsn	2-9	1-4	0-1	1-2	0-2	0-0	22.2	+3.50
Stratford	1-2	0-0	0-0	0-0	1-2	0-0	50.0	+11.00
Bangor	1-6	0-2	1-1	0-1	0-2	0-0	16.7	-1.50
Southwell	1-11	0-2	0-0	0-3	1-6	0-0	9.1	+1.00
Wetherby	1-11	0-4	0-0	1-5	0-1	0-1	9.1	-4.00
Sedgefield	1-14	0-6	1-1	0-1	0-4	0-2	7.1	-11.00

WINNING HORSES

Horse	Races Run	1st	2nd	3rd	£
Sheepclose	6	1	1	1	3899
Shadows Lengthen	7	2	1	1	7538
City Ground	5	1	0	1	3249
Lightening Rod	4	1	1	1	3119

*Rear Admiral	2	1	1	0	2599
Saints And Sinners	8	2	2	0	5068
Carlton Jack	1	1	0	0	1437
Total winning prize-money					**£26909**
Favourites	**1-5**		**20.0%**		**1.00**

DAVID M EASTERBY

SHERIFF HUTTON, N YORKS

	No. of Hrs	Races Run	1st	2nd	3rd	Unpl	Per cent	£1 Level Stake
NH Flat	0	0	0	0	0	0	0.0	0.00
Hurdles	0	0	0	0	0	0	0.0	0.00
Chases	1	4	1	0	0	3	25.0	+2.00
Totals	1	4	1	0	0	3	25.0	+2.00
11-12	2	2	1	0	1	0	50.0	+0.10
10-11	1	1	0	0	0	1	0.0	-1.00

JOCKEYS

	W-R	Per cent	£1 Level Stake
Mr T Greenall	1-3	33.3	+3.00

COURSE RECORD

	Total W-R	Non-Hndcps Hurdles	Chases	Hndcps Hurdles	Chases	NH Flat	Per cent	£1 Level Stake
Bangor	1-1	0-0	1-1	0-0	0-0	0-0	100.0	+5.00

WINNING HORSES

Horse	Races Run	1st	2nd	3rd	£
Classinaglass	4	1	0	0	2560
Total winning prize-money					**£2560**
Favourites	**0-0**		**0.0%**		**0.00**

BRIAN ECKLEY

LLANSPYDDID, POWYS

	No. of Hrs	Races Run	1st	2nd	3rd	Unpl	Per cent	£1 Level Stake
NH Flat	5	8	0	0	2	6	0.0	-8.00
Hurdles	3	24	1	2	2	19	4.2	-17.00
Chases	0	0	0	0	0	0	0.0	0.00
Totals	7	32	1	2	4	25	3.1	-25.00
11-12	3	8	0	0	0	8	0.0	-8.00
10-11	4	6	0	1	0	5	0.0	-6.00

JOCKEYS

	W-R	Per cent	£1 Level Stake
Gary Derwin	1-19	5.3	-12.00

COURSE RECORD

	Total W-R	Non-Hndcps Hurdles	Chases	Hndcps Hurdles	Chases	NH Flat	Per cent	£1 Level Stake
Ffos Las	1-6	0-2	0-0	1-2	0-0	0-2	16.7	+1.00

WINNING HORSES

Horse	Races Run	1st	2nd	3rd	£
Lucky Prince	9	1	2	0	2599
Total winning prize-money					**£2599**
Favourites	**0-0**		**0.0%**		**0.00**

CHARLES EGERTON

CHADDLEWORTH, BERKS

	No. of Hrs	Races Run	1st	2nd	3rd	Unpl	Per cent	£1 Level Stake
NH Flat	4	9	0	1	0	8	0.0	-9.00
Hurdles	7	22	3	5	1	13	13.6	-1.00
Chases	4	9	0	1	1	7	0.0	-9.00
Totals	12	40	3	7	2	28	7.5	-19.00
11-12	16	40	4	4	3	29	10.0	0.00
10-11	19	56	5	4	6	41	8.9	-31.65

JOCKEYS

	W-R	Per cent	£1 Level Stake
Gavin Sheehan	1-2	50.0	+5.00
Jimmy McCarthy	1-6	16.7	-1.00
Sam Twiston-Davies	1-15	6.7	-6.00

COURSE RECORD

	Total W-R	Non-Hndcps Hurdles	Chases	Hndcps Hurdles	Chases	NH Flat	Per cent	£1 Level Stake
Lingfield	1-3	0-1	0-0	1-2	0-0	0-0	33.3	+6.00
Mrket Rsn	1-3	1-1	0-1	0-0	0-1	0-0	33.3	+2.00
Plumpton	1-6	0-1	0-0	1-2	0-2	0-1	16.7	+1.00

WINNING HORSES

Horse	Races Run	1st	2nd	3rd	£
Gee Hi	3	1	1	0	3249
Seedsman	5	1	2	1	2669
Capellini	7	1	2	0	2053
Total winning prize-money					**£7971**
Favourites	**0-20**		**0.0%**		**-20.00**

BRIAN ELLISON

NORTON, N YORKS

	No. of Hrs	Races Run	1st	2nd	3rd	Unpl	Per cent	£1 Level Stake
NH Flat	4	8	0	0	1	7	0.0	-8.00
Hurdles	59	207	29	34	26	118	14.0	-5.11
Chases	14	51	10	7	3	31	19.6	-3.88
Totals	64	266	39	41	30	156	14.7	-16.99
11-12	54	219	35	32	40	112	16.0	-58.14
10-11	29	107	21	13	17	56	19.6	+26.56

Class 5	8-36	22.2	-11.09	Totals	10-64 15.6 +12.10
Class 6	0-7	0.0	-7.00		

BY MONTH

NH Flat	W-R	Per cent	£1 Level Stake	Hurdles	W-R	Per cent	£1 Level Stake
May	0-0	0.0	0.00	May	0-10	0.0	-10.00
June	0-0	0.0	0.00	June	2-10	20.0	-0.90
July	0-0	0.0	0.00	July	1-8	12.5	+26.00
August	0-0	0.0	0.00	August	5-12	41.7	+1.95
September	0-0	0.0	0.00	September	2-11	18.2	-4.27
October	0-0	0.0	0.00	October	2-18	11.1	+19.25
November	0-2	0.0	-2.00	November	1-25	4.0	-10.00
December	0-2	0.0	-2.00	December	2-26	7.7	-14.90
January	0-1	0.0	-1.00	January	1-12	8.3	-5.00
February	0-3	0.0	-3.00	February	2-22	9.1	-15.00
March	0-0	0.0	0.00	March	5-33	15.2	-1.63
April	0-0	0.0	0.00	April	6-20	30.0	+9.39

Chases	W-R	Per cent	£1 Level Stake	Totals	W-R	Per cent	£1 Level Stake
May	0-0	0.0	0.00	May	0-10	0.0	-10.00
June	1-1	100.0	+4.00	June	3-11	27.3	+3.10
July	0-5	0.0	-5.00	July	1-13	7.7	+21.00
August	0-2	0.0	-2.00	August	5-14	35.7	-0.05
September	1-2	50.0	0.00	September	3-13	23.1	-4.27
October	1-3	33.3	+1.00	October	3-21	14.3	+20.25
November	1-6	16.7	-3.75	November	2-33	6.1	-15.75
December	1-7	14.3	-4.13	December	3-35	8.6	-21.03
January	2-6	33.3	+8.00	January	3-19	15.8	+2.00
February	1-7	14.3	-1.50	February	3-32	9.4	-19.50
March	1-6	16.7	-1.50	March	6-39	15.4	-3.13
April	1-6	16.7	+1.00	April	7-26	26.9	+10.39

DISTANCE

Hurdles	W-R	Per cent	£1 Level Stake	Chases	W-R	Per cent	£1 Level Stake
2m-2m3f	21-153	13.7	-32.80	2m-2m3f	1-17	5.9	-14.75
2m4f-2m7f	7-44	15.9	+36.25	2m4f-2m7f	7-21	33.3	+16.50
3m+	1-10	10.0	-8.56	3m+	2-13	15.4	-5.63

TYPE OF RACE

Non-Handicaps	W-R	Per cent	£1 Level Stake	Handicaps	W-R	Per cent	£1 Level Stake
Nov Hrdls	10-37	27.0	+29.57	Nov Hrdls	0-9	0.0	-9.00
Hrdls	4-39	10.3	-25.07	Hrdls	13-110	11.8	+6.53
Nov Chs	4-14	28.6	+4.75	Nov Chs	0-1	0.0	-1.00
Chases	0-0	0.0	0.00	Chases	6-36	16.7	-7.63
Sell/Claim	2-13	15.4	-8.13	Sell/Claim	0-0	0.0	0.00

RACE CLASS

	W-R	Per cent	£1 Level Stake
Class 1	0-15	0.0	-15.00
Class 2	4-35	11.4	+29.00
Class 3	9-60	15.0	-5.79
Class 4	18-113	15.9	-7.11

FIRST TIME OUT

	W-R	Per cent	£1 Level Stake
Bumpers	0-4	0.0	-4.00
Hurdles	7-55	12.7	+10.85
Chases	3-5	60.0	+5.25

JOCKEYS

	W-R	Per cent	£1 Level Stake
Danny Cook	23-142	16.2	-35.08
Craig Gallagher	3-8	37.5	+14.00
Denis O'Regan	3-15	20.0	-5.65
Aidan Coleman	2-8	25.0	+30.00
Miss H Bethell	2-8	25.0	+29.00
Kyle James	2-15	13.3	-3.25
Tom Bellamy	1-2	50.0	0.00
James Reveley	1-4	25.0	+3.00
Tom Scudamore	1-5	20.0	+2.00
Harry Haynes	1-7	14.3	+1.00

COURSE RECORD

	Total W-R	Non-Hndcps Hurdles	Non-Hndcps Chases	Hndcps Hurdles	Hndcps Chases	NH Flat	Per cent	£1 Level Stake
Wetherby	6-26	4-8	1-3	1-13	0-1	0-1	23.1	+1.11
Musselbgh	5-25	1-4	2-2	0-12	2-5	0-2	20.0	-0.52
Worcester	4-7	2-4	0-1	1-1	1-1	0-0	57.1	+2.48
Mrket Rsn	4-23	3-13	1-1	0-7	0-2	0-0	17.4	+24.50
Hexham	3-10	3-7	0-0	0-3	0-0	0-0	30.0	+0.54
Haydock	3-21	0-1	0-0	3-14	0-6	0-0	14.3	+11.00
Ayr	2-9	0-1	0-0	1-4	1-4	0-0	22.2	+5.50
Carlisle	2-10	0-3	0-0	1-5	1-2	0-0	20.0	-1.75
Ludlow	2-11	1-7	0-1	1-3	0-0	0-0	18.2	-3.42
Sedgefield	2-25	1-8	0-0	1-12	0-3	0-2	8.0	-20.30
Fakenham	1-5	0-1	0-0	0-3	1-1	0-0	20.0	-1.00
Southwell	1-7	0-2	0-1	1-3	0-1	0-0	14.3	+5.00
Doncaster	1-8	0-2	0-2	1-4	0-0	0-0	12.5	-5.38
Kelso	1-8	1-3	0-0	0-3	0-2	0-0	12.5	-4.75
Aintree	1-8	0-4	0-0	1-3	0-1	0-0	12.5	+26.00
Catterick	1-12	0-8	0-0	1-2	0-1	0-1	8.3	-5.00

WINNING HORSES

Horse	Races Run	1st	2nd	3rd	£
Fleet Dawn	7	3	1	1	37558
*Yesyoucan	7	3	2	0	33131
Bocciani	9	2	2	1	28636
Simonside	9	1	2	1	9697
Dusky Bob	7	2	0	1	12021
*Viva Colonia	4	2	0	0	11696
Mubrook	6	1	1	0	6498
Phase Shift	10	2	3	2	11723
*Local Present	9	2	0	0	7765
Red Inca	6	1	1	0	5848
Neptune Equester	4	2	0	0	7668
*Fine Kingdom	8	1	2	3	3574
*Discovery Bay	3	2	1	0	5235
Powerful Ambition	7	1	3	1	3285
*Porgy	4	2	0	1	3249
Forgotten Symphony	3	1	1	0	3249
*Totalize	4	2	1	0	6498

Musnad	4	2	0	0	5172
Stormy Weather	5	1	0	1	3080
Andreo Bambaleo	10	1	0	0	3054
Dilizan	1	1	0	0	2395
Rano Pano	9	1	0	3	2274
*Floral Patches	3	1	0	0	2053
Dream Risk	4	2	0	0	3469
Total winning prize-money					£218828
Favourites	14-40		35.0%		-5.94

GERRY ENRIGHT

LEWES, E SUSSEX

	No. of Hrs	Races Run	1st	2nd	3rd	Unpl	Per cent	£1 Level Stake
NH Flat	0	0	0	0	0	0	0.0	0.00
Hurdles	5	9	0	0	0	9	0.0	-9.00
Chases	2	6	1	1	0	4	16.7	+2.50
Totals	6	15	1	1	0	13	6.7	-6.50
11-12	6	14	0	1	2	11	0.0	-14.00
10-11	4	15	0	1	1	13	0.0	-15.00

JOCKEYS

	W-R	Per cent	£1 Level Stake
Colin Bolger	1-10	10.0	-1.50

COURSE RECORD

	Total W-R	Non-Hndcps Hurdles	Chases	Hndcps Hurdles	Chases	NH Flat	Per cent	£1 Level Stake
Fontwell	1-6	0-2	0-0	0-1	1-3	0-0	16.7	+2.50

WINNING HORSES

Horse	Races Run	1st	2nd	3rd	£
Doctor Ric	5	1	1	0	1819
Total winning prize-money					£1819
Favourites	0-0		0.0%		0.00

JAMES EUSTACE

NEWMARKET, SUFFOLK

	No. of Hrs	Races Run	1st	2nd	3rd	Unpl	Per cent	£1 Level Stake
NH Flat	1	1	0	0	0	1	0.0	-1.00
Hurdles	5	17	3	0	2	12	17.6	-4.50
Chases	1	1	0	0	0	1	0.0	-1.00
Totals	6	19	3	0	2	14	15.8	-6.50
11-12	9	42	0	4	8	30	0.0	-42.00
10-11	8	29	2	2	7	18	6.9	-4.50

JOCKEYS

	W-R	Per cent	£1 Level Stake
Paddy Brennan	1-2	50.0	+2.50
Paul Moloney	1-5	20.0	-2.00
Jack Quinlan	1-7	14.3	-2.00

COURSE RECORD

	Total W-R	Non-Hndcps Hurdles	Chases	Hndcps Hurdles	Chases	NH Flat	Per cent	£1 Level Stake
Mrket Rsn	1-1	0-0	0-0	1-1	0-0	0-0	100.0	+4.00
Folkestone	1-2	0-1	0-0	1-1	0-0	0-0	50.0	+2.50
Fontwell	1-3	1-1	0-0	0-1	0-0	0-1	33.3	0.00

WINNING HORSES

Horse	Races Run	1st	2nd	3rd	£
Wily Fox	7	2	0	1	5302
Iron Butterfly	3	1	0	0	3119
Total winning prize-money					£8421
Favourites	1-2		50.0%		3.00

DAVID EVANS

PANDY, MONMOUTHS

	No. of Hrs	Races Run	1st	2nd	3rd	Unpl	Per cent	£1 Level Stake
NH Flat	5	10	2	1	1	6	20.0	-1.50
Hurdles	24	77	6	7	14	50	7.8	-24.76
Chases	5	16	2	2	2	10	12.5	-4.00
Totals	28	103	10	10	17	66	9.7	-30.26
11-12	22	77	10	8	4	55	13.0	-11.75
10-11	24	60	10	3	6	41	16.7	+5.70

BY MONTH

NH Flat	W-R	Per cent	£1 Level Stake	Hurdles	W-R	Per cent	£1 Level Stake
May	0-0	0.0	0.00	May	0-2	0.0	-2.00
June	0-0	0.0	0.00	June	0-9	0.0	-9.00
July	0-0	0.0	0.00	July	1-11	9.1	-6.67
August	0-0	0.0	0.00	August	2-10	20.0	+25.91
September	1-4	25.0	+2.00	September	1-15	6.7	-10.50
October	0-0	0.0	0.00	October	2-10	20.0	-2.50
November	1-1	100.0	+1.50	November	0-6	0.0	-6.00
December	0-0	0.0	0.00	December	0-6	0.0	-6.00
January	0-1	0.0	-1.00	January	0-2	0.0	-2.00
February	0-0	0.0	0.00	February	0-1	0.0	-1.00
March	0-0	0.0	0.00	March	0-3	0.0	-3.00
April	0-3	0.0	-3.00	April	0-2	0.0	-2.00

Chases	W-R	Per cent	£1 Level Stake	Totals	W-R	Per cent	£1 Level Stake
May	0-2	0.0	-2.00	May	0-4	0.0	-4.00
June	0-0	0.0	0.00	June	0-9	0.0	-9.00
July	0-3	0.0	-3.00	July	1-14	7.1	-9.67
August	0-0	0.0	0.00	August	2-10	20.0	+25.91
September	2-3	66.7	+9.00	September	4-22	18.2	+0.50
October	0-3	0.0	-3.00	October	2-13	15.4	-5.50
November	0-3	0.0	-3.00	November	1-10	10.0	-7.50
December	0-1	0.0	-1.00	December	0-8	0.0	-8.00
January	0-0	0.0	0.00	January	0-3	0.0	-3.00
February	0-0	0.0	0.00	February	0-1	0.0	-1.00

March	0-1	0.0	-1.00
April	0-0	0.0	0.00

DISTANCE

Hurdles	W-R	Per cent	£1 Level Stake
2m-2m3f	5-49	10.2	-0.51
2m4f-2m7f	1-20	5.0	-16.25
3m+	0-8	0.0	-8.00

TYPE OF RACE

Non-Handicaps

	W-R	Per cent	£1 Level Stake
Nov Hrdls	0-5	0.0	-5.00
Hrdls	3-29	10.3	+13.83
Nov Chs	1-4	25.0	-2.00
Chases	0-0	0.0	0.00
Sell/Claim	1-4	25.0	-2.09

RACE CLASS

	W-R	Per cent	£1 Level Stake
Class 1	0-1	0.0	-1.00
Class 2	0-2	0.0	-2.00
Class 3	0-8	0.0	-8.00
Class 4	7-67	10.4	-4.67
Class 5	1-18	5.6	-16.09
Class 6	2-7	28.6	+1.50

JOCKEYS

	W-R	Per cent	£1 Level Stake
Aidan Coleman	10-48	20.8	+24.74

COURSE RECORD

	Total W-R	Non-Hndcps Hurdles	Chases	Hndcps Hurdles	Chases	NH Flat	Per cent	£1 Level Stake
Stratford	3-13	2-6	0-0	0-4	1-2	0-1	23.1	+3.24
Hereford	2-13	0-1	1-1	0-9	0-1	1-1	15.4	-5.00
Exeter	1-1	0-0	0-0	1-1	0-0	0-0	100.0	+2.75
Fontwell	1-4	1-3	0-0	0-1	0-0	0-0	25.0	+0.50
Nton Abbot	1-7	1-3	0-0	0-4	0-0	0-0	14.3	+27.00
Ludlow	1-15	0-5	0-1	1-5	0-2	0-2	6.7	-11.25
Ffos Las	1-18	0-5	0-2	0-6	0-3	1-2	5.6	-15.50

WINNING HORSES

Horse	Races Run	1st	2nd	3rd	£
Shabak Hom	8	1	1	2	4224
Aviso	10	1	1	0	3899
King's Wharf	7	2	1	2	6498
Bajan Hero	5	1	0	1	3080
Scotsbrook Cloud	6	1	2	0	2599
Annaluna	8	1	0	4	2599
Choisirez	6	1	0	1	1949
John Reel	3	1	1	1	1754

March	0-4	0.0	-4.00
April	0-5	0.0	-5.00

Chases

Chases	W-R	Per cent	£1 Level Stake
2m-2m3f	1-5	20.0	+5.00
2m4f-2m7f	0-5	0.0	-5.00
3m+	1-6	16.7	-4.00

Handicaps

	W-R	Per cent	£1 Level Stake
Nov Hrdls	1-7	14.3	-3.25
Hrdls	1-32	3.1	-28.25
Nov Chs	0-3	0.0	-3.00
Chases	1-9	11.1	+1.00
Sell/Claim	0-0	0.0	0.00

FIRST TIME OUT

	W-R	Per cent	£1 Level Stake
Bumpers	2-5	40.0	+3.50
Hurdles	0-22	0.0	-22.00
Chases	0-1	0.0	-1.00
Totals	2-28	7.1	-19.50

Third Of The Third		3	1	1	0	1365
Total winning prize-money						£27967
Favourites	4-13		30.8%			-1.01

JAMES EVANS

BROADWAS, WORCS

	No. of Hrs	Races Run	1st	2nd	3rd	Unpl	Per cent	£1 Level Stake
NH Flat	2	2	0	0	0	2	0.0	-2.00
Hurdles	11	35	5	5	5	20	14.3	+9.50
Chases	5	21	3	1	3	14	14.3	-8.42
Totals	14	58	8	6	8	36	13.8	-0.92
11-12	17	63	6	4	9	43	9.5	-30.43
10-11	17	96	6	11	8	71	6.3	-46.17

JOCKEYS

	W-R	Per cent	£1 Level Stake
Liam Treadwell	3-14	21.4	+13.50
Mark Quinlan	2-13	15.4	+3.75
Felix De Giles	1-4	25.0	+0.50
Robert Kirk	1-6	16.7	-2.00
Timmy Murphy	1-13	7.7	-8.67

COURSE RECORD

	Total W-R	Non-Hndcps Hurdles	Chases	Hndcps Hurdles	Chases	NH Flat	Per cent	£1 Level Stake
Stratford	2-2	0-0	0-0	1-1	1-1	0-0	100.0	+15.33
Worcester	2-13	0-5	0-1	2-3	0-4	0-0	15.4	0.00
Uttoxeter	1-2	0-1	0-0	1-1	0-0	0-0	50.0	+3.50
Huntingdon	1-3	0-0	0-0	1-2	0-1	0-0	33.3	+10.00
Mrket Rsn	1-3	0-0	0-0	0-1	1-2	0-0	33.3	+1.50
Fontwell	1-6	0-0	0-0	0-4	1-2	0-0	16.7	-2.25

WINNING HORSES

Horse	Races Run	1st	2nd	3rd	£
Prophete De Guye	9	1	1	1	3249
Trackmate	8	2	3	1	5783
Roc De Guye	8	1	1	1	2599
Mexican Bob	3	2	0	0	4289
Heezagrey	13	2	1	4	3509
Total winning prize-money					£19429
Favourites	1-4		25.0%		-0.25

JAMES EWART

LANGHOLM, DUMFRIES & G'WAY

	No. of Hrs	Races Run	1st	2nd	3rd	Unpl	Per cent	£1 Level Stake
NH Flat	8	13	0	1	2	10	0.0	-13.00
Hurdles	19	54	1	5	11	37	1.9	-52.27
Chases	13	62	14	8	7	33	22.6	-19.20
Totals	34	129	15	14	20	80	11.6	-84.47

11-12	40	153	23	22	21	87	15.0	-24.12
10-11	42	126	16	8	12	90	12.7	+21.14

Class 5	4-27	14.8	-15.15	Totals	3-34	8.8 -23.87
Class 6	0-13	0.0	-13.00			

BY MONTH

NH Flat	W-R	Per cent	£1 Level Stake	Hurdles	W-R	Per cent	£1 Level Stake
May	0-2	0.0	-2.00	May	0-6	0.0	-6.00
June	0-0	0.0	0.00	June	0-0	0.0	0.00
July	0-0	0.0	0.00	July	0-0	0.0	0.00
August	0-0	0.0	0.00	August	0-0	0.0	0.00
September	0-0	0.0	0.00	September	0-0	0.0	0.00
October	0-0	0.0	0.00	October	0-1	0.0	-1.00
November	0-3	0.0	-3.00	November	0-3	0.0	-3.00
December	0-3	0.0	-3.00	December	1-11	9.1	-9.27
January	0-1	0.0	-1.00	January	0-9	0.0	-9.00
February	0-1	0.0	-1.00	February	0-5	0.0	-5.00
March	0-0	0.0	0.00	March	0-12	0.0	-12.00
April	0-3	0.0	-3.00	April	0-7	0.0	-7.00

Chases	W-R	Per cent	£1 Level Stake	Totals	W-R	Per cent	£1 Level Stake
May	0-0	0.0	0.00	May	0-8	0.0	-8.00
June	0-0	0.0	0.00	June	0-0	0.0	0.00
July	0-0	0.0	0.00	July	0-0	0.0	0.00
August	0-0	0.0	0.00	August	0-0	0.0	0.00
September	0-0	0.0	0.00	September	0-0	0.0	0.00
October	1-1	100.0	+1.38	October	1-2	50.0	+0.38
November	2-4	50.0	+3.75	November	2-10	20.0	-2.25
December	1-12	8.3	-9.38	December	2-26	7.7	-21.65
January	1-9	11.1	-6.50	January	1-19	5.3	-16.50
February	3-9	33.3	+0.10	February	3-15	20.0	-5.90
March	3-12	25.0	-4.63	March	3-24	12.5	-16.63
April	3-15	20.0	-3.93	April	3-25	12.0	-13.93

DISTANCE

Hurdles	W-R	Per cent	£1 Level Stake	Chases	W-R	Per cent	£1 Level Stake
2m-2m3f	0-26	0.0	-26.00	2m-2m3f	12-29	41.4	+7.30
2m4f-2m7f	1-16	6.3	-14.27	2m4f-2m7f	1-15	6.7	-11.00
3m+	0-12	0.0	-12.00	3m+	1-18	5.6	-15.50

TYPE OF RACE

Non-Handicaps	W-R	Per cent	£1 Level Stake	Handicaps	W-R	Per cent	£1 Level Stake
Nov Hrdls	0-16	0.0	-16.00	Nov Hrdls	0-6	0.0	-6.00
Hrdls	1-13	7.7	-11.27	Hrdls	0-17	0.0	-17.00
Nov Chs	4-12	33.3	+2.00	Nov Chs	0-5	0.0	-5.00
Chases	0-1	0.0	-1.00	Chases	10-44	22.7	-15.20
Sell/Claim	0-2	0.0	-2.00	Sell/Claim	0-0	0.0	0.00

RACE CLASS / FIRST TIME OUT

	W-R	Per cent	£1 Level Stake		W-R	Per cent	£1 Level Stake
Class 1	0-3	0.0	-3.00	Bumpers	0-8	0.0	-8.00
Class 2	0-5	0.0	-5.00	Hurdles	0-16	0.0	-16.00
Class 3	1-21	4.8	-18.63	Chases	3-10	30.0	+0.13
Class 4	10-60	16.7	-29.70				

JOCKEYS

	W-R	Per cent	£1 Level Stake
Brian Hughes	10-89	11.2	-59.85
Dale Irving	3-19	15.8	-9.75
Ryan Mania	1-2	50.0	+1.75
Graham Watters	1-3	33.3	-0.63

COURSE RECORD

	Total W-R	Non-Hndcps Hurdles	Chases	Hndcps Hurdles	Chases	NH Flat	Per cent	£1 Level Stake
Newcastle	3-21	0-7	1-2	0-3	2-6	0-3	14.3	-11.13
Kelso	2-10	0-2	0-0	0-1	2-5	0-2	20.0	-5.13
Musselbgh	2-19	1-6	1-2	0-1	0-6	0-4	10.5	-13.27
Ayr	2-23	0-7	0-2	0-5	2-7	0-2	8.7	-18.52
Catterick	1-5	0-1	1-2	0-0	0-2	0-0	20.0	-1.25
Carlisle	1-6	0-1	0-0	0-1	1-3	0-1	16.7	-4.43
Hexham	1-6	0-2	0-0	0-1	1-3	0-0	16.7	-1.50
Sedgefield	1-7	0-0	0-0	0-3	1-4	0-0	14.3	-4.25
Wetherby	1-9	0-3	0-2	0-1	1-2	0-1	11.1	-5.75
Doncaster	1-12	0-1	1-3	0-2	0-6	0-0	8.3	-8.25

WINNING HORSES

Horse	Races Run	1st	2nd	3rd	£
Wilde Pastures	6	3	1	1	15465
Sacre Toi	8	4	1	2	14296
Zaru	4	1	0	0	3769
Sleep In First	8	4	1	1	7538
Civil Unrest	7	1	1	0	3249
Lord Wishes	5	1	2	1	3249
*Lets Get Serious	4	1	0	0	3054
Total winning prize-money					**£50620**
Favourites	10-24		41.7%		1.27

RICHARD FAHEY

MUSLEY BANK, N YORKS

	No. of Hrs	Races Run	1st	2nd	3rd	Unpl	Per cent	£1 Level Stake
NH Flat	1	3	2	0	0	1	66.7	+3.00
Hurdles	8	26	0	5	4	17	0.0	-26.00
Chases	0	0	0	0	0	0	0.0	0.00
Totals	9	29	2	5	4	18	6.9	-23.00
11-12	12	36	4	6	2	24	11.1	-24.75
10-11	12	38	1	5	4	28	2.6	-28.00

JOCKEYS

	W-R	Per cent	£1 Level Stake
Brian Hughes	2-22	9.1	-16.00

COURSE RECORD

	Total W-R	Non-Hndcps Hurdles	Chases	Hndcps Hurdles	Chases	NH Flat	Per cent	£1 Level Stake
Huntingdon	1-2	0-1	0-0	0-0	0-0	1-1	50.0	0.00
Wetherby	1-4	0-3	0-0	0-0	0-0	1-1	25.0	0.00

WINNING HORSES

Horse	Races Run	1st	2nd	3rd	£
Dakar Run	3	2	0	0	3202
Total winning prize-money					£3202
Favourites	1-2		50.0%		0.00

CHRIS FAIRHURST

MIDDLEHAM MOOR, N YORKS

	No. of Hrs	Races Run	1st	2nd	3rd	Unpl	Per cent	£1 Level Stake
NH Flat	1	1	0	0	0	1	0.0	-1.00
Hurdles	4	14	2	1	1	10	14.3	-4.50
Chases	0	0	0	0	0	0	0.0	0.00
Totals	5	15	2	1	1	11	13.3	-5.50
11-12	3	12	0	2	1	9	0.0	-12.00
10-11	5	13	1	1	1	10	7.7	+38.00

JOCKEYS

	W-R	Per cent	£1 Level Stake
Jonathan England	2-3	66.7	+6.50

COURSE RECORD

	Total W-R	Non-Hndcps Hurdles	Chases	Hndcps Hurdles	Chases	NH Flat	Per cent	£1 Level Stake
Newcastle	1-1	0-0	0-0	1-1	0-0	0-0	100.0	+3.50
Sedgefield	1-1	0-0	0-0	1-1	0-0	0-0	100.0	+4.00

WINNING HORSES

Horse	Races Run	1st	2nd	3rd	£
Mootabar	7	2	0	0	3899
Total winning prize-money					£3899
Favourites	1-3		33.3%		1.50

JOHN FERGUSON

COWLINGE, SUFFOLK

	No. of Hrs	Races Run	1st	2nd	3rd	Unpl	Per cent	£1 Level Stake
NH Flat	7	10	2	0	0	8	20.0	-6.00
Hurdles	41	94	17	13	16	48	18.1	-41.01
Chases	10	21	4	4	1	12	19.0	-0.25
Totals	54	125	23	17	17	68	18.4	-47.26
11-12	26	77	24	11	6	36	31.2	+33.03
10-11	3	6	0	0	1	5	0.0	-6.00

BY MONTH

NH Flat	W-R	Per cent	£1 Level Stake		Hurdles	W-R	Per cent	£1 Level Stake
May	0-0	0.0	0.00		May	0-1	0.0	-1.00
June	0-0	0.0	0.00		June	1-4	25.0	+0.33
July	0-0	0.0	0.00		July	0-2	0.0	-2.00
August	0-0	0.0	0.00		August	0-1	0.0	-1.00
September	0-1	0.0	-1.00		September	1-2	50.0	+1.00
October	0-1	0.0	-1.00		October	1-17	5.9	-14.80
November	1-1	100.0	+1.00		November	0-0	0.0	0.00
December	0-1	0.0	-1.00		December	4-16	25.0	+0.63
January	0-0	0.0	0.00		January	4-10	40.0	+5.76
February	1-1	100.0	+1.00		February	4-16	25.0	-9.15
March	0-2	0.0	-2.00		March	1-12	8.3	-10.78
April	0-3	0.0	-3.00		April	1-13	7.7	-10.00

Chases	W-R	Per cent	£1 Level Stake		Totals	W-R	Per cent	£1 Level Stake
May	0-0	0.0	0.00		May	0-1	0.0	-1.00
June	0-1	0.0	-1.00		June	1-5	20.0	-0.67
July	0-0	0.0	0.00		July	0-2	0.0	-2.00
August	0-0	0.0	0.00		August	0-1	0.0	-1.00
September	0-0	0.0	0.00		September	1-3	33.3	0.00
October	1-4	25.0	+3.50		October	2-22	9.1	-12.30
November	0-1	0.0	-1.00		November	1-2	50.0	0.00
December	1-6	16.7	-2.75		December	5-23	21.7	-3.12
January	0-2	0.0	-2.00		January	4-12	33.3	+3.76
February	1-3	33.3	+3.50		February	6-20	30.0	-4.65
March	0-2	0.0	-2.00		March	1-16	6.3	-14.78
April	1-2	50.0	+1.50		April	2-18	11.1	-11.50

DISTANCE

Hurdles	W-R	Per cent	£1 Level Stake		Chases	W-R	Per cent	£1 Level Stake
2m-2m3f	15-75	20.0	-26.54		2m-2m3f	3-12	25.0	+5.25
2m4f-2m7f	2-18	11.1	-13.47		2m4f-2m7f	0-6	0.0	-6.00
3m+	0-1	0.0	-1.00		3m+	1-3	33.3	+0.50

TYPE OF RACE

Non-Handicaps	W-R	Per cent	£1 Level Stake		Handicaps	W-R	Per cent	£1 Level Stake
Nov Hrdls	10-38	26.3	-11.63		Nov Hrdls	0-3	0.0	-3.00
Hrdls	6-32	18.8	-9.72		Hrdls	1-21	4.8	-16.67
Nov Chs	1-8	12.5	-0.50		Nov Chs	0-2	0.0	-2.00
Chases	1-4	25.0	-0.50		Chases	2-6	33.3	+3.75
Sell/Claim	0-0	0.0	0.00		Sell/Claim	0-0	0.0	0.00

RACE CLASS

	W-R	Per cent	£1 Level Stake
Class 1	1-15	6.7	-10.67
Class 2	0-7	0.0	-7.00
Class 3	1-13	7.7	-11.78
Class 4	17-67	25.4	-8.31

FIRST TIME OUT

	W-R	Per cent	£1 Level Stake
Bumpers	2-7	28.6	-3.00
Hurdles	6-40	15.0	-16.69
Chases	1-7	14.3	-3.50

Class 5	1-12	8.3	-6.00	Totals	9-54 16.7	-23.19
Class 6	3-11	27.3	-3.50			

JOCKEYS

	W-R	Per cent	£1 Level Stake
Denis O'Regan	16-83	19.3	-31.70
Jack Quinlan	6-31	19.4	-8.06
Mr James Ferguson	1-3	33.3	+0.50

COURSE RECORD

	Total W-R	Non-Hndcps Hurdles Chases	Hndcps Hurdles Chases	NH Flat	Per cent	£1 Level Stake
Doncaster	5-11	2-5 0-2	0-0 1-1	2-3	45.5	+3.78
Catterick	3-4	3-4 0-0	0-0 0-0	0-0	75.0	+7.16
Leicester	2-2	2-2 0-0	0-0 0-0	0-0	100.0	+1.93
Musselbgh	2-9	1-4 0-1	0-2 1-2	0-0	22.2	+1.75
Ayr	1-1	1-1 0-0	0-0 0-0	0-0	100.0	+0.22
Chepstow	1-2	1-2 0-0	0-0 0-0	0-0	50.0	+2.33
Plumpton	1-2	1-2 0-0	0-0 0-0	0-0	50.0	+1.00
Towcester	1-3	0-2 1-1	0-0 0-0	0-0	33.3	+4.50
Hereford	1-5	0-2 0-1	1-2 0-0	0-0	20.0	-0.67
Mrket Rsn	1-5	1-3 0-1	0-0 0-1	0-1	20.0	-3.50
Wetherby	1-5	1-2 0-0	0-2 0-0	0-1	20.0	-3.47
Stratford	1-6	1-3 0-1	0-2 0-0	0-0	16.7	-3.00
Ludlow	1-7	1-5 0-1	0-0 0-1	0-0	14.3	-4.80
Aintree	1-8	1-3 0-0	0-4 0-0	0-1	12.5	-3.00
Fakenham	1-11	0-7 1-2	0-1 0-1	0-0	9.1	-7.50

WINNING HORSES

Horse	Races Run	1st	2nd	3rd	£
*Ruacana	4	2	0	0	22532
*Zuider Zee	3	1	1	1	5393
Monarch's Way	4	1	0	0	4431
*Darley Sun	3	1	1	1	3899
*Buthelezi	3	2	0	0	7148
Pine Creek	4	2	0	1	7148
Memorabilia	3	1	1	0	3769
Once More Dubai	2	1	0	0	3422
Whispering Gallery	2	2	0	0	6368
Cayman Islands	7	1	1	0	3249
Red Devil Boys	2	2	0	0	4874
*Haymarket	4	1	0	2	3249
*Bordoni	4	1	1	0	3249
Dubawi Phantom	3	1	0	0	2599
Chat Room	1	1	0	0	2274
Creekside	4	1	0	0	2274
*Macklin	1	1	0	0	1647
Purple Bay	3	1	0	0	1560
Total winning prize-money					**£89085**
Favourites	11-27		40.7%		-6.42

MARJORIE FIFE

STILLINGTON, N YORKS

	No. of Hrs	Races Run	1st	2nd	3rd	Unpl	Per cent	£1 Level Stake
NH Flat	0	0	0	0	0	0	0.0	0.00
Hurdles	5	25	2	0	3	20	8.0	+31.00
Chases	0	0	0	0	0	0	0.0	0.00
Totals	5	25	2	0	3	20	8.0	+31.00
11-12	5	37	1	3	5	28	2.7	-29.50
10-11	3	15	1	1	2	11	6.7	-6.50

JOCKEYS

	W-R	Per cent	£1 Level Stake
Kyle James	2-17	11.8	+39.00

COURSE RECORD

	Total W-R	Non-Hndcps Hurdles Chases	Hndcps Hurdles Chases	NH Flat	Per cent	£1 Level Stake
Wetherby	1-3	1-1 0-0	0-2 0-0	0-0	33.3	+48.00
Mrket Rsn	1-6	0-0 0-0	1-6 0-0	0-0	16.7	-1.00

WINNING HORSES

Horse	Races Run	1st	2nd	3rd	£
King Mak	10	1	0	1	2534
Ritsi	8	1	0	1	1779
Total winning prize-money					**£4313**
Favourites	0-0		0.0%		0.00

TIM FITZGERALD

NORTON, N YORKS

	No. of Hrs	Races Run	1st	2nd	3rd	Unpl	Per cent	£1 Level Stake
NH Flat	1	2	0	0	0	2	0.0	-2.00
Hurdles	3	6	0	0	0	6	0.0	-6.00
Chases	3	16	2	3	2	9	12.5	+3.50
Totals	7	24	2	3	2	17	8.3	-4.50
11-12	4	11	1	3	0	7	9.1	-5.00
10-11	5	16	1	2	0	13	6.3	-12.00

JOCKEYS

	W-R	Per cent	£1 Level Stake
Brian Hughes	2-14	14.3	+5.50

COURSE RECORD

	Total W-R	Non-Hndcps Hurdles Chases	Hndcps Hurdles Chases	NH Flat	Per cent	£1 Level Stake
Carlisle	1-1	0-0 0-0	0-0 1-1	0-0	100.0	+11.00
Cartmel	1-1	0-0 0-0	0-0 1-1	0-0	100.0	+6.50

WINNING HORSES

Horse	Races Run	1st	2nd	3rd	£
Acrai Rua	10	2	1	1	10072
Total winning prize-money					£10072
Favourites	0-0		0.0%		0.00

JOHN FLINT

KENFIG HILL, BRIDGEND

	No. of Hrs	Races Run	1st	2nd	3rd	Unpl	Per cent	£1 Level Stake
NH Flat	7	13	0	3	1	9	0.0	-13.00
Hurdles	28	83	11	9	11	52	13.3	-19.75
Chases	11	31	0	2	4	25	0.0	-31.00
Totals	40	127	11	14	16	86	8.7	-63.75
11-12	39	125	15	8	10	92	12.0	+26.33
10-11	37	107	10	12	14	71	9.3	+14.38

BY MONTH

NH Flat	W-R	Per cent	£1 Level Stake	Hurdles	W-R	Per cent	£1 Level Stake
May	0-0	0.0	0.00	May	2-13	15.4	-4.50
June	0-1	0.0	-1.00	June	1-9	11.1	-5.25
July	0-0	0.0	0.00	July	1-9	11.1	-1.00
August	0-1	0.0	-1.00	August	4-9	44.4	+12.75
September	0-0	0.0	0.00	September	0-5	0.0	-5.00
October	0-2	0.0	-2.00	October	1-11	9.1	-5.50
November	0-2	0.0	-2.00	November	1-6	16.7	-3.25
December	0-2	0.0	-2.00	December	0-4	0.0	-4.00
January	0-0	0.0	0.00	January	0-2	0.0	-2.00
February	0-2	0.0	-2.00	February	0-5	0.0	-5.00
March	0-2	0.0	-2.00	March	1-6	16.7	+7.00
April	0-1	0.0	-1.00	April	0-4	0.0	-4.00

Chases	W-R	Per cent	£1 Level Stake	Totals	W-R	Per cent	£1 Level Stake
May	0-3	0.0	-3.00	May	2-16	12.5	-7.50
June	0-2	0.0	-2.00	June	1-12	8.3	-8.25
July	0-2	0.0	-2.00	July	1-11	9.1	-3.00
August	0-5	0.0	-5.00	August	4-15	26.7	+6.75
September	0-0	0.0	0.00	September	0-5	0.0	-5.00
October	0-5	0.0	-5.00	October	1-18	5.6	-12.50
November	0-2	0.0	-2.00	November	1-10	10.0	-7.25
December	0-5	0.0	-5.00	December	0-11	0.0	-11.00
January	0-0	0.0	0.00	January	0-2	0.0	-2.00
February	0-4	0.0	-4.00	February	0-11	0.0	-11.00
March	0-2	0.0	-2.00	March	1-10	10.0	+3.00
April	0-1	0.0	-1.00	April	0-6	0.0	-6.00

DISTANCE

Hurdles	W-R	Per cent	£1 Level Stake	Chases	W-R	Per cent	£1 Level Stake
2m-2m3f	5-43	11.6	-5.75	2m-2m3f	0-13	0.0	-13.00
2m4f-2m7f	4-30	13.3	-15.75	2m4f-2m7f	0-12	0.0	-12.00
3m+	2-10	20.0	+1.75	3m+	0-6	0.0	-6.00

TYPE OF RACE

	Non-Handicaps W-R	Per cent	£1 Level Stake	Handicaps W-R	Per cent	£1 Level Stake
Nov Hrdls	2-10	20.0	-2.00	1-3	33.3	-0.25
Hrdls	0-6	0.0	-6.00	5-52	9.6	-14.00
Nov Chs	0-7	0.0	-7.00	0-5	0.0	-5.00
Chases	0-0	0.0	0.00	0-19	0.0	-19.00
Sell/Claim	2-9	22.2	-2.50	1-4	25.0	+4.00

RACE CLASS

	W-R	Per cent	£1 Level Stake
Class 1	0-4	0.0	-4.00
Class 2	0-0	0.0	0.00
Class 3	2-14	14.3	+4.00
Class 4	4-58	6.9	-36.25
Class 5	5-41	12.2	-17.50
Class 6	0-10	0.0	-10.00

FIRST TIME OUT

	W-R	Per cent	£1 Level Stake
Bumpers	0-7	0.0	-7.00
Hurdles	3-26	11.5	-12.00
Chases	0-7	0.0	-7.00
Totals	3-40	7.5	-26.00

JOCKEYS

	W-R	Per cent	£1 Level Stake
Thomas Flint	8-66	12.1	-24.25
Sam Thomas	1-2	50.0	+3.00
Micheal Nolan	1-4	25.0	-0.50
Rhys Flint	1-25	4.0	-12.00

COURSE RECORD

	Total W-R	Non-Hndcps Hurdles	Chases	Hndcps Hurdles	Chases	NH Flat	Per cent	£1 Level Stake
Fakenham	2-5	1-3	0-0	1-2	0-0	0-0	40.0	+13.00
Ffos Las	2-18	0-1	0-1	2-7	0-5	0-4	11.1	-6.50
Hexham	1-2	1-1	0-0	0-0	0-1	0-0	50.0	+1.75
Leicester	1-2	1-1	0-0	0-0	0-1	0-0	50.0	+0.75
Towcester	1-5	0-0	0-0	1-1	0-2	0-2	20.0	+0.50
Worcester	1-5	0-0	0-0	1-3	0-1	0-1	20.0	+3.00
Fontwell	1-7	0-1	0-1	1-3	0-2	0-0	14.3	-4.25
Uttoxeter	1-7	0-1	0-0	1-4	0-1	0-1	14.3	+1.00
Stratford	1-10	1-2	0-0	0-7	0-1	0-0	10.0	-7.00

WINNING HORSES

Horse	Races Run	1st	2nd	3rd	£
Rowlestone Lad	5	2	0	1	9487
Enter Milan	3	1	0	0	5198
Patsy Cline	4	2	1	0	5496
First Beauty	9	1	2	2	2599
Captain Scarlett	10	2	0	1	4074
Kapdor	7	1	1	1	1779
*Bracken House	2	1	0	0	1689
Kilmore West	5	1	0	0	1622
Total winning prize-money					£31944
Favourites	4-56		7.1%		-44.00

S FLOOK

LEOMINSTER, HEREFORDSHIRE

	No. of Hrs	Races Run	1st	2nd	3rd	Unpl	Per cent	£1 Level Stake
NH Flat	0	0	0	0	0	0	0.0	0.00
Hurdles	0	0	0	0	0	0	0.0	0.00
Chases	8	32	5	6	3	18	15.6	-10.09
Totals	8	32	5	6	3	18	15.6	-10.09
11-12	7	26	8	3	3	12	30.8	+27.73
10-11	5	16	2	1	4	9	12.5	-1.00

JOCKEYS

	W-R	Per cent	£1 Level Stake
Mr R Jarrett	3-18	16.7	-4.72
Ben Poste	1-2	50.0	+0.63
Mr Matthew Barber	1-4	25.0	+2.00

COURSE RECORD

	Total W-R	Non-Hndcps Hurdles	Chases	Hndcps Hurdles	Chases	NH Flat	Per cent	£1 Level Stake
Ludlow	2-8	0-0	2-8	0-0	0-0	0-0	25.0	-3.22
Warwick	1-1	0-0	1-1	0-0	0-0	0-0	100.0	+5.00
Southwell	1-2	0-0	1-2	0-0	0-0	0-0	50.0	+0.63
Stratford	1-2	0-0	1-2	0-0	0-0	0-0	50.0	+6.50

WINNING HORSES

Horse	Races Run	1st	2nd	3rd	£
Rumbury Grey	6	1	2	1	10793
I Have Dreamed	3	1	0	1	2184
Island Life	5	2	0	0	3301
Gentle George	7	1	2	0	1248
Total winning prize-money					£17526
Favourites	2-8		25.0%		-3.84

RICHARD FORD

GARSTANG, LANCS

	No. of Hrs	Races Run	1st	2nd	3rd	Unpl	Per cent	£1 Level Stake
NH Flat	5	7	0	0	0	7	0.0	-7.00
Hurdles	10	20	2	3	0	15	10.0	-10.00
Chases	4	14	3	3	1	7	21.4	+2.25
Totals	17	41	5	6	1	29	12.2	-14.75
11-12	18	39	5	5	4	25	12.8	-6.50
10-11	11	33	3	1	2	27	9.1	-12.00

JOCKEYS

	W-R	Per cent	£1 Level Stake
Harry Challoner	3-27	11.1	-9.50
Richard Johnson	1-1	100.0	+1.75
Lucy Alexander	1-7	14.3	-1.00

COURSE RECORD

	Total W-R	Non-Hndcps Hurdles	Chases	Hndcps Hurdles	Chases	NH Flat	Per cent	£1 Level Stake
Bangor	2-6	0-0	0-0	1-4	1-2	0-0	33.3	+5.25
Perth	1-2	0-0	0-0	0-0	1-2	0-0	50.0	+4.00
Musselbgh	1-3	0-0	0-0	0-0	1-1	0-2	33.3	+4.50
Hexham	1-4	1-1	0-0	0-0	0-1	0-2	25.0	-2.50

WINNING HORSES

Horse	Races Run	1st	2nd	3rd	£
*Swaledale Lad	5	2	1	0	6404
Silver Steel	8	2	1	1	5848
Colditz	3	1	0	0	3054
Total winning prize-money					£15306
Favourites	1-1		100.0%		0.50

RICHENDA FORD

BROCKHAMPTON GREEN, DORSET

	No. of Hrs	Races Run	1st	2nd	3rd	Unpl	Per cent	£1 Level Stake
NH Flat	0	0	0	0	0	0	0.0	0.00
Hurdles	0	0	0	0	0	0	0.0	0.00
Chases	4	15	1	1	1	12	6.7	-9.50
Totals	4	15	1	1	1	12	6.7	-9.50
11-12	3	7	0	0	0	7	0.0	-7.00

JOCKEYS

	W-R	Per cent	£1 Level Stake
Andrew Thornton	1-8	12.5	-2.50

COURSE RECORD

	Total W-R	Non-Hndcps Hurdles	Chases	Hndcps Hurdles	Chases	NH Flat	Per cent	£1 Level Stake
Lingfield	1-3	0-0	0-1	0-0	1-2	0-0	33.3	+2.50

WINNING HORSES

Horse	Races Run	1st	2nd	3rd	£
Somerby	9	1	1	1	2669
Total winning prize-money					£2669
Favourites	0-0		0.0%		0.00

BRIAN FORSEY

ASH PRIORS, SOMERSET

	No. of Hrs	Races Run	1st	2nd	3rd	Unpl	Per cent	£1 Level Stake
NH Flat	1	1	0	0	0	1	0.0	-1.00
Hurdles	6	19	1	0	2	16	5.3	-10.00
Chases	1	6	1	1	0	4	16.7	0.00

Totals	6	26	2	1	2	21	7.7	-11.00
11-12	7	27	0	2	2	23	0.0	-27.00
10-11	4	16	0	1	1	14	0.0	-16.00

JOCKEYS

	W-R	Per cent	£1 Level Stake
Conor O'Farrell	1-1	100.0	+5.00
Wayne Kavanagh	1-16	6.3	-7.00

COURSE RECORD

	Total W-R	Non-Hndcps Hurdles	Chases	Hndcps Hurdles	Chases	NH Flat	Per cent	£1 Level Stake
Fontwell	1-2	0-0	0-0	1-1	0-1	0-0	50.0	+7.00
Taunton	1-4	0-1	0-0	0-1	1-2	0-0	25.0	+2.00

WINNING HORSES

Horse	Races Run	1st	2nd	3rd	£
Solitary Palm	7	1	1	0	3182
Aureate	9	1	0	1	1689
Total winning prize-money					£4871
Favourites	0-0		0.0%		0.00

JOANNE FOSTER

MENSTON, W YORKS

	No. of Hrs	Races Run	1st	2nd	3rd	Unpl	Per cent	£1 Level Stake
NH Flat	0	0	0	0	0	0	0.0	0.00
Hurdles	11	36	4	5	8	19	11.1	+47.50
Chases	6	31	6	4	7	14	19.4	+9.50
Totals	13	67	10	9	15	33	14.9	+57.00
11-12	6	20	2	0	7	11	10.0	-2.50
10-11	8	24	2	0	2	20	8.3	+9.00

BY MONTH

NH Flat	W-R	Per cent	£1 Level Stake	Hurdles	W-R	Per cent	£1 Level Stake
May	0-0	0.0	0.00	May	0-2	0.0	-2.00
June	0-0	0.0	0.00	June	1-5	20.0	+3.50
July	0-0	0.0	0.00	July	0-5	0.0	-5.00
August	0-0	0.0	0.00	August	0-1	0.0	-1.00
September	0-0	0.0	0.00	September	0-1	0.0	-1.00
October	0-0	0.0	0.00	October	0-2	0.0	-2.00
November	0-0	0.0	0.00	November	0-4	0.0	-4.00
December	0-0	0.0	0.00	December	0-3	0.0	-3.00
January	0-0	0.0	0.00	January	0-1	0.0	-1.00
February	0-0	0.0	0.00	February	1-5	20.0	+62.00
March	0-0	0.0	0.00	March	1-2	50.0	+1.50
April	0-0	0.0	0.00	April	1-5	20.0	-0.50

Chases	W-R	Per cent	£1 Level Stake	Totals	W-R	Per cent	£1 Level Stake
May	0-0	0.0	0.00	May	0-2	0.0	-2.00
June	0-0	0.0	0.00	June	1-5	20.0	+3.50
July	0-2	0.0	-2.00	July	0-7	0.0	-7.00

August	0-1	0.0	-1.00	August	0-2	0.0	-2.00
September	0-0	0.0		September	0-1	0.0	-1.00
October	0-5	0.0	-5.00	October	0-7	0.0	-7.00
November	1-3	33.3	+2.50	November	1-7	14.3	-1.50
December	0-2	0.0	-2.00	December	0-5	0.0	-5.00
January	0-3	0.0	-3.00	January	0-4	0.0	-4.00
February	2-3	66.7	+14.00	February	3-8	37.5	+76.00
March	3-8	37.5	+10.00	March	4-10	40.0	+11.50
April	0-4	0.0	-4.00	April	1-9	11.1	-4.50

DISTANCE

Hurdles	W-R	Per cent	£1 Level Stake	Chases	W-R	Per cent	£1 Level Stake
2m-2m3f	2-19	10.5	+51.50	2m-2m3f	1-4	25.0	+3.00
2m4f-2m7f	2-14	14.3	-1.00	2m4f-2m7f	1-8	12.5	-3.00
3m+	0-3	0.0	-3.00	3m+	4-19	21.1	+9.50

TYPE OF RACE

Non-Handicaps	W-R	Per cent	£1 Level Stake	Handicaps	W-R	Per cent	£1 Level Stake
Nov Hrdls	0-1	0.0	-1.00	Nov Hrdls	0-2	0.0	-2.00
Hrdls	0-1	0.0	-1.00	Hrdls	4-25	16.0	+58.50
Nov Chs	1-2	50.0	+3.00	Nov Chs	0-2	0.0	-2.00
Chases	0-0	0.0	0.00	Chases	5-27	18.5	+8.50
Sell/Claim	0-6	0.0	-6.00	Sell/Claim	0-1	0.0	-1.00

RACE CLASS / FIRST TIME OUT

	W-R	Per cent	£1 Level Stake		W-R	Per cent	£1 Level Stake
Class 1	0-0	0.0	0.00	Bumpers	0-0	0.0	0.00
Class 2	0-2	0.0	-2.00	Hurdles	0-10	0.0	-10.00
Class 3	0-7	0.0	-7.00	Chases	0-3	0.0	-3.00
Class 4	4-22	18.2	+0.50	---			
Class 5	6-36	16.7	+65.50	Totals	0-13	0.0	-13.00
Class 6	0-0	0.0	0.00				

JOCKEYS

	W-R	Per cent	£1 Level Stake
Samantha Drake	8-58	13.8	-8.00
Miss L Egerton	1-1	100.0	+66.00
Ryan Mania	1-2	50.0	+5.00

COURSE RECORD

	Total W-R	Non-Hndcps Hurdles	Chases	Hndcps Hurdles	Chases	NH Flat	Per cent	£1 Level Stake
Sedgefield	3-9	0-1	1-1	1-4	1-3	0-0	33.3	+4.50
Hexham	2-7	0-0	0-0	1-3	1-4	0-0	28.6	+7.00
Southwell	1-1	0-0	0-0	1-1	0-0	0-0	100.0	+2.50
Towcester	1-2	0-0	0-0	0-1	1-1	0-0	50.0	+7.00
Catterick	1-4	0-0	0-1	1-1	0-2	0-0	25.0	+63.00
Newcastle	1-4	0-0	0-0	0-2	1-2	0-0	25.0	+3.00
Mrket Rsn	1-10	0-2	0-0	0-2	1-6	0-0	10.0	0.00

WINNING HORSES

Horse	Races Run	1st	2nd	3rd	£
*Peaks Of Fire	6	1	0	2	3769
Leac An Scail	14	2	4	3	3171
Marino Prince	9	1	0	1	3119
*Keeverfield	10	2	1	2	4938
Cara Court	6	3	0	1	6728
Vardas Supreme	8	1	1	3	2144
Total winning prize-money					£23869
Favourites	2-6		33.3%		2.00

DEREK FRANKLAND

MIXBURY, OXON

	No. of Hrs	Races Run	1st	2nd	3rd	Unpl	Per cent	£1 Level Stake
NH Flat	0	0	0	0	0	0	0.0	0.00
Hurdles	3	11	1	0	1	9	9.1	+4.00
Chases	2	7	0	2	2	3	0.0	-7.00
Totals	4	18	1	2	3	12	5.6	-3.00
11-12	3	23	0	0	2	21	0.0	-23.00
10-11	5	17	0	1	3	13	0.0	-17.00

JOCKEYS

	W-R	Per cent	£1 Level Stake
David Bass	1-11	9.1	+4.00

COURSE RECORD

	Total W-R	Non-Hndcps Hurdles	Chases	Hndcps Hurdles	Chases	NH Flat	Per cent	£1 Level Stake
Uttoxeter	1-3	0-1	0-0	1-2	0-0	0-0	33.3	+12.00

WINNING HORSES

Horse	Races Run	1st	2nd	3rd	£
*Small Fly	3	1	0	1	2859
Total winning prize-money					£2859
Favourites	0-0		0.0%		0.00

JAMES FROST

SCORRITON, DEVON

	No. of Hrs	Races Run	1st	2nd	3rd	Unpl	Per cent	£1 Level Stake
NH Flat	0	0	0	0	0	0	0.0	0.00
Hurdles	17	47	2	2	1	42	4.3	-5.00
Chases	9	17	0	1	2	14	0.0	-17.00
Totals	21	64	2	3	3	56	3.1	-22.00
11-12	19	79	3	8	10	58	3.8	-51.50
10-11	24	107	6	11	10	80	5.6	-70.30

JOCKEYS

	W-R	Per cent	£1 Level Stake
Hadden Frost	2-57	3.5	-15.00

COURSE RECORD

	Total W-R	Non-Hndcps Hurdles	Chases	Hndcps Hurdles	Chases	NH Flat	Per cent	£1 Level Stake
Uttoxeter	1-5	0-3	0-0	1-1	0-1	0-0	20.0	+29.00
Exeter	1-7	0-3	0-0	1-2	0-2	0-0	14.3	+1.00

WINNING HORSES

Horse	Races Run	1st	2nd	3rd	£
Union Saint	11	2	2	1	5068
Total winning prize-money					£5068
Favourites	0-0		0.0%		0.00

HARRY FRY

SEABOROUGH, DORSET

	No. of Hrs	Races Run	1st	2nd	3rd	Unpl	Per cent	£1 Level Stake
NH Flat	8	11	2	3	2	4	18.2	-2.75
Hurdles	16	39	10	5	5	19	25.6	+15.85
Chases	7	20	7	3	2	8	35.0	+27.92
Totals	27	70	19	11	9	31	27.1	+41.02

BY MONTH

NH Flat	W-R	Per cent	£1 Level Stake	Hurdles	W-R	Per cent	£1 Level Stake
May	0-0	0.0	0.00	May	0-0	0.0	0.00
June	0-0	0.0	0.00	June	0-0	0.0	0.00
July	0-0	0.0	0.00	July	0-0	0.0	0.00
August	0-0	0.0	0.00	August	0-0	0.0	0.00
September	0-0	0.0	0.00	September	0-0	0.0	0.00
October	0-1	0.0	-1.00	October	2-7	28.6	+11.00
November	1-3	33.3	+1.50	November	2-7	28.6	-0.50
December	0-0	0.0	0.00	December	0-7	0.0	-7.00
January	0-0	0.0	0.00	January	0-1	0.0	-1.00
February	1-2	50.0	+1.75	February	2-6	33.3	-0.13
March	0-1	0.0	-1.00	March	3-6	50.0	+16.75
April	0-4	0.0	-4.00	April	1-5	20.0	-3.27

Chases	W-R	Per cent	£1 Level Stake	Totals	W-R	Per cent	£1 Level Stake
May	0-0	0.0	0.00	May	0-0	0.0	0.00
June	0-0	0.0	0.00	June	0-0	0.0	0.00
July	0-0	0.0	0.00	July	0-0	0.0	0.00
August	0-0	0.0	0.00	August	0-0	0.0	0.00
September	0-0	0.0	0.00	September	0-0	0.0	0.00
October	0-1	0.0	-1.00	October	2-9	22.2	+9.00
November	0-2	0.0	-2.00	November	3-12	25.0	-1.00
December	1-4	25.0	+17.00	December	1-11	9.1	+10.00
January	2-4	50.0	+2.75	January	2-5	40.0	+1.75

	W-R	Per cent	£1 Level Stake		W-R	Per cent	£1 Level Stake
February	3-3	100.0	+12.83	February	6-11	54.5	+14.45
March	0-0	0.0	0.00	March	3-7	42.9	+15.75
April	1-6	16.7	-1.67	April	2-15	13.3	-8.94

DISTANCE

Hurdles	W-R	Per cent	£1 Level Stake	Chases	W-R	Per cent	£1 Level Stake
2m-2m3f	4-16	25.0	+7.60	2m-2m3f	0-5	0.0	-5.00
2m4f-2m7f	5-21	23.8	+7.00	2m4f-2m7f	6-12	50.0	+22.92
3m+	1-2	50.0	+1.25	3m+	1-3	33.3	+10.00

TYPE OF RACE

Non-Handicaps	W-R	Per cent	£1 Level Stake	Handicaps	W-R	Per cent	£1 Level Stake
Nov Hrdls	7-16	43.8	+16.98	Nov Hrdls	0-1	0.0	-1.00
Hrdls	3-9	33.3	+12.88	Hrdls	0-13	0.0	-13.00
Nov Chs	4-9	44.4	+17.58	Nov Chs	1-3	33.3	+1.00
Chases	0-0	0.0	0.00	Chases	2-8	25.0	+9.33
Sell/Claim	0-0	0.0	0.00	Sell/Claim	0-0	0.0	0.00

RACE CLASS / FIRST TIME OUT

	W-R	Per cent	£1 Level Stake		W-R	Per cent	£1 Level Stake
Class 1	3-10	30.0	+9.38	Bumpers	0-8	0.0	-8.00
Class 2	0-5	0.0	-5.00	Hurdles	3-15	20.0	+6.25
Class 3	5-19	26.3	+16.83	Chases	0-4	0.0	-4.00
Class 4	10-25	40.0	+26.31				
Class 5	0-4	0.0	-4.00	Totals	3-27	11.1	-5.75
Class 6	1-7	14.3	-2.50				

JOCKEYS

	W-R	Per cent	£1 Level Stake
Noel Fehily	14-43	32.6	+30.19
Ryan Mahon	4-12	33.3	+14.83
Mr J Barber	1-4	25.0	+7.00

COURSE RECORD

	Total W-R	Non-Hndcps Hurdles	Chases	Hndcps Hurdles	Chases	NH Flat	Per cent	£1 Level Stake
Plumpton	4-4	2-2	2-2	0-0	0-0	0-0	100.0	+25.08
Newbury	4-5	1-1	1-1	0-0	0-1	2-2	80.0	+9.25
Taunton	3-7	2-3	0-0	0-1	1-1	0-2	42.9	+2.31
Wincanton	3-16	2-6	0-2	0-2	1-2	0-4	18.8	+7.25
Bangor	1-1	0-0	1-1	0-0	0-0	0-0	100.0	+0.50
Doncaster	1-3	1-2	0-0	0-0	0-0	0-0	33.3	-0.38
Ludlow	1-3	1-1	0-0	0-1	0-1	0-0	33.3	+4.00
Kempton	1-6	0-1	0-0	0-2	1-2	0-0	16.7	+7.00
Exeter	1-7	1-2	0-2	0-3	0-0	0-0	14.3	+4.00

WINNING HORSES

Horse	Races Run	1st	2nd	3rd	£
*Opening Batsman	6	3	1	0	69187
Violin Davis	7	4	0	1	24522
Rock On Ruby	3	1	1	1	10571
*Oscar Rock	3	2	1	0	10492
Highland Retreat	7	2	1	3	8994
*Dancingtilmidnight	3	2	0	0	10397
Henryville	4	1	1	1	4874
Karinga Dancer	3	2	0	0	7798
*Chemistry Master	4	1	0	0	3249
*Billy Merriott	2	1	0	0	2669
Total winning prize-money					£152753
Favourites	7-13		53.8%		4.64

CAROLINE FRYER

WYMONDHAM, NORFOLK

	No. of Hrs	Races Run	1st	2nd	3rd	Unpl	Per cent	£1 Level Stake
NH Flat	0	0	0	0	0	0	0.0	0.00
Hurdles	6	19	2	2	3	12	10.5	-3.25
Chases	4	7	0	0	1	6	0.0	-7.00
Totals	10	26	2	2	4	18	7.7	-10.25
11-12	5	6	1	3	0	2	16.7	-3.50
10-11	3	3	0	0	0	3	0.0	-3.00

JOCKEYS

	W-R	Per cent	£1 Level Stake
Miss B Andrews	1-7	14.3	+5.00
Harry Skelton	1-12	8.3	-8.25

COURSE RECORD

	Total W-R	Non-Hndcps Hurdles	Chases	Hndcps Hurdles	Chases	NH Flat	Per cent	£1 Level Stake
Fakenham	2-9	1-5	0-1	1-3	0-0	0-0	22.2	+6.75

WINNING HORSES

Horse	Races Run	1st	2nd	3rd	£
Riddlestown	7	1	2	1	3899
County Zen	4	1	0	0	2738
Total winning prize-money					£6637
Favourites	1-1		100.0%		2.75

SUSAN GARDNER

LONGDOWN, DEVON

	No. of Hrs	Races Run	1st	2nd	3rd	Unpl	Per cent	£1 Level Stake
NH Flat	10	20	2	2	3	13	10.0	+38.50
Hurdles	25	121	13	13	9	86	10.7	-11.55
Chases	6	23	6	4	3	10	26.1	+17.70
Totals	34	164	21	19	15	109	12.8	+44.45
11-12	26	98	11	5	5	77	11.2	-27.25
10-11	17	52	7	2	1	42	13.5	+8.50

	W-R	Per cent	£1 Level Stake	Totals	W-R	Per cent	£1 Level Stake
Class 5	7-52	13.5	+23.50	Totals	1-34	2.9	-29.50
Class 6	1-18	5.6	-10.50				

BY MONTH

NH Flat	W-R	Per cent	£1 Level Stake	Hurdles	W-R	Per cent	£1 Level Stake
May	0-2	0.0	-2.00	May	0-11	0.0	-11.00
June	0-1	0.0	-1.00	June	2-7	28.6	+1.25
July	0-3	0.0	-3.00	July	1-9	11.1	-5.25
August	1-3	33.3	+4.50	August	0-9	0.0	-9.00
September	0-0	0.0	0.00	September	1-6	16.7	0.00
October	0-1	0.0	-1.00	October	2-14	14.3	+34.00
November	0-3	0.0	-3.00	November	1-10	10.0	-6.50
December	0-1	0.0	-1.00	December	2-8	25.0	+2.00
January	0-0	0.0	0.00	January	1-6	16.7	-2.75
February	0-2	0.0	-2.00	February	0-9	0.0	-9.00
March	0-2	0.0	-2.00	March	0-16	0.0	-16.00
April	1-2	50.0	+49.00	April	3-16	18.8	+10.50

Chases	W-R	Per cent	£1 Level Stake	Totals	W-R	Per cent	£1 Level Stake
May	1-4	25.0	+0.50	May	1-17	5.9	-12.50
June	2-3	66.7	+11.50	June	4-11	36.4	+11.75
July	0-2	0.0	-2.00	July	1-14	7.1	-10.25
August	0-0	0.0	0.00	August	1-12	8.3	-4.50
September	0-0	0.0	0.00	September	1-6	16.7	0.00
October	0-0	0.0	0.00	October	2-15	13.3	+33.00
November	0-0	0.0	0.00	November	1-13	7.7	-9.50
December	1-2	50.0	+0.20	December	3-11	27.3	+1.20
January	1-5	20.0	+1.50	January	2-11	18.2	-1.25
February	0-2	0.0	-2.00	February	0-13	0.0	-13.00
March	0-2	0.0	-2.00	March	0-20	0.0	-20.00
April	1-3	33.3	+10.00	April	5-21	23.8	+69.50

DISTANCE

Hurdles	W-R	Per cent	£1 Level Stake	Chases	W-R	Per cent	£1 Level Stake
2m-2m3f	5-62	8.1	+2.00	2m-2m3f	0-1	0.0	-1.00
2m4f-2m7f	8-48	16.7	-2.75	2m4f-2m7f	1-6	16.7	+0.50
3m+	0-11	0.0	-11.00	3m+	5-16	31.3	+18.20

TYPE OF RACE

Non-Handicaps	W-R	Per cent	£1 Level Stake	Handicaps	W-R	Per cent	£1 Level Stake
Nov Hrdls	1-22	4.5	+19.00	Nov Hrdls	4-18	22.2	+0.75
Hrdls	0-11	0.0	-11.00	Hrdls	7-68	10.3	-23.50
Nov Chs	0-2	0.0	-2.00	Nov Chs	1-3	33.3	+3.50
Chases	0-0	0.0	0.00	Chases	5-18	27.8	+16.20
Sell/Claim	0-0	0.0	0.00	Sell/Claim	1-2	50.0	+3.00

RACE CLASS / FIRST TIME OUT

	W-R	Per cent	£1 Level Stake		W-R	Per cent	£1 Level Stake
Class 1	0-3	0.0	-3.00	Bumpers	0-10	0.0	-10.00
Class 2	0-2	0.0	-2.00	Hurdles	0-20	0.0	-20.00
Class 3	3-15	20.0	+12.50	Chases	1-4	25.0	+0.50
Class 4	10-74	13.5	+23.95				

JOCKEYS

	W-R	Per cent	£1 Level Stake
Miss Lucy Gardner	10-58	17.2	+55.95
Micheal Nolan	4-25	16.0	-6.00
Matt Griffiths	3-19	15.8	+34.50
Jack Doyle	1-3	33.3	+3.50
James Best	1-5	20.0	-0.50
Aidan Coleman	1-14	7.1	-8.00
D P Fahy	1-16	6.3	-11.00

COURSE RECORD

	Total W-R	Non-Hndcps Hurdles	Chases	Hndcps Hurdles	Chases	NH Flat	Per cent	£1 Level Stake
Exeter	5-31	1-8	0-0	2-17	2-5	0-1	16.1	+30.75
Nton Abbot	3-29	0-4	0-0	3-21	0-2	0-2	10.3	-1.00
Bangor	2-3	0-1	0-0	1-1	1-1	0-0	66.7	+3.70
Worcester	2-7	0-3	0-0	1-3	1-1	0-0	28.6	+5.00
Cartmel	1-2	0-1	0-0	0-0	1-1	0-0	50.0	+6.00
Mrket Rsn	1-2	0-0	0-0	0-1	0-0	1-1	50.0	+5.50
Fontwell	1-3	0-0	0-0	1-3	0-0	0-0	33.3	+0.50
Perth	1-3	0-0	0-0	0-2	1-1	0-0	33.3	+10.00
Ffos Las	1-5	0-1	0-0	1-4	0-0	0-0	20.0	-2.25
Stratford	1-9	0-2	0-0	0-3	0-1	1-3	11.1	+42.00
Taunton	1-9	0-1	0-0	1-7	0-0	0-1	11.1	-4.00
Uttoxeter	1-12	0-1	0-0	1-7	0-1	0-3	8.3	-8.25
Wincanton	1-15	0-5	0-0	1-6	0-2	0-2	6.7	-9.50

WINNING HORSES

Horse	Races Run	1st	2nd	3rd	£
Flying Award	8	3	1	0	22743
Sea Saffron	9	2	1	2	11047
Miss Saffron	3	1	1	0	7148
Look For Love	11	2	1	2	3899
Call Me Sir	10	3	1	0	9530
Southway Star	13	4	2	1	9520
Rafafie	2	1	0	0	2599
Storm Alert	7	2	2	2	4419
Bach On Tow	7	1	1	0	2060
Majestic Bull	9	1	1	1	1779
Youngstar	3	1	0	0	1365
Total winning prize-money					**£76109**
Favourites	7-13	53.8%			13.70

ROSEMARY GASSON

BALSCOTE, OXON

	No. of Hrs	Races Run	1st	2nd	3rd	Unpl	Per cent	£1 Level Stake
NH Flat	1	1	0	0	0	1	0.0	-1.00
Hurdles	2	9	0	2	2	5	0.0	-9.00
Chases	6	33	2	8	2	21	6.1	-22.00

Totals	8	43	2	10	4	27	4.7	-32.00
11-12	7	28	3	1	8	16	10.7	-14.13
10-11	3	16	2	2	2	10	12.5	-0.50

JOCKEYS

	W-R	Per cent	£1 Level Stake
Ben Poste	2-35	5.7	-24.00

COURSE RECORD

	Total W-R	Non-Hndcps Hurdles	Chases	Hndcps Hurdles	Chases	NH Flat	Per cent	£1 Level Stake
Uttoxeter	1-5	0-1	0-0	0-1	1-3	0-0	20.0	-0.50
Stratford	1-7	0-0	0-1	0-1	1-5	0-0	14.3	-0.50

WINNING HORSES

Horse	Races Run	1st	2nd	3rd	£
Gentleman Anshan	5	1	1	0	7596
Kilcascan	10	1	4	2	1819
Total winning prize-money					**£9415**
Favourites	0-4		0.0%		**-4.00**

MICHAEL GATES

CLIFFORD CHAMBERS, WARWICKS

	No. of Hrs	Races Run	1st	2nd	3rd	Unpl	Per cent	£1 Level Stake
NH Flat	1	4	0	0	0	4	0.0	-4.00
Hurdles	5	19	0	0	1	18	0.0	-19.00
Chases	4	19	2	1	1	15	10.5	-8.75
Totals	6	42	2	1	2	37	4.8	-31.75
11-12	7	26	3	0	3	20	11.5	-3.00
10-11	9	30	0	1	2	27	0.0	-30.00

JOCKEYS

	W-R	Per cent	£1 Level Stake
Nico de Boinville	2-25	8.0	-14.75

COURSE RECORD

	Total W-R	Non-Hndcps Hurdles	Chases	Hndcps Hurdles	Chases	NH Flat	Per cent	£1 Level Stake
Fakenham	1-4	0-0	0-2	0-1	1-1	0-0	25.0	-0.75
Worcester	1-7	0-2	0-0	0-2	1-2	0-1	14.3	0.00

WINNING HORSES

Horse	Races Run	1st	2nd	3rd	£
Full Ov Beans	14	2	1	1	6383
Total winning prize-money					**£6383**
Favourites	0-1		0.0%		**-1.00**

JONATHAN GEAKE

MARLBOROUGH, WILTS

	No. of Hrs	Races Run	1st	2nd	3rd	Unpl	Per cent	£1 Level Stake
NH Flat	1	1	0	0	0	1	0.0	-1.00
Hurdles	6	10	0	0	0	10	0.0	-10.00
Chases	3	17	2	7	2	6	11.8	-10.67
Totals	9	28	2	7	2	17	7.1	-21.67
11-12	10	19	1	1	1	16	5.3	-12.00
10-11	6	22	3	2	1	16	13.6	-7.50

JOCKEYS

	W-R	Per cent	£1 Level Stake
Mark Grant	2-26	7.7	-19.67

COURSE RECORD

	Total W-R	Non-Hndcps Hurdles	Chases	Hndcps Hurdles	Chases	NH Flat	Per cent	£1 Level Stake
Plumpton	2-14	0-1	0-0	0-0	2-12	0-1	14.3	-7.67

WINNING HORSES

Horse	Races Run	1st	2nd	3rd	£
Ballyman	7	1	4	2	1949
Beware Chalk Pit	7	1	3	0	1949
Total winning prize-money					**£3898**
Favourites	0-3		0.0%		**-3.00**

TOM GEORGE

SLAD, GLOUCS

	No. of Hrs	Races Run	1st	2nd	3rd	Unpl	Per cent	£1 Level Stake
NH Flat	8	9	0	2	0	7	0.0	-9.00
Hurdles	32	80	7	14	14	45	8.8	-44.70
Chases	41	155	32	23	16	84	20.6	+2.95
Totals	69	244	39	39	30	136	16.0	-50.75
11-12	61	245	40	41	29	135	16.3	-22.52
10-11	70	228	20	31	26	151	8.8	-97.47

BY MONTH

NH Flat	W-R	Per cent	£1 Level Stake	Hurdles	W-R	Per cent	£1 Level Stake
May	0-0	0.0	0.00	May	0-2	0.0	-2.00
June	0-0	0.0	0.00	June	0-1	0.0	-1.00
July	0-0	0.0	0.00	July	0-0	0.0	0.00
August	0-0	0.0	0.00	August	0-0	0.0	0.00
September	0-0	0.0	0.00	September	0-0	0.0	0.00
October	0-2	0.0	-2.00	October	0-6	0.0	-6.00
November	0-2	0.0	-2.00	November	3-21	14.3	-0.50
December	0-1	0.0	-1.00	December	1-9	11.1	-3.00
January	0-0	0.0	0.00	January	1-7	14.3	-4.80
February	0-2	0.0	-2.00	February	1-14	7.1	-11.90

March	0-1	0.0	-1.00	March	1-11	9.1	-6.50
April	0-1	0.0	-1.00	April	0-9	0.0	-9.00

Chases	W-R	Per cent	£1 Level Stake	Totals	W-R	Per cent	£1 Level Stake
May	1-6	16.7	0.00	May	1-8	12.5	-2.00
June	0-2	0.0	-2.00	June	0-3	0.0	-3.00
July	0-4	0.0	-4.00	July	0-4	0.0	-4.00
August	0-1	0.0	-1.00	August	0-1	0.0	-1.00
September	0-0	0.0	0.00	September	0-0	0.0	0.00
October	3-17	17.6	-4.63	October	3-25	12.0	-12.63
November	6-20	30.0	+14.00	November	9-43	20.9	+11.50
December	4-19	21.1	+0.38	December	5-29	17.2	-3.62
January	8-24	33.3	+13.07	January	9-31	29.0	+8.27
February	4-21	19.0	-8.88	February	5-37	13.5	-22.78
March	3-23	13.0	-0.50	March	4-35	11.4	-8.00
April	3-18	16.7	-3.50	April	3-28	10.7	-13.50

DISTANCE

Hurdles	W-R	Per cent	£1 Level Stake	Chases	W-R	Per cent	£1 Level Stake
2m-2m3f	5-44	11.4	-16.80	2m-2m3f	18-58	31.0	+21.75
2m4f-2m7f	1-22	4.5	-19.90	2m4f-2m7f	5-53	9.4	-28.55
3m+	1-14	7.1	-8.00	3m+	9-44	20.5	+9.75

TYPE OF RACE

Non-Handicaps	W-R	Per cent	£1 Level Stake	Handicaps	W-R	Per cent	£1 Level Stake
Nov Hrdls	6-28	21.4	-1.70	Nov Hrdls	0-10	0.0	-10.00
Hrdls	0-19	0.0	-19.00	Hrdls	1-22	4.5	-13.00
Nov Chs	8-31	25.8	-2.88	Nov Chs	5-21	23.8	+4.25
Chases	0-3	0.0	-3.00	Chases	19-100	19.0	+4.58
Sell/Claim	0-0	0.0	0.00	Sell/Claim	0-0	0.0	0.00

RACE CLASS / FIRST TIME OUT

	W-R	Per cent	£1 Level Stake		W-R	Per cent	£1 Level Stake
Class 1	2-32	6.3	-20.00	Bumpers	0-8	0.0	-8.00
Class 2	4-19	21.1	+4.00	Hurdles	2-25	8.0	-9.00
Class 3	15-63	23.8	+15.20	Chases	6-36	16.7	-5.00
Class 4	16-106	15.1	-38.95				
Class 5	2-15	13.3	-2.00	Totals	8-69	11.6	-22.00
Class 6	0-9	0.0	-9.00				

JOCKEYS

	W-R	Per cent	£1 Level Stake
Paddy Brennan	29-172	16.9	-37.25
Alain Cawley	3-9	33.3	+14.50
Mr F Tett	2-3	66.7	+8.50
Denis O'Regan	2-4	50.0	+2.50
Liam Heard	2-19	10.5	-5.00
Jason Maguire	1-2	50.0	+1.00

COURSE RECORD

	Total W-R	Non-Hndcps Hurdles	Non-Hndcps Chases	Hndcps Hurdles	Hndcps Chases	NH Flat	Per cent	£1 Level Stake
Wincanton	6-20	0-0	0-1	0-2	6-15	0-2	30.0	+7.07
Haydock	4-7	0-0	1-1	0-2	3-4	0-0	57.1	+23.50
Leicester	4-7	0-0	1-2	0-0	3-5	0-0	57.1	+10.88
Kempton	3-13	1-3	0-0	0-2	2-8	0-0	23.1	+5.00
Doncaster	2-8	1-2	0-0	0-2	1-4	0-0	25.0	+2.00
Warwick	2-9	0-2	1-3	0-2	1-2	0-0	22.2	+0.50
Exeter	2-11	1-4	1-5	0-0	0-2	0-0	18.2	-0.30
Chepstow	2-12	1-3	0-1	0-1	1-6	0-1	16.7	-2.00
Newbury	2-17	0-3	1-2	0-3	1-9	0-0	11.8	-9.00
Musselbgh	1-1	1-1	0-0	0-0	0-0	0-0	100.0	+1.10
Towcester	1-1	0-0	0-0	0-0	1-1	0-0	100.0	+5.00
Mrket Rsn	1-3	0-0	1-1	0-0	0-2	0-0	33.3	-1.00
Stratford	1-4	0-0	0-0	0-0	1-4	0-0	25.0	-1.50
Ffos Las	1-4	0-1	0-0	0-0	1-3	0-0	25.0	0.00
Southwell	1-5	0-2	0-0	0-0	1-3	0-0	20.0	-2.13
Taunton	1-5	0-1	1-2	0-1	0-1	0-0	20.0	-2.00
Aintree	1-7	0-0	1-1	0-0	0-6	0-0	14.3	-4.63
Perth	1-7	0-0	0-0	0-1	1-6	0-0	14.3	+1.50
Ludlow	1-10	0-3	0-1	0-3	1-3	0-0	10.0	-7.75
Wetherby	1-12	1-4	0-3	0-1	0-3	0-1	8.3	-5.00
Cheltenham	1-24	0-6	0-4	1-5	0-9	0-0	4.2	-15.00

WINNING HORSES

Horse	Races Run	1st	2nd	3rd	£
Olofi	3	1	0	0	56950
Majala	4	3	0	0	38643
Monsieur Cadou	5	2	0	1	24368
Big Fella Thanks	6	1	1	1	12512
Chartreux	6	2	3	0	24068
Rody	6	3	1	0	23725
Ballyallia Man	6	1	1	3	9384
Morgan's Bay	6	2	0	0	12346
Good Order	4	1	2	0	7798
Forgotten Gold	6	2	1	1	14111
Module	4	2	0	0	11047
Parsnip Pete	5	2	0	0	10131
Arthur's Pass	6	3	0	1	14128
*Lordofthehouse	4	2	0	0	9097
God's Own	5	2	1	2	7798
Back Bob Back	4	1	0	0	3769
Seigneur Des Bois	3	1	1	1	3769
Overnight Fame	4	1	0	1	3769
High Ho Sheriff	5	1	1	1	3607
Moscow Chancer	3	1	0	0	3249
Big Society	6	1	4	0	3249
Desperate Dex	6	2	3	0	5328
Be Definite	7	1	0	2	3054
The Darling Boy	4	1	2	1	1949
Total winning prize-money					£307849
Favourites	12-45		26.7%		-14.38

KAREN GEORGE

HIGHER EASTINGTON, DEVON

	No. of Hrs	Races Run	1st	2nd	3rd	Unpl	Per cent	£1 Level Stake
NH Flat	2	4	0	0	0	4	0.0	-4.00
Hurdles	6	26	1	3	5	17	3.8	-21.00
Chases	0	0	0	0	0	0	0.0	0.00
Totals	8	30	1	3	5	21	3.3	-25.00
11-12	7	15	1	1	4	9	6.7	-9.50
10-11	6	20	0	4	3	13	0.0	-20.00

JOCKEYS

	W-R	Per cent	£1 Level Stake
James Cowley	1-7	14.3	-2.00

COURSE RECORD

	Total W-R	Non-Hndcps Hurdles	Chases	Hndcps Hurdles	Chases	NH Flat	Per cent	£1 Level Stake
Warwick	1-6	0-2	0-0	1-4	0-0	0-0	16.7	-1.00

WINNING HORSES

Horse	Races Run	1st	2nd	3rd	£
Gizzit	14	1	3	3	1949
Total winning prize-money					£1949
Favourites	1-4		25.0%		1.00

NICK GIFFORD

FINDON, W SUSSEX

	No. of Hrs	Races Run	1st	2nd	3rd	Unpl	Per cent	£1 Level Stake
NH Flat	3	6	1	0	2	3	16.7	-4.09
Hurdles	15	42	5	5	6	26	11.9	+15.83
Chases	16	53	4	5	6	38	7.5	-22.00
Totals	26	101	10	10	14	67	9.9	-10.26
11-12	28	96	7	16	11	62	7.3	-67.89
10-11	34	130	17	18	14	81	13.1	-29.25

BY MONTH

NH Flat	W-R	Per cent	£1 Level Stake	Hurdles	W-R	Per cent	£1 Level Stake
May	0-1	0.0	-1.00	May	1-3	33.3	+1.50
June	0-2	0.0	-2.00	June	0-1	0.0	-1.00
July	0-0	0.0	0.00	July	0-0	0.0	0.00
August	0-0	0.0	0.00	August	0-0	0.0	0.00
September	0-0	0.0	0.00	September	0-1	0.0	-1.00
October	1-1	100.0	+0.91	October	0-6	0.0	-6.00
November	0-0	0.0	0.00	November	1-5	20.0	+6.00
December	0-0	0.0	0.00	December	0-6	0.0	-6.00
January	0-0	0.0	0.00	January	0-1	0.0	-1.00
February	0-1	0.0	-1.00	February	2-7	28.6	+28.83
March	0-1	0.0	-1.00	March	0-4	0.0	-4.00
April	0-0	0.0	0.00	April	1-8	12.5	-1.50

Chases	W-R	Per cent	£1 Level Stake	Totals	W-R	Per cent	£1 Level Stake
May	1-2	50.0	+3.00	May	2-6	33.3	+3.50
June	0-1	0.0	-1.00	June	0-4	0.0	-4.00
July	0-0	0.0	0.00	July	0-0	0.0	0.00
August	0-0	0.0	0.00	August	0-0	0.0	0.00
September	0-2	0.0	-2.00	September	0-3	0.0	-3.00
October	0-5	0.0	-5.00	October	1-12	8.3	-10.09
November	1-5	20.0	+1.00	November	2-10	20.0	+7.00
December	0-8	0.0	-8.00	December	0-14	0.0	-14.00
January	0-5	0.0	-5.00	January	0-6	0.0	-6.00
February	1-6	16.7	+2.00	February	3-14	21.4	+29.83
March	0-8	0.0	-8.00	March	0-13	0.0	-13.00
April	1-11	9.1	+1.00	April	2-19	10.5	-0.50

DISTANCE

Hurdles	W-R	Per cent	£1 Level Stake	Chases	W-R	Per cent	£1 Level Stake
2m-2m3f	4-25	16.0	+28.33	2m-2m3f	1-20	5.0	-8.00
2m4f-2m7f	1-15	6.7	-10.50	2m4f-2m7f	2-18	11.1	-7.00
3m+	0-2	0.0	-2.00	3m+	1-15	6.7	-7.00

TYPE OF RACE

Non-Handicaps	W-R	Per cent	£1 Level Stake	Handicaps	W-R	Per cent	£1 Level Stake
Nov Hrdls	0-12	0.0	-12.00	Nov Hrdls	0-2	0.0	-2.00
Hrdls	3-11	27.3	+8.33	Hrdls	2-17	11.8	+21.50
Nov Chs	0-7	0.0	-7.00	Nov Chs	1-9	11.1	+3.00
Chases	0-2	0.0	-2.00	Chases	3-35	8.6	-16.00
Sell/Claim	0-0	0.0	0.00	Sell/Claim	0-0	0.0	0.00

RACE CLASS / FIRST TIME OUT

RACE CLASS	W-R	Per cent	£1 Level Stake	FIRST TIME OUT	W-R	Per cent	£1 Level Stake
Class 1	0-5	0.0	-5.00	Bumpers	0-3	0.0	-3.00
Class 2	3-15	20.0	+39.00	Hurdles	0-11	0.0	-11.00
Class 3	1-17	5.9	-12.50	Chases	1-12	8.3	-7.00
Class 4	4-54	7.4	-34.67				
Class 5	1-5	20.0	+6.00	Totals	1-26	3.8	-21.00
Class 6	1-5	20.0	-3.09				

JOCKEYS

	W-R	Per cent	£1 Level Stake
Tom Cannon	4-29	13.8	-0.67
Denis O'Regan	3-23	13.0	-1.00
Thomas Garner	2-4	50.0	+34.50
A P McCoy	1-13	7.7	-11.09

COURSE RECORD

	Total W-R	Non-Hndcps Hurdles	Chases	Hndcps Hurdles	Chases	NH Flat	Per cent	£1 Level Stake
Ascot	2-9	0-0	0-1	1-4	1-3	0-1	22.2	+37.00
Plumpton	2-16	1-3	0-1	1-6	0-5	0-1	12.5	-5.00
Fontwell	2-18	0-8	0-1	0-3	1-3	1-3	11.1	-11.09

Ludlow	1-2	1-1	0-0	0-0	0-1	0-0	50.0	-0.17
Wincanton	1-3	0-0	0-0	0-1	1-2	0-0	33.3	+3.00
Folkestone	1-6	1-4	0-0	0-0	0-2	0-0	16.7	+5.00
Sandown	1-11	0-1	0-1	0-1	1-8	0-0	9.1	-3.00

WINNING HORSES

Horse	Races Run	1st	2nd	3rd	£
Fairy Rath	8	2	1	1	46136
On Trend	6	1	1	1	31280
Kuilsriver	5	2	1	0	29958
*Dollar Bill	8	2	0	3	5952
Utopian	4	1	1	0	3249
General Kutuzov	2	1	0	0	3054
Old Dreams	9	1	2	3	1437
Total winning prize-money					**£121066**
Favourites	2-4		50.0%		-0.26

ED DE GILES
LEDBURY, H'FORDS

	No. of Hrs	Races Run	1st	2nd	3rd	Unpl	Per cent	£1 Level Stake
NH Flat	1	2	0	0	0	2	0.0	-2.00
Hurdles	3	5	1	0	2	2	20.0	+3.00
Chases	3	12	1	2	1	8	8.3	-4.50
Totals	6	19	2	2	3	12	10.5	-3.50
11-12	9	32	2	3	8	19	6.3	-14.13
10-11	5	11	1	2	1	7	9.1	-6.50

JOCKEYS

	W-R	Per cent	£1 Level Stake
Liam Treadwell	1-6	16.7	+2.00
Felix De Giles	1-10	10.0	-2.50

COURSE RECORD

	Total W-R	Non-Hndcps Hurdles	Chases	Hndcps Hurdles	Chases	NH Flat	Per cent	£1 Level Stake
Musselbgh	1-1	0-0	0-0	0-0	1-1	0-0	100.0	+6.50
Southwell	1-1	0-0	0-0	1-1	0-0	0-0	100.0	+7.00

WINNING HORSES

Horse	Races Run	1st	2nd	3rd	£
Prince Of Dreams	8	1	2	1	12996
Mutanaker	4	1	0	1	1949
Total winning prize-money					**£14945**
Favourites	0-0		0.0%		0.00

JONATHEN DE GILES
STANTON FITZWARREN, WILTS

	No. of Hrs	Races Run	1st	2nd	3rd	Unpl	Per cent	£1 Level Stake
NH Flat	1	1	0	0	0	1	0.0	-1.00
Hurdles	3	7	1	1	0	5	14.3	-2.50

Chases	2	2	0	1	0	1	0.0	-2.00
Totals	4	10	1	2	0	7	10.0	-5.50
11-12	4	12	0	0	3	9	0.0	-12.00
10-11	8	27	1	0	3	23	3.7	-21.50

JOCKEYS

	W-R	Per cent	£1 Level Stake
Felix De Giles	1-5	20.0	-0.50

COURSE RECORD

	Total W-R	Non-Hndcps Hurdles	Chases	Hndcps Hurdles	Chases	NH Flat	Per cent	£1 Level Stake
Hereford	1-1	0-0	0-0	1-1	0-0	0-0	100.0	+3.50

WINNING HORSES

Horse	Races Run	1st	2nd	3rd	£
Daarth	2	1	1	0	0
Total winning prize-money					**£0**
Favourites	0-0		0.0%		0.00

MARK GILLARD
HOLWELL, DORSET

	No. of Hrs	Races Run	1st	2nd	3rd	Unpl	Per cent	£1 Level Stake
NH Flat	3	5	0	0	0	5	0.0	-5.00
Hurdles	12	50	4	7	8	31	8.0	-17.50
Chases	8	34	5	3	2	24	14.7	-10.50
Totals	19	89	9	10	10	60	10.1	-33.00
11-12	12	52	4	8	7	33	7.7	-31.75
10-11	9	62	4	8	7	43	6.5	-26.13

JOCKEYS

	W-R	Per cent	£1 Level Stake
Tommy Phelan	5-57	8.8	-17.25
Tom Cannon	2-8	25.0	+1.75
Nico de Boinville	1-3	33.3	+0.25
Jake Hodson	1-11	9.1	-7.75

COURSE RECORD

	Total W-R	Non-Hndcps Hurdles	Chases	Hndcps Hurdles	Chases	NH Flat	Per cent	£1 Level Stake
Chepstow	4-12	0-2	0-0	3-6	1-3	0-1	33.3	+7.25
Nton Abbot	2-10	0-3	0-1	0-2	2-4	0-0	20.0	+2.00
Exeter	2-11	0-3	1-2	0-3	1-2	0-1	18.2	-3.25
Wincanton	1-9	0-0	0-0	1-6	0-1	0-2	11.1	+8.00

WINNING HORSES

Horse	Races Run	1st	2nd	3rd	£
Ice 'N' Easy	4	2	1	0	7760
Petito	5	1	2	0	3574

Border Lad	4	1	0	0	2599
Red Law	7	1	0	2	2395
*Bravo Bravo	11	2	4	1	3639
Lady Bridget	8	1	0	2	1949
Sir Roger	3	1	0	0	1949
Total winning prize-money					£23865
Favourites	2-5		40.0%		1.50

Chases	7	15	0	0	4	11	0.0	-15.00
Totals	17	68	5	3	7	53	7.4	+23.25
11-12	27	125	8	17	17	83	6.4	-50.03
10-11	30	150	17	26	14	91	11.3	-21.97

JOCKEYS

	W-R	Per cent	£1 Level Stake
A P McCoy	4-6	66.7	+18.25
Rachael Green	1-4	25.0	+63.00

COURSE RECORD

	Total W-R	Non-Hndcps Hurdles Chases		Hndcps Hurdles Chases		NH Flat	Per cent	£1 Level Stake
Nton Abbot	2-3	1-1	0-0	0-1	0-0	1-1	66.7	+14.00
Worcester	2-11	1-4	0-0	0-3	0-2	1-2	18.2	-3.75
Ludlow	1-6	0-0	0-0	1-4	0-1	0-1	16.7	+61.00

WINNING HORSES

Horse	Races Run	1st	2nd	3rd	£
Hills Of Aran	4	1	0	0	5198
Tenby Jewel	7	1	0	1	2924
Cock Of The Rock	2	1	0	0	1949
Sir Benfro	9	2	0	0	3182
Total winning prize-money					£13253
Favourites	0-2		0.0%		-2.00

JIM GOLDIE

UPLAWMOOR, E RENFREWS

	No. of Hrs	Races Run	1st	2nd	3rd	Unpl	Per cent	£1 Level Stake
NH Flat	5	15	2	3	3	7	13.3	-3.00
Hurdles	28	106	6	7	15	78	5.7	-61.63
Chases	6	13	1	0	0	12	7.7	-2.00
Totals	34	134	9	10	18	97	6.7	-66.63
11-12	38	150	16	25	19	90	10.7	-47.00
10-11	39	158	21	20	22	95	13.3	-30.77

JOCKEYS

	W-R	Per cent	£1 Level Stake
Henry Brooke	4-44	9.1	-14.38
Lucy Alexander	4-44	9.1	-17.25
Richie McGrath	1-13	7.7	-2.00

COURSE RECORD

	Total W-R	Non-Hndcps Hurdles Chases		Hndcps Hurdles Chases		NH Flat	Per cent	£1 Level Stake
Ayr	5-43	0-8	0-0	4-23	1-7	0-5	11.6	-2.38
Perth	2-25	0-7	0-1	1-15	0-0	1-2	8.0	-15.25
Mrket Rsn	1-3	1-2	0-0	0-1	0-0	0-0	33.3	+8.00
Kelso	1-18	0-5	0-0	0-10	0-1	1-2	5.6	-12.00

WINNING HORSES

Horse	Races Run	1st	2nd	3rd	£
Bene Lad	8	1	0	0	7798
Seven Is Lucky	6	1	0	0	3249
Jonny Delta	5	1	0	2	3249
A Southside Boy	5	1	0	0	3249
*Spirit Of A Nation	6	1	1	2	3165
Too Cool To Fool	8	1	0	0	3119
LilliofthebaIlet	8	1	0	3	2534
Mister Pagan	5	1	1	1	2053
Caledonia	5	1	1	2	1819
Total winning prize-money					£30235
Favourites	1-2		50.0%		0.63

KEITH GOLDSWORTHY

YERBESTON, PEMBROKES

	No. of Hrs	Races Run	1st	2nd	3rd	Unpl	Per cent	£1 Level Stake
NH Flat	4	6	2	0	0	4	33.3	+7.00
Hurdles	14	47	3	3	3	38	6.4	+31.25

STEVE GOLLINGS

SCAMBLESBY, LINCS

	No. of Hrs	Races Run	1st	2nd	3rd	Unpl	Per cent	£1 Level Stake
NH Flat	5	6	0	0	0	6	0.0	-6.00
Hurdles	10	32	7	4	1	20	21.9	+0.38
Chases	7	33	9	6	4	14	27.3	+10.50
Totals	19	71	16	10	5	40	22.5	+4.88
11-12	20	85	10	8	16	51	11.8	-44.34
10-11	23	97	16	13	15	53	16.5	-17.32

BY MONTH

NH Flat	W-R	Per cent	£1 Level Stake	Hurdles	W-R	Per cent	£1 Level Stake
May	0-0	0.0	0.00	May	0-3	0.0	-3.00
June	0-0	0.0	0.00	June	0-1	0.0	-1.00
July	0-0	0.0	0.00	July	1-1	100.0	+4.50
August	0-1	0.0	-1.00	August	0-0	0.0	0.00
September	0-0	0.0	0.00	September	1-1	100.0	+4.50
October	0-1	0.0	-1.00	October	0-1	0.0	-1.00
November	0-0	0.0	0.00	November	1-8	12.5	-5.25
December	0-0	0.0	0.00	December	1-6	16.7	-2.25
January	0-0	0.0	0.00	January	0-1	0.0	-1.00
February	0-2	0.0	-2.00	February	0-1	0.0	-1.00
March	0-1	0.0	-1.00	March	2-2	100.0	+5.88
April	0-1	0.0	-1.00	April	1-7	14.3	0.00

Chases	W-R	Per cent	£1 Level Stake	Totals	W-R	Per cent	£1 Level Stake
May	0-3	0.0	-3.00	May	0-6	0.0	-6.00
June	1-1	100.0	+6.00	June	1-2	50.0	+5.00
July	0-0	0.0	0.00	July	1-1	100.0	+4.50
August	1-1	100.0	+8.00	August	1-2	50.0	+7.00
September	0-1	0.0	-1.00	September	1-2	50.0	+3.50
October	0-0	0.0	0.00	October	0-2	0.0	-2.00
November	2-3	66.7	+5.50	November	3-11	27.3	+0.25
December	2-5	40.0	+3.25	December	3-11	27.3	+1.00
January	0-2	0.0	-2.00	January	0-3	0.0	-3.00
February	0-3	0.0	-3.00	February	0-6	0.0	-6.00
March	2-6	33.3	-1.25	March	4-9	44.4	+3.63
April	1-8	12.5	-2.00	April	2-16	12.5	-3.00

	W-R						Per cent	£1 Level Stake
Mrket Rsn	3-10	0-2	0-1	2-2	1-3	0-2	30.0	+5.50
Doncaster	2-6	0-0	1-2	0-0	1-4	0-0	33.3	+2.75
Leicester	1-1	0-0	0-0	1-1	0-0	0-0	100.0	+2.75
Ayr	1-3	0-0	0-0	0-2	1-1	0-0	33.3	+3.00
Huntingdon	1-3	0-0	0-0	0-0	1-2	0-1	33.3	+0.50
Haydock	1-5	0-1	0-0	1-3	0-1	0-0	20.0	-2.25
Perth	1-5	0-0	0-0	1-2	0-3	0-0	20.0	+2.00

WINNING HORSES

Horse	Races Run	1st	2nd	3rd	£
Conquisto	9	4	2	2	34822
Local Hero	5	2	0	0	34170
Walkabout Creek	5	2	2	0	14823
Laterly	7	1	0	1	6498
Bar De Ligne	6	1	1	0	6498
Shan Blue	4	2	0	0	6953
Soudain	7	2	2	1	6823
Honest John	6	2	0	0	6108
Total winning prize-money					£116695
Favourites	4-10		40.0%		1.38

DISTANCE

Hurdles	W-R	Per cent	£1 Level Stake	Chases	W-R	Per cent	£1 Level Stake
2m-2m3f	4-23	17.4	-5.50	2m-2m3f	3-8	37.5	+3.25
2m4f-2m7f	3-6	50.0	+8.88	2m4f-2m7f	2-11	18.2	+5.00
3m+	0-3	0.0	-3.00	3m+	4-14	28.6	+2.25

TYPE OF RACE

Non-Handicaps	W-R	Per cent	£1 Level Stake	Handicaps	W-R	Per cent	£1 Level Stake
Nov Hrdls	1-7	14.3	-1.50	Nov Hrdls	1-2	50.0	+0.38
Hrdls	0-0	0.0	0.00	Hrdls	5-23	21.7	+1.50
Nov Chs	2-5	40.0	+0.25	Nov Chs	2-7	28.6	+1.50
Chases	0-0	0.0	0.00	Chases	5-21	23.8	+8.75
Sell/Claim	0-0	0.0	0.00	Sell/Claim	0-0	0.0	0.00

CHRIS GORDON

MORESTEAD, HANTS

	No. of Hrs	Races Run	1st	2nd	3rd	Unpl	Per cent	£1 Level Stake
NH Flat	5	6	0	0	0	6	0.0	-6.00
Hurdles	25	102	12	11	9	70	11.8	+37.75
Chases	16	60	3	9	10	38	5.0	-51.38
Totals	33	168	15	20	19	114	8.9	-19.63
11-12	33	182	22	21	24	115	12.1	-37.03
10-11	34	134	9	9	17	99	6.7	+66.33

RACE CLASS

	W-R	Per cent	£1 Level Stake
Class 1	3-12	25.0	+5.00
Class 2	1-8	12.5	-5.63
Class 3	4-25	16.0	-10.00
Class 4	8-19	42.1	+22.50
Class 5	0-1	0.0	-1.00
Class 6	0-6	0.0	-6.00

FIRST TIME OUT

	W-R	Per cent	£1 Level Stake
Bumpers	0-5	0.0	-5.00
Hurdles	1-10	10.0	-4.50
Chases	1-4	25.0	-0.50
Totals	2-19	10.5	-10.00

BY MONTH

NH Flat	W-R	Per cent	£1 Level Stake	Hurdles	W-R	Per cent	£1 Level Stake
May	0-0	0.0	0.00	May	1-11	9.1	+6.00
June	0-0	0.0	0.00	June	0-5	0.0	-5.00
July	0-0	0.0	0.00	July	0-2	0.0	-2.00
August	0-0	0.0	0.00	August	2-8	25.0	+14.00
September	0-0	0.0	0.00	September	3-8	37.5	+22.00
October	0-1	0.0	-1.00	October	0-4	0.0	-4.00
November	0-0	0.0	0.00	November	1-12	8.3	-8.00
December	0-0	0.0	0.00	December	0-12	0.0	-12.00
January	0-0	0.0	0.00	January	0-8	0.0	-8.00
February	0-1	0.0	-1.00	February	0-8	0.0	-8.00
March	0-2	0.0	-2.00	March	1-8	12.5	-4.25
April	0-2	0.0	-2.00	April	4-16	25.0	+47.00

Chases	W-R	Per cent	£1 Level Stake	Totals	W-R	Per cent	£1 Level Stake
May	0-6	0.0	-6.00	May	1-17	5.9	0.00
June	0-3	0.0	-3.00	June	0-8	0.0	-8.00
July	0-1	0.0	-1.00	July	0-3	0.0	-3.00
August	0-3	0.0	-3.00	August	2-11	18.2	+11.00
September	0-2	0.0	-2.00	September	3-10	30.0	+20.00
October	0-8	0.0	-8.00	October	0-13	0.0	-13.00

JOCKEYS

	W-R	Per cent	£1 Level Stake
Paul Bohan	6-19	31.6	+6.25
Tom Scudamore	4-14	28.6	+0.75
James Reveley	2-3	66.7	+4.88
Brian Hughes	2-13	15.4	+3.00
Denis O'Regan	1-1	100.0	+4.00
Jason Maguire	1-2	50.0	+5.00

COURSE RECORD

	Total W-R	Non-Hndcps Hurdles	Chases	Hndcps Hurdles	Chases	NH Flat	Per cent	£1 Level Stake
Southwell	3-3	0-0	1-1	0-0	2-2	0-0	100.0	+14.50
Sedgefield	3-4	1-1	0-0	1-1	1-2	0-0	75.0	+7.13

November	1-9	11.1	-6.63	November	2-21	9.5	-14.63
December	0-3	0.0	-3.00	December	0-15	0.0	-15.00
January	0-3	0.0	-3.00	January	0-11	0.0	-11.00
February	0-6	0.0	-6.00	February	0-15	0.0	-15.00
March	0-5	0.0	-5.00	March	1-15	6.7	-11.25
April	2-11	18.2	-4.75	April	6-29	20.7	+40.25

DISTANCE

Hurdles	W-R	Per cent	£1 Level Stake	Chases	W-R	Per cent	£1 Level Stake
2m-2m3f	3-36	8.3	+15.50	2m-2m3f	2-32	6.3	-26.38
2m4f-2m7f	5-46	10.9	+18.50	2m4f-2m7f	0-9	0.0	-9.00
3m+	4-20	20.0	+3.75	3m+	1-19	5.3	-16.00

TYPE OF RACE

Non-Handicaps	W-R	Per cent	£1 Level Stake	Handicaps	W-R	Per cent	£1 Level Stake
Nov Hrdls	0-14	0.0	-14.00	Nov Hrdls	1-2	50.0	+32.00
Hrdls	0-10	0.0	-10.00	Hrdls	9-72	12.5	+8.75
Nov Chs	0-3	0.0	-3.00	Nov Chs	0-0	0.0	0.00
Chases	0-1	0.0	-1.00	Chases	3-56	5.4	-47.38
Sell/Claim	1-2	50.0	+2.00	Sell/Claim	1-2	50.0	+19.00

RACE CLASS / FIRST TIME OUT

	W-R	Per cent	£1 Level Stake		W-R	Per cent	£1 Level Stake
Class 1	0-1	0.0	-1.00	Bumpers	0-5	0.0	-5.00
Class 2	0-9	0.0	-9.00	Hurdles	1-18	5.6	-1.00
Class 3	1-12	8.3	-8.75	Chases	2-10	20.0	-4.63
Class 4	4-73	5.5	-51.75				
Class 5	10-70	14.3	+53.88	Totals	3-33	9.1	-10.63
Class 6	0-3	0.0	-3.00				

JOCKEYS

	W-R	Per cent	£1 Level Stake
Tom Cannon	13-138	9.4	-7.13
Joshua Moore	1-1	100.0	+12.00
Micheal Nolan	1-1	100.0	+3.50

COURSE RECORD

	Total W-R	Non-Hndcps Hurdles	Chases	Hndcps Hurdles	Chases	NH Flat	Per cent	£1 Level Stake
Plumpton	5-32	0-3	0-0	4-22	1-7	0-0	15.6	+25.50
Fontwell	5-47	0-6	0-0	5-20	0-18	0-3	10.6	+9.50
Newbury	1-4	0-2	0-0	1-1	0-1	0-0	25.0	-0.25
Stratford	1-4	0-0	0-0	1-3	0-1	0-0	25.0	+17.00
Southwell	1-5	1-2	0-0	0-0	0-3	0-0	20.0	-1.00
Huntingdon	1-6	0-0	0-0	0-4	1-2	0-0	16.7	-3.63
Wincanton	1-9	0-3	0-0	0-3	1-2	0-1	11.1	-5.75

WINNING HORSES

Horse	Races Run	1st	2nd	3rd	£
King Edmund	8	1	4	0	7596
Promised Wings	8	1	4	1	3119

Akbabend	7	3	0	1	6563
Gilded Age	6	1	0	1	2395
*Superciliary	8	1	0	1	2395
Benny The Swinger	4	1	2	0	2339
Osmosia	10	2	1	2	2259
Princely Hero	17	2	3	4	4198
Absolute Shambles	14	1	4	1	1949
Marie Deja La	10	1	0	2	1949
Manjam	2	1	0	0	1689
Total winning prize-money					£36451
Favourites	2-39		5.1%		-32.75

HARRIET GRAHAM

PHILIP LAW, BORDERS

	No. of Hrs	Races Run	1st	2nd	3rd	Unpl	Per cent	£1 Level Stake
NH Flat	3	4	0	0	0	4	0.0	-4.00
Hurdles	4	16	2	0	2	12	12.5	+0.50
Chases	2	17	1	3	2	11	5.9	-14.75
Totals	7	37	3	3	4	27	8.1	-18.25
11-12	11	54	11	3	4	36	20.4	+10.62
10-11	11	44	0	1	3	40	0.0	-43.00

JOCKEYS

	W-R	Per cent	£1 Level Stake
Lucy Alexander	1-1	100.0	+10.00
Jonathan England	1-3	33.3	+2.50
Gary Rutherford	1-22	4.5	-19.75

COURSE RECORD

	Total W-R	Non-Hndcps Hurdles	Chases	Hndcps Hurdles	Chases	NH Flat	Per cent	£1 Level Stake
Cartmel	2-7	0-2	0-0	1-2	1-3	0-0	28.6	+0.75
Newcastle	1-9	0-2	0-0	1-2	0-5	0-0	11.1	+2.00

WINNING HORSES

Horse	Races Run	1st	2nd	3rd	£
Soul Magic	6	1	1	0	3249
Scotswell	6	2	0	0	6173
Total winning prize-money					£9422
Favourites	1-1	100.0%			1.25

CHRIS GRANT

NEWTON BEWLEY, CO DURHAM

	No. of Hrs	Races Run	1st	2nd	3rd	Unpl	Per cent	£1 Level Stake
NH Flat	11	18	0	0	2	16	0.0	-18.00
Hurdles	32	109	9	13	15	72	8.3	-30.63
Chases	22	86	11	17	13	45	12.8	-10.75
Totals	54	213	20	30	30	133	9.4	-59.38
11-12	56	233	23	24	25	161	9.9	-52.82
10-11	47	140	13	12	18	97	9.3	-48.54

	W-R		
Class 5	6-42	14.3	+7.13
Class 6	0-19	0.0	-19.00

(Totals 5-54 9.3 -32.38)

BY MONTH

NH Flat	W-R	Per cent	£1 Level Stake	Hurdles	W-R	Per cent	£1 Level Stake
May	0-0	0.0	0.00	May	2-14	14.3	-1.00
June	0-2	0.0	-2.00	June	0-2	0.0	-2.00
July	0-0	0.0	0.00	July	0-3	0.0	-3.00
August	0-0	0.0	0.00	August	0-6	0.0	-6.00
September	0-0	0.0	0.00	September	0-4	0.0	-4.00
October	0-0	0.0	0.00	October	1-12	8.3	-4.00
November	0-2	0.0	-2.00	November	1-14	7.1	-5.00
December	0-3	0.0	-3.00	December	2-15	13.3	-1.13
January	0-2	0.0	-2.00	January	1-8	12.5	-2.00
February	0-2	0.0	-2.00	February	0-10	0.0	-10.00
March	0-3	0.0	-3.00	March	2-13	15.4	+15.50
April	0-4	0.0	-4.00	April	0-8	0.0	-8.00

Chases	W-R	Per cent	£1 Level Stake	Totals	W-R	Per cent	£1 Level Stake
May	0-12	0.0	-12.00	May	2-26	7.7	-13.00
June	1-5	20.0	+16.00	June	1-9	11.1	+12.00
July	0-3	0.0	-3.00	July	0-6	0.0	-6.00
August	0-6	0.0	-6.00	August	0-12	0.0	-12.00
September	0-3	0.0	-3.00	September	0-7	0.0	-7.00
October	1-8	12.5	-5.38	October	2-20	10.0	-9.38
November	3-9	33.3	0.00	November	4-25	16.0	-7.00
December	1-10	10.0	+16.00	December	3-28	10.7	+11.87
January	0-7	0.0	-7.00	January	1-17	5.9	-11.00
February	1-7	14.3	-3.50	February	1-19	5.3	-15.50
March	1-6	16.7	-2.50	March	3-22	13.6	+10.00
April	3-10	30.0	-0.38	April	3-22	13.6	-12.38

DISTANCE

Hurdles	W-R	Per cent	£1 Level Stake	Chases	W-R	Per cent	£1 Level Stake
2m-2m3f	4-55	7.3	-25.50	2m-2m3f	3-22	13.6	+9.75
2m4f-2m7f	3-35	8.6	-3.13	2m4f-2m7f	4-33	12.1	-20.38
3m+	2-19	10.5	-2.00	3m+	4-31	12.9	-0.13

TYPE OF RACE

Non-Handicaps	W-R	Per cent	£1 Level Stake	Handicaps	W-R	Per cent	£1 Level Stake
Nov Hrdls	2-32	6.3	-22.13	Nov Hrdls	0-4	0.0	-4.00
Hrdls	1-14	7.1	-6.00	Hrdls	5-50	10.0	+5.00
Nov Chs	2-16	12.5	-10.50	Nov Chs	2-8	25.0	-1.00
Chases	0-0	0.0	0.00	Chases	7-62	11.3	+0.75
Sell/Claim	1-9	11.1	-3.50	Sell/Claim	0-1	0.0	-1.00

RACE CLASS | ## FIRST TIME OUT

	W-R	Per cent	£1 Level Stake		W-R	Per cent	£1 Level Stake
Class 1	0-2	0.0	-2.00	Bumpers	0-11	0.0	-11.00
Class 2	0-4	0.0	-4.00	Hurdles	3-26	11.5	-10.13
Class 3	3-28	10.7	+7.75	Chases	2-17	11.8	-11.25
Class 4	11-118	9.3	-49.25				

JOCKEYS

	W-R	Per cent	£1 Level Stake
Samantha Drake	4-12	33.3	+29.50
Diarmuid O'Regan	3-21	14.3	-9.38
Wilson Renwick	3-45	6.7	-2.00
Henry Brooke	2-11	18.2	+14.63
Denis O'Regan	2-36	5.6	-30.25
Timmy Murphy	1-2	50.0	+1.75
A P McCoy	1-4	25.0	-0.75
Ryan Mania	1-4	25.0	-1.13
Barry Keniry	1-6	16.7	0.00
Brian Hughes	1-17	5.9	-13.75
Alexander Voy	1-23	4.3	-16.00

COURSE RECORD

	Total W-R	Non-Hndcps Hurdles	Chases	Hndcps Hurdles	Chases	NH Flat	Per cent	£1 Level Stake
Wetherby	4-30	1-9	1-4	2-10	0-6	0-1	13.3	-3.00
Ayr	3-12	0-0	0-1	1-6	2-3	0-2	25.0	+18.50
Kelso	3-18	1-4	0-4	1-4	1-5	0-1	16.7	-6.50
Carlisle	2-11	0-2	1-2	0-1	1-3	0-3	18.2	-4.25
Sedgefield	2-24	1-5	0-1	0-6	1-11	0-1	8.3	-13.75
Fakenham	1-1	1-1	0-0	0-0	0-0	0-0	100.0	+4.50
Haydock	1-3	0-0	0-0	0-1	1-2	0-0	33.3	+0.50
Hexham	1-11	0-2	0-0	0-3	1-4	0-2	9.1	+10.00
Musselbgh	1-17	0-6	0-1	1-4	0-5	0-1	5.9	-8.00
Newcastle	1-20	0-6	0-0	0-4	1-7	0-3	5.0	-17.38
Catterick	1-21	0-7	0-0	0-7	1-6	0-0	4.8	+5.00

WINNING HORSES

Horse	Races Run	1st	2nd	3rd	£
Ulysse Collonges	5	2	1	0	11792
Nine Stories	3	1	0	0	6498
Rock Relief	8	1	2	1	5523
Overyou	9	2	5	1	9309
Overquest	3	1	0	0	5198
Micro Mission	6	2	2	0	7624
Emirate Isle	7	1	0	0	4224
William Money	9	1	4	1	3769
Notonebuttwo	8	1	1	0	3249
Alpha One	9	1	1	2	3129
Lucematic	5	1	2	1	2924
Muwalla	5	1	1	2	2534
Lutin Du Moulin	3	1	0	1	2079
Tears From Heaven	2	1	0	0	2053
Molaise Lad	8	1	3	2	2053
Bob Will	10	1	1	1	1949
Asteroid Belt	5	1	1	1	1779
Total winning prize-money					**£75686**
Favourites	5-14		35.7%		-0.63

LIAM GRASSICK

CLEEVE HILL, GLOUCS

	No. of Hrs	Races Run	1st	2nd	3rd	Unpl	Per cent	£1 Level Stake
NH Flat	0	0	0	0	0	0	0.0	0.00
Hurdles	6	19	1	1	0	17	5.3	+32.00
Chases	1	2	0	0	1	1	0.0	-2.00
Totals	6	21	1	1	1	18	4.8	+30.00
11-12	2	7	0	0	0	7	0.0	-7.00

JOCKEYS

	W-R	Per cent	£1 Level Stake
Liam Treadwell	1-12	8.3	+39.00

COURSE RECORD

	Total W-R	Non-Hndcps Hurdles	Chases	Hndcps Hurdles	Chases	NH Flat	Per cent	£1 Level Stake
Worcester	1-4	0-2	0-0	1-2	0-0	0-0	25.0	+47.00

WINNING HORSES

Horse	Races Run	1st	2nd	3rd	£
Commanche Dream	4	1	1	0	1949
Total winning prize-money					£1949
Favourites	0-0		0.0%		0.00

CARROLL GRAY

MOORLAND, SOMERSET

	No. of Hrs	Races Run	1st	2nd	3rd	Unpl	Per cent	£1 Level Stake
NH Flat	2	3	0	0	0	3	0.0	-3.00
Hurdles	6	11	0	0	0	11	0.0	-11.00
Chases	5	18	1	3	4	10	5.6	-14.25
Totals	10	32	1	3	4	24	3.1	-28.25
11-12	12	36	2	3	4	27	5.6	-17.00
10-11	13	56	3	3	9	41	5.4	-11.67

JOCKEYS

	W-R	Per cent	£1 Level Stake
Micheal Nolan	1-13	7.7	-9.25

COURSE RECORD

	Total W-R	Non-Hndcps Hurdles	Chases	Hndcps Hurdles	Chases	NH Flat	Per cent	£1 Level Stake
Sedgefield	1-2	0-0	0-0	0-0	1-2	0-0	50.0	+1.75

WINNING HORSES

Horse	Races Run	1st	2nd	3rd	£
Mon Chevalier	9	1	2	3	3054
Total winning prize-money					£3054
Favourites	0-3		0.0%		-3.00

WARREN GREATREX

UPPER LAMBOURN, BERKS

	No. of Hrs	Races Run	1st	2nd	3rd	Unpl	Per cent	£1 Level Stake
NH Flat	8	17	2	5	1	9	11.8	+7.00
Hurdles	23	71	7	6	8	50	9.9	-35.63
Chases	8	23	4	5	2	12	17.4	-7.68
Totals	28	111	13	16	11	71	11.7	-36.31
11-12	41	132	20	18	16	78	15.2	-29.13
10-11	37	101	13	13	9	66	12.9	-36.59

BY MONTH

NH Flat	W-R	Per cent	£1 Level Stake	Hurdles	W-R	Per cent	£1 Level Stake
May	0-0	0.0	0.00	May	0-1	0.0	-1.00
June	0-0	0.0	0.00	June	0-0	0.0	0.00
July	0-0	0.0	0.00	July	0-0	0.0	0.00
August	0-0	0.0	0.00	August	0-0	0.0	0.00
September	0-0	0.0	0.00	September	0-0	0.0	0.00
October	1-2	50.0	+15.00	October	0-4	0.0	-4.00
November	0-4	0.0	-4.00	November	1-9	11.1	-6.63
December	0-1	0.0	-1.00	December	1-9	11.1	-5.75
January	0-2	0.0	-2.00	January	0-6	0.0	-6.00
February	1-3	33.3	+4.00	February	3-18	16.7	+4.75
March	0-1	0.0	-1.00	March	1-11	9.1	-8.00
April	0-4	0.0	-4.00	April	1-13	7.7	-9.00

Chases	W-R	Per cent	£1 Level Stake	Totals	W-R	Per cent	£1 Level Stake
May	0-0	0.0	0.00	May	0-1	0.0	-1.00
June	0-0	0.0	0.00	June	0-0	0.0	0.00
July	0-0	0.0	0.00	July	0-0	0.0	0.00
August	0-0	0.0	0.00	August	0-0	0.0	0.00
September	0-2	0.0	-2.00	September	0-2	0.0	-2.00
October	0-1	0.0	-1.00	October	1-7	14.3	+10.00
November	0-6	0.0	-6.00	November	1-19	5.3	-16.63
December	0-4	0.0	-4.00	December	1-14	7.1	-10.75
January	0-3	0.0	-3.00	January	0-11	0.0	-11.00
February	0-2	0.0	-2.00	February	4-23	17.4	+6.75
March	1-2	50.0	+4.00	March	2-14	14.3	-5.00
April	3-3	100.0	+6.32	April	4-20	20.0	-6.68

DISTANCE

Hurdles	W-R	Per cent	£1 Level Stake	Chases	W-R	Per cent	£1 Level Stake
2m-2m3f	1-23	4.3	-18.50	2m-2m3f	2-7	28.6	-2.18
2m4f-2m7f	4-34	11.8	-10.38	2m4f-2m7f	2-8	25.0	+2.50
3m+	2-14	14.3	-6.75	3m+	0-8	0.0	-8.00

TYPE OF RACE

Non-Handicaps	W-R	Per cent	£1 Level Stake	Handicaps	W-R	Per cent	£1 Level Stake
Nov Hrdls	1-17	5.9	-2.00	Nov Hrdls	0-2	0.0	-2.00
Hrdls	3-13	23.1	-2.13	Hrdls	3-39	7.7	-29.50

Nov Chs	1-11	9.1	-9.43	Nov Chs	1-3	33.3	+1.50
Chases	0-0	0.0	0.00	Chases	2-9	22.2	+0.25
Sell/Claim	0-0	0.0	0.00	Sell/Claim	0-0	0.0	0.00

RACE CLASS

	W-R	Per cent	£1 Level Stake
Class 1	0-5	0.0	-5.00
Class 2	0-8	0.0	-8.00
Class 3	3-28	10.7	-6.50
Class 4	5-46	10.9	-27.68
Class 5	3-9	33.3	+1.88
Class 6	2-15	13.3	+9.00

FIRST TIME OUT

	W-R	Per cent	£1 Level Stake
Bumpers	2-8	25.0	+16.00
Hurdles	0-16	0.0	-16.00
Chases	0-4	0.0	-4.00
Totals	2-28	7.1	-4.00

JOCKEYS

	W-R	Per cent	£1 Level Stake
Noel Fehily	4-31	12.9	-16.63
A P McCoy	3-9	33.3	-0.93
Thomas Garner	2-12	16.7	+1.00
Wayne Hutchinson	2-26	7.7	-18.75
Tom Scudamore	1-2	50.0	+15.00
Jason Maguire	1-9	11.1	+6.00

COURSE RECORD

	Total W-R	Non-Hndcps Hurdles	Chases	Hndcps Hurdles	Chases	NH Flat	Per cent	£1 Level Stake
Plumpton	2-9	0-0	0-0	1-6	1-1	0-2	22.2	-1.25
Worcester	1-1	0-0	0-0	0-0	0-0	1-1	100.0	+16.00
Carlisle	1-2	0-0	1-1	0-0	0-0	0-1	50.0	-0.43
Chepstow	1-2	0-0	0-0	0-1	1-1	0-0	50.0	+1.25
Sedgefield	1-2	0-0	0-0	1-1	0-0	0-1	50.0	+1.25
Southwell	1-2	1-1	0-0	0-1	0-0	0-0	50.0	+2.50
Warwick	1-2	1-1	0-0	0-1	0-0	0-0	50.0	+13.00
Bangor	1-3	0-0	0-0	0-2	0-0	1-1	33.3	+4.00
Ffos Las	1-3	1-2	0-1	0-0	0-0	0-0	33.3	+1.00
Wetherby	1-4	0-1	0-0	1-3	0-0	0-0	25.0	-1.00
Folkestone	1-5	1-3	0-1	0-0	0-0	0-1	20.0	-2.63
Huntingdon	1-7	0-1	0-1	0-1	1-2	0-2	14.3	-1.00

WINNING HORSES

Horse	Races Run	1st	2nd	3rd	£
Five Rivers	6	2	0	1	10267
Dolatulo	8	2	3	0	10267
Westward Point	6	2	1	1	7935
Bunglasha Lady	4	1	0	0	5198
Turbo Du Ranch	8	1	1	1	3119
Umadachar	5	2	0	1	5172
Ballyculla	4	1	0	2	1949
Mixologist	4	1	1	2	1949
Tamarina Bay	3	1	0	0	1643
Total winning prize-money					£47499
Favourites	6-21		28.6%		-3.05

TOM GRETTON

INKBERROW, WORCESTERSHIRE

	No. of Hrs	Races Run	1st	2nd	3rd	Unpl	Per cent	£1 Level Stake
NH Flat	3	3	0	1	0	2	0.0	-3.00
Hurdles	10	16	0	0	1	15	0.0	-16.00
Chases	6	22	5	3	3	11	22.7	-5.58
Totals	17	41	5	4	4	28	12.2	-24.58
11-12	14	36	0	3	1	32	0.0	-36.00
10-11	14	36	3	2	3	28	8.3	-7.00

JOCKEYS

	W-R	Per cent	£1 Level Stake
Felix De Giles	4-21	19.0	-10.08
James Reveley	1-1	100.0	+4.50

COURSE RECORD

	Total W-R	Non-Hndcps Hurdles	Chases	Hndcps Hurdles	Chases	NH Flat	Per cent	£1 Level Stake
Lingfield	2-3	0-0	0-0	0-0	2-3	0-0	66.7	+3.00
Newcastle	1-2	0-0	0-0	0-1	1-1	0-0	50.0	+3.50
Wincanton	1-3	0-0	0-0	0-1	1-2	0-0	33.3	-1.33
Towcester	1-4	0-1	0-0	0-1	1-2	0-0	25.0	-0.75

WINNING HORSES

Horse	Races Run	1st	2nd	3rd	£
Little Jimmy	7	3	1	1	3899
Armedanddangerous	4	2	0	0	6108
Total winning prize-money					£10007
Favourites	3-5		60.0%		2.67

DAVID C GRIFFITHS

BAWTRY, S YORKS

	No. of Hrs	Races Run	1st	2nd	3rd	Unpl	Per cent	£1 Level Stake
NH Flat	2	6	1	1	1	3	16.7	+9.00
Hurdles	0	0	0	0	0	0	0.0	0.00
Chases	0	0	0	0	0	0	0.0	0.00
Totals	2	6	1	1	1	3	16.7	+9.00

JOCKEYS

	W-R	Per cent	£1 Level Stake
Peter Carberry	1-2	50.0	+13.00

COURSE RECORD

	Total W-R	Non-Hndcps Hurdles	Chases	Hndcps Hurdles	Chases	NH Flat	Per cent	£1 Level Stake
Catterick	1-2	0-0	0-0	0-0	0-0	1-2	50.0	+13.00

WINNING HORSES

Horse	Races Run	1st	2nd	3rd	£
*Bypass	4	1	1	1	1643
Total winning prize-money					£1643
Favourites	0-0		0.0%		0.00

DIANA GRISSELL

BRIGHTLING, E SUSSEX

	No. of Hrs	Races Run	1st	2nd	3rd	Unpl	Per cent	£1 Level Stake
NH Flat	0	0	0	0	0	0	0.0	0.00
Hurdles	7	15	0	0	2	13	0.0	-15.00
Chases	6	22	5	1	3	13	22.7	+8.50
Totals	12	37	5	1	5	26	13.5	-6.50
11-12	11	28	1	4	1	22	3.6	-15.00
10-11	15	35	4	1	3	27	11.4	+16.94

JOCKEYS

	W-R	Per cent	£1 Level Stake
Sam Thomas	3-9	33.3	+3.25
Marc Goldstein	2-11	18.2	+7.25

COURSE RECORD

	Total W-R	Non-Hndcps Hurdles	Chases	Hndcps Hurdles	Chases	NH Flat	Per cent	£1 Level Stake
Newbury	1-1	0-0	0-0	0-0	1-1	0-0	100.0	+4.00
Sandown	1-1	0-0	0-0	0-0	1-1	0-0	100.0	+2.75
Huntingdon	1-2	0-0	0-0	0-1	1-1	0-0	50.0	+1.50
Folkestone	1-4	0-2	0-1	0-0	1-1	0-0	25.0	+11.00
Plumpton	1-10	0-3	0-1	0-0	1-6	0-0	10.0	-6.75

WINNING HORSES

Horse	Races Run	1st	2nd	3rd	£
Arbeo	7	3	1	0	18194
Quartz Du Montceau	7	2	0	2	4328
Total winning prize-money					£22522
Favourites	1-3		33.3%		0.50

JOHN BRYAN GROUCOTT

BOURTON, SHROPSHIRE

	No. of Hrs	Races Run	1st	2nd	3rd	Unpl	Per cent	£1 Level Stake
NH Flat	0	0	0	0	0	0	0.0	0.00
Hurdles	3	9	1	1	1	6	11.1	-2.00
Chases	5	10	1	0	1	8	10.0	-2.00
Totals	5	19	2	1	2	14	10.5	-4.00
11-12	9	24	2	3	1	18	8.3	+8.13
10-11	7	33	4	3	1	25	12.1	-4.25

JOCKEYS

	W-R	Per cent	£1 Level Stake
Nick Slatter	1-1	100.0	+7.00
Harry Challoner	1-15	6.7	-8.00

COURSE RECORD

	Total W-R	Non-Hndcps Hurdles	Chases	Hndcps Hurdles	Chases	NH Flat	Per cent	£1 Level Stake
Wetherby	1-2	0-0	0-0	1-1	0-1	0-0	50.0	+5.00
Ludlow	1-3	0-0	0-0	0-1	1-2	0-0	33.3	+5.00

WINNING HORSES

Horse	Races Run	1st	2nd	3rd	£
One More Dinar	3	1	0	1	2599
Waywood Princess	5	1	0	0	1949
Total winning prize-money					£4548
Favourites	0-0		0.0%		0.00

RICHARD GUEST

WETHERBY, W YORKS

	No. of Hrs	Races Run	1st	2nd	3rd	Unpl	Per cent	£1 Level Stake
NH Flat	0	0	0	0	0	0	0.0	0.00
Hurdles	11	37	0	3	2	32	0.0	-37.00
Chases	3	14	4	3	1	6	28.6	+4.00
Totals	12	51	4	6	3	38	7.8	-33.00
11-12	25	106	5	5	11	85	4.7	-54.50
10-11	19	66	5	4	7	50	7.6	-34.50

JOCKEYS

	W-R	Per cent	£1 Level Stake
Denis O'Regan	3-5	60.0	+11.00
Nico de Boinville	1-2	50.0	0.00

COURSE RECORD

	Total W-R	Non-Hndcps Hurdles	Chases	Hndcps Hurdles	Chases	NH Flat	Per cent	£1 Level Stake
Leicester	2-3	0-0	0-0	0-0	2-3	0-0	66.7	+5.00
Doncaster	1-8	0-4	0-0	0-3	1-1	0-0	12.5	-2.50
Mrket Rsn	1-14	0-3	0-0	0-8	1-3	0-0	7.1	-9.50

WINNING HORSES

Horse	Races Run	1st	2nd	3rd	£
Be My Deputy	12	4	3	1	11332
Total winning prize-money					£11332
Favourites	1-560		0.2%		-558.00

POLLY GUNDRY

OTTERY ST MARY, DEVON

	No. of Hrs	Races Run	1st	2nd	3rd	Unpl	Per cent	£1 Level Stake
NH Flat	1	2	1	0	1	0	50.0	+6.50
Hurdles	15	31	0	1	3	27	0.0	-31.00
Chases	5	10	0	0	1	9	0.0	-10.00
Totals	19	43	1	1	5	36	2.3	-34.50
11-12	19	76	7	7	4	58	9.2	-33.70
10-11	4	8	3	1	0	4	37.5	+17.50

JOCKEYS

	W-R	Per cent	£1 Level Stake
Tom O'Brien	1-16	6.3	-7.50

COURSE RECORD

	Total W-R	Non-Hndcps Hurdles	Chases	Hndcps Hurdles	Chases	NH Flat	Per cent	£1 Level Stake
Fontwell	1-5	0-1	0-0	0-2	0-1	1-1	20.0	+3.50

WINNING HORSES

Horse	Races Run	1st	2nd	3rd	£
*Harry's Farewell	2	1	0	1	1560
Total winning prize-money					£1560
Favourites	0-5		0.0%		-5.00

BEN DE HAAN

LAMBOURN, BERKS

	No. of Hrs	Races Run	1st	2nd	3rd	Unpl	Per cent	£1 Level Stake
NH Flat	2	2	0	0	0	2	0.0	-2.00
Hurdles	7	14	1	4	1	8	7.1	-3.00
Chases	3	5	0	2	0	3	0.0	-5.00
Totals	9	21	1	6	1	13	4.8	-10.00
11-12	7	22	4	3	2	13	18.2	-2.90
10-11	11	34	5	4	4	21	14.7	-13.64

JOCKEYS

	W-R	Per cent	£1 Level Stake
Daryl Jacob	1-11	9.1	0.00

COURSE RECORD

	Total W-R	Non-Hndcps Hurdles	Chases	Hndcps Hurdles	Chases	NH Flat	Per cent	£1 Level Stake
Aintree	1-4	0-0	0-0	1-3	0-0	0-1	25.0	+7.00

WINNING HORSES

Horse	Races Run	1st	2nd	3rd	£
Native Gallery	2	1	0	0	10010
Total winning prize-money					£10010
Favourites	0-1		0.0%		-1.00

ALEX HALES

EDGCOTE, NORTHANTS

	No. of Hrs	Races Run	1st	2nd	3rd	Unpl	Per cent	£1 Level Stake
NH Flat	3	4	0	0	1	3	0.0	-4.00
Hurdles	8	32	3	1	3	25	9.4	0.00
Chases	8	32	3	5	5	19	9.4	-20.25
Totals	17	68	6	6	9	47	8.8	-24.25
11-12	29	93	7	5	7	74	7.5	+3.00
10-11	35	124	13	7	10	94	10.5	+15.88

JOCKEYS

	W-R	Per cent	£1 Level Stake
Killian Moore	3-27	11.1	-7.25
Will Kennedy	2-18	11.1	+2.50
Peter Buchanan	1-6	16.7	-2.50

COURSE RECORD

	Total W-R	Non-Hndcps Hurdles	Chases	Hndcps Hurdles	Chases	NH Flat	Per cent	£1 Level Stake
Mrket Rsn	2-6	0-2	0-0	1-1	1-3	0-0	33.3	+12.50
Fontwell	1-4	0-0	0-0	1-1	0-3	0-0	25.0	+4.00
Towcester	1-6	0-2	0-0	0-0	1-4	0-0	16.7	-3.25
Uttoxeter	1-8	0-1	0-1	0-3	1-3	0-0	12.5	-2.50
Fakenham	1-11	1-1	0-0	0-5	0-5	0-0	9.1	-2.00

WINNING HORSES

Horse	Races Run	1st	2nd	3rd	£
*Crafty Roberto	6	1	0	0	3574
Salut Honore	8	1	0	2	2164
Lilac Belle	6	1	0	0	2053
Royaume Bleu	7	1	2	1	1997
Farewellatmidnight	7	1	1	1	1949
Gilzean	7	1	1	1	1949
Total winning prize-money					£13686
Favourites	1-3		33.3%		-0.25

GERALD HAM

ROOKS BRIDGE, SOMERSET

	No. of Hrs	Races Run	1st	2nd	3rd	Unpl	Per cent	£1 Level Stake
NH Flat	0	0	0	0	0	0	0.0	0.00
Hurdles	1	1	0	0	0	1	0.0	-1.00

Chases	1	2	1	0	0	1	50.0	+8.00
Totals	**2**	**3**	**1**	**0**	**0**	**2**	**33.3**	**+7.00**
11-12	*7*	*14*	*2*	*0*	*0*	*12*	*14.3*	*-0.50*
10-11	*18*	*68*	*3*	*5*	*6*	*54*	*4.4*	*+8.50*

JOCKEYS

	W-R	Per cent	£1 Level Stake
Paddy Brennan	1-1	100.0	+9.00

COURSE RECORD

	Total W-R	Non-Hndcps Hurdles	Chases	Hndcps Hurdles	Chases	NH Flat	Per cent	£1 Level Stake
Nton Abbot	1-1	0-0	0-0	0-0	1-1	0-0	100.0	+9.00

WINNING HORSES

Horse	Races Run	1st	2nd	3rd	£
Lansdowne Princess	2	1	0	0	3899
Total winning prize-money					**£3899**
Favourites	0-0		0.0%		0.00

DEBRA HAMER

NANTYCAWS, CARMARTHENS

	No. of Hrs	Races Run	1st	2nd	3rd	Unpl	Per cent	£1 Level Stake
NH Flat	4	6	0	0	2	4	0.0	-6.00
Hurdles	10	18	0	0	1	17	0.0	-18.00
Chases	4	14	4	1	1	8	28.6	+3.83
Totals	**15**	**38**	**4**	**1**	**4**	**29**	**10.5**	**-20.17**
11-12	*13*	*60*	*6*	*4*	*8*	*42*	*10.0*	*-24.52*
10-11	*13*	*41*	*4*	*2*	*3*	*32*	*9.8*	*-13.25*

JOCKEYS

	W-R	Per cent	£1 Level Stake
Aodhagan Conlon	2-13	15.4	-4.67
Tom O'Brien	1-2	50.0	+3.00
Paddy Brennan	1-2	50.0	+2.50

COURSE RECORD

	Total W-R	Non-Hndcps Hurdles	Chases	Hndcps Hurdles	Chases	NH Flat	Per cent	£1 Level Stake
Ffos Las	2-12	0-5	1-1	0-1	1-3	0-2	16.7	-3.17
Chepstow	1-4	0-0	0-0	0-1	1-3	0-0	25.0	+1.00
Hereford	1-8	0-2	0-0	0-0	1-4	0-2	12.5	-4.00

WINNING HORSES

Horse	Races Run	1st	2nd	3rd	£
Bendant	7	2	0	0	7018
Prime Edition	3	1	1	0	1949
Michigan Assassin	3	1	0	1	1864
Total winning prize-money					**£10831**
Favourites	1-1		100.0%		3.33

ANN HAMILTON

GREAT BAVINGTON, NORTHUMBLAND

	No. of Hrs	Races Run	1st	2nd	3rd	Unpl	Per cent	£1 Level Stake
NH Flat	2	3	0	1	0	2	0.0	-3.00
Hurdles	6	20	4	4	4	8	20.0	+6.00
Chases	5	15	2	0	1	12	13.3	-6.25
Totals	**9**	**38**	**6**	**5**	**5**	**22**	**15.8**	**-3.25**
11-12	*8*	*55*	*8*	*5*	*7*	*35*	*14.5*	*+0.33*
10-11	*9*	*39*	*5*	*6*	*5*	*23*	*12.8*	*-1.67*

JOCKEYS

	W-R	Per cent	£1 Level Stake
Wilson Renwick	2-14	14.3	-1.00
Graham Watters	1-1	100.0	+4.00
Ryan Mania	1-2	50.0	+7.00
Nick Slatter	1-2	50.0	+1.75
Callum Whillans	1-2	50.0	+2.00

COURSE RECORD

	Total W-R	Non-Hndcps Hurdles	Chases	Hndcps Hurdles	Chases	NH Flat	Per cent	£1 Level Stake
Kelso	3-8	0-2	0-0	1-1	2-5	0-0	37.5	+9.75
Sedgefield	1-4	1-2	0-0	0-0	0-1	0-1	25.0	+5.00
Newcastle	1-5	1-1	0-0	0-2	0-2	0-0	20.0	-1.00
Hexham	1-8	0-4	0-0	1-1	0-3	0-0	12.5	-4.00

WINNING HORSES

Horse	Races Run	1st	2nd	3rd	£
Rolecarr	6	2	0	1	13361
Dr Flynn	4	2	0	0	5733
*Runswick Royal	4	2	2	0	6238
Total winning prize-money					**£25332**
Favourites	0-0		0.0%		0.00

MICKY HAMMOND

MIDDLEHAM MOOR, N YORKS

	No. of Hrs	Races Run	1st	2nd	3rd	Unpl	Per cent	£1 Level Stake
NH Flat	5	7	0	0	1	6	0.0	-7.00
Hurdles	23	76	4	6	5	61	5.3	-47.50
Chases	8	25	3	2	1	19	12.0	+5.00
Totals	**32**	**108**	**7**	**8**	**7**	**86**	**6.5**	**-49.50**
11-12	*33*	*140*	*14*	*16*	*22*	*88*	*10.0*	*-42.54*
10-11	*28*	*129*	*18*	*19*	*17*	*75*	*14.0*	*+18.25*

JOCKEYS

	W-R	Per cent	£1 Level Stake
Jason Maguire	3-13	23.1	+17.00
Joe Colliver	3-52	5.8	-34.50
Wilson Renwick	1-18	5.6	-7.00

COURSE RECORD

	Total W-R	Non-Hndcps Hurdles	Chases	Hndcps Hurdles	Chases	NH Flat	Per cent	£1 Level Stake
Catterick	2-25	1-9	0-4	1-9	0-2	0-1	8.0	-12.50
Haydock	1-1	1-1	0-0	0-0	0-0	0-0	100.0	+10.00
Hexham	1-4	0-1	0-0	1-1	0-1	0-1	25.0	+1.00
Mrket Rsn	1-4	0-0	0-0	0-1	1-3	0-0	25.0	+11.00
Sedgefield	1-16	0-4	0-1	0-5	1-3	0-3	6.3	-12.00
Wetherby	1-27	0-7	0-0	0-14	1-4	0-2	3.7	-16.00

WINNING HORSES

Horse	Races Run	1st	2nd	3rd	£
Only Orsenfoolsies	4	2	1	0	12996
Gonow	7	1	1	2	3119
La Pantera Rosa	4	3	0	0	9083
Danceintothelight	6	1	0	0	2395
Total winning prize-money					£27593
Favourites	1-165	0.6%			-161.00

G D HANMER

NANTWICH, CHESHIRE

	No. of Hrs	Races Run	1st	2nd	3rd	Unpl	Per cent	£1 Level Stake
NH Flat	0	0	0	0	0	0	0.0	0.00
Hurdles	0	0	0	0	0	0	0.0	0.00
Chases	6	8	2	1	1	4	25.0	+2.63
Totals	6	8	2	1	1	4	25.0	+2.63
11-12	1	1	0	0	1	0	0.0	-1.00
10-11	4	5	0	1	1	3	0.0	-5.00

JOCKEYS

	W-R	Per cent	£1 Level Stake
Josh Hamer	1-2	50.0	+0.63
Mr W Biddick	1-2	50.0	+6.00

COURSE RECORD

	Total W-R	Non-Hndcps Hurdles	Chases	Hndcps Hurdles	Chases	NH Flat	Per cent	£1 Level Stake
Leicester	1-3	0-0	1-3	0-0	0-0	0-0	33.3	+5.00
Bangor	1-4	0-0	1-4	0-0	0-0	0-0	25.0	-1.38

WINNING HORSES

Horse	Races Run	1st	2nd	3rd	£
*Sorted	1	1	0	0	9105
What A Laugh	3	1	1	0	717
Total winning prize-money					£9822
Favourites	1-2	50.0%			0.63

MRS PAULINE HARKIN

CHIPPING WARDEN, NORTHANTS

	No. of Hrs	Races Run	1st	2nd	3rd	Unpl	Per cent	£1 Level Stake
NH Flat	0	0	0	0	0	0	0.0	0.00
Hurdles	0	0	0	0	0	0	0.0	0.00
Chases	1	2	1	0	0	1	50.0	+3.00
Totals	1	2	1	0	0	1	50.0	+3.00
10-11	4	6	0	0	0	6	0.0	-6.00

JOCKEYS

	W-R	Per cent	£1 Level Stake
Mr P Mann	1-2	50.0	+3.00

COURSE RECORD

	Total W-R	Non-Hndcps Hurdles	Chases	Hndcps Hurdles	Chases	NH Flat	Per cent	£1 Level Stake
Cheltenham	1-2	0-0	1-2	0-0	0-0	0-0	50.0	+3.00

WINNING HORSES

Horse	Races Run	1st	2nd	3rd	£
Doctor Kingsley	2	1	0	0	4367
Total winning prize-money					£4367
Favourites	1-1	100.0%			4.00

SHAUN HARRIS

CARBURTON, NOTTS

	No. of Hrs	Races Run	1st	2nd	3rd	Unpl	Per cent	£1 Level Stake
NH Flat	0	0	0	0	0	0	0.0	0.00
Hurdles	6	22	0	1	3	18	0.0	-22.00
Chases	2	10	1	1	3	5	10.0	-5.00
Totals	7	32	1	2	6	23	3.1	-27.00
11-12	4	15	0	0	0	15	0.0	-15.00
10-11	7	20	0	0	3	17	0.0	-20.00

JOCKEYS

	W-R	Per cent	£1 Level Stake
Trevor Whelan	1-10	10.0	-5.00

COURSE RECORD

	Total W-R	Non-Hndcps Hurdles	Chases	Hndcps Hurdles	Chases	NH Flat	Per cent	£1 Level Stake
Musselbgh	1-2	0-0	0-0	0-1	1-1	0-0	50.0	+3.00

WINNING HORSES

Horse	Races Run	1st	2nd	3rd	£
*Father Shine	11	1	0	3	4431
Total winning prize-money					£4431
Favourites	0-0		0.0%		0.00

LISA HARRISON

ALDOTH, CUMBRIA

	No. of Hrs	Races Run	1st	2nd	3rd	Unpl	Per cent	£1 Level Stake
NH Flat	3	4	0	0	1	3	0.0	-4.00
Hurdles	8	30	1	2	0	27	3.3	-18.00
Chases	2	10	0	1	1	8	0.0	-10.00
Totals	8	44	1	3	2	38	2.3	-32.00
11-12	11	45	3	7	3	32	6.7	-14.00
10-11	13	52	6	2	1	43	11.5	-6.25

JOCKEYS

	W-R	Per cent	£1 Level Stake
Stephen Mulqueen	1-17	5.9	-5.00

COURSE RECORD

	Total W-R	Non-Hndcps Hurdles	Chases	Hndcps Hurdles	Chases	NH Flat	Per cent	£1 Level Stake
Sedgefield	1-2	0-0	0-0	1-2	0-0	0-0	50.0	+10.00

WINNING HORSES

Horse	Races Run	1st	2nd	3rd	£
Solway Dornal	8	1	1	1	1689
Total winning prize-money					£1689
Favourites	0-1		0.0%		-1.00

BEN HASLAM

MIDDLEHAM MOOR, N YORKS

	No. of Hrs	Races Run	1st	2nd	3rd	Unpl	Per cent	£1 Level Stake
NH Flat	0	0	0	0	0	0	0.0	0.00
Hurdles	8	13	1	1	1	10	7.7	0.00
Chases	1	1	0	0	0	1	0.0	-1.00
Totals	8	14	1	1	1	11	7.1	-1.00
11-12	14	51	7	8	5	31	13.7	-21.15
10-11	12	42	5	3	4	30	11.9	-2.10

JOCKEYS

	W-R	Per cent	£1 Level Stake
Craig Gallagher	1-8	12.5	+5.00

COURSE RECORD

	Total W-R	Non-Hndcps Hurdles	Chases	Hndcps Hurdles	Chases	NH Flat	Per cent	£1 Level Stake
Wetherby	1-3	0-0	0-0	1-3	0-0	0-0	33.3	+10.00

WINNING HORSES

Horse	Races Run	1st	2nd	3rd	£
Hi Dancer	2	1	0	0	4549
Total winning prize-money					£4549
Favourites	0-0		0.0%		0.00

FLEUR HAWES

DISS, NORFOLK

	No. of Hrs	Races Run	1st	2nd	3rd	Unpl	Per cent	£1 Level Stake
NH Flat	1	1	0	0	0	1	0.0	-1.00
Hurdles	4	8	0	0	1	7	0.0	-8.00
Chases	3	9	1	2	0	6	11.1	-6.13
Totals	7	18	1	2	1	14	5.6	-15.13
11-12	4	4	0	0	2	2	0.0	-4.00
10-11	6	10	0	0	1	9	0.0	-10.00

JOCKEYS

	W-R	Per cent	£1 Level Stake
Leighton Aspell	1-1	100.0	+1.88

COURSE RECORD

	Total W-R	Non-Hndcps Hurdles	Chases	Hndcps Hurdles	Chases	NH Flat	Per cent	£1 Level Stake
Mrket Rsn	1-1	0-0	0-0	0-0	1-1	0-0	100.0	+1.88

WINNING HORSES

Horse	Races Run	1st	2nd	3rd	£
*Flaming Gorge	5	1	2	0	6498
Total winning prize-money					£6498
Favourites	0-2		0.0%		-2.00

NIGEL HAWKE

STOODLEIGH, DEVON

	No. of Hrs	Races Run	1st	2nd	3rd	Unpl	Per cent	£1 Level Stake
NH Flat	4	6	0	0	0	6	0.0	-6.00
Hurdles	12	38	1	6	5	26	2.6	-35.00

Chases	3	21	5	3	2	11	23.8	+15.88
Totals	**14**	**65**	**6**	**9**	**7**	**43**	**9.2**	**-25.12**
11-12	*16*	*67*	*4*	*6*	*2*	*55*	*6.0*	*-34.67*
10-11	*19*	*70*	*7*	*5*	*4*	*54*	*10.0*	*+13.50*

JOCKEYS

	W-R	Per cent	£1 Level Stake
Mark Quinlan	5-52	9.6	-23.13
Kieron Edgar	1-2	50.0	+9.00

COURSE RECORD

	Total W-R	Non-Hndcps Hurdles	Chases	Hndcps Hurdles	Chases	NH Flat	Per cent	£1 Level Stake
Uttoxeter	2-6	0-1	1-1	0-0	1-3	0-1	33.3	+6.38
Cheltenham	1-1	0-0	0-0	0-0	1-1	0-0	100.0	+10.00
Perth	1-2	0-0	0-0	0-1	1-1	0-0	50.0	+2.50
Southwell	1-2	0-0	0-0	1-1	0-0	0-1	50.0	+1.00
Chepstow	1-14	0-3	0-0	0-6	1-4	0-1	7.1	-5.00

WINNING HORSES

Horse	Races Run	1st	2nd	3rd	£
Anay Turge	11	4	2	1	19577
Master Neo	5	1	1	0	3833
Samingarry	11	1	3	0	0
Total winning prize-money					**£23410**
Favourites	**0-2**		**0.0%**		**-2.00**

RICHARD HAWKER

RODE, SOMERSET

	No. of Hrs	Races Run	1st	2nd	3rd	Unpl	Per cent	£1 Level Stake
NH Flat	3	5	0	1	1	3	0.0	-5.00
Hurdles	7	19	0	0	1	18	0.0	-19.00
Chases	2	8	1	1	0	6	12.5	-2.50
Totals	**9**	**32**	**1**	**2**	**2**	**27**	**3.1**	**-26.50**
11-12	*7*	*23*	*2*	*2*	*4*	*15*	*8.7*	*-8.25*
10-11	*5*	*18*	*0*	*0*	*1*	*17*	*0.0*	*-18.00*

JOCKEYS

	W-R	Per cent	£1 Level Stake
Paddy Brennan	1-3	33.3	+2.50

COURSE RECORD

	Total W-R	Non-Hndcps Hurdles	Chases	Hndcps Hurdles	Chases	NH Flat	Per cent	£1 Level Stake
Stratford	1-2	0-0	0-0	0-0	1-2	0-0	50.0	+3.50

WINNING HORSES

Horse	Races Run	1st	2nd	3rd	£
Lidjo De Rouge	7	1	1	0	2339

Total winning prize-money		£2339
Favourites	0-0 0.0%	0.00

MISS C M E HAYDON

AYLESBURY, BUCKS

	No. of Hrs	Races Run	1st	2nd	3rd	Unpl	Per cent	£1 Level Stake
NH Flat	0	0	0	0	0	0	0.0	0.00
Hurdles	0	0	0	0	0	0	0.0	0.00
Chases	1	1	1	0	0	0	100.0	+5.00
Totals	**1**	**1**	**1**	**0**	**0**	**0**	**100.0**	**+5.00**
10-11	*1*	*2*	*0*	*0*	*1*	*1*	*0.0*	*-2.00*

JOCKEYS

	W-R	Per cent	£1 Level Stake
Miss C Haydon	1-1	100.0	+5.00

COURSE RECORD

	Total W-R	Non-Hndcps Hurdles	Chases	Hndcps Hurdles	Chases	NH Flat	Per cent	£1 Level Stake
Folkestone	1-1	0-0	1-1	0-0	0-0	0-0	100.0	+5.00

WINNING HORSES

Horse	Races Run	1st	2nd	3rd	£
Little Legend	1	1	0	0	1153
Total winning prize-money					**£1153**
Favourites	**0-0**		**0.0%**		**0.00**

JONATHAN HAYNES

LOW ROW, CUMBRIA

	No. of Hrs	Races Run	1st	2nd	3rd	Unpl	Per cent	£1 Level Stake
NH Flat	4	6	0	0	0	6	0.0	-6.00
Hurdles	5	11	0	0	0	11	0.0	-11.00
Chases	1	7	1	1	2	3	14.3	-2.00
Totals	**7**	**24**	**1**	**1**	**2**	**20**	**4.2**	**-19.00**
11-12	*4*	*23*	*2*	*0*	*2*	*19*	*8.7*	*+41.00*
10-11	*2*	*20*	*0*	*2*	*2*	*16*	*0.0*	*-20.00*

JOCKEYS

	W-R	Per cent	£1 Level Stake
John Kington	1-16	6.3	-11.00

COURSE RECORD

	Total W-R	Non-Hndcps Hurdles	Chases	Hndcps Hurdles	Chases	NH Flat	Per cent	£1 Level Stake
Hexham	1-7	0-2	0-0	0-0	1-4	0-1	14.3	-2.00

WINNING HORSES

Horse	Races Run	1st	2nd	3rd	£
Panthers Run	7	1	1	2	2339
Total winning prize-money					£2339
Favourites	0-0		0.0%		0.00

PETER HEDGER

DOGMERSFIELD, HAMPSHIRE

	No. of Hrs	Races Run	1st	2nd	3rd	Unpl	Per cent	£1 Level Stake
NH Flat	0	0	0	0	0	0	0.0	0.00
Hurdles	3	12	1	2	0	9	8.3	-9.63
Chases	0	0	0	0	0	0	0.0	0.00
Totals	3	12	1	2	0	9	8.3	-9.63
11-12	7	11	0	0	0	11	0.0	-11.00
10-11	6	10	1	0	1	8	10.0	-4.00

JOCKEYS

	W-R	Per cent	£1 Level Stake
Leighton Aspell	1-4	25.0	-1.63

COURSE RECORD

	Total W-R	Non-Hndcps Hurdles	Chases	Hndcps Hurdles	Chases	NH Flat	Per cent	£1 Level Stake
Fontwell	1-3	1-3	0-0	0-0	0-0	0-0	33.3	-0.63

WINNING HORSES

Horse	Races Run	1st	2nd	3rd	£
Whipcrackaway	8	1	2	0	2534
Total winning prize-money					£2534
Favourites	1-3		33.3%		-0.63

PAUL HENDERSON

WHITSBURY, HANTS

	No. of Hrs	Races Run	1st	2nd	3rd	Unpl	Per cent	£1 Level Stake
NH Flat	6	11	2	0	1	8	18.2	+0.50
Hurdles	26	65	3	6	4	52	4.6	-28.00
Chases	12	55	11	4	4	36	20.0	+38.13
Totals	29	131	16	10	9	96	12.2	+10.63
11-12	19	98	13	8	8	69	13.3	-2.50
10-11	16	59	3	4	9	43	5.1	-24.75

BY MONTH

Month	NH Flat W-R	Per cent	£1 Level Stake	Hurdles W-R	Per cent	£1 Level Stake
May	0-1	0.0	-1.00	1-5	20.0	+18.00
June	0-1	0.0	-1.00	0-3	0.0	-3.00
July	0-3	0.0	-3.00	0-4	0.0	-4.00
August	0-0	0.0	0.00	0-5	0.0	-5.00
September	0-0	0.0	0.00	0-7	0.0	-7.00
October	0-0	0.0	0.00	0-1	0.0	-1.00
November	0-1	0.0	-1.00	0-6	0.0	-6.00
December	1-1	100.0	+5.50	0-8	0.0	-8.00
January	0-0	0.0	0.00	1-5	20.0	+3.00
February	0-2	0.0	-2.00	0-7	0.0	-7.00
March	1-1	100.0	+4.00	0-6	0.0	-6.00
April	0-1	0.0	-1.00	1-8	12.5	-2.00

Month	Chases W-R	Per cent	£1 Level Stake	Totals W-R	Per cent	£1 Level Stake
May	0-4	0.0	-4.00	1-10	10.0	+13.00
June	0-1	0.0	-1.00	0-5	0.0	-5.00
July	0-3	0.0	-3.00	0-10	0.0	-10.00
August	1-5	20.0	+18.00	1-10	10.0	+13.00
September	2-6	33.3	+11.50	2-13	15.4	+4.50
October	3-9	33.3	+9.50	3-10	30.0	+8.50
November	2-7	28.6	+3.38	2-14	14.3	-3.62
December	0-4	0.0	-4.00	1-13	7.7	-6.50
January	0-2	0.0	-2.00	1-7	14.3	+1.00
February	0-7	0.0	-7.00	0-16	0.0	-16.00
March	2-3	66.7	+3.75	3-10	30.0	+1.75
April	1-4	25.0	+13.00	2-13	15.4	+10.00

DISTANCE

Hurdles	W-R	Per cent	£1 Level Stake	Chases	W-R	Per cent	£1 Level Stake
2m-2m3f	0-32	0.0	-32.00	2m-2m3f	4-13	30.8	+37.50
2m4f-2m7f	3-32	9.4	+5.00	2m4f-2m7f	3-26	11.5	-14.75
3m+	0-1	0.0	-1.00	3m+	4-16	25.0	+15.38

TYPE OF RACE

Non-Handicaps	W-R	Per cent	£1 Level Stake	Handicaps	W-R	Per cent	£1 Level Stake
Nov Hrdls	0-16	0.0	-16.00	Nov Hrdls	0-10	0.0	-10.00
Hrdls	0-8	0.0	-8.00	Hrdls	3-31	9.7	+6.00
Nov Chs	0-2	0.0	-2.00	Nov Chs	1-8	12.5	+15.00
Chases	0-0	0.0	0.00	Chases	10-45	22.2	+25.13
Sell/Claim	0-0	0.0	0.00	Sell/Claim	0-0	0.0	0.00

RACE CLASS

	W-R	Per cent	£1 Level Stake
Class 1	0-4	0.0	-4.00
Class 2	1-6	16.7	+11.00
Class 3	1-29	3.4	-21.00
Class 4	6-54	11.1	+3.50
Class 5	6-30	20.0	+17.63
Class 6	2-8	25.0	+3.50

FIRST TIME OUT

	W-R	Per cent	£1 Level Stake
Bumpers	0-6	0.0	-6.00
Hurdles	0-17	0.0	-17.00
Chases	1-6	16.7	-2.00
Totals	1-29	3.4	-25.00

JOCKEYS

	W-R	Per cent	£1 Level Stake
Tom O'Brien	8-51	15.7	+24.75
James Best	2-7	28.6	+3.38

Richard Johnson	2-12	16.7	-3.50
Nick Scholfield	2-17	11.8	-3.00
David Bass	1-4	25.0	+19.00
Paddy Brennan	1-6	16.7	+4.00

COURSE RECORD

	Total W-R	Non-Hndcps Hurdles	Hndcps Chases	Hndcps Hurdles	Chases	NH Flat	Per cent	£1 Level Stake
Plumpton	4-9	0-0	0-0	1-2	3-7	0-0	44.4	+10.38
Nton Abbot	2-21	0-6	0-1	0-6	2-7	0-1	9.5	+5.75
Wincanton	2-24	0-4	0-0	1-12	1-7	0-1	8.3	+3.50
Uttoxeter	1-2	0-0	0-0	0-0	1-2	0-0	50.0	+5.50
Ffos Las	1-2	0-1	0-0	0-0	0-0	1-1	50.0	+3.00
Exeter	1-3	0-0	0-0	0-1	1-2	0-0	33.3	+1.00
Folkestone	1-3	0-1	0-0	0-0	0-1	1-1	33.3	+3.50
Hereford	1-3	0-1	0-0	0-1	1-1	0-0	33.3	+7.00
Cheltenham	1-5	0-0	0-0	0-1	1-4	0-0	20.0	+12.00
Fakenham	1-5	0-0	0-1	1-2	0-2	0-0	20.0	+3.00
Kempton	1-10	0-1	0-0	0-4	1-4	0-1	10.0	0.00

WINNING HORSES

Horse	Races Run	1st	2nd	3rd	£
Life Of A Luso	9	1	1	1	12512
Lucy's Legend	11	2	1	1	13394
Minella Special	4	2	0	0	11372
Chasers Chance	6	2	0	0	6498
Doheny Bar	3	1	0	0	3249
Minella Ranger	8	1	1	1	3249
Carleton Place	9	2	0	0	4938
Dushy Valley	11	2	1	1	3947
Pierre Dubh	7	1	0	0	1949
Steel City	4	1	0	1	1560
Rule Of Thumb	5	1	0	0	1437
Total winning prize-money					**£64105**
Favourites	**2-6**		**33.3%**		**-0.13**

NICKY HENDERSON

UPPER LAMBOURN, BERKS

	No. of Hrs	Races Run	1st	2nd	3rd	Unpl	Per cent	£1 Level Stake
NH Flat	*35*	*51*	*20*	*6*	*7*	*18*	*39.2*	*+4.96*
Hurdles	*104*	*299*	*69*	*46*	*31*	*152*	*23.1*	*-30.87*
Chases	*47*	*147*	*34*	*23*	*15*	*75*	*23.1*	*-10.11*
Totals	**159**	**497**	**123**	**75**	**53**	**245**	**24.7**	**-36.02**
11-12	*191*	*611*	*161*	*107*	*48*	*295*	*26.4*	*-9.14*
10-11	*201*	*609*	*152*	*75*	*68*	*314*	*25.0*	*-87.39*

BY MONTH

NH Flat	W-R	Per cent	£1 Level Stake	Hurdles	W-R	Per cent	£1 Level Stake
May	4-11	36.4	-3.18	May	6-22	27.3	+7.16
June	4-6	66.7	+6.89	June	1-8	12.5	-5.13
July	1-3	33.3	-1.33	July	2-9	22.2	-5.21
August	0-2	0.0	-2.00	August	3-6	50.0	+2.54

	W-R	Per cent	£1 Level Stake		W-R	Per cent	£1 Level Stake
September	0-1	0.0	-1.00	September	0-4	0.0	-4.00
October	1-2	50.0	+2.00	October	4-15	26.7	-3.15
November	1-2	50.0	+2.50	November	10-39	25.6	-12.93
December	1-1	100.0	+2.75	December	9-36	25.0	-1.80
January	1-2	50.0	-0.20	January	5-21	23.8	-5.73
February	2-5	40.0	+3.40	February	15-46	32.6	+6.66
March	2-4	50.0	-0.20	March	6-39	15.4	-15.90
April	3-12	25.0	-4.67	April	8-54	14.8	+6.61

Chases	W-R	Per cent	£1 Level Stake	Totals	W-R	Per cent	£1 Level Stake
May	1-7	14.3	+0.50	May	11-40	27.5	+4.48
June	1-3	33.3	-0.80	June	6-17	35.3	+0.96
July	0-0	0.0	0.00	July	3-12	25.0	-6.54
August	0-0	0.0	0.00	August	3-8	37.5	+0.54
September	0-0	0.0	0.00	September	0-5	0.0	-5.00
October	2-8	25.0	+5.00	October	7-25	28.0	+3.85
November	5-22	22.7	-3.10	November	16-63	25.4	-13.53
December	8-28	28.6	-2.80	December	18-65	27.7	-1.85
January	3-13	23.1	-8.40	January	9-36	25.0	-14.33
February	5-19	26.3	-1.15	February	22-70	31.4	+8.91
March	4-22	18.2	+1.53	March	12-65	18.5	-14.57
April	5-25	20.0	-0.90	April	16-91	17.6	+1.04

DISTANCE

Hurdles	W-R	Per cent	£1 Level Stake	Chases	W-R	Per cent	£1 Level Stake
2m-2m3f	46-177	26.0	-20.85	2m-2m3f	13-52	25.0	-30.87
2m4f-2m7f	22-94	23.4	+15.23	2m4f-2m7f	14-53	26.4	+22.13
3m+	1-28	3.6	-25.25	3m+	7-42	16.7	-1.38

TYPE OF RACE

Non-Handicaps	W-R	Per cent	£1 Level Stake	Handicaps	W-R	Per cent	£1 Level Stake
Nov Hrdls	30-82	36.6	-6.62	Nov Hrdls	4-14	28.6	+35.25
Hrdls	20-72	27.8	-17.83	Hrdls	15-130	11.5	-40.67
Nov Chs	16-48	33.3	-14.87	Nov Chs	2-11	18.2	+10.00
Chases	7-25	28.0	-11.70	Chases	9-62	14.5	+7.45
Sell/Claim	0-0	0.0	0.00	Sell/Claim	0-0	0.0	0.00

RACE CLASS

	W-R	Per cent	£1 Level Stake
Class 1	36-175	20.6	+4.64
Class 2	11-58	19.0	-8.70
Class 3	15-92	16.3	-40.16
Class 4	38-112	33.9	+3.68
Class 5	9-27	33.3	+0.21
Class 6	14-33	42.4	+5.31

FIRST TIME OUT

	W-R	Per cent	£1 Level Stake
Bumpers	15-35	42.9	+5.63
Hurdles	24-84	28.6	+3.59
Chases	13-40	32.5	+10.49
Totals	52-159	32.7	+19.71

JOCKEYS

	W-R	Per cent	£1 Level Stake
Barry Geraghty	53-187	28.3	-1.57
A P McCoy	20-66	30.3	-3.59
Andrew Tinkler	19-94	20.2	-41.41
David Bass	14-54	25.9	+13.90

Jeremiah McGrath	7-40	17.5	-7.29
Mr S Waley-Cohen	5-12	41.7	+17.27
Nico de Boinville	2-11	18.2	+9.00
Gary Derwin	1-4	25.0	-2.33
Edmond Linehan	1-5	20.0	-0.50
Jack Sherwood	1-6	16.7	-1.50

COURSE RECORD

	Total W-R	Non-Hndcps Hurdles	Chases	Hndcps Hurdles	Chases	NH Flat	Per cent	£1 Level Stake
Kempton	15-47	5-14	3-11	3-11	2-8	2-3	31.9	+38.14
Sandown	12-45	3-8	3-9	5-20	1-5	0-3	26.7	+14.28
Cheltenham	10-81	3-24	5-11	0-22	2-23	0-1	12.3	-35.22
Ascot	9-33	3-9	3-6	1-12	1-4	1-2	27.3	-4.98
Huntingdon	8-15	5-7	3-5	0-2	0-0	0-1	53.3	+2.91
Aintree	7-41	1-10	2-3	3-16	1-9	0-3	17.1	-0.60
Fontwell	6-8	3-4	0-0	1-1	1-1	1-2	75.0	+7.87
Newbury	6-43	2-11	0-6	2-14	1-10	1-2	14.0	-17.25
Bangor	5-8	3-4	0-1	1-1	0-0	1-2	62.5	+5.66
Fakenham	5-9	3-4	0-1	0-2	0-0	2-2	55.6	+1.62
Mrket Rsn	5-12	1-2	0-0	1-3	1-3	2-4	41.7	+11.30
Ffos Las	4-10	2-2	0-1	0-4	0-0	2-3	40.0	+1.21
Doncaster	4-17	3-10	1-4	0-3	0-0	0-0	23.5	-5.14
Ludlow	4-19	3-10	0-1	0-4	0-1	1-3	21.1	-6.45
Warwick	3-4	1-2	0-0	0-0	1-1	1-1	75.0	+3.67
Hereford	3-6	2-2	0-0	0-1	0-0	1-3	50.0	+2.58
Southwell	3-11	1-2	0-0	0-4	0-1	2-4	27.3	-1.08
Nton Abbot	2-5	0-1	0-0	1-2	0-1	1-1	40.0	+1.75
Taunton	2-8	1-3	1-1	0-3	0-1	0-0	25.0	-4.86
Stratford	2-12	1-2	0-0	1-5	0-3	0-2	16.7	-5.30
Perth	1-3	1-1	0-1	0-1	0-0	0-0	33.3	-0.25
Wetherby	1-3	1-2	0-1	0-0	0-0	0-0	33.3	-0.38
Plumpton	1-4	0-2	1-2	0-0	0-0	0-0	25.0	-2.70
Ayr	1-5	0-0	1-1	0-2	0-1	0-1	20.0	-1.00
Haydock	1-7	1-2	0-1	0-4	0-0	0-0	14.3	-5.70
Towcester	1-7	0-3	0-1	0-0	0-0	1-3	14.3	-4.00
Uttoxeter	1-7	1-2	0-1	0-2	0-0	1-2	14.3	-6.27
Worcester	1-8	1-4	0-1	0-2	0-0	0-0	12.5	-6.83

WINNING HORSES

Horse	Races Run	1st	2nd	3rd	£
Bobs Worth	2	2	0	0	398650
Sprinter Sacre	4	4	0	0	429101
Long Run	3	1	1	1	113900
My Tent Or Yours	6	4	2	0	131970
Simonsig	3	3	0	0	118418
Triolo D'Alene	5	1	1	1	67524
Roberto Goldback	6	1	0	1	56270
Oscar Whisky	5	2	1	0	73423
Darlan	2	1	0	0	48408
Captain Conan	5	4	0	0	100802
Rajdhani Express	6	3	1	0	65124
Close Touch	5	4	1	0	46965
Nadiya De La Vega	5	1	0	2	31280
Minella Forfitness	5	3	1	1	34648
Oscara Dara	5	1	1	0	25628
Molotof	7	2	2	1	23441
Lyvius	5	1	0	0	19933
Polly Peachum	6	3	0	0	24503
Petit Robin	7	2	1	0	24592
Rolling Star	3	1	0	0	17085
Ma Filleule	6	2	3	0	20984
Forgotten Voice	5	3	1	0	20730
Gibb River	1	1	0	0	15640
Bear's Affair	3	1	0	0	12825
Tetlami	5	2	1	0	18072
Utopie Des Bordes	5	3	1	0	24440
Une Artiste	4	2	0	0	22780
Whisper	5	3	0	0	16183
River Maigue	4	1	2	0	9697
Open Hearted	3	1	0	1	9384
First In The Queue	8	1	1	0	8058
Top Of The Range	6	1	0	1	7798
State Benefit	5	1	0	0	7795
Minella Class	5	1	0	1	7577
Hadrian's Approach	6	1	2	1	6882
Malt Master	3	1	2	0	6498
Chatterbox	3	2	0	0	9626
Cape Express	5	4	0	0	12632
Captain Cutter	2	1	0	1	6265
Prince Of Pirates	3	1	0	1	6256
Broadbackbob	2	1	0	0	5848
Zama Zama	1	1	0	0	5198
Golden Hoof	7	3	2	0	8447
Ericht	5	2	0	0	7148
Who's Cross	2	1	0	1	3899
Private Equity	5	1	3	1	3769
Otto The Great	4	1	1	0	3769
*Little Dutch Girl	6	1	1	2	3422
Carabinier	1	1	0	0	3249
Master Of The Game	3	1	0	2	3249
Miss Ballantyne	4	1	1	1	3249
Heronry	5	3	0	1	7733
One Conemara	4	2	1	0	3249
Shernando	4	1	1	2	3119
Definite Ruby	6	1	1	2	3119
Springinherstep	4	2	1	0	3119
West Wizard	1	1	0	0	2989
Makari	3	1	1	0	2924
Laudatory	6	1	1	0	2599
Pippa Greene	1	1	0	0	2534
Lieutenant Miller	5	1	3	0	2534
City Press	1	1	0	0	2534
Vasco Du Ronceray	6	1	2	0	2534
Rackham Lerouge	2	1	0	0	2404
Mayfair Music	1	1	0	0	2395
Karazhan	3	2	1	0	3639
Free Thinking	3	1	0	1	2053
Glorious Twelfth	4	1	1	0	1949
Tradewinds	2	1	1	0	1949
Oscar Hoof	3	2	0	1	3509
Billy Twyford	2	1	1	1	1745
Fabrika	3	1	1	0	1560

Act Four	2	1	0	0	1560
Spartan Angel	1	1	0	0	1437
Seaham Hall	1	1	0	0	1365
Your Tepee Or Mine	3	1	0	0	1365
Cevaro	6	1	2	1	1365
Total winning prize-money					**£2220316**
Favourites	**108-196**		**55.1%**		**19.70**

LADY HERRIES

PATCHING, W SUSSEX

	No. of Hrs	Races Run	1st	2nd	3rd	Unpl	Per cent	£1 Level Stake
NH Flat	1	1	0	0	0	1	0.0	-1.00
Hurdles	0	0	0	0	0	0	0.0	0.00
Chases	1	3	1	1	1	0	33.3	-1.27
Totals	**2**	**4**	**1**	**1**	**1**	**1**	**25.0**	**-2.27**
11-12	*5*	*16*	*4*	*2*	*1*	*9*	*25.0*	*-1.70*
10-11	*3*	*8*	*0*	*3*	*0*	*5*	*0.0*	*-8.00*

JOCKEYS

	W-R	Per cent	£1 Level Stake
Richard Johnson	1-3	33.3	-1.27

COURSE RECORD

	Total W-R	Non-Hndcps Hurdles	Chases	Hndcps Hurdles	Chases	NH Flat	Per cent	£1 Level Stake
Stratford	1-1	0-0	1-1	0-0	0-0	0-0	100.0	+0.73

WINNING HORSES

Horse	Races Run	1st	2nd	3rd	£
Geneva Geyser	3	1	1	1	3899
Total winning prize-money					**£3899**
Favourites	**1-1**		**100.0%**		**0.73**

PETER HIATT

HOOK NORTON, OXON

	No. of Hrs	Races Run	1st	2nd	3rd	Unpl	Per cent	£1 Level Stake
NH Flat	1	2	0	0	0	2	0.0	-2.00
Hurdles	5	12	3	1	0	8	25.0	+15.25
Chases	2	4	0	0	0	4	0.0	-4.00
Totals	**8**	**18**	**3**	**1**	**0**	**14**	**16.7**	**+9.25**
11-12	*13*	*44*	*2*	*4*	*3*	*35*	*4.5*	*+4.00*
10-11	*14*	*39*	*2*	*4*	*5*	*28*	*5.1*	*-17.00*

JOCKEYS

	W-R	Per cent	£1 Level Stake
Trevor Whelan	2-3	66.7	+3.25
Liam Treadwell	1-10	10.0	+11.00

COURSE RECORD

	Total W-R	Non-Hndcps Hurdles	Chases	Hndcps Hurdles	Chases	NH Flat	Per cent	£1 Level Stake
Doncaster	1-1	0-0	0-0	1-1	0-0	0-0	100.0	+20.00
Mrket Rsn	1-1	0-0	0-0	1-1	0-0	0-0	100.0	+2.00
Lingfield	1-2	0-0	0-0	1-2	0-0	0-0	50.0	+1.25

WINNING HORSES

Horse	Races Run	1st	2nd	3rd	£
Killimore Cottage	7	3	1	0	5328
Total winning prize-money					**£5328**
Favourites	**1-1**		**100.0%**		**2.25**

ALAN HILL

ASTON ROWANT, OXFORDSHIRE

	No. of Hrs	Races Run	1st	2nd	3rd	Unpl	Per cent	£1 Level Stake
NH Flat	0	0	0	0	0	0	0.0	0.00
Hurdles	0	0	0	0	0	0	0.0	0.00
Chases	4	9	2	2	2	3	22.2	-3.65
Totals	**4**	**9**	**2**	**2**	**2**	**3**	**22.2**	**-3.65**
11-12	*5*	*8*	*3*	*2*	*1*	*2*	*37.5*	*+3.90*
10-11	*3*	*5*	*2*	*1*	*1*	*1*	*40.0*	*-0.46*

JOCKEYS

	W-R	Per cent	£1 Level Stake
Mr P York	1-2	50.0	+0.10
Mr Joe Hill	1-3	33.3	+0.25

COURSE RECORD

	Total W-R	Non-Hndcps Hurdles	Chases	Hndcps Hurdles	Chases	NH Flat	Per cent	£1 Level Stake
Doncaster	1-1	0-0	1-1	0-0	0-0	0-0	100.0	+1.10
Fakenham	1-1	0-0	1-1	0-0	0-0	0-0	100.0	+2.25

WINNING HORSES

Horse	Races Run	1st	2nd	3rd	£
*Dante's Storm	2	1	0	0	1248
*Ravethebrave	3	1	0	2	1185
Total winning prize-money					**£2433**
Favourites	**2-3**		**66.7%**		**2.35**

LAWNEY HILL

ASTON ROWANT, OXON

	No. of Hrs	Races Run	1st	2nd	3rd	Unpl	Per cent	£1 Level Stake
NH Flat	3	5	1	1	0	3	20.0	+1.50
Hurdles	27	67	8	7	2	50	11.9	-28.80
Chases	22	58	6	7	10	35	10.3	-16.90

Totals	41	130	15	15	12	88	11.5	-44.20
11-12	45	141	22	16	16	87	15.6	-11.52
10-11	46	143	27	19	12	85	18.9	+30.66

	W-R	Per cent	£1 Level Stake				
Class 3	1-19	5.3	-13.50	Chases	3-15	20.0	+9.00
Class 4	6-60	10.0	-20.63				
Class 5	6-39	15.4	-14.57	Totals	5-41	12.2	-8.13
Class 6	1-5	20.0	+1.50				

BY MONTH

NH Flat	W-R	Per cent	£1 Level Stake	Hurdles	W-R	Per cent	£1 Level Stake
May	1-2	50.0	+4.50	May	0-3	0.0	-3.00
June	0-0	0.0	0.00	June	0-5	0.0	-5.00
July	0-0	0.0	0.00	July	1-5	20.0	-2.63
August	0-0	0.0	0.00	August	0-5	0.0	-5.00
September	0-1	0.0	-1.00	September	0-6	0.0	-6.00
October	0-1	0.0	-1.00	October	1-8	12.5	+4.00
November	0-0	0.0	0.00	November	2-4	50.0	+1.13
December	0-0	0.0	0.00	December	0-7	0.0	-7.00
January	0-0	0.0	0.00	January	1-7	14.3	-4.00
February	0-0	0.0	0.00	February	2-9	22.2	+1.20
March	0-1	0.0	-1.00	March	1-4	25.0	+1.50
April	0-0	0.0	0.00	April	0-4	0.0	-4.00

Chases	W-R	Per cent	£1 Level Stake	Totals	W-R	Per cent	£1 Level Stake
May	1-2	50.0	+0.10	May	2-7	28.6	+1.60
June	0-4	0.0	-4.00	June	0-9	0.0	-9.00
July	3-9	33.3	+15.00	July	4-14	28.6	+12.37
August	0-8	0.0	-8.00	August	0-13	0.0	-13.00
September	1-4	25.0	+5.00	September	1-11	9.1	-2.00
October	0-8	0.0	-8.00	October	1-17	5.9	-5.00
November	0-7	0.0	-7.00	November	2-11	18.2	-5.87
December	0-4	0.0	-4.00	December	0-11	0.0	-11.00
January	0-0	0.0	0.00	January	1-7	14.3	-4.00
February	0-5	0.0	-5.00	February	2-14	14.3	-3.80
March	0-2	0.0	-2.00	March	1-7	14.3	-1.50
April	1-5	20.0	+1.00	April	1-9	11.1	-3.00

DISTANCE

Hurdles	W-R	Per cent	£1 Level Stake	Chases	W-R	Per cent	£1 Level Stake
2m-2m3f	2-21	9.5	-10.80	2m-2m3f	1-4	25.0	+4.50
2m4f-2m7f	2-22	9.1	-13.50	2m4f-2m7f	2-21	9.5	-5.50
3m+	4-24	16.7	-4.50	3m+	3-33	9.1	-15.90

TYPE OF RACE

Non-Handicaps	W-R	Per cent	£1 Level Stake	Handicaps	W-R	Per cent	£1 Level Stake
Nov Hrdls	0-8	0.0	-8.00	Nov Hrdls	0-3	0.0	-3.00
Hrdls	0-5	0.0	-5.00	Hrdls	6-49	12.2	-16.00
Nov Chs	0-8	0.0	-8.00	Nov Chs	2-7	28.6	+7.00
Chases	1-2	50.0	+0.10	Chases	3-41	7.3	-16.00
Sell/Claim	2-2	100.0	+3.20	Sell/Claim	0-0	0.0	0.00

RACE CLASS / FIRST TIME OUT

	W-R	Per cent	£1 Level Stake		W-R	Per cent	£1 Level Stake
Class 1	1-5	20.0	+5.00	Bumpers	1-3	33.3	+3.50
Class 2	0-2	0.0	-2.00	Hurdles	1-23	4.3	-20.63

JOCKEYS

	W-R	Per cent	£1 Level Stake
David Bass	8-67	11.9	-13.50
Harry Skelton	3-23	13.0	-5.88
Miss G Andrews	1-2	50.0	+0.10
Joshua Moore	1-3	33.3	-0.80
Dougie Costello	1-5	20.0	+3.50
Aidan Coleman	1-12	8.3	-9.63

COURSE RECORD

	Total W-R	Non-Hndcps Hurdles	Chases	Hndcps Hurdles	Chases	NH Flat	Per cent	£1 Level Stake
Fontwell	4-16	0-1	0-3	3-8	1-3	0-1	25.0	+0.63
Mrket Rsn	3-7	0-1	0-0	0-2	3-4	0-0	42.9	+17.50
Catterick	1-1	1-1	0-0	0-0	0-0	0-0	100.0	+1.20
Fakenham	1-2	1-1	0-0	0-1	0-0	0-0	50.0	+1.00
Wetherby	1-2	0-1	0-0	1-1	0-0	0-0	50.0	+6.00
Folkestone	1-3	0-0	1-1	0-0	0-2	0-0	33.3	-0.90
Plumpton	1-8	0-1	0-1	0-3	0-2	1-1	12.5	-1.50
Stratford	1-8	0-0	0-0	0-2	1-6	0-0	12.5	+0.50
Uttoxeter	1-8	0-0	0-0	1-4	0-4	0-0	12.5	-5.63
Huntingdon	1-11	0-2	0-0	1-8	0-0	0-1	9.1	+1.00

WINNING HORSES

Horse	Races Run	1st	2nd	3rd	£
*I Have Dreamed	1	1	0	0	28475
*Billy Twyford	3	2	1	0	8678
Giant O Murchu	5	1	0	0	3899
*Bellaboosh	1	1	0	0	3899
Quarl Ego	5	1	1	1	3769
Baily Storm	6	1	2	1	3249
*Ocean Du Moulin	2	1	1	0	2599
*Overlay	6	3	0	0	5978
Minella Theatre	6	1	1	0	2053
Aghill	5	1	1	1	2053
Mid Div And Creep	2	1	0	0	1872
Come On Laurie	2	1	0	0	1437
Total winning prize-money					**£67961**
Favourites	5-12		41.7%		-0.20

MARTIN HILL

LITTLEHEMPSTON, DEVON

	No. of Hrs	Races Run	1st	2nd	3rd	Unpl	Per cent	£1 Level Stake
NH Flat	3	5	0	0	0	5	0.0	-5.00
Hurdles	9	25	3	1	2	19	12.0	+38.00
Chases	2	6	0	0	0	6	0.0	-6.00
Totals	**14**	**36**	**3**	**1**	**2**	**30**	**8.3**	**+27.00**

11-12	10	34	1	5	0	28	2.9	-27.00
10-11	11	29	4	1	4	20	13.8	+47.00

JOCKEYS

	W-R	Per cent	£1 Level Stake
Hadden Frost	3-26	11.5	+37.00

COURSE RECORD

	Total W-R	Non-Hndcps Hurdles	Chases	Hndcps Hurdles	Chases	NH Flat	Per cent	£1 Level Stake
Exeter	2-7	1-1	0-0	1-5	0-1	0-0	28.6	+22.00
Stratford	1-7	0-1	0-0	1-4	0-1	0-1	14.3	+27.00

WINNING HORSES

Horse	Races Run	1st	2nd	3rd	£
Tzora	6	1	0	2	5848
Kim Tian Road	2	2	0	0	3899
Total winning prize-money					£9747
Favourites	0-0		0.0%		0.00

ANDY HOBBS

HANLEY SWAN, WORCS

	No. of Hrs	Races Run	1st	2nd	3rd	Unpl	Per cent	£1 Level Stake
NH Flat	2	2	0	0	0	2	0.0	-2.00
Hurdles	14	32	1	2	1	28	3.1	-17.00
Chases	9	26	1	4	2	19	3.8	-23.13
Totals	19	60	2	6	3	49	3.3	-42.13
11-12	3	4	1	0	0	3	25.0	+3.00
10-11	2	4	2	1	1	0	50.0	-0.33

JOCKEYS

	W-R	Per cent	£1 Level Stake
Charlie Huxley	1-9	11.1	+6.00
D P Fahy	1-28	3.6	-25.13

COURSE RECORD

	Total W-R	Non-Hndcps Hurdles	Chases	Hndcps Hurdles	Chases	NH Flat	Per cent	£1 Level Stake
Ffos Las	1-4	0-1	0-0	0-1	1-2	0-0	25.0	-1.13
Huntingdon	1-8	1-3	0-0	0-2	0-2	0-1	12.5	+7.00

WINNING HORSES

Horse	Races Run	1st	2nd	3rd	£
Waltzing Tornado	7	1	1	0	2144
*Nether Stream	2	1	0	0	1689
Total winning prize-money					£3833
Favourites	1-11		9.1%		-8.13

MRS K HOBBS

HUNGERFORD, SHROP

	No. of Hrs	Races Run	1st	2nd	3rd	Unpl	Per cent	£1 Level Stake
NH Flat	0	0	0	0	0	0	0.0	0.00
Hurdles	0	0	0	0	0	0	0.0	0.00
Chases	1	1	1	0	0	0	100.0	+1.50
Totals	1	1	1	0	0	0	100.0	+1.50
11-12	1	1	0	1	0	0	0.0	-1.00
10-11	2	2	0	0	1	1	0.0	-2.00

JOCKEYS

	W-R	Per cent	£1 Level Stake
Thomas Cheesman	1-1	100.0	+1.50

COURSE RECORD

	Total W-R	Non-Hndcps Hurdles	Chases	Hndcps Hurdles	Chases	NH Flat	Per cent	£1 Level Stake
Folkestone	1-1	0-0	1-1	0-0	0-0	0-0	100.0	+1.50

WINNING HORSES

Horse	Races Run	1st	2nd	3rd	£
Commander Kev	1	1	0	0	1153
Total winning prize-money					£1153
Favourites	1-1		100.0%		1.50

PHILIP HOBBS

WITHYCOMBE, SOMERSET

	No. of Hrs	Races Run	1st	2nd	3rd	Unpl	Per cent	£1 Level Stake
NH Flat	31	48	6	10	8	24	12.5	-25.40
Hurdles	98	275	33	37	25	180	12.0	-42.89
Chases	54	184	29	29	26	99	15.8	-18.99
Totals	138	507	68	76	59	303	13.4	-87.28
11-12	142	507	73	72	56	306	14.4	-140.80
10-11	152	556	86	76	79	315	15.5	-154.06

BY MONTH

NH Flat	W-R	Per cent	£1 Level Stake	Hurdles	W-R	Per cent	£1 Level Stake
May	0-5	0.0	-5.00	May	4-15	26.7	-0.07
June	0-2	0.0	-2.00	June	0-10	0.0	-10.00
July	0-0	0.0	0.00	July	0-11	0.0	-11.00
August	0-0	0.0	0.00	August	0-6	0.0	-6.00
September	0-0	0.0	0.00	September	0-4	0.0	-4.00
October	1-3	33.3	+1.50	October	4-33	12.1	0.00
November	0-5	0.0	-5.00	November	5-37	13.5	+22.25
December	2-8	25.0	+0.75	December	6-32	18.8	-5.20
January	0-3	0.0	-3.00	January	3-24	12.5	-18.68
February	0-9	0.0	-9.00	February	6-34	17.6	-1.95
March	2-9	22.2	-2.90	March	2-42	4.8	+1.25

April	1-4	25.0	-0.75

Chases	W-R	Per cent	£1 Level Stake
May	3-8	37.5	+12.50
June	0-7	0.0	-7.00
July	1-6	16.7	0.00
August	4-7	57.1	+35.00
September	1-10	10.0	-0.50
October	3-19	15.8	-2.88
November	5-23	21.7	-2.27
December	2-23	8.7	-14.00
January	2-14	14.3	-2.75
February	4-27	14.8	-9.33
March	1-17	5.9	-14.50
April	3-23	13.0	-13.25

April	3-27	11.1	-9.50

Totals	W-R	Per cent	£1 Level Stake
May	7-28	25.0	+7.43
June	0-19	0.0	-19.00
July	1-17	5.9	-11.00
August	4-13	30.8	+29.00
September	1-14	7.1	-4.50
October	8-55	14.5	-1.38
November	10-65	15.4	+14.98
December	10-63	15.9	-18.45
January	5-41	12.2	-24.43
February	10-70	14.3	-20.28
March	5-68	7.4	-16.15
April	7-54	13.0	-23.50

Course	W-R						Per cent	£1 Level Stake
Chepstow	5-29	2-10	1-4	1-7	1-8	0-0	17.2	-1.89
Lingfield	4-4	2-2	1-1	0-0	1-1	0-0	100.0	+6.82
Bangor	4-11	0-1	0-1	1-2	3-4	0-3	36.4	+11.50
Newbury	4-24	2-3	1-4	1-7	0-9	0-1	16.7	+57.80
Exeter	4-44	2-17	1-7	0-9	0-5	1-6	9.1	-33.57
Fontwell	3-10	2-4	0-0	1-5	0-1	0-0	30.0	+12.75
Towcester	3-10	2-5	0-2	1-2	0-0	0-1	30.0	-0.58
Ascot	3-18	1-5	1-3	1-4	0-2	0-4	16.7	-3.00
Ffos Las	3-21	0-7	1-2	0-2	1-5	1-5	14.3	-5.40
Nton Abbot	3-27	0-8	0-0	0-7	3-11	0-1	11.1	-11.75
Cheltenham	3-41	0-7	1-6	1-15	1-12	0-1	7.3	-23.27
Mrket Rsn	2-7	0-1	0-0	1-3	1-3	0-0	28.6	+5.00
Uttoxeter	2-10	1-4	0-1	0-2	0-0	1-3	20.0	-2.25
Worcester	2-16	1-4	0-1	0-5	1-5	0-1	12.5	+14.00
Sandown	2-24	1-3	0-2	0-9	1-10	0-0	8.3	-17.40
Kempton	2-26	0-8	2-5	0-6	0-4	0-3	7.7	-14.00
Leicester	1-3	0-1	0-1	1-1	0-0	0-0	33.3	-1.09
Plumpton	1-6	0-2	0-1	1-2	0-0	0-1	16.7	-2.50
Hereford	1-7	1-3	0-0	0-2	0-2	0-0	14.3	-2.00
Warwick	1-8	0-1	1-1	0-3	0-1	0-2	12.5	-1.50
Doncaster	1-9	0-1	0-3	1-3	0-2	0-0	11.1	+12.00
Haydock	1-13	0-2	0-0	0-7	0-3	1-1	7.7	-9.00
Aintree	1-16	0-1	0-2	0-5	1-8	0-0	6.3	-11.50
Taunton	1-31	0-10	0-2	1-10	0-3	0-6	3.2	-29.20

DISTANCE

Hurdles	W-R	Per cent	£1 Level Stake
2m-2m3f	17-128	13.3	-66.39
2m4f-2m7f	11-103	10.7	-3.50
3m+	5-44	11.4	+27.00

Chases	W-R	Per cent	£1 Level Stake
2m-2m3f	6-44	13.6	-18.66
2m4f-2m7f	14-68	20.6	+16.92
3m+	9-72	12.5	-17.25

TYPE OF RACE

Non-Handicaps	W-R	Per cent	£1 Level Stake
Nov Hrdls	11-89	12.4	-1.35
Hrdls	9-53	17.0	-9.37
Nov Chs	9-46	19.6	-9.72
Chases	4-18	22.2	-2.27
Sell/Claim	0-0	0.0	0.00

Handicaps	W-R	Per cent	£1 Level Stake
Nov Hrdls	1-12	8.3	-8.00
Hrdls	12-121	9.9	-24.18
Nov Chs	2-14	14.3	-5.00
Chases	14-105	13.3	-1.00
Sell/Claim	0-1	0.0	-1.00

RACE CLASS

	W-R	Per cent	£1 Level Stake
Class 1	5-64	7.8	-36.00
Class 2	5-48	10.4	-21.27
Class 3	12-113	10.6	+3.72
Class 4	35-199	17.6	-2.23
Class 5	7-48	14.6	-11.85
Class 6	4-35	11.4	-19.65

FIRST TIME OUT

	W-R	Per cent	£1 Level Stake
Bumpers	3-31	9.7	-17.00
Hurdles	12-74	16.2	+17.93
Chases	7-33	21.2	+8.12
Totals	22-138	15.9	+9.05

JOCKEYS

	W-R	Per cent	£1 Level Stake
Richard Johnson	42-274	15.3	+16.03
Tom O'Brien	15-103	14.6	-13.18
A P McCoy	6-24	25.0	-10.88
James Best	3-51	5.9	-34.00
Micheal Nolan	2-28	7.1	-18.25

COURSE RECORD

	Total W-R	Non-Hndcps Hurdles	Chases	Hndcps Hurdles	Chases	NH Flat	Per cent	£1 Level Stake
Wincanton	6-28	2-9	1-4	1-6	0-4	2-5	21.4	+2.00
Ludlow	5-22	1-9	2-4	0-0	2-8	0-1	22.7	+2.75

WINNING HORSES

Horse	Races Run	1st	2nd	3rd	£
Wishfull Thinking	7	2	1	2	56908
Balthazar King	4	1	1	0	31280
The Disengager	8	4	0	0	43420
Captain Chris	4	1	2	0	28475
Menorah	6	1	2	2	22780
Lamb Or Cod	3	1	0	0	19933
*Ballygarvey	6	3	0	0	23363
Marufo	2	1	1	0	12512
Big Easy	5	1	0	0	10010
Fair Along	4	1	0	1	8758
Rob Conti	5	2	1	1	10589
Fingal Bay	3	1	1	0	7323
Fairoak Lad	4	1	0	0	6963
Thunderstorm	6	5	0	0	22392
Roll The Dice	9	2	2	3	10229
De La Bech	7	3	1	0	12824
*Pistol	4	2	1	0	9097
Doctor Foxtrot	1	1	0	0	5393
Ballytober	5	1	1	0	5005
Tony Star	8	1	2	2	4549
Thomas Wild	4	1	1	0	4289
Uncle Jimmy	5	2	1	0	7473
Calusa Caldera	4	2	0	0	7148
Filbert	4	1	0	0	3899
Carrigmorna King	6	1	1	1	3899
Orabora	3	1	0	1	3899
Berkeley Barron	2	1	0	0	3899
Pateese	6	1	0	2	3769
Al Alfa	6	1	1	0	3769

Bright Abbey	4	1	0	1	3574
Return Spring	6	1	2	0	3574
Quick Decisson	3	2	0	1	4776
Reste Gosse	2	1	0	0	3249
So Fine	6	1	0	3	3249
Sammys Gone	3	1	1	0	3249
If In Doubt	5	1	2	1	3119
Western Jo	3	2	0	0	4762
Woodford County	2	1	0	0	2669
Princely Player	5	1	1	0	2599
Bold Henry	3	1	1	1	2599
Gas Line Boy	5	1	1	1	2599
Marchand D'Argent	7	1	1	0	2534
Lord Lescribaa	6	1	1	0	2395
Joseph Mercer	5	1	0	1	2144
Irish Buccaneer	4	1	2	1	2053
The Skyfarmer	3	1	1	1	1949
Royal Regatta	1	1	0	0	1949
Horizontal Speed	4	1	2	0	1430
Garde La Victoire	1	1	0	0	1365
Total winning prize-money					**£449684**
Favourites	**23-80**		**28.7%**		**-22.03**

RACHEL HOBBS

HANLEY SWAN, WORCS

	No. of Hrs	Races Run	1st	2nd	3rd	Unpl	Per cent	£1 Level Stake
NH Flat	3	4	0	0	0	4	0.0	-4.00
Hurdles	13	21	1	1	2	17	4.8	-11.00
Chases	3	5	2	0	1	2	40.0	+16.33
Totals	**17**	**30**	**3**	**1**	**3**	**23**	**10.0**	**+1.33**
11-12	29	107	7	9	26	65	6.5	-31.00
10-11	27	100	7	14	14	65	7.0	-28.75

JOCKEYS

	W-R	Per cent	£1 Level Stake
Peter Carberry	1-3	33.3	+14.00
D P Fahy	1-4	25.0	+6.00
Sean Quinlan	1-8	12.5	-3.67

COURSE RECORD

	Total W-R	Non-Hndcps Hurdles	Chases	Hndcps Hurdles	Chases	NH Flat	Per cent	£1 Level Stake
Worcester	2-12	1-3	0-0	0-5	1-2	0-2	16.7	+15.00
Hereford	1-3	0-1	0-0	0-1	1-1	0-0	33.3	+1.33

WINNING HORSES

Horse	Races Run	1st	2nd	3rd	£
Unwanted Gift	2	1	0	0	2020
Bennys Quest	4	1	0	0	1916
Faith Jicaro	2	1	0	1	1779
Total winning prize-money					**£5715**
Favourites	**0-0**		**0.0%**		**0.00**

RON HODGES

CHARLTON MACKRELL, SOMERSET

	No. of Hrs	Races Run	1st	2nd	3rd	Unpl	Per cent	£1 Level Stake
NH Flat	3	5	0	0	0	5	0.0	-5.00
Hurdles	7	21	0	0	0	21	0.0	-21.00
Chases	3	10	1	0	1	8	10.0	-1.50
Totals	**12**	**36**	**1**	**0**	**1**	**34**	**2.8**	**-27.50**
11-12	18	72	7	2	8	55	9.7	+45.68
10-11	29	88	3	9	9	67	3.4	-67.38

JOCKEYS

	W-R	Per cent	£1 Level Stake
Jack Doyle	1-5	20.0	+3.50

COURSE RECORD

	Total W-R	Non-Hndcps Hurdles	Chases	Hndcps Hurdles	Chases	NH Flat	Per cent	£1 Level Stake
Wincanton	1-5	0-1	0-0	0-2	1-1	0-1	20.0	+3.50

WINNING HORSES

Horse	Races Run	1st	2nd	3rd	£
Miss Tenacious	6	1	0	0	4161
Total winning prize-money					**£4161**
Favourites	**0-1**		**0.0%**		**-1.00**

SIMON HODGSON

YEOVIL, SOMERSET

	No. of Hrs	Races Run	1st	2nd	3rd	Unpl	Per cent	£1 Level Stake
NH Flat	3	5	2	0	0	3	40.0	+28.00
Hurdles	2	11	0	3	0	8	0.0	-11.00
Chases	0	0	0	0	0	0	0.0	0.00
Totals	**5**	**16**	**2**	**3**	**0**	**11**	**12.5**	**+17.00**

JOCKEYS

	W-R	Per cent	£1 Level Stake
James Davies	2-7	28.6	+26.00

COURSE RECORD

	Total W-R	Non-Hndcps Hurdles	Chases	Hndcps Hurdles	Chases	NH Flat	Per cent	£1 Level Stake
Towcester	1-1	0-0	0-0	0-0	0-0	1-1	100.0	+22.00
Taunton	1-3	0-0	0-0	0-1	0-0	1-2	33.3	+7.00

WINNING HORSES

Horse	Races Run	1st	2nd	3rd	£
Neston Grace	3	2	0	0	3931
Total winning prize-money					£3931
Favourites	0-0		0.0%		0.00

HENRY HOGARTH

STILLINGTON, N YORKS

	No. of Hrs	Races Run	1st	2nd	3rd	Unpl	Per cent	£1 Level Stake
NH Flat	0	0	0	0	0	0	0.0	0.00
Hurdles	9	18	0	2	1	15	0.0	-18.00
Chases	10	33	2	0	10	21	6.1	-15.00
Totals	13	51	2	2	11	36	3.9	-33.00
11-12	14	54	1	6	9	38	1.9	-46.50
10-11	15	57	5	6	3	43	8.8	-25.13

JOCKEYS

	W-R	Per cent	£1 Level Stake
Brian Hughes	1-9	11.1	0.00
Fearghal Davis	1-22	4.5	-13.00

COURSE RECORD

	Total W-R	Non-Hndcps Hurdles	Chases	Hndcps Hurdles	Chases	NH Flat	Per cent	£1 Level Stake
Cartmel	1-2	0-0	0-0	0-0	1-2	0-0	50.0	+7.00
Hexham	1-11	0-0	0-2	0-3	1-6	0-0	9.1	-2.00

WINNING HORSES

Horse	Races Run	1st	2nd	3rd	£
Mysterious World	4	1	0	2	2599
Finbin	6	1	1	0	2498
Total winning prize-money					£5097
Favourites	0-2		0.0%		-2.00

REG HOLLINSHEAD

UPPER LONGDON, STAFFS

	No. of Hrs	Races Run	1st	2nd	3rd	Unpl	Per cent	£1 Level Stake
NH Flat	3	6	0	0	0	6	0.0	-6.00
Hurdles	10	21	1	1	3	16	4.8	+5.00
Chases	0	0	0	0	0	0	0.0	0.00
Totals	13	27	1	1	3	22	3.7	-1.00
11-12	10	27	0	2	2	23	0.0	-27.00
10-11	11	46	3	2	3	38	6.5	-22.25

JOCKEYS

	W-R	Per cent	£1 Level Stake
Paul Moloney	1-9	11.1	+17.00

COURSE RECORD

	Total W-R	Non-Hndcps Hurdles	Chases	Hndcps Hurdles	Chases	NH Flat	Per cent	£1 Level Stake
Bangor	1-6	1-5	0-0	0-0	0-0	0-1	16.7	+20.00

WINNING HORSES

Horse	Races Run	1st	2nd	3rd	£
Rapid Heat Lad	3	1	0	1	2669
Total winning prize-money					£2669
Favourites	0-0		0.0%		0.00

ANTHONY HONEYBALL

MOSTERTON, DORSET

	No. of Hrs	Races Run	1st	2nd	3rd	Unpl	Per cent	£1 Level Stake
NH Flat	18	29	4	5	4	16	13.8	-7.88
Hurdles	19	48	4	6	6	31	8.3	-33.42
Chases	10	28	11	1	1	15	39.3	+24.54
Totals	35	105	19	12	11	62	18.1	-16.76
11-12	31	83	22	11	12	38	26.5	+45.88
10-11	19	61	14	6	10	30	23.0	+62.25

BY MONTH

NH Flat	W-R	Per cent	£1 Level Stake	Hurdles	W-R	Per cent	£1 Level Stake
May	0-2	0.0	-2.00	May	0-2	0.0	-2.00
June	0-1	0.0	-1.00	June	0-0	0.0	0.00
July	0-0	0.0	0.00	July	1-4	25.0	+1.50
August	0-3	0.0	-3.00	August	1-3	33.3	+3.00
September	0-0	0.0	0.00	September	0-0	0.0	0.00
October	1-3	33.3	-0.63	October	1-8	12.5	-6.17
November	1-3	33.3	+9.00	November	0-10	0.0	-10.00
December	0-3	0.0	-3.00	December	0-5	0.0	-5.00
January	0-2	0.0	-2.00	January	1-1	100.0	+0.25
February	1-5	20.0	-3.75	February	0-7	0.0	-7.00
March	0-2	0.0	-2.00	March	0-4	0.0	-4.00
April	1-5	20.0	+0.50	April	0-4	0.0	-4.00

Chases	W-R	Per cent	£1 Level Stake	Totals	W-R	Per cent	£1 Level Stake
May	0-0	0.0	0.00	May	0-4	0.0	-4.00
June	0-1	0.0	-1.00	June	0-2	0.0	-2.00
July	1-2	50.0	+5.00	July	2-6	33.3	+6.50
August	2-3	66.7	+1.75	August	3-9	33.3	+1.75
September	0-0	0.0	0.00	September	0-0	0.0	0.00
October	0-1	0.0	-1.00	October	2-12	16.7	-7.80
November	0-0	0.0	0.00	November	1-13	7.7	-1.00
December	2-3	66.7	+7.50	December	2-11	18.2	-0.50
January	0-1	0.0	-1.00	January	1-4	25.0	-2.75
February	1-3	33.3	+6.00	February	2-15	13.3	-4.75
March	3-6	50.0	+6.67	March	3-12	25.0	+0.67
April	2-8	25.0	+0.63	April	3-17	17.6	-2.87

DISTANCE

Hurdles	W-R	Per cent	£1 Level Stake	Chases	W-R	Per cent	£1 Level Stake
2m-2m3f	3-24	12.5	-11.25	2m-2m3f	5-10	50.0	+7.75
2m4f-2m7f	1-17	5.9	-15.17	2m4f-2m7f	4-11	36.4	+12.67
3m+	0-7	0.0	-7.00	3m+	2-7	28.6	+4.13

TYPE OF RACE

Non-Handicaps	W-R	Per cent	£1 Level Stake	Handicaps	W-R	Per cent	£1 Level Stake
Nov Hrdls	1-25	4.0	-23.17	Nov Hrdls	0-3	0.0	-3.00
Hrdls	1-10	10.0	-8.75	Hrdls	2-11	18.2	+0.50
Nov Chs	8-16	50.0	+25.29	Nov Chs	2-8	25.0	-2.75
Chases	0-0	0.0	0.00	Chases	1-3	33.3	+3.00
Sell/Claim	0-0	0.0	0.00	Sell/Claim	0-0	0.0	0.00

RACE CLASS / FIRST TIME OUT

	W-R	Per cent	£1 Level Stake		W-R	Per cent	£1 Level Stake
Class 1	0-10	0.0	-10.00	Bumpers	3-18	16.7	-2.38
Class 2	0-3	0.0	-3.00	Hurdles	2-12	16.7	-4.67
Class 3	5-17	29.4	+11.00	Chases	0-5	0.0	-5.00
Class 4	9-44	20.5	-6.13				
Class 5	1-10	10.0	-8.75	Totals	5-35	14.3	-12.05
Class 6	4-21	19.0	+0.13				

JOCKEYS

	W-R	Per cent	£1 Level Stake
Rachael Green	7-61	11.5	-22.00
Aidan Coleman	5-20	25.0	-7.25
Charlie Huxley	3-5	60.0	+12.00
Noel Fehily	2-6	33.3	+5.13
Denis O'Regan	1-2	50.0	+4.00
A P McCoy	1-3	33.3	-0.63

COURSE RECORD

	Total W-R	Non-Hndcps Hurdles	Chases	Hndcps Hurdles	Chases	NH Flat	Per cent	£1 Level Stake
Wetherby	2-2	0-0	2-2	0-0	0-0	0-0	100.0	+9.63
Catterick	2-3	0-0	1-2	0-0	0-0	1-1	66.7	+3.25
Stratford	2-6	0-1	1-1	1-2	0-1	0-1	33.3	+2.00
Wincanton	2-9	0-4	1-1	0-0	1-1	0-3	22.2	+5.50
Worcester	2-9	0-3	1-1	1-2	0-0	0-3	22.2	+3.50
Carlisle	1-1	1-1	0-0	0-0	0-0	0-0	100.0	+0.83
Mrket Rsn	1-1	0-0	1-1	0-0	0-0	0-0	100.0	+4.50
Plumpton	1-1	0-0	0-0	0-0	0-0	1-1	100.0	+11.00
Ffos Las	1-2	0-0	0-0	0-0	0-0	1-2	50.0	+3.50
Warwick	1-3	0-1	1-1	0-0	0-0	0-1	33.3	-1.33
Chepstow	1-6	0-1	0-0	0-2	0-2	1-1	16.7	-3.63
Doncaster	1-7	1-3	0-1	0-1	0-0	0-2	14.3	-5.75
Fontwell	1-7	0-2	0-0	0-0	1-2	0-3	14.3	-4.25
Newbury	1-8	0-4	0-1	0-1	1-1	0-1	12.5	-5.50

WINNING HORSES

Horse	Races Run	1st	2nd	3rd	£
Jackies Solitaire	6	2	0	1	12346
*Danimix	5	3	0	0	13400
Marie Des Anges	10	4	0	2	15595
Velator	4	1	1	0	6330
Hes Our Lad	4	2	0	1	8487
Dorset Naga	3	1	0	0	3054
Ballybough Pat	6	1	1	1	2599
Eleven Fifty Nine	4	1	1	0	1949
Regal Encore	2	1	1	0	1754
Midnight Minx	2	1	0	0	1643
Chill Factor	3	1	0	2	1643
Fountains Mary	3	1	0	0	1437
Total winning prize-money					£70237
Favourites	8-21		38.1%		-5.38

STUART HOWE

OAKFORD, DEVON

	No. of Hrs	Races Run	1st	2nd	3rd	Unpl	Per cent	£1 Level Stake
NH Flat	1	2	0	0	0	2	0.0	-2.00
Hurdles	4	17	2	0	2	13	11.8	-4.17
Chases	0	0	0	0	0	0	0.0	0.00
Totals	4	19	2	0	2	15	10.5	-6.17
11-12	4	13	0	0	1	12	0.0	-13.00
10-11	9	39	1	3	2	33	2.6	-5.00

JOCKEYS

	W-R	Per cent	£1 Level Stake
Tom Scudamore	2-3	66.7	+9.83

COURSE RECORD

	Total W-R	Non-Hndcps Hurdles	Chases	Hndcps Hurdles	Chases	NH Flat	Per cent	£1 Level Stake
Nton Abbot	2-6	2-2	0-0	0-4	0-0	0-0	33.3	+6.83

WINNING HORSES

Horse	Races Run	1st	2nd	3rd	£
My Legal Lady	4	2	0	0	6004
Total winning prize-money					£6004
Favourites	0-0		0.0%		0.00

JO HUGHES

LAMBOURN. BERKS

	No. of Hrs	Races Run	1st	2nd	3rd	Unpl	Per cent	£1 Level Stake
NH Flat	4	8	1	2	2	3	12.5	-2.00
Hurdles	13	22	2	2	0	18	9.1	+0.50
Chases	8	20	2	3	2	13	10.0	-10.00

Totals	19	50	5	7	4	34	10.0	-11.50
11-12	18	64	9	8	5	42	14.1	+200.50

JOCKEYS

	W-R	Per cent	£1 Level Stake
Mark Grant	5-44	11.4	-5.50

COURSE RECORD

	Total W-R	Non-Hndcps Hurdles	Chases	Hndcps Hurdles	Chases	NH Flat	Per cent	£1 Level Stake
Uttoxeter	2-2	0-0	0-0	1-1	1-1	0-0	100.0	+16.50
Cartmel	1-3	0-1	0-0	1-2	0-0	0-0	33.3	+6.50
Sandown	1-3	0-1	0-0	0-0	1-2	0-0	33.3	+1.50
Fontwell	1-5	0-0	0-1	0-2	0-0	1-2	20.0	+1.00

WINNING HORSES

Horse	Races Run	1st	2nd	3rd	£
Soll	4	1	0	0	12686
Pensnett Bay	5	1	2	0	4431
Douglas	6	2	1	0	4744
Gentleman Jon	2	1	0	0	1560
Total winning prize-money					£23421
Favourites	0-1		0.0%		-1.00

MARK HUGHES

WIGTON, CUMBRIA

	No. of Hrs	Races Run	1st	2nd	3rd	Unpl	Per cent	£1 Level Stake
NH Flat	0	0	0	0	0	0	0.0	0.00
Hurdles	0	0	0	0	0	0	0.0	0.00
Chases	1	8	2	1	1	4	25.0	-1.00
Totals	1	8	2	1	1	4	25.0	-1.00
11-12	1	7	3	2	2	0	42.9	-1.89
10-11	1	3	2	0	0	1	66.7	+19.91

JOCKEYS

	W-R	Per cent	£1 Level Stake
Mr P Gerety	1-2	50.0	+1.50
Mr W Kinsey	1-5	20.0	-1.50

COURSE RECORD

	Total W-R	Non-Hndcps Hurdles	Chases	Hndcps Hurdles	Chases	NH Flat	Per cent	£1 Level Stake
Cheltenham	1-1	0-0	1-1	0-0	0-0	0-0	100.0	+2.50
Perth	1-1	0-0	1-1	0-0	0-0	0-0	100.0	+2.50

WINNING HORSES

Horse	Races Run	1st	2nd	3rd	£
Special Portrait	8	2	1	1	5927
Total winning prize-money					£5927
Favourites	1-1		100.0%		2.50

SARAH HUMPHREY

WEST WRATTING, CAMBS

	No. of Hrs	Races Run	1st	2nd	3rd	Unpl	Per cent	£1 Level Stake
NH Flat	5	7	1	0	0	6	14.3	0.00
Hurdles	16	40	3	3	8	26	7.5	-25.09
Chases	12	25	1	1	3	20	4.0	-19.00
Totals	26	72	5	4	11	52	6.9	-44.09
11-12	22	93	22	6	15	50	23.7	+28.01
10-11	23	75	10	8	7	50	13.3	-15.09

JOCKEYS

	W-R	Per cent	£1 Level Stake
Jack Doyle	4-48	8.3	-27.09
Charlie Huxley	1-5	20.0	+2.00

COURSE RECORD

	Total W-R	Non-Hndcps Hurdles	Chases	Hndcps Hurdles	Chases	NH Flat	Per cent	£1 Level Stake
Newbury	1-1	1-1	0-0	0-0	0-0	0-0	100.0	+7.00
Fontwell	1-6	1-3	0-0	0-2	0-1	0-0	16.7	-1.00
Huntingdon	1-7	1-4	0-1	0-1	0-1	0-0	14.3	-5.09
Southwell	1-7	0-2	0-0	0-2	0-1	1-2	14.3	0.00
Uttoxeter	1-7	0-1	0-1	0-2	1-3	0-0	14.3	-1.00

WINNING HORSES

Horse	Races Run	1st	2nd	3rd	£
Vasco D'Ycy	4	1	1	0	5198
*Tornade D'Estruval	4	1	1	0	3292
*Reve De Nuit	5	1	1	1	2599
Presenting Paddy	3	1	1	0	2534
Brass Monkey	5	1	0	0	1437
Total winning prize-money					£15060
Favourites	1-4		25.0%		-2.09

LAURA HURLEY

KINETON, WARWICKS

	No. of Hrs	Races Run	1st	2nd	3rd	Unpl	Per cent	£1 Level Stake
NH Flat	0	0	0	0	0	0	0.0	0.00
Hurdles	2	2	0	0	0	2	0.0	-2.00
Chases	4	17	1	1	2	13	5.9	-5.00
Totals	5	19	1	1	2	15	5.3	-7.00
11-12	5	19	0	2	1	16	0.0	-19.00
10-11	3	10	1	3	2	4	10.0	-4.00

JOCKEYS

	W-R	Per cent	£1 Level Stake
Kieron Edgar	1-4	25.0	+8.00

COURSE RECORD

	Total W-R	Non-Hndcps Hurdles	Chases	Hndcps Hurdles	Chases	NH Flat	Per cent	£1 Level Stake
Huntingdon 1-2.	0-0	0-0	0-0	1-2	0-0		50.0	+10.00

WINNING HORSES

Horse	Races Run	1st	2nd	3rd	£
Orang Outan	4	1	0	1	2144
Total winning prize-money					£2144
Favourites	0-0		0.0%		0.00

F A HUTSBY

STRATFORD-UPON-AVON, WARWICKS

	No. of Hrs	Races Run	1st	2nd	3rd	Unpl	Per cent	£1 Level Stake
NH Flat	0	0	0	0	0	0	0.0	0.00
Hurdles	0	0	0	0	0	0	0.0	0.00
Chases	4	16	4	3	3	6	25.0	-3.89
Totals	4	16	4	3	3	6	25.0	-3.89
11-12	2	3	0	1	0	2	0.0	-3.00
10-11	2	3	1	2	0	0	33.3	+0.75

JOCKEYS

	W-R	Per cent	£1 Level Stake
Mr T Ellis	4-12	33.3	+0.11

COURSE RECORD

	Total W-R	Non-Hndcps Hurdles	Chases	Hndcps Hurdles	Chases	NH Flat	Per cent	£1 Level Stake
Fakenham	2-2	0-0	2-2	0-0	0-0	0-0	100.0	+2.41
Wetherby	1-1	0-0	1-1	0-0	0-0	0-0	100.0	+0.20
Cheltenham	1-2	0-0	1-2	0-0	0-0	0-0	50.0	+4.50

WINNING HORSES

Horse	Races Run	1st	2nd	3rd	£
Rash Move	6	2	2	2	3040
*Penmore Mill	4	2	1	0	2371
Total winning prize-money					£5411
Favourites	2-4		50.0%		-1.27

TINA JACKSON

LIVERTON, CLEVELAND

	No. of Hrs	Races Run	1st	2nd	3rd	Unpl	Per cent	£1 Level Stake
NH Flat	0	0	0	0	0	0	0.0	0.00
Hurdles	2	2	0	0	0	2	0.0	-2.00

Chases	2	6	1	1	0	4	16.7	+7.00
Totals	2	8	1	1	0	6	12.5	+5.00
11-12	8	20	1	0	2	17	5.0	-16.25
10-11	7	24	2	0	1	21	8.3	-13.25

JOCKEYS

	W-R	Per cent	£1 Level Stake
Richie McGrath	1-5	20.0	+8.00

COURSE RECORD

	Total W-R	Non-Hndcps Hurdles	Chases	Hndcps Hurdles	Chases	NH Flat	Per cent	£1 Level Stake
Newcastle 1-3	0-0	0-0	0-0	1-3	0-0		33.3	+10.00

WINNING HORSES

Horse	Races Run	1st	2nd	3rd	£
Boris The Blade	6	1	1	0	2339
Total winning prize-money					£2339
Favourites	0-0		0.0%		0.00

VALERIE JACKSON

BELSAY, NORTHUMBERLAND

	No. of Hrs	Races Run	1st	2nd	3rd	Unpl	Per cent	£1 Level Stake
NH Flat	0	0	0	0	0	0	0.0	0.00
Hurdles	2	9	1	2	1	5	11.1	-4.50
Chases	1	5	1	1	1	2	20.0	-2.13
Totals	3	14	2	3	2	7	14.3	-6.63
11-12	1	2	0	0	0	2	0.0	-2.00
10-11	2	6	1	1	0	4	16.7	+9.00

JOCKEYS

	W-R	Per cent	£1 Level Stake
Brian Hughes	2-12	16.7	-4.63

COURSE RECORD

	Total W-R	Non-Hndcps Hurdles	Chases	Hndcps Hurdles	Chases	NH Flat	Per cent	£1 Level Stake
Hexham	2-4	0-0	1-2	1-2	0-0	0-0	50.0	+3.38

WINNING HORSES

Horse	Races Run	1st	2nd	3rd	£
Wheyaye	8	1	2	1	3256
Wave Power	5	1	1	1	3249
Total winning prize-money					£6505
Favourites	0-0		0.0%		0.00

IAIN JARDINE

BONCHESTER BRIDGE, BORDERS

	No. of Hrs	Races Run	1st	2nd	3rd	Unpl	Per cent	£1 Level Stake
NH Flat	3	4	0	0	1	3	0.0	-4.00
Hurdles	11	30	4	2	1	23	13.3	-4.13
Chases	5	8	0	2	1	5	0.0	-8.00
Totals	15	42	4	4	3	31	9.5	-16.13
11-12	6	23	2	4	3	14	8.7	-10.50

JOCKEYS

	W-R	Per cent	£1 Level Stake
Callum Whillans	2-5	40.0	+8.38
Brian Toomey	1-2	50.0	+5.00
Adrian Lane	1-18	5.6	-12.50

COURSE RECORD

	Total W-R	Non-Hndcps Hurdles	Chases	Hndcps Hurdles	Chases	NH Flat	Per cent	£1 Level Stake
Catterick	1-1	0-0	0-0	1-1	0-0	0-0	100.0	+6.00
Hexham	1-2	1-1	0-0	0-1	0-0	0-0	50.0	+0.38
Wetherby	1-3	1-1	0-0	0-1	0-0	0-1	33.3	+8.00
Kelso	1-6	0-2	0-2	1-1	0-1	0-0	16.7	-0.50

WINNING HORSES

Horse	Races Run	1st	2nd	3rd	£
Rowan Road	9	2	1	0	4549
Nelson Du Ronceray	5	2	1	1	4339
Total winning prize-money					£8888
Favourites		1-6	16.7%		-3.63

ALAN JARVIS

TWYFORD, BUCKS

	No. of Hrs	Races Run	1st	2nd	3rd	Unpl	Per cent	£1 Level Stake
NH Flat	0	0	0	0	0	0	0.0	0.00
Hurdles	1	1	1	0	0	0	100.0	+2.75
Chases	0	0	0	0	0	0	0.0	0.00
Totals	1	1	1	0	0	0	100.0	+2.75
11-12	2	3	2	0	0	1	66.7	+8.25
10-11	3	5	0	0	1	4	0.0	-5.00

JOCKEYS

	W-R	Per cent	£1 Level Stake
Harry Derham	1-1	100.0	+2.75

COURSE RECORD

	Total W-R	Non-Hndcps Hurdles	Chases	Hndcps Hurdles	Chases	NH Flat	Per cent	£1 Level Stake
Stratford	1-1	0-0	0-0	1-1	0-0	0-0	100.0	+2.75

WINNING HORSES

Horse	Races Run	1st	2nd	3rd	£
Bow To No One	1	1	0	0	3899
Total winning prize-money					£3899
Favourites	170-170		100.0%		467.50

MALCOLM JEFFERSON

NORTON, N YORKS

	No. of Hrs	Races Run	1st	2nd	3rd	Unpl	Per cent	£1 Level Stake
NH Flat	11	21	3	4	3	11	14.3	-13.08
Hurdles	21	56	5	9	7	35	8.9	-27.90
Chases	17	77	16	9	8	44	20.8	+55.58
Totals	38	154	24	22	18	90	15.6	+14.60
11-12	44	173	25	13	26	109	14.5	+85.63
10-11	59	212	26	29	23	134	12.3	-10.20

BY MONTH

NH Flat	W-R	Per cent	£1 Level Stake	Hurdles	W-R	Per cent	£1 Level Stake
May	0-1	0.0	-1.00	May	1-6	16.7	+2.00
June	0-0	0.0	0.00	June	0-2	0.0	-2.00
July	0-0	0.0	0.00	July	0-0	0.0	0.00
August	0-0	0.0	0.00	August	0-3	0.0	-3.00
September	0-0	0.0	0.00	September	0-1	0.0	-1.00
October	0-4	0.0	-4.00	October	1-6	16.7	-2.50
November	0-3	0.0	-3.00	November	1-7	14.3	+2.00
December	2-3	66.7	+2.67	December	2-8	25.0	-0.40
January	0-1	0.0	-1.00	January	0-1	0.0	-1.00
February	0-2	0.0	-2.00	February	0-10	0.0	-10.00
March	0-4	0.0	-4.00	March	0-7	0.0	-7.00
April	1-3	33.3	-0.75	April	0-5	0.0	-5.00

Chases	W-R	Per cent	£1 Level Stake	Totals	W-R	Per cent	£1 Level Stake
May	1-4	25.0	+1.00	May	2-11	18.2	+2.00
June	1-3	33.3	+6.00	June	1-5	20.0	+4.00
July	1-6	16.7	+2.00	July	1-6	16.7	+2.00
August	1-2	50.0	+21.00	August	1-5	20.0	+18.00
September	1-3	33.3	+10.00	September	1-4	25.0	+9.00
October	1-7	14.3	-3.50	October	2-17	11.8	-10.00
November	0-7	0.0	-7.00	November	1-17	5.9	-8.00
December	3-8	37.5	+16.50	December	7-19	36.8	+18.77
January	2-6	33.3	+6.50	January	2-8	25.0	+4.50
February	0-7	0.0	-7.00	February	0-19	0.0	-19.00
March	3-9	33.3	+16.33	March	3-20	15.0	+5.33
April	2-15	13.3	-6.25	April	3-23	13.0	-12.00

DISTANCE

Hurdles	W-R	Per cent	£1 Level Stake	Chases	W-R	Per cent	£1 Level Stake
2m-2m3f	3-25	12.0	-9.40	2m-2m3f	4-16	25.0	+20.83
2m4f-2m7f	1-21	4.8	-17.50	2m4f-2m7f	9-35	25.7	+44.75
3m+	1-10	10.0	-1.00	3m+	3-26	11.5	-10.00

TYPE OF RACE

Non-Handicaps

	W-R	Per cent	£1 Level Stake
Nov Hrdls	2-20	10.0	-14.40
Hrdls	1-5	20.0	+3.00
Nov Chs	2-12	16.7	+9.00
Chases	1-4	25.0	+4.00
Sell/Claim	0-0	0.0	0.00

Handicaps

	W-R	Per cent	£1 Level Stake
Nov Hrdls	1-10	10.0	-4.50
Hrdls	1-21	4.8	-12.00
Nov Chs	2-6	33.3	+8.00
Chases	11-55	20.0	+34.58
Sell/Claim	0-0	0.0	0.00

RACE CLASS

	W-R	Per cent	£1 Level Stake
Class 1	2-12	16.7	+0.50
Class 2	1-10	10.0	+5.00
Class 3	4-34	11.8	-15.25
Class 4	12-62	19.4	+38.43
Class 5	2-16	12.5	-2.00
Class 6	3-20	15.0	-12.08

FIRST TIME OUT

	W-R	Per cent	£1 Level Stake
Bumpers	1-11	9.1	-8.75
Hurdles	2-17	11.8	-3.50
Chases	1-10	10.0	-5.00
Totals	4-38	10.5	-17.25

JOCKEYS

	W-R	Per cent	£1 Level Stake
Harry Haynes	13-93	14.0	-1.42
Brian Hughes	7-30	23.3	+16.52
Denis O'Regan	2-12	16.7	+5.00
Jack Doyle	1-2	50.0	+2.50
Ryan Mania	1-3	33.3	+6.00

COURSE RECORD

	Total W-R	Non-Hndcps Hurdles	Chases	Hndcps Hurdles	Chases	NH Flat	Per cent	£1 Level Stake
Sedgefield	5-15	1-1	0-0	0-3	3-9	1-2	33.3	+23.67
Wetherby	4-24	1-9	0-1	1-2	2-9	0-3	16.7	-3.40
Perth	3-7	0-0	1-1	0-1	2-5	0-0	42.9	+16.00
Carlisle	2-12	0-0	0-3	0-2	2-5	0-2	16.7	-4.17
Newcastle	2-12	0-5	0-1	0-1	2-3	0-2	16.7	+6.75
Mrket Rsn	2-16	0-1	0-1	0-8	1-5	1-1	12.5	-4.75
Uttoxeter	1-3	0-0	1-1	0-0	0-1	0-1	33.3	+5.00
Cheltenham	1-5	0-0	1-2	0-1	0-2	0-0	20.0	+3.00
Kelso	1-5	1-2	0-0	0-1	0-1	0-1	20.0	+3.00
Catterick	1-7	0-2	0-0	0-1	0-2	1-2	14.3	-3.00
Haydock	1-8	0-1	0-0	0-1	1-5	0-1	12.5	+7.00
Doncaster	1-9	0-1	0-2	1-2	0-4	0-0	11.1	-3.50

WINNING HORSES

Horse	Races Run	1st	2nd	3rd	£
Cape Tribulation	5	2	0	0	80735
Mcmurrough	10	4	0	0	29891
Aneyeforaneye	6	3	1	0	15526
Quite The Man	7	2	1	1	10072
Schinken Otto	11	2	1	1	6823
Renoyr	3	1	1	1	3249
The Magic Bishop	11	1	2	2	3054
*Silent Snow	4	1	1	0	3054

King Of The Wolds	6	1	2	2	2738
Hi George	7	2	0	1	5133
Sun Cloud	6	1	2	2	2534
Milan Royale	7	1	0	0	2339
Pair Of Jacks	2	1	1	0	1437
Enchanted Garden	4	1	2	0	1365
Shuh Shuh Gah	2	1	1	0	1365
Total winning prize-money					**£169315**
Favourites	6-17		35.3%		1.10

L JEFFORD

KENTISBEARE, DEVON

	No. of Hrs	Races Run	1st	2nd	3rd	Unpl	Per cent	£1 Level Stake
NH Flat	0	0	0	0	0	0	0.0	0.00
Hurdles	0	0	0	0	0	0	0.0	0.00
Chases	3	7	1	1	2	3	14.3	+14.00
Totals	3	7	1	1	2	3	14.3	+14.00
11-12	1	1	0	0	0	1	0.0	-1.00
10-11	1	2	0	0	0	2	0.0	-2.00

JOCKEYS

	W-R	Per cent	£1 Level Stake
Mr W Biddick	1-2	50.0	+19.00

COURSE RECORD

	Total W-R	Non-Hndcps Hurdles	Chases	Hndcps Hurdles	Chases	NH Flat	Per cent	£1 Level Stake
Exeter	1-1	0-0	1-1	0-0	0-0	0-0	100.0	+20.00

WINNING HORSES

Horse	Races Run	1st	2nd	3rd	£
*Regal Rumpus	3	1	0	1	936
Total winning prize-money					**£936**
Favourites	0-1		0.0%		-1.00

J R JENKINS

ROYSTON, HERTS

	No. of Hrs	Races Run	1st	2nd	3rd	Unpl	Per cent	£1 Level Stake
NH Flat	2	3	0	0	0	3	0.0	-3.00
Hurdles	6	28	3	0	4	21	10.7	+4.50
Chases	1	2	0	0	0	2	0.0	-2.00
Totals	8	33	3	0	4	26	9.1	-0.50
11-12	11	38	6	2	4	26	15.8	-2.25
10-11	10	31	3	2	1	25	9.7	-14.50

JOCKEYS

	W-R	Per cent	£1 Level Stake
A P McCoy	1-1	100.0	+2.50
Tom Cannon	1-2	50.0	+1.00
Jack Sherwood	1-5	20.0	+21.00

COURSE RECORD

	Total W-R	Non-Hndcps Hurdles Chases		Hndcps Hurdles	Chases	NH Flat	Per cent	£1 Level Stake
Hereford	1-1	1-1	0-0	0-0	0-0	0-0	100.0	+2.00
Stratford	1-1	1-1	0-0	0-0	0-0	0-0	100.0	+2.50
Southwell	1-8	1-3	0-0	0-4	0-0	0-1	12.5	+18.00

WINNING HORSES

Horse	Races Run	1st	2nd	3rd	£
Not Til Monday	3	2	0	0	4744
Frolic Along	3	1	0	0	2053
Total winning prize-money					**£6797**
Favourites	0-0		0.0%		0.00

MISS SAMANTHA JENNINGS

BRIDGEND, BRIDGEND

	No. of Hrs	Races Run	1st	2nd	3rd	Unpl	Per cent	£1 Level Stake
NH Flat	0	0	0	0	0	0	0.0	0.00
Hurdles	0	0	0	0	0	0	0.0	0.00
Chases	1	1	1	0	0	0	100.0	+3.50
Totals	1	1	1	0	0	0	100.0	+3.50

JOCKEYS

	W-R	Per cent	£1 Level Stake
Miss H Lewis	1-1	100.0	+3.50

COURSE RECORD

	Total W-R	Non-Hndcps Hurdles Chases		Hndcps Hurdles	Chases	NH Flat	Per cent	£1 Level Stake
Stratford	1-1	0-0	1-1	0-0	0-0	0-0	100.0	+3.50

WINNING HORSES

Horse	Races Run	1st	2nd	3rd	£
*Overlut	1	1	0	0	1872
Total winning prize-money					**£1872**
Favourites	1-1		100.0%		3.50

ALAN JESSOP

SOUTH HANNINGFIELD, ESSEX

	No. of Hrs	Races Run	1st	2nd	3rd	Unpl	Per cent	£1 Level Stake
NH Flat	0	0	0	0	0	0	0.0	0.00
Hurdles	2	2	1	0	0	1	50.0	+10.00
Chases	1	1	0	0	0	1	0.0	-1.00
Totals	3	3	1	0	0	2	33.3	+9.00
11-12	2	6	1	0	1	4	16.7	+2.50
10-11	3	6	1	0	0	5	16.7	+9.00

JOCKEYS

	W-R	Per cent	£1 Level Stake
Tom O'Brien	1-1	100.0	+11.00

COURSE RECORD

	Total W-R	Non-Hndcps Hurdles Chases		Hndcps Hurdles	Chases	NH Flat	Per cent	£1 Level Stake
Stratford	1-1	1-1	0-0	0-0	0-0	0-0	100.0	+11.00

WINNING HORSES

Horse	Races Run	1st	2nd	3rd	£
Max Milano	1	1	0	0	2534
Total winning prize-money					**£2534**
Favourites	0-0		0.0%		0.00

LINDA JEWELL

SUTTON VALENCE, KENT

	No. of Hrs	Races Run	1st	2nd	3rd	Unpl	Per cent	£1 Level Stake
NH Flat	3	6	0	0	0	6	0.0	-6.00
Hurdles	11	18	0	0	0	18	0.0	-18.00
Chases	4	17	2	2	2	11	11.8	+21.00
Totals	14	41	2	2	2	35	4.9	-3.00
11-12	14	45	1	5	7	32	2.2	-39.00
10-11	12	36	3	1	1	31	8.3	-11.00

JOCKEYS

	W-R	Per cent	£1 Level Stake
Tom Cannon	1-3	33.3	+14.00
Andrew Thornton	1-13	7.7	+8.00

COURSE RECORD

	Total W-R	Non-Hndcps Hurdles Chases		Hndcps Hurdles	Chases	NH Flat	Per cent	£1 Level Stake
Lingfield	1-6	0-2	0-0	0-0	1-4	0-0	16.7	+15.00
Fontwell	1-10	0-3	0-0	0-3	1-2	0-2	10.0	+7.00

WINNING HORSES

Horse	Races Run	1st	2nd	3rd	£
Red Anchor	6	2	0	0	6027
Total winning prize-money					**£6027**
Favourites	0-0		0.0%		0.00

SUSAN JOHNSON
MADLEY, H'FORDS

	No. of Hrs	Races Run	1st	2nd	3rd	Unpl	Per cent	£1 Level Stake
NH Flat	1	1	0	0	0	1	0.0	-1.00
Hurdles	2	7	3	0	0	4	42.9	+16.25
Chases	2	4	1	1	0	2	25.0	+0.33
Totals	3	12	4	1	0	7	33.3	+15.58
11-12	1	1	0	1	0	0	0.0	-1.00
10-11	1	2	0	0	0	2	0.0	-2.00

JOCKEYS

	W-R	Per cent	£1 Level Stake
Richard Johnson	3-6	50.0	+16.58
Adam Wedge	1-6	16.7	-1.00

COURSE RECORD

	Total W-R	Non-Hndcps Hurdles	Chases	Hndcps Hurdles	Chases	NH Flat	Per cent	£1 Level Stake
Taunton	1-1	0-0	0-0	1-1	0-0	0-0	100.0	+14.00
Ffos Las	1-1	0-0	0-0	0-0	1-1	0-0	100.0	+3.33
Worcester	1-2	0-1	0-0	1-1	0-0	0-0	50.0	+3.00
Hereford	1-3	0-1	0-0	1-1	0-1	0-0	33.3	+0.25

WINNING HORSES

Horse	Races Run	1st	2nd	3rd	£
The Last Bridge	7	2	1	0	4540
Themanfromfraam	4	2	0	0	3469
Total winning prize-money					**£8009**
Favourites	2-3		66.7%		4.58

ALAN JONES
BICKHAM, SOMERSET

	No. of Hrs	Races Run	1st	2nd	3rd	Unpl	Per cent	£1 Level Stake
NH Flat	3	5	0	0	0	5	0.0	-5.00
Hurdles	15	31	1	3	1	26	3.2	-26.00
Chases	6	17	2	3	1	11	11.8	-4.75
Totals	21	53	3	6	2	42	5.7	-35.75
11-12	15	54	6	8	5	35	11.1	-29.00
10-11	20	52	6	5	5	36	11.5	+3.50

JOCKEYS

	W-R	Per cent	£1 Level Stake
James Best	2-8	25.0	+6.00
Nick Scholfield	1-16	6.3	-12.75

COURSE RECORD

	Total W-R	Non-Hndcps Hurdles	Chases	Hndcps Hurdles	Chases	NH Flat	Per cent	£1 Level Stake
Perth	1-1	0-0	0-0	0-0	1-1	0-0	100.0	+8.00
Uttoxeter	1-5	0-0	0-0	1-5	0-0	0-0	20.0	0.00
Bangor	1-6	0-1	0-1	0-1	1-3	0-0	16.7	-2.75

WINNING HORSES

Horse	Races Run	1st	2nd	3rd	£
Quincy Des Pictons	5	1	1	1	16245
Humbel Ben	4	1	1	0	3422
Murfreesboro	3	1	0	1	2144
Total winning prize-money					**£21811**
Favourites	1-1		100.0%		2.25

LUCY JONES
KILGETTY, PEMBROKESHIRE

	No. of Hrs	Races Run	1st	2nd	3rd	Unpl	Per cent	£1 Level Stake
NH Flat	1	1	0	0	0	1	0.0	-1.00
Hurdles	9	26	2	1	4	19	7.7	-7.00
Chases	4	14	1	3	2	8	7.1	-10.50
Totals	13	41	3	4	6	28	7.3	-18.50
11-12	13	41	6	5	3	27	14.6	-15.63
10-11	5	22	1	1	4	16	4.5	-17.50

JOCKEYS

	W-R	Per cent	£1 Level Stake
Tom Bellamy	1-1	100.0	+10.00
A P McCoy	1-4	25.0	-0.50
Will Kennedy	1-5	20.0	+3.00

COURSE RECORD

	Total W-R	Non-Hndcps Hurdles	Chases	Hndcps Hurdles	Chases	NH Flat	Per cent	£1 Level Stake
Newbury	1-3	0-0	0-0	1-1	0-2	0-0	33.3	+8.00
Worcester	1-4	0-1	1-1	0-2	0-0	0-0	25.0	-0.50
Stratford	1-5	0-0	0-0	1-4	0-1	0-0	20.0	+3.00

WINNING HORSES

Horse	Races Run	1st	2nd	3rd	£
Supreme Bob	1	1	0	0	3119
*Gentleman Jeff	6	1	2	0	2599
*Noble Media	4	1	0	1	1689
Total winning prize-money					**£7407**
Favourites	0-2		0.0%		-2.00

MISS KAYLEY JONES

SOUTH MOLTON, DEVON

	No. of Hrs	Races Run	1st	2nd	3rd	Unpl	Per cent	£1 Level Stake
NH Flat	0	0	0	0	0	0	0.0	0.00
Hurdles	0	0	0	0	0	0	0.0	0.00
Chases	5	7	2	0	3	2	28.6	+9.50
Totals	5	7	2	0	3	2	28.6	+9.50

JOCKEYS

	W-R	Per cent	£1 Level Stake
Mr M Ennis	1-1	100.0	+10.00
Mr Joshua Guerriero	1-1	100.0	+4.50

COURSE RECORD

	Total W-R	Non-Hndcps Hurdles	Non-Hndcps Chases	Hndcps Hurdles	Hndcps Chases	NH Flat	Per cent	£1 Level Stake
Leicester	1-1	0-0	1-1	0-0	0-0	0-0	100.0	+4.50
Nton Abbot	1-2	0-0	1-1	0-0	0-1	0-0	50.0	+9.00

WINNING HORSES

Horse	Races Run	1st	2nd	3rd	£
*Robin Will	1	1	0	0	1560
*Parkam Jack	1	1	0	0	1383
Total winning prize-money					£2943
Favourites	0-0		0.0%		0.00

CAROLINE KEEVIL

MOTCOMBE, DORSET

	No. of Hrs	Races Run	1st	2nd	3rd	Unpl	Per cent	£1 Level Stake
NH Flat	8	11	0	0	1	10	0.0	-11.00
Hurdles	22	69	3	0	5	61	4.3	-51.50
Chases	8	32	3	4	7	18	9.4	-21.25
Totals	29	112	6	4	13	89	5.4	-83.75
11-12	39	160	6	5	16	133	3.8	-114.00
10-11	27	89	7	10	10	62	7.9	+2.50

JOCKEYS

	W-R	Per cent	£1 Level Stake
Ian Popham	3-42	7.1	-28.25
James Best	2-37	5.4	-25.50
Joe Tizzard	1-1	100.0	+2.00

COURSE RECORD

	Total W-R	Non-Hndcps Hurdles	Non-Hndcps Chases	Hndcps Hurdles	Hndcps Chases	NH Flat	Per cent	£1 Level Stake
Taunton	2-14	0-5	0-1	1-5	1-2	0-1	14.3	-4.00
Towcester	1-2	1-1	0-1	0-0	0-0	0-0	50.0	+3.50
Kempton	1-4	0-1	0-0	0-1	1-2	0-0	25.0	-0.75

Plumpton	1-6	0-0	0-0	1-4	0-1	0-1	16.7	-1.00
Chepstow	1-8	0-3	0-0	0-3	1-1	0-1	12.5	-3.50

WINNING HORSES

Horse	Races Run	1st	2nd	3rd	£
Bally Legend	7	1	2	1	6256
Marshal Zhukov	8	2	1	3	9747
Midnight Lira	8	1	0	3	3422
Darkestbeforedawn	7	1	0	1	3119
Cinevator	6	1	0	1	2738
Total winning prize-money					£25282
Favourites	4-7		57.1%		8.75

MARTIN KEIGHLEY

CONDICOTE, GLOUCS

	No. of Hrs	Races Run	1st	2nd	3rd	Unpl	Per cent	£1 Level Stake
NH Flat	14	17	3	3	3	8	17.6	-5.75
Hurdles	32	118	17	15	15	71	14.4	-24.92
Chases	18	62	9	6	6	41	14.5	-8.52
Totals	46	197	29	24	24	120	14.7	-39.19
11-12	52	242	34	38	33	137	14.0	-7.50
10-11	44	177	19	22	19	117	10.7	-68.47

BY MONTH

NH Flat	W-R	Per cent	£1 Level Stake	Hurdles	W-R	Per cent	£1 Level Stake
May	1-3	33.3	+1.50	May	1-12	8.3	-8.25
June	0-0	0.0	0.00	June	0-5	0.0	-5.00
July	0-3	0.0	-3.00	July	1-12	8.3	-2.00
August	0-1	0.0	-1.00	August	1-5	20.0	+10.00
September	0-0	0.0	0.00	September	0-6	0.0	-6.00
October	1-3	33.3	0.00	October	2-10	20.0	-3.50
November	0-1	0.0	-1.00	November	2-12	16.7	+2.50
December	0-1	0.0	-1.00	December	3-15	20.0	-1.25
January	1-1	100.0	+2.75	January	1-6	16.7	-1.50
February	0-2	0.0	-2.00	February	4-10	40.0	+7.83
March	0-0	0.0	0.00	March	1-9	11.1	-5.75
April	0-2	0.0	-2.00	April	1-16	6.3	-12.00

Chases	W-R	Per cent	£1 Level Stake	Totals	W-R	Per cent	£1 Level Stake
May	2-11	18.2	-3.77	May	4-26	15.4	-10.52
June	1-4	25.0	+13.00	June	1-9	11.1	+8.00
July	0-4	0.0	-4.00	July	1-19	5.3	-9.00
August	1-4	25.0	-0.50	August	2-10	20.0	+8.50
September	0-3	0.0	-3.00	September	0-9	0.0	-9.00
October	1-7	14.3	+0.50	October	4-20	20.0	-3.00
November	0-5	0.0	-5.00	November	2-18	11.1	-3.50
December	2-6	33.3	+6.50	December	5-22	22.7	+4.25
January	0-5	0.0	-5.00	January	2-12	16.7	-3.75
February	1-3	33.3	-0.13	February	5-15	33.3	+5.70
March	0-3	0.0	-3.00	March	1-12	8.3	-8.75
April	1-7	14.3	-4.13	April	2-25	8.0	-18.13

DISTANCE

Hurdles	W-R	Per cent	£1 Level Stake	Chases	W-R	Per cent	£1 Level Stake
2m-2m3f	3-30	10.0	-13.25	2m-2m3f	3-12	25.0	-1.90
2m4f-2m7f	6-51	11.8	-13.00	2m4f-2m7f	3-23	13.0	+0.38
3m+	8-37	21.6	+1.33	3m+	3-27	11.1	-7.00

TYPE OF RACE

Non-Handicaps	W-R	Per cent	£1 Level Stake	Handicaps	W-R	Per cent	£1 Level Stake
Nov Hrdls	1-18	5.6	-14.75	Nov Hrdls	2-8	25.0	-0.75
Hrdls	2-12	16.7	-5.67	Hrdls	10-75	13.3	-5.50
Nov Chs	1-10	10.0	-8.27	Nov Chs	0-1	0.0	-1.00
Chases	0-3	0.0	-3.00	Chases	8-48	16.7	+3.75
Sell/Claim	1-2	50.0	+1.75	Sell/Claim	1-4	25.0	-1.00

RACE CLASS / FIRST TIME OUT

	W-R	Per cent	£1 Level Stake		W-R	Per cent	£1 Level Stake
Class 1	1-14	7.1	-11.13	Bumpers	3-14	21.4	-2.75
Class 2	2-16	12.5	+5.50	Hurdles	1-19	5.3	-14.00
Class 3	3-28	10.7	-13.00	Chases	1-13	7.7	-11.27
Class 4	12-78	15.4	-21.56				
Class 5	8-46	17.4	+4.75	Totals	5-46	10.9	-28.02
Class 6	3-15	20.0	-3.75				

JOCKEYS

	W-R	Per cent	£1 Level Stake
Ian Popham	11-59	18.6	-11.42
Alain Cawley	9-72	12.5	-13.77
Daniel Hiskett	3-29	10.3	-16.75
Aidan Coleman	2-8	25.0	+12.50
Killian Moore	1-1	100.0	+2.25
Robert Thornton	1-1	100.0	+5.50
Christopher Ward	1-2	50.0	+3.00
Nick Slatter	1-10	10.0	-5.50

COURSE RECORD

	Total W-R	Non-Hndcps Hurdles	Non-Hndcps Chases	Hndcps Hurdles	Hndcps Chases	NH Flat	Per cent	£1 Level Stake
Hereford	5-11	0-1	1-1	2-4	2-3	0-2	45.5	+23.73
Towcester	4-12	0-2	0-0	2-4	1-4	1-2	33.3	+7.25
Haydock	2-5	1-2	0-0	1-3	0-0	0-0	40.0	+2.75
Catterick	2-6	0-1	0-1	0-1	1-2	1-1	33.3	+0.63
Fontwell	2-7	0-0	0-0	1-6	0-0	1-1	28.6	-0.50
Ludlow	2-7	2-3	0-0	0-2	0-2	0-0	28.6	-1.42
Chepstow	2-11	1-2	0-1	1-8	0-0	0-0	18.2	-2.00
Ayr	1-2	0-0	0-0	1-2	0-0	0-0	50.0	+2.00
Southwell	1-4	0-1	0-0	1-2	0-0	0-1	25.0	+6.00
Taunton	1-4	0-0	0-0	1-4	0-0	0-0	25.0	+4.00
Fakenham	1-5	0-0	0-0	1-3	0-2	0-0	20.0	-2.00
Huntingdon	1-5	0-1	0-0	1-3	0-1	0-0	20.0	+2.00
Wincanton	1-7	0-2	0-0	0-2	1-3	0-0	14.3	+0.50
Mrket Rsn	1-9	0-0	0-0	0-3	1-6	0-0	11.1	-5.50
Stratford	1-9	0-1	0-0	0-5	1-2	0-1	11.1	+8.00
Uttoxeter	1-13	0-2	0-0	1-7	0-3	0-1	7.7	-7.50
Cheltenham	1-14	0-2	0-1	0-5	1-5	0-1	7.1	-11.13

WINNING HORSES

Horse	Races Run	1st	2nd	3rd	£
Champion Court	5	1	2	0	28475
Seymour Eric	6	5	0	1	26447
Pilgrims Lane	7	2	1	0	13641
Any Currency	8	1	0	1	6498
The Fox's Decree	15	1	2	5	5326
Annacotty	4	2	0	1	7798
Always Bold	9	2	2	0	5848
Sky Calling	9	1	1	1	3249
Faultless Feelings	6	1	1	1	3249
Mauricetheathlete	10	1	1	2	3119
Brimham Boy	3	1	1	0	2599
Court In Session	6	1	1	1	2599
Benbane Head	9	1	1	0	2534
Ukrainian Star	7	1	1	1	2339
Junior Jack	3	1	0	0	2274
Typhon De Guye	8	1	1	2	2060
*Tower	8	1	0	2	2053
Monty's Revenge	10	1	1	1	1949
Creepy	6	1	2	0	1754
Midnight Myth	6	1	0	0	1689
Johnny Og	1	1	0	0	1643
Buddy Love	6	1	0	0	1437
Total winning prize-money					£128580
Favourites	8-23		34.8%		-0.19

NICK KENT
BRIGG, LINCS

	No. of Hrs	Races Run	1st	2nd	3rd	Unpl	Per cent	£1 Level Stake
NH Flat	4	9	0	0	2	7	0.0	-9.00
Hurdles	13	46	2	7	3	34	4.3	-35.75
Chases	3	13	0	1	2	10	0.0	-13.00
Totals	17	68	2	8	7	51	2.9	-57.75
11-12	13	42	0	5	5	32	0.0	-42.00
10-11	5	12	1	2	1	8	8.3	-9.50

JOCKEYS

	W-R	Per cent	£1 Level Stake
Henry Brooke	1-1	100.0	+6.00
Charles Greene	1-19	5.3	-15.75

COURSE RECORD

	Total W-R	Non-Hndcps Hurdles	Non-Hndcps Chases	Hndcps Hurdles	Hndcps Chases	NH Flat	Per cent	£1 Level Stake
Mrket Rsn	2-22	0-5	0-0	2-12	0-2	0-3	9.1	-11.75

WINNING HORSES

Horse	Races Run	1st	2nd	3rd	£
Around A Pound	9	2	1	0	5198
Total winning prize-money					£5198
Favourites	1-3		33.3%		0.25

SARAH KERSWELL

KINGSBRIDGE, DEVON

	No. of Hrs	Races Run	1st	2nd	3rd	Unpl	Per cent	£1 Level Stake
NH Flat	0	0	0	0	0	0	0.0	0.00
Hurdles	4	11	1	0	4	6	9.1	+2.00
Chases	2	7	1	0	0	6	14.3	+19.00
Totals	5	18	2	0	4	12	11.1	+21.00

JOCKEYS

	W-R	Per cent	£1 Level Stake
Lucy Alexander	1-3	33.3	+23.00
Brendan Powell	1-11	9.1	+2.00

COURSE RECORD

	Total W-R	Non-Hndcps Hurdles	Chases	Hndcps Hurdles	Chases	NH Flat	Per cent	£1 Level Stake
Nton Abbot	1-2	0-1	0-0	1-1	0-0	0-0	50.0	+11.00
Stratford	1-3	0-1	0-0	0-0	1-2	0-0	33.3	+23.00

WINNING HORSES

Horse	Races Run	1st	2nd	3rd	£
Magical Legend	5	1	0	0	6963
Romance Dance	4	1	0	2	2924
Total winning prize-money					£9887
Favourites	0-0		0.0%		0.00

NEIL KING

NEWMARKET, SUFFOLK

	No. of Hrs	Races Run	1st	2nd	3rd	Unpl	Per cent	£1 Level Stake
NH Flat	5	9	0	1	2	6	0.0	-9.00
Hurdles	31	92	10	14	11	57	10.9	+8.00
Chases	14	74	12	11	3	48	16.2	+29.00
Totals	40	175	22	26	16	111	12.6	+28.00
11-12	43	196	16	27	28	123	8.2	-47.08
10-11	47	192	19	13	18	142	9.9	-52.68

BY MONTH

NH Flat	W-R	Per cent	£1 Level Stake
May	0-1	0.0	-1.00
June	0-1	0.0	-1.00
July	0-0	0.0	0.00
August	0-0	0.0	0.00
September	0-0	0.0	0.00
October	0-0	0.0	0.00
November	0-0	0.0	0.00
December	0-1	0.0	-1.00
January	0-1	0.0	-1.00
February	0-0	0.0	0.00
March	0-1	0.0	-1.00
April	0-4	0.0	-4.00

Hurdles	W-R	Per cent	£1 Level Stake
May	1-9	11.1	-2.00
June	0-6	0.0	-6.00
July	2-9	22.2	+19.00
August	0-9	0.0	-9.00
September	0-6	0.0	-6.00
October	2-9	22.2	+8.00
November	2-13	15.4	-1.50
December	1-11	9.1	+15.00
January	0-3	0.0	-3.00
February	0-2	0.0	-2.00
March	1-4	25.0	+0.50
April	1-11	9.1	-5.00

Chases	W-R	Per cent	£1 Level Stake
May	5-15	33.3	+11.00
June	1-6	16.7	+1.50
July	0-4	0.0	-4.00
August	0-3	0.0	-3.00
September	1-4	25.0	+6.00
October	0-5	0.0	-5.00
November	0-6	0.0	-6.00
December	2-12	16.7	-3.50
January	1-5	20.0	-1.00
February	0-4	0.0	-4.00
March	0-5	0.0	-5.00
April	2-5	40.0	+42.00

Totals	W-R	Per cent	£1 Level Stake
May	6-25	24.0	+8.00
June	1-13	7.7	-5.50
July	2-13	15.4	+15.00
August	0-12	0.0	-12.00
September	1-10	10.0	0.00
October	2-14	14.3	+3.00
November	2-19	10.5	-7.50
December	3-24	12.5	+10.50
January	1-9	11.1	-5.00
February	0-6	0.0	-6.00
March	1-10	10.0	-5.50
April	3-20	15.0	+33.00

DISTANCE

Hurdles	W-R	Per cent	£1 Level Stake	Chases	W-R	Per cent	£1 Level Stake
2m-2m3f	5-53	9.4	-7.00	2m-2m3f	2-18	11.1	-4.50
2m4f-2m7f	3-24	12.5	+14.50	2m4f-2m7f	4-29	13.8	-9.50
3m+	2-15	13.3	+0.50	3m+	6-27	22.2	+43.00

TYPE OF RACE

Non-Handicaps	W-R	Per cent	£1 Level Stake	Handicaps	W-R	Per cent	£1 Level Stake
Nov Hrdls	1-18	5.6	-12.50	Nov Hrdls	0-5	0.0	-5.00
Hrdls	3-14	21.4	+31.00	Hrdls	6-48	12.5	+1.50
Nov Chs	1-3	33.3	+0.50	Nov Chs	0-3	0.0	-3.00
Chases	0-1	0.0	-1.00	Chases	11-67	16.4	+32.50
Sell/Claim	0-5	0.0	-5.00	Sell/Claim	0-2	0.0	-2.00

RACE CLASS / FIRST TIME OUT

	W-R	Per cent	£1 Level Stake		W-R	Per cent	£1 Level Stake
Class 1	0-3	0.0	-3.00	Bumpers	0-5	0.0	-5.00
Class 2	0-3	0.0	-3.00	Hurdles	4-25	16.0	+18.00
Class 3	3-27	11.1	+14.50	Chases	3-10	30.0	+34.50
Class 4	12-92	13.0	-1.00				
Class 5	7-43	16.3	+27.50	Totals	7-40	17.5	+47.50
Class 6	0-7	0.0	-7.00				

JOCKEYS

	W-R	Per cent	£1 Level Stake
Trevor Whelan	11-65	16.9	+68.00
Alex Merriam	9-98	9.2	-39.00

Miss Carey Williamson	1-1	100.0	+6.00
Miss C Twemlow	1-4	25.0	0.00

COURSE RECORD

	Total W-R	Non-Hndcps Hurdles	Chases	Hndcps Hurdles	Chases	NH Flat	Per cent	£1 Level Stake
Leicester	3-9	1-4	1-1	0-0	1-4	0-0	33.3	+5.50
Plumpton	3-17	0-1	0-0	1-5	2-11	0-0	17.6	+4.50
Uttoxeter	3-19	0-3	0-0	1-8	2-7	0-1	15.8	+6.00
Sedgefield	2-4	0-0	0-0	1-2	1-2	0-0	50.0	+5.50
Fontwell	2-10	0-0	0-0	0-1	2-8	0-1	20.0	+4.00
Fakenham	2-14	0-1	0-1	1-4	1-8	0-0	14.3	-3.00
Stratford	2-18	0-3	0-0	2-11	0-4	0-0	11.1	+3.00
Perth	1-3	0-0	0-0	0-1	1-2	0-0	33.3	+31.00
Towcester	1-3	0-0	0-0	0-0	1-2	0-0	33.3	+5.00
Folkestone	1-4	1-1	0-0	0-2	0-1	0-0	25.0	+22.00
Kempton	1-6	1-3	0-0	0-1	0-1	0-1	16.7	-0.50
Huntingdon	1-21	1-8	0-1	0-5	0-5	0-2	4.8	-8.00

WINNING HORSES

Horse	Races Run	1st	2nd	3rd	£
Cerium	7	1	1	0	12984
Fashionable Gal	7	2	2	3	8296
A Little Swifter	4	1	0	0	4549
Delgany Gunner	13	4	3	1	11112
*Ironically	7	2	1	2	7018
Kaysersberg	5	1	2	0	3899
Evella	11	1	3	4	3697
The Red Laird	3	1	0	0	3422
*Outback	5	1	1	0	3249
Ballyvoneen	10	4	0	0	11056
Hi Ho Silvia	2	1	0	0	2634
Pairc Na Gcapall	9	1	2	0	2599
Zepnove	7	1	0	1	2339
Milansbar	1	1	0	0	2053
Total winning prize-money					**£78907**
Favourites	**2-7**		**28.6%**		**0.50**

ALAN KING

BARBURY CASTLE, WILTS

	No. of Hrs	Races Run	1st	2nd	3rd	Unpl	Per cent	£1 Level Stake
NH Flat	22	36	0	7	4	25	0.0	-36.00
Hurdles	90	271	49	34	37	151	18.1	+42.29
Chases	31	98	9	25	21	43	9.2	-55.75
Totals	125	405	58	66	62	219	14.3	-49.46
11-12	141	512	80	79	70	283	15.6	-132.60
10-11	171	595	84	102	80	328	14.1	-172.49

BY MONTH

NH Flat	W-R	Per cent	£1 Level Stake	Hurdles	W-R	Per cent	£1 Level Stake
May	0-3	0.0	-3.00	May	3-25	12.0	-10.76
June	0-0	0.0	0.00	June	1-3	33.3	+6.00
July	0-0	0.0	0.00	July	0-4	0.0	-4.00
August	0-0	0.0	0.00	August	0-4	0.0	-4.00
September	0-0	0.0	0.00	September	0-4	0.0	-4.00
October	0-1	0.0	-1.00	October	6-17	35.3	+18.00
November	0-2	0.0	-2.00	November	9-43	20.9	+5.62
December	0-3	0.0	-3.00	December	8-40	20.0	+4.62
January	0-3	0.0	-3.00	January	4-21	19.0	-5.95
February	0-6	0.0	-6.00	February	2-34	5.9	-24.13
March	0-4	0.0	-4.00	March	4-32	12.5	+14.90
April	0-14	0.0	-14.00	April	12-44	27.3	+45.98

Chases	W-R	Per cent	£1 Level Stake	Totals	W-R	Per cent	£1 Level Stake
May	0-9	0.0	-9.00	May	3-37	8.1	-22.76
June	0-1	0.0	-1.00	June	1-4	25.0	+5.00
July	0-3	0.0	-3.00	July	0-7	0.0	-7.00
August	0-1	0.0	-1.00	August	0-5	0.0	-5.00
September	1-1	100.0	+3.50	September	1-5	20.0	-0.50
October	0-6	0.0	-6.00	October	6-24	25.0	+11.00
November	3-17	17.6	-6.00	November	12-62	19.4	-2.38
December	1-17	5.9	-13.75	December	9-60	15.0	-12.13
January	1-8	12.5	-5.50	January	5-32	15.6	-14.45
February	2-12	16.7	-4.00	February	4-52	7.7	-34.13
March	0-11	0.0	-11.00	March	4-47	8.5	-0.10
April	1-12	8.3	+1.00	April	13-70	18.6	+32.98

DISTANCE

Hurdles	W-R	Per cent	£1 Level Stake	Chases	W-R	Per cent	£1 Level Stake
2m-2m3f	28-144	19.4	+26.03	2m-2m3f	3-29	10.3	-19.25
2m4f-2m7f	17-93	18.3	+28.88	2m4f-2m7f	3-45	6.7	-30.75
3m+	4-34	11.8	-12.63	3m+	3-24	12.5	-5.75

TYPE OF RACE

Non-Handicaps	W-R	Per cent	£1 Level Stake	Handicaps	W-R	Per cent	£1 Level Stake
Nov Hrdls	18-88	20.5	-4.47	Nov Hrdls	0-12	0.0	-12.00
Hrdls	18-69	26.1	+46.88	Hrdls	13-102	12.7	+11.88
Nov Chs	3-21	14.3	-13.25	Nov Chs	0-8	0.0	-8.00
Chases	1-7	14.3	-4.25	Chases	5-62	8.1	-30.25
Sell/Claim	0-0	0.0	0.00	Sell/Claim	0-0	0.0	0.00

RACE CLASS

	W-R	Per cent	£1 Level Stake
Class 1	7-76	9.2	+0.50
Class 2	6-50	12.0	-18.25
Class 3	8-64	12.5	-27.00
Class 4	31-163	19.0	+15.63
Class 5	6-31	19.4	+0.65
Class 6	0-21	0.0	-21.00

FIRST TIME OUT

	W-R	Per cent	£1 Level Stake
Bumpers	0-22	0.0	-22.00
Hurdles	13-80	16.3	-6.22
Chases	0-23	0.0	-23.00
Totals	13-125	10.4	-51.22

JOCKEYS

	W-R	Per cent	£1 Level Stake
Wayne Hutchinson	29-143	20.3	+91.06
Robert Thornton	26-211	12.3	-99.63

Charlie Huxley	2-12	16.7	-7.40
Fergus Sweeney	1-1	100.0	+4.50

COURSE RECORD

	Total W-R	Non-Hndcps Hurdles	Chases	Hndcps Hurdles	Chases	NH Flat	Per cent	£1 Level Stake
Plumpton	5-13	4-7	1-2	0-2	0-1	0-1	38.5	-1.33
Huntingdon	5-19	3-7	0-0	2-7	0-3	0-2	26.3	+4.10
Kempton	5-37	3-16	0-3	1-11	1-5	0-2	13.5	-12.20
Haydock	4-9	2-2	1-1	1-3	0-3	0-0	44.4	+3.13
Hereford	3-6	3-4	0-1	0-1	0-0	0-0	50.0	+16.33
Chepstow	3-13	2-6	0-0	1-4	0-3	0-0	23.1	-0.50
Aintree	3-19	3-7	0-0	0-6	0-3	0-3	15.8	-1.13
Wincanton	3-26	1-11	0-0	2-9	0-3	0-3	11.5	-10.50
Newbury	3-38	2-13	0-2	0-11	1-8	0-4	7.9	-24.75
Towcester	2-4	2-2	0-1	0-1	0-0	0-0	50.0	+2.41
Wetherby	2-11	0-4	0-0	1-4	1-2	0-1	18.2	-4.38
Taunton	2-13	2-8	0-0	0-3	0-0	0-2	15.4	+6.38
Ascot	2-15	1-5	0-1	1-5	0-4	0-0	13.3	+35.00
Warwick	2-15	1-4	1-1	0-3	0-2	0-5	13.3	-9.00
Mrket Rsn	2-17	2-6	0-2	0-3	0-6	0-0	11.8	0.00
Folkestone	1-1	0-0	1-1	0-0	0-0	0-0	100.0	+2.25
Ffos Las	1-2	0-0	0-0	1-2	0-0	0-0	50.0	+5.00
Lingfield	1-3	0-1	0-0	1-2	0-0	0-0	33.3	+2.50
Ayr	1-4	0-0	0-0	0-1	1-2	0-1	25.0	+9.00
Ludlow	1-6	1-4	0-0	0-1	0-1	0-0	16.7	+3.00
Fontwell	1-8	1-4	0-1	0-2	0-0	0-1	12.5	-6.09
Stratford	1-8	0-1	0-1	0-2	1-4	0-0	12.5	-3.50
Bangor	1-10	1-5	0-1	0-1	0-2	0-1	10.0	-5.50
Uttoxeter	1-12	1-9	0-0	0-1	0-1	0-1	8.3	-10.09
Sandown	1-13	0-1	0-1	1-6	0-3	0-2	7.7	-2.00
Doncaster	1-25	1-13	0-1	0-6	0-2	0-3	4.0	-23.60
Cheltenham	1-36	0-11	0-2	1-11	0-10	0-2	2.8	-2.00

WINNING HORSES

Horse	Races Run	1st	2nd	3rd	£
Godsmejudge	7	3	2	1	115342
L'Unique	4	3	0	1	71559
Medinas	6	2	2	0	76840
Raya Star	5	1	2	0	28135
Bless The Wings	5	2	0	0	38407
Balder Succes	7	1	0	2	25024
Two Rockers	4	3	0	0	22179
Kumbeshwar	7	1	3	0	16245
Bakbenscher	7	1	1	1	14296
Araldur	5	2	1	0	15716
Salden Licht	2	1	1	0	6498
Midnight Sail	8	1	4	0	6498
Midnight Prayer	4	2	0	0	7993
*Mcvicar	7	2	1	0	9097
Kenai Peninsula	5	2	0	0	8586
Turn Over Sivola	7	3	1	1	9839
Forresters Folly	5	1	1	0	5005
Henry San	7	1	2	3	3899
Handazan	5	1	2	1	3899
Call Me A Star	6	2	2	1	5588

Salmanazar	5	1	2	0	3899
Uxizandre	6	2	1	2	7798
*Fair Trade	4	1	1	1	3574
Midnight Appeal	6	2	1	1	5956
Valdez	7	2	2	1	5956
*King Of Dudes	5	2	1	0	5891
Ulys Du Charmil	4	2	1	0	5819
Compton Blue	6	2	0	1	5263
*Kuda Huraa	3	1	0	0	3119
*Seventh Sign	4	2	1	0	6238
Miss Exhibitionist	7	1	3	1	2738
Hollow Penny	5	1	1	2	2669
Genstone Trail	2	1	0	0	2534
The Mumper	5	1	0	1	2534
Desert Joe	1	1	0	0	2144
Hindon Road	2	1	0	0	1689
Total winning prize-money					**£558466**
Favourites	21-60	35.0%			-10.51

WILLIAM KINSEY

ASHTON, CHESHIRE

	No. of Hrs	Races Run	1st	2nd	3rd	Unpl	Per cent	£1 Level Stake
NH Flat	8	14	0	2	1	11	0.0	-14.00
Hurdles	15	47	6	5	6	30	12.8	+10.38
Chases	7	15	2	3	0	10	13.3	+16.00
Totals	22	76	8	10	7	51	10.5	+12.38
11-12	6	14	2	0	4	8	14.3	+24.00
10-11	1	1	0	0	0	1	0.0	-1.00

JOCKEYS

	W-R	Per cent	£1 Level Stake
Charlie Huxley	4-52	7.7	-10.38
Harry Challoner	2-10	20.0	+8.00
Samantha Drake	1-1	100.0	+25.00
Mr W Kinsey	1-3	33.3	-0.25

COURSE RECORD

	Total W-R	Non-Hndcps Hurdles	Chases	Hndcps Hurdles	Chases	NH Flat	Per cent	£1 Level Stake
Sedgefield	2-13	0-4	0-0	2-5	0-1	0-3	15.4	-6.38
Haydock	1-2	0-0	0-0	1-1	0-1	0-0	50.0	+10.00
Hexham	1-2	0-0	0-0	1-1	0-1	0-0	50.0	+0.75
Worcester	1-2	0-0	0-0	0-0	1-1	0-1	50.0	+24.00
Aintree	1-3	0-1	0-0	1-1	0-0	0-1	33.3	+20.00
Wetherby	1-7	0-2	0-0	0-2	1-2	0-1	14.3	-2.00
Catterick	1-10	1-3	0-1	0-4	0-0	0-2	10.0	+3.00

WINNING HORSES

Horse	Races Run	1st	2nd	3rd	£
Alpha Victor	5	2	0	0	9495
Kykate	9	2	3	0	6265
Gwladys Street	7	2	2	1	5198

*Amber Cloud	2	1	1	0	3249
Le Seychellois	4	1	0	0	1916
Total winning prize-money					£26123
Favourites	2-3		66.7%		2.63

PHILIP KIRBY

MIDDLEHAM, N YORKS

	No. of Hrs	Races Run	1st	2nd	3rd	Unpl	Per cent	£1 Level Stake
NH Flat	9	18	2	4	2	10	11.1	-9.63
Hurdles	41	127	17	14	7	89	13.4	+33.33
Chases	11	23	6	1	1	15	26.1	+13.50
Totals	53	168	25	19	10	114	14.9	+37.20
11-12	30	122	11	13	12	86	9.0	-67.86
10-11	27	113	9	13	12	79	8.0	-42.38

BY MONTH

NH Flat	W-R	Per cent	£1 Level Stake	Hurdles	W-R	Per cent	£1 Level Stake
May	0-0	0.0	0.00	May	1-13	7.7	+13.00
June	0-0	0.0	0.00	June	1-4	25.0	-0.25
July	0-0	0.0	0.00	July	2-7	28.6	+9.50
August	0-0	0.0	0.00	August	0-11	0.0	-11.00
September	0-0	0.0	0.00	September	1-7	14.3	+0.50
October	0-1	0.0	-1.00	October	1-7	14.3	-2.67
November	0-0	0.0	0.00	November	0-7	0.0	-7.00
December	0-1	0.0	-1.00	December	1-7	14.3	-3.00
January	0-3	0.0	-3.00	January	0-7	0.0	-7.00
February	0-2	0.0	-2.00	February	3-25	12.0	+12.50
March	1-5	20.0	-2.13	March	1-11	9.1	-6.50
April	1-6	16.7	-0.50	April	6-21	28.6	+35.25

Chases	W-R	Per cent	£1 Level Stake	Totals	W-R	Per cent	£1 Level Stake
May	0-4	0.0	-4.00	May	1-17	5.9	+9.00
June	0-0	0.0	0.00	June	1-4	25.0	-0.25
July	0-1	0.0	-1.00	July	2-8	25.0	+8.50
August	0-0	0.0	0.00	August	0-11	0.0	-11.00
September	0-0	0.0	0.00	September	1-7	14.3	+0.50
October	0-0	0.0	0.00	October	1-8	12.5	-3.67
November	2-3	66.7	+10.00	November	2-10	20.0	+3.00
December	1-3	33.3	+4.50	December	2-11	18.2	+0.50
January	1-1	100.0	+6.50	January	1-11	9.1	-3.50
February	1-3	33.3	+0.50	February	4-30	13.3	+11.00
March	0-3	0.0	-3.00	March	2-19	10.5	-11.63
April	1-5	20.0	0.00	April	8-32	25.0	+34.75

DISTANCE

Hurdles	W-R	Per cent	£1 Level Stake	Chases	W-R	Per cent	£1 Level Stake
2m-2m3f	9-76	11.8	+10.08	2m-2m3f	0-5	0.0	-5.00
2m4f-2m7f	5-41	12.2	+3.25	2m4f-2m7f	3-10	30.0	+6.50
3m+	3-10	30.0	+20.00	3m+	3-8	37.5	+12.00

TYPE OF RACE

Non-Handicaps	W-R	Per cent	£1 Level Stake	Handicaps	W-R	Per cent	£1 Level Stake
Nov Hrdls	2-16	12.5	+9.00	Nov Hrdls	3-19	15.8	+5.08
Hrdls	0-4	0.0	-4.00	Hrdls	12-87	13.8	+24.25
Nov Chs	0-1	0.0	-1.00	Nov Chs	0-2	0.0	-2.00
Chases	0-0	0.0	0.00	Chases	6-20	30.0	+16.50
Sell/Claim	0-0	0.0	0.00	Sell/Claim	0-1	0.0	-1.00

RACE CLASS

	W-R	Per cent	£1 Level Stake
Class 1	0-3	0.0	-3.00
Class 2	1-3	33.3	+20.00
Class 3	2-15	13.3	-5.00
Class 4	15-72	20.8	+57.00
Class 5	5-59	8.5	-24.17
Class 6	2-16	12.5	-7.63

FIRST TIME OUT

	W-R	Per cent	£1 Level Stake
Bumpers	1-9	11.1	-3.50
Hurdles	4-38	10.5	+32.00
Chases	1-6	16.7	+1.50
Totals	6-53	11.3	+30.00

JOCKEYS

	W-R	Per cent	£1 Level Stake
Richie McGrath	9-53	17.0	+28.25
Adam Nicol	8-36	22.2	+32.58
Kyle James	5-24	20.8	-0.63
Jonathan England	1-1	100.0	+16.00
James Reveley	1-2	50.0	+2.00
Barry Keniry	1-11	9.1	0.00

COURSE RECORD

	Total W-R	Non-Hndcps Hurdles	Chases	Hndcps Hurdles	Chases	NH Flat	Per cent	£1 Level Stake
Mrket Rsn	5-19	0-1	0-0	3-15	1-2	1-1	26.3	+14.50
Newcastle	4-12	1-2	0-0	3-7	0-2	0-1	33.3	+14.75
Aintree	2-3	0-0	0-0	2-2	0-0	0-1	66.7	+26.75
Huntingdon	2-4	0-0	0-0	1-3	1-1	0-0	50.0	+5.50
Carlisle	2-5	1-1	0-0	0-1	1-1	0-2	40.0	+25.50
Bangor	1-1	0-0	0-0	1-1	0-0	0-0	100.0	+3.33
Sandown	1-1	0-0	0-0	1-1	0-0	0-0	100.0	+22.00
Ayr	1-6	0-0	0-0	1-3	0-1	0-2	16.7	0.00
Doncaster	1-7	0-1	0-0	0-4	0-0	1-2	14.3	-4.13
Musselbgh	1-9	0-0	0-1	0-6	1-2	0-0	11.1	-1.50
Catterick	1-11	0-3	0-0	1-7	0-0	0-1	9.1	-2.50
Kelso	1-11	0-4	0-0	1-6	0-1	0-0	9.1	-7.00
Uttoxeter	1-13	0-1	0-0	0-9	1-3	0-0	7.7	-4.00
Wetherby	1-13	0-1	0-0	1-10	0-0	0-2	7.7	-6.50
Sedgefield	1-24	0-4	0-0	0-12	1-5	0-3	4.2	-20.50

WINNING HORSES

Horse	Races Run	1st	2nd	3rd	£
*Stopped Out	3	2	0	0	18889
Call It On	6	2	0	1	9617
Goldan Jess	6	1	0	0	6043
*Rumble Of Thunder	3	1	0	0	5393

*Everaard	4	2	0	0	8447
Cool Operator	5	2	0	0	6953
Full Speed	3	1	1	1	3798
Pickworth	8	3	0	0	8642
*Mrs Eff	2	2	0	0	5235
Matthew Riley	3	1	1	0	3119
*Picks Milan	1	1	0	0	3119
Avanos	7	1	0	2	2534
Iktiview	11	1	2	0	2534
Ancient Times	8	2	2	0	4094
*Avidity	3	1	1	0	1949
Next Edition	2	1	0	0	1689
Little Poppet	1	1	0	0	1560
Total winning prize-money					£93615
Favourites	6-15		40.0%		5.46

T LACEY

CHIPPING NORTON, OXON

	No. of Hrs	Races Run	1st	2nd	3rd	Unpl	Per cent	£1 Level Stake
NH Flat	0	0	0	0	0	0	0.0	0.00
Hurdles	0	0	0	0	0	0	0.0	0.00
Chases	1	2	1	0	0	1	50.0	+5.00
Totals	**1**	**2**	**1**	**0**	**0**	**1**	**50.0**	**+5.00**

JOCKEYS

	W-R	Per cent	£1 Level Stake
Mr S Drinkwater	1-2	50.0	+5.00

COURSE RECORD

	Total W-R	Non-Hndcps Hurdles	Chases	Hndcps Hurdles	Chases	NH Flat	Per cent	£1 Level Stake
Lingfield	1-1	0-0	1-1	0-0	0-0	0-0	100.0	+6.00

WINNING HORSES

Horse	Races Run	1st	2nd	3rd	£
*Trouble Digger	2	1	0	0	988
Total winning prize-money					£988
Favourites	0-0		0.0%		0.00

NICK LAMPARD

CLATFORD, WILTS

	No. of Hrs	Races Run	1st	2nd	3rd	Unpl	Per cent	£1 Level Stake
NH Flat	2	2	0	0	0	2	0.0	-2.00
Hurdles	2	8	3	2	1	2	37.5	+34.00
Chases	2	4	0	0	1	3	0.0	-4.00
Totals	**6**	**14**	**3**	**2**	**2**	**7**	**21.4**	**+28.00**
11-12	6	21	0	0	1	20	0.0	-21.00
10-11	2	4	1	0	0	3	25.0	+11.00

JOCKEYS

	W-R	Per cent	£1 Level Stake
Gerard Tumelty	2-5	40.0	+34.50
Mr Joshua Newman	1-5	20.0	-2.50

COURSE RECORD

	Total W-R	Non-Hndcps Hurdles	Chases	Hndcps Hurdles	Chases	NH Flat	Per cent	£1 Level Stake
Fontwell	1-2	0-0	0-1	1-1	0-0	0-0	50.0	+0.50
Plumpton	1-3	0-0	0-0	1-3	0-0	0-0	33.3	+31.00
Wincanton	1-4	0-0	0-0	1-3	0-1	0-0	25.0	+1.50

WINNING HORSES

Horse	Races Run	1st	2nd	3rd	£
Goochypoochyprader	6	3	2	1	5952
Total winning prize-money					£5952
Favourites	2-4		50.0%		1.00

EMMA LAVELLE

HATHERDEN, HANTS

	No. of Hrs	Races Run	1st	2nd	3rd	Unpl	Per cent	£1 Level Stake
NH Flat	13	20	1	4	3	12	5.0	+1.00
Hurdles	29	86	5	10	14	57	5.8	-52.50
Chases	21	66	6	11	9	40	9.1	-44.00
Totals	**57**	**172**	**12**	**25**	**26**	**109**	**7.0**	**-95.50**
11-12	69	213	40	25	28	120	18.8	+24.08
10-11	64	207	30	22	21	134	14.5	-47.04

BY MONTH

NH Flat	W-R	Per cent	£1 Level Stake	Hurdles	W-R	Per cent	£1 Level Stake
May	0-0	0.0	0.00	May	0-4	0.0	-4.00
June	0-0	0.0	0.00	June	0-2	0.0	-2.00
July	0-0	0.0	0.00	July	0-3	0.0	-3.00
August	0-0	0.0	0.00	August	0-0	0.0	0.00
September	0-0	0.0	0.00	September	0-2	0.0	-2.00
October	0-2	0.0	-2.00	October	1-13	7.7	-1.00
November	0-3	0.0	-3.00	November	2-14	14.3	-1.75
December	0-2	0.0	-2.00	December	1-13	7.7	-7.50
January	0-4	0.0	-4.00	January	0-8	0.0	-8.00
February	0-5	0.0	-5.00	February	0-11	0.0	-11.00
March	0-2	0.0	-2.00	March	0-8	0.0	-8.00
April	1-2	50.0	+19.00	April	1-8	12.5	-4.25

Chases	W-R	Per cent	£1 Level Stake	Totals	W-R	Per cent	£1 Level Stake
May	1-3	33.3	+1.50	May	1-7	14.3	-2.50
June	0-2	0.0	-2.00	June	0-4	0.0	-4.00
July	0-1	0.0	-1.00	July	0-4	0.0	-4.00
August	0-1	0.0	-1.00	August	0-1	0.0	-1.00
September	0-0	0.0	0.00	September	0-2	0.0	-2.00

October	0-13	0.0	-13.00	October	1-28	3.6	-16.00
November	1-9	11.1	-6.50	November	3-26	11.5	-11.25
December	4-10	40.0	+5.00	December	5-25	20.0	-4.50
January	0-7	0.0	-7.00	January	0-19	0.0	-19.00
February	0-9	0.0	-9.00	February	0-25	0.0	-25.00
March	0-3	0.0	-3.00	March	0-13	0.0	-13.00
April	0-8	0.0	-8.00	April	2-18	11.1	+6.75

DISTANCE

Hurdles	W-R	Per cent	£1 Level Stake	Chases	W-R	Per cent	£1 Level Stake
2m-2m3f	1-23	4.3	-19.25	2m-2m3f	1-9	11.1	-6.00
2m4f-2m7f	4-40	10.0	-10.25	2m4f-2m7f	0-18	0.0	-18.00
3m+	0-23	0.0	-23.00	3m+	5-39	12.8	-20.00

TYPE OF RACE

Non-Handicaps	W-R	Per cent	£1 Level Stake	Handicaps	W-R	Per cent	£1 Level Stake
Nov Hrdls	1-22	4.5	-10.00	Nov Hrdls	0-0	0.0	0.00
Hrdls	1-18	5.6	-14.25	Hrdls	3-46	6.5	-28.25
Nov Chs	2-22	9.1	-16.50	Nov Chs	0-3	0.0	-3.00
Chases	0-1	0.0	-1.00	Chases	3-39	7.7	-24.50
Sell/Claim	0-0	0.0	0.00	Sell/Claim	0-0	0.0	0.00

RACE CLASS / FIRST TIME OUT

	W-R	Per cent	£1 Level Stake		W-R	Per cent	£1 Level Stake
Class 1	2-26	7.7	-3.00	Bumpers	0-13	0.0	-13.00
Class 2	3-22	13.6	-3.50	Hurdles	3-26	11.5	-4.75
Class 3	4-34	11.8	-19.25	Chases	1-18	5.6	-15.50
Class 4	2-63	3.2	-46.50				
Class 5	1-10	10.0	-6.25	Totals	4-57	7.0	-33.25
Class 6	0-17	0.0	-17.00				

JOCKEYS

	W-R	Per cent	£1 Level Stake
Dominic Elsworth	5-65	7.7	-45.75
Dougie Costello	4-52	7.7	-20.75
Leighton Aspell	1-2	50.0	0.00
Noel Fehily	1-5	20.0	+16.00
Barry Geraghty	1-7	14.3	-4.00

COURSE RECORD

	Total W-R	Non-Hndcps Hurdles	Chases	Hndcps Hurdles	Chases	NH Flat	Per cent	£1 Level Stake
Doncaster	2-4	0-0	0-0	0-0	2-4	0-0	50.0	+6.00
Kempton	2-7	1-2	0-0	1-2	0-2	0-1	28.6	+13.50
Lingfield	1-1	0-0	1-1	0-0	0-0	0-0	100.0	+1.00
Chepstow	1-3	1-2	0-0	0-1	0-0	0-0	33.3	+0.75
Towcester	1-3	0-1	1-1	0-0	0-1	0-0	33.3	-0.50
Aintree	1-4	0-0	0-0	0-1	0-2	1-1	25.0	+17.00
Sandown	1-5	0-2	0-0	1-2	0-1	0-0	20.0	+0.50
Stratford	1-5	0-1	0-1	1-1	0-2	0-0	20.0	-1.25
Uttoxeter	1-12	0-3	0-3	0-4	1-2	0-0	8.3	-7.50
Cheltenham	1-20	0-4	1-2	0-7	0-7	0-0	5.0	-17.00

WINNING HORSES

Horse	Races Run	1st	2nd	3rd	£
Killyglass	2	1	0	0	17085
Court In Motion	3	1	1	1	13742
Court By Surprise	4	1	0	1	12996
Highland Lodge	6	2	0	2	18019
Fox Appeal	3	1	0	1	10010
Kentford Grey Lady	6	1	0	3	9384
Easter Meteor	3	1	1	0	7148
Claret Cloak	4	1	0	1	6498
Shotgun Paddy	4	1	1	2	3899
Tim The Chair	7	1	1	0	3249
Le Bec	4	1	1	0	3249
Total winning prize-money					£105279
Favourites	4-19		21.1%		-7.75

BARRY LEAVY

FORSBROOK, STAFFS

	No. of Hrs	Races Run	1st	2nd	3rd	Unpl	Per cent	£1 Level Stake
NH Flat	1	1	0	0	0	1	0.0	-1.00
Hurdles	12	32	4	2	4	22	12.5	+5.55
Chases	3	12	1	2	1	8	8.3	-4.00
Totals	13	45	5	4	5	31	11.1	+0.55
11-12	10	43	4	5	5	29	9.3	-10.00
10-11	14	63	8	7	11	37	12.7	+1.00

JOCKEYS

	W-R	Per cent	£1 Level Stake
Harry Challoner	2-8	25.0	+3.80
Jason Maguire	1-1	100.0	+1.75
Sam Jones	1-2	50.0	+6.00
Richard Killoran	1-4	25.0	+19.00

COURSE RECORD

	Total W-R	Non-Hndcps Hurdles	Chases	Hndcps Hurdles	Chases	NH Flat	Per cent	£1 Level Stake
Bangor	2-5	0-0	0-0	1-4	1-1	0-0	40.0	+13.00
Uttoxeter	2-20	0-5	0-1	2-10	0-3	0-1	10.0	+4.80
Mrket Rsn	1-5	1-1	0-0	0-3	0-1	0-0	20.0	-2.25

WINNING HORSES

Horse	Races Run	1st	2nd	3rd	£
On The Right Path	3	1	0	0	6498
Mohi Rahrere	6	1	1	0	3769
Lean Burn	12	2	1	1	3834
*Westlin' Winds	5	1	0	1	1689
Total winning prize-money					£15790
Favourites	1-5		20.0%		-3.20

RICHARD LEE

BYTON, H'FORDS

	No. of Hrs	Races Run	1st	2nd	3rd	Unpl	Per cent	£1 Level Stake
NH Flat	2	3	0	0	0	3	0.0	-3.00
Hurdles	21	65	8	7	7	43	12.3	-7.90
Chases	22	94	13	10	13	58	13.8	-21.79
Totals	31	162	21	17	20	104	13.0	-32.69
11-12	34	148	17	13	14	104	11.5	-31.79
10-11	39	163	25	18	21	99	15.3	+30.74

BY MONTH

NH Flat	W-R	Per cent	£1 Level Stake	Hurdles	W-R	Per cent	£1 Level Stake
May	0-1	0.0	-1.00	May	0-9	0.0	-9.00
June	0-0	0.0	0.00	June	0-0	0.0	0.00
July	0-0	0.0	0.00	July	0-4	0.0	-4.00
August	0-0	0.0	0.00	August	0-1	0.0	-1.00
September	0-0	0.0	0.00	September	0-1	0.0	-1.00
October	0-1	0.0	-1.00	October	1-7	14.3	-2.50
November	0-0	0.0	0.00	November	3-8	37.5	+27.25
December	0-0	0.0	0.00	December	1-5	20.0	+2.00
January	0-0	0.0	0.00	January	0-6	0.0	-6.00
February	0-0	0.0	0.00	February	1-12	8.3	-9.90
March	0-0	0.0	0.00	March	2-7	28.6	+1.25
April	0-1	0.0	-1.00	April	0-5	0.0	-5.00

Chases	W-R	Per cent	£1 Level Stake	Totals	W-R	Per cent	£1 Level Stake
May	1-4	25.0	-1.00	May	1-14	7.1	-11.00
June	0-3	0.0	-3.00	June	0-3	0.0	-3.00
July	0-3	0.0	-3.00	July	0-7	0.0	-7.00
August	0-2	0.0	-2.00	August	0-3	0.0	-3.00
September	0-1	0.0	-1.00	September	0-2	0.0	-2.00
October	1-10	10.0	-4.00	October	2-18	11.1	-7.50
November	1-13	7.7	-8.50	November	4-21	19.0	+18.75
December	2-10	20.0	-1.50	December	3-15	20.0	+0.50
January	2-10	20.0	-1.50	January	2-16	12.5	-7.50
February	2-15	13.3	-5.17	February	3-27	11.1	-15.07
March	3-13	23.1	+9.88	March	5-20	25.0	+11.13
April	1-10	10.0	-1.00	April	1-16	6.3	-7.00

DISTANCE

Hurdles	W-R	Per cent	£1 Level Stake	Chases	W-R	Per cent	£1 Level Stake
2m-2m3f	7-33	21.2	-1.90	2m-2m3f	4-24	16.7	-7.50
2m4f-2m7f	0-20	0.0	-20.00	2m4f-2m7f	2-30	6.7	-16.50
3m+	1-12	8.3	+14.00	3m+	7-40	17.5	+2.21

TYPE OF RACE

Non-Handicaps	W-R	Per cent	£1 Level Stake	Handicaps	W-R	Per cent	£1 Level Stake
Nov Hrdls	2-9	22.2	-1.25	Nov Hrdls	1-7	14.3	-2.50
Hrdls	2-20	10.0	-10.90	Hrdls	3-29	10.3	+6.75

Nov Chs	4-19	21.1	-3.17	Nov Chs	0-3	0.0	-3.00
Chases	0-0	0.0	0.00	Chases	9-71	12.7	-14.63
Sell/Claim	0-0	0.0	0.00	Sell/Claim	0-1	0.0	-1.00

RACE CLASS

	W-R	Per cent	£1 Level Stake
Class 1	0-8	0.0	-8.00
Class 2	0-12	0.0	-12.00
Class 3	9-45	20.0	+12.88
Class 4	9-62	14.5	-6.32
Class 5	3-33	9.1	-16.25
Class 6	0-2	0.0	-2.00

FIRST TIME OUT

	W-R	Per cent	£1 Level Stake
Bumpers	0-2	0.0	-2.00
Hurdles	1-14	7.1	-9.50
Chases	2-15	13.3	-6.00
Totals	3-31	9.7	-17.50

JOCKEYS

	W-R	Per cent	£1 Level Stake
Micheal Nolan	9-40	22.5	-1.54
Charlie Poste	5-22	22.7	+21.10
Jake Greenall	2-16	12.5	+8.00
Jamie Moore	2-20	10.0	-8.00
Denis O'Regan	1-5	20.0	+0.50
Richard Johnson	1-9	11.1	-5.75
Tom Scudamore	1-20	5.0	-17.00

COURSE RECORD

	Total W-R	Non-Hndcps Hurdles	Chases	Hndcps Hurdles	Chases	NH Flat	Per cent	£1 Level Stake
Ludlow	3-28	1-11	1-5	0-3	1-7	0-2	10.7	-17.57
Hereford	2-6	0-1	0-0	1-2	1-3	0-0	33.3	+3.00
Towcester	2-6	1-2	1-1	0-1	0-2	0-0	33.3	+6.00
Ffos Las	2-13	0-1	0-1	1-5	1-6	0-0	15.4	+15.88
Chepstow	2-14	0-2	1-2	0-1	1-9	0-0	14.3	+6.50
Doncaster	1-1	0-0	0-0	0-0	1-1	0-0	100.0	+4.50
Fontwell	1-2	0-0	0-0	0-0	1-2	0-0	50.0	+2.50
Carlisle	1-3	0-0	1-2	0-0	0-1	0-0	33.3	0.00
Plumpton	1-4	0-1	0-1	0-0	1-2	0-0	25.0	+5.00
Stratford	1-4	0-1	0-0	0-2	1-1	0-0	25.0	+5.00
Taunton	1-4	0-0	0-0	1-2	0-2	0-0	25.0	-0.25
Exeter	1-9	1-2	0-1	0-3	0-3	0-0	11.1	-5.75
Uttoxeter	1-9	0-2	0-1	1-4	0-2	0-0	11.1	-4.50
Bangor	1-11	0-1	0-2	0-1	1-6	0-1	9.1	-5.00
Worcester	1-11	1-2	0-0	0-3	0-6	0-0	9.1	-6.50

WINNING HORSES

Horse	Races Run	1st	2nd	3rd	£
Simply Wings	6	2	1	1	15254
Mountainous	5	2	2	0	13536
Grey Gold	2	1	0	0	7148
Incentivise	7	2	1	0	9938
The Chazer	10	2	0	3	10397
Le Beau Bai	6	1	0	0	5848
Big News	5	1	1	1	4549
*Dropzone	5	1	1	0	4224
Chiquilline	5	1	0	1	3899
Victory Gunner	6	1	1	0	3861

Tresor De Bontee	7	2	0	1	5487
Young Victoria	2	2	0	0	5133
*Scales	6	1	0	3	2053
*Goodtoknow	6	1	0	1	1689
Milo Milan	4	1	0	3	0
Total winning prize-money					**£93016**
Favourites	**6-16**		**37.5%**		**3.97**

C R LEECH

WESTBURY-ON-SEVERN, GLOUS

	No. of Hrs	Races Run	1st	2nd	3rd	Unpl	Per cent	£1 Level Stake
NH Flat	0	0	0	0	0	0	0.0	0.00
Hurdles	0	0	0	0	0	0	0.0	0.00
Chases	1	2	1	0	0	1	50.0	+8.00
Totals	**1**	**2**	**1**	**0**	**0**	**1**	**50.0**	**+8.00**

JOCKEYS

	W-R	Per cent	£1 Level Stake
Miss Hannah Watson	1-2	50.0	+8.00

COURSE RECORD

	Total W-R	Non-Hndcps Hurdles	Hndcps Chases	Hndcps Hurdles	Chases	NH Flat	Per cent	£1 Level Stake
Towcester	1-1	0-0	1-1	0-0	0-0	0-0	100.0	+9.00

WINNING HORSES

Horse	Races Run	1st	2nd	3rd	£
*Soulard	2	1	0	0	936
Total winning prize-money					**£936**
Favourites	**0-0**		**0.0%**		**0.00**

SOPHIE LEECH

ELTON, GLOUCS

	No. of Hrs	Races Run	1st	2nd	3rd	Unpl	Per cent	£1 Level Stake
NH Flat	2	2	1	0	0	1	50.0	+1.75
Hurdles	24	87	11	9	8	59	12.6	-16.13
Chases	13	57	6	10	8	33	10.5	+2.00
Totals	**33**	**146**	**18**	**19**	**16**	**93**	**12.3**	**-12.38**
11-12	42	134	10	13	11	100	7.5	-52.38
10-11	37	123	9	16	11	87	7.3	-46.08

BY MONTH

NH Flat	W-R	Per cent	£1 Level Stake	Hurdles	W-R	Per cent	£1 Level Stake
May	0-0	0.0	0.00	May	1-5	20.0	+3.50
June	0-1	0.0	-1.00	June	1-6	16.7	-1.00
July	0-0	0.0	0.00	July	2-7	28.6	+6.50
August	0-0	0.0	0.00	August	2-13	15.4	+4.38
September	0-0	0.0	0.00	September	1-7	14.3	-3.00
October	0-0	0.0	0.00	October	0-11	0.0	-11.00
November	0-0	0.0	0.00	November	1-10	10.0	-1.00
December	0-0	0.0	0.00	December	0-9	0.0	-9.00
January	0-0	0.0	0.00	January	0-5	0.0	-5.00
February	1-1	100.0	+2.75	February	0-3	0.0	-3.00
March	0-0	0.0	0.00	March	1-3	33.3	+1.50
April	0-0	0.0	0.00	April	2-8	25.0	+1.00

Chases	W-R	Per cent	£1 Level Stake	Totals	W-R	Per cent	£1 Level Stake
May	0-5	0.0	-5.00	May	1-10	10.0	-1.50
June	1-2	50.0	+10.00	June	2-9	22.2	+8.00
July	1-9	11.1	-4.00	July	3-16	18.8	+2.50
August	2-5	40.0	+3.00	August	4-18	22.2	+7.38
September	0-4	0.0	-4.00	September	1-11	9.1	-7.00
October	0-7	0.0	-7.00	October	0-18	0.0	-18.00
November	0-3	0.0	-3.00	November	1-13	7.7	-4.00
December	0-7	0.0	-7.00	December	0-16	0.0	-16.00
January	0-1	0.0	-1.00	January	0-6	0.0	-6.00
February	2-6	33.3	+28.00	February	3-10	30.0	+27.75
March	0-4	0.0	-4.00	March	1-7	14.3	-2.50
April	0-4	0.0	-4.00	April	2-12	16.7	-3.00

DISTANCE

Hurdles	W-R	Per cent	£1 Level Stake	Chases	W-R	Per cent	£1 Level Stake
2m-2m3f	4-43	9.3	-14.00	2m-2m3f	2-16	12.5	+18.00
2m4f-2m7f	5-33	15.2	+2.50	2m4f-2m7f	2-18	11.1	-1.00
3m+	2-11	18.2	-4.63	3m+	2-23	8.7	-15.00

TYPE OF RACE

Non-Handicaps	W-R	Per cent	£1 Level Stake	Handicaps	W-R	Per cent	£1 Level Stake
Nov Hrdls	2-13	15.4	+6.50	Nov Hrdls	0-9	0.0	-9.00
Hrdls	0-4	0.0	-4.00	Hrdls	7-56	12.5	-15.63
Nov Chs	1-6	16.7	-1.00	Nov Chs	2-11	18.2	-3.00
Chases	0-1	0.0	-1.00	Chases	3-39	7.7	+7.00
Sell/Claim	1-2	50.0	+0.50	Sell/Claim	1-3	33.3	+5.50

RACE CLASS / FIRST TIME OUT

	W-R	Per cent	£1 Level Stake		W-R	Per cent	£1 Level Stake
Class 1	0-4	0.0	-4.00	Bumpers	1-2	50.0	+1.75
Class 2	0-1	0.0	-1.00	Hurdles	1-20	5.0	-11.50
Class 3	1-26	3.8	-18.00	Chases	0-11	0.0	-11.00
Class 4	8-70	11.4	-11.00				
Class 5	8-43	18.6	+19.88	Totals	2-33	6.1	-20.75
Class 6	1-2	50.0	+1.75				

JOCKEYS

	W-R	Per cent	£1 Level Stake
Paul Moloney	10-60	16.7	+20.25
James Best	3-23	13.0	+3.38
Jason Maguire	2-6	33.3	+3.00
Paddy Brennan	1-3	33.3	+1.50
Miss Hannah Watson	1-3	33.3	+5.50
Richie McLernon	1-21	4.8	-16.00

COURSE RECORD

	Total W-R	Non-Hndcps Hurdles	Chases	Hndcps Hurdles	Chases	NH Flat	Per cent	£1 Level Stake
Chepstow	3-10	0-0	0-0	2-5	1-5	0-0	30.0	+29.50
Nton Abbot	3-12	0-2	0-0	2-6	1-4	0-0	25.0	+12.50
Southwell	2-7	0-1	0-0	1-4	1-2	0-0	28.6	+7.00
Bangor	2-8	0-0	0-1	1-5	1-2	0-0	25.0	-2.63
Worcester	2-8	2-5	0-0	0-1	0-1	0-1	25.0	+11.50
Carlisle	1-1	0-0	0-0	1-1	0-0	0-0	100.0	+5.50
Plumpton	1-2	0-0	0-0	0-1	0-0	1-1	50.0	+1.75
Wetherby	1-2	1-1	0-0	0-1	0-0	0-0	50.0	+0.50
Sandown	1-6	0-0	0-0	0-2	1-4	0-0	16.7	+2.00
Cartmel	1-7	0-0	1-1	0-3	0-3	0-0	14.3	-2.00
Fontwell	1-10	0-1	0-0	1-5	0-4	0-0	10.0	-5.00

WINNING HORSES

Horse	Races Run	1st	2nd	3rd	£
Olympian Boy	10	2	3	1	10072
Tasheba	6	2	0	1	6823
*Nicene Creed	8	2	0	0	5068
Is It Me	7	1	2	0	3080
Tamarillo Grove	7	1	0	0	2534
Le Grand Chene	12	3	2	2	6238
Kings Story	2	1	0	0	2053
Keenes Day	11	2	2	1	4003
Prince Pippin	8	1	2	0	2053
*Keltic Crisis	4	1	1	1	1779
*Anteros	1	1	0	0	1711
Old Magic	9	1	0	2	1689
Total winning prize-money					£47103
Favourites	3-23		13.0%		-15.13

D H LLEWELLYN

PEMBROKE, PEMBROKESHIRE

	No. of Hrs	Races Run	1st	2nd	3rd	Unpl	Per cent	£1 Level Stake
NH Flat	0	0	0	0	0	0	0.0	0.00
Hurdles	0	0	0	0	0	0	0.0	0.00
Chases	1	2	1	0	0	1	50.0	+0.25
Totals	1	2	1	0	0	1	50.0	+0.25
11-12	1	1	0	0	0	1	0.0	-1.00
10-11	1	1	0	0	0	1	0.0	-1.00

JOCKEYS

	W-R	Per cent	£1 Level Stake
Mr J E Tudor	1-2	50.0	+0.25

COURSE RECORD

	Total W-R	Non-Hndcps Hurdles	Chases	Hndcps Hurdles	Chases	NH Flat	Per cent	£1 Level Stake
Ffos Las	1-1	0-0	1-1	0-0	0-0	0-0	100.0	+1.25

WINNING HORSES

Horse	Races Run	1st	2nd	3rd	£
*Rosies Peacock	2	1	0	0	1317
Total winning prize-money					£1317
Favourites	1-1		100.0%		1.25

BERNARD LLEWELLYN

FOCHRIW, CAERPHILLY

	No. of Hrs	Races Run	1st	2nd	3rd	Unpl	Per cent	£1 Level Stake
NH Flat	3	4	0	0	0	4	0.0	-4.00
Hurdles	29	103	9	10	11	73	8.7	+59.63
Chases	7	21	0	0	3	18	0.0	-21.00
Totals	34	128	9	10	14	95	7.0	+34.63
11-12	37	170	17	23	23	107	10.0	-33.50
10-11	28	109	8	20	12	68	7.3	-42.00

JOCKEYS

	W-R	Per cent	£1 Level Stake
Robert Williams	6-69	8.7	+6.63
Mark Quinlan	2-8	25.0	+64.00
D P Fahy	1-19	5.3	-4.00

COURSE RECORD

	Total W-R	Non-Hndcps Hurdles	Chases	Hndcps Hurdles	Chases	NH Flat	Per cent	£1 Level Stake
Nton Abbot	3-14	1-1	0-0	2-12	0-1	0-0	21.4	+35.00
Ffos Las	2-26	1-5	0-0	1-12	0-8	0-1	7.7	+54.00
Worcester	1-3	0-0	0-0	1-1	0-2	0-0	33.3	+6.00
Exeter	1-4	1-1	0-0	0-1	0-1	0-1	25.0	+13.00
Plumpton	1-4	0-0	0-0	1-4	0-0	0-0	25.0	-1.38
Taunton	1-5	0-0	0-0	1-5	0-0	0-0	20.0	0.00

WINNING HORSES

Horse	Races Run	1st	2nd	3rd	£
Sweet World	2	1	0	1	3574
Come On Annie	7	2	2	0	4687
*Surprise Us	2	1	0	0	2395
Bazart	5	1	0	0	2259
Going Nowhere Fast	4	1	1	0	2053
*Rime Avec Gentil	7	1	3	0	2053
*Fuzzy Logic	6	1	0	0	1949
Dancewiththedevil	6	1	0	0	1689
Total winning prize-money					£20659
Favourites	2-7		28.6%		0.63

CHARLIE LONGSDON

OVER NORTON, OXON

	No. of Hrs	Races Run	1st	2nd	3rd	Unpl	Per cent	£1 Level Stake
NH Flat	29	48	8	7	5	28	16.7	-5.11
Hurdles	67	195	18	25	20	132	9.2	-78.29
Chases	39	144	25	14	19	86	17.4	-20.06
Totals	115	387	51	46	44	246	13.2	-103.46
11-12	92	344	68	48	31	197	19.8	+53.19
10-11	61	236	44	40	27	125	18.6	+50.80

BY MONTH

NH Flat	W-R	Per cent	£1 Level Stake	Hurdles	W-R	Per cent	£1 Level Stake
May	1-4	25.0	-2.09	May	0-11	0.0	-11.00
June	0-1	0.0	-1.00	June	0-3	0.0	-3.00
July	0-2	0.0	-2.00	July	0-4	0.0	-4.00
August	0-0	0.0	0.00	August	0-4	0.0	-4.00
September	2-4	50.0	+2.23	September	0-6	0.0	-6.00
October	1-6	16.7	-1.50	October	4-36	11.1	-23.55
November	1-6	16.7	+15.00	November	4-30	13.3	-15.48
December	1-3	33.3	-0.13	December	4-23	17.4	+5.57
January	0-1	0.0	-1.00	January	1-14	7.1	-1.00
February	0-5	0.0	-5.00	February	3-20	15.0	+23.00
March	2-10	20.0	-3.63	March	1-18	5.6	-14.50
April	0-6	0.0	-6.00	April	1-26	3.8	-24.33

Chases	W-R	Per cent	£1 Level Stake	Totals	W-R	Per cent	£1 Level Stake
May	3-12	25.0	+18.75	May	4-27	14.8	+5.66
June	0-3	0.0	-3.00	June	0-7	0.0	-7.00
July	1-3	33.3	-0.50	July	1-9	11.1	-6.50
August	0-0	0.0	0.00	August	0-4	0.0	-4.00
September	0-3	0.0	-3.00	September	2-13	15.4	-6.77
October	4-27	14.8	-13.38	October	9-69	13.0	-38.43
November	7-22	31.8	-1.68	November	12-58	20.7	-2.16
December	5-23	21.7	-5.75	December	10-49	20.4	-0.31
January	1-12	8.3	-6.00	January	2-27	7.4	-8.00
February	1-17	5.9	-2.00	February	4-42	9.5	+16.00
March	2-10	20.0	+1.50	March	5-38	13.2	-16.63
April	1-12	8.3	-5.00	April	2-44	4.5	-35.33

DISTANCE

Hurdles	W-R	Per cent	£1 Level Stake	Chases	W-R	Per cent	£1 Level Stake
2m-2m3f	7-86	8.1	-56.96	2m-2m3f	10-27	37.0	+11.21
2m4f-2m7f	8-83	9.6	-24.83	2m4f-2m7f	9-56	16.1	+12.88
3m+	3-26	11.5	+3.50	3m+	6-61	9.8	-44.14

TYPE OF RACE

Non-Handicaps	W-R	Per cent	£1 Level Stake	Handicaps	W-R	Per cent	£1 Level Stake
Nov Hrdls	5-47	10.6	-23.26	Nov Hrdls	1-15	6.7	0.00
Hrdls	5-41	12.2	-19.91	Hrdls	7-91	7.7	-34.13
Nov Chs	5-31	16.1	-13.88	Nov Chs	2-9	22.2	-1.25

Chases	0-1	0.0	-1.00	Chases	18-103	17.5	-3.93
Sell/Claim	0-1	0.0	-1.00	Sell/Claim	0-0	0.0	0.00

RACE CLASS

	W-R	Per cent	£1 Level Stake
Class 1	0-28	0.0	-28.00
Class 2	2-27	7.4	-8.50
Class 3	10-85	11.8	-5.25
Class 4	26-163	16.0	-47.91
Class 5	5-46	10.9	-18.69
Class 6	8-38	21.1	+4.89

FIRST TIME OUT

	W-R	Per cent	£1 Level Stake
Bumpers	8-29	27.6	+13.89
Hurdles	6-55	10.9	-15.94
Chases	7-31	22.6	+27.13
Totals	21-115	18.3	+25.08

JOCKEYS

	W-R	Per cent	£1 Level Stake
Noel Fehily	30-189	15.9	-8.70
Kielan Woods	8-64	12.5	-15.40
Richard Johnson	5-28	17.9	+4.82
A P McCoy	4-11	36.4	-1.04
Felix De Giles	2-26	7.7	-18.25
Gavin Sheehan	1-1	100.0	+1.20
Paddy Brennan	1-10	10.0	-8.09

COURSE RECORD

	Total W-R	Non-Hndcps Hurdles	Chases	Hndcps Hurdles	Chases	NH Flat	Per cent	£1 Level Stake
Warwick	6-18	1-2	1-3	2-4	0-5	2-4	33.3	+39.25
Plumpton	5-20	2-6	0-1	0-6	2-5	1-2	25.0	-4.40
Hereford	4-8	0-1	1-1	0-0	2-5	1-1	50.0	+4.63
Mrket Rsn	4-18	0-4	1-2	0-2	2-8	1-2	22.2	-2.27
Fontwell	4-19	2-5	0-0	0-4	1-6	1-4	21.1	-10.09
Huntingdon	3-18	1-4	2-3	0-4	0-2	0-5	16.7	-2.25
Fakenham	2-5	0-1	0-1	1-1	1-2	0-0	40.0	+0.25
Lingfield	2-9	0-2	0-1	0-1	2-5	0-0	22.2	-4.17
Kempton	2-10	0-1	0-0	2-5	0-3	0-1	20.0	+4.00
Southwell	2-11	0-2	0-0	0-2	1-2	1-5	18.2	-4.13
Stratford	2-14	0-6	0-1	0-3	1-2	1-2	14.3	+13.50
Towcester	2-15	0-4	0-1	0-4	2-6	0-0	13.3	-3.50
Bangor	2-16	1-4	0-4	0-3	1-4	0-1	12.5	-8.00
Ludlow	2-19	1-8	0-2	1-3	0-4	0-2	10.5	-2.09
Uttoxeter	2-23	1-9	0-1	0-7	1-3	0-3	8.7	-18.55
Folkestone	1-2	0-0	0-0	0-1	1-1	0-0	50.0	+1.25
Leicester	1-4	0-0	0-1	0-0	1-3	0-0	25.0	+11.00
Sandown	1-7	0-1	0-0	0-3	1-2	0-1	14.3	-3.25
Musselbgh	1-8	1-3	0-0	0-3	0-2	0-0	12.5	+3.00
Aintree	1-8	0-0	0-0	1-6	0-0	0-1	12.5	-2.50
Doncaster	1-10	0-3	0-1	1-4	0-2	0-0	10.0	+7.00
Newbury	1-13	0-3	0-0	0-2	1-6	0-2	7.7	-10.13

WINNING HORSES

Horse	Races Run	1st	2nd	3rd	£
Ely Brown	5	2	0	1	21583
Vulcanite	5	2	1	1	14101
Loose Chips	6	2	0	1	13988
Ostland	1	1	0	0	9384

Cross Of Honour	3	1	1	1	7988
Superior Quality	3	2	0	0	11047
Pete The Feat	8	5	0	1	23888
Time For Spring	5	1	0	1	6882
*Kellys Brow	1	1	0	0	6498
Hildisvini	3	2	0	0	9552
Hazy Tom	6	1	1	0	5653
Little Chip	9	1	1	0	5198
Great's Autrechene	3	1	0	0	4549
Pendra	4	2	1	0	6160
No No Bingo	9	3	1	0	10722
Newton Tonic	5	2	0	0	6336
Topaze Collonges	8	3	2	0	7635
Fennis Boy	2	1	0	0	3607
Brassick	3	1	1	1	3249
Tatispout	5	1	0	0	3129
Up To Something	7	2	3	0	5263
Loudmouth	3	1	0	1	3119
Onefourfun	4	1	0	0	3054
Spanish Arch	7	1	0	2	2924
*Tidal Way	6	2	1	1	5133
Pure Style	4	1	3	0	2053
Overdante	6	1	1	0	1949
Spirit Of Shankly	4	1	1	2	1754
Ready Token	2	1	0	0	1643
Court Appeal	1	1	0	0	1560
Hannibal The Great	2	1	0	1	1437
No No Charlie	2	1	1	0	1365
Venceremos	2	1	0	0	1365
Wadswick Court	2	1	0	0	1365
Total winning prize-money					**£215133**
Favourites	**23-57**		**40.4%**		**-3.09**

DANIEL MARK LOUGHNANE

BALDWIN'S GATE, STAFFS

	No. of Hrs	Races Run	1st	2nd	3rd	Unpl	Per cent	£1 Level Stake
NH Flat	1	2	1	0	0	1	50.0	+13.00
Hurdles	6	14	0	1	1	12	0.0	-14.00
Chases	1	1	0	0	0	1	0.0	-1.00
Totals	**6**	**17**	**1**	**1**	**1**	**14**	**5.9**	**-2.00**
11-12	*3*	*8*	*1*	*2*	*0*	*5*	*12.5*	*+18.00*

JOCKEYS

	W-R	Per cent	£1 Level Stake
Alain Cawley	1-12	8.3	+3.00

COURSE RECORD

	Total W-R	Non-Hndcps Hurdles Chases	Hndcps Hurdles Chases	NH Flat	Per cent	£1 Level Stake
Stratford	1-2	0-0 0-0	0-1 0-0	1-1	50.0	+13.00

WINNING HORSES

Horse	Races Run	1st	2nd	3rd	£
Ma Toolan	7	1	1	1	1754
Total winning prize-money					**£1754**
Favourites	**0-1**		**0.0%**		**-1.00**

MRS ROSE LOXTON

BRUTON, SOMERSET

	No. of Hrs	Races Run	1st	2nd	3rd	Unpl	Per cent	£1 Level Stake
NH Flat	0	0	0	0	0	0	0.0	0.00
Hurdles	0	0	0	0	0	0	0.0	0.00
Chases	1	1	1	0	0	0	100.0	+25.00
Totals	**1**	**1**	**1**	**0**	**0**	**0**	**100.0**	**+25.00**

JOCKEYS

	W-R	Per cent	£1 Level Stake
Miss Leanda Tickle	1-1	100.0	+25.00

COURSE RECORD

	Total W-R	Non-Hndcps Hurdles Chases	Hndcps Hurdles Chases	NH Flat	Per cent	£1 Level Stake
Stratford	1-1	0-0 1-1	0-0 0-0	0-0	100.0	+25.00

WINNING HORSES

Horse	Races Run	1st	2nd	3rd	£
*Oslot	1	1	0	0	1872
Total winning prize-money					**£1872**
Favourites	**0-0**		**0.0%**		**0.00**

SHAUN LYCETT

CLAPTON-ON-THE-HILL, GLOUCS

	No. of Hrs	Races Run	1st	2nd	3rd	Unpl	Per cent	£1 Level Stake
NH Flat	2	3	0	0	0	3	0.0	-3.00
Hurdles	12	27	1	5	3	18	3.7	-20.00
Chases	4	6	0	0	1	5	0.0	-6.00
Totals	**13**	**36**	**1**	**5**	**4**	**26**	**2.8**	**-29.00**
11-12	*17*	*64*	*7*	*16*	*7*	*34*	*10.9*	*-21.80*
10-11	*16*	*60*	*4*	*11*	*2*	*43*	*6.7*	*+3.50*

JOCKEYS

	W-R	Per cent	£1 Level Stake
Tom Scudamore	1-1	100.0	+6.00

	No. of Hrs	Races Run	1st	2nd	3rd	Unpl	Per cent	£1 Level Stake
11-12	2	5	0	1	0	4	0.0	-5.00
10-11	2	6	0	0	1	5	0.0	-5.00

JOCKEYS

	W-R	Per cent	£1 Level Stake
Brian Harding	1-6	16.7	+1.00

COURSE RECORD

	Total W-R	Non-Hndcps Hurdles	Chases	Hndcps Hurdles	Chases	NH Flat	Per cent	£1 Level Stake
Carlisle	1-3	0-0	0-0	0-0	1-3	0-0	33.3	+4.00

WINNING HORSES

Horse	Races Run	1st	2nd	3rd	£
Royal Mackintosh	5	1	1	2	3054
Total winning prize-money					£3054
Favourites	0-1		0.0%		-1.00

MICHAEL MADGWICK
DENMEAD, HANTS

	No. of Hrs	Races Run	1st	2nd	3rd	Unpl	Per cent	£1 Level Stake
NH Flat	1	1	0	0	0	1	0.0	-1.00
Hurdles	8	21	2	0	3	16	9.5	-10.50
Chases	3	11	2	0	1	8	18.2	+13.00
Totals	9	33	4	0	4	25	12.1	+1.50
11-12	9	24	1	2	2	19	4.2	-17.50
10-11	9	30	3	2	4	21	10.0	-6.50

JOCKEYS

	W-R	Per cent	£1 Level Stake
Marc Goldstein	4-24	16.7	+10.50

COURSE RECORD

	Total W-R	Non-Hndcps Hurdles	Chases	Hndcps Hurdles	Chases	NH Flat	Per cent	£1 Level Stake
Plumpton	2-8	0-3	0-1	2-2	0-2	0-0	25.0	+2.50
Stratford	1-2	0-0	0-0	0-0	1-2	0-0	50.0	+7.00
Fontwell	1-10	0-5	0-0	0-2	1-3	0-0	10.0	+5.00

WINNING HORSES

Horse	Races Run	1st	2nd	3rd	£
Ray Diamond	10	2	0	0	8561
Peyekashe	6	2	0	1	4175
Total winning prize-money					£12736
Favourites	1-3		33.3%		1.00

COURSE RECORD

	Total W-R	Non-Hndcps Hurdles	Chases	Hndcps Hurdles	Chases	NH Flat	Per cent	£1 Level Stake
Fakenham	1-3	0-0	0-0	1-3	0-0	0-0	33.3	+4.00

WINNING HORSES

Horse	Races Run	1st	2nd	3rd	£
Ironical	5	1	3	0	1949
Total winning prize-money					£1949
Favourites	0-2		0.0%		-2.00

JOHN MACKIE
CHURCH BROUGHTON , DERBYS

	No. of Hrs	Races Run	1st	2nd	3rd	Unpl	Per cent	£1 Level Stake
NH Flat	3	5	0	0	0	5	0.0	-5.00
Hurdles	10	39	2	3	4	30	5.1	-0.50
Chases	0	0	0	0	0	0	0.0	0.00
Totals	13	44	2	3	4	35	4.5	-5.50
11-12	16	54	2	7	7	38	3.7	-36.00
10-11	20	61	3	0	6	52	4.9	-12.50

JOCKEYS

	W-R	Per cent	£1 Level Stake
Peter Carberry	1-5	20.0	-0.50
Brian Hughes	1-6	16.7	+28.00

COURSE RECORD

	Total W-R	Non-Hndcps Hurdles	Chases	Hndcps Hurdles	Chases	NH Flat	Per cent	£1 Level Stake
Wetherby	1-6	0-0	0-0	1-4	0-0	0-2	16.7	-1.50
Uttoxeter	1-13	0-1	0-0	1-11	0-0	0-1	7.7	+21.00

WINNING HORSES

Horse	Races Run	1st	2nd	3rd	£
Knight In Purple	5	1	0	1	2599
Bosamcliff	4	1	0	1	1949
Total winning prize-money					£4548
Favourites	1-2		50.0%		2.50

ALAN MACTAGGART
BEDRULE, BORDERS

	No. of Hrs	Races Run	1st	2nd	3rd	Unpl	Per cent	£1 Level Stake
NH Flat	1	2	0	0	0	2	0.0	-2.00
Hurdles	1	1	0	0	0	1	0.0	-1.00
Chases	1	5	1	1	2	1	20.0	+2.00
Totals	2	8	1	1	2	4	12.5	-1.00

CHARLIE MANN

UPPER LAMBOURN, BERKS

	No. of Hrs	Races Run	1st	2nd	3rd	Unpl	Per cent	£1 Level Stake
NH Flat	2	3	0	0	0	3	0.0	-3.00
Hurdles	25	90	13	10	10	57	14.4	-18.75
Chases	20	57	3	10	7	37	5.3	-18.63
Totals	36	150	16	20	17	97	10.7	-40.38
11-12	47	199	21	24	22	132	10.6	-14.11
10-11	50	205	21	28	26	130	10.2	-40.00

BY MONTH

NH Flat	W-R	Per cent	£1 Level Stake	Hurdles	W-R	Per cent	£1 Level Stake
May	0-0	0.0	0.00	May	4-10	40.0	+11.08
June	0-0	0.0	0.00	June	2-6	33.3	+0.17
July	0-0	0.0	0.00	July	0-3	0.0	-3.00
August	0-0	0.0	0.00	August	1-4	25.0	-0.25
September	0-0	0.0	0.00	September	0-2	0.0	-2.00
October	0-0	0.0	0.00	October	0-6	0.0	-6.00
November	0-0	0.0	0.00	November	1-10	10.0	-6.00
December	0-0	0.0	0.00	December	3-13	23.1	+6.50
January	0-0	0.0	0.00	January	1-8	12.5	+5.00
February	0-0	0.0	0.00	February	0-10	0.0	-10.00
March	0-1	0.0	-1.00	March	1-11	9.1	-7.25
April	0-2	0.0	-2.00	April	0-7	0.0	-7.00

Chases	W-R	Per cent	£1 Level Stake	Totals	W-R	Per cent	£1 Level Stake
May	0-9	0.0	-9.00	May	4-19	21.1	+2.08
June	2-7	28.6	+14.38	June	4-13	30.8	+14.55
July	0-4	0.0	-4.00	July	0-7	0.0	-7.00
August	0-2	0.0	-2.00	August	1-6	16.7	-2.25
September	0-0	0.0	0.00	September	0-2	0.0	-2.00
October	0-1	0.0	-1.00	October	0-7	0.0	-7.00
November	0-7	0.0	-7.00	November	1-17	5.9	-13.00
December	0-6	0.0	-6.00	December	3-19	15.8	+0.50
January	0-3	0.0	-3.00	January	1-11	9.1	+2.00
February	0-6	0.0	-6.00	February	0-16	0.0	-16.00
March	0-5	0.0	-5.00	March	1-17	5.9	-13.25
April	1-7	14.3	+10.00	April	1-16	6.3	+1.00

DISTANCE

Hurdles	W-R	Per cent	£1 Level Stake	Chases	W-R	Per cent	£1 Level Stake
2m-2m3f	6-44	13.6	-10.33	2m-2m3f	0-6	0.0	-6.00
2m4f-2m7f	5-24	20.8	+5.83	2m4f-2m7f	2-21	9.5	+15.00
3m+	2-22	9.1	-14.25	3m+	1-30	3.3	-27.63

TYPE OF RACE

Non-Handicaps

	W-R	Per cent	£1 Level Stake
Nov Hrdls	4-19	21.1	-2.00
Hrdls	0-16	0.0	-16.00
Nov Chs	1-16	6.3	+1.00

Handicaps

	W-R	Per cent	£1 Level Stake
Nov Hrdls	1-4	25.0	-0.25
Hrdls	8-51	15.7	-0.50
Nov Chs	1-6	16.7	-3.63

Chases	0-2	0.0	-2.00	Chases	1-33	3.0	-14.00
Sell/Claim	0-0	0.0	0.00	Sell/Claim	0-0	0.0	0.00

RACE CLASS

	W-R	Per cent	£1 Level Stake
Class 1	0-2	0.0	-2.00
Class 2	1-9	11.1	+4.00
Class 3	4-50	8.0	-23.08
Class 4	11-72	15.3	-2.29
Class 5	0-14	0.0	-14.00
Class 6	0-3	0.0	-3.00

FIRST TIME OUT

	W-R	Per cent	£1 Level Stake
Bumpers	0-2	0.0	-2.00
Hurdles	4-22	18.2	-0.92
Chases	0-12	0.0	-12.00
Totals	4-36	11.1	-14.92

JOCKEYS

	W-R	Per cent	£1 Level Stake
Gavin Sheehan	10-43	23.3	+13.00
Noel Fehily	3-16	18.8	+11.75
Sam Thomas	2-50	4.0	-28.63
Paul N O'Brien	1-18	5.6	-13.50

COURSE RECORD

	Total W-R	Non-Hndcps Hurdles	Non-Hndcps Chases	Hndcps Hurdles	Hndcps Chases	NH Flat	Per cent	£1 Level Stake
Warwick	3-6	1-2	0-0	2-4	0-0	0-0	50.0	+9.75
Mrket Rsn	3-13	0-2	0-1	2-6	1-4	0-0	23.1	+14.25
Folkestone	2-3	1-1	0-1	1-1	0-0	0-0	66.7	+12.00
Uttoxeter	1-3	1-3	0-0	0-0	0-0	0-0	33.3	+1.33
Nton Abbot	1-4	1-2	0-0	0-1	0-1	0-0	25.0	-2.33
Taunton	1-4	0-1	0-1	1-1	0-1	0-0	25.0	-0.25
Ascot	1-5	0-2	1-1	0-2	0-0	0-0	20.0	+12.00
Fakenham	1-5	0-0	0-1	1-1	0-3	0-0	20.0	-0.50
Sandown	1-8	0-0	0-2	1-4	0-2	0-0	12.5	+5.00
Southwell	1-9	0-0	0-0	1-4	0-4	0-1	11.1	-4.00
Fontwell	1-12	0-5	0-1	0-2	1-4	0-0	8.3	-9.63

WINNING HORSES

Horse	Races Run	1st	2nd	3rd	£
Lord Of House	6	2	0	1	18378
Victor Leudorum	6	3	1	0	14790
Who Owns Me	8	3	0	2	10682
Greyfriars Drummer	4	3	0	0	11631
Seventh Sky	8	1	2	0	3422
Western King	5	1	1	1	3249
Airmen's Friend	4	1	0	2	3054
Duke Of Monmouth	7	1	1	1	2534
Charming Lad	6	1	2	1	2404
Total winning prize-money					£70144
Favourites	4-14		28.6%		-2.46

ANDREW J MARTIN

CHIPPING NORTON, OXON

	No. of Hrs	Races Run	1st	2nd	3rd	Unpl	Per cent	£1 Level Stake
NH Flat	1	4	0	0	1	3	0.0	-4.00
Hurdles	6	15	0	0	1	14	0.0	-15.00
Chases	4	15	3	3	4	5	20.0	+9.00
Totals	7	34	3	3	6	22	8.8	-10.00
11-12	5	17	2	2	1	12	11.8	-5.75
10-11	2	12	0	1	2	9	0.0	-12.00

JOCKEYS

	W-R	Per cent	£1 Level Stake
Mr J Martin	2-31	6.5	-20.00
Ben Poste	1-1	100.0	+12.00

COURSE RECORD

	Total W-R	Non-Hndcps Hurdles	Chases	Hndcps Hurdles	Chases	NH Flat	Per cent	£1 Level Stake
Fontwell	1-1	0-0	0-0	0-0	1-1	0-0	100.0	+4.00
Lingfield	1-1	0-0	1-1	0-0	0-0	0-0	100.0	+5.00
Ludlow	1-4	0-2	0-0	0-0	1-2	0-0	25.0	+9.00

WINNING HORSES

Horse	Races Run	1st	2nd	3rd	£
*Oranger	6	2	2	1	9424
Sunny Ledgend	6	1	1	1	3861
Total winning prize-money					£13285
Favourites	0-1		0.0%		-1.00

I M MASON

MALTON, NORTH YORKS

	No. of Hrs	Races Run	1st	2nd	3rd	Unpl	Per cent	£1 Level Stake
NH Flat	0	0	0	0	0	0	0.0	0.00
Hurdles	0	0	0	0	0	0	0.0	0.00
Chases	3	4	1	1	0	2	25.0	+0.50
Totals	3	4	1	1	0	2	25.0	+0.50
11-12	2	3	0	1	0	2	0.0	-3.00
10-11	1	3	0	2	0	1	0.0	-3.00

JOCKEYS

	W-R	Per cent	£1 Level Stake
Miss Joanna Mason	1-4	25.0	+0.50

COURSE RECORD

	Total W-R	Non-Hndcps Hurdles	Chases	Hndcps Hurdles	Chases	NH Flat	Per cent	£1 Level Stake
Hexham	1-1	0-0	1-1	0-0	0-0	0-0	100.0	+3.50

WINNING HORSES

Horse	Races Run	1st	2nd	3rd	£
Impact Zone	2	1	0	0	1373
Total winning prize-money					£1373
Favourites	0-0		0.0%		0.00

ROBIN MATHEW

LITTLE BARRINGTON, GLOUCS

	No. of Hrs	Races Run	1st	2nd	3rd	Unpl	Per cent	£1 Level Stake
NH Flat	1	1	0	0	0	1	0.0	-1.00
Hurdles	5	18	3	1	1	13	16.7	+19.50
Chases	2	5	1	0	0	4	20.0	+1.00
Totals	6	24	4	1	1	18	16.7	+19.50
11-12	6	15	0	1	2	12	0.0	-15.00
10-11	7	20	0	0	0	20	0.0	-20.00

JOCKEYS

	W-R	Per cent	£1 Level Stake
Ed Cookson	2-6	33.3	+13.00
Lee Edwards	2-12	16.7	+12.50

COURSE RECORD

	Total W-R	Non-Hndcps Hurdles	Chases	Hndcps Hurdles	Chases	NH Flat	Per cent	£1 Level Stake
Towcester	2-6	0-0	0-1	2-4	0-1	0-0	33.3	+18.50
Warwick	1-1	0-0	0-0	0-0	1-1	0-0	100.0	+5.00
Uttoxeter	1-3	0-0	0-0	1-2	0-0	0-1	33.3	+10.00

WINNING HORSES

Horse	Races Run	1st	2nd	3rd	£
Bally Sands	6	2	0	0	11436
Bravo Riquet	11	2	1	1	3639
Total winning prize-money					£15075
Favourites	0-1		0.0%		-1.00

DONALD MCCAIN

CHOLMONDELEY, CHESHIRE

	No. of Hrs	Races Run	1st	2nd	3rd	Unpl	Per cent	£1 Level Stake
NH Flat	56	76	20	17	12	27	26.3	-28.22
Hurdles	144	465	91	67	56	251	19.6	-112.26
Chases	48	191	34	32	28	97	17.8	-59.92
Totals	195	732	145	116	96	375	19.8	-200.40
11-12	165	699	148	116	85	350	21.2	+15.37
10-11	137	586	100	98	64	324	17.1	-171.00

Class 5   26-89   29.2   +5.27   Totals   46-195 23.6   -42.51
Class 6   19-66   28.8   -19.32

BY MONTH

NH Flat	W-R	Per cent	£1 Level Stake	Hurdles	W-R	Per cent	£1 Level Stake
May	2-8	25.0	-4.00	May	11-42	26.2	-0.57
June	2-3	66.7	+2.38	June	9-24	37.5	+12.60
July	1-5	20.0	-2.75	July	5-27	18.5	-6.38
August	0-3	0.0	-3.00	August	9-28	32.1	+0.27
September	0-0	0.0	0.00	September	3-16	18.8	-9.20
October	1-8	12.5	-6.20	October	6-42	14.3	-20.32
November	2-9	22.2	-5.94	November	9-47	19.1	-14.16
December	3-8	37.5	+0.41	December	14-57	24.6	+9.32
January	1-6	16.7	-3.75	January	5-32	15.6	-21.51
February	4-9	44.4	+1.41	February	5-52	9.6	-33.45
March	2-10	20.0	-4.40	March	4-42	9.5	-24.77
April	2-7	28.6	-2.38	April	11-56	19.6	-4.08

Chases	W-R	Per cent	£1 Level Stake	Totals	W-R	Per cent	£1 Level Stake
May	2-11	18.2	-2.17	May	15-61	24.6	-6.74
June	1-4	25.0	-1.63	June	12-31	38.7	+13.35
July	0-1	0.0	-1.00	July	6-33	18.2	-10.13
August	1-2	50.0	-0.47	August	10-33	30.3	-3.20
September	1-3	33.3	+1.00	September	4-19	21.1	-8.20
October	2-16	12.5	-8.38	October	9-66	13.6	-34.90
November	5-28	17.9	-13.68	November	16-84	19.0	-33.78
December	10-23	43.5	+23.17	December	27-88	30.7	+32.90
January	5-22	22.7	-11.73	January	11-60	18.3	-36.99
February	3-29	10.3	-19.18	February	12-90	13.3	-51.22
March	2-20	10.0	-14.36	March	8-72	11.1	-43.53
April	2-32	6.3	-11.50	April	15-95	15.8	-17.96

DISTANCE

Hurdles	W-R	Per cent	£1 Level Stake	Chases	W-R	Per cent	£1 Level Stake
2m-2m3f	50-251	19.9	-49.80	2m-2m3f	15-58	25.9	-3.04
2m4f-2m7f	33-156	21.2	-44.69	2m4f-2m7f	11-64	17.2	-11.10
3m+	8-58	13.8	-17.77	3m+	8-69	11.6	-45.77

TYPE OF RACE

Non-Handicaps	W-R	Per cent	£1 Level Stake	Handicaps	W-R	Per cent	£1 Level Stake
Nov Hrdls	45-167	26.9	-23.19	Nov Hrdls	3-23	13.0	-8.00
Hrdls	23-98	23.5	-6.74	Hrdls	16-159	10.1	-69.20
Nov Chs	18-65	27.7	-24.45	Nov Chs	3-23	13.0	+4.50
Chases	1-15	6.7	-13.09	Chases	12-88	13.6	-26.88
Sell/Claim	6-20	30.0	+0.51	Sell/Claim	0-1	0.0	-1.00

RACE CLASS

	W-R	Per cent	£1 Level Stake
Class 1	6-65	9.2	-23.67
Class 2	7-62	11.3	-36.39
Class 3	22-128	17.2	-18.28
Class 4	65-322	20.2	-107.00

FIRST TIME OUT

	W-R	Per cent	£1 Level Stake
Bumpers	14-56	25.0	-22.36
Hurdles	24-105	22.9	-9.93
Chases	8-34	23.5	-10.22

JOCKEYS

	W-R	Per cent	£1 Level Stake
Jason Maguire	108-476	22.7	-102.43
Henry Brooke	23-130	17.7	-43.61
Richard Johnson	3-3	100.0	+11.98
John Kington	2-11	18.2	-3.70
Paul O'Brien	2-13	15.4	-0.50
Nick Slatter	2-15	13.3	-7.30
Callum Whillans	2-18	11.1	-5.50
Lucy Alexander	1-1	100.0	+2.75
Sam Thomas	1-2	50.0	-0.09
A P McCoy	1-6	16.7	+5.00

COURSE RECORD

	Total W-R	Non-Hndcps Hurdles	Chases	Hndcps Hurdles	Chases	NH Flat	Per cent	£1 Level Stake
Sedgefield	14-45	8-22	0-2	3-9	0-3	3-9	31.1	-8.69
Bangor	13-60	7-27	1-6	3-14	0-6	2-7	21.7	-13.53
Kelso	12-26	5-12	2-5	0-2	4-6	1-1	46.2	+24.98
Uttoxeter	12-56	8-29	1-3	1-12	0-4	2-8	21.4	-8.93
Ayr	10-34	4-11	2-6	1-5	2-9	1-3	29.4	-8.15
Musselbgh	9-32	4-11	2-5	0-8	2-7	1-1	28.1	+6.49
Haydock	8-32	4-8	0-4	2-9	1-6	1-5	25.0	+6.68
Carlisle	8-42	3-10	3-10	0-13	0-3	2-6	19.0	-27.47
Cartmel	7-18	4-9	1-1	2-7	0-1	0-0	38.9	-0.37
Perth	6-31	4-12	1-1	1-9	0-6	0-3	19.4	-10.50
Wetherby	6-37	3-14	0-5	1-9	1-6	1-3	16.2	-16.27
Towcester	5-21	1-10	2-5	0-1	0-2	2-3	23.8	-7.04
Newcastle	5-28	3-11	0-2	1-5	1-6	0-4	17.9	-3.50
Mrket Rsn	5-29	3-13	0-0	0-11	0-2	2-3	17.2	-11.44
Sandown	3-12	0-2	1-2	1-5	1-3	0-0	25.0	+2.18
Catterick	3-25	2-12	0-2	0-4	1-4	0-3	12.0	-15.14
Cheltenham	3-28	1-4	1-5	0-11	1-6	0-2	10.7	-0.25
Chepstow	2-10	0-2	1-1	0-4	0-2	1-1	20.0	-5.36
Southwell	2-14	1-6	0-0	1-4	0-2	0-2	14.3	-6.38
Aintree	2-35	1-9	0-4	0-11	1-10	0-1	5.7	-30.82
Fontwell	1-1	1-1	0-0	0-0	0-0	0-0	100.0	+1.25
Warwick	1-5	0-1	0-1	1-2	0-1	0-0	20.0	+1.00
Ascot	1-6	1-1	0-1	0-4	0-0	0-0	16.7	-3.13
Hereford	1-6	1-3	0-0	0-0	0-1	0-2	16.7	-4.09
Leicester	1-6	1-5	0-0	0-0	0-1	0-0	16.7	+3.50
Newbury	1-10	1-4	0-1	0-4	0-1	0-0	10.0	+1.00
Kempton	1-11	0-2	0-1	1-4	0-4	0-0	9.1	-1.00
Worcester	1-11	0-7	0-0	0-0	0-2	1-2	9.1	-8.50
Stratford	1-12	1-2	0-1	0-5	0-1	0-3	8.3	-9.13
Doncaster	1-14	0-9	1-2	0-2	0-1	0-0	7.1	-12.78

WINNING HORSES

Horse	Races Run	1st	2nd	3rd	£
Red Merlin	1	1	0	0	31323
Across The Bay	6	3	1	0	40543
Lively Baron	8	2	0	2	22282

Lexi's Boy	1	1	0	0	15640	*Right To Rule	6	1	2	0	2599
Up And Go	5	3	0	0	21033	Star In Flight	4	1	0	0	2534
Super Duty	6	1	4	0	12558	Amron Lad	3	1	0	0	2534
She Ranks Me	9	4	3	1	28390	Dj Milan	5	1	1	1	2534
Doyly Carte	5	3	0	2	18386	Oscatara	2	1	0	0	2534
Clondaw Kaempfer	3	2	0	0	16762	Salto Chisco	3	1	2	0	2259
Dunowen Point	5	2	1	0	14570	Orlittlebylittle	3	2	1	0	4094
Peddlers Cross	2	1	0	0	10128	Deise Dynamo	5	1	1	2	2144
Bourne	8	1	0	0	9747	Tick Tocker	5	1	1	0	2079
Desert Cry	7	2	1	2	17545	*Trend Is My Friend	4	1	0	1	1949
Constant Contact	4	1	0	0	9747	Plan Again	1	1	0	0	1949
Ballybriggan	4	1	0	1	8123	Moscow Presents	6	1	2	1	1949
Storming Gale	6	1	0	1	7798	Vinstar	3	1	2	0	1848
Overturn	5	3	1	0	14881	Ghaabesh	6	1	1	1	1779
Red Rocco	4	2	1	0	11696	Mountain Hiker	2	1	0	1	1779
Kie	7	2	4	1	12845	*Hit The Switch	6	2	0	3	3379
Bhaltair	13	2	1	3	12996	Witness In Court	6	1	1	3	1689
Swift Arrow	7	3	1	1	13321	Hellorboston	4	2	1	0	3072
*Kruzhlinin	6	2	2	0	12151	Sealous Scout	3	1	1	1	1643
Grouse Lodge	9	6	0	2	19970	Diamond King	2	2	0	0	3285
Cygnet	4	1	0	0	5848	*Master Red	2	1	1	0	1560
Charminster	3	1	0	1	5697	Tonvadosa	3	2	0	0	2924
Real Milan	6	2	1	1	9552	Cordillera	2	1	0	0	1506
Beeves	5	2	1	0	7213	Halo Moon	2	1	1	0	1437
Call Back	6	2	1	0	4431	Baltimoar	3	1	1	0	1365
Golden Call	1	1	0	0	3899	Mount Hope	6	1	1	0	1365
Bunclody	2	1	0	0	3899	Sea The Fire	1	1	0	0	1365
Nodform Richard	5	1	0	1	3899	Blue Article	1	1	0	0	0
Kellys Brow	5	2	0	0	6433	**Total winning prize-money**					**£633557**
Smadynium	6	2	0	1	6758	**Favourites**	79-195		40.5%		-33.33
Brady	8	3	4	0	3899						
Bit Of A Jig	4	1	0	1	3899						
Sydney Paget	8	2	2	1	7474						
Swatow Typhoon	3	3	0	0	8137						
Absinthe	4	1	1	0	3249						
*Veloce	5	2	2	0	6368						
Dungeel	3	2	0	0	6498						
Abbey Storm	3	1	1	0	3249						
Ifyousayso	3	1	0	0	3249						
*Indepub	4	2	1	0	4938						
Mulligan's Man	5	4	0	0	9812						
Keeneland	2	2	0	0	6498						
Hurraboru	8	1	2	1	3249						
Corrin Wood	6	1	3	2	3249						
Blackwater King	5	1	3	0	3249						
Dreams Of Milan	5	2	1	1	5848						
Supreme Asset	5	2	0	2	6498						
Woodpole Academy	3	1	1	1	3249						
*Counsel	7	3	0	0	8648						
Indian Castle	3	1	2	0	3119						
Cuban Piece	5	2	0	0	4614						
Boruler	4	1	1	0	2924						
Halogen	6	2	1	0	5203						
Seedless	7	2	1	1	4289						
Sud Pacifique	10	2	3	2	5198						
The Weatherman	2	1	0	0	2599						
An Capall Mor	8	2	1	0	5133						

IAN MCINNES

CATWICK, E YORKS

	No. of Hrs	Races Run	1st	2nd	3rd	Unpl	Per cent	£1 Level Stake
NH Flat	1	1	0	0	0	1	0.0	-1.00
Hurdles	3	8	1	0	0	7	12.5	+9.00
Chases	0	0	0	0	0	0	0.0	0.00
Totals	4	9	1	0	0	8	11.1	+8.00
11-12	4	13	1	1	0	11	7.7	+16.00
10-11	6	11	0	1	0	10	0.0	-11.00

JOCKEYS

	W-R	Per cent	£1 Level Stake
Barry Keniry	1-4	25.0	+13.00

COURSE RECORD

	Total W-R	Non-Hndcps Hurdles	Chases	Hndcps Hurdles	Chases	NH Flat	Per cent	£1 Level Stake
Mrket Rsn	1-6	0-1	0-0	1-4	0-0	0-1	16.7	+11.00

WINNING HORSES

Horse	Races Run	1st	2nd	3rd	£
Carlitos Spirit	2	1	0	0	2534
Total winning prize-money					£2534
Favourites	0-0		0.0%		0.00

KAREN MCLINTOCK

INGOE, NORTHUMBERLAND

	No. of Hrs	Races Run	1st	2nd	3rd	Unpl	Per cent	£1 Level Stake
NH Flat	12	28	5	5	2	16	17.9	-1.09
Hurdles	5	15	0	1	2	12	0.0	-15.00
Chases	4	14	4	4	2	4	28.6	+1.88
Totals	20	57	9	10	6	32	15.8	-14.21
11-12	9	20	2	2	3	13	10.0	-14.75
10-11	14	41	6	9	4	22	14.6	+34.61

JOCKEYS

	W-R	Per cent	£1 Level Stake
Brian Hughes	6-40	15.0	-13.63
Paddy Brennan	1-2	50.0	+8.00
James Reveley	1-2	50.0	+2.50
Richard Johnson	1-2	50.0	-0.09

COURSE RECORD

	Total W-R	Non-Hndcps Hurdles	Chases	Hndcps Hurdles	Chases	NH Flat	Per cent	£1 Level Stake
Cartmel	1-1	0-0	1-1	0-0	0-0	0-0	100.0	+1.88
Carlisle	1-2	0-0	0-0	0-0	0-0	1-2	50.0	+8.00
Towcester	1-2	0-0	0-0	0-0	0-0	1-2	50.0	-0.09
Catterick	1-3	0-0	1-2	0-0	0-0	0-1	33.3	+1.50
Uttoxeter	1-3	0-1	0-0	0-0	0-0	1-2	33.3	+7.00
Sedgefield	1-4	0-1	0-0	0-0	1-2	0-1	25.0	+0.50
Hexham	1-5	0-0	0-0	0-0	0-0	1-5	20.0	-2.00
Southwell	1-5	0-1	0-0	0-1	0-0	1-3	20.0	-3.00
Perth	1-7	0-2	0-0	0-1	1-2	0-2	14.3	-3.00

WINNING HORSES

Horse	Races Run	1st	2nd	3rd	£
Nodforms Violet	6	2	2	0	9097
Bridlingtonbygones	10	2	2	3	8317
Mason David Brown	2	1	1	0	1643
Devenish Island	2	2	0	0	3119
Absolutely Bygones	4	1	1	0	1369
Omani Rebel	3	1	0	0	1365
Total winning prize-money					£24910
Favourites	3-5		60.0%		2.91

GRAEME MCPHERSON

UPPER ODDINGTON, GLOUCS

	No. of Hrs	Races Run	1st	2nd	3rd	Unpl	Per cent	£1 Level Stake
NH Flat	10	12	3	0	2	7	25.0	+5.83
Hurdles	30	72	4	10	7	51	5.6	-48.50
Chases	12	26	1	2	6	17	3.8	+3.00
Totals	39	110	8	12	15	75	7.3	-39.67
11-12	35	125	10	15	18	82	8.0	+10.75
10-11	25	94	9	12	10	63	9.6	+31.33

JOCKEYS

	W-R	Per cent	£1 Level Stake
Killian Moore	3-28	10.7	+8.88
Tom Molloy	3-51	5.9	-28.54
Jason Maguire	1-1	100.0	+7.00
Wayne Hutchinson	1-10	10.0	-7.00

COURSE RECORD

	Total W-R	Non-Hndcps Hurdles	Chases	Hndcps Hurdles	Chases	NH Flat	Per cent	£1 Level Stake
Chepstow	2-5	1-3	0-0	0-1	1-1	0-0	40.0	+26.38
Sandown	1-3	0-0	0-0	0-2	0-0	1-1	33.3	+5.00
Warwick	1-5	0-3	0-0	0-1	0-0	1-1	20.0	-0.67
Mrket Rsn	1-7	1-5	0-0	0-2	0-0	0-0	14.3	-4.00
Towcester	1-8	0-4	0-0	0-3	0-0	1-1	12.5	-2.50
Uttoxeter	1-9	1-2	0-0	0-4	0-1	0-2	11.1	-5.88
Stratford	1-10	0-0	0-0	1-6	0-3	0-1	10.0	+5.00

WINNING HORSES

Horse	Races Run	1st	2nd	3rd	£
Kilcrea Asla	4	1	0	1	6498
Harry Hunt	5	1	1	0	5630
Timesishard	6	1	1	2	3574
Wychwoods Brook	5	1	2	0	2599
Westlin' Winds	3	1	0	2	2144
*Red Admirable	3	1	0	0	1949
Werenearlyoutofit	2	1	0	1	1754
Glacial Rock	1	1	0	0	1365
Total winning prize-money					£25513
Favourites	17-21		81.0%		22.71

H A MCWILLIAMS

PILLING, LANCS

	No. of Hrs	Races Run	1st	2nd	3rd	Unpl	Per cent	£1 Level Stake
NH Flat	0	0	0	0	0	0	0.0	0.00
Hurdles	0	0	0	0	0	0	0.0	0.00
Chases	1	4	1	1	2	0	25.0	0.00
Totals	1	4	1	1	2	0	25.0	0.00
11-12	2	6	2	1	0	3	33.3	+50.00
10-11	1	3	0	0	1	2	0.0	-3.00

JOCKEYS

	W-R	Per cent	£1 Level Stake
Kielan Woods	1-3	33.3	+1.00

COURSE RECORD

	Total W-R	Non-Hndcps Hurdles	Chases	Hndcps Hurdles	Chases	NH Flat	Per cent	£1 Level Stake
Cartmel	1-1	0-0	0-0	0-0	1-1	0-0	100.0	+3.00

WINNING HORSES

Horse	Races Run	1st	2nd	3rd	£
Gougane	4	1	1	2	3899
Total winning prize-money					£3899
Favourites	1-1		100.0%		3.00

N MECHIE

THIRSK, NORTH YORKS

	No. of Hrs	Races Run	1st	2nd	3rd	Unpl	Per cent	£1 Level Stake
NH Flat	0	0	0	0	0	0	0.0	0.00
Hurdles	0	0	0	0	0	0	0.0	0.00
Chases	1	2	1	0	0	1	50.0	+19.00
Totals	1	2	1	0	0	1	50.0	+19.00

JOCKEYS

	W-R	Per cent	£1 Level Stake
Miss C Walton	1-2	50.0	+19.00

COURSE RECORD

	Total W-R	Non-Hndcps Hurdles	Chases	Hndcps Hurdles	Chases	NH Flat	Per cent	£1 Level Stake
Carlisle	1-1	0-0	1-1	0-0	0-0	0-0	100.0	+20.00

WINNING HORSES

Horse	Races Run	1st	2nd	3rd	£
*Kildonnan	2	1	0	0	1647
Total winning prize-money					£1647
Favourites	0-0		0.0%		0.00

PHIL MIDDLETON

DORTON, BUCKS

	No. of Hrs	Races Run	1st	2nd	3rd	Unpl	Per cent	£1 Level Stake
NH Flat	0	0	0	0	0	0	0.0	0.00
Hurdles	7	43	4	8	3	28	9.3	-3.00
Chases	3	11	2	3	3	3	18.2	-2.00
Totals	8	54	6	11	6	31	11.1	-5.00

11-12	9	53	7	4	6	36	13.2	+1.00
10-11	5	32	2	7	3	20	6.3	-16.75

JOCKEYS

	W-R	Per cent	£1 Level Stake
A P McCoy	2-6	33.3	+6.50
Thomas Garner	2-16	12.5	+5.50
Kielan Woods	2-17	11.8	-2.00

COURSE RECORD

	Total W-R	Non-Hndcps Hurdles	Chases	Hndcps Hurdles	Chases	NH Flat	Per cent	£1 Level Stake
Uttoxeter	3-7	0-0	0-0	3-6	0-1	0-0	42.9	+26.50
Towcester	2-8	1-2	0-0	0-5	1-1	0-0	25.0	+4.50
Stratford	1-8	0-1	0-0	0-4	1-3	0-0	12.5	-5.00

WINNING HORSES

Horse	Races Run	1st	2nd	3rd	£
Olympian	8	2	2	1	7603
Like Ice	3	1	1	1	3249
Sail And Return	9	2	0	1	4289
Marju King	9	1	3	0	1689
Total winning prize-money					£16830
Favourites	0-2		0.0%		-2.00

ANTHONY MIDDLETON

GRANBOROUGH, BUCKS

	No. of Hrs	Races Run	1st	2nd	3rd	Unpl	Per cent	£1 Level Stake
NH Flat	8	12	0	0	0	12	0.0	-12.00
Hurdles	20	85	5	6	10	64	5.9	-38.00
Chases	7	23	2	1	6	14	8.7	-13.50
Totals	26	120	7	7	16	90	5.8	-63.50
11-12	5	14	2	1	4	7	14.3	+1.00
10-11	8	29	1	2	4	22	3.4	-24.00

JOCKEYS

	W-R	Per cent	£1 Level Stake
James Banks	4-31	12.9	-3.00
Charlie Deutsch	1-1	100.0	+9.00
Paul Moloney	1-7	14.3	+6.00
Mark Marris	1-11	9.1	-5.50

COURSE RECORD

	Total W-R	Non-Hndcps Hurdles	Chases	Hndcps Hurdles	Chases	NH Flat	Per cent	£1 Level Stake
Lingfield	3-6	1-1	1-1	1-3	0-1	0-0	50.0	+18.50
Folkestone	1-1	1-1	0-0	0-0	0-0	0-0	100.0	+9.00
Towcester	1-3	1-2	0-0	0-1	0-0	0-0	33.3	+2.50
Bangor	1-4	1-3	0-0	0-1	0-0	0-0	25.0	+9.00
Leicester	1-4	0-1	0-0	0-2	1-1	0-0	25.0	-0.50

WINNING HORSES

Horse	Races Run	1st	2nd	3rd	£
*Grafite	8	1	2	1	6498
American Life	10	1	1	3	4106
*Va'Vite	5	2	0	1	6238
Lough Coi	9	2	0	2	4403
*Fitandproperjob	9	1	0	1	1712
Total winning prize-money					£22957
Favourites	0-3		0.0%		-3.00

M G MILLER

BLANDFORD FORUM, DORSET

	No. of Hrs	Races Run	1st	2nd	3rd	Unpl	Per cent	£1 Level Stake
NH Flat	0	0	0	0	0	0	0.0	0.00
Hurdles	0	0	0	0	0	0	0.0	0.00
Chases	1	3	1	1	0	1	33.3	+14.00
Totals	1	3	1	1	0	1	33.3	+14.00
10-11	1	1	0	0	0	1	0.0	-1.00

JOCKEYS

	W-R	Per cent	£1 Level Stake
Mr W Biddick	1-2	50.0	+15.00

COURSE RECORD

	Total W-R	Non-Hndcps Hurdles Chases		Hndcps Hurdles Chases		NH Flat	Per cent	£1 Level Stake
Wincanton	1-1	0-0	1-1	0-0	0-0	0-0	100.0	+16.00

WINNING HORSES

Horse	Races Run	1st	2nd	3rd	£
*Vintage Class	3	1	1	0	936
Total winning prize-money					£936
Favourites	0-0		0.0%		0.00

NICK MITCHELL

PIDDLETRENTHIDE, DORSET

	No. of Hrs	Races Run	1st	2nd	3rd	Unpl	Per cent	£1 Level Stake
NH Flat	5	6	0	0	0	6	0.0	-6.00
Hurdles	10	38	1	3	5	29	2.6	-28.00
Chases	6	17	1	3	2	11	5.9	+9.00
Totals	18	61	2	6	7	46	3.3	-25.00
11-12	23	84	5	1	10	68	6.0	-40.50
10-11	22	80	6	10	9	55	7.5	-32.46

JOCKEYS

	W-R	Per cent	£1 Level Stake
Daryl Jacob	2-15	13.3	+21.00

COURSE RECORD

	Total W-R	Non-Hndcps Hurdles Chases		Hndcps Hurdles Chases		NH Flat	Per cent	£1 Level Stake
Nton Abbot	1-6	0-1	0-1	1-4	0-0	0-0	16.7	+4.00
Worcester	1-7	0-2	1-1	0-3	0-1	0-0	14.3	+19.00

WINNING HORSES

Horse	Races Run	1st	2nd	3rd	£
*Johnny's Way	3	1	1	1	2599
Kayfrou	5	1	1	0	2053
Total winning prize-money					£4652
Favourites	0-1		0.0%		-1.00

RICHARD MITCHELL

PIDDLETRENTHIDE, DORSET

	No. of Hrs	Races Run	1st	2nd	3rd	Unpl	Per cent	£1 Level Stake
NH Flat	0	0	0	0	0	0	0.0	0.00
Hurdles	4	12	2	1	2	7	16.7	+25.00
Chases	5	22	0	3	3	16	0.0	-22.00
Totals	9	34	2	4	5	23	5.9	+3.00
11-12	8	28	1	2	5	20	3.6	-11.00
10-11	12	47	2	2	7	36	4.3	-28.50

JOCKEYS

	W-R	Per cent	£1 Level Stake
Tom Bellamy	2-5	40.0	+32.00

COURSE RECORD

	Total W-R	Non-Hndcps Hurdles Chases		Hndcps Hurdles Chases		NH Flat	Per cent	£1 Level Stake
Sandown	1-1	0-0	0-0	1-1	0-0	0-0	100.0	+7.00
Kempton	1-2	0-0	0-0	1-2	0-0	0-0	50.0	+27.00

WINNING HORSES

Horse	Races Run	1st	2nd	3rd	£
Thundering Home	8	2	1	2	5848
Total winning prize-money					£5848
Favourites	0-1		0.0%		-1.00

JAMES MOFFATT

CARTMEL, CUMBRIA

	No. of Hrs	Races Run	1st	2nd	3rd	Unpl	Per cent	£1 Level Stake
NH Flat	4	5	0	0	0	5	0.0	-5.00
Hurdles	15	53	6	7	3	37	11.3	+28.41
Chases	4	10	1	2	2	5	10.0	-3.00
Totals	20	68	7	9	5	47	10.3	+20.41

| 11-12 | 26 | 112 | 9 | 9 | 15 | 79 | 8.0 | -59.75 |
| 10-11 | 30 | 119 | 2 | 17 | 12 | 88 | 1.7 | -95.00 |

JOCKEYS

	W-R	Per cent	£1 Level Stake
Brian Harding	6-43	14.0	-5.59
Lucy Alexander	1-4	25.0	+47.00

COURSE RECORD

	Total W-R	Non-Hndcps Hurdles	Chases	Hndcps Hurdles	Chases	NH Flat	Per cent	£1 Level Stake
Carlisle	2-5	2-2	0-0	0-2	0-0	0-1	40.0	+2.91
Sedgefield	2-8	0-1	0-0	2-5	0-1	0-1	25.0	+7.00
Cartmel	2-12	2-5	0-0	0-5	0-2	0-0	16.7	+46.50
Newcastle	1-6	0-0	0-0	0-2	1-3	0-1	16.7	+1.00

WINNING HORSES

Horse	Races Run	1st	2nd	3rd	£
Dun Masc	3	1	0	1	6389
Morning Royalty	6	2	0	2	5783
Sam Lord	8	2	0	1	5393
Bollin Dolly	5	1	0	0	2599
Itstooearly	5	1	0	0	2599
Total winning prize-money					**£22763**
Favourites	1-4	25.0%			**-2.09**

LAURA MONGAN

EPSOM, SURREY

	No. of Hrs	Races Run	1st	2nd	3rd	Unpl	Per cent	£1 Level Stake
NH Flat	3	4	0	1	0	3	0.0	-4.00
Hurdles	16	42	1	4	5	32	2.4	-21.00
Chases	5	15	0	2	6	7	0.0	-15.00
Totals	18	61	1	7	11	42	1.6	-40.00
11-12	17	52	3	3	6	40	5.8	-25.50
10-11	15	36	5	3	5	23	13.9	+8.79

JOCKEYS

	W-R	Per cent	£1 Level Stake
Nathan Adams	1-25	4.0	-4.00

COURSE RECORD

	Total W-R	Non-Hndcps Hurdles	Chases	Hndcps Hurdles	Chases	NH Flat	Per cent	£1 Level Stake
Sandown	1-4	0-0	0-1	1-3	0-0	0-0	25.0	+17.00

WINNING HORSES

Horse	Races Run	1st	2nd	3rd	£
First Avenue	5	1	0	1	39865
Total winning prize-money					**£39865**
Favourites	0-1	0.0%			**-1.00**

GARY MOORE

LOWER BEEDING, W SUSSEX

	No. of Hrs	Races Run	1st	2nd	3rd	Unpl	Per cent	£1 Level Stake
NH Flat	9	11	1	2	0	8	9.1	+4.00
Hurdles	60	181	18	18	16	129	9.9	-9.25
Chases	25	85	15	15	6	49	17.6	+14.60
Totals	78	277	34	35	22	186	12.3	+9.35
11-12	75	307	29	39	42	196	9.4	-152.22
10-11	100	383	45	53	40	245	11.7	-23.36

BY MONTH

NH Flat	W-R	Per cent	£1 Level Stake	Hurdles	W-R	Per cent	£1 Level Stake
May	0-3	0.0	-3.00	May	1-12	8.3	-5.50
June	0-0	0.0	0.00	June	2-11	18.2	-2.25
July	0-0	0.0	0.00	July	2-9	22.2	+7.00
August	0-0	0.0	0.00	August	1-7	14.3	+6.00
September	0-0	0.0	0.00	September	0-6	0.0	-6.00
October	0-0	0.0	0.00	October	0-16	0.0	-16.00
November	1-2	50.0	+13.00	November	1-24	4.2	-16.50
December	0-1	0.0	-1.00	December	1-17	5.9	-8.00
January	0-1	0.0	-1.00	January	4-10	40.0	+36.50
February	0-0	0.0	0.00	February	2-24	8.3	-5.00
March	0-2	0.0	-2.00	March	1-23	4.3	-17.00
April	0-2	0.0	-2.00	April	3-22	13.6	+17.50

Chases	W-R	Per cent	£1 Level Stake	Totals	W-R	Per cent	£1 Level Stake
May	1-8	12.5	-4.50	May	2-23	8.7	-13.00
June	1-7	14.3	-0.50	June	3-18	16.7	-2.75
July	0-1	0.0	-1.00	July	2-10	20.0	+6.00
August	0-1	0.0	-1.00	August	1-8	12.5	+5.00
September	0-0	0.0	0.00	September	0-6	0.0	-6.00
October	1-9	11.1	-7.17	October	1-25	4.0	-23.17
November	2-13	15.4	+1.67	November	4-39	10.3	-1.83
December	1-7	14.3	+5.00	December	2-25	8.0	-4.00
January	3-10	30.0	+26.75	January	7-21	33.3	+62.25
February	2-8	25.0	+1.25	February	4-32	12.5	-3.75
March	0-7	0.0	-7.00	March	1-32	3.1	-26.00
April	4-14	28.6	+1.10	April	7-38	18.4	+16.60

DISTANCE

Hurdles	W-R	Per cent	£1 Level Stake	Chases	W-R	Per cent	£1 Level Stake
2m-2m3f	10-120	8.3	-10.50	2m-2m3f	7-34	20.6	-7.20
2m4f-2m7f	6-52	11.5	+0.25	2m4f-2m7f	4-37	10.8	+7.55
3m+	2-9	22.2	+1.00	3m+	4-14	28.6	+14.25

TYPE OF RACE

Non-Handicaps	W-R	Per cent	£1 Level Stake	Handicaps	W-R	Per cent	£1 Level Stake
Nov Hrdls	4-36	11.1	+5.00	Nov Hrdls	0-19	0.0	-19.00
Hrdls	7-43	16.3	+35.00	Hrdls	7-78	9.0	-25.25

Nov Chs	3-18	16.7	-13.20	Nov Chs	1-8	12.5	+18.00
Chases	1-2	50.0	+5.00	Chases	10-57	17.5	+4.80
Sell/Claim	0-4	0.0	-4.00	Sell/Claim	0-1	0.0	-1.00

Panjo Bere	2	1	0	0	3054
Dynamic Idol	4	1	0	0	2259
Petit Ecuyer	8	2	1	0	4003
Gigondas	6	1	0	1	2014
Lajidaal	8	1	0	3	1819
Sunny Spells	5	2	1	0	3379
Total winning prize-money					**£286464**
Favourites	**7-24**		**29.2%**		**-3.15**

RACE CLASS

	W-R	Per cent	£1 Level Stake
Class 1	4-24	16.7	+15.25
Class 2	2-14	14.3	+25.00
Class 3	5-47	10.6	-9.70
Class 4	14-134	10.4	-31.70
Class 5	8-49	16.3	+4.50
Class 6	1-9	11.1	+6.00

FIRST TIME OUT

	W-R	Per cent	£1 Level Stake
Bumpers	1-9	11.1	+6.00
Hurdles	4-53	7.5	-9.50
Chases	3-16	18.8	-5.67
Totals	8-78	10.3	-9.17

JOCKEYS

	W-R	Per cent	£1 Level Stake
Jamie Moore	19-154	12.3	+1.85
Joshua Moore	15-94	16.0	+36.50

COURSE RECORD

	Total W-R	Non-Hndcps Hurdles	Chases	Hndcps Hurdles	Chases	NH Flat	Per cent	£1 Level Stake
Fontwell	8-54	2-16	0-4	2-16	4-16	0-2	14.8	+9.55
Lingfield	4-15	1-3	1-2	0-5	2-5	0-0	26.7	+11.42
Plumpton	4-38	1-7	0-1	1-18	2-11	0-1	10.5	-13.00
Sandown	3-29	1-9	1-2	1-12	0-5	0-1	10.3	+5.00
Nton Abbot	2-6	2-6	0-0	0-0	0-0	0-0	33.3	+10.00
Stratford	2-9	0-4	1-1	1-3	0-1	0-0	22.2	-2.70
Huntingdon	2-13	1-5	0-1	0-1	0-3	1-3	15.4	+15.00
Kempton	2-17	0-8	1-1	1-6	0-2	0-0	11.8	-4.17
Bangor	1-1	1-1	0-0	0-0	0-0	0-0	100.0	+2.50
Haydock	1-2	0-1	0-0	0-0	1-1	0-0	50.0	+3.50
Aintree	1-3	1-1	0-2	0-0	0-0	0-0	33.3	+20.00
Uttoxeter	1-4	0-1	0-0	1-2	0-1	0-0	25.0	+2.50
Newbury	1-10	1-4	0-0	0-4	0-1	0-1	10.0	-4.00
Cheltenham	1-11	0-3	0-1	0-3	1-4	0-0	9.1	+15.00
Ascot	1-13	0-4	0-0	0-4	1-4	0-1	7.7	-9.25

WINNING HORSES

Horse	Races Run	1st	2nd	3rd	£
Sire De Grugy	6	4	1	0	68614
Well Refreshed	7	4	0	0	64712
Ubak	4	1	0	1	34170
Vino Griego	9	2	3	0	38420
Chris Pea Green	5	3	0	0	13062
De Blacksmith	6	2	0	0	9032
Fruity O'Rooney	7	1	2	1	6389
Whitby Jack	6	1	1	0	5848
Be All Man	4	1	1	2	5198
Knight Of Pleasure	5	1	0	0	5198
Dalmo	3	1	0	1	3607
Ballyfoy	1	1	0	0	3249
Kambis	4	1	0	2	3119
*Leo Luna	4	2	0	1	6238
Cabimas	9	1	3	1	3080

GEORGE MOORE

MIDDLEHAM MOOR, N YORKS

	No. of Hrs	Races Run	1st	2nd	3rd	Unpl	Per cent	£1 Level Stake
NH Flat	4	6	0	0	0	6	0.0	-6.00
Hurdles	8	24	2	1	1	20	8.3	-12.75
Chases	2	15	1	4	2	8	6.7	-9.50
Totals	**13**	**45**	**3**	**5**	**3**	**34**	**6.7**	**-28.25**
11-12	23	79	8	10	3	58	10.1	-28.46
10-11	27	103	14	8	13	68	13.6	+33.38

JOCKEYS

	W-R	Per cent	£1 Level Stake
Barry Keniry	3-32	9.4	-15.25

COURSE RECORD

	Total W-R	Non-Hndcps Hurdles	Chases	Hndcps Hurdles	Chases	NH Flat	Per cent	£1 Level Stake
Hexham	1-3	1-3	0-0	0-0	0-0	0-0	33.3	+0.25
Kelso	1-3	0-1	0-0	0-1	1-1	0-0	33.3	+2.50
Newcastle	1-4	0-1	0-0	1-1	0-1	0-1	25.0	+4.00

WINNING HORSES

Horse	Races Run	1st	2nd	3rd	£
Jack The Gent	7	1	3	1	5198
Wolf Shield	5	1	0	1	3798
Kealshore Again	6	1	1	0	1916
Total winning prize-money					**£10912**
Favourites	**0-1**		**0.0%**		**-1.00**

KEVIN MORGAN

GAZELEY, SUFFOLK

	No. of Hrs	Races Run	1st	2nd	3rd	Unpl	Per cent	£1 Level Stake
NH Flat	1	1	0	0	0	1	0.0	-1.00
Hurdles	2	4	1	0	0	3	25.0	+30.00
Chases	2	3	0	0	1	2	0.0	-3.00
Totals	**4**	**8**	**1**	**0**	**1**	**6**	**12.5**	**+26.00**
11-12	9	25	3	1	7	14	12.0	+11.00
10-11	6	19	1	1	1	16	5.3	-12.50

JOCKEYS

	W-R	Per cent	£1 Level Stake
Adam Wedge	1-4	25.0	+30.00

COURSE RECORD

	Total W-R	Non-Hndcps Hurdles	Chases	Hndcps Hurdles	Chases	NH Flat	Per cent	£1 Level Stake
Worcester	1-5	0-0	0-0	1-2	0-3	0-0	20.0	+29.00

WINNING HORSES

Horse	Races Run	1st	2nd	3rd	£
My Farmer Girl	2	1	0	0	1779
Total winning prize-money					£1779
Favourites	0-11		0.0%		-11.00

HUGHIE MORRISON

EAST ILSLEY, BERKS

	No. of Hrs	Races Run	1st	2nd	3rd	Unpl	Per cent	£1 Level Stake
NH Flat	2	3	0	2	0	1	0.0	-3.00
Hurdles	7	15	2	1	3	9	13.3	-3.00
Chases	2	3	0	2	0	1	0.0	-3.00
Totals	10	21	2	5	3	11	9.5	-9.00
11-12	9	28	4	2	2	20	14.3	-10.63
10-11	9	23	5	3	2	13	21.7	+6.58

JOCKEYS

	W-R	Per cent	£1 Level Stake
Brendan Powell	1-2	50.0	+4.00
A P McCoy	1-5	20.0	+1.00

COURSE RECORD

	Total W-R	Non-Hndcps Hurdles	Chases	Hndcps Hurdles	Chases	NH Flat	Per cent	£1 Level Stake
Hereford	1-2	0-0	0-0	1-2	0-0	0-0	50.0	+4.00
Huntingdon	1-2	0-0	0-0	1-1	0-0	0-1	50.0	+4.00

WINNING HORSES

Horse	Races Run	1st	2nd	3rd	£
Stravita	7	2	1	2	3469
Total winning prize-money					£3469
Favourites	0-5		0.0%		-5.00

WILLIAM MUIR

LAMBOURN, BERKS

	No. of Hrs	Races Run	1st	2nd	3rd	Unpl	Per cent	£1 Level Stake
NH Flat	1	1	0	0	0	1	0.0	-1.00
Hurdles	2	10	2	1	3	4	20.0	-6.38

Chases	0	0	0	0	0	0	0.0	0.00
Totals	3	11	2	1	3	5	18.2	-7.38
11-12	4	8	0	3	1	4	0.0	-8.00
10-11	1	5	0	2	1	2	0.0	-5.00

JOCKEYS

	W-R	Per cent	£1 Level Stake
Paddy Brennan	2-9	22.2	-5.38

COURSE RECORD

	Total W-R	Non-Hndcps Hurdles	Chases	Hndcps Hurdles	Chases	NH Flat	Per cent	£1 Level Stake
Towcester	1-1	1-1	0-0	0-0	0-0	0-0	100.0	+1.00
Uttoxeter	1-1	1-1	0-0	0-0	0-0	0-0	100.0	+0.61

WINNING HORSES

Horse	Races Run	1st	2nd	3rd	£
Enroller	5	2	1	1	3639
Total winning prize-money					£3639
Favourites	1-2		50.0%		-0.39

NEIL MULHOLLAND

LIMPLEY STOKE, WILTS

	No. of Hrs	Races Run	1st	2nd	3rd	Unpl	Per cent	£1 Level Stake
NH Flat	11	12	0	1	1	10	0.0	-12.00
Hurdles	41	122	15	7	9	91	12.3	+11.17
Chases	18	51	3	7	12	29	5.9	-24.50
Totals	54	185	18	15	22	130	9.7	-25.33
11-12	41	181	16	20	27	118	8.8	-42.25
10-11	46	205	21	33	10	141	10.2	-65.67

BY MONTH

NH Flat	W-R	Per cent	£1 Level Stake	Hurdles	W-R	Per cent	£1 Level Stake
May	0-0	0.0	0.00	May	3-15	20.0	+10.67
June	0-0	0.0	0.00	June	0-6	0.0	-6.00
July	0-0	0.0	0.00	July	0-5	0.0	-5.00
August	0-0	0.0	0.00	August	0-3	0.0	-3.00
September	0-0	0.0	0.00	September	0-0	0.0	0.00
October	0-3	0.0	-3.00	October	2-18	11.1	+1.00
November	0-3	0.0	-3.00	November	3-13	23.1	+18.75
December	0-1	0.0	-1.00	December	2-14	14.3	-3.25
January	0-1	0.0	-1.00	January	2-12	16.7	+16.50
February	0-1	0.0	-1.00	February	2-18	11.1	-9.50
March	0-1	0.0	-1.00	March	1-5	20.0	+4.00
April	0-2	0.0	-2.00	April	0-13	0.0	-13.00

Chases	W-R	Per cent	£1 Level Stake	Totals	W-R	Per cent	£1 Level Stake
May	0-3	0.0	-3.00	May	3-18	16.7	+7.67
June	1-6	16.7	+1.50	June	1-12	8.3	-4.50
July	0-3	0.0	-3.00	July	0-8	0.0	-8.00

	W-R	Per cent	£1 Level Stake		W-R	Per cent	£1 Level Stake
August	0-8	0.0	-8.00	August	0-11	0.0	-11.00
September	0-3	0.0	-3.00	September	0-3	0.0	-3.00
October	0-7	0.0	-7.00	October	2-28	7.1	-9.00
November	1-7	14.3	+3.00	November	4-23	17.4	+18.75
December	0-1	0.0	-1.00	December	2-16	12.5	-5.25
January	0-5	0.0	-5.00	January	2-18	11.1	+10.50
February	0-2	0.0	-2.00	February	2-21	9.5	-12.50
March	0-1	0.0	-1.00	March	1-7	14.3	+2.00
April	1-5	20.0	+4.00	April	1-20	5.0	-11.00

	Total W-R	Non-Hndcps Hurdles	Chases	Hndcps Hurdles	Chases	NH Flat	Per cent	£1 Level Stake
Newbury	1-3	0-1	0-0	1-2	0-0	0-0	33.3	+6.00
Cheltenham	1-7	0-0	0-1	1-3	0-3	0-0	14.3	+1.00
Kempton	1-8	1-4	0-0	0-2	0-1	0-1	12.5	+13.00
Plumpton	1-9	1-3	0-0	0-1	0-4	0-1	11.1	-6.25
Southwell	1-9	0-4	0-0	1-3	0-2	0-0	11.1	-4.67
Taunton	1-12	0-3	1-1	0-6	0-1	0-1	8.3	-2.00
Fontwell	1-18	0-2	0-0	1-10	0-6	0-0	5.6	-11.00

WINNING HORSES

Horse	Races Run	1st	2nd	3rd	£
*Buck Magic	6	2	0	1	16604
Mabel Tasman	2	1	0	0	5848
Pass The Time	4	2	0	1	6927
Minella Definitely	5	2	0	0	6498
Coronea Lilly	4	2	0	0	3249
Matrow's Lady	7	2	2	1	6368
Adiynara	6	1	2	0	2599
King Helissio	4	1	0	0	2339
Hobb's Dream	10	1	0	4	2144
Wait No More	8	1	2	0	1949
Uimhir A Seacht	7	2	0	0	3509
Meet Me At Dawn	7	1	1	1	1779
Total winning prize-money					**£59813**
Favourites	1-10		10.0%		**-7.50**

DISTANCE

Hurdles	W-R	Per cent	£1 Level Stake	Chases	W-R	Per cent	£1 Level Stake
2m-2m3f	7-57	12.3	+1.33	2m-2m3f	0-12	0.0	-12.00
2m4f-2m7f	7-48	14.6	+17.83	2m4f-2m7f	2-21	9.5	-3.50
3m+	1-17	5.9	-8.00	3m+	1-18	5.6	-9.00

TYPE OF RACE

Non-Handicaps	W-R	Per cent	£1 Level Stake	Handicaps	W-R	Per cent	£1 Level Stake
Nov Hrdls	5-34	14.7	+16.83	Nov Hrdls	1-8	12.5	-5.50
Hrdls	2-9	22.2	+32.00	Hrdls	6-65	9.2	-28.92
Nov Chs	1-3	33.3	+7.00	Nov Chs	0-7	0.0	-7.00
Chases	0-2	0.0	-2.00	Chases	2-39	5.1	-22.50
Sell/Claim	1-4	25.0	-1.25	Sell/Claim	0-1	0.0	-1.00

RACE CLASS / FIRST TIME OUT

	W-R	Per cent	£1 Level Stake		W-R	Per cent	£1 Level Stake
Class 1	0-8	0.0	-8.00	Bumpers	0-11	0.0	-11.00
Class 2	0-4	0.0	-4.00	Hurdles	5-33	15.2	+15.67
Class 3	3-12	25.0	+20.00	Chases	0-10	0.0	-10.00
Class 4	8-76	10.5	-7.42				
Class 5	7-76	9.2	-16.92	Totals	5-54	9.3	-5.33
Class 6	0-9	0.0	-9.00				

JOCKEYS

	W-R	Per cent	£1 Level Stake
Michael Byrne	5-24	20.8	+8.75
Chris Meehan	4-22	18.2	-4.75
Dougie Costello	4-79	5.1	-42.17
Noel Fehily	2-7	28.6	+23.50
Tom Scudamore	1-3	33.3	+14.00
Daryl Jacob	1-10	10.0	+11.00
Andrias Guerin	1-23	4.3	-18.67

COURSE RECORD

	Total W-R	Non-Hndcps Hurdles	Chases	Hndcps Hurdles	Chases	NH Flat	Per cent	£1 Level Stake
Ludlow	3-9	3-4	0-0	0-3	0-1	0-1	33.3	+38.00
Ffos Las	2-6	0-1	0-0	1-3	1-1	0-1	33.3	+5.50
Chepstow	2-8	0-2	0-0	1-3	1-2	0-1	25.0	+3.50
Wincanton	2-18	2-6	0-0	0-9	0-1	0-2	11.1	-9.17
Fakenham	1-2	1-1	0-0	0-0	0-1	0-0	50.0	+13.00
Doncaster	1-3	0-0	0-0	1-2	0-1	0-0	33.3	+0.75

MICHAEL MULLINEAUX

ALPRAHAM, CHESHIRE

	No. of Hrs	Races Run	1st	2nd	3rd	Unpl	Per cent	£1 Level Stake
NH Flat	4	7	0	0	0	7	0.0	-7.00
Hurdles	9	44	2	2	6	34	4.5	-23.50
Chases	3	12	0	1	1	10	0.0	-12.00
Totals	13	63	2	3	7	51	3.2	-42.50
11-12	15	63	2	3	8	50	3.2	-7.50
10-11	20	78	1	4	7	66	1.3	-57.00

JOCKEYS

	W-R	Per cent	£1 Level Stake
Kielan Woods	1-6	16.7	+3.50
Sean Quinlan	1-31	3.2	-20.00

COURSE RECORD

	Total W-R	Non-Hndcps Hurdles	Chases	Hndcps Hurdles	Chases	NH Flat	Per cent	£1 Level Stake
Sedgefield	1-2	0-0	0-0	1-1	0-1	0-0	50.0	+7.50
Hereford	1-12	0-0	0-0	1-6	0-4	0-2	8.3	-1.00

WINNING HORSES

Horse	Races Run	1st	2nd	3rd	£
Sacco D'Oro	12	1	1	3	2144
Phoenix Eye	8	1	0	0	1689
Total winning prize-money					**£3833**
Favourites	0-1		0.0%		**-1.00**

SEAMUS MULLINS

WILSFORD-CUM-LAKE, WILTS

	No. of Hrs	Races Run	1st	2nd	3rd	Unpl	Per cent	£1 Level Stake
NH Flat	19	21	3	1	1	16	14.3	+46.00
Hurdles	37	99	12	17	6	64	12.1	+2.08
Chases	20	63	5	5	12	41	7.9	-40.00
Totals	56	183	20	23	19	121	10.9	+8.08
11-12	56	231	22	23	39	147	9.5	-24.72
10-11	61	233	21	26	22	163	9.0	-94.49

BY MONTH

NH Flat	W-R	Per cent	£1 Level Stake
May	0-2	0.0	-2.00
June	0-1	0.0	-1.00
July	1-1	100.0	+20.00
August	0-0	0.0	0.00
September	0-0	0.0	0.00
October	0-3	0.0	-3.00
November	0-1	0.0	-1.00
December	1-5	20.0	+12.00
January	1-2	50.0	+27.00
February	0-3	0.0	-3.00
March	0-1	0.0	-1.00
April	0-2	0.0	-2.00

Hurdles	W-R	Per cent	£1 Level Stake
May	1-15	6.7	-8.50
June	5-9	55.6	+9.25
July	0-2	0.0	-2.00
August	0-1	0.0	-1.00
September	0-2	0.0	-2.00
October	0-0	0.0	0.00
November	2-7	28.6	+40.00
December	0-8	0.0	-8.00
January	0-5	0.0	-5.00
February	2-14	14.3	-2.00
March	2-20	10.0	-2.67
April	0-16	0.0	-16.00

Chases	W-R	Per cent	£1 Level Stake
May	1-13	7.7	-7.00
June	1-7	14.3	-3.50
July	0-2	0.0	-2.00
August	0-1	0.0	-1.00
September	0-2	0.0	-2.00
October	0-2	0.0	-2.00
November	0-6	0.0	-6.00
December	0-5	0.0	-5.00
January	0-5	0.0	-5.00
February	1-7	14.3	-2.00
March	1-6	16.7	-1.50
April	1-7	14.3	-3.00

Totals	W-R	Per cent	£1 Level Stake
May	2-30	6.7	-17.50
June	6-17	35.3	+4.75
July	1-5	20.0	+16.00
August	0-2	0.0	-2.00
September	0-4	0.0	-4.00
October	0-5	0.0	-5.00
November	2-14	14.3	+33.00
December	1-18	5.6	-1.00
January	1-12	8.3	+17.00
February	3-24	12.5	-7.00
March	3-27	11.1	-5.17
April	1-25	4.0	-21.00

DISTANCE

Hurdles	W-R	Per cent	£1 Level Stake
2m-2m3f	7-47	14.9	+21.00
2m4f-2m7f	3-37	8.1	-16.42
3m+	2-15	13.3	-2.50

Chases	W-R	Per cent	£1 Level Stake
2m-2m3f	1-15	6.7	-10.50
2m4f-2m7f	3-23	13.0	-8.50
3m+	1-25	4.0	-21.00

TYPE OF RACE

Non-Handicaps	W-R	Per cent	£1 Level Stake
Nov Hrdls	3-32	9.4	+2.33
Hrdls	2-18	11.1	-8.00

Handicaps	W-R	Per cent	£1 Level Stake
Nov Hrdls	1-9	11.1	+4.00
Hrdls	6-40	15.0	+3.75

Nov Chs	1-13	7.7	-7.00	Nov Chs	1-10	10.0	-6.50
Chases	0-2	0.0	-2.00	Chases	3-38	7.9	-24.50
Sell/Claim	0-1	0.0	-1.00	Sell/Claim	0-0	0.0	0.00

RACE CLASS

	W-R	Per cent	£1 Level Stake
Class 1	0-9	0.0	-9.00
Class 2	0-6	0.0	-6.00
Class 3	2-18	11.1	+7.00
Class 4	11-85	12.9	-4.42
Class 5	4-49	8.2	-30.50
Class 6	3-16	18.8	+51.00

FIRST TIME OUT

	W-R	Per cent	£1 Level Stake
Bumpers	3-19	15.8	+48.00
Hurdles	1-23	4.3	+3.00
Chases	0-14	0.0	-14.00
Totals	4-56	7.1	+37.00

JOCKEYS

	W-R	Per cent	£1 Level Stake
Andrew Thornton	15-95	15.8	+54.08
Mne Kevin Jones	3-16	18.8	+16.00
Dominic Elsworth	1-6	16.7	0.00
Wayne Kavanagh	1-40	2.5	-36.00

COURSE RECORD

	Total W-R	Non-Hndcps Hurdles	Chases	Hndcps Hurdles	Chases	NH Flat	Per cent	£1 Level Stake
Fontwell	5-34	1-7	0-3	1-6	2-14	1-4	14.7	+14.50
Nton Abbot	3-10	0-0	0-1	2-5	0-2	1-2	30.0	+19.50
Worcester	2-5	0-0	1-1	1-2	0-1	0-1	40.0	+4.25
Chepstow	2-8	0-2	0-0	0-2	1-3	1-1	25.0	+25.50
Towcester	2-12	0-3	0-0	2-5	0-3	0-1	16.7	-1.00
Wincanton	2-21	2-9	0-0	0-6	0-4	0-2	9.5	-12.67
Ffos Las	1-4	1-1	0-0	0-1	0-2	0-0	25.0	+4.00
Exeter	1-5	0-1	0-1	1-2	0-1	0-0	20.0	+8.00
Lingfield	1-6	1-3	0-1	0-0	0-2	0-0	16.7	+20.00
Plumpton	1-25	0-5	0-1	0-6	1-10	0-3	4.0	-21.00

WINNING HORSES

Horse	Races Run	1st	2nd	3rd	£
Romeo Americo	12	3	3	0	15054
Time To Think	4	2	0	0	8642
Alder Mairi	5	2	1	1	6568
Ugly Bug	6	2	1	0	7310
Brunette'Sonly	7	1	2	0	3249
Wilde Ruby	9	2	3	0	5614
Top Smart	6	1	0	2	2924
Might As Well	6	1	0	3	2599
Catch The Rascal	4	1	0	2	2339
Anteros	1	1	0	0	2177
Homer Run	2	1	1	0	1949
Dat's The Plan	1	1	0	0	1745
Well Green	2	1	1	0	1622
The Informant	3	1	0	1	1365
Total winning prize-money					**£63157**
Favourites	2-9		22.2%		**-3.50**

PAT MURPHY

EAST GARSTON, BERKS

	No. of Hrs	Races Run	1st	2nd	3rd	Unpl	Per cent	£1 Level Stake
NH Flat	1	1	0	0	0	1	0.0	-1.00
Hurdles	3	13	1	2	1	9	7.7	-5.00
Chases	0	0	0	0	0	0	0.0	0.00
Totals	4	14	1	2	1	10	7.1	-6.00
11-12	12	34	1	3	8	22	2.9	-26.00
10-11	13	48	0	3	3	42	0.0	-48.00

JOCKEYS

	W-R	Per cent	£1 Level Stake
Colin Bolger	1-10	10.0	-2.00

COURSE RECORD

	Total W-R	Non-Hndcps Hurdles	Chases	Hndcps Hurdles	Chases	NH Flat	Per cent	£1 Level Stake
Warwick	1-2	0-1	0-0	1-1	0-0	0-0	50.0	+6.00

WINNING HORSES

Horse	Races Run	1st	2nd	3rd	£
Cloudy Bob	8	1	2	1	4874
Total winning prize-money					£4874
Favourites	0-0		0.0%		0.00

FERDY MURPHY

WEST WITTON, N YORKS

	No. of Hrs	Races Run	1st	2nd	3rd	Unpl	Per cent	£1 Level Stake
NH Flat	6	9	1	0	0	8	11.1	+17.00
Hurdles	25	81	5	9	6	61	6.2	-23.25
Chases	31	142	7	19	26	90	4.9	-86.25
Totals	53	232	13	28	32	159	5.6	-92.50
11-12	72	326	22	30	47	227	6.7	-166.13
10-11	84	306	28	38	33	207	9.2	-122.13

BY MONTH

NH Flat	W-R	Per cent	£1 Level Stake	Hurdles	W-R	Per cent	£1 Level Stake
May	0-3	0.0	-3.00	May	0-5	0.0	-5.00
June	1-1	100.0	+25.00	June	0-2	0.0	-2.00
July	0-0	0.0	0.00	July	0-1	0.0	-1.00
August	0-0	0.0	0.00	August	0-2	0.0	-2.00
September	0-0	0.0	0.00	September	0-1	0.0	-1.00
October	0-0	0.0	0.00	October	1-15	6.7	-11.25
November	0-1		-1.00	November	1-11	9.1	-6.00
December	0-1		-1.00	December	0-9	0.0	-9.00
January	0-2	0.0	-2.00	January	1-9	11.1	+8.00
February	0-0	0.0	0.00	February	0-8	0.0	-8.00
March	0-0	0.0	0.00	March	1-6	16.7	+20.00
April	0-1	0.0	-1.00	April	1-12	8.3	-6.00

Chases	W-R	Per cent	£1 Level Stake	Totals	W-R	Per cent	£1 Level Stake
May	1-17	5.9	-11.00	May	1-25	4.0	-19.00
June	0-3	0.0	-3.00	June	1-6	16.7	+20.00
July	0-1	0.0	-1.00	July	0-2	0.0	-2.00
August	0-2	0.0	-2.00	August	0-4	0.0	-4.00
September	0-0	0.0	0.00	September	0-1	0.0	-1.00
October	0-14	0.0	-14.00	October	1-29	3.4	-25.25
November	4-21	19.0	+10.25	November	5-33	15.2	+3.25
December	0-23	0.0	-23.00	December	0-33	0.0	-33.00
January	1-13	7.7	-9.50	January	2-24	8.3	-3.50
February	0-15	0.0	-15.00	February	0-23	0.0	-23.00
March	0-12	0.0	-12.00	March	1-18	5.6	+8.00
April	1-21	4.8	-6.00	April	2-34	5.9	-13.00

DISTANCE

Hurdles	W-R	Per cent	£1 Level Stake	Chases	W-R	Per cent	£1 Level Stake
2m-2m3f	1-38	2.6	-12.00	2m-2m3f	1-32	3.1	-19.00
2m4f-2m7f	4-36	11.1	-4.25	2m4f-2m7f	4-59	6.8	-25.75
3m+	0-7	0.0	-7.00	3m+	2-51	3.9	-41.50

TYPE OF RACE

Non-Handicaps	W-R	Per cent	£1 Level Stake	Handicaps	W-R	Per cent	£1 Level Stake
Nov Hrdls	1-22	4.5	-17.00	Nov Hrdls	1-6	16.7	+20.00
Hrdls	0-10	0.0	-10.00	Hrdls	2-38	5.3	-15.00
Nov Chs	0-11	0.0	-11.00	Nov Chs	2-12	16.7	+5.75
Chases	0-2	0.0	-2.00	Chases	5-117	4.3	-79.00
Sell/Claim	1-4	25.0	-0.25	Sell/Claim	0-1	0.0	-1.00

RACE CLASS

	W-R	Per cent	£1 Level Stake
Class 1	0-5	0.0	-5.00
Class 2	0-19	0.0	-19.00
Class 3	1-34	2.9	-17.00
Class 4	4-93	4.3	-41.00
Class 5	7-72	9.7	-27.50
Class 6	1-9	11.1	+17.00

FIRST TIME OUT

	W-R	Per cent	£1 Level Stake
Bumpers	1-6	16.7	+20.00
Hurdles	1-21	4.8	-17.25
Chases	2-26	7.7	-7.00
Totals	4-53	7.5	-4.25

JOCKEYS

	W-R	Per cent	£1 Level Stake
James Reveley	4-72	5.6	-43.75
Tony Kelly	3-56	5.4	-11.00
John Winston	2-20	10.0	+9.75
Lucy Alexander	2-35	5.7	-17.00
Miss C Walton	1-4	25.0	+11.00
Sam Twiston-Davies	1-5	20.0	-1.50

COURSE RECORD

	Total W-R	Non-Hndcps Hurdles	Chases	Hndcps Hurdles	Chases	NH Flat	Per cent	£1 Level Stake
Hexham	6-28	1-5	0-5	1-2	3-14	1-2	21.4	+27.00
Sedgefield	3-31	1-6	0-1	0-4	2-19	0-1	9.7	-5.00

Ayr	2-22	0-4	0-1	1-5	1-11	0-1	9.1	+7.00
Carlisle	1-7	0-0	0-0	1-3	0-4	0-0	14.3	+19.00
Kelso	1-13	0-2	0-2	0-2	1-7	0-0	7.7	-9.50

WINNING HORSES

Horse	Races Run	1st	2nd	3rd	£
Hollo Ladies	8	1	1	1	5393
Chavoy	4	2	0	1	7343
Badgers Retreat	5	1	0	0	3861
Secret Desert	9	1	0	1	2924
Mansonien L'As	7	2	2	1	4419
Vuvuzela	5	1	0	1	2534
Samson Collonges	9	2	0	2	3769
Ibn Hiyyan	3	1	0	1	1916
Ockey De Neulliac	3	1	0	1	1779
Loxendor	2	1	0	0	1369
Total winning prize-money					**£35307**
Favourites	**2-5**		**40.0%**		**1.50**

ANABEL K MURPHY

WILMCOTE, WARWICKS

	No. of Hrs	Races Run	1st	2nd	3rd	Unpl	Per cent	£1 Level Stake
NH Flat	2	2	0	0	0	2	0.0	-2.00
Hurdles	11	43	4	5	2	32	9.3	-24.75
Chases	4	8	1	0	2	5	12.5	-4.00
Totals	15	53	5	5	4	39	9.4	-30.75
11-12	20	64	5	3	3	53	7.8	-4.00
10-11	22	73	8	6	11	48	11.0	-21.05

JOCKEYS

	W-R	Per cent	£1 Level Stake
A P McCoy	2-7	28.6	+3.50
Josh Hamer	1-2	50.0	+1.75
Richie McLernon	1-11	9.1	-7.00
Tom Messenger	1-18	5.6	-14.00

COURSE RECORD

	Total W-R	Non-Hndcps Hurdles	Chases	Hndcps Hurdles	Chases	NH Flat	Per cent	£1 Level Stake
Fakenham	1-2	0-0	0-0	1-2	0-0	0-0	50.0	+2.00
Taunton	1-2	0-0	0-0	1-2	0-0	0-0	50.0	+3.00
Huntingdon	1-5	0-0	0-0	1-5	0-0	0-0	20.0	-1.25
Mrket Rsn	1-6	0-0	1-2	0-3	0-1	0-0	16.7	-2.00
Warwick	1-6	0-1	0-0	1-4	0-0	0-1	16.7	-0.50

WINNING HORSES

Horse	Races Run	1st	2nd	3rd	£
Dormouse	12	2	2	1	5956
Prince Of Denial	4	1	0	1	3129
King's Road	7	2	1	1	4003
Total winning prize-money					**£13088**
Favourites	**2-5**		**40.0%**		**3.75**

BARRY MURTAGH

LOW BRAITHWAITE, CUMBRIA

	No. of Hrs	Races Run	1st	2nd	3rd	Unpl	Per cent	£1 Level Stake
NH Flat	6	7	0	0	0	7	0.0	-7.00
Hurdles	13	43	2	4	4	33	4.7	-24.00
Chases	6	30	3	3	4	20	10.0	+5.00
Totals	21	80	5	7	8	60	6.3	-26.00
11-12	20	113	13	8	11	81	11.5	+21.08
10-11	16	72	5	10	8	49	6.9	-46.75

JOCKEYS

	W-R	Per cent	£1 Level Stake
Tony Kelly	1-1	100.0	+10.00
James Reveley	1-5	20.0	+1.50
Richie McGrath	1-6	16.7	+1.50
Peter Carberry	1-6	16.7	+2.00
Lucy Alexander	1-41	2.4	-20.00

COURSE RECORD

	Total W-R	Non-Hndcps Hurdles	Chases	Hndcps Hurdles	Chases	NH Flat	Per cent	£1 Level Stake
Cartmel	2-5	0-0	0-0	0-2	2-3	0-0	40.0	+23.50
Perth	1-6	0-0	0-0	1-3	0-3	0-0	16.7	+6.00
Carlisle	1-12	0-1	1-2	0-5	0-3	0-1	8.3	-5.50
Sedgefield	1-15	0-0	0-1	1-9	0-4	0-1	6.7	-7.00

WINNING HORSES

Horse	Races Run	1st	2nd	3rd	£
Kealigolane	10	1	1	1	6498
Danny John Boy	3	1	0	0	3899
King's Chorister	9	1	1	2	3899
Pete	14	1	0	2	3249
Stanley Bridge	9	1	2	0	3119
Total winning prize-money					**£20664**
Favourites	**0-1**		**0.0%**		**-1.00**

WILLIE MUSSON

NEWMARKET, SUFFOLK

	No. of Hrs	Races Run	1st	2nd	3rd	Unpl	Per cent	£1 Level Stake
NH Flat	1	2	0	0	0	2	0.0	-2.00
Hurdles	6	13	1	0	1	11	7.7	-8.00
Chases	0	0	0	0	0	0	0.0	0.00
Totals	6	15	1	0	1	13	6.7	-10.00
11-12	9	15	2	1	1	11	13.3	-7.00
10-11	5	11	2	1	1	7	18.2	+8.00

JOCKEYS

	W-R	Per cent	£1 Level Stake
Leighton Aspell	1-4	25.0	+1.00

COURSE RECORD

	Total W-R	Non-Hndcps Hurdles Chases	Hndcps Hurdles Chases	NH Flat	Per cent	£1 Level Stake
Warwick	1-1	0-0 0-0	1-1 0-0	0-0	100.0	+4.00

WINNING HORSES

Horse	Races Run	1st	2nd	3rd	£
Madame Allsorts	4	1	0	0	3119
Total winning prize-money					**£3119**
Favourites	0-0		0.0%		0.00

MISS MARIA D MYCO

SEDGEFIELD, CLEVELAND

	No. of Hrs	Races Run	1st	2nd	3rd	Unpl	Per cent	£1 Level Stake
NH Flat	0	0	0	0	0	0	0.0	0.00
Hurdles	0	0	0	0	0	0	0.0	0.00
Chases	1	1	1	0	0	0	100.0	+5.50
Totals	1	1	1	0	0	0	100.0	+5.50
11-12	1	2	0	0	0	2	0.0	-2.00
10-11	1	1	0	0	0	1	0.0	-1.00

JOCKEYS

	W-R	Per cent	£1 Level Stake
John Dawson	1-1	100.0	+5.50

COURSE RECORD

	Total W-R	Non-Hndcps Hurdles Chases	Hndcps Hurdles Chases	NH Flat	Per cent	£1 Level Stake
Cartmel	1-1	0-0 1-1	0-0 0-0	0-0	100.0	+5.50

WINNING HORSES

Horse	Races Run	1st	2nd	3rd	£
*Yes I Can	1	1	0	0	1248
Total winning prize-money					**£1248**
Favourites	0-0		0.0%		0.00

JOHN NEEDHAM

LUDLOW, SHROPSHIRE

	No. of Hrs	Races Run	1st	2nd	3rd	Unpl	Per cent	£1 Level Stake
NH Flat	0	0	0	0	0	0	0.0	0.00
Hurdles	3	3	0	0	0	3	0.0	-3.00
Chases	4	11	1	2	0	8	9.1	+2.00
Totals	6	14	1	2	0	11	7.1	-1.00
11-12	10	30	4	3	2	21	13.3	-12.38
10-11	7	14	0	0	2	12	0.0	-14.00

JOCKEYS

	W-R	Per cent	£1 Level Stake
Mr P John	1-9	11.1	+4.00

COURSE RECORD

	Total W-R	Non-Hndcps Hurdles Chases	Hndcps Hurdles Chases	NH Flat	Per cent	£1 Level Stake
Kelso	1-2	0-0 0-0	0-0 1-2	0-0	50.0	+11.00

WINNING HORSES

Horse	Races Run	1st	2nd	3rd	£
Mortimers Cross	6	1	2	0	16266
Total winning prize-money					**£16266**
Favourites	0-0		0.0%		0.00

HELEN NELMES

WARMWELL, DORSET

	No. of Hrs	Races Run	1st	2nd	3rd	Unpl	Per cent	£1 Level Stake
NH Flat	3	6	1	3	1	1	16.7	+9.00
Hurdles	8	19	0	1	2	16	0.0	-19.00
Chases	6	17	4	3	1	9	23.5	+30.00
Totals	13	42	5	7	4	26	11.9	+20.00
11-12	15	49	3	2	6	38	6.1	+7.00
10-11	10	41	3	0	4	34	7.3	+18.00

JOCKEYS

	W-R	Per cent	£1 Level Stake
Paul Moloney	2-5	40.0	+23.00
Chris Davies	2-14	14.3	+7.00
Sam Thomas	1-7	14.3	+6.00

COURSE RECORD

	Total W-R	Non-Hndcps Hurdles Chases	Hndcps Hurdles Chases	NH Flat	Per cent	£1 Level Stake
Exeter	2-5	0-1 0-2	0-0 2-2	0-0	40.0	+23.00
Fontwell	2-14	0-2 0-1	0-2 1-6	1-3	14.3	+7.00
Lingfield	1-2	0-1 0-0	0-0 1-1	0-0	50.0	+11.00

WINNING HORSES

Horse	Races Run	1st	2nd	3rd	£
The Clyda Rover	6	3	3	0	16062
Cranky Corner	4	1	0	0	3054
Unowhatimeanharry	2	1	0	0	1625
Total winning prize-money					**£20741**
Favourites	1-2		50.0%		3.00

DR RICHARD NEWLAND

CLAINES, WORCS

	Nov Chs	1-12	8.3	-9.25	Nov Chs	0-3	0.0	-3.00
	Chases	0-1	0.0	-1.00	Chases	8-32	25.0	-5.56
	Sell/Claim	5-9	55.6	+12.63	Sell/Claim	0-0	0.0	0.00

	No. of Hrs	Races Run	1st	2nd	3rd	Unpl	Per cent	£1 Level Stake
NH Flat	2	2	0	2	0	0	0.0	-2.00
Hurdles	22	97	26	15	14	42	26.8	+12.34
Chases	12	48	9	9	5	25	18.8	-18.81
Totals	26	147	35	26	19	67	23.8	-8.47
11-12	22	137	21	14	23	79	15.3	-29.09
10-11	24	108	22	9	13	64	20.4	+23.17

RACE CLASS

	W-R	Per cent	£1 Level Stake
Class 1	0-16	0.0	-16.00
Class 2	5-27	18.5	-3.00
Class 3	5-27	18.5	-8.50
Class 4	14-50	28.0	+9.52
Class 5	11-24	45.8	+12.52
Class 6	0-3	0.0	-3.00

FIRST TIME OUT

	W-R	Per cent	£1 Level Stake
Bumpers	0-2	0.0	-2.00
Hurdles	4-20	20.0	-3.50
Chases	0-4	0.0	-4.00
Totals	4-26	15.4	-9.50

BY MONTH

NH Flat	W-R	Per cent	£1 Level Stake	Hurdles	W-R	Per cent	£1 Level Stake
May	0-0	0.0	0.00	May	0-5	0.0	-5.00
June	0-0	0.0	0.00	June	3-10	30.0	+2.50
July	0-1	0.0	-1.00	July	6-13	46.2	+6.89
August	0-0	0.0	0.00	August	1-8	12.5	-4.25
September	0-0	0.0	0.00	September	3-6	50.0	+6.63
October	0-1	0.0	-1.00	October	3-7	42.9	+3.50
November	0-0	0.0	0.00	November	4-8	50.0	+0.07
December	0-0	0.0	0.00	December	1-11	9.1	-7.00
January	0-0	0.0	0.00	January	1-5	20.0	+12.00
February	0-0	0.0	0.00	February	1-7	14.3	0.00
March	0-0	0.0	0.00	March	2-9	22.2	+2.25
April	0-0	0.0	0.00	April	1-8	12.5	-5.25

Chases	W-R	Per cent	£1 Level Stake	Totals	W-R	Per cent	£1 Level Stake
May	0-2	0.0	-2.00	May	0-7	0.0	-7.00
June	1-1	100.0	+4.50	June	4-11	36.4	+7.00
July	1-4	25.0	+1.00	July	7-18	38.9	+6.89
August	1-5	20.0	-3.00	August	2-13	15.4	-7.25
September	0-2	0.0	-2.00	September	3-8	37.5	+4.63
October	2-4	50.0	-0.56	October	5-12	41.7	+1.94
November	1-5	20.0	-2.25	November	5-13	38.5	-2.18
December	0-4	0.0	-4.00	December	1-15	6.7	-11.00
January	1-4	25.0	-1.50	January	2-9	22.2	+10.50
February	1-7	14.3	-2.00	February	2-14	14.3	-2.00
March	0-4	0.0	-4.00	March	2-13	15.4	-1.75
April	1-6	16.7	-3.00	April	2-14	14.3	-8.25

JOCKEYS

	W-R	Per cent	£1 Level Stake
Tom O'Brien	15-41	36.6	+18.60
Christopher Ward	9-52	17.3	-23.39
A P McCoy	4-9	44.4	+0.83
Richard Johnson	2-11	18.2	-4.25
Jason Maguire	1-1	100.0	+2.75
Joshua Moore	1-2	50.0	+3.00
Tom Scudamore	1-3	33.3	-0.50
Sam Jones	1-4	25.0	+1.50
Jamie Moore	1-5	20.0	+12.00

DISTANCE

Hurdles	W-R	Per cent	£1 Level Stake	Chases	W-R	Per cent	£1 Level Stake
2m-2m3f	17-55	30.9	+25.89	2m-2m3f	4-12	33.3	+4.25
2m4f-2m7f	8-33	24.2	-7.30	2m4f-2m7f	4-25	16.0	-13.97
3m+	1-9	11.1	-6.25	3m+	1-11	9.1	-9.09

COURSE RECORD

	Total W-R	Non-Hndcps Hurdles	Chases	Hndcps Hurdles	Chases	NH Flat	Per cent	£1 Level Stake
Uttoxeter	6-13	4-7	0-1	2-4	0-0	0-1	46.2	+11.50
Fontwell	3-5	1-1	0-0	1-1	1-2	0-1	60.0	+3.16
Ffos Las	3-7	0-0	0-0	2-4	1-3	0-0	42.9	+10.00
Stratford	3-10	1-3	0-1	2-3	0-3	0-0	30.0	+0.77
Plumpton	2-4	0-0	0-0	1-2	1-2	0-0	50.0	+0.73
Ludlow	2-5	2-4	0-0	0-0	0-1	0-0	40.0	+16.00
Towcester	2-5	1-2	0-0	0-2	1-1	0-0	40.0	-0.84
Huntingdon	2-6	0-2	0-2	2-2	0-0	0-0	33.3	-1.03
Nton Abbot	2-6	0-2	0-0	2-2	0-2	0-0	33.3	+0.25
Sedgefield	1-1	1-1	0-0	0-0	0-0	0-0	100.0	+3.00
Carlisle	1-2	0-0	0-0	1-2	0-0	0-0	50.0	+0.75
Chepstow	1-2	0-1	0-0	1-1	0-0	0-0	50.0	+0.75
Perth	1-2	0-0	0-0	0-1	1-1	0-0	50.0	0.00
Southwell	1-4	1-2	0-0	0-2	0-0	0-0	25.0	-0.75
Taunton	1-4	1-2	0-0	0-1	0-1	0-0	25.0	+3.00
Mrket Rsn	1-5	0-0	0-0	0-3	1-2	0-0	20.0	0.00
Wetherby	1-5	0-2	0-1	0-1	1-1	0-0	20.0	-2.50
Leicester	1-6	0-3	1-1	0-0	0-2	0-0	16.7	-3.25
Sandown	1-7	0-2	0-1	0-2	1-2	0-0	14.3	-2.00

TYPE OF RACE

Non-Handicaps	W-R	Per cent	£1 Level Stake	Handicaps	W-R	Per cent	£1 Level Stake
Nov Hrdls	5-19	26.3	-3.21	Nov Hrdls	0-1	0.0	-1.00
Hrdls	2-12	16.7	+9.00	Hrdls	14-56	25.0	-5.08

WINNING HORSES

Horse	Races Run	1st	2nd	3rd	£
Dashing George	10	2	1	1	19467
Stage Acclaim	10	3	3	0	15891
Smalib Monterg	10	4	2	1	22649
Connectivity	4	1	0	1	12021

Rowan Tiger	3	1	0	0	9812
Bobowen	13	5	3	1	14426
Act Of Kalanisi	9	1	0	1	5697
Ahyaknowyerself	8	4	1	1	12782
Angelot Du Berlais	4	1	0	1	3249
Changing The Guard	13	3	4	1	7888
*Dalmo	3	1	0	0	2599
Ardkilly Witness	6	1	2	1	2534
Young Hurricane	7	1	1	2	2534
Bellflower Boy	9	2	1	3	4449
Royale Knight	7	4	0	1	7901
Callhimwhatyouwant	7	1	1	1	2274
Total winning prize-money					**£146173**
Favourites	30-44		68.2%		36.03

ANNA NEWTON-SMITH

JEVINGTON, E SUSSEX

	No. of Hrs	Races Run	1st	2nd	3rd	Unpl	Per cent	£1 Level Stake
NH Flat	2	2	0	0	0	2	0.0	-2.00
Hurdles	6	36	0	4	4	28	0.0	-36.00
Chases	4	22	2	2	2	16	9.1	-1.75
Totals	11	60	2	6	6	46	3.3	-39.75
11-12	16	67	3	8	9	47	4.5	-46.33
10-11	15	71	8	8	12	43	11.3	-35.50

JOCKEYS

	W-R	Per cent	£1 Level Stake
Andrew Thornton	2-10	20.0	+10.25

COURSE RECORD

	Total W-R	Non-Hndcps Hurdles	Chases	Hndcps Hurdles	Chases	NH Flat	Per cent	£1 Level Stake
Sandown	1-2	0-0	0-0	0-0	1-2	0-0	50.0	+15.00
Wincanton	1-3	0-0	0-0	0-0	1-3	0-0	33.3	+0.25

WINNING HORSES

Horse	Races Run	1st	2nd	3rd	£
Goring One	8	2	1	0	9827
Total winning prize-money					**£9827**
Favourites	0-3		0.0%		-3.00

PAUL NICHOLLS

DITCHEAT, SOMERSET

	No. of Hrs	Races Run	1st	2nd	3rd	Unpl	Per cent	£1 Level Stake
NH Flat	25	31	6	6	6	13	19.4	-9.88
Hurdles	100	267	60	50	33	124	22.5	-55.66
Chases	74	260	65	45	33	117	25.0	-32.63
Totals	170	558	131	101	72	254	23.5	-98.17
11-12	182	592	136	97	74	285	23.0	-70.62
10-11	186	576	132	86	80	278	22.9	-81.99

BY MONTH

NH Flat	W-R	Per cent	£1 Level Stake	Hurdles	W-R	Per cent	£1 Level Stake
May	1-4	25.0	-1.00	May	4-16	25.0	+1.25
June	0-0	0.0	0.00	June	0-5	0.0	-5.00
July	0-0	0.0	0.00	July	0-3	0.0	-3.00
August	0-0	0.0	0.00	August	1-3	33.3	-1.47
September	0-0	0.0	0.00	September	0-0	0.0	0.00
October	2-5	40.0	+0.38	October	10-30	33.3	-1.29
November	1-5	20.0	+0.50	November	8-38	21.1	-12.79
December	0-3	0.0	-3.00	December	7-29	24.1	-1.09
January	0-0	0.0	0.00	January	3-17	17.6	-5.42
February	0-4	0.0	-4.00	February	13-46	28.3	-4.59
March	0-2	0.0	-2.00	March	6-35	17.1	-6.93
April	2-8	25.0	-0.75	April	8-45	17.8	-15.34

Chases	W-R	Per cent	£1 Level Stake	Totals	W-R	Per cent	£1 Level Stake
May	5-13	38.5	+1.68	May	10-33	30.3	+1.93
June	2-9	22.2	-4.75	June	2-14	14.3	-9.75
July	1-6	16.7	-0.50	July	1-9	11.1	-3.50
August	1-5	20.0	-2.90	August	2-8	25.0	-4.37
September	3-5	60.0	+1.49	September	3-5	60.0	+1.49
October	6-29	20.7	-9.30	October	18-64	28.1	-10.21
November	8-39	20.5	-5.21	November	17-82	20.7	-17.50
December	10-34	29.4	+0.61	December	17-66	25.8	-3.48
January	4-18	22.2	-9.26	January	7-35	20.0	-14.68
February	9-29	31.0	-7.18	February	22-79	27.8	-15.77
March	10-32	31.3	+18.15	March	16-69	23.2	+9.22
April	6-41	14.6	-15.46	April	16-94	17.0	-31.55

DISTANCE

Hurdles	W-R	Per cent	£1 Level Stake	Chases	W-R	Per cent	£1 Level Stake
2m-2m3f	30-132	22.7	-48.22	2m-2m3f	17-79	21.5	-25.46
2m4f-2m7f	26-90	28.9	+17.35	2m4f-2m7f	24-94	25.5	+12.72
3m+	4-45	8.9	-24.79	3m+	24-87	27.6	-19.89

TYPE OF RACE

Non-Handicaps	W-R	Per cent	£1 Level Stake	Handicaps	W-R	Per cent	£1 Level Stake
Nov Hrdls	26-83	31.3	-2.79	Nov Hrdls	1-7	14.3	-4.80
Hrdls	22-77	28.6	-15.78	Hrdls	11-99	11.1	-31.29
Nov Chs	36-89	40.4	+3.49	Nov Chs	1-11	9.1	-6.00
Chases	11-39	28.2	-12.21	Chases	17-120	14.2	-16.92
Sell/Claim	0-2	0.0	-2.00	Sell/Claim	0-0	0.0	0.00

RACE CLASS

	W-R	Per cent	£1 Level Stake
Class 1	24-158	15.2	-55.19
Class 2	20-107	18.7	-19.81
Class 3	35-131	26.7	-18.41
Class 4	38-117	32.5	-1.68

FIRST TIME OUT

	W-R	Per cent	£1 Level Stake
Bumpers	5-25	20.0	-7.88
Hurdles	21-82	25.6	-7.46
Chases	18-63	28.6	+3.22

Class 5 9-25 36.0 -0.63 Totals 44-170 25.9 -12.12
Class 6 5-20 25.0 -2.45

JOCKEYS

	W-R	Per cent	£1 Level Stake
Daryl Jacob	55-193	28.5	-6.93
R Walsh	51-185	27.6	-36.51
Harry Derham	10-90	11.1	-26.72
Ryan Mahon	6-39	15.4	+4.50
Mr J Sole	3-4	75.0	+2.72
A P McCoy	2-5	40.0	-0.30
Nick Scholfield	2-11	18.2	-7.18
Harry Skelton	1-7	14.3	-5.56
Mr S Clements	1-9	11.1	-7.20

COURSE RECORD

	Total W-R	Non-Hndcps Hurdles	Chases	Hndcps Hurdles	Chases	NH Flat	Per cent	£1 Level Stake
Wincanton	18-56	10-18	3-6	2-13	1-13	2-6	32.1	+6.20
Cheltenham	14-89	5-20	1-17	3-27	4-21	1-4	15.7	-13.67
Nton Abbot	10-22	2-7	6-8	0-0	1-6	1-1	45.5	+6.59
Exeter	9-25	5-9	3-8	1-3	0-2	0-3	36.0	+7.23
Kempton	8-33	2-12	4-10	0-4	2-6	0-1	24.2	-10.52
Newbury	8-39	1-9	3-7	0-10	4-12	0-1	20.5	+0.86
Fontwell	7-16	2-7	4-7	0-0	0-1	1-1	43.8	+5.50
Taunton	7-34	4-13	0-1	2-6	0-10	1-4	20.6	-6.90
Sandown	7-41	0-4	5-14	1-8	1-13	0-2	17.1	-11.48
Doncaster	5-13	0-5	3-4	1-1	1-3	0-0	38.5	-1.78
Ascot	5-23	2-6	2-6	0-4	1-7	0-0	21.7	-11.52
Chepstow	5-33	2-12	2-4	1-8	0-7	0-2	15.2	-23.05
Worcester	4-20	2-6	1-5	0-3	1-4	0-2	20.0	-8.30
Wetherby	3-3	2-2	1-1	0-0	0-0	0-0	100.0	+6.10
Huntingdon	3-4	1-2	2-2	0-0	0-0	0-0	75.0	+0.86
Haydock	3-12	0-3	2-3	0-4	1-1	0-1	25.0	+5.50
Southwell	2-2	1-1	1-1	0-0	0-0	0-0	100.0	+2.35
Musselbgh	2-3	1-2	0-0	1-1	0-0	0-0	66.7	+2.00
Ffos Las	2-8	2-5	0-3	0-0	0-0	0-0	25.0	-2.13
Ludlow	2-9	1-3	0-1	0-1	1-3	0-1	22.2	+0.25
Stratford	2-11	1-4	1-2	0-1	0-4	0-0	18.2	-7.22
Aintree	2-37	1-8	1-6	0-9	0-12	0-2	5.4	-28.30
Hereford	1-2	1-1	0-0	0-0	0-1	0-0	50.0	+1.00
Warwick	1-4	0-0	1-3	0-0	0-1	0-0	25.0	-1.25
Fakenham	1-7	0-2	1-4	0-0	0-1	0-0	14.3	-4.50

WINNING HORSES

Horse	Races Run	1st	2nd	3rd	£
Zarkandar	5	4	0	0	253491
Silviniaco Conti	5	3	0	1	195118
Al Ferof	1	1	0	0	91120
Tidal Bay	3	2	1	0	103649
Unioniste	5	3	0	1	72036
Sanctuaire	6	2	0	1	42713
Cedre Bleu	6	2	0	0	48515
Salubrious	6	2	1	0	37778
Prospect Wells	5	1	1	0	28609
Pacha Du Polder	5	1	1	0	28475
Shooters Wood	9	2	3	0	46920
Big Buck's	1	1	0	0	19933
Rocky Creek	5	3	1	1	34755
Dodging Bullets	5	2	0	1	33006
Grandioso	5	3	1	0	32664
Poungach	6	2	2	0	24043
Irish Saint	4	2	1	1	21509
Ulck Du Lin	6	2	0	2	28152
Ptit Zig	3	2	0	1	15640
Hinterland	4	1	3	0	14296
Far West	5	4	1	0	40932
*Aaim To Prosper	7	1	3	1	12996
Toubab	5	1	0	1	12996
Michel Le Bon	5	1	1	0	12512
Sametegal	6	2	2	2	21095
Wonderful Charm	2	1	0	0	12073
Easter Day	6	3	2	0	25796
Sire Collonges	5	2	1	1	10783
Ghizao	6	1	0	3	10749
There's No Panic	9	2	1	1	11177
Benvolio	4	2	0	1	11047
Dark Lover	5	2	0	1	13763
Rolling Aces	5	2	1	1	13160
Oscargo	2	1	1	0	7148
Prince Tom	6	3	1	0	15856
Mr Mole	5	2	1	1	9422
Minella Stars	6	1	3	0	6657
Rebel Rebellion	7	2	1	1	12346
Jump City	7	2	2	2	10159
No Loose Change	3	1	0	0	6498
Hawkes Point	4	1	2	0	6498
Empire Levant	3	1	0	0	6498
Criqtonic	4	1	0	0	6498
Gwanako	5	2	0	0	6239
Merrion Square	5	3	0	0	6239
Current Event	5	1	0	0	5653
Elenika	8	1	2	1	5653
Landscape	8	2	0	2	9747
Buck's Bond	4	2	1	0	8317
Ruben Cotter	4	2	0	0	8447
Southfield Theatre	4	3	0	1	11047
Atlantic Roller	2	1	1	0	4549
Fox Run	4	2	1	0	6003
Saphir Du Rheu	3	1	0	1	4106
Virak	1	1	0	0	4061
Domtaline	6	1	2	2	3994
Spock	3	1	0	0	3899
*Keppols Hill	5	1	2	0	3899
Sound Investment	5	2	0	1	6636
Minellahalfcentury	1	1	0	0	3899
Themilanhorse	4	1	1	1	3769
Fago	4	1	1	0	3769
Sidney Melbourne	4	1	2	0	3574
Flaming Gorge	1	1	0	0	3249
Cowards Close	2	1	0	0	3249
Oscar Amy	2	1	0	0	3249

Whisky Yankee	3	2	1	0	5068
Wilton Milan	4	2	0	1	4898
Wiffy Chatsby	5	2	0	0	5679
Indian Daudaie	4	2	1	1	5328
Provo	2	1	1	0	2599
Dualla Lord	1	1	0	0	2534
Howlongisafoot	1	1	0	0	2094
*Urubu D'Irlande	1	1	0	0	2060
Suerte Al Salto	8	2	4	1	2053
Billy Merriott	1	1	0	0	2014
Foggy's Wall	2	2	0	0	3465
Tricky Trickster	3	1	1	0	988
Total winning prize-money					**£1631108**
Favourites	76-187		**40.6%**		**-14.61**

PETER NIVEN

BARTON-LE-STREET, N YORKS

	No. of Hrs	Races Run	1st	2nd	3rd	Unpl	Per cent	£1 Level Stake
NH Flat	9	12	2	1	3	6	16.7	-1.75
Hurdles	7	23	0	3	4	16	0.0	-23.00
Chases	2	12	0	1	3	8	0.0	-12.00
Totals	16	47	2	5	10	30	4.3	-36.75
11-12	16	40	5	4	2	29	12.5	+15.50
10-11	15	44	4	4	3	33	9.1	-19.00

JOCKEYS

	W-R	Per cent	£1 Level Stake
Wilson Renwick	1-10	10.0	-3.50
Brian Hughes	1-15	6.7	-11.25

COURSE RECORD

	Total W-R	Non-Hndcps Hurdles	Chases	Hndcps Hurdles	Chases	NH Flat	Per cent	£1 Level Stake
Bangor	1-1	0-0	0-0	0-0	0-0	1-1	100.0	+2.75
Musselbgh	1-10	0-4	0-0	0-3	0-1	1-2	10.0	-3.50

WINNING HORSES

Horse	Races Run	1st	2nd	3rd	£
Clever Cookie	1	1	0	0	1949
Baltimore Rock	1	1	0	0	1437
Total winning prize-money					**£3386**
Favourites	0-1		0.0%		-1.00

RAYSON NIXON

ETTRICKBRIDGE, BORDERS

	No. of Hrs	Races Run	1st	2nd	3rd	Unpl	Per cent	£1 Level Stake
NH Flat	0	0	0	0	0	0	0.0	0.00
Hurdles	2	17	1	2	1	13	5.9	+109.00
Chases	2	5	0	0	0	5	0.0	-5.00

Totals	3	22	1	2	1	18	4.5	+104.00
11-12	9	47	0	2	5	40	0.0	-47.00
10-11	9	48	3	2	3	40	6.3	+19.00

JOCKEYS

	W-R	Per cent	£1 Level Stake
Barry Keniry	1-13	7.7	+113.00

COURSE RECORD

	Total W-R	Non-Hndcps Hurdles	Chases	Hndcps Hurdles	Chases	NH Flat	Per cent	£1 Level Stake
Hexham	1-4	1-1	0-0	0-2	0-1	0-0	25.0	+122.00

WINNING HORSES

Horse	Races Run	1st	2nd	3rd	£
Gymdoli	9	1	1	1	2599
Total winning prize-money					**£2599**
Favourites	0-0		0.0%		0.00

SUSAN NOCK

ICOMB, GLOUCS

	No. of Hrs	Races Run	1st	2nd	3rd	Unpl	Per cent	£1 Level Stake
NH Flat	0	0	0	0	0	0	0.0	0.00
Hurdles	2	9	2	1	1	5	22.2	-1.09
Chases	1	1	0	0	0	1	0.0	-1.00
Totals	3	10	2	1	1	6	20.0	-2.09
11-12	6	22	3	1	2	16	13.6	+19.50
10-11	7	22	0	2	2	18	0.0	-22.00

JOCKEYS

	W-R	Per cent	£1 Level Stake
Brendan Powell	1-1	100.0	+5.00
Sam Twiston-Davies	1-4	25.0	-2.09

COURSE RECORD

	Total W-R	Non-Hndcps Hurdles	Chases	Hndcps Hurdles	Chases	NH Flat	Per cent	£1 Level Stake
Nton Abbot	1-1	1-1	0-0	0-0	0-0	0-0	100.0	+0.91
Wincanton	1-1	0-0	0-0	1-1	0-0	0-0	100.0	+5.00

WINNING HORSES

Horse	Races Run	1st	2nd	3rd	£
Hatters River	5	1	1	1	3899
Royal Guardsman	4	1	0	0	2464
Total winning prize-money					**£6363**
Favourites	1-2		50.0%		-0.09

LUCY NORMILE

DUNCRIEVIE, PERTH & KINROSS

	No. of Hrs	Races Run	1st	2nd	3rd	Unpl	Per cent	£1 Level Stake
NH Flat	5	12	0	1	1	10	0.0	-12.00
Hurdles	19	51	2	1	5	43	3.9	-6.00
Chases	7	21	2	0	3	16	9.5	+9.00
Totals	24	84	4	2	9	69	4.8	-9.00
11-12	18	74	4	1	8	61	5.4	-38.75
10-11	21	67	5	0	4	58	7.5	-27.75

JOCKEYS

	W-R	Per cent	£1 Level Stake
Ryan Mania	2-21	9.5	+9.00
Jimmy McCarthy	1-4	25.0	+7.00
Alexander Voy	1-22	4.5	+12.00

COURSE RECORD

	Total W-R	Non-Hndcps Hurdles	Chases	Hndcps Hurdles	Chases	NH Flat	Per cent	£1 Level Stake
Bangor	1-2	0-0	0-0	0-0	1-2	0-0	50.0	+7.00
Uttoxeter	1-2	0-0	0-0	1-2	0-0	0-0	50.0	+9.00
Musselbgh	1-8	0-3	0-0	1-3	0-0	0-2	12.5	+26.00
Sedgefield	1-16	0-2	0-1	0-6	1-7	0-0	6.3	+5.00

WINNING HORSES

Horse	Races Run	1st	2nd	3rd	£
Parson's Punch	6	1	0	2	3899
Strobe	9	2	0	0	3736
Agricultural	7	1	1	1	1689
Total winning prize-money					£9324
Favourites	0-0		0.0%		0.00

JOHN NORTON

HIGH HOYLAND, S YORKS

	No. of Hrs	Races Run	1st	2nd	3rd	Unpl	Per cent	£1 Level Stake
NH Flat	2	3	0	0	1	2	0.0	-3.00
Hurdles	3	8	0	0	0	8	0.0	-8.00
Chases	1	6	1	0	1	4	16.7	-2.00
Totals	5	17	1	0	2	14	5.9	-13.00
11-12	6	20	0	1	1	18	0.0	-20.00
10-11	6	16	0	1	0	15	0.0	-16.00

JOCKEYS

	W-R	Per cent	£1 Level Stake
Adrian Lane	1-3	33.3	+1.00

COURSE RECORD

	Total W-R	Non-Hndcps Hurdles	Chases	Hndcps Hurdles	Chases	NH Flat	Per cent	£1 Level Stake
Mrket Rsn	1-2	0-0	0-0	0-0	1-1	0-1	50.0	+2.00

WINNING HORSES

Horse	Races Run	1st	2nd	3rd	£
Gorey Lane	6	1	0	1	3054
Total winning prize-money					£3054
Favourites	0-1		0.0%		-1.00

DANIEL O'BRIEN

CAPEL, KENT

	No. of Hrs	Races Run	1st	2nd	3rd	Unpl	Per cent	£1 Level Stake
NH Flat	0	0	0	0	0	0	0.0	0.00
Hurdles	7	21	2	1	4	14	9.5	+31.00
Chases	4	9	2	0	0	7	22.2	-4.09
Totals	10	30	4	1	4	21	13.3	+26.91
11-12	8	23	1	0	2	20	4.3	-21.09
10-11	8	16	0	1	3	12	0.0	-16.00

JOCKEYS

	W-R	Per cent	£1 Level Stake
Tom Cannon	2-4	50.0	+0.91
Ben Poste	1-4	25.0	+22.00
Mattie Batchelor	1-4	25.0	+22.00

COURSE RECORD

	Total W-R	Non-Hndcps Hurdles	Chases	Hndcps Hurdles	Chases	NH Flat	Per cent	£1 Level Stake
Plumpton	3-11	0-0	0-0	1-9	2-2	0-0	27.3	+19.91
Fontwell	1-4	0-0	0-0	1-3	0-1	0-0	25.0	+22.00

WINNING HORSES

Horse	Races Run	1st	2nd	3rd	£
Sacrilege	3	1	0	0	2534
Inthejungle	4	2	0	0	4003
Golden Games	1	1	0	0	2053
Total winning prize-money					£8590
Favourites	1-2		50.0%		-0.09

FERGAL O'BRIEN

COLN ST. DENNIS, GLOUCS

	No. of Hrs	Races Run	1st	2nd	3rd	Unpl	Per cent	£1 Level Stake
NH Flat	17	27	3	1	3	20	11.1	+12.00
Hurdles	39	117	11	20	12	74	9.4	-25.63
Chases	20	83	14	15	10	44	16.9	-15.59

Totals	60	227	28	36	25	138	12.3	-29.22
11-12	36	118	11	14	19	74	9.3	-52.63
10-11	4	7	2	2	0	3	28.6	+12.63

Class 3	5-24	20.8	+32.25		Chases	5-12	41.7	+16.88
Class 4	12-103	11.7	-34.50					
Class 5	9-63	14.3	-11.97		Totals	9-60	15.0	-4.25
Class 6	2-19	10.5	+3.00					

BY MONTH

NH Flat	W-R	Per cent	£1 Level Stake		Hurdles	W-R	Per cent	£1 Level Stake
May	0-0	0.0	0.00		May	2-16	12.5	-9.63
June	0-1	0.0	-1.00		June	0-10	0.0	-10.00
July	0-0	0.0	0.00		July	0-5	0.0	-5.00
August	0-0	0.0	0.00		August	0-7	0.0	-7.00
September	0-0	0.0	0.00		September	1-7	14.3	+1.00
October	0-1	0.0	-1.00		October	1-14	7.1	-5.50
November	1-4	25.0	+3.00		November	3-11	27.3	+1.25
December	0-1	0.0	-1.00		December	1-8	12.5	-4.75
January	0-5	0.0	-5.00		January	0-6	0.0	-6.00
February	0-6	0.0	-6.00		February	0-14	0.0	-14.00
March	1-2	50.0	+13.00		March	1-11	9.1	+23.00
April	1-7	14.3	+10.00		April	2-8	25.0	+11.00

Chases	W-R	Per cent	£1 Level Stake		Totals	W-R	Per cent	£1 Level Stake
May	2-4	50.0	+8.00		May	4-20	20.0	-1.63
June	1-7	14.3	-4.38		June	1-18	5.6	-15.38
July	0-8	0.0	-8.00		July	0-13	0.0	-13.00
August	0-6	0.0	-6.00		August	0-13	0.0	-13.00
September	2-6	33.3	+12.00		September	3-13	23.1	+13.00
October	2-11	18.2	+0.88		October	3-26	11.5	-5.62
November	0-7	0.0	-7.00		November	4-22	18.2	-2.75
December	1-4	25.0	-1.38		December	2-13	15.4	-7.13
January	0-4	0.0	-4.00		January	0-15	0.0	-15.00
February	1-5	20.0	0.00		February	1-25	4.0	-20.00
March	3-10	30.0	+0.50		March	5-23	21.7	+36.50
April	2-11	18.2	-6.22		April	5-26	19.2	+14.78

JOCKEYS

	W-R	Per cent	£1 Level Stake
Paddy Brennan	9-83	10.8	-48.25
Timmy Murphy	6-39	15.4	+35.63
Miss A E Stirling	3-5	60.0	+14.00
Alain Cawley	3-23	13.0	+12.00
Conor Shoemark	3-25	12.0	-14.59
Mr M Wall	1-1	100.0	+1.00
Sam Twiston-Davies	1-1	100.0	+2.00
William Twiston-Davies	1-1	100.0	+9.00
Paul Moloney	1-5	20.0	+4.00

DISTANCE

Hurdles	W-R	Per cent	£1 Level Stake		Chases	W-R	Per cent	£1 Level Stake
2m-2m3f	6-52	11.5	-13.63		2m-2m3f	3-22	13.6	-11.25
2m4f-2m7f	5-50	10.0	+3.00		2m4f-2m7f	7-25	28.0	+15.53
3m+	0-15	0.0	-15.00		3m+	4-36	11.1	-19.88

COURSE RECORD

	Total W-R	Non-Hndcps Hurdles	Chases	Hndcps Hurdles	Chases	NH Flat	Per cent	£1 Level Stake
Towcester	4-11	2-3	1-1	0-2	1-3	0-2	36.4	+1.25
Uttoxeter	4-24	0-6	0-1	2-10	2-7	0-0	16.7	+8.63
Ascot	3-6	0-1	1-1	1-1	0-1	1-2	50.0	+6.16
Mrket Rsn	3-11	0-2	0-0	3-5	0-2	0-2	27.3	+3.50
Newbury	2-6	1-1	0-0	0-1	1-3	0-1	33.3	+33.00
Cheltenham	2-17	0-1	1-3	0-3	0-6	1-4	11.8	+2.00
Musselbgh	1-1	0-0	1-1	0-0	0-0	0-0	100.0	+4.00
Plumpton	1-1	1-1	0-0	0-0	1-1	0-0	100.0	+1.50
Sedgefield	1-3	0-0	0-0	1-2	0-1	0-0	33.3	+5.50
Taunton	1-4	0-1	0-0	0-2	0-0	1-1	25.0	+11.00
Nton Abbot	1-7	0-2	0-0	0-1	1-4	0-0	14.3	+2.00
Wetherby	1-7	0-2	0-1	0-2	1-2	0-0	14.3	+2.00
Exeter	1-9	0-3	0-1	1-3	0-2	0-0	11.1	-5.25
Southwell	1-9	0-3	0-0	0-1	1-3	0-0	11.1	+1.00
Hereford	1-10	0-3	0-0	0-4	1-3	0-0	10.0	-7.38
Bangor	1-11	0-3	0-1	0-2	1-5	0-0	9.1	-8.13

TYPE OF RACE

Non-Handicaps	W-R	Per cent	£1 Level Stake		Handicaps	W-R	Per cent	£1 Level Stake
Nov Hrdls	2-30	6.7	-23.63		Nov Hrdls	1-13	7.7	-5.00
Hrdls	1-12	8.3	+22.00		Hrdls	6-54	11.1	-17.00
Nov Chs	1-9	11.1	-6.13		Nov Chs	4-13	30.8	+4.25
Chases	3-5	60.0	+3.91		Chases	6-56	10.7	-17.63
Sell/Claim	0-9	0.0	-9.00		Sell/Claim	1-1	100.0	+5.00

WINNING HORSES

Horse	Races Run	1st	2nd	3rd	£
Silver Roque	6	2	1	1	9552
Farmer Matt	7	2	1	0	8855
Creevytennant	3	2	0	0	9047
*Alvarado	5	1	0	1	5443
Manballandall	2	1	0	0	5393
Down Ace	1	1	0	0	4874
Bradley	6	1	1	0	4679
Beggar's Velvet	6	3	0	0	9487
Queen Of Mantua	7	2	0	1	5725
Jacks Grey	7	1	0	0	3054
*Dark Energy	6	2	0	1	4156
Young Mags	5	1	1	1	2534
Allerton	3	1	2	0	2395
Fiddlers Bid	6	1	2	2	2283
Gemini Ahhs	6	1	2	3	2274
Doubletoiltrouble	9	2	3	1	3964

RACE CLASS / FIRST TIME OUT

	W-R	Per cent	£1 Level Stake			W-R	Per cent	£1 Level Stake
Class 1	0-9	0.0	-9.00		Bumpers	1-17	5.9	0.00
Class 2	0-9	0.0	-9.00		Hurdles	3-31	9.7	-21.13

Gud Day	11	1	2	2	2144
*Super Collider	4	1	0	0	2079
*Kayfton Pete	4	1	1	1	2053
Gallic Warrior	3	1	0	0	2053
Total winning prize-money					**£92044**
Favourites	**9-32**		**28.1%**		**-7.84**

JEDD O'KEEFFE

MIDDLEHAM MOOR, N YORKS

	No. of Hrs	Races Run	1st	2nd	3rd	Unpl	Per cent	£1 Level Stake
NH Flat	0	0	0	0	0	0	0.0	0.00
Hurdles	3	12	1	2	0	9	8.3	+1.00
Chases	1	4	0	0	0	4	0.0	-4.00
Totals	**3**	**16**	**1**	**2**	**0**	**13**	**6.3**	**-3.00**
11-12	*3*	*10*	*0*	*2*	*1*	*7*	*0.0*	*-10.00*
10-11	*3*	*5*	*0*	*0*	*1*	*4*	*0.0*	*-5.00*

JOCKEYS

	W-R	Per cent	£1 Level Stake
Brian Harding	1-8	12.5	+5.00

COURSE RECORD

	Total W-R	Non-Hndcps Hurdles	Chases	Hndcps Hurdles	Chases	NH Flat	Per cent	£1 Level Stake
Sedgefield	1-4	0-0	0-0	1-3	0-1	0-0	25.0	+9.00

WINNING HORSES

Horse	Races Run	1st	2nd	3rd	£
Highland Love	11	1	2	0	1689
Total winning prize-money					**£1689**
Favourites	**0-0**		**0.0%**		**0.00**

DAVID O'MEARA

NAWTON, N YORKS

	No. of Hrs	Races Run	1st	2nd	3rd	Unpl	Per cent	£1 Level Stake
NH Flat	4	9	0	2	3	4	0.0	-9.00
Hurdles	15	36	4	3	2	27	11.1	-11.25
Chases	4	10	3	1	0	6	30.0	+5.91
Totals	**22**	**55**	**7**	**6**	**5**	**37**	**12.7**	**-14.34**
11-12	*24*	*92*	*15*	*13*	*11*	*53*	*16.3*	*+3.50*
10-11	*13*	*33*	*1*	*5*	*4*	*23*	*3.0*	*-22.00*

JOCKEYS

	W-R	Per cent	£1 Level Stake
Timmy Murphy	2-7	28.6	+5.50
Jake Greenall	2-7	28.6	+0.41
Jason Maguire	1-2	50.0	+1.25
Barry Keniry	1-10	10.0	-1.00
Denis O'Regan	1-15	6.7	-6.50

COURSE RECORD

	Total W-R	Non-Hndcps Hurdles	Chases	Hndcps Hurdles	Chases	NH Flat	Per cent	£1 Level Stake
Catterick	2-8	0-3	1-1	1-2	0-1	0-1	25.0	+9.50
Musselbgh	1-2	0-0	0-0	1-2	0-0	0-0	50.0	+2.00
Newcastle	1-4	1-2	0-0	0-1	0-0	0-1	25.0	-0.75
Sedgefield	1-4	0-0	1-1	0-3	0-0	0-0	25.0	-2.09
Cheltenham	1-5	0-0	0-1	1-3	0-1	0-0	20.0	+3.50
Wetherby	1-7	0-1	1-2	0-2	0-0	0-2	14.3	-1.50

WINNING HORSES

Horse	Races Run	1st	2nd	3rd	£
Ifandbutwhynot	7	3	0	1	18229
Rose Of The Moon	4	2	0	0	9627
Classical Mist	4	1	1	0	3899
White Fusion	5	1	0	0	3422
Total winning prize-money					**£35177**
Favourites	**1-10**		**10.0%**		**-8.09**

JOHN O'NEILL

STRATTON AUDLEY, OXON

	No. of Hrs	Races Run	1st	2nd	3rd	Unpl	Per cent	£1 Level Stake
NH Flat	1	3	1	0	1	1	33.3	+20.00
Hurdles	1	1	0	0	0	1	0.0	-1.00
Chases	1	8	0	1	0	7	0.0	-8.00
Totals	**3**	**12**	**1**	**1**	**1**	**9**	**8.3**	**+11.00**
11-12	*3*	*5*	*0*	*0*	*0*	*5*	*0.0*	*-5.00*
10-11	*3*	*13*	*2*	*1*	*1*	*9*	*15.4*	*+4.33*

JOCKEYS

	W-R	Per cent	£1 Level Stake
Andrew Thornton	1-7	14.3	+16.00

COURSE RECORD

	Total W-R	Non-Hndcps Hurdles	Chases	Hndcps Hurdles	Chases	NH Flat	Per cent	£1 Level Stake
Huntingdon	1-3	0-0	0-0	0-0	0-2	1-1	33.3	+20.00

WINNING HORSES

Horse	Races Run	1st	2nd	3rd	£
Cabaret Girl	3	1	0	1	1643
Total winning prize-money					**£1643**
Favourites	**0-0**		**0.0%**		**0.00**

JONJO O'NEILL

CHELTENHAM, GLOUCS

	No. of Hrs	Races Run	1st	2nd	3rd	Unpl	Per cent	£1 Level Stake
NH Flat	29	37	4	6	6	21	10.8	-24.88
Hurdles	133	403	49	23	31	300	12.2	-125.40
Chases	62	250	35	28	27	160	14.0	-57.08
Totals	180	690	88	57	64	481	12.8	-207.36
11-12	*156*	*647*	*97*	*81*	*53*	*416*	*15.0*	*-105.02*
10-11	*189*	*750*	*93*	*70*	*75*	*512*	*12.4*	*-167.11*

Chases	0-1	0.0	-1.00	Chases	26-193	13.5	-50.06
Sell/Claim	0-0	0.0	0.00	Sell/Claim	0-1	0.0	-1.00

RACE CLASS

	W-R	Per cent	£1 Level Stake
Class 1	3-43	7.0	-11.50
Class 2	7-33	21.2	+26.75
Class 3	13-100	13.0	-24.13
Class 4	46-375	12.3	-152.98
Class 5	15-108	13.9	-26.63
Class 6	4-31	12.9	-18.88

FIRST TIME OUT

	W-R	Per cent	£1 Level Stake
Bumpers	2-29	6.9	-23.00
Hurdles	13-102	12.7	-34.56
Chases	7-49	14.3	-22.67
Totals	22-180	12.2	-80.23

BY MONTH

NH Flat	W-R	Per cent	£1 Level Stake
May	1-7	14.3	-5.50
June	0-2	0.0	-2.00
July	0-1	0.0	-1.00
August	1-3	33.3	-0.63
September	0-1	0.0	-1.00
October	0-4	0.0	-4.00
November	0-2	0.0	-2.00
December	1-3	33.3	+1.50
January	0-3	0.0	-3.00
February	0-7	0.0	-7.00
March	0-2	0.0	-2.00
April	1-2	50.0	+1.75

Hurdles	W-R	Per cent	£1 Level Stake
May	9-33	27.3	+4.32
June	3-19	15.8	-8.88
July	2-19	10.5	-10.00
August	2-16	12.5	-10.20
September	4-19	21.1	+7.00
October	6-49	12.2	-27.42
November	2-54	3.7	-39.50
December	6-46	13.0	+8.88
January	5-35	14.3	-18.95
February	5-52	9.6	-25.75
March	4-35	11.4	+14.10
April	1-26	3.8	-19.00

Chases	W-R	Per cent	£1 Level Stake
May	7-16	43.8	+3.42
June	3-17	17.6	-4.25
July	1-16	6.3	-12.50
August	1-19	5.3	-11.00
September	2-18	11.1	-5.50
October	3-33	9.1	-8.00
November	2-28	7.1	-18.63
December	6-25	24.0	+20.00
January	1-25	4.0	-18.50
February	3-20	15.0	-1.75
March	4-19	21.1	+5.38
April	2-14	14.3	-5.75

Totals	W-R	Per cent	£1 Level Stake
May	17-56	30.4	+2.24
June	6-38	15.8	-15.13
July	3-36	8.3	-23.50
August	4-38	10.5	-21.83
September	6-38	15.8	+0.50
October	9-86	10.5	-39.42
November	4-84	4.8	-60.13
December	13-74	17.6	+30.38
January	6-63	9.5	-40.45
February	8-79	10.1	-34.50
March	8-56	14.3	+17.48
April	4-42	9.5	-23.00

DISTANCE

Hurdles	W-R	Per cent	£1 Level Stake
2m-2m3f	18-202	8.9	-118.85
2m4f-2m7f	19-133	14.3	-45.08
3m+	12-68	17.6	+38.53

Chases	W-R	Per cent	£1 Level Stake
2m-2m3f	9-51	17.6	-12.11
2m4f-2m7f	17-117	14.5	-22.34
3m+	9-82	11.0	-22.63

TYPE OF RACE

Non-Handicaps	W-R	Per cent	£1 Level Stake
Nov Hrdls	16-128	12.5	-78.13
Hrdls	8-86	9.3	-29.00
Nov Chs	3-24	12.5	-14.02

Handicaps	W-R	Per cent	£1 Level Stake
Nov Hrdls	2-19	10.5	0.00
Hrdls	23-168	13.7	-16.28
Nov Chs	6-32	18.8	+8.00

JOCKEYS

	W-R	Per cent	£1 Level Stake
A P McCoy	61-334	18.3	-77.95
Richie McLernon	16-195	8.2	-64.66
Maurice Linehan	8-79	10.1	+4.88
Jason Maguire	1-1	100.0	+4.00
Dougie Costello	1-19	5.3	-16.13
Mr A J Berry	1-26	3.8	-21.50

COURSE RECORD

	Total W-R	Non-Hndcps Hurdles	Chases	Hndcps Hurdles	Chases	NH Flat	Per cent	£1 Level Stake
Uttoxeter	10-55	4-14	1-3	4-23	1-14	0-1	18.2	-7.50
Ffos Las	8-29	1-9	0-1	4-7	2-10	1-2	27.6	+7.74
Bangor	7-37	1-11	0-0	2-11	2-10	2-5	18.9	-5.88
Wetherby	5-18	2-6	1-2	1-4	0-5	1-1	27.8	-4.56
Stratford	5-20	0-4	0-1	1-2	4-12	0-1	25.0	+8.25
Sandown	4-21	2-4	0-0	0-7	2-9	0-1	19.0	-0.88
Huntingdon	4-23	0-7	0-0	1-9	3-6	0-1	17.4	-9.43
Nton Abbot	4-24	0-5	0-0	2-8	2-9	0-2	16.7	-6.00
Southwell	4-28	2-11	0-0	1-10	1-7	0-0	14.3	-11.97
Folkestone	3-6	2-3	0-0	0-1	1-2	0-0	50.0	+20.25
Kempton	3-24	2-11	0-0	0-2	1-9	0-2	12.5	-12.50
Warwick	3-26	1-9	0-1	1-11	1-2	0-3	11.5	+1.75
Mrket Rsn	3-41	1-12	0-3	0-6	2-16	0-4	7.3	-34.08
Worcester	3-44	0-14	1-3	1-10	1-13	0-4	6.8	-26.00
Catterick	2-3	1-1	0-0	0-1	1-1	0-0	66.7	+3.75
Hereford	2-9	1-3	0-0	0-4	1-1	0-1	22.2	-3.00
Carlisle	2-13	0-1	0-1	2-4	0-7	0-0	15.4	-5.40
Leicester	2-17	0-4	0-2	1-1	1-10	0-0	11.8	-8.00
Exeter	2-18	1-4	0-3	0-4	1-7	0-0	11.1	+10.00
Newbury	2-18	1-8	0-0	0-0	1-7	0-2	11.1	-4.38
Towcester	2-29	0-14	0-0	1-7	1-7	0-1	6.9	-18.09
Cheltenham	2-31	0-5	0-2	2-11	0-13	0-0	6.5	-1.25
Ascot	1-9	0-4	0-0	0-2	1-2	0-1	11.1	+1.00
Ludlow	1-16	0-6	0-1	0-2	1-7	0-0	6.3	-9.50
Plumpton	1-16	1-7	0-0	0-6	0-3	0-0	6.3	-13.90
Chepstow	1-17	0-5	0-0	0-4	1-7	0-1	5.9	-4.00
Wincanton	1-17	1-10	0-0	0-4	0-3	0-0	5.9	-15.80
Doncaster	1-19	0-8	0-0	1-6	0-4	0-0	5.3	+4.00

WINNING HORSES

Horse	Races Run	1st	2nd	3rd	£
Holywell	6	1	5	0	45560
Mister Hyde	7	3	0	1	33471
Taquin Du Seuil	5	3	1	0	31986
Mr Watson	6	2	0	0	19667
Eastlake	13	5	2	1	43244
Lost Glory	7	4	0	0	27513
Storm Survivor	11	2	1	0	15465
Shutthefrontdoor	5	3	0	1	17162
Arbor Supreme	8	1	0	0	10128
Get Me Out Of Here	5	1	0	0	9697
Kandari	4	1	1	1	7798
See U Bob	7	1	2	1	6498
Twirling Magnet	3	1	0	0	6498
Johns Spirit	8	1	1	2	6498
Cloudy Copper	2	2	0	0	9747
Open Day	5	2	1	0	9942
O'Callaghan Strand	11	3	0	2	11242
Dream Again Boys	4	2	0	0	7993
Balinroab	5	1	0	1	4549
Upswing	4	1	0	1	4224
Very Stylish	4	1	0	0	3899
*Tominator	4	2	0	0	6433
Mission Complete	6	1	0	0	3899
Sentimentaljourney	10	2	1	1	7064
Amuse Me	10	3	0	0	8707
Get Back In Line	2	1	1	0	3574
Rum And Butter	5	1	0	1	3509
Titchwood	3	1	0	0	3444
Wild Rhubarb	6	2	1	0	5783
Coffee	9	2	0	0	5473
American Legend	6	1	0	1	3249
Merry King	5	1	2	0	3217
Cloudingstar	3	1	0	0	3119
Forty Five	5	1	1	1	3054
I'm The Decider	5	1	0	0	3054
Another Trump	12	1	0	1	3054
Point Blank	1	1	0	0	3054
Caddie Master	2	1	0	0	2924
Well Sharp	3	2	0	1	5272
Minella For Steak	4	1	0	1	2738
Sagredo	6	1	2	0	2599
Larks Lad	4	1	1	0	2599
Prompter	5	1	2	1	2599
Wheres The Hare	5	1	0	2	2599
Dursey Sound	4	2	1	0	4744
The Mad Robertson	3	1	0	1	2534
Spate River	2	1	0	1	2144
Blackwell Synergy	6	1	0	1	2144
Rollinrollinrollin	4	1	0	1	2144
My Mate Vinnie	5	1	0	0	2144
Whistling Senator	10	1	1	1	2079
Space Telescope	3	1	0	0	2053
Spot The Ball	4	1	1	0	2053
Listen And Learn	5	1	1	0	2053
More Of That	1	1	0	0	1779
Oscar Fortune	2	1	0	0	1711
Glan Lady	5	1	0	0	1689
Mythical Warrior	4	1	0	0	1689
Lookout Mountain	4	1	0	0	1437
Even If	3	1	0	0	1437
Total winning prize-money					**£457632**
Favourites	**37-107**		**34.6%**		**-2.94**

J J O'SHEA
FARNWORTH, GT MANCHESTER

	No. of Hrs	Races Run	1st	2nd	3rd	Unpl	Per cent	£1 Level Stake
NH Flat	0	0	0	0	0	0	0.0	0.00
Hurdles	0	0	0	0	0	0	0.0	0.00
Chases	3	7	2	1	1	3	28.6	0.00
Totals	3	7	2	1	1	3	28.6	0.00
11-12	1	2	1	0	0	1	50.0	+21.00

JOCKEYS

	W-R	Per cent	£1 Level Stake
Mr P Gerety	2-3	66.7	+4.00

COURSE RECORD

	Total W-R	Non-Hndcps Hurdles	Chases	Hndcps Hurdles	Chases	NH Flat	Per cent	£1 Level Stake
Haydock	1-1	0-0	1-1	0-0	0-0	0-0	100.0	+2.25
Kelso	1-1	0-0	1-1	0-0	0-0	0-0	100.0	+2.75

WINNING HORSES

Horse	Races Run	1st	2nd	3rd	£
*Cottage Oak	4	2	0	1	6551
Total winning prize-money					**£6551**
Favourites	1-1		100.0%		2.25

JOHN O'SHEA
ELTON, GLOUCS

	No. of Hrs	Races Run	1st	2nd	3rd	Unpl	Per cent	£1 Level Stake
NH Flat	0	0	0	0	0	0	0.0	0.00
Hurdles	13	67	6	7	9	45	9.0	-40.90
Chases	3	9	1	1	1	6	11.1	+12.00
Totals	13	76	7	8	10	51	9.2	-28.90
11-12	17	86	7	9	8	62	8.1	-19.93
10-11	19	96	4	9	5	78	4.2	-17.00

JOCKEYS

	W-R	Per cent	£1 Level Stake
Ciaran Mckee	3-22	13.6	-3.00
A P McCoy	2-5	40.0	-1.40
James Banks	1-1	100.0	+2.50
Mark Quinlan	1-3	33.3	+18.00

COURSE RECORD

	Total W-R	Non-Hndcps Hurdles Chases	Hndcps Hurdles Chases	NH Flat	Per cent	£1 Level Stake
Towcester	2-11	1-3 0-0	1-6 0-2	0-0	18.2	-1.50
Exeter	1-1	1-1 0-0	0-0 0-0	0-0	100.0	+4.00
Leicester	1-1	1-1 0-0	0-0 0-0	0-0	100.0	+2.50
Worcester	1-2	0-0 0-0	0-1 1-1	0-0	50.0	+19.00
Fontwell	1-5	1-3 0-0	0-2 0-0	0-0	20.0	-2.90
Bangor	1-7	0-2 0-0	1-5 0-0	0-0	14.3	-1.00

WINNING HORSES

Horse	Races Run	1st	2nd	3rd	£
Staccato Valtat	4	1	0	0	3119
Littledean Jimmy	4	1	3	0	2014
Nicky Nutjob	12	2	1	2	3899
My Viking Bay	15	2	1	5	3729
Stafford Charlie	7	1	1	0	1689
Total winning prize-money					£14450
Favourites	3-6		50.0%		1.10

JIM OLD

BARBURY CASTLE, WILTS

	No. of Hrs	Races Run	1st	2nd	3rd	Unpl	Per cent	£1 Level Stake
NH Flat	3	4	0	0	0	4	0.0	-4.00
Hurdles	9	20	2	4	0	14	10.0	-2.50
Chases	6	18	4	2	2	10	22.2	+7.75
Totals	12	42	6	6	2	28	14.3	+1.25
11-12	9	32	3	3	3	23	9.4	-5.75
10-11	20	53	5	3	3	42	9.4	-8.75

JOCKEYS

	W-R	Per cent	£1 Level Stake
Mark Grant	6-36	16.7	+7.25

COURSE RECORD

	Total W-R	Non-Hndcps Hurdles Chases	Hndcps Hurdles Chases	NH Flat	Per cent	£1 Level Stake
Taunton	2-4	0-0 0-0	2-3 0-1	0-0	50.0	+13.50
Leicester	1-2	0-0 0-0	0-0 1-2	0-0	50.0	+1.25
Folkestone	1-3	0-0 0-0	0-1 1-2	0-0	33.3	+12.00
Uttoxeter	1-3	0-0 0-0	0-1 1-2	0-0	33.3	0.00
Towcester	1-6	0-0 0-1	0-0 1-5	0-0	16.7	-1.50

WINNING HORSES

Horse	Races Run	1st	2nd	3rd	£
Okafranca	6	2	1	0	6981
Round The Horn	4	1	0	0	3379
Witch's Hat	4	1	1	0	2339
Thedreamstillalive	5	1	1	0	2053
Todareistodo	7	1	2	2	1997
Total winning prize-money					£16749
Favourites	0-1		0.0%		-1.00

HENRY OLIVER

BROOMHALL, WORCS

	No. of Hrs	Races Run	1st	2nd	3rd	Unpl	Per cent	£1 Level Stake
NH Flat	2	3	0	0	0	3	0.0	-3.00
Hurdles	5	12	2	0	0	10	16.7	+1.50
Chases	0	0	0	0	0	0	0.0	0.00
Totals	5	15	2	0	0	13	13.3	-1.50

JOCKEYS

	W-R	Per cent	£1 Level Stake
Henry Oliver	2-15	13.3	-1.50

COURSE RECORD

	Total W-R	Non-Hndcps Hurdles Chases	Hndcps Hurdles Chases	NH Flat	Per cent	£1 Level Stake
Bangor	1-1	0-0 0-0	1-1 0-0	0-0	100.0	+3.50
Chepstow	1-2	0-1 0-0	1-1 0-0	0-0	50.0	+7.00

WINNING HORSES

Horse	Races Run	1st	2nd	3rd	£
*Signed Request	5	2	0	0	4003
Total winning prize-money					£4003
Favourites	1-1		100.0%		3.50

JOHN PANVERT

STOODLEIGH, DEVON

	No. of Hrs	Races Run	1st	2nd	3rd	Unpl	Per cent	£1 Level Stake
NH Flat	0	0	0	0	0	0	0.0	0.00
Hurdles	5	19	1	3	0	15	5.3	+7.00
Chases	1	1	0	0	0	1	0.0	-1.00
Totals	6	20	1	3	0	16	5.0	+6.00
11-12	8	31	0	5	1	25	0.0	-31.00
10-11	10	36	2	1	4	29	5.6	-11.00

JOCKEYS

	W-R	Per cent	£1 Level Stake
Charlie Wallis	1-6	16.7	+20.00

COURSE RECORD

	Total W-R	Non-Hndcps Hurdles Chases	Hndcps Hurdles Chases	NH Flat	Per cent	£1 Level Stake
Nton Abbot	1-3	0-0 0-0	1-2 0-1	0-0	33.3	+23.00

WINNING HORSES

Horse	Races Run	1st	2nd	3rd	£
Cladding	5	1	0	0	2843
Total winning prize-money					£2843
Favourites	0-1		0.0%		-1.00

HILARY PARROTT

COOMBE HILL, GLOS

	No. of Hrs	Races Run	1st	2nd	3rd	Unpl	Per cent	£1 Level Stake
NH Flat	1	1	0	0	0	1	0.0	-1.00
Hurdles	2	2	0	0	0	2	0.0	-2.00
Chases	2	7	2	1	0	4	28.6	+1.25
Totals	5	10	2	1	0	7	20.0	-1.75
11-12	*3*	*5*	*1*	*0*	*0*	*4*	*20.0*	*+16.00*
10-11	*3*	*7*	*0*	*0*	*0*	*7*	*0.0*	*-7.00*

JOCKEYS

	W-R	Per cent	£1 Level Stake
Mr S Drinkwater	1-3	33.3	+0.25
Jack Doyle	1-5	20.0	0.00

COURSE RECORD

	Total W-R	Non-Hndcps Hurdles Chases	Hndcps Hurdles Chases	NH Flat	Per cent	£1 Level Stake
Ludlow	1-1	0-0 1-1	0-0 0-0	0-0	100.0	+2.25
Aintree	1-2	0-0 1-2	0-0 0-0	0-0	50.0	+3.00

WINNING HORSES

Horse	Races Run	1st	2nd	3rd	£
Wayward Prince	5	1	1	0	17085
Bob 'N' You	2	1	0	0	2184
Total winning prize-money					£19269
Favourites	1-1		100.0%		2.25

S J PARTRIDGE

NEWTON ABBOT, DEVON

	No. of Hrs	Races Run	1st	2nd	3rd	Unpl	Per cent	£1 Level Stake
NH Flat	0	0	0	0	0	0	0.0	0.00
Hurdles	0	0	0	0	0	0	0.0	0.00
Chases	1	3	1	1	0	1	33.3	-1.00
Totals	1	3	1	1	0	1	33.3	-1.00

JOCKEYS

	W-R	Per cent	£1 Level Stake
Mr D Edwards	1-2	50.0	0.00

COURSE RECORD

	Total W-R	Non-Hndcps Hurdles Chases	Hndcps Hurdles Chases	NH Flat	Per cent	£1 Level Stake
Exeter	1-2	0-0 1-2	0-0 0-0	0-0	50.0	0.00

WINNING HORSES

Horse	Races Run	1st	2nd	3rd	£
Lucette Annie	3	1	1	0	936
Total winning prize-money					£936
Favourites	1-1		100.0%		1.00

JAMES PAYNE

BROMPTON REGIS, SOMERSET

	No. of Hrs	Races Run	1st	2nd	3rd	Unpl	Per cent	£1 Level Stake
NH Flat	0	0	0	0	0	0	0.0	0.00
Hurdles	0	0	0	0	0	0	0.0	0.00
Chases	2	11	1	2	0	8	9.1	+15.00
Totals	2	11	1	2	0	8	9.1	+15.00
11-12	*1*	*6*	*1*	*2*	*1*	*2*	*16.7*	*-2.75*
10-11	*3*	*7*	*1*	*2*	*0*	*4*	*14.3*	*-2.00*

JOCKEYS

	W-R	Per cent	£1 Level Stake
Liam Treadwell	1-7	14.3	+19.00

COURSE RECORD

	Total W-R	Non-Hndcps Hurdles Chases	Hndcps Hurdles Chases	NH Flat	Per cent	£1 Level Stake
Exeter	1-1	0-0 0-0	0-0 1-1	0-0	100.0	+25.00

WINNING HORSES

Horse	Races Run	1st	2nd	3rd	£
Knapp Bridge Boy	6	1	1	0	3899
Total winning prize-money					£3899
Favourites	0-0		0.0%		0.00

LYDIA PEARCE

NEWMARKET, SUFFOLK

	No. of Hrs	Races Run	1st	2nd	3rd	Unpl	Per cent	£1 Level Stake
NH Flat	2	3	1	0	0	2	33.3	+31.00
Hurdles	2	3	0	0	0	3	0.0	-3.00
Chases	0	0	0	0	0	0	0.0	0.00
Totals	4	6	1	0	0	5	16.7	+28.00
11-12	4	8	1	2	0	5	12.5	-3.00
10-11	1	1	0	0	0	1	0.0	-1.00

JOCKEYS

	W-R	Per cent	£1 Level Stake
Charlie Wallis	1-2	50.0	+32.00

COURSE RECORD

	Total W-R	Non-Hndcps Hurdles Chases	Hndcps Hurdles Chases	NH Flat	Per cent	£1 Level Stake
Towcester	1-1	0-0 0-0	0-0 0-0	1-1	100.0	+33.00

WINNING HORSES

Horse	Races Run	1st	2nd	3rd	£
Salbatore	2	1	0	0	1365
Total winning prize-money					**£1365**
Favourites	0-0		0.0%		0.00

DAVID PHELAN

BEAUWORTH, HANTS

	No. of Hrs	Races Run	1st	2nd	3rd	Unpl	Per cent	£1 Level Stake
NH Flat	0	0	0	0	0	0	0.0	0.00
Hurdles	0	0	0	0	0	0	0.0	0.00
Chases	4	4	1	1	1	1	25.0	+6.00
Totals	4	4	1	1	1	1	25.0	+6.00
11-12	2	2	0	0	0	2	0.0	-2.00
10-11	5	8	0	2	1	5	0.0	-8.00

JOCKEYS

	W-R	Per cent	£1 Level Stake
Mr P York	1-1	100.0	+9.00

COURSE RECORD

	Total W-R	Non-Hndcps Hurdles Chases	Hndcps Hurdles Chases	NH Flat	Per cent	£1 Level Stake
Huntingdon	1-1	0-0 1-1	0-0 0-0	0-0	100.0	+9.00

WINNING HORSES

Horse	Races Run	1st	2nd	3rd	£
Oscar The Myth	1	1	0	0	811
Total winning prize-money					**£811**
Favourites	0-0		0.0%		0.00

RICHARD PHILLIPS

ADLESTROP, GLOUCS

	No. of Hrs	Races Run	1st	2nd	3rd	Unpl	Per cent	£1 Level Stake
NH Flat	7	15	2	3	2	8	13.3	-5.25
Hurdles	24	96	8	8	10	70	8.3	-38.50
Chases	7	15	2	2	1	10	13.3	+4.88
Totals	33	126	12	13	13	88	9.5	-38.87
11-12	33	115	4	16	17	78	3.5	-91.25
10-11	40	161	8	13	13	127	5.0	-110.27

BY MONTH

NH Flat	W-R	Per cent	£1 Level Stake	Hurdles	W-R	Per cent	£1 Level Stake
May	0-0	0.0	0.00	May	1-11	9.1	-3.50
June	0-0	0.0	0.00	June	4-8	50.0	+23.50
July	0-0	0.0	0.00	July	0-7	0.0	-7.00
August	0-0	0.0	0.00	August	1-10	10.0	-6.50
September	1-2	50.0	+4.50	September	0-2	0.0	-2.00
October	0-4	0.0	-4.00	October	0-4	0.0	-4.00
November	0-1	0.0	-1.00	November	0-8	0.0	-8.00
December	0-2	0.0	-2.00	December	0-11	0.0	-11.00
January	1-2	50.0	+1.25	January	0-9	0.0	-9.00
February	0-1	0.0	-1.00	February	1-8	12.5	+1.00
March	0-1	0.0	-1.00	March	0-8	0.0	-8.00
April	0-2	0.0	-2.00	April	1-10	10.0	-4.00

Chases	W-R	Per cent	£1 Level Stake	Totals	W-R	Per cent	£1 Level Stake
May	0-3	0.0	-3.00	May	1-14	7.1	-6.50
June	0-3	0.0	-3.00	June	4-11	36.4	+20.50
July	0-0	0.0	0.00	July	0-7	0.0	-7.00
August	0-0	0.0	0.00	August	1-10	10.0	-6.50
September	0-0	0.0	0.00	September	1-4	25.0	+2.50
October	0-0	0.0	0.00	October	0-8	0.0	-8.00
November	1-3	33.3	-0.13	November	1-12	8.3	-9.13
December	0-2	0.0	-2.00	December	0-15	0.0	-15.00
January	0-1	0.0	-1.00	January	1-12	8.3	-8.75
February	0-1	0.0	-1.00	February	1-10	10.0	-1.00
March	1-1	100.0	+16.00	March	1-10	10.0	+7.00
April	0-1	0.0	-1.00	April	1-13	7.7	-7.00

DISTANCE

Hurdles	W-R	Per cent	£1 Level Stake	Chases	W-R	Per cent	£1 Level Stake
2m-2m3f	0-32	0.0	-32.00	2m-2m3f	0-1	0.0	-1.00
2m4f-2m7f	5-37	13.5	+3.50	2m4f-2m7f	1-9	11.1	-6.13
3m+	3-27	11.1	-10.00	3m+	1-5	20.0	+12.00

Total winning prize-money			£31136
Favourites	5-9	55.6%	15.25

TYPE OF RACE

Non-Handicaps	W-R	Per cent	£1 Level Stake	Handicaps	W-R	Per cent	£1 Level Stake
Nov Hrdls	0-15	0.0	-15.00	Nov Hrdls	2-6	33.3	+4.00
Hrdls	1-11	9.1	-2.00	Hrdls	5-63	7.9	-24.50
Nov Chs	0-3	0.0	-3.00	Nov Chs	0-0	0.0	0.00
Chases	0-0	0.0	0.00	Chases	2-12	16.7	+7.88
Sell/Claim	0-0	0.0	0.00	Sell/Claim	0-0	0.0	0.00

RACE CLASS

	W-R	Per cent	£1 Level Stake
Class 1	0-0	0.0	0.00
Class 2	0-1	0.0	-1.00
Class 3	2-13	15.4	+3.00
Class 4	4-62	6.5	-26.50
Class 5	4-35	11.4	-9.13
Class 6	2-15	13.3	-5.25

FIRST TIME OUT

	W-R	Per cent	£1 Level Stake
Bumpers	1-7	14.3	-0.50
Hurdles	0-21	0.0	-21.00
Chases	0-5	0.0	-5.00
Totals	1-33	3.0	-26.50

JOCKEYS

	W-R	Per cent	£1 Level Stake
Richard Johnson	6-34	17.6	+20.50
Ian Popham	1-1	100.0	+5.00
Peter Carberry	1-3	33.3	+3.50
A P McCoy	1-7	14.3	-2.00
Jason Maguire	1-7	14.3	-3.75
Wayne Hutchinson	1-12	8.3	-3.00
Sean Quinlan	1-28	3.6	-25.13

COURSE RECORD

	Total W-R	Non-Hndcps Hurdles	Chases	Hndcps Hurdles	Chases	NH Flat	Per cent	£1 Level Stake
Worcester	4-16	1-3	0-0	3-10	0-2	0-1	25.0	+15.50
Huntingdon	2-13	0-3	0-0	1-8	1-2	0-0	15.4	+13.00
Wetherby	1-1	0-0	0-0	0-0	0-0	1-1	100.0	+2.25
Lingfield	1-3	0-0	0-0	0-2	1-1	0-0	33.3	-0.13
Bangor	1-5	0-1	0-1	1-3	0-0	0-0	20.0	-1.50
Fontwell	1-10	0-0	0-0	0-6	0-2	1-2	10.0	-3.50
Towcester	1-10	0-3	0-0	1-5	0-0	0-2	10.0	-2.50
Uttoxeter	1-10	0-0	0-1	1-8	0-1	0-0	10.0	-4.00

WINNING HORSES

Horse	Races Run	1st	2nd	3rd	£
King Jack	3	1	0	0	3769
Rich Buddy	6	2	0	0	5451
Saticon	4	2	0	0	7148
Crystal Swing	9	1	0	1	3249
Mr Tingle	3	2	0	0	4517
Captain Tidds	5	1	2	0	1916
Miss Lilly Lewis	2	1	0	0	1754
Stop The Show	8	1	0	3	1689
Ifits A Fiddle	3	1	1	0	1643

DAVID PIPE

NICHOLASHAYNE, DEVON

	No. of Hrs	Races Run	1st	2nd	3rd	Unpl	Per cent	£1 Level Stake
NH Flat	31	51	18	9	1	23	35.3	-2.12
Hurdles	116	376	51	39	45	241	13.6	-150.52
Chases	58	203	36	25	19	123	17.7	-31.81
Totals	159	630	105	73	65	387	16.7	-184.45
11-12	156	625	100	73	69	383	16.0	-145.53
10-11	133	503	66	62	47	328	13.1	-95.14

BY MONTH

NH Flat	W-R	Per cent	£1 Level Stake	Hurdles	W-R	Per cent	£1 Level Stake
May	1-4	25.0	+2.00	May	5-29	17.2	-7.34
June	1-1	100.0	+4.00	June	1-20	5.0	-18.17
July	0-1	0.0	-1.00	July	3-23	13.0	-7.00
August	0-1	0.0	-1.00	August	1-23	4.3	-17.00
September	1-1	100.0	+0.67	September	1-16	6.3	-1.00
October	1-3	33.3	+1.50	October	5-36	13.9	-16.75
November	0-3	0.0	-3.00	November	2-33	6.1	-21.00
December	4-11	36.4	-1.82	December	9-41	22.0	-2.13
January	3-4	75.0	+4.00	January	5-27	18.5	-11.47
February	6-11	54.5	+1.97	February	9-50	18.0	-13.48
March	0-6	0.0	-6.00	March	3-39	7.7	-29.02
April	1-5	20.0	-3.43	April	7-39	17.9	-6.17

Chases	W-R	Per cent	£1 Level Stake	Totals	W-R	Per cent	£1 Level Stake
May	2-10	20.0	-7.30	May	8-43	18.6	-12.64
June	0-7	0.0	-7.00	June	2-28	7.1	-21.17
July	1-4	25.0	-0.25	July	4-28	14.3	-8.25
August	1-5	20.0	-1.75	August	2-29	6.9	-19.75
September	1-6	16.7	-0.50	September	3-23	13.0	-0.83
October	3-7	42.9	+7.75	October	9-46	19.6	-7.50
November	5-25	20.0	+3.94	November	7-61	11.5	-20.06
December	7-33	21.2	+4.61	December	20-85	23.5	+0.66
January	5-30	16.7	-4.84	January	13-61	21.3	-12.31
February	7-25	28.0	+3.27	February	22-86	25.6	-8.24
March	1-28	3.6	-21.00	March	4-73	5.5	-56.02
April	3-23	13.0	-8.75	April	11-67	16.4	-18.35

DISTANCE

Hurdles	W-R	Per cent	£1 Level Stake	Chases	W-R	Per cent	£1 Level Stake
2m-2m3f	26-192	13.5	-99.90	2m-2m3f	3-39	7.7	-21.00
2m4f-2m7f	20-131	15.3	-28.62	2m4f-2m7f	12-75	16.0	-38.19
3m+	5-53	9.4	-22.00	3m+	21-89	23.6	+27.38

	Total W-R	Non-Hndcps Hurdles	Chases	Hndcps Hurdles	Chases	NH Flat	Per cent	£1 Level Stake
Sandown	3-22	1-1	0-3	1-14	0-2	1-2	13.6	-13.68
Newbury	3-29	0-4	1-3	1-11	0-10	1-1	10.3	-20.47
Nton Abbot	3-32	0-6	0-2	1-19	1-4	1-1	9.4	-9.83
Musselbgh	2-4	0-1	0-0	2-2	0-1	0-0	50.0	+2.50
Newcastle	2-5	1-1	0-0	0-1	1-3	0-0	40.0	+0.73
Leicester	2-8	0-0	0-0	0-1	2-7	0-0	25.0	-3.22
Southwell	2-9	0-0	1-1	0-6	1-1	0-1	22.2	-0.25
Ayr	2-10	0-1	0-1	1-3	1-4	0-1	20.0	-2.25
Warwick	2-12	1-3	0-1	0-5	1-3	0-0	16.7	-7.75
Hexham	1-2	0-0	1-1	0-0	0-1	0-0	50.0	-0.67
Fakenham	1-3	1-3	0-0	0-0	0-0	0-0	33.3	+8.00
Kelso	1-4	0-2	0-1	1-1	0-0	0-0	25.0	-1.00
Bangor	1-7	0-2	0-0	0-3	1-2	0-0	14.3	+1.50
Hereford	1-8	0-1	1-2	0-4	0-1	0-0	12.5	-6.64
Ludlow	1-10	0-1	0-0	0-5	0-2	1-2	10.0	-7.50
Kempton	1-12	0-1	1-5	0-4	0-1	0-1	8.3	-10.39
Ascot	1-13	0-1	0-0	0-6	0-4	1-2	7.7	-11.33
Haydock	1-15	1-1	0-0	0-10	0-4	0-0	6.7	-11.00
Mrket Rsn	1-16	0-1	0-1	1-7	0-7	0-0	6.3	-8.50
Uttoxeter	1-18	0-6	0-1	0-7	1-3	0-1	5.6	-11.00

TYPE OF RACE

Non-Handicaps

	W-R	Per cent	£1 Level Stake
Nov Hrdls	15-72	20.8	-14.48
Hrdls	6-34	17.6	-15.69
Nov Chs	13-46	28.3	-4.84
Chases	0-10	0.0	-10.00
Sell/Claim	1-9	11.1	-4.50

Handicaps

	W-R	Per cent	£1 Level Stake
Nov Hrdls	3-26	11.5	-11.00
Hrdls	27-237	11.4	-102.34
Nov Chs	0-12	0.0	-12.00
Chases	23-135	17.0	-4.97
Sell/Claim	0-1	0.0	-1.00

RACE CLASS

	W-R	Per cent	£1 Level Stake
Class 1	10-93	10.8	-40.79
Class 2	13-89	14.6	-10.92
Class 3	14-119	11.8	-44.51
Class 4	40-223	17.9	-78.64
Class 5	14-72	19.4	-13.55
Class 6	14-34	41.2	+4.96

FIRST TIME OUT

	W-R	Per cent	£1 Level Stake
Bumpers	10-31	32.3	-0.70
Hurdles	12-89	13.5	-33.92
Chases	10-39	25.6	-2.14
Totals	32-159	20.1	-36.76

JOCKEYS

	W-R	Per cent	£1 Level Stake
Tom Scudamore	53-290	18.3	-91.13
Conor O'Farrell	18-104	17.3	-27.16
Mr M Ennis	5-23	21.7	+19.00
Timmy Murphy	5-31	16.1	-13.08
Kieron Edgar	5-48	10.4	-33.17
A P McCoy	4-14	28.6	+7.73
Tom Bellamy	4-49	8.2	-30.00
Mr M Heard	3-14	21.4	+1.38
Samuel Welton	2-4	50.0	+8.00
Noel Fehily	1-3	33.3	-0.25
Nick Scholfield	1-3	33.3	+5.00
Andrew Glassonbury	1-4	25.0	+2.00
Paddy Brennan	1-5	20.0	-1.25
Hadden Frost	1-8	12.5	-4.00
Francis Hayes	1-15	6.7	-12.50

COURSE RECORD

	Total W-R	Non-Hndcps Hurdles	Chases	Hndcps Hurdles	Chases	NH Flat	Per cent	£1 Level Stake
Towcester	8-17	3-4	0-0	1-5	2-2	2-6	47.1	+17.13
Taunton	8-39	2-9	0-2	4-20	1-4	1-4	20.5	-6.40
Wincanton	7-54	1-11	0-1	4-31	2-10	0-1	13.0	-16.92
Exeter	6-33	0-7	1-4	3-15	0-3	2-4	18.2	-8.04
Ffos Las	6-34	1-11	0-0	1-11	1-7	3-5	17.6	-15.07
Cheltenham	6-63	0-3	3-11	1-21	2-24	0-4	9.5	-13.50
Plumpton	5-10	2-2	0-0	2-5	0-2	1-1	50.0	+0.30
Chepstow	5-20	1-3	0-3	1-5	3-8	0-1	25.0	+6.50
Worcester	5-33	1-6	0-2	2-14	0-8	2-3	15.2	-13.67
Wetherby	4-12	1-2	2-3	0-1	1-3	0-3	33.3	-0.10
Stratford	4-16	2-7	0-0	1-7	1-1	0-1	25.0	+3.25
Lingfield	3-8	0-1	0-0	2-3	1-4	0-0	37.5	+5.75
Fontwell	3-13	1-3	1-1	0-6	0-1	1-2	23.1	-1.68
Aintree	3-16	1-3	1-2	0-4	0-5	1-2	18.8	-6.25

WINNING HORSES

Horse	Races Run	1st	2nd	3rd	£
Big Occasion	8	1	2	3	45560
Dynaste	5	4	1	0	92053
The Package	4	1	0	0	34331
Master Overseer	5	2	0	0	37769
Swing Bowler	3	1	0	1	19494
Ballynagour	2	1	0	0	18768
Goulanes	4	2	1	0	32828
Weekend Millionair	10	2	1	2	18424
Premier Dane	3	3	0	0	32844
Junior	4	1	0	0	15377
Shoegazer	14	5	2	1	35819
Sona Sasta	4	1	1	0	12996
His Excellency	13	1	3	2	12512
Our Father	3	1	1	0	12512
Swing Bill	7	1	0	0	11992
Close House	4	1	1	0	10128
Shotavodka	5	3	0	0	17870
Buddy Bolero	3	2	0	0	10732
Consigliere	5	1	1	0	6498
No Secrets	4	2	0	0	12346
Bygones Sovereign	6	1	0	1	6498
Amigo	4	2	0	2	6498
Gevrey Chamberlin	5	3	0	0	15270
Tanerko Emery	7	3	2	1	11372
Edmund Kean	4	2	0	1	10072
Home Run	12	5	2	1	15589
Katchmore	6	1	0	1	4549
African Broadway	5	1	0	2	4549
Franklin Roosevelt	7	2	1	1	6855
Alderluck	5	1	0	0	3899
E Street Boy	5	2	0	0	7148
Take Over Sivola	4	1	0	0	3899
Broadway Buffalo	6	5	0	0	13826

Horse	Races Run	1st	2nd	3rd	£
Top Gamble	3	2	1	0	5328
Shaking Hands	5	2	0	0	6823
Decoy	3	1	0	0	3574
Qalinas	10	2	2	2	6707
Too Generous	5	4	0	0	7701
War Singer	2	1	0	0	3379
Bathwick Man	7	2	1	2	6498
Midnight Tuesday	5	1	0	2	3249
Red Sherlock	2	2	0	0	4809
Weather Babe	2	2	0	0	5718
Western Warhorse	2	1	0	0	3119
Diamond's Return	4	2	1	0	4516
I Shot The Sheriff	4	1	1	0	2599
Doctor Harper	3	2	0	0	4659
Barton Stacey	2	1	0	0	2534
Royal Mile	6	1	1	1	2339
Oddjob	4	1	1	0	2144
Beattie Green	2	1	0	0	2144
Henok	6	1	0	0	2144
Martial Law	4	1	1	0	2112
*Centasia	3	1	0	0	1949
Heath Hunter	1	1	0	0	1949
Vieux Lion Rouge	4	3	0	0	4697
The Liquidator	3	1	1	0	1625
Seven Nation Army	1	1	0	0	1560
Volt Face	1	1	0	0	1560
Kings Palace	3	1	1	0	1437
Total winning prize-money					£697750
Favourites	47-132		35.6%		-22.28

JACKIE DU PLESSIS

TREHAN, CORNWALL

	No. of Hrs	Races Run	1st	2nd	3rd	Unpl	Per cent	£1 Level Stake
NH Flat	2	4	0	0	0	4	0.0	-4.00
Hurdles	4	11	1	2	0	8	9.1	-5.50
Chases	4	8	1	4	2	1	12.5	-2.50
Totals	9	23	2	6	2	13	8.7	-12.00
11-12	7	11	3	1	2	5	27.3	+36.00
10-11	3	10	2	1	1	6	20.0	-5.15

JOCKEYS

	W-R	Per cent	£1 Level Stake
James Best	2-16	12.5	-5.00

COURSE RECORD

	Total W-R	Non-Hndcps Hurdles	Chases	Hndcps Hurdles	Chases	NH Flat	Per cent	£1 Level Stake
Ludlow	1-3	0-2	0-0	0-0	1-1	0-0	33.3	+2.50
Nton Abbot	1-6	1-3	0-1	0-1	0-1	0-0	16.7	-0.50

WINNING HORSES

Horse	Races Run	1st	2nd	3rd	£
Armenian Boy	2	1	1	0	9384
Fear Glic	3	1	1	0	3249
Total winning prize-money					£12633
Favourites	0-3		0.0%		-3.00

MRS DAVID PLUNKETT

BANBURY, OXON

	No. of Hrs	Races Run	1st	2nd	3rd	Unpl	Per cent	£1 Level Stake
NH Flat	0	0	0	0	0	0	0.0	0.00
Hurdles	0	0	0	0	0	0	0.0	0.00
Chases	1	4	1	0	0	3	25.0	+8.00
Totals	1	4	1	0	0	3	25.0	+8.00
10-11	1	1	0	0	0	1	0.0	-1.00

JOCKEYS

	W-R	Per cent	£1 Level Stake
Mr J Martin	1-4	25.0	+8.00

COURSE RECORD

	Total W-R	Non-Hndcps Hurdles	Chases	Hndcps Hurdles	Chases	NH Flat	Per cent	£1 Level Stake
Nton Abbot	1-1	0-0	1-1	0-0	0-0	0-0	100.0	+11.00

WINNING HORSES

Horse	Races Run	1st	2nd	3rd	£
Himalayan Express	4	1	0	0	1153
Total winning prize-money					£1153
Favourites	0-0		0.0%		0.00

CHARLES POGSON

FARNSFIELD, NOTTS

	No. of Hrs	Races Run	1st	2nd	3rd	Unpl	Per cent	£1 Level Stake
NH Flat	1	1	0	0	0	1	0.0	-1.00
Hurdles	5	23	0	1	1	21	0.0	-23.00
Chases	4	16	1	2	3	10	6.3	-11.67
Totals	8	40	1	3	4	32	2.5	-35.67
11-12	14	74	4	3	8	59	5.4	-24.00
10-11	19	77	3	6	14	54	3.9	-62.42

JOCKEYS

	W-R	Per cent	£1 Level Stake
Adam Pogson	1-40	2.5	-35.67

COURSE RECORD

	Total W-R	Non-Hndcps Hurdles	Chases	Hndcps Hurdles	Chases	NH Flat	Per cent	£1 Level Stake
Catterick	1-2	0-0	0-0	0-0	1-2	0-0	50.0	+2.33

WINNING HORSES

Horse	Races Run	1st	2nd	3rd	£
Noble Witness	10	1	2	1	3899
Total winning prize-money					£3899
Favourites	0-0		0.0%		0.00

JAMIE POULTON

TELSCOMBE, E SUSSEX

	No. of Hrs	Races Run	1st	2nd	3rd	Unpl	Per cent	£1 Level Stake
NH Flat	1	2	0	0	0	2	0.0	-2.00
Hurdles	5	12	3	0	1	8	25.0	+10.75
Chases	1	1	0	0	0	1	0.0	-1.00
Totals	6	15	3	0	1	11	20.0	+7.75
11-12	7	20	1	2	1	16	5.0	-15.50
10-11	6	29	2	2	3	22	6.9	+2.00

JOCKEYS

	W-R	Per cent	£1 Level Stake
Jeremiah McGrath	3-7	42.9	+15.75

COURSE RECORD

	Total W-R	Non-Hndcps Hurdles	Chases	Hndcps Hurdles	Chases	NH Flat	Per cent	£1 Level Stake
Kempton	1-1	0-0	0-0	1-1	0-0	0-0	100.0	+5.50
Lingfield	1-1	0-0	0-0	1-1	0-0	0-0	100.0	+12.00
Fontwell	1-6	0-2	0-0	1-3	0-0	0-1	16.7	-2.75

WINNING HORSES

Horse	Races Run	1st	2nd	3rd	£
Farbreaga	6	3	0	1	6992
Total winning prize-money					£6992
Favourites	0-40		0.0%		-40.00

BRENDAN POWELL

UPPER LAMBOURN, BERKS

	No. of Hrs	Races Run	1st	2nd	3rd	Unpl	Per cent	£1 Level Stake
NH Flat	21	33	7	3	5	18	21.2	+17.25
Hurdles	52	183	12	18	17	136	6.6	-100.10
Chases	19	68	7	12	14	35	10.3	+8.50
Totals	71	284	26	33	36	189	9.2	-74.35
11-12	66	260	29	27	30	174	11.2	-64.79
10-11	47	221	23	25	24	149	10.4	-80.05

BY MONTH

NH Flat	W-R	Per cent	£1 Level Stake	Hurdles	W-R	Per cent	£1 Level Stake
May	0-6	0.0	-6.00	May	1-20	5.0	-15.50
June	0-3	0.0	-3.00	June	0-11	0.0	-11.00
July	0-0	0.0	0.00	July	1-9	11.1	+2.00
August	1-1	100.0	+5.00	August	2-8	25.0	+3.00
September	0-1	0.0	-1.00	September	0-5	0.0	-5.00
October	1-3	33.3	+8.00	October	4-17	23.5	+14.82
November	2-4	50.0	+7.50	November	0-21	0.0	-21.00
December	2-3	66.7	+11.75	December	1-21	4.8	-19.67
January	1-3	33.3	+4.00	January	0-10	0.0	-10.00
February	0-2	0.0	-2.00	February	0-19	0.0	-19.00
March	0-6	0.0	-6.00	March	1-19	5.3	-12.00
April	0-1	0.0	-1.00	April	2-23	8.7	-6.75

Chases	W-R	Per cent	£1 Level Stake	Totals	W-R	Per cent	£1 Level Stake
May	0-9	0.0	-9.00	May	1-35	2.9	-30.50
June	2-5	40.0	+12.50	June	2-19	10.5	-1.50
July	0-5	0.0	-5.00	July	1-14	7.1	-3.00
August	0-3	0.0	-3.00	August	3-12	25.0	+5.00
September	0-2	0.0	-2.00	September	0-8	0.0	-8.00
October	0-7	0.0	-7.00	October	5-27	18.5	+15.82
November	1-7	14.3	+10.00	November	3-32	9.4	-3.50
December	1-8	12.5	+2.00	December	4-32	12.5	-5.92
January	1-5	20.0	+10.00	January	2-18	11.1	+4.00
February	0-7	0.0	-7.00	February	0-28	0.0	-28.00
March	1-6	16.7	+4.00	March	2-31	6.5	-14.00
April	1-4	25.0	+3.00	April	3-28	10.7	-4.75

DISTANCE

Hurdles	W-R	Per cent	£1 Level Stake	Chases	W-R	Per cent	£1 Level Stake
2m-2m3f	10-123	8.1	-43.92	2m-2m3f	2-23	8.7	+4.00
2m4f-2m7f	2-48	4.2	-44.18	2m4f-2m7f	3-22	13.6	+10.50
3m+	0-12	0.0	-12.00	3m+	2-23	8.7	-6.00

TYPE OF RACE

Non-Handicaps	W-R	Per cent	£1 Level Stake	Handicaps	W-R	Per cent	£1 Level Stake
Nov Hrdls	1-30	3.3	-26.00	Nov Hrdls	3-14	21.4	+17.00
Hrdls	2-39	5.1	-33.17	Hrdls	6-94	6.4	-51.93
Nov Chs	3-17	17.6	+18.00	Nov Chs	0-8	0.0	-8.00
Chases	0-1	0.0	-1.00	Chases	4-42	9.5	-0.50
Sell/Claim	0-5	0.0	-5.00	Sell/Claim	0-1	0.0	-1.00

RACE CLASS

	W-R	Per cent	£1 Level Stake
Class 1	0-3	0.0	-3.00
Class 2	0-5	0.0	-5.00
Class 3	3-31	9.7	-10.50
Class 4	13-160	8.1	-43.85

FIRST TIME OUT

	W-R	Per cent	£1 Level Stake
Bumpers	5-21	23.8	+12.25
Hurdles	2-43	4.7	-17.50
Chases	0-7	0.0	-7.00

Class 5	4-57	7.0	-28.25	Totals	7-71	9.9	-12.25
Class 6	6-28	21.4	+16.25				

JOCKEYS

	W-R	Per cent	£1 Level Stake
Brendan Powell	10-135	7.4	-50.00
Andrew Tinkler	4-30	13.3	-1.00
A P McCoy	3-20	15.0	-14.85
Sam Jones	2-9	22.2	+4.75
Richard Killoran	2-15	13.3	+3.00
Patrick Corbett	1-1	100.0	+2.25
Sam Twiston-Davies	1-1	100.0	+12.00
Micheal Nolan	1-4	25.0	+17.00
Leighton Aspell	1-5	20.0	+12.00
Nick Scholfield	1-5	20.0	-0.50

COURSE RECORD

	Total W-R	Non-Hndcps Hurdles Chases	Hndcps Hurdles Chases	NH Flat	Per cent	£1 Level Stake
Wincanton	4-19	0-3 1-1	2-10 1-4	0-1	21.1	+26.25
Warwick	3-8	1-4 1-1	0-1 1-2	0-0	37.5	+23.50
Worcester	3-15	0-3 0-0	0-7 2-3	1-2	20.0	+13.50
Nton Abbot	2-6	0-0 0-0	1-4 0-1	1-1	33.3	+7.00
Towcester	2-13	0-3 0-1	0-2 0-3	2-4	15.4	-4.75
Fontwell	2-35	0-3 0-2	2-15 0-11	0-4	5.7	-26.43
Doncaster	1-3	0-0 1-1	0-0 0-1	0-1	33.3	+7.00
Exeter	1-7	0-2 0-0	0-3 0-0	1-2	14.3	0.00
Hereford	1-7	1-2 0-0	0-4 0-0	0-1	14.3	-3.00
Ludlow	1-8	0-5 0-0	1-2 0-0	0-1	12.5	-1.00
Ffos Las	1-8	0-2 0-0	1-3 0-3	0-0	12.5	-4.75
Uttoxeter	1-11	0-2 0-2	1-5 0-1	0-1	9.1	0.00
Newbury	1-12	0-8 0-0	0-0 0-0	1-4	8.3	-1.00
Plumpton	1-14	1-7 0-1	0-6 0-0	0-0	7.1	-12.67
Stratford	1-17	0-4 0-2	1-7 0-3	0-1	5.9	-4.00
Huntingdon	1-18	0-6 0-1	0-6 0-4	1-1	5.6	-11.00

WINNING HORSES

Horse	Races Run	1st	2nd	3rd	£
Va'Vite	3	1	1	1	6330
*Canadian Diamond	6	2	1	0	9097
The Lemonpie	9	3	3	0	8902
Milans Well	5	2	2	0	8552
Shoreacres	3	1	0	0	3899
Night Force	3	1	1	1	3899
*Sir Fredlot	7	2	1	1	6636
Fulgora	3	1	0	0	3639
Dark And Dangerous	9	1	0	4	3119
Morestead	15	1	1	1	3054
Violets Boy	8	1	0	2	2599
Award Winner	15	2	0	0	4484
Glen Countess	7	1	3	1	2259
Bennys Well	8	1	1	0	2014
King Spirit	6	1	0	2	1754
Reach The Beach	3	2	0	0	3076
Guanciale	5	1	1	0	1711

Bob Tucker	2	1	0	1	1437
Shipton	3	1	0	0	1365
Total winning prize-money					£77826
Favourites	3-16		18.8%		-10.85

JOHN PRICE
EBBW VALE, BLAENAU GWENT

	No. of Hrs	Races Run	1st	2nd	3rd	Unpl	Per cent	£1 Level Stake
NH Flat	0	0	0	0	0	0	0.0	0.00
Hurdles	3	7	2	0	1	4	28.6	+2.50
Chases	0	0	0	0	0	0	0.0	0.00
Totals	3	7	2	0	1	4	28.6	+2.50
11-12	3	6	2	1	0	3	33.3	+16.00
10-11	3	7	0	0	0	7	0.0	-7.00

JOCKEYS

	W-R	Per cent	£1 Level Stake
Robert Dunne	2-2	100.0	+7.50

COURSE RECORD

	Total W-R	Non-Hndcps Hurdles Chases	Hndcps Hurdles Chases	NH Flat	Per cent	£1 Level Stake
Ludlow	2-3	2-2 0-0	0-1 0-0	0-0	66.7	+6.50

WINNING HORSES

Horse	Races Run	1st	2nd	3rd	£
*Descaro	4	2	0	1	7148
Total winning prize-money					£7148
Favourites	0-0		0.0%		0.00

ANDREW PRICE
LEOMINSTER, H'FORDS

	No. of Hrs	Races Run	1st	2nd	3rd	Unpl	Per cent	£1 Level Stake
NH Flat	4	9	0	1	0	8	0.0	-9.00
Hurdles	4	6	1	0	0	5	16.7	+61.00
Chases	2	11	1	2	2	6	9.1	-5.00
Totals	6	26	2	3	2	19	7.7	+47.00
11-12	6	14	0	0	0	14	0.0	-14.00
10-11	6	17	1	1	0	15	5.9	-9.50

JOCKEYS

	W-R	Per cent	£1 Level Stake
Robert Dunne	2-21	9.5	+52.00

COURSE RECORD

	Total W-R	Non-Hndcps Hurdles Chases	Hndcps Hurdles Chases	NH Flat	Per cent	£1 Level Stake
Huntingdon	1-1	0-0 0-0	0-0 1-1	0-0	100.0	+5.00
Chepstow	1-3	1-1 0-0	0-0 0-1	0-1	33.3	+64.00

WINNING HORSES

Horse	Races Run	1st	2nd	3rd	£
Bobby Dove	7	1	1	2	3899
Flora Lea	3	1	0	0	3899
Total winning prize-money					£7798
Favourites	0-0		0.0%		0.00

RICHARD PRICE

ULLINGSWICK, H'FORDS

	No. of Hrs	Races Run	1st	2nd	3rd	Unpl	Per cent	£1 Level Stake
NH Flat	2	3	0	0	1	2	0.0	-3.00
Hurdles	9	20	2	0	3	15	10.0	-1.50
Chases	1	1	0	0	0	1	0.0	-1.00
Totals	11	24	2	0	4	18	8.3	-5.50
11-12	13	45	0	2	6	37	0.0	-45.00
10-11	15	47	3	3	4	37	6.4	+50.00

JOCKEYS

	W-R	Per cent	£1 Level Stake
David Bass	2-11	18.2	+7.50

COURSE RECORD

	Total W-R	Non-Hndcps Hurdles	Chases	Hndcps Hurdles	Chases	NH Flat	Per cent	£1 Level Stake
Wincanton	1-2	0-1	0-0	1-1	0-0	0-0	50.0	+9.00
Warwick	1-3	1-2	0-0	0-0	0-0	0-1	33.3	+4.50

WINNING HORSES

Horse	Races Run	1st	2nd	3rd	£
*In The Crowd	6	2	0	1	8772
Total winning prize-money					£8772
Favourites	0-0		0.0%		0.00

DAVID PRICHARD

BRIDGWATER, SOMERSET

	No. of Hrs	Races Run	1st	2nd	3rd	Unpl	Per cent	£1 Level Stake
NH Flat	0	0	0	0	0	0	0.0	0.00
Hurdles	0	0	0	0	0	0	0.0	0.00
Chases	1	3	1	0	2	0	33.3	+0.50
Totals	1	3	1	0	2	0	33.3	+0.50

JOCKEYS

	W-R	Per cent	£1 Level Stake
Mr David Prichard	1-2	50.0	+1.50

COURSE RECORD

	Total W-R	Non-Hndcps Hurdles	Chases	Hndcps Hurdles	Chases	NH Flat	Per cent	£1 Level Stake
Ludlow	1-1	0-0	1-1	0-0	0-0	0-0	100.0	+2.50

WINNING HORSES

Horse	Races Run	1st	2nd	3rd	£
Martys Mission	3	1	0	2	1872
Total winning prize-money					£1872
Favourites	1-1		100.0%		2.50

PETER PRITCHARD

WHATCOTE, WARWICKS

	No. of Hrs	Races Run	1st	2nd	3rd	Unpl	Per cent	£1 Level Stake
NH Flat	2	3	0	0	0	3	0.0	-3.00
Hurdles	7	28	5	1	0	22	17.9	+52.50
Chases	2	5	0	1	0	4	0.0	-5.00
Totals	8	36	5	2	0	29	13.9	+44.50
11-12	10	49	1	6	5	37	2.0	-43.50
10-11	12	64	3	3	3	55	4.7	-39.38

JOCKEYS

	W-R	Per cent	£1 Level Stake
Jack Doyle	3-21	14.3	+17.50
Nico de Boinville	1-1	100.0	+28.00
Ryan Mahon	1-4	25.0	+9.00

COURSE RECORD

	Total W-R	Non-Hndcps Hurdles	Chases	Hndcps Hurdles	Chases	NH Flat	Per cent	£1 Level Stake
Hereford	1-2	0-0	0-0	1-2	0-0	0-0	50.0	+2.50
Southwell	1-2	0-0	0-0	1-2	0-0	0-0	50.0	+11.00
Chepstow	1-4	0-1	0-0	1-2	0-1	0-0	25.0	+19.00
Ludlow	1-5	0-3	0-0	1-1	0-0	0-1	20.0	+24.00
Towcester	1-10	0-0	0-0	1-6	0-3	0-1	10.0	+1.00

WINNING HORSES

Horse	Races Run	1st	2nd	3rd	£
Tisfreetdream	7	2	0	0	4445
Earcomesthedream	10	3	0	0	4094
Total winning prize-money					£8539
Favourites	0-0		0.0%		0.00

NOEL QUINLAN

NEWMARKET, SUFFOLK

	No. of Hrs	Races Run	1st	2nd	3rd	Unpl	Per cent	£1 Level Stake
NH Flat	3	6	1	1	0	4	16.7	+1.00
Hurdles	12	28	0	2	2	24	0.0	-28.00
Chases	2	7	1	1	0	5	14.3	-1.00
Totals	15	41	2	4	2	33	4.9	-28.00
11-12	11	34	5	10	3	16	14.7	+18.50
10-11	3	6	0	1	1	4	0.0	-6.00

JOCKEYS

	W-R	Per cent	£1 Level Stake
Jack Quinlan	2-35	5.7	-22.00

COURSE RECORD

	Total W-R	Non-Hndcps Hurdles	Chases	Hndcps Hurdles	Chases	NH Flat	Per cent	£1 Level Stake
Fontwell	1-1	0-0	0-0	0-0	0-0	1-1	100.0	+6.00
Mrket Rsn	1-3	0-0	0-1	0-0	1-1	0-1	33.3	+3.00

WINNING HORSES

Horse	Races Run	1st	2nd	3rd	£
Park Lane	4	1	1	0	4874
Petie McSweetie	6	1	0	1	1365
Total winning prize-money					£6239
Favourites	0-0		0.0%		0.00

JOHN QUINN

SETTRINGTON, N YORKS

	No. of Hrs	Races Run	1st	2nd	3rd	Unpl	Per cent	£1 Level Stake
NH Flat	4	5	1	0	1	3	20.0	-1.75
Hurdles	23	63	19	7	8	29	30.2	+30.02
Chases	1	1	0	1	0	0	0.0	-1.00
Totals	26	69	20	8	9	32	29.0	+27.27
11-12	21	74	17	17	9	31	23.0	+35.28
10-11	29	80	15	7	7	51	18.8	-12.94

BY MONTH

NH Flat	W-R	Per cent	£1 Level Stake	Hurdles	W-R	Per cent	£1 Level Stake
May	0-0	0.0	0.00	May	1-4	25.0	+1.00
June	0-0	0.0	0.00	June	0-6	0.0	-6.00
July	0-0	0.0	0.00	July	0-4	0.0	-4.00
August	0-0	0.0	0.00	August	3-3	100.0	+10.50
September	0-0	0.0	0.00	September	1-1	100.0	+4.50
October	0-0	0.0	0.00	October	1-5	20.0	-2.63
November	0-1	0.0	-1.00	November	1-5	20.0	-2.90
December	0-2	0.0	-2.00	December	4-10	40.0	+14.08
January	0-0	0.0	0.00	January	1-3	33.3	+12.00
February	0-0	0.0	0.00	February	1-8	12.5	-6.20
March	0-0	0.0	0.00	March	4-10	40.0	+2.66
April	1-2	50.0	+1.25	April	2-4	50.0	+7.00

Chases	W-R	Per cent	£1 Level Stake	Totals	W-R	Per cent	£1 Level Stake
May	0-0	0.0	0.00	May	1-4	25.0	+1.00
June	0-0	0.0	0.00	June	0-6	0.0	-6.00
July	0-0	0.0	0.00	July	0-4	0.0	-4.00
August	0-0	0.0	0.00	August	3-3	100.0	+10.50
September	0-0	0.0	0.00	September	1-1	100.0	+4.50
October	0-1	0.0	-1.00	October	1-6	16.7	-3.63
November	0-0	0.0	0.00	November	1-6	16.7	-3.90
December	0-0	0.0	0.00	December	4-12	33.3	+12.08
January	0-0	0.0	0.00	January	1-3	33.3	+12.00
February	0-0	0.0	0.00	February	1-8	12.5	-6.20
March	0-0	0.0	0.00	March	4-10	40.0	+2.66
April	0-0	0.0	0.00	April	3-6	50.0	+8.25

DISTANCE

Hurdles	W-R	Per cent	£1 Level Stake	Chases	W-R	Per cent	£1 Level Stake
2m-2m3f	17-51	33.3	+30.52	2m-2m3f	0-0	0.0	0.00
2m4f-2m7f	1-6	16.7	+0.50	2m4f-2m7f	0-1	0.0	-1.00
3m+	1-6	16.7	-1.00	3m+	0-0	0.0	0.00

TYPE OF RACE

Non-Handicaps	W-R	Per cent	£1 Level Stake	Handicaps	W-R	Per cent	£1 Level Stake
Nov Hrdls	2-10	20.0	-2.75	Nov Hrdls	0-2	0.0	-2.00
Hrdls	9-26	34.6	+24.86	Hrdls	6-18	33.3	+13.00
Nov Chs	0-1	0.0	-1.00	Nov Chs	0-0	0.0	0.00
Chases	0-0	0.0	0.00	Chases	0-0	0.0	0.00
Sell/Claim	2-7	28.6	-3.09	Sell/Claim	0-0	0.0	0.00

RACE CLASS | FIRST TIME OUT

Race Class	W-R	Per cent	£1 Level Stake	First Time Out	W-R	Per cent	£1 Level Stake
Class 1	2-9	22.2	+2.75	Bumpers	1-4	25.0	-0.75
Class 2	1-5	20.0	+1.00	Hurdles	7-22	31.8	+25.35
Class 3	3-8	37.5	+5.50	Chases	0-0	0.0	0.00
Class 4	9-27	33.3	+23.02				
Class 5	4-15	26.7	-3.26	Totals	8-26	30.8	+24.60
Class 6	1-5	20.0	-1.75				

JOCKEYS

	W-R	Per cent	£1 Level Stake
Dougie Costello	15-48	31.3	+28.39
Dean Pratt	3-9	33.3	+4.75
Jason Maguire	1-1	100.0	+1.38
Denis O'Regan	1-6	16.7	-2.25

COURSE RECORD

	Total W-R	Non-Hndcps Hurdles	Chases	Hndcps Hurdles	Chases	NH Flat	Per cent	£1 Level Stake
Doncaster	5-9	5-8	0-0	0-1	0-0	0-0	55.6	+22.58
Cartmel	3-4	1-2	0-0	2-2	0-0	0-0	75.0	+9.50

Mrket Rsn	2-4	2-4	0-0	0-0	0-0	0-0	50.0	+3.60
Catterick	2-7	2-6	0-0	0-0	0-0	0-1	28.6	-3.29
Ascot	1-1	0-0	0-0	1-1	0-0	0-0	100.0	+4.00
Hexham	1-2	0-0	0-0	0-1	0-0	1-1	50.0	+1.25
Kelso	1-2	1-2	0-0	0-0	0-0	0-0	50.0	+0.38
Newcastle	1-2	1-1	0-0	0-1	0-0	0-0	50.0	+1.75
Sandown	1-2	0-0	0-0	1-2	0-0	0-0	50.0	+1.50
Stratford	1-3	0-0	0-0	1-3	0-0	0-0	33.3	+2.00
Aintree	1-6	0-3	0-1	1-2	0-0	0-0	16.7	0.00
Wetherby	1-9	1-5	0-0	0-3	0-0	0-1	11.1	+2.00

WINNING HORSES

Horse	Races Run	1st	2nd	3rd	£
Countrywide Flame	5	1	1	1	58521
*Cockney Sparrow	5	3	2	0	32822
Kashmir Peak	4	2	0	0	18331
*Calculated Risk	6	3	0	1	15882
Royal Bonsai	1	1	0	0	6498
Red Tyke	3	2	0	0	7083
Massini Lotto	5	1	0	0	3574
Tartan Tiger	2	1	0	1	3249
*Hidden Justice	3	2	0	0	5848
Zaplamation	4	1	1	1	2599
Luccombe Chine	5	1	0	0	2599
King Fingal	3	1	1	0	2190
Zermatt	1	1	0	0	1643
Total winning prize-money					£160839
Favourites	10-260		3.8%		-233.98

DAVID REES

CLARBESTON, PEMBROKES

	No. of Hrs	Races Run	1st	2nd	3rd	Unpl	Per cent	£1 Level Stake
NH Flat	1	1	0	0	0	1	0.0	-1.00
Hurdles	20	53	7	3	6	37	13.2	+24.50
Chases	10	27	4	3	8	12	14.8	+8.00
Totals	26	81	11	6	14	50	13.6	+31.50
11-12	14	58	7	8	4	39	12.1	-6.25
10-11	15	70	14	7	6	43	20.0	+14.25

BY MONTH

NH Flat	W-R	Per cent	£1 Level Stake	Hurdles	W-R	Per cent	£1 Level Stake
May	0-0	0.0	0.00	May	1-5	20.0	+2.00
June	0-1	0.0	-1.00	June	1-6	16.7	+7.00
July	0-0	0.0	0.00	July	0-11	0.0	-11.00
August	0-0	0.0	0.00	August	0-5	0.0	-5.00
September	0-0	0.0	0.00	September	0-3	0.0	-3.00
October	0-0	0.0	0.00	October	1-3	33.3	+0.50
November	0-0	0.0	0.00	November	0-4	0.0	-4.00
December	0-0	0.0	0.00	December	1-4	25.0	+22.00
January	0-0	0.0	0.00	January	0-0	0.0	0.00
February	0-0	0.0	0.00	February	0-1	0.0	-1.00
March	0-0	0.0	0.00	March	2-7	28.6	+6.00
April	0-0	0.0	0.00	April	1-4	25.0	+11.00

Chases	W-R	Per cent	£1 Level Stake	Totals	W-R	Per cent	£1 Level Stake
May	0-1	0.0	-1.00	May	1-6	16.7	+1.00
June	1-1	100.0	+14.00	June	2-8	25.0	+20.00
July	0-2	0.0	-2.00	July	0-13	0.0	-13.00
August	0-3	0.0	-3.00	August	0-8	0.0	-8.00
September	0-3	0.0	-3.00	September	0-6	0.0	-6.00
October	1-3	33.3	+2.00	October	2-6	33.3	+2.50
November	0-3	0.0	-3.00	November	0-7	0.0	-7.00
December	0-2	0.0	-2.00	December	1-6	16.7	+20.00
January	0-0	0.0	0.00	January	0-0	0.0	0.00
February	0-2	0.0	-2.00	February	0-3	0.0	-3.00
March	0-2	0.0	-2.00	March	2-9	22.2	+4.00
April	2-5	40.0	+10.00	April	3-9	33.3	+21.00

DISTANCE

Hurdles	W-R	Per cent	£1 Level Stake	Chases	W-R	Per cent	£1 Level Stake
2m-2m3f	5-27	18.5	+30.50	2m-2m3f	0-7	0.0	-7.00
2m4f-2m7f	2-22	9.1	-2.00	2m4f-2m7f	0-7	0.0	-7.00
3m+	0-4	0.0	-4.00	3m+	4-13	30.8	+22.00

TYPE OF RACE

Non-Handicaps	W-R	Per cent	£1 Level Stake	Handicaps	W-R	Per cent	£1 Level Stake
Nov Hrdls	1-12	8.3	+14.00	Nov Hrdls	1-4	25.0	+4.00
Hrdls	2-8	25.0	+0.50	Hrdls	3-28	10.7	+7.00
Nov Chs	0-4	0.0	-4.00	Nov Chs	0-0	0.0	0.00
Chases	0-0	0.0	0.00	Chases	4-23	17.4	+12.00
Sell/Claim	0-3	0.0	-3.00	Sell/Claim	0-0	0.0	0.00

RACE CLASS

	W-R	Per cent	£1 Level Stake
Class 1	0-3	0.0	-3.00
Class 2	0-2	0.0	-2.00
Class 3	0-10	0.0	-10.00
Class 4	7-40	17.5	+31.50
Class 5	4-25	16.0	+16.00
Class 6	0-1	0.0	-1.00

FIRST TIME OUT

	W-R	Per cent	£1 Level Stake
Bumpers	0-1	0.0	-1.00
Hurdles	4-19	21.1	+25.50
Chases	1-6	16.7	+9.00
Totals	5-26	19.2	+33.50

JOCKEYS

	W-R	Per cent	£1 Level Stake
Adam Wedge	3-9	33.3	+19.00
Paul Moloney	3-39	7.7	-20.50
Mr J F Mathias	2-3	66.7	+19.00
Nick Scholfield	1-2	50.0	+24.00
Mr B Gibbs	1-4	25.0	+1.00
Tom Scudamore	1-8	12.5	+5.00

COURSE RECORD

	Total W-R	Non-Hndcps Hurdles	Chases	Hndcps Hurdles	Chases	NH Flat	Per cent	£1 Level Stake
Ffos Las	5-19	3-7	0-2	0-3	2-7	0-0	26.3	+30.50
Chepstow	2-4	0-0	0-1	2-3	0-0	0-0	50.0	+19.00

Nton Abbot	2-9	0-3	0-0	1-4	1-2	0-0	22.2	+13.00
Ludlow	1-3	0-1	0-0	0-0	1-2	0-0	33.3	+2.00
Stratford	1-5	0-0	0-0	1-5	0-0	0-0	20.0	+8.00

WINNING HORSES

Horse	Races Run	1st	2nd	3rd	£
Accordingtopalm	3	1	0	0	3899
Sir Mattie	7	2	0	1	7538
Smiling Lady	5	1	0	1	3249
Changing Lanes	5	1	0	2	3120
Molon Labe	4	2	1	0	3119
Fishing Bridge	2	1	0	0	3119
Superman De La Rue	4	1	1	0	3080
Major Decision	2	1	0	0	2395
Cresswell Bramble	4	1	0	2	1949
Total winning prize-money					£31468
Favourites	1-6		16.7%		-1.00

January	2-4	50.0	-0.60	January	6-15	40.0	+18.60
February	0-5	0.0	-5.00	February	3-17	17.6	-4.63
March	2-8	25.0	+10.25	March	4-19	21.1	+12.13
April	1-3	33.3	-1.00	April	3-10	30.0	-0.70

DISTANCE

Hurdles	W-R	Per cent	£1 Level Stake	Chases	W-R	Per cent	£1 Level Stake
2m-2m3f	13-44	29.5	+46.95	2m-2m3f	5-15	33.3	+1.15
2m4f-2m7f	4-26	15.4	-15.93	2m4f-2m7f	1-14	7.1	-12.00
3m+	4-15	26.7	+2.20	3m+	3-24	12.5	+7.50

TYPE OF RACE

Non-Handicaps	W-R	Per cent	£1 Level Stake	Handicaps	W-R	Per cent	£1 Level Stake
Nov Hrdls	9-32	28.1	-6.15	Nov Hrdls	1-2	50.0	+8.00
Hrdls	1-11	9.1	+4.00	Hrdls	9-38	23.7	+22.38
Nov Chs	1-7	14.3	-5.00	Nov Chs	1-6	16.7	-4.60
Chases	0-0	0.0	0.00	Chases	7-40	17.5	+6.25
Sell/Claim	0-1	0.0	-1.00	Sell/Claim	0-0	0.0	0.00

KEITH REVELEY

LINGDALE, REDCAR & CLEVELAND

	No. of Hrs	Races Run	1st	2nd	3rd	Unpl	Per cent	£1 Level Stake
NH Flat	7	15	4	2	2	7	26.7	+1.38
Hurdles	26	85	21	14	11	39	24.7	+33.22
Chases	16	53	9	5	4	35	17.0	-3.35
Totals	39	153	34	21	17	81	22.2	+31.25
11-12	44	197	30	37	25	105	15.2	-16.18
10-11	42	167	23	25	24	95	13.8	+27.83

BY MONTH

NH Flat	W-R	Per cent	£1 Level Stake	Hurdles	W-R	Per cent	£1 Level Stake
May	0-0	0.0	0.00	May	2-10	20.0	-0.60
June	0-0	0.0	0.00	June	1-2	50.0	+0.75
July	0-0	0.0	0.00	July	3-7	42.9	+2.58
August	0-0	0.0	0.00	August	1-3	33.3	+1.00
September	0-0	0.0	0.00	September	0-0	0.0	0.00
October	0-1	0.0	-1.00	October	0-2	0.0	-2.00
November	0-1	0.0	-1.00	November	3-14	21.4	+3.50
December	0-2	0.0	-2.00	December	4-17	23.5	+11.63
January	2-4	50.0	+4.00	January	2-7	28.6	+15.20
February	1-4	25.0	-1.63	February	2-8	25.0	+2.00
March	0-1	0.0	-1.00	March	2-10	20.0	+2.88
April	1-2	50.0	+4.00	April	1-5	20.0	-3.70

Chases	W-R	Per cent	£1 Level Stake	Totals	W-R	Per cent	£1 Level Stake
May	1-8	12.5	+0.50	May	3-18	16.7	-0.10
June	0-1	0.0	-1.00	June	1-3	33.3	-0.25
July	0-1	0.0	-1.00	July	3-8	37.5	+1.58
August	0-0	0.0	0.00	August	1-3	33.3	+1.00
September	0-0	0.0	0.00	September	0-0	0.0	0.00
October	1-1	100.0	+7.00	October	1-4	25.0	+4.00
November	1-12	8.3	-8.00	November	4-27	14.8	-5.50
December	1-10	10.0	-4.50	December	5-29	17.2	+5.13

RACE CLASS

	W-R	Per cent	£1 Level Stake
Class 1	0-5	0.0	-5.00
Class 2	2-14	14.3	-3.13
Class 3	5-28	17.9	-2.25
Class 4	20-68	29.4	+37.25
Class 5	3-24	12.5	+2.00
Class 6	4-14	28.6	+2.38

FIRST TIME OUT

	W-R	Per cent	£1 Level Stake
Bumpers	1-7	14.3	-3.50
Hurdles	4-18	22.2	+2.13
Chases	1-14	7.1	-6.00
Totals	6-39	15.4	-7.37

JOCKEYS

	W-R	Per cent	£1 Level Stake
James Reveley	29-114	25.4	+47.05
Jonathan England	3-9	33.3	+2.70
Mr Colm McCormack	1-7	14.3	-1.00
Mr R Lindsay	1-11	9.1	-5.50

COURSE RECORD

	Total W-R	Non-Hndcps Hurdles	Chases	Hndcps Hurdles	Chases	NH Flat	Per cent	£1 Level Stake
Southwell	8-22	4-6	0-0	2-9	1-5	1-2	36.4	+20.00
Doncaster	7-26	0-4	0-1	4-9	2-10	1-2	26.9	+28.25
Catterick	7-32	2-13	0-2	2-3	3-9	0-5	21.9	-7.77
Kelso	3-8	1-1	1-1	0-2	1-3	0-1	37.5	+3.90
Newcastle	3-12	1-4	0-0	0-3	1-3	1-2	25.0	+0.80
Uttoxeter	2-7	0-1	0-1	1-3	0-1	1-1	28.6	+4.00
Perth	1-1	1-1	0-0	0-0	0-0	0-0	100.0	+1.20
Haydock	1-4	0-1	0-0	1-3	0-0	0-0	25.0	-1.13
Musselbgh	1-8	1-5	0-1	0-0	0-2	0-0	12.5	+7.00
Sedgefield	1-17	1-6	0-1	0-3	0-6	0-1	5.9	-9.00

WINNING HORSES

Horse	Races Run	1st	2nd	3rd	£
Crowning Jewel	7	2	2	2	14621
Benny Be Good	2	1	1	0	9812
Night In Milan	8	2	2	2	11696
Brave Spartacus	10	4	0	1	18965
Robbie	8	4	0	0	14301
Kings Grey	4	1	1	1	5653
Cue To Cue	3	1	1	0	4431
Categorical	7	1	0	0	3861
Broctune Papa Gio	4	1	0	0	3249
*Waltz Darling	2	1	0	1	3249
Special Catch	5	2	0	0	6173
Vinetta	6	1	1	0	3249
Tekthelot	6	1	2	2	3165
Harvey's Hope	8	2	1	1	5788
Victor Hewgo	5	3	1	0	8187
Mr Puck	4	1	1	2	3119
Seren Gris	1	1	0	0	2534
Flora's Pride	4	1	1	1	2496
Dance Of Time	4	2	0	0	3202
Flemens Pride	2	1	0	0	1560
Delta Forty	2	1	1	0	1560
Total winning prize-money					**£130871**
Favourites	12-25		48.0%		-0.13

LYDIA RICHARDS

FUNTINGTON, W SUSSEX

	No. of Hrs	Races Run	1st	2nd	3rd	Unpl	Per cent	£1 Level Stake
NH Flat	1	1	0	0	0	1	0.0	-1.00
Hurdles	4	9	0	2	1	6	0.0	-9.00
Chases	2	14	4	4	3	3	28.6	+3.50
Totals	6	24	4	6	4	10	16.7	-6.50
11-12	6	23	0	1	5	17	0.0	-23.00
10-11	4	17	1	2	1	13	5.9	-12.00

JOCKEYS

	W-R	Per cent	£1 Level Stake
Marc Goldstein	4-15	26.7	+2.50

COURSE RECORD

	Total W-R	Non-Hndcps Hurdles	Chases	Hndcps Hurdles	Chases	NH Flat	Per cent	£1 Level Stake
Fontwell	4-17	0-1	0-1	0-4	4-10	0-1	23.5	+0.50

WINNING HORSES

Horse	Races Run	1st	2nd	3rd	£
Venetian Lad	12	4	3	2	10592
Total winning prize-money					**£10592**
Favourites	0-33		0.0%		-33.00

NICKY RICHARDS

GREYSTOKE, CUMBRIA

	No. of Hrs	Races Run	1st	2nd	3rd	Unpl	Per cent	£1 Level Stake
NH Flat	6	10	1	3	1	5	10.0	-6.00
Hurdles	30	106	18	9	10	69	17.0	-2.53
Chases	12	39	6	7	7	19	15.4	+0.67
Totals	45	155	25	19	18	93	16.1	-7.86
11-12	51	170	29	28	23	90	17.1	-18.65
10-11	52	190	18	17	20	135	9.5	-69.66

BY MONTH

NH Flat	W-R	Per cent	£1 Level Stake		Hurdles	W-R	Per cent	£1 Level Stake
May	0-1	0.0	-1.00		May	0-11	0.0	-11.00
June	0-0	0.0	0.00		June	1-6	16.7	-4.17
July	0-0	0.0	0.00		July	1-6	16.7	+2.50
August	0-0	0.0	0.00		August	2-6	33.3	+2.75
September	0-0	0.0	0.00		September	1-2	50.0	+3.50
October	0-0	0.0	0.00		October	2-10	20.0	+1.38
November	0-1	0.0	-1.00		November	2-8	25.0	-0.40
December	0-2	0.0	-2.00		December	3-14	21.4	+19.53
January	0-1	0.0	-1.00		January	2-13	15.4	-7.75
February	1-1	100.0	+3.00		February	3-9	33.3	+1.13
March	0-1	0.0	-1.00		March	1-7	14.3	+4.00
April	0-3	0.0	-3.00		April	0-14	0.0	-14.00

Chases	W-R	Per cent	£1 Level Stake		Totals	W-R	Per cent	£1 Level Stake
May	2-5	40.0	+13.50		May	2-17	11.8	+1.50
June	1-4	25.0	-2.33		June	2-10	20.0	-6.50
July	0-1	0.0	-1.00		July	1-7	14.3	+1.50
August	0-0	0.0	0.00		August	2-6	33.3	+2.75
September	1-3	33.3	+3.00		September	2-5	40.0	+6.50
October	0-3	0.0	-3.00		October	2-13	15.4	-1.62
November	0-4	0.0	-4.00		November	2-13	15.4	-5.40
December	1-7	14.3	+4.00		December	4-23	17.4	+21.53
January	0-0	0.0	0.00		January	2-14	14.3	-8.75
February	1-4	25.0	-1.50		February	5-14	35.7	+2.63
March	0-5	0.0	-5.00		March	1-13	7.7	-2.00
April	0-3	0.0	-3.00		April	0-20	0.0	-20.00

DISTANCE

Hurdles	W-R	Per cent	£1 Level Stake		Chases	W-R	Per cent	£1 Level Stake
2m-2m3f	9-49	18.4	-15.40		2m-2m3f	1-10	10.0	-4.00
2m4f-2m7f	8-42	19.0	+19.37		2m4f-2m7f	3-19	15.8	-0.83
3m+	1-15	6.7	-6.50		3m+	2-10	20.0	+5.50

TYPE OF RACE

Non-Handicaps	W-R	Per cent	£1 Level Stake		Handicaps	W-R	Per cent	£1 Level Stake
Nov Hrdls	7-35	20.0	-5.12		Nov Hrdls	1-4	25.0	+7.00
Hrdls	2-17	11.8	-11.67		Hrdls	8-50	16.0	+7.25

Nov Chs	2-11	18.2	-3.33	Nov Chs	2-3	66.7	+10.50
Chases	1-2	50.0	+11.00	Chases	1-23	4.3	-17.50
Sell/Claim	0-2	0.0	-2.00	Sell/Claim	0-0	0.0	0.00

RACE CLASS

	W-R	Per cent	£1 Level Stake
Class 1	0-7	0.0	-7.00
Class 2	1-8	12.5	-4.50
Class 3	3-32	9.4	+0.50
Class 4	14-74	18.9	-6.37
Class 5	6-27	22.2	+12.50
Class 6	1-7	14.3	-3.00

FIRST TIME OUT

	W-R	Per cent	£1 Level Stake
Bumpers	0-6	0.0	-6.00
Hurdles	3-29	10.3	-15.79
Chases	3-10	30.0	+14.50
Totals	6-45	13.3	-7.29

JOCKEYS

	W-R	Per cent	£1 Level Stake
Brian Harding	10-67	14.9	-6.15
Dougie Costello	6-38	15.8	+0.75
B T Treanor	3-9	33.3	+2.03
Davy Russell	2-7	28.6	-3.50
Fearghal Davis	2-13	15.4	+1.00
Richard Johnson	1-1	100.0	+5.00
Miss J R Richards	1-9	11.1	+4.00

COURSE RECORD

	Total W-R	Non-Hndcps Hurdles	Chases	Hndcps Hurdles	Chases	NH Flat	Per cent	£1 Level Stake
Kelso	5-21	3-12	1-4	0-2	0-2	1-1	23.8	+11.25
Sedgefield	4-9	1-3	0-1	1-2	2-2	0-1	44.4	+20.03
Newcastle	3-12	2-6	0-0	1-4	0-1	0-1	25.0	-5.03
Carlisle	2-6	2-2	0-0	0-1	0-2	0-1	33.3	+6.13
Mrket Rsn	2-10	0-1	0-2	2-5	0-2	0-0	20.0	-1.75
Musselbgh	2-16	0-3	0-0	2-8	0-2	0-3	12.5	+10.50
Ayr	2-22	0-5	0-0	1-7	1-8	0-2	9.1	-14.00
Hexham	1-2	0-0	1-1	0-1	0-0	0-0	50.0	-0.33
Southwell	1-3	0-1	0-0	1-2	0-0	0-0	33.3	+5.50
Cartmel	1-4	1-3	0-0	0-0	0-1	0-0	25.0	-2.17
Worcester	1-4	0-1	1-1	0-2	0-0	0-0	25.0	+2.00
Perth	1-7	0-3	0-1	1-2	0-1	0-0	14.3	-1.00

WINNING HORSES

Horse	Races Run	1st	2nd	3rd	£
Duke Of Navan	4	3	0	0	17220
Parc Des Princes	9	2	1	0	9422
Simply Ned	5	1	0	1	5523
Glingerbank	4	2	0	0	7733
Streams Of Whiskey	5	1	0	1	3899
And The Man	4	1	0	0	3769
Itzacliche	3	1	0	0	3120
One For Harry	7	2	0	0	4809
Scarlet Fire	4	1	0	0	3119
Eduard	6	2	2	1	5978
Peachey Moment	6	1	1	0	3054
Hannah Jacques	6	2	1	0	5319
Benmadigan	7	2	0	1	4744

Houston Dynimo	6	1	1	3	2599
Flinty Bay	3	1	1	0	2372
Tutchec	7	1	1	1	2079
Brijomi Queen	4	1	1	0	1949
Total winning prize-money					£86708
Favourites	8-22		36.4%		-5.99

DAVID RICHARDS

LLANTILIO CROSSENNY,MONMOUTHS

	No. of Hrs	Races Run	1st	2nd	3rd	Unpl	Per cent	£1 Level Stake
NH Flat	1	3	0	0	0	3	0.0	-3.00
Hurdles	1	7	1	0	1	5	14.3	-2.67
Chases	1	1	0	0	1	0	0.0	-1.00
Totals	2	11	1	0	2	8	9.1	-6.67
11-12	1	5	2	0	0	3	40.0	+7.00
10-11	2	8	2	1	0	5	25.0	-1.00

JOCKEYS

	W-R	Per cent	£1 Level Stake
Robert Williams	1-5	20.0	-0.67

COURSE RECORD

	Total W-R	Non-Hndcps Hurdles	Chases	Hndcps Hurdles	Chases	NH Flat	Per cent	£1 Level Stake
Hereford	1-2	0-0	0-0	1-2	0-0	0-0	50.0	+2.33

WINNING HORSES

Horse	Races Run	1st	2nd	3rd	£
Another Kate	8	1	0	2	2469
Total winning prize-money					£2469
Favourites	0-0		0.0%		0.00

MARK RIMELL

LEAFIELD, OXON

	No. of Hrs	Races Run	1st	2nd	3rd	Unpl	Per cent	£1 Level Stake
NH Flat	6	8	2	1	0	5	25.0	+19.00
Hurdles	7	15	3	0	2	10	20.0	+5.00
Chases	2	5	0	1	0	4	0.0	-5.00
Totals	11	28	5	2	2	19	17.9	+19.00
11-12	18	80	4	7	10	58	5.0	-62.13
10-11	16	70	6	8	6	50	8.6	-11.09

JOCKEYS

	W-R	Per cent	£1 Level Stake
Tom Scudamore	3-13	23.1	+13.00
Nick Scholfield	2-2	100.0	+19.00

COURSE RECORD

	Total W-R	Non-Hndcps Hurdles Chases	Hndcps Hurdles	Chases	NH Flat	Per cent	£1 Level Stake
Plumpton	1-1	0-0 0-0	1-1	0-0	0-0	100.0	+7.00
Uttoxeter	1-1	0-0 0-0	0-0	0-0	1-1	100.0	+15.00
Fontwell	1-2	0-1 0-0	1-1	0-0	0-0	50.0	+3.00
Mrket Rsn	1-2	0-0 0-0	0-1	0-0	1-1	50.0	+9.00
Wincanton	1-2	0-0 0-0	1-1	0-0	0-1	50.0	+5.00

WINNING HORSES

Horse	Races Run	1st	2nd	3rd	£
Azulada Bay	4	2	0	1	5203
Definite Lady	2	1	0	0	1689
Benefit Cut	1	1	0	0	1365
Jazz Man	2	1	0	0	0
Total winning prize-money					£8257
Favourites	0-0		0.0%		0.00

BETH ROBERTS

BLAENGARW, BRIDGEND

	No. of Hrs	Races Run	1st	2nd	3rd	Unpl	Per cent	£1 Level Stake
NH Flat	2	3	0	0	1	2	0.0	-3.00
Hurdles	3	9	1	0	0	8	11.1	-1.00
Chases	0	0	0	0	0	0	0.0	0.00
Totals	4	12	1	0	1	10	8.3	-4.00
11-12	1	3	0	0	0	3	0.0	-3.00
10-11	1	1	0	1	0	0	0.0	-1.00

JOCKEYS

	W-R	Per cent	£1 Level Stake
James Cowley	1-1	100.0	+7.00

COURSE RECORD

	Total W-R	Non-Hndcps Hurdles Chases	Hndcps Hurdles	Chases	NH Flat	Per cent	£1 Level Stake
Ffos Las	1-4	0-3 0-0	1-1	0-0	0-0	25.0	+4.00

WINNING HORSES

Horse	Races Run	1st	2nd	3rd	£
Copper Carroll	6	1	0	0	2144
Total winning prize-money					£2144
Favourites	0-0		0.0%		0.00

DAVE ROBERTS

KENLEY, SHROPSHIRE

	No. of Hrs	Races Run	1st	2nd	3rd	Unpl	Per cent	£1 Level Stake
NH Flat	1	1	0	0	0	1	0.0	-1.00
Hurdles	9	21	1	1	3	16	4.8	-4.00

Chases	4	11	1	1	3	6	9.1	-1.00
Totals	12	33	2	2	6	23	6.1	-6.00
11-12	9	31	4	5	4	18	12.9	+8.50

JOCKEYS

	W-R	Per cent	£1 Level Stake
Lee Edwards	2-32	6.3	-5.00

COURSE RECORD

	Total W-R	Non-Hndcps Hurdles Chases	Hndcps Hurdles	Chases	NH Flat	Per cent	£1 Level Stake
Hexham	1-2	0-0 0-0	1-1	0-1	0-0	50.0	+15.00
Uttoxeter	1-3	0-0 0-0	0-2	1-1	0-0	33.3	+7.00

WINNING HORSES

Horse	Races Run	1st	2nd	3rd	£
Bellaboosh	2	1	0	1	2703
Highland River	6	1	0	2	1997
Total winning prize-money					£4700
Favourites	0-1		0.0%		-1.00

RENEE ROBESON

TYRINGHAM, BUCKS

	No. of Hrs	Races Run	1st	2nd	3rd	Unpl	Per cent	£1 Level Stake
NH Flat	4	4	0	0	2	2	0.0	-4.00
Hurdles	15	58	7	8	6	37	12.1	-8.75
Chases	3	7	0	0	3	4	0.0	-7.00
Totals	17	69	7	8	11	43	10.1	-19.75
11-12	17	69	9	11	8	41	13.0	+69.25
10-11	21	67	8	7	10	42	11.9	-21.38

JOCKEYS

	W-R	Per cent	£1 Level Stake
Jimmy McCarthy	3-14	21.4	+4.25
Brendan Powell	2-4	50.0	+16.00
Joshua Moore	1-7	14.3	-0.50
Tom O'Brien	1-9	11.1	-4.50

COURSE RECORD

	Total W-R	Non-Hndcps Hurdles Chases	Hndcps Hurdles	Chases	NH Flat	Per cent	£1 Level Stake
Haydock	1-2	0-0 0-0	1-2	0-0	0-0	50.0	+2.50
Kempton	1-2	1-1 0-0	0-0	0-1	0-0	50.0	+8.00
Ludlow	1-2	0-1 0-0	1-1	0-0	0-0	50.0	+8.00
Fakenham	1-4	0-1 0-0	1-3	0-0	0-0	25.0	+2.50
Worcester	1-4	0-1 0-0	1-2	0-0	0-1	25.0	+6.00
Southwell	1-7	0-1 0-0	1-5	0-0	0-1	14.3	-3.25
Uttoxeter	1-7	0-1 0-0	1-3	0-2	0-1	14.3	-2.50

WINNING HORSES

Horse	Races Run	1st	2nd	3rd	£
Grassfinch	4	2	0	0	8382
*Benefit Cut	4	1	1	0	3899
Ogee	5	1	0	0	3574
San Telm	4	1	0	2	3249
Smart Exit	6	1	0	1	3249
The Fonz	6	1	1	1	2669
Total winning prize-money					£25022
Favourites	2-6		33.3%		2.25

PAULINE ROBSON

KIRKHARLE, NORTHUMBERLAND

	No. of Hrs	Races Run	1st	2nd	3rd	Unpl	Per cent	£1 Level Stake
NH Flat	2	3	2	0	0	1	66.7	+6.25
Hurdles	6	18	3	3	2	10	16.7	-2.75
Chases	6	15	5	4	0	6	33.3	+4.73
Totals	11	36	10	7	2	17	27.8	+8.23
11-12	6	25	5	5	3	12	20.0	-3.29
10-11	10	41	4	9	6	22	9.8	-21.50

BY MONTH

NH Flat	W-R	Per cent	£1 Level Stake	Hurdles	W-R	Per cent	£1 Level Stake
May	2-2	100.0	+7.25	May	2-2	100.0	+10.00
June	0-0	0.0	0.00	June	0-1	0.0	-1.00
July	0-0	0.0	0.00	July	0-0	0.0	0.00
August	0-0	0.0	0.00	August	0-0	0.0	0.00
September	0-0	0.0	0.00	September	0-0	0.0	0.00
October	0-0	0.0	0.00	October	0-1	0.0	-1.00
November	0-0	0.0	0.00	November	0-2	0.0	-2.00
December	0-0	0.0	0.00	December	0-4	0.0	-4.00
January	0-0	0.0	0.00	January	0-0	0.0	0.00
February	0-0	0.0	0.00	February	0-1	0.0	-1.00
March	0-0	0.0	0.00	March	0-3	0.0	-3.00
April	0-1	0.0	-1.00	April	1-4	25.0	-0.75

Chases	W-R	Per cent	£1 Level Stake	Totals	W-R	Per cent	£1 Level Stake
May	0-2	0.0	-2.00	May	4-6	66.7	+15.25
June	0-1	0.0	-1.00	June	0-2	0.0	-2.00
July	0-0	0.0	0.00	July	0-0	0.0	0.00
August	0-0	0.0	0.00	August	0-0	0.0	0.00
September	0-0	0.0	0.00	September	0-0	0.0	0.00
October	1-2	50.0	+3.50	October	1-3	33.3	+2.50
November	1-2	50.0	+5.00	November	1-4	25.0	+3.00
December	1-1	100.0	+0.73	December	1-5	20.0	-3.27
January	0-1	0.0	-1.00	January	0-1	0.0	-1.00
February	0-0	0.0	0.00	February	0-1	0.0	-1.00
March	2-4	50.0	+1.50	March	2-7	28.6	-1.50
April	0-2	0.0	-2.00	April	1-7	14.3	-3.75

DISTANCE

Hurdles	W-R	Per cent	£1 Level Stake	Chases	W-R	Per cent	£1 Level Stake
2m-2m3f	0-6	0.0	-6.00	2m-2m3f	0-3	0.0	-3.00
2m4f-2m7f	3-10	30.0	+5.25	2m4f-2m7f	5-7	71.4	+12.73
3m+	0-2	0.0	-2.00	3m+	0-5	0.0	-5.00

TYPE OF RACE

Non-Handicaps	W-R	Per cent	£1 Level Stake	Handicaps	W-R	Per cent	£1 Level Stake
Nov Hrdls	0-2	0.0	-2.00	Nov Hrdls	1-2	50.0	+1.25
Hrdls	0-4	0.0	-4.00	Hrdls	2-10	20.0	+2.00
Nov Chs	3-6	50.0	+3.23	Nov Chs	0-0	0.0	0.00
Chases	0-1	0.0	-1.00	Chases	2-8	25.0	+2.50
Sell/Claim	0-0	0.0	0.00	Sell/Claim	0-0	0.0	0.00

RACE CLASS

	W-R	Per cent	£1 Level Stake
Class 1	0-1	0.0	-1.00
Class 2	1-3	33.3	-1.27
Class 3	5-11	45.5	+13.50
Class 4	2-11	18.2	-2.25
Class 5	0-8	0.0	-8.00
Class 6	2-2	100.0	+7.25

FIRST TIME OUT

	W-R	Per cent	£1 Level Stake
Bumpers	1-2	50.0	+4.00
Hurdles	2-5	40.0	+4.25
Chases	1-4	25.0	+1.50
Totals	4-11	36.4	+9.75

JOCKEYS

	W-R	Per cent	£1 Level Stake
Timmy Murphy	7-13	53.8	+19.25
Richie McGrath	3-10	30.0	+1.98

COURSE RECORD

	Total W-R	Non-Hndcps Hurdles	Chases	Hndcps Hurdles	Chases	NH Flat	Per cent	£1 Level Stake
Carlisle	3-6	0-0	2-4	0-1	1-1	0-0	50.0	+5.00
Perth	3-6	0-0	0-1	2-4	0-0	1-1	50.0	+6.50
Kelso	2-9	0-1	1-1	1-5	0-2	0-0	22.2	-1.27
Musselbgh	1-1	0-0	0-0	0-0	1-1	0-0	100.0	+6.00
Sedgefield	1-3	0-1	0-0	0-0	0-1	1-1	33.3	+3.00

WINNING HORSES

Horse	Races Run	1st	2nd	3rd	£
Rival D'Estruval	5	2	1	0	13228
Humbie	3	2	1	0	14296
Locked Inthepocket	7	3	1	0	14945
Upsilon Bleu	3	1	2	0	6498
Shanen	6	2	1	1	3418
Total winning prize-money					£52385
Favourites	3-12		25.0%		-5.02

BRIAN ROTHWELL

NORTON, N YORKS

	No. of Hrs	Races Run	1st	2nd	3rd	Unpl	Per cent	£1 Level Stake
NH Flat	4	5	0	0	0	5	0.0	-5.00
Hurdles	10	30	3	3	3	21	10.0	-15.77
Chases	0	0	0	0	0	0	0.0	0.00
Totals	**14**	**35**	**3**	**3**	**3**	**26**	**8.6**	**-20.77**
11-12	6	23	0	3	4	16	0.0	-23.00
10-11	7	16	0	0	2	14	0.0	-16.00

JOCKEYS

	W-R	Per cent	£1 Level Stake
A P McCoy	1-1	100.0	+2.00
Harry Haynes	1-2	50.0	+7.50
Dougie Costello	1-14	7.1	-12.27

COURSE RECORD

	Total W-R	Non-Hndcps Hurdles	Chases	Hndcps Hurdles	Chases	NH Flat	Per cent	£1 Level Stake
Wetherby	2-9	0-4	0-0	2-4	0-0	0-1	22.2	-4.27
Ayr	1-2	1-1	0-0	0-1	0-0	0-0	50.0	+7.50

WINNING HORSES

Horse	Races Run	1st	2nd	3rd	£
Bonnie Burnett	8	1	1	2	2599
Tinseltown	7	2	2	0	3559
Total winning prize-money					**£6158**
Favourites	**2-5**		**40.0%**		**-0.27**

RICHARD ROWE

SULLINGTON, W SUSSEX

	No. of Hrs	Races Run	1st	2nd	3rd	Unpl	Per cent	£1 Level Stake
NH Flat	3	4	0	0	0	4	0.0	-4.00
Hurdles	9	21	0	5	2	14	0.0	-21.00
Chases	9	29	1	2	0	26	3.4	-25.25
Totals	**18**	**54**	**1**	**7**	**2**	**44**	**1.9**	**-50.25**
11-12	18	78	7	8	6	57	9.0	-43.97
10-11	28	112	6	8	13	85	5.4	-56.75

JOCKEYS

	W-R	Per cent	£1 Level Stake
Andrew Glassonbury	1-7	14.3	-3.25

COURSE RECORD

	Total W-R	Non-Hndcps Hurdles	Chases	Hndcps Hurdles	Chases	NH Flat	Per cent	£1 Level Stake
Plumpton	1-17	0-2	0-1	0-6	1-7	0-1	5.9	-13.25

WINNING HORSES

Horse	Races Run	1st	2nd	3rd	£
Alteranthela	4	1	1	0	3329
Total winning prize-money					**£3329**
Favourites	**0-5**		**0.0%**		**-5.00**

PHILIP ROWLEY

BRIDGNORTH, SHORPSHIRE

	No. of Hrs	Races Run	1st	2nd	3rd	Unpl	Per cent	£1 Level Stake
NH Flat	0	0	0	0	0	0	0.0	0.00
Hurdles	0	0	0	0	0	0	0.0	0.00
Chases	4	7	3	1	2	1	42.9	+16.38
Totals	**4**	**7**	**3**	**1**	**2**	**1**	**42.9**	**+16.38**
11-12	4	13	2	3	0	8	15.4	+5.00
10-11	3	6	1	1	0	4	16.7	+3.00

JOCKEYS

	W-R	Per cent	£1 Level Stake
Mr Alex Edwards	2-2	100.0	+17.88
Miss J C Williams	1-4	25.0	-0.50

COURSE RECORD

	Total W-R	Non-Hndcps Hurdles	Chases	Hndcps Hurdles	Chases	NH Flat	Per cent	£1 Level Stake
Ludlow	3-5	0-0	3-5	0-0	0-0	0-0	60.0	+18.38

WINNING HORSES

Horse	Races Run	1st	2nd	3rd	£
*Surenaga	2	1	0	1	2496
The General Lee	3	1	0	1	2184
*Forest Walker	1	1	0	0	1872
Total winning prize-money					**£6552**
Favourites	**2-3**		**66.7%**		**3.38**

LUCINDA RUSSELL

ARLARY, PERTH & KINROSS

	No. of Hrs	Races Run	1st	2nd	3rd	Unpl	Per cent	£1 Level Stake
NH Flat	24	33	7	4	7	15	21.2	+8.38
Hurdles	66	230	26	27	32	145	11.3	-97.19
Chases	54	219	26	38	25	130	11.9	-100.75
Totals	**104**	**482**	**59**	**69**	**64**	**290**	**12.2**	**-189.56**
11-12	94	453	57	69	66	261	12.6	-122.17
10-11	78	348	42	43	40	223	12.1	-112.50

	W-R	Per cent	£1 Level Stake			
Class 5	14-99	14.1	-32.77	Totals	14-104	13.5	-27.40
Class 6	6-27	22.2	+7.38			

BY MONTH

NH Flat	W-R	Per cent	£1 Level Stake	Hurdles	W-R	Per cent	£1 Level Stake
May	1-2	50.0	+3.50	May	2-22	9.1	-12.50
June	0-2	0.0	-2.00	June	3-16	18.8	+2.00
July	0-0	0.0	0.00	July	1-11	9.1	-5.00
August	0-1	0.0	-1.00	August	4-22	18.2	-2.88
September	0-2	0.0	-2.00	September	1-10	10.0	-4.00
October	1-4	25.0	+7.00	October	3-18	16.7	-8.03
November	3-5	60.0	+11.00	November	3-21	14.3	-2.38
December	0-3	0.0	-3.00	December	2-25	8.0	-13.50
January	0-4	0.0	-4.00	January	4-17	23.5	-4.42
February	1-2	50.0	+4.00	February	0-16	0.0	-16.00
March	0-3	0.0	-3.00	March	0-22	0.0	-22.00
April	1-5	20.0	-2.13	April	3-30	10.0	-8.50

Chases	W-R	Per cent	£1 Level Stake	Totals	W-R	Per cent	£1 Level Stake
May	2-11	18.2	+2.00	May	5-35	14.3	-7.00
June	1-11	9.1	-8.13	June	4-29	13.8	-8.13
July	1-7	14.3	-3.00	July	2-18	11.1	-8.00
August	4-16	25.0	-3.75	August	8-39	20.5	-7.63
September	0-12	0.0	-12.00	September	1-24	4.2	-18.00
October	3-23	13.0	-8.88	October	7-45	15.6	-9.91
November	3-28	10.7	-13.25	November	9-54	16.7	-4.63
December	2-21	9.5	-15.40	December	4-49	8.2	-31.90
January	2-19	10.5	-13.06	January	6-40	15.0	-21.48
February	3-21	14.3	-8.63	February	4-39	10.3	-20.63
March	4-20	20.0	+9.83	March	4-45	8.9	-15.17
April	1-30	3.3	-26.50	April	5-65	7.7	-37.13

DISTANCE

Hurdles	W-R	Per cent	£1 Level Stake	Chases	W-R	Per cent	£1 Level Stake
2m-2m3f	10-115	8.7	-62.63	2m-2m3f	8-54	14.8	-20.93
2m4f-2m7f	7-68	10.3	-40.82	2m4f-2m7f	13-85	15.3	-20.00
3m+	9-47	19.1	+6.25	3m+	5-80	6.3	-59.82

TYPE OF RACE

Non-Handicaps

	W-R	Per cent	£1 Level Stake	Handicaps	W-R	Per cent	£1 Level Stake
Nov Hrdls	9-71	12.7	-30.04	Nov Hrdls	1-25	4.0	-16.00
Hrdls	5-28	17.9	-10.78	Hrdls	11-99	11.1	-33.38
Nov Chs	5-33	15.2	-13.68	Nov Chs	3-24	12.5	-13.00
Chases	2-5	40.0	+1.60	Chases	16-157	10.2	-75.67
Sell/Claim	0-8	0.0	-8.00	Sell/Claim	0-0	0.0	0.00

RACE CLASS

	W-R	Per cent	£1 Level Stake
Class 1	1-20	5.0	-17.90
Class 2	2-18	11.1	-8.00
Class 3	8-78	10.3	-31.92
Class 4	28-240	11.7	-106.35

FIRST TIME OUT

	W-R	Per cent	£1 Level Stake
Bumpers	6-24	25.0	+14.50
Hurdles	4-44	9.1	-29.90
Chases	4-36	11.1	-12.00

JOCKEYS

	W-R	Per cent	£1 Level Stake
Peter Buchanan	27-199	13.6	-76.38
Craig Nichol	7-52	13.5	-17.25
Grant Cockburn	7-55	12.7	-14.75
Campbell Gillies	4-23	17.4	-2.63
Graham Watters	4-44	9.1	-20.63
A P McCoy	3-8	37.5	-0.68
Tom Scudamore	3-22	13.6	-5.25
Steven Fox	3-52	5.8	-31.00
Miss C Walton	1-6	16.7	0.00

COURSE RECORD

	Total W-R	Non-Hndcps Hurdles	Chases	Hndcps Hurdles	Chases	NH Flat	Per cent	£1 Level Stake
Perth	17-107	5-21	1-4	6-38	5-38	0-6	15.9	-13.88
Ayr	12-53	3-14	3-8	1-12	3-12	2-7	22.6	-12.02
Hexham	11-42	4-11	0-2	2-12	3-13	2-4	26.2	-2.27
Carlisle	5-43	0-6	1-3	0-7	2-22	2-5	11.6	-7.50
Newcastle	4-35	1-10	0-1	2-6	1-16	0-2	11.4	+2.50
Uttoxeter	2-6	0-0	1-1	0-1	1-4	0-0	33.3	+3.25
Haydock	2-10	0-1	0-1	0-2	1-5	1-1	20.0	+0.50
Sandown	1-1	0-0	1-1	0-0	0-0	0-0	100.0	+1.10
Sedgefield	1-10	1-2	0-0	0-4	0-4	0-0	10.0	-6.25
Cartmel	1-20	0-3	0-2	0-7	1-8	0-0	5.0	-16.50
Wetherby	1-22	0-6	0-3	0-4	1-8	0-1	4.5	-18.50
Musselbgh	1-44	0-9	0-5	0-10	1-16	0-4	2.3	-37.00
Kelso	1-54	0-18	0-4	1-14	0-18	0-0	1.9	-48.00

WINNING HORSES

Horse	Races Run	1st	2nd	3rd	£
Bold Sir Brian	5	2	0	0	21947
Prosecco	5	2	1	1	16245
Green Flag	7	3	3	0	15740
Do It For Dalkey	3	1	2	0	7798
Nuts N Bolts	7	2	0	1	11566
Tap Night	7	3	2	0	7798
Devotion To Duty	6	1	0	0	6498
Kris Cross	7	2	1	0	9097
Tito Bustillo	4	1	1	0	5653
Wild Geese	5	1	1	2	5198
Eyre Apparent	12	2	3	1	9653
Etxalar	7	1	1	0	4874
Degas Art	5	1	0	0	4791
Ballyben	5	1	0	2	4549
Vallani	9	2	0	0	6706
Lucky Sunny	6	2	0	0	6844
Fog Patches	9	2	5	1	6478
Navy List	5	1	0	1	3899
*Lone Foot Laddie	5	1	0	1	3899
Blazin White Face	6	2	1	0	7047
Samstown	7	2	0	0	6678

Dotties Dilema	6	2	1	0	5065
On Broadway	9	1	4	1	3256
Cadore	5	1	2	1	3249
Ryton Runner	10	1	2	3	3249
Urban Kode	12	2	0	4	5883
Rhymers Ha'	6	1	2	0	3249
Stormion	9	2	0	1	3119
*Saphir River	7	1	0	2	3054
Livvy Inn	7	1	1	2	2669
Quinder Spring	9	2	2	1	2599
Glenora Gale	7	1	1	2	2534
Lord Of Drums	11	1	1	2	2259
Rhymers Stone	4	1	0	0	2122
No Deal	2	2	0	0	3418
Imjoeking	5	2	2	1	3490
Delightfully	7	1	0	3	1884
Simarthur	2	1	1	0	1711
Island Confusion	3	1	0	1	1643
Total winning prize-money					**£227411**
Favourites	17-59		28.8%		-9.69

JOHN RYAN
NEWMARKET, SUFFOLK

	No. of Hrs	Races Run	1st	2nd	3rd	Unpl	Per cent	£1 Level Stake
NH Flat	0	0	0	0	0	0	0.0	0.00
Hurdles	2	7	2	2	0	3	28.6	+11.00
Chases	0	0	0	0	0	0	0.0	0.00
Totals	2	7	2	2	0	3	28.6	+11.00
11-12	2	5	0	0	0	5	0.0	-5.00
10-11	4	11	1	0	1	9	9.1	-2.00

JOCKEYS

	W-R	Per cent	£1 Level Stake
Colin Bolger	1-2	50.0	+9.00
Jack Doyle	1-5	20.0	+2.00

COURSE RECORD

	Total W-R	Non-Hndcps Hurdles	Chases	Hndcps Hurdles	Chases	NH Flat	Per cent	£1 Level Stake
Doncaster	1-1	1-1	0-0	0-0	0-0	0-0	100.0	+6.00
Warwick	1-1	1-1	0-0	0-0	0-0	0-0	100.0	+10.00

WINNING HORSES

Horse	Races Run	1st	2nd	3rd	£
Somemothersdohavem	5	1	2	0	3119
Masters Blazing	2	1	0	0	3119
Total winning prize-money					**£6238**
Favourites	0-0		0.0%		0.00

JOHN RYALL
RIMPTON, SOMERSET

	No. of Hrs	Races Run	1st	2nd	3rd	Unpl	Per cent	£1 Level Stake
NH Flat	0	0	0	0	0	0	0.0	0.00
Hurdles	2	2	0	0	0	2	0.0	-2.00
Chases	4	13	1	3	1	8	7.7	-4.50
Totals	5	15	1	3	1	10	6.7	-6.50
11-12	4	16	1	0	3	12	6.3	-12.50
10-11	6	18	0	0	1	17	0.0	-18.00

JOCKEYS

	W-R	Per cent	£1 Level Stake
Nick Scholfield	1-4	25.0	+4.50

COURSE RECORD

	Total W-R	Non-Hndcps Hurdles	Chases	Hndcps Hurdles	Chases	NH Flat	Per cent	£1 Level Stake
Fontwell	1-2	0-0	0-0	0-0	1-2	0-0	50.0	+6.50

WINNING HORSES

Horse	Races Run	1st	2nd	3rd	£
Cypress Grove	6	1	1	1	2339
Total winning prize-money					**£2339**
Favourites	0-0		0.0%		0.00

KEVIN RYAN
HAMBLETON, N YORKS

	No. of Hrs	Races Run	1st	2nd	3rd	Unpl	Per cent	£1 Level Stake
NH Flat	2	3	0	0	1	2	0.0	-3.00
Hurdles	4	9	4	2	1	2	44.4	+8.88
Chases	0	0	0	0	0	0	0.0	0.00
Totals	5	12	4	2	2	4	33.3	+5.88
11-12	6	15	2	4	1	8	13.3	+3.50
10-11	5	8	2	0	1	5	25.0	+6.00

JOCKEYS

	W-R	Per cent	£1 Level Stake
Brian Toomey	3-10	30.0	-3.12
Brian Hughes	1-2	50.0	+9.00

COURSE RECORD

	Total W-R	Non-Hndcps Hurdles	Chases	Hndcps Hurdles	Chases	NH Flat	Per cent	£1 Level Stake
Fakenham	1-1	1-1	0-0	0-0	0-0	0-0	100.0	+1.88
Hexham	1-1	1-1	0-0	0-0	0-0	0-0	100.0	+0.91

Kelso	1-1	0-0	0-0	1-1	0-0	0-0	100.0	+10.00
Carlisle	1-2	0-0	0-0	1-1	0-0	0-1	50.0	+0.10

WINNING HORSES

Horse	Races Run	1st	2nd	3rd	£
Flaming Arrow	4	2	1	1	6404
*Mwaleshi	2	2	0	0	3989
Total winning prize-money					£10393
Favourites	2-3		66.7%		1.01

AYTACH SADIK

WOLVERLEY, WORCS

	No. of Hrs	Races Run	1st	2nd	3rd	Unpl	Per cent	£1 Level Stake
NH Flat	1	2	0	0	0	2	0.0	-2.00
Hurdles	4	15	2	0	0	13	13.3	-8.63
Chases	4	17	2	1	3	11	11.8	+20.50
Totals	5	34	4	1	3	26	11.8	+9.87
11-12	5	33	2	3	1	27	6.1	-19.38
10-11	5	34	2	3	5	24	5.9	-10.00

JOCKEYS

	W-R	Per cent	£1 Level Stake
A P McCoy	2-3	66.7	+3.38
Peter Carberry	1-3	33.3	+5.50
Tommy Phelan	1-6	16.7	+23.00

COURSE RECORD

	Total W-R	Non-Hndcps Hurdles	Chases	Hndcps Hurdles	Chases	NH Flat	Per cent	£1 Level Stake
Bangor	1-1	0-0	0-0	1-1	0-0	0-0	100.0	+2.50
Taunton	1-1	0-0	1-1	0-0	0-0	0-0	100.0	+28.00
Hereford	1-2	0-0	0-0	1-1	0-1	0-0	50.0	+0.88
Nton Abbot	1-2	0-0	0-0	0-1	1-1	0-0	50.0	+6.50

WINNING HORSES

Horse	Races Run	1st	2nd	3rd	£
Apache Dawn	11	1	1	2	4094
*Finch Flyer	10	2	0	0	4684
How's D Strawboss	7	1	0	1	2395
Total winning prize-money					£11173
Favourites	1-1		100.0%		1.88

T F SAGE

TETBURY, GLOUCESTERSHIRE

	No. of Hrs	Races Run	1st	2nd	3rd	Unpl	Per cent	£1 Level Stake
NH Flat	0	0	0	0	0	0	0.0	0.00
Hurdles	0	0	0	0	0	0	0.0	0.00
Chases	1	3	1	0	1	1	33.3	+1.00
Totals	1	3	1	0	1	1	33.3	+1.00
11-12	1	2	1	0	0	1	50.0	+0.50
10-11	1	2	1	1	0	0	50.0	+3.00

JOCKEYS

	W-R	Per cent	£1 Level Stake
Mr M Wall	1-2	50.0	+2.00

COURSE RECORD

	Total W-R	Non-Hndcps Hurdles	Chases	Hndcps Hurdles	Chases	NH Flat	Per cent	£1 Level Stake
Stratford	1-1	0-0	1-1	0-0	0-0	0-0	100.0	+3.00

WINNING HORSES

Horse	Races Run	1st	2nd	3rd	£
*Presentandcorrect	3	1	0	1	1560
Total winning prize-money					£1560
Favourites	0-0		0.0%		0.00

DIANNE SAYER

HACKTHORPE, CUMBRIA

	No. of Hrs	Races Run	1st	2nd	3rd	Unpl	Per cent	£1 Level Stake
NH Flat	3	4	0	1	1	2	0.0	-4.00
Hurdles	24	135	14	9	15	97	10.4	-26.58
Chases	13	49	6	6	7	30	12.2	+9.60
Totals	28	188	20	16	23	129	10.6	-20.98
11-12	28	185	16	22	14	132	8.6	-31.50
10-11	23	134	11	15	8	100	8.2	-65.75

BY MONTH

NH Flat	W-R	Per cent	£1 Level Stake	Hurdles	W-R	Per cent	£1 Level Stake
May	0-0	0.0	0.00	May	3-13	23.1	+12.75
June	0-1	0.0	-1.00	June	2-9	22.2	+4.50
July	0-1	0.0	-1.00	July	2-9	22.2	+6.00
August	0-0	0.0	0.00	August	0-8	0.0	-8.00
September	0-1	0.0	-1.00	September	0-6	0.0	-6.00
October	0-0	0.0	0.00	October	0-14	0.0	-14.00
November	0-0	0.0	0.00	November	0-13	0.0	-13.00
December	0-1	0.0	-1.00	December	1-13	7.7	+8.00
January	0-0	0.0	0.00	January	0-14	0.0	-14.00
February	0-0	0.0	0.00	February	0-11	0.0	-11.00
March	0-0	0.0	0.00	March	1-9	11.1	0.00
April	0-0	0.0	0.00	April	5-16	31.3	+8.17

Chases	W-R	Per cent	£1 Level Stake	Totals	W-R	Per cent	£1 Level Stake
May	0-6	0.0	-6.00	May	3-19	15.8	+6.75
June	0-3	0.0	-3.00	June	2-13	15.4	+0.50
July	1-5	20.0	+6.00	July	3-15	20.0	+11.00
August	1-4	25.0	-1.90	August	1-12	8.3	-9.90
September	0-2	0.0	-2.00	September	0-9	0.0	-9.00
October	0-4	0.0	-4.00	October	0-18	0.0	-18.00

November	1-3	33.3	+0.50	November	1-16	6.3	-12.50
December	0-3	0.0	-3.00	December	1-17	5.9	+4.00
January	1-3	33.3	+1.00	January	1-17	5.9	-13.00
February	1-5	20.0	+12.00	February	1-16	6.3	+1.00
March	0-4	0.0	-4.00	March	1-13	7.7	-4.00
April	1-7	14.3	+14.00	April	6-23	26.1	+22.17

Wetherby	1-11	0-1	0-0	1-10	0-0	0-0	9.1	-4.50

WINNING HORSES

Horse	Races Run	1st	2nd	3rd	£
Cool Baranca	17	3	0	3	14195
Red Kingdom	11	2	2	1	8447
Sergeant Pink	8	1	1	1	3899
Stags Leap	8	1	0	0	3899
Markadam	8	2	1	2	7018
My Friend George	4	1	0	0	3769
*Solis	17	2	2	4	6368
Endeavor	16	2	3	1	6368
Oh Right	8	1	1	3	2599
Worth A King'S	8	2	1	0	3834
Goodlukin Lucy	6	1	0	1	2053
Shoal Bay Dreamer	6	1	0	0	1819
Talk Of Saafend	9	1	2	0	1689
Total winning prize-money					**£65957**
Favourites	3-10		30.0%		-2.98

DISTANCE

Hurdles	W-R	Per cent	£1 Level Stake	Chases	W-R	Per cent	£1 Level Stake
2m-2m3f	9-79	11.4	+3.17	2m-2m3f	1-16	6.3	-12.00
2m4f-2m7f	4-42	9.5	-20.75	2m4f-2m7f	3-22	13.6	-5.40
3m+	1-14	7.1	-9.00	3m+	2-11	18.2	+27.00

TYPE OF RACE

Non-Handicaps	W-R	Per cent	£1 Level Stake	Handicaps	W-R	Per cent	£1 Level Stake
Nov Hrdls	0-11	0.0	-11.00	Nov Hrdls	4-17	23.5	+22.00
Hrdls	0-6	0.0	-6.00	Hrdls	10-99	10.1	-29.58
Nov Chs	0-4	0.0	-4.00	Nov Chs	1-6	16.7	+11.00
Chases	0-0	0.0	0.00	Chases	5-39	12.8	+2.60
Sell/Claim	0-1	0.0	-1.00	Sell/Claim	0-1	0.0	-1.00

RACE CLASS

	W-R	Per cent	£1 Level Stake
Class 1	0-0	0.0	0.00
Class 2	0-3	0.0	-3.00
Class 3	3-27	11.1	+3.00
Class 4	9-96	9.4	-8.23
Class 5	8-58	13.8	-8.75
Class 6	0-4	0.0	-4.00

FIRST TIME OUT

	W-R	Per cent	£1 Level Stake
Bumpers	0-3	0.0	-3.00
Hurdles	1-20	5.0	-18.33
Chases	0-5	0.0	-5.00
Totals	1-28	3.6	-26.33

JOCKEYS

	W-R	Per cent	£1 Level Stake
Miss E C Sayer	10-79	12.7	-12.08
Ryan Mania	3-36	8.3	-16.50
Jason Maguire	2-4	50.0	+9.10
Tony Kelly	2-5	40.0	+5.50
James Reveley	2-29	6.9	+9.00
Henry Brooke	1-10	10.0	+9.00

COURSE RECORD

	Total W-R	Non-Hndcps Hurdles	Chases	Hndcps Hurdles	Chases	NH Flat	Per cent	£1 Level Stake
Cartmel	3-16	0-1	0-0	2-9	1-6	0-0	18.8	+9.50
Mrket Rsn	3-21	0-0	0-0	3-16	0-4	0-0	14.3	-9.08
Sedgefield	2-10	0-1	0-0	2-6	0-3	0-0	20.0	+4.00
Ayr	2-15	0-1	0-1	1-10	1-3	0-0	13.3	-7.00
Carlisle	2-16	0-2	0-1	1-6	1-7	0-0	12.5	+22.00
Kelso	2-20	0-3	0-0	2-10	0-7	0-0	10.0	+6.00
Perth	2-24	0-0	0-0	1-17	1-6	0-1	8.3	-14.90
Newcastle	1-8	0-0	0-0	0-6	1-2	0-0	12.5	+13.00
Uttoxeter	1-9	0-0	0-0	1-7	0-2	0-0	11.1	-5.50
Hexham	1-11	0-3	0-1	0-2	1-4	0-0	9.1	-7.50

JEREMY SCOTT

BROMPTON REGIS, SOMERSET

	No. of Hrs	Races Run	1st	2nd	3rd	Unpl	Per cent	£1 Level Stake
NH Flat	14	23	3	3	3	14	13.0	+19.00
Hurdles	33	144	24	22	24	74	16.7	-43.03
Chases	15	44	3	7	6	28	6.8	-21.25
Totals	47	211	30	32	33	116	14.2	-45.28
11-12	35	138	24	18	15	81	17.4	+25.30
10-11	28	93	14	8	15	56	15.1	+33.46

BY MONTH

NH Flat	W-R	Per cent	£1 Level Stake	Hurdles	W-R	Per cent	£1 Level Stake
May	0-5	0.0	-5.00	May	0-7	0.0	-7.00
June	0-0	0.0	0.00	June	1-2	50.0	+1.25
July	0-0	0.0	0.00	July	2-4	50.0	+4.25
August	0-1	0.0	-1.00	August	2-6	33.3	-1.00
September	0-1	0.0	-1.00	September	1-3	33.3	-0.90
October	1-3	33.3	+5.00	October	1-19	5.3	-16.13
November	1-2	50.0	+7.00	November	2-20	10.0	-12.38
December	0-0	0.0	0.00	December	5-18	27.8	+9.25
January	0-2	0.0	-2.00	January	2-15	13.3	-8.00
February	0-2	0.0	-2.00	February	1-18	5.6	-15.75
March	1-1	100.0	+24.00	March	3-11	27.3	+5.13
April	0-6	0.0	-6.00	April	4-21	19.0	-1.75

Chases	W-R	Per cent	£1 Level Stake	Totals	W-R	Per cent	£1 Level Stake
May	0-1	0.0	-1.00	May	0-13	0.0	-13.00
June	0-2	0.0	-2.00	June	1-4	25.0	-0.75
July	0-2	0.0	-2.00	July	2-6	33.3	+2.25
August	0-0	0.0	0.00	August	2-7	28.6	-2.00
September	1-3	33.3	-0.75	September	2-7	28.6	-2.65
October	1-2	50.0	+1.50	October	3-24	12.5	-9.63

November	0-9	0.0	-9.00	November	3-31	9.7	-14.38
December	0-5	0.0	-5.00	December	5-23	21.7	+4.25
January	0-9	0.0	-9.00	January	2-26	7.7	-19.00
February	0-4	0.0	-4.00	February	1-24	4.2	-21.75
March	0-2	0.0	-2.00	March	4-14	28.6	+27.13
April	1-5	20.0	+12.00	April	5-32	15.6	+4.25

DISTANCE

Hurdles	W-R	Per cent	£1 Level Stake	Chases	W-R	Per cent	£1 Level Stake
2m-2m3f	10-63	15.9	-15.52	2m-2m3f	0-12	0.0	-12.00
2m4f-2m7f	12-61	19.7	-15.00	2m4f-2m7f	1-21	4.8	-18.75
3m+	2-20	10.0	-12.50	3m+	2-11	18.2	+9.50

TYPE OF RACE

Non-Handicaps	W-R	Per cent	£1 Level Stake	Handicaps	W-R	Per cent	£1 Level Stake
Nov Hrdls	8-43	18.6	-9.77	Nov Hrdls	3-12	25.0	-0.50
Hrdls	4-16	25.0	-2.75	Hrdls	9-73	12.3	-30.00
Nov Chs	0-8	0.0	-8.00	Nov Chs	1-9	11.1	-6.75
Chases	0-0	0.0	0.00	Chases	2-27	7.4	-6.50
Sell/Claim	0-0	0.0	0.00	Sell/Claim	0-0	0.0	0.00

RACE CLASS / FIRST TIME OUT

	W-R	Per cent	£1 Level Stake		W-R	Per cent	£1 Level Stake
Class 1	2-8	25.0	-1.25	Bumpers	2-14	14.3	+19.00
Class 2	0-11	0.0	-11.00	Hurdles	4-26	15.4	-11.75
Class 3	5-50	10.0	-23.63	Chases	0-7	0.0	-7.00
Class 4	14-106	13.2	-36.65				
Class 5	7-19	36.8	+11.25	Totals	6-47	12.8	+0.25
Class 6	2-17	11.8	+17.00				

JOCKEYS

	W-R	Per cent	£1 Level Stake
Nick Scholfield	26-146	17.8	-20.65
Matt Griffiths	2-45	4.4	-32.00
Brendan Powell	1-2	50.0	+23.00
Ian Popham	1-4	25.0	-1.63

COURSE RECORD

	Total W-R	Non-Hndcps Hurdles	Chases	Hndcps Hurdles	Chases	NH Flat	Per cent	£1 Level Stake
Wincanton	8-35	3-13	0-1	4-10	0-6	1-5	22.9	+23.63
Nton Abbot	4-10	2-3	0-0	2-5	0-0	0-2	40.0	+0.85
Worcester	3-8	1-1	0-0	1-4	1-2	0-1	37.5	+2.50
Taunton	3-16	1-4	0-1	1-8	0-1	1-2	18.8	+11.00
Exeter	3-32	1-14	0-3	1-8	1-5	0-2	9.4	-9.88
Chepstow	2-12	2-7	0-0	0-3	0-1	0-1	16.7	-4.50
Ludlow	2-12	0-3	0-1	1-3	1-4	0-1	16.7	-5.63
Hereford	1-3	0-0	0-0	1-3	0-0	0-0	33.3	-0.38
Sandown	1-7	1-1	0-0	0-5	0-0	0-1	14.3	-2.50
Cheltenham	1-8	1-2	0-0	0-5	0-0	0-1	12.5	-3.00
Fontwell	1-8	0-1	0-1	1-3	0-3	0-0	12.5	-5.38
Huntingdon	1-12	0-4	0-0	0-3	0-3	1-2	8.3	-4.00

WINNING HORSES

Horse	Races Run	1st	2nd	3rd	£
Melodic Rendezvous	4	3	1	0	38830
Decimus	7	2	1	1	11657
Pericoloso	10	2	1	0	8447
Quaddick Lake	14	3	3	3	11800
Addiction	6	1	2	0	4549
*On The Bridge	7	5	2	0	12775
*Special Account	5	3	0	0	7528
Kilmurvy	8	2	2	3	5482
Mystic Appeal	6	1	0	0	3249
Pyleigh Lass	5	1	1	1	3249
Notarfbad	6	1	1	0	3249
Ballinahow Star	5	2	1	0	5133
Moorlands Mist	5	1	1	1	1949
Alberobello	6	1	2	0	1949
Empiracle	1	1	0	0	1365
Miner Distraction	2	1	0	0	0
Total winning prize-money					£121211
Favourites	14-40		35.0%		-3.52

MISS KATIE SCOTT

GALASHEILS, SCOTTISH BORDERS

	No. of Hrs	Races Run	1st	2nd	3rd	Unpl	Per cent	£1 Level Stake
NH Flat	0	0	0	0	0	0	0.0	0.00
Hurdles	0	0	0	0	0	0	0.0	0.00
Chases	1	1	1	0	0	0	100.0	+4.50
Totals	1	1	1	0	0	0	100.0	+4.50
11-12	1	1	1	0	0	0	100.0	+6.00
10-11	2	2	0	1	0	1	0.0	-2.00

JOCKEYS

	W-R	Per cent	£1 Level Stake
Mr J Hamilton	1-1	100.0	+4.50

COURSE RECORD

	Total W-R	Non-Hndcps Hurdles	Chases	Hndcps Hurdles	Chases	NH Flat	Per cent	£1 Level Stake
Kelso	1-1	0-0	1-1	0-0	0-0	0-0	100.0	+4.50

WINNING HORSES

Horse	Races Run	1st	2nd	3rd	£
*Moscow Menace	1	1	0	0	3120
Total winning prize-money					£3120
Favourites	0-0		0.0%		0.00

MICHAEL SCUDAMORE

BROMSASH, H'FORDS

	No. of Hrs	Races Run	1st	2nd	3rd	Unpl	Per cent	£1 Level Stake
NH Flat	5	8	1	1	0	6	12.5	+13.00
Hurdles	21	48	0	2	4	42	0.0	-48.00
Chases	12	50	6	6	5	33	12.0	+4.75
Totals	29	106	7	9	9	81	6.6	-30.25
11-12	35	123	9	6	13	95	7.3	-58.00
10-11	43	171	9	18	10	134	5.3	-67.00

JOCKEYS

	W-R	Per cent	£1 Level Stake
Tom Scudamore	4-45	8.9	-27.25
Jamie Moore	1-1	100.0	+25.00
P Carberry	1-2	50.0	+9.00
Jack Sherwood	1-5	20.0	+16.00

COURSE RECORD

	Total W-R	Non-Hndcps Hurdles	Chases	Hndcps Hurdles	Chases	NH Flat	Per cent	£1 Level Stake
Chepstow	2-7	0-0	0-0	0-3	1-3	1-1	28.6	+25.00
Southwell	2-10	0-0	0-1	0-2	2-7	0-0	20.0	-2.75
Cheltenham	1-6	0-1	0-1	0-1	1-3	0-0	16.7	+20.00
Fontwell	1-6	0-0	0-0	0-0	1-6	0-0	16.7	-0.50
Ffos Las	1-7	0-0	0-0	0-2	1-3	0-2	14.3	-2.00

WINNING HORSES

Horse	Races Run	1st	2nd	3rd	£
Monbeg Dude	5	2	0	1	79730
Bounds And Leaps	5	2	1	0	7668
Arumun	7	1	0	1	3054
Gunner Rose	5	1	1	0	2534
Sankyouplease	3	1	0	0	1560
Total winning prize-money					£94546
Favourites	1-2		50.0%		1.75

P SENTER

BELBROUGHTON, WORCS

	No. of Hrs	Races Run	1st	2nd	3rd	Unpl	Per cent	£1 Level Stake
NH Flat	0	0	0	0	0	0	0.0	0.00
Hurdles	0	0	0	0	0	0	0.0	0.00
Chases	1	1	1	0	0	0	100.0	+100.00
Totals	1	1	1	0	0	0	100.0	+100.00
11-12	1	1	0	0	0	1	0.0	-1.00

JOCKEYS

	W-R	Per cent	£1 Level Stake
Ben Poste	1-1	100.0	+100.00

COURSE RECORD

	Total W-R	Non-Hndcps Hurdles	Chases	Hndcps Hurdles	Chases	NH Flat	Per cent	£1 Level Stake
Worcester	1-1	0-0	1-1	0-0	0-0	0-0	100.0	+100.00

WINNING HORSES

Horse	Races Run	1st	2nd	3rd	£
The Wife's Sister	1	1	0	0	790
Total winning prize-money					£790
Favourites	0-0		0.0%		0.00

DEREK SHAW

SPROXTON, LEICS

	No. of Hrs	Races Run	1st	2nd	3rd	Unpl	Per cent	£1 Level Stake
NH Flat	1	2	0	0	0	2	0.0	-2.00
Hurdles	3	9	0	1	0	8	0.0	-9.00
Chases	1	7	1	1	3	2	14.3	+2.00
Totals	5	18	1	2	3	12	5.6	-9.00
11-12	7	23	0	1	2	20	0.0	-23.00
10-11	3	4	0	1	2	1	0.0	-4.00

JOCKEYS

	W-R	Per cent	£1 Level Stake
Ollie Garner	1-12	8.3	-3.00

COURSE RECORD

	Total W-R	Non-Hndcps Hurdles	Chases	Hndcps Hurdles	Chases	NH Flat	Per cent	£1 Level Stake
Wetherby	1-3	0-1	0-0	0-0	1-1	0-1	33.3	+6.00

WINNING HORSES

Horse	Races Run	1st	2nd	3rd	£
Thorncliffer	7	1	1	3	2339
Total winning prize-money					£2339
Favourites	0-0		0.0%		0.00

MATT SHEPPARD

EASTNOR, H'FORDS

	No. of Hrs	Races Run	1st	2nd	3rd	Unpl	Per cent	£1 Level Stake
NH Flat	0	0	0	0	0	0	0.0	0.00
Hurdles	11	30	1	1	1	27	3.3	-27.00
Chases	8	37	4	3	6	24	10.8	-18.50
Totals	14	67	5	4	7	51	7.5	-45.50
11-12	14	56	6	4	6	40	10.7	-5.50
10-11	19	65	2	4	5	54	3.1	-26.00

Month	W-R	Per cent	£1 Level Stake		Month	W-R	Per cent	£1 Level Stake
July	0-1	0.0	-1.00		July	0-6	0.0	-6.00
August	0-1	0.0	-1.00		August	0-2	0.0	-2.00
September	0-0	0.0	0.00		September	0-0	0.0	0.00
October	1-3	33.3	0.00		October	2-8	25.0	+3.00
November	2-7	28.6	-1.38		November	9-22	40.9	+9.87
December	1-12	8.3	-7.67		December	4-25	16.0	-4.73
January	1-4	25.0	0.00		January	2-12	16.7	+0.50
February	3-12	25.0	+0.58		February	4-24	16.7	-8.42
March	0-6	0.0	-6.00		March	2-17	11.8	-6.17
April	0-9	0.0	-9.00		April	1-30	3.3	-26.25

JOCKEYS

	W-R	Per cent	£1 Level Stake
Charlie Poste	3-48	6.3	-37.00
Micheal Nolan	1-1	100.0	+5.50
Mr J M Ridley	1-8	12.5	-4.00

COURSE RECORD

	Total W-R	Non-Hndcps Hurdles	Chases	Hndcps Hurdles	Chases	NH Flat	Per cent	£1 Level Stake
Chepstow	3-7	0-1	0-1	0-2	3-3	0-0	42.9	+7.50
Uttoxeter	1-6	0-1	0-1	1-3	0-1	0-0	16.7	-3.00
Hereford	1-10	0-0	0-0	0-4	1-6	0-0	10.0	-6.00

WINNING HORSES

Horse	Races Run	1st	2nd	3rd	£
Munlochy Bay	5	1	0	1	2599
Loughalder	10	3	1	1	6433
*Daneva	9	1	1	2	1819
Total winning prize-money					£10851
Favourites	2-3		66.7%		2.50

OLIVER SHERWOOD

UPPER LAMBOURN, BERKS

	No. of Hrs	Races Run	1st	2nd	3rd	Unpl	Per cent	£1 Level Stake
NH Flat	11	16	4	3	2	7	25.0	+1.21
Hurdles	30	86	13	15	6	52	15.1	-25.32
Chases	14	59	8	11	7	33	13.6	-29.46
Totals	46	161	25	29	15	92	15.5	-53.57
11-12	53	176	17	21	22	116	9.7	-65.05
10-11	52	213	25	36	22	141	11.7	+112.25

BY MONTH

NH Flat	W-R	Per cent	£1 Level Stake		Hurdles	W-R	Per cent	£1 Level Stake
May	0-2	0.0	-2.00		May	0-4	0.0	-4.00
June	0-0	0.0	0.00		June	1-5	20.0	-3.38
July	0-2	0.0	-2.00		July	0-3	0.0	-3.00
August	0-0	0.0	0.00		August	0-1	0.0	-1.00
September	0-0	0.0	0.00		September	0-0	0.0	0.00
October	0-1	0.0	-1.00		October	1-4	25.0	+4.00
November	1-3	33.3	-0.38		November	6-12	50.0	+11.63
December	0-1	0.0	-1.00		December	3-12	25.0	+3.94
January	0-0	0.0	0.00		January	1-8	12.5	+0.50
February	0-0	0.0	0.00		February	1-12	8.3	-9.00
March	2-3	66.7	+7.83		March	0-8	0.0	-8.00
April	1-4	25.0	-0.25		April	0-17	0.0	-17.00

Chases	W-R	Per cent	£1 Level Stake		Totals	W-R	Per cent	£1 Level Stake
May	0-1	0.0	-1.00		May	0-7	0.0	-7.00
June	0-3	0.0	-3.00		June	1-8	12.5	-6.38

DISTANCE

Hurdles	W-R	Per cent	£1 Level Stake		Chases	W-R	Per cent	£1 Level Stake
2m-2m3f	10-36	27.8	+5.68		2m-2m3f	3-20	15.0	-7.58
2m4f-2m7f	1-41	2.4	-33.00		2m4f-2m7f	4-24	16.7	-10.88
3m+	2-9	22.2	+2.00		3m+	1-15	6.7	-11.00

TYPE OF RACE

Non-Handicaps	W-R	Per cent	£1 Level Stake		Handicaps	W-R	Per cent	£1 Level Stake
Nov Hrdls	6-36	16.7	-13.19		Nov Hrdls	0-1	0.0	-1.00
Hrdls	3-16	18.8	-0.63		Hrdls	3-31	9.7	-12.00
Nov Chs	2-17	11.8	-10.00		Nov Chs	0-9	0.0	-9.00
Chases	0-0	0.0	0.00		Chases	6-33	18.2	-10.46
Sell/Claim	1-2	50.0	+1.50		Sell/Claim	0-0	0.0	0.00

RACE CLASS

	W-R	Per cent	£1 Level Stake
Class 1	2-7	28.6	+0.94
Class 2	0-11	0.0	-11.00
Class 3	4-35	11.4	-19.88
Class 4	12-79	15.2	-28.18
Class 5	3-15	20.0	+1.33
Class 6	4-14	28.6	+3.21

FIRST TIME OUT

	W-R	Per cent	£1 Level Stake
Bumpers	3-11	27.3	+2.46
Hurdles	3-24	12.5	-8.00
Chases	2-11	18.2	-3.67
Totals	8-46	17.4	-9.21

JOCKEYS

	W-R	Per cent	£1 Level Stake
Leighton Aspell	14-84	16.7	-25.08
Thomas Garner	4-21	19.0	-1.25
Barry Geraghty	2-2	100.0	+2.07
A P McCoy	2-8	25.0	+0.12
Sam Jones	2-28	7.1	-19.92
Wayne Hutchinson	1-1	100.0	+7.50

COURSE RECORD

	Total W-R	Non-Hndcps Hurdles	Chases	Hndcps Hurdles	Chases	NH Flat	Per cent	£1 Level Stake
Ascot	3-6	2-2	0-0	0-2	0-1	1-1	50.0	+2.57
Exeter	3-6	1-2	0-0	0-1	1-2	1-1	50.0	+4.50
Fakenham	2-6	2-3	0-0	0-2	0-1	0-0	33.3	+10.50
Huntingdon	2-9	0-5	0-0	0-1	1-1	1-2	22.2	+2.00
Fontwell	2-14	0-3	1-3	0-3	1-4	0-1	14.3	-8.00
Folkestone	1-2	0-1	0-0	0-0	1-1	0-0	50.0	+2.33

Lingfield	1-2	0-0	1-1	0-0	0-1	0-0	50.0	+2.00
Plumpton	1-2	0-1	0-0	0-0	1-1	0-0	50.0	+0.63
Stratford	1-2	1-1	0-1	0-0	0-0	0-0	50.0	+1.50
Bangor	1-3	1-1	0-0	0-0	0-1	0-1	33.3	-0.75
Hereford	1-3	0-0	0-1	1-1	0-1	0-0	33.3	+1.50
Taunton	1-3	1-2	0-0	0-1	0-0	0-0	33.3	+3.50
Leicester	1-4	0-1	0-0	0-0	1-3	0-0	25.0	+0.33
Worcester	1-4	0-1	0-1	1-1	0-0	0-1	25.0	+4.00
Kempton	1-6	0-2	0-1	1-1	0-2	0-0	16.7	+0.50
Newbury	1-6	1-2	0-0	0-1	0-3	0-0	16.7	-3.63
Towcester	1-7	1-3	0-3	0-0	0-1	0-0	14.3	-5.38
Uttoxeter	1-8	0-1	0-1	0-2	0-2	1-2	12.5	-3.67

WINNING HORSES

Horse	Races Run	1st	2nd	3rd	£
Puffin Billy	6	3	1	0	24762
Mischievous Milly	4	2	2	0	16420
Rouge Et Blanc	10	3	2	1	15447
Many Clouds	6	2	3	0	10805
Arkose	7	2	0	1	7148
Milgen Bay	3	1	0	0	4549
Camden	6	2	1	0	6823
Kaituna	4	1	0	2	3054
Global Power	7	1	1	2	3054
Greenlaw	2	1	0	0	2599
Florafern	5	1	1	0	2534
Drum Valley	5	1	2	1	2534
Ubaldo Des Menhies	5	1	3	0	2053
Deputy Dan	2	2	0	0	3574
Dune Shine	1	1	0	0	1689
Lemony Bay	1	1	0	0	1560
Total winning prize-money					£108605
Favourites	9-25		36.0%		-0.98

SIMON SHIRLEY-BEAVAN

ABBOTRULE, BORDERS

	No. of Hrs	Races Run	1st	2nd	3rd	Unpl	Per cent	£1 Level Stake
NH Flat	2	2	0	0	0	2	0.0	-2.00
Hurdles	2	6	0	0	1	5	0.0	-6.00
Chases	1	5	3	0	0	2	60.0	+13.08
Totals	4	13	3	0	1	9	23.1	+5.08
11-12	1	1	0	0	0	1	0.0	-1.00
10-11	6	11	4	0	0	7	36.4	+2.66

JOCKEYS

	W-R	Per cent	£1 Level Stake
Barry Keniry	3-9	33.3	+9.08

COURSE RECORD

	Total W-R	Non-Hndcps Hurdles Chases		Hndcps Hurdles Chases		NH Flat	Per cent	£1 Level Stake
Catterick	3-3	0-0	2-2	0-0	1-1	0-0	100.0	+15.08

WINNING HORSES

Horse	Races Run	1st	2nd	3rd	£
Rapidolyte De Ladalka	5	3	0	0	14884
Total winning prize-money					£14884
Favourites	0-0		0.0%		0.00

LYNN SIDDALL

COLTON, N YORKS

	No. of Hrs	Races Run	1st	2nd	3rd	Unpl	Per cent	£1 Level Stake
NH Flat	2	3	0	0	0	3	0.0	-3.00
Hurdles	9	38	4	1	2	31	10.5	+114.50
Chases	0	0	0	0	0	0	0.0	0.00
Totals	11	41	4	1	2	34	9.8	+111.50
11-12	9	39	0	1	2	36	0.0	-39.00
10-11	11	37	1	0	2	34	2.7	-14.00

JOCKEYS

	W-R	Per cent	£1 Level Stake
Tom Siddall	2-37	5.4	+81.00
Micheal Nolan	1-1	100.0	+7.50
Brian Harding	1-2	50.0	+24.00

COURSE RECORD

	Total W-R	Non-Hndcps Hurdles Chases		Hndcps Hurdles Chases		NH Flat	Per cent	£1 Level Stake
Uttoxeter	2-12	0-4	0-0	2-7	0-0	0-1	16.7	+31.00
Hexham	1-4	0-2	0-0	1-2	0-0	0-0	25.0	+4.50
Wetherby	1-8	0-3	0-0	1-4	0-0	0-1	12.5	+93.00

WINNING HORSES

Horse	Races Run	1st	2nd	3rd	£
Prize Fighter	6	1	1	1	3119
*I Know The Code	6	1	0	1	2209
Lisdonagh House	4	2	0	0	3639
Total winning prize-money					£8967
Favourites	0-0		0.0%		0.00

EVELYN SLACK

HILTON, CUMBRIA

	No. of Hrs	Races Run	1st	2nd	3rd	Unpl	Per cent	£1 Level Stake
NH Flat	0	0	0	0	0	0	0.0	0.00
Hurdles	5	20	1	1	0	18	5.0	-9.00
Chases	1	3	1	0	2	0	33.3	+8.00
Totals	5	23	2	1	2	18	8.7	-1.00
11-12	10	38	1	5	1	31	2.6	-33.75
10-11	9	46	3	5	3	35	6.5	-4.00

JOCKEYS

	W-R	Per cent	£1 Level Stake
Alexander Voy	1-4	25.0	+7.00
Stephen Mulqueen	1-11	9.1	0.00

COURSE RECORD

	Total W-R	Non-Hndcps Hurdles	Chases	Hndcps Hurdles	Chases	NH Flat	Per cent	£1 Level Stake
Cartmel	1-4	0-0	0-0	0-2	1-2	0-0	25.0	+7.00
Sedgefield	1-8	0-2	0-0	1-6	0-0	0-0	12.5	+3.00

WINNING HORSES

Horse	Races Run	1st	2nd	3rd	£
Hathamore	5	1	0	2	2599
Scriptwriter	12	1	1	0	2534
Total winning prize-money					**£5133**
Favourites	0-1		0.0%		-1.00

PAM SLY

THORNEY, CAMBS

	No. of Hrs	Races Run	1st	2nd	3rd	Unpl	Per cent	£1 Level Stake
NH Flat	4	5	0	1	2	2	0.0	-5.00
Hurdles	12	50	3	7	7	33	6.0	-27.00
Chases	3	5	0	0	0	5	0.0	-5.00
Totals	17	60	3	8	9	40	5.0	-37.00
11-12	21	91	7	7	12	65	7.7	-34.13
10-11	18	84	9	12	9	54	10.7	-30.26

JOCKEYS

	W-R	Per cent	£1 Level Stake
Miss G Andrews	2-14	14.3	+2.00
Gavin Sheehan	1-1	100.0	+6.00

COURSE RECORD

	Total W-R	Non-Hndcps Hurdles	Chases	Hndcps Hurdles	Chases	NH Flat	Per cent	£1 Level Stake
Towcester	1-4	0-1	0-0	1-3	0-0	0-0	25.0	+3.00
Wetherby	1-6	0-0	0-0	1-6	0-0	0-0	16.7	-1.00
Fakenham	1-11	0-2	0-2	1-5	0-1	0-1	9.1	0.00

WINNING HORSES

Horse	Races Run	1st	2nd	3rd	£
Pheidias	4	1	0	0	3249
Chicklemix	4	1	1	0	2599
Arkaim	11	1	3	1	1949
Total winning prize-money					**£7797**
Favourites	0-1		0.0%		-1.00

SUE SMITH

HIGH ELDWICK, W YORKS

	No. of Hrs	Races Run	1st	2nd	3rd	Unpl	Per cent	£1 Level Stake
NH Flat	11	20	1	1	4	14	5.0	-5.00
Hurdles	38	106	11	8	5	82	10.4	-29.61
Chases	29	152	19	21	27	85	12.5	+28.92
Totals	58	278	31	30	36	181	11.2	-5.69
11-12	66	328	43	37	46	201	13.1	-36.37
10-11	84	367	42	29	31	265	11.4	-23.96

BY MONTH

NH Flat	W-R	Per cent	£1 Level Stake	Hurdles	W-R	Per cent	£1 Level Stake
May	0-1	0.0	-1.00	May	1-6	16.7	-1.50
June	0-3	0.0	-3.00	June	0-1	0.0	-1.00
July	1-1	100.0	+14.00	July	0-3	0.0	-3.00
August	0-1	0.0	-1.00	August	0-5	0.0	-5.00
September	0-1	0.0	-1.00	September	0-3	0.0	-3.00
October	0-2	0.0	-2.00	October	1-9	11.1	-6.63
November	0-3	0.0	-3.00	November	1-10	10.0	+16.00
December	0-3	0.0	-3.00	December	1-17	5.9	-12.00
January	0-0	0.0	0.00	January	1-6	16.7	0.00
February	0-1	0.0	-1.00	February	5-22	22.7	-6.49
March	0-1	0.0	-1.00	March	1-15	6.7	+2.00
April	0-3	0.0	-3.00	April	0-9	0.0	-9.00

Chases	W-R	Per cent	£1 Level Stake	Totals	W-R	Per cent	£1 Level Stake
May	2-6	33.3	+3.50	May	3-13	23.1	+1.00
June	0-2	0.0	-2.00	June	0-6	0.0	-6.00
July	0-4	0.0	-4.00	July	1-8	12.5	+7.00
August	0-2	0.0	-2.00	August	0-8	0.0	-8.00
September	0-2	0.0	-2.00	September	0-6	0.0	-6.00
October	3-14	21.4	+16.50	October	4-25	16.0	+7.87
November	4-23	17.4	-7.88	November	5-36	13.9	+5.12
December	3-23	13.0	+7.13	December	4-43	9.3	-7.87
January	1-5	20.0	-3.33	January	2-11	18.2	-3.33
February	2-23	8.7	-12.50	February	7-46	15.2	-19.99
March	1-27	3.7	-25.00	March	2-43	4.7	-24.00
April	3-21	14.3	+60.50	April	3-33	9.1	+48.50

DISTANCE

Hurdles	W-R	Per cent	£1 Level Stake	Chases	W-R	Per cent	£1 Level Stake
2m-2m3f	8-49	16.3	+14.85	2m-2m3f	6-30	20.0	-1.38
2m4f-2m7f	2-39	5.1	-31.47	2m4f-2m7f	8-61	13.1	-2.88
3m+	1-18	5.6	-13.00	3m+	5-61	8.2	+33.17

TYPE OF RACE

Non-Handicaps				Handicaps			
	W-R	Per cent	£1 Level Stake		W-R	Per cent	£1 Level Stake
Nov Hrdls	2-31	6.5	+12.00	Nov Hrdls	0-7	0.0	-7.00
Hrdls	0-6	0.0	-6.00	Hrdls	9-61	14.8	-27.61

Nov Chs	7-30	23.3	+5.17	Nov Chs	2-19	10.5	-11.38
Chases	0-3	0.0	-3.00	Chases	10-100	10.0	+38.13
Sell/Claim	0-1	0.0	-1.00	Sell/Claim	0-0	0.0	0.00

RACE CLASS

	W-R	Per cent	£1 Level Stake
Class 1	2-24	8.3	+60.00
Class 2	2-25	8.0	+1.50
Class 3	8-58	13.8	-5.00
Class 4	13-118	11.0	-43.07
Class 5	5-33	15.2	-14.13
Class 6	1-20	5.0	-5.00

FIRST TIME OUT

	W-R	Per cent	£1 Level Stake
Bumpers	0-11	0.0	-11.00
Hurdles	3-24	12.5	-9.50
Chases	3-23	13.0	-7.50
Totals	6-58	10.3	-28.00

JOCKEYS

	W-R	Per cent	£1 Level Stake
Ryan Mania	16-161	9.9	+34.29
Jonathan England	10-65	15.4	-13.62
Timmy Murphy	1-2	50.0	+3.50
Brian Harding	1-2	50.0	+4.00
Wilson Renwick	1-2	50.0	+4.50
Lucy Alexander	1-2	50.0	+0.63
Wayne Hutchinson	1-5	20.0	0.00

COURSE RECORD

	Total W-R	Non-Hndcps Hurdles	Chases	Hndcps Hurdles	Chases	NH Flat	Per cent	£1 Level Stake
Sedgefield	7-33	1-7	1-2	1-5	4-17	0-2	21.2	+22.63
Wetherby	6-39	0-6	1-4	4-13	1-14	0-2	15.4	-8.75
Kelso	5-14	1-3	1-3	1-1	2-6	0-1	35.7	+30.35
Hexham	3-11	0-2	2-2	1-2	0-3	0-2	27.3	+6.88
Carlisle	2-30	0-1	1-10	0-6	1-12	0-1	6.7	-11.00
Southwell	1-1	0-0	0-0	0-0	1-1	0-0	100.0	+5.00
Aintree	1-6	0-0	0-0	0-1	1-5	0-0	16.7	+61.00
Bangor	1-8	0-2	0-1	1-3	0-1	0-1	12.5	-6.47
Haydock	1-18	0-2	0-0	0-6	1-10	0-0	5.6	-13.00
Uttoxeter	1-18	0-3	0-0	0-6	0-6	1-3	5.6	-3.00
Catterick	1-21	0-3	1-2	0-7	0-5	0-4	4.8	-19.33
Doncaster	1-21	0-3	0-4	1-4	0-9	0-1	4.8	-16.00
Newcastle	1-22	0-4	0-1	0-5	1-11	0-1	4.5	-18.00

WINNING HORSES

Horse	Races Run	1st	2nd	3rd	£
Auroras Encore	9	1	0	0	547268
*Mwaleshi	4	2	0	0	23583
Cloudy Too	7	3	0	1	25349
Douglas Julian	7	1	0	0	11394
Lackamon	7	1	0	2	9384
No Planning	9	2	1	3	10397
Yurok	6	1	0	3	6256
Rebel Swing	9	1	1	1	5653
Herdsman	5	2	0	0	10787
Vintage Star	5	1	3	0	4549
Tahiti Pearl	10	4	2	0	12494
*Swiss Art	8	1	1	1	3422

Highrate	8	1	1	2	3249
*Coverholder	7	4	0	0	10474
Daldini	1	1	0	0	3054
Fill The Power	9	1	4	1	3054
Twice Lucky	9	1	1	0	2885
Grate Fella	4	1	1	1	2859
Alba King	2	1	0	0	1689
Rattlin	4	1	0	0	1365
Total winning prize-money					**£699165**
Favourites	10-27		37.0%		1.05

SUZY SMITH

LEWES, E SUSSEX

	No. of Hrs	Races Run	1st	2nd	3rd	Unpl	Per cent	£1 Level Stake
NH Flat	4	4	1	1	0	2	25.0	+9.00
Hurdles	10	40	6	5	4	25	15.0	+11.75
Chases	4	6	2	1	0	3	33.3	+6.00
Totals	14	50	9	7	4	30	18.0	+26.75
11-12	17	57	5	4	10	38	8.8	-15.50
10-11	18	71	9	11	5	46	12.7	-14.25

JOCKEYS

	W-R	Per cent	£1 Level Stake
Gavin Sheehan	5-18	27.8	+28.50
Paddy Brennan	2-6	33.3	+10.25
Micheal Nolan	1-1	100.0	+6.50
Colin Bolger	1-15	6.7	-8.50

COURSE RECORD

	Total W-R	Non-Hndcps Hurdles	Chases	Hndcps Hurdles	Chases	NH Flat	Per cent	£1 Level Stake
Plumpton	3-20	0-7	0-0	3-11	0-0	0-2	15.0	+13.50
Fontwell	2-9	0-0	0-1	1-5	0-1	1-2	22.2	+10.50
Mrket Rsn	1-2	0-0	0-0	1-2	0-0	0-0	50.0	+1.25
Uttoxeter	1-2	0-0	0-0	0-1	1-1	0-0	50.0	+5.00
Stratford	1-3	0-0	0-0	1-3	0-0	0-0	33.3	+5.50
Kempton	1-6	0-2	0-0	0-3	1-1	0-0	16.7	-1.00

WINNING HORSES

Horse	Races Run	1st	2nd	3rd	£
Emmaslegend	2	2	0	0	15939
Quipe Me Posted	2	1	1	0	4549
*Laughton Park	2	1	0	0	2738
Madame Jasmine	7	1	2	0	2669
Natural Spring	5	1	0	0	2534
Invicta Lake	11	1	2	3	2534
Royal Kicks	8	1	0	1	2053
Ourmanmassini	5	1	0	0	1437
Total winning prize-money					**£34453**
Favourites	1-2		50.0%		1.25

JULIAN SMITH

TIRLEY, GLOUCS

	No. of Hrs	Races Run	1st	2nd	3rd	Unpl	Per cent	£1 Level Stake
NH Flat	3	4	0	0	0	4	0.0	-4.00
Hurdles	5	14	0	4	2	8	0.0	-14.00
Chases	5	17	2	4	2	9	11.8	+15.75
Totals	12	35	2	8	4	21	5.7	-2.25
11-12	7	23	2	4	6	11	8.7	-11.88
10-11	7	27	2	4	1	20	7.4	+3.00

JOCKEYS

	W-R	Per cent	£1 Level Stake
Sam Twiston-Davies	1-8	12.5	-4.25
Wayne Hutchinson	1-19	5.3	+10.00

COURSE RECORD

	Total W-R	Non-Hndcps Hurdles	Chases	Hndcps Hurdles	Chases	NH Flat	Per cent	£1 Level Stake
Mrket Rsn	1-2	0-0	0-0	0-0	1-2	0-0	50.0	+1.75
Worcester	1-9	0-0	0-0	0-1	1-5	0-3	11.1	+20.00

WINNING HORSES

Horse	Races Run	1st	2nd	3rd	£
Iona Days	8	1	3	1	5653
Midnight Gold	5	1	0	1	2122
Total winning prize-money					£7775
Favourites	0-1		0.0%		-1.00

R MIKE SMITH

GALSTON, E AYRSHIRE

	No. of Hrs	Races Run	1st	2nd	3rd	Unpl	Per cent	£1 Level Stake
NH Flat	2	2	0	0	0	2	0.0	-2.00
Hurdles	5	11	0	0	0	11	0.0	-11.00
Chases	3	12	1	0	0	11	8.3	+5.00
Totals	9	25	1	0	0	24	4.0	-8.00
11-12	7	23	2	1	4	16	8.7	-14.50
10-11	3	12	1	2	1	8	8.3	+3.00

JOCKEYS

	W-R	Per cent	£1 Level Stake
Mr C Bewley	1-14	7.1	+3.00

COURSE RECORD

	Total W-R	Non-Hndcps Hurdles	Chases	Hndcps Hurdles	Chases	NH Flat	Per cent	£1 Level Stake
Musselbgh	1-6	0-1	0-0	0-0	1-4	0-1	16.7	+11.00

WINNING HORSES

Horse	Races Run	1st	2nd	3rd	£
Knight Woodsman	7	1	0	0	2496
Total winning prize-money					£2496
Favourites	0-0		0.0%		0.00

MICHAEL SMITH

KIRKHEATON, NORTHUMBERLAND

	No. of Hrs	Races Run	1st	2nd	3rd	Unpl	Per cent	£1 Level Stake
NH Flat	4	8	1	0	0	7	12.5	0.00
Hurdles	10	31	6	3	8	14	19.4	+11.16
Chases	0	0	0	0	0	0	0.0	0.00
Totals	11	39	7	3	8	21	17.9	+11.16
11-12	5	14	2	1	0	11	14.3	-6.00
10-11	8	23	3	3	5	12	13.0	+31.00

JOCKEYS

	W-R	Per cent	£1 Level Stake
Danny Cook	6-24	25.0	+19.66
Denis O'Regan	1-6	16.7	+0.50

COURSE RECORD

	Total W-R	Non-Hndcps Hurdles	Chases	Hndcps Hurdles	Chases	NH Flat	Per cent	£1 Level Stake
Musselbgh	3-9	2-6	0-0	0-1	0-0	1-2	33.3	+4.16
Catterick	2-3	2-3	0-0	0-0	0-0	0-0	66.7	+8.50
Ayr	1-3	0-1	0-0	1-1	0-0	0-1	33.3	+16.00
Wetherby	1-4	1-2	0-0	0-2	0-0	0-0	25.0	+2.50

WINNING HORSES

Horse	Races Run	1st	2nd	3rd	£
Orsippus	3	1	0	1	14296
Imperial Vic	6	3	0	2	9270
Dante's Frolic	5	1	0	1	2738
War On	4	1	0	1	2669
Amisfield Lad	3	1	0	0	1949
Total winning prize-money					£30922
Favourites	2-4		50.0%		0.41

GILES SMYLY

WORMINGTON, WORCS

	No. of Hrs	Races Run	1st	2nd	3rd	Unpl	Per cent	£1 Level Stake
NH Flat	5	9	0	1	0	8	0.0	-9.00
Hurdles	4	5	1	0	2	2	20.0	+20.00
Chases	3	7	0	1	0	6	0.0	-7.00
Totals	10	21	1	2	2	16	4.8	+4.00

11-12	10	31	3	1	3	24	9.7	-4.75
10-11	14	33	1	2	5	25	3.0	-16.00

JOCKEYS

	W-R	Per cent	£1 Level Stake
David England	1-20	5.0	+5.00

COURSE RECORD

	Total W-R	Non-Hndcps Hurdles	Chases	Hndcps Hurdles	Chases	NH Flat	Per cent	£1 Level Stake
Southwell	1-2	0-0	0-0	1-1	0-0	0-1	50.0	+23.00

WINNING HORSES

Horse	Races Run	1st	2nd	3rd	£
*Taigan	1	1	0	0	0
Total winning prize-money					£0
Favourites	0-0		0.0%		0.00

JAMIE SNOWDEN

LAMBOURN, BERKS

	No. of Hrs	Races Run	1st	2nd	3rd	Unpl	Per cent	£1 Level Stake
NH Flat	5	10	1	0	3	6	10.0	-5.67
Hurdles	28	82	6	10	12	54	7.3	-45.75
Chases	13	36	7	4	3	22	19.4	-10.15
Totals	36	128	14	14	18	82	10.9	-61.57
11-12	29	118	19	19	15	65	16.1	+0.98
10-11	28	115	6	4	17	88	5.2	-80.81

BY MONTH

NH Flat	W-R	Per cent	£1 Level Stake	Hurdles	W-R	Per cent	£1 Level Stake
May	0-0	0.0	0.00	May	2-8	25.0	+0.50
June	0-0	0.0	0.00	June	0-4	0.0	-4.00
July	0-0	0.0	0.00	July	0-3	0.0	-3.00
August	0-0	0.0	0.00	August	0-3	0.0	-3.00
September	0-0	0.0	0.00	September	0-3	0.0	-3.00
October	0-0	0.0	0.00	October	1-10	10.0	-1.50
November	0-0	0.0	0.00	November	1-9	11.1	-1.50
December	0-3	0.0	-3.00	December	0-8	0.0	-8.00
January	0-1	0.0	-1.00	January	1-3	33.3	+5.00
February	0-3	0.0	-3.00	February	1-8	12.5	-4.25
March	0-1	0.0	-1.00	March	0-6	0.0	-6.00
April	1-2	50.0	+2.33	April	0-17	0.0	-17.00

Chases	W-R	Per cent	£1 Level Stake	Totals	W-R	Per cent	£1 Level Stake
May	2-3	66.7	+1.98	May	4-11	36.4	+2.48
June	2-2	100.0	+3.38	June	2-6	33.3	-0.62
July	0-2	0.0	-2.00	July	0-5	0.0	-5.00
August	0-2	0.0	-2.00	August	0-5	0.0	-5.00
September	0-2	0.0	-2.00	September	0-5	0.0	-5.00
October	1-4	25.0	+0.50	October	2-14	14.3	-1.00
November	0-5	0.0	-5.00	November	1-14	7.1	-6.50

December	0-2	0.0	-2.00	December	0-13	0.0	-13.00
January	0-0	0.0	0.00	January	1-4	25.0	+4.00
February	0-3	0.0	-3.00	February	1-14	7.1	-10.25
March	1-4	25.0	+1.00	March	1-11	9.1	-6.00
April	1-7	14.3	-1.00	April	2-26	7.7	-15.67

DISTANCE

Hurdles	W-R	Per cent	£1 Level Stake	Chases	W-R	Per cent	£1 Level Stake
2m-2m3f	4-44	9.1	-18.25	2m-2m3f	4-13	30.8	-0.90
2m4f-2m7f	2-31	6.5	-20.50	2m4f-2m7f	2-13	15.4	-4.25
3m+	0-7	0.0	-7.00	3m+	1-10	10.0	-5.00

TYPE OF RACE

Non-Handicaps	W-R	Per cent	£1 Level Stake	Handicaps	W-R	Per cent	£1 Level Stake
Nov Hrdls	2-26	7.7	-19.25	Nov Hrdls	0-8	0.0	-8.00
Hrdls	1-16	6.3	-8.00	Hrdls	3-29	10.3	-7.50
Nov Chs	2-11	18.2	-6.52	Nov Chs	0-5	0.0	-5.00
Chases	0-1	0.0	-1.00	Chases	5-19	26.3	+2.38
Sell/Claim	0-2	0.0	-2.00	Sell/Claim	0-1	0.0	-1.00

RACE CLASS

	W-R	Per cent	£1 Level Stake
Class 1	0-7	0.0	-7.00
Class 2	2-7	28.6	+5.00
Class 3	1-14	7.1	-10.75
Class 4	5-59	8.5	-42.77
Class 5	5-32	15.6	-1.38
Class 6	1-9	11.1	-4.67

FIRST TIME OUT

	W-R	Per cent	£1 Level Stake
Bumpers	0-5	0.0	-5.00
Hurdles	3-24	12.5	-6.75
Chases	1-7	14.3	-5.27
Totals	4-36	11.1	-17.02

JOCKEYS

	W-R	Per cent	£1 Level Stake
Tom O'Brien	6-44	13.6	-21.52
Brendan Powell	2-16	12.5	-6.17
Harry Skelton	2-19	10.5	-8.88
Gavin Sheehan	1-1	100.0	+5.00
Dave Crosse	1-3	33.3	+2.00
Sam Twiston-Davies	1-8	12.5	-3.50
Mr Matthew Stanley	1-9	11.1	-0.50

COURSE RECORD

	Total W-R	Non-Hndcps Hurdles	Chases	Hndcps Hurdles	Chases	NH Flat	Per cent	£1 Level Stake
Towcester	3-9	1-5	0-3	2-3	0-0	0-1	33.3	+13.00
Worcester	2-6	1-3	1-1	0-2	0-0	0-0	33.3	-0.25
Wincanton	2-8	0-5	0-0	1-2	1-1	0-0	25.0	+4.50
Huntingdon	2-10	0-4	1-1	0-3	0-1	1-1	20.0	-3.94
Hereford	1-2	0-0	0-0	0-0	1-2	0-0	50.0	+0.63
Lingfield	1-2	1-1	0-0	0-0	1-1	0-0	50.0	+1.75
Nton Abbot	1-2	0-0	0-1	0-0	1-1	0-0	50.0	+1.25
Fontwell	1-11	0-4	0-1	0-3	1-1	0-2	9.1	-6.50
Plumpton	1-11	0-4	0-0	0-3	1-3	0-1	9.1	-5.00

WINNING HORSES

Horse	Races Run	1st	2nd	3rd	£
Miss Milborne	7	1	1	0	15014
Marodima	7	2	1	0	16310
Sandy's Double	3	1	0	1	4061
Jean Fleming	3	1	1	1	3285
Ixora	6	2	2	0	5653
Jamesson	4	1	0	1	2274
Knighton Combe	5	1	0	0	1949
Niki Royal	4	1	0	0	1949
Millers Reef	4	1	1	1	1819
Jawhary	9	2	0	1	3379
Joanne One	2	1	0	0	1560
Total winning prize-money					£57253
Favourites	5-18		27.8%		-3.06

MIKE SOWERSBY

GOODMANHAM, E YORKS

	No. of Hrs	Races Run	1st	2nd	3rd	Unpl	Per cent	£1 Level Stake
NH Flat	5	8	0	0	0	8	0.0	-8.00
Hurdles	12	63	1	1	4	57	1.6	-58.00
Chases	4	17	3	0	1	13	17.6	+19.00
Totals	16	88	4	1	5	78	4.5	-47.00
11-12	21	91	6	7	7	71	6.6	+2.50
10-11	15	77	2	2	9	64	2.6	-45.00

JOCKEYS

	W-R	Per cent	£1 Level Stake
Denis O'Regan	2-5	40.0	+5.00
Samantha Drake	1-5	20.0	+21.00
Edmond Linehan	1-17	5.9	-12.00

COURSE RECORD

	Total W-R	Non-Hndcps Hurdles	Chases	Hndcps Hurdles	Chases	NH Flat	Per cent	£1 Level Stake
Sedgefield	3-11	0-3	0-1	0-3	3-3	0-1	27.3	+25.00
Catterick	1-11	0-2	0-0	1-9	0-0	0-0	9.1	-6.00

WINNING HORSES

Horse	Races Run	1st	2nd	3rd	£
Tregaro	5	2	0	1	6029
Carmela Maria	11	1	0	1	2924
Moon Melody	8	1	0	1	1819
Total winning prize-money					£10772
Favourites	0-2		0.0%		-2.00

JOHN SPEARING

KINNERSLEY, WORCS

	No. of Hrs	Races Run	1st	2nd	3rd	Unpl	Per cent	£1 Level Stake
NH Flat	3	5	0	0	0	5	0.0	-5.00
Hurdles	8	41	5	6	6	24	12.2	-10.00
Chases	0	0	0	0	0	0	0.0	0.00
Totals	11	46	5	6	6	29	10.9	-15.00
11-12	10	28	0	1	2	25	0.0	-28.00
10-11	12	35	2	2	3	28	5.7	-16.00

JOCKEYS

	W-R	Per cent	£1 Level Stake
Jamie Moore	3-16	18.8	+5.00
Paddy Brennan	1-3	33.3	+3.00
Nico de Boinville	1-4	25.0	0.00

COURSE RECORD

	Total W-R	Non-Hndcps Hurdles	Chases	Hndcps Hurdles	Chases	NH Flat	Per cent	£1 Level Stake
Ffos Las	1-1	0-0	0-0	1-1	0-0	0-0	100.0	+3.00
Fontwell	1-2	0-1	0-0	1-1	0-0	0-0	50.0	+3.00
Catterick	1-4	1-2	0-0	0-1	0-0	0-1	25.0	+2.00
Ludlow	1-4	0-1	0-0	1-2	0-0	0-1	25.0	+9.00
Worcester	1-6	1-3	0-0	0-3	0-0	0-0	16.7	-3.00

WINNING HORSES

Horse	Races Run	1st	2nd	3rd	£
Pearls Legend	8	2	2	2	9902
Miss Conduct	10	1	3	3	3899
Starlight Air	4	1	0	0	1949
Barton Gift	6	1	1	1	1872
Total winning prize-money					£17622
Favourites	1-4		25.0%		0.00

BRIAN STOREY

BOLTONFELLEND, CUMBRIA

	No. of Hrs	Races Run	1st	2nd	3rd	Unpl	Per cent	£1 Level Stake
NH Flat	3	3	1	0	0	2	33.3	0.00
Hurdles	13	24	0	0	0	24	0.0	-24.00
Chases	5	9	0	0	0	9	0.0	-9.00
Totals	17	36	1	0	0	35	2.8	-33.00
11-12	28	91	1	6	6	78	1.1	-78.00
10-11	15	57	1	3	2	51	1.8	-49.50

JOCKEYS

	W-R	Per cent	£1 Level Stake
Brian Toomey	1-1	100.0	+2.00

COURSE RECORD

	Total W-R	Non-Hndcps Hurdles	Chases	Hndcps Hurdles	Chases	NH Flat	Per cent	£1 Level Stake
Sedgefield	1-7	0-0	0-0	0-4	0-2	1-1	14.3	-4.00

WINNING HORSES

Horse	Races Run	1st	2nd	3rd	£
Cole Harden	1	1	0	0	1560
Total winning prize-money					£1560
Favourites	1-1		100.0%		2.00

ROB SUMMERS

TANWORTH-IN-ARDEN, WARWICKS

	No. of Hrs	Races Run	1st	2nd	3rd	Unpl	Per cent	£1 Level Stake
NH Flat	2	5	0	0	1	4	0.0	-5.00
Hurdles	6	16	1	1	0	14	6.3	-3.00
Chases	4	14	2	2	2	8	14.3	+7.00
Totals	10	35	3	3	3	26	8.6	-1.00
11-12	9	33	1	1	4	27	3.0	-28.67
10-11	7	20	1	2	0	17	5.0	-7.00

JOCKEYS

	W-R	Per cent	£1 Level Stake
Charlie Wallis	2-19	10.5	+7.00
Tom Messenger	1-3	33.3	+5.00

COURSE RECORD

	Total W-R	Non-Hndcps Hurdles	Chases	Hndcps Hurdles	Chases	NH Flat	Per cent	£1 Level Stake
Hereford	1-3	0-0	0-0	1-3	0-0	0-0	33.3	+10.00
Uttoxeter	1-4	0-1	0-0	0-1	1-1	0-1	25.0	+4.00
Worcester	1-6	0-0	0-1	0-3	1-2	0-0	16.7	+7.00

WINNING HORSES

Horse	Races Run	1st	2nd	3rd	£
Arctic Echo	4	1	0	0	3054
Fintan	6	1	0	1	3054
Red Whisper	7	1	1	0	1689
Total winning prize-money					£7797
Favourites	0-0		0.0%		0.00

ALAN SWINBANK

MELSONBY, N YORKS

	No. of Hrs	Races Run	1st	2nd	3rd	Unpl	Per cent	£1 Level Stake
NH Flat	11	22	3	6	3	10	13.6	-4.50
Hurdles	12	40	7	7	4	22	17.5	+2.95
Chases	3	6	0	0	0	6	0.0	-6.00

Totals	21	68	10	13	7	38	14.7	-7.55
11-12	29	83	10	15	12	46	12.0	-43.59
10-11	40	114	25	19	20	50	21.9	-15.18

BY MONTH

NH Flat	W-R	Per cent	£1 Level Stake	Hurdles	W-R	Per cent	£1 Level Stake
May	0-1	0.0	-1.00	May	0-2	0.0	-2.00
June	1-1	100.0	+3.00	June	0-2	0.0	-2.00
July	0-2	0.0	-2.00	July	0-0	0.0	0.00
August	0-2	0.0	-2.00	August	0-1	0.0	-1.00
September	0-0	0.0	0.00	September	0-0	0.0	0.00
October	0-0	0.0	0.00	October	0-5	0.0	-5.00
November	0-2	0.0	-2.00	November	3-5	60.0	+14.10
December	0-3	0.0	-3.00	December	0-9	0.0	-9.00
January	0-4	0.0	-4.00	January	0-5	0.0	-5.00
February	1-3	33.3	+8.00	February	0-3	0.0	-3.00
March	0-2	0.0	-2.00	March	3-7	42.9	+13.10
April	1-2	50.0	+0.50	April	1-1	100.0	+2.75

Chases	W-R	Per cent	£1 Level Stake	Totals	W-R	Per cent	£1 Level Stake
May	0-0	0.0	0.00	May	0-3	0.0	-3.00
June	0-1	0.0	-1.00	June	1-4	25.0	0.00
July	0-0	0.0	0.00	July	0-2	0.0	-2.00
August	0-0	0.0	0.00	August	0-3	0.0	-3.00
September	0-0	0.0	0.00	September	0-0	0.0	0.00
October	0-0	0.0	0.00	October	0-5	0.0	-5.00
November	0-2	0.0	-2.00	November	3-9	33.3	+10.10
December	0-0	0.0	0.00	December	0-12	0.0	-12.00
January	0-2	0.0	-2.00	January	0-11	0.0	-11.00
February	0-1	0.0	-1.00	February	1-7	14.3	+4.00
March	0-0	0.0	0.00	March	3-9	33.3	+11.10
April	0-0	0.0	0.00	April	2-3	66.7	+3.25

DISTANCE

Hurdles	W-R	Per cent	£1 Level Stake	Chases	W-R	Per cent	£1 Level Stake
2m-2m3f	7-25	28.0	+17.95	2m-2m3f	0-4	0.0	-4.00
2m4f-2m7f	0-13	0.0	-13.00	2m4f-2m7f	0-2	0.0	-2.00
3m+	0-2	0.0	-2.00	3m+	0-0	0.0	0.00

TYPE OF RACE

Non-Handicaps	W-R	Per cent	£1 Level Stake	Handicaps	W-R	Per cent	£1 Level Stake
Nov Hrdls	2-19	10.5	-13.15	Nov Hrdls	3-5	60.0	+23.00
Hrdls	0-1	0.0	-1.00	Hrdls	2-14	14.3	-4.90
Nov Chs	0-1	0.0	-1.00	Nov Chs	0-1	0.0	-1.00
Chases	0-0	0.0	0.00	Chases	0-4	0.0	-4.00
Sell/Claim	0-1	0.0	-1.00	Sell/Claim	0-0	0.0	0.00

RACE CLASS · FIRST TIME OUT

	W-R	Per cent	£1 Level Stake		W-R	Per cent	£1 Level Stake
Class 1	0-0	0.0	0.00	Bumpers	2-11	18.2	+4.00
Class 2	0-2	0.0	-2.00	Hurdles	1-8	12.5	-2.00

Class 3	0-8	0.0	-8.00	Chases	0-2	0.0	-2.00
Class 4	5-31	16.1	+3.85				
Class 5	2-6	33.3	+2.10	Totals	3-21	14.3	0.00
Class 6	3-21	14.3	-3.50				

January	0-1	0.0	-1.00	January	1-8	12.5	+1.50
February	0-4	0.0	-4.00	February	0-8	0.0	-8.00
March	0-3	0.0	-3.00	March	2-7	28.6	-2.59
April	0-5	0.0	-5.00	April	0-16	0.0	-16.00

JOCKEYS

	W-R	Per cent	£1 Level Stake
Fearghal Davis	4-32	12.5	-1.90
Joe Colliver	3-11	27.3	+5.85
Thomas Garner	1-2	50.0	+5.00
A P McCoy	1-3	33.3	-0.50
Brian Hughes	1-12	8.3	-8.00

COURSE RECORD

	Total W-R	Non-Hndcps Hurdles	Chases	Hndcps Hurdles	Chases	NH Flat	Per cent	£1 Level Stake
Carlisle	5-16	1-7	0-0	3-6	0-0	1-3	31.3	+17.60
Sedgefield	2-11	0-4	0-0	1-1	0-0	1-6	18.2	+2.10
Kelso	2-12	1-8	0-0	1-3	0-0	0-1	16.7	-2.25
Mrket Rsn	1-6	0-1	0-0	0-1	0-0	1-4	16.7	-2.00

WINNING HORSES

Horse	Races Run	1st	2nd	3rd	£
Big Water	3	1	2	0	3899
Phoenix Returns	7	1	1	2	3249
Anna's Arch	6	3	1	0	7138
Mitchell's Way	8	2	1	1	5788
Master Rajeem	3	2	1	0	3119
The Ferick	5	1	0	1	1365
Total winning prize-money					£24558
Favourites	3-10		30.0%		-3.30

Chases

	W-R	Per cent	£1 Level Stake
May	0-1	0.0	-1.00
June	0-0	0.0	0.00
July	0-0	0.0	0.00
August	0-0	0.0	0.00
September	0-0	0.0	0.00
October	1-5	20.0	+29.00
November	0-1	0.0	-1.00
December	0-3	0.0	-3.00
January	2-4	50.0	+8.00
February	0-4	0.0	-4.00
March	0-3	0.0	-3.00
April	0-6	0.0	-6.00

Totals

	W-R	Per cent	£1 Level Stake
May	0-3	0.0	-3.00
June	0-2	0.0	-2.00
July	0-3	0.0	-3.00
August	0-1	0.0	-1.00
September	0-3	0.0	-3.00
October	1-20	5.0	+14.00
November	2-14	14.3	+22.38
December	2-18	11.1	+18.00
January	3-13	23.1	+8.50
February	0-16	0.0	-16.00
March	2-13	15.4	-8.59
April	0-27	0.0	-27.00

DISTANCE

Hurdles	W-R	Per cent	£1 Level Stake	Chases	W-R	Per cent	£1 Level Stake
2m-2m3f	2-40	5.0	-18.63	2m-2m3f	0-4	0.0	-4.00
2m4f-2m7f	3-32	9.4	+14.00	2m4f-2m7f	3-19	15.8	+27.00
3m+	2-9	22.2	+9.91	3m+	0-4	0.0	-4.00

TYPE OF RACE

Non-Handicaps	W-R	Per cent	£1 Level Stake	Handicaps	W-R	Per cent	£1 Level Stake
Nov Hrdls	3-31	9.7	-7.72	Nov Hrdls	0-9	0.0	-9.00
Hrdls	0-15	0.0	-15.00	Hrdls	4-26	15.4	+37.00
Nov Chs	2-10	20.0	+27.00	Nov Chs	0-6	0.0	-6.00
Chases	0-0	0.0	0.00	Chases	1-11	9.1	-2.00
Sell/Claim	0-0	0.0	0.00	Sell/Claim	0-0	0.0	0.00

TOM SYMONDS

HAREWOOD END, H'FORDS

	No. of Hrs	Races Run	1st	2nd	3rd	Unpl	Per cent	£1 Level Stake
NH Flat	16	25	0	5	4	16	0.0	-25.00
Hurdles	21	81	7	4	9	61	8.6	+5.28
Chases	6	27	3	5	4	15	11.1	+19.00
Totals	37	133	10	14	17	92	7.5	-0.72
11-12	33	107	7	10	9	81	6.5	-20.00

RACE CLASS

	W-R	Per cent	£1 Level Stake
Class 1	1-7	14.3	-5.09
Class 2	1-1	100.0	+16.00
Class 3	1-15	6.7	+19.00
Class 4	7-67	10.4	+12.38
Class 5	0-23	0.0	-23.00
Class 6	0-20	0.0	-20.00

FIRST TIME OUT

	W-R	Per cent	£1 Level Stake
Bumpers	0-16	0.0	-16.00
Hurdles	0-17	0.0	-17.00
Chases	0-4	0.0	-4.00
Totals	0-37	0.0	-37.00

BY MONTH

NH Flat	W-R	Per cent	£1 Level Stake	Hurdles	W-R	Per cent	£1 Level Stake
May	0-0	0.0	0.00	May	0-2	0.0	-2.00
June	0-0	0.0	0.00	June	0-2	0.0	-2.00
July	0-0	0.0	0.00	July	0-3	0.0	-3.00
August	0-1	0.0	-1.00	August	0-0	0.0	0.00
September	0-2	0.0	-2.00	September	0-1	0.0	-1.00
October	0-3	0.0	-3.00	October	0-12	0.0	-12.00
November	0-3	0.0	-3.00	November	2-10	20.0	+26.38
December	0-3	0.0	-3.00	December	2-12	16.7	+24.00

JOCKEYS

	W-R	Per cent	£1 Level Stake
Ben Poste	7-39	17.9	+47.91
Felix De Giles	3-67	4.5	-21.63

COURSE RECORD

	Total W-R	Non-Hndcps Hurdles	Chases	Hndcps Hurdles	Chases	NH Flat	Per cent	£1 Level Stake
Ludlow	2-12	0-2	1-3	1-2	0-2	0-3	16.7	+0.50
Uttoxeter	2-16	1-8	1-2	0-4	0-0	0-2	12.5	+20.38

Ascot	1-2	0-0	0-0	1-2	0-0	0-0	50.0	+32.00
Doncaster	1-3	1-1	0-0	0-1	0-0	0-1	33.3	-1.09
Kempton	1-5	0-2	0-0	1-1	0-2	0-0	20.0	+12.00
Warwick	1-6	0-1	0-1	1-3	0-0	0-1	16.7	-3.50
Huntingdon	1-12	0-4	0-1	0-3	1-4	0-0	8.3	-3.00
Towcester	1-12	1-8	0-0	0-1	0-0	0-3	8.3	+7.00

WINNING HORSES

Horse	Races Run	1st	2nd	3rd	£
Tweedledrum	9	3	1	0	30677
Valmari	9	2	2	0	8347
Trojan Sun	8	1	2	3	3899
Midnight Belle	8	2	0	1	6368
Scholastica	5	1	1	2	2663
Abruzzi	6	1	2	1	2534
Total winning prize-money					£54488
Favourites	3-9		33.3%		-1.59

MISS L THOMAS

WROUGHTON, OXON

	No. of Hrs	Races Run	1st	2nd	3rd	Unpl	Per cent	£1 Level Stake
NH Flat	0	0	0	0	0	0	0.0	0.00
Hurdles	0	0	0	0	0	0	0.0	0.00
Chases	1	1	1	0	0	0	100.0	+3.00
Totals	1	1	1	0	0	0	100.0	+3.00
11-12	1	1	0	0	0	1	0.0	-1.00
10-11	2	2	0	0	0	2	0.0	-2.00

JOCKEYS

	W-R	Per cent	£1 Level Stake
Mr Joshua Newman	1-1	100.0	+3.00

COURSE RECORD

	Total W-R	Non-Hndcps Hurdles Chases	Hndcps Hurdles Chases	NH Flat	Per cent	£1 Level Stake
Towcester	1-1	0-0 1-1	0-0 0-0	0-0	100.0	+3.00

WINNING HORSES

Horse	Races Run	1st	2nd	3rd	£
Shrewd Investment	1	1	0	0	988
Total winning prize-money					£988
Favourites	0-0		0.0%		0.00

DAVID THOMPSON

BOLAM, CO DURHAM

	No. of Hrs	Races Run	1st	2nd	3rd	Unpl	Per cent	£1 Level Stake
NH Flat	6	12	0	0	1	11	0.0	-12.00
Hurdles	12	43	3	4	4	32	7.0	-19.38

Chases	3	8	0	1	2	5	0.0	-8.00
Totals	17	63	3	5	7	48	4.8	-39.38
11-12	22	69	5	5	3	56	7.2	-15.00
10-11	12	37	0	1	7	29	0.0	-37.00

JOCKEYS

	W-R	Per cent	£1 Level Stake
Tony Kelly	3-41	7.3	-17.38

COURSE RECORD

	Total W-R	Non-Hndcps Hurdles Chases	Hndcps Hurdles Chases	NH Flat	Per cent	£1 Level Stake
Musselbgh	1-1	0-0 0-0	1-1 0-0	0-0	100.0	+9.00
Fakenham	1-5	0-0 0-0	1-4 0-1	0-0	20.0	-2.38
Catterick	1-6	0-0 0-0	1-4 0-1	0-1	16.7	+5.00

WINNING HORSES

Horse	Races Run	1st	2nd	3rd	£
*Everdon Brook	7	3	2	1	11150
Total winning prize-money					£11150
Favourites	0-2		0.0%		-2.00

VICTOR THOMPSON

ALNWICK, NORTHUMBRIA

	No. of Hrs	Races Run	1st	2nd	3rd	Unpl	Per cent	£1 Level Stake
NH Flat	0	0	0	0	0	0	0.0	0.00
Hurdles	3	3	0	0	0	3	0.0	-3.00
Chases	3	10	3	0	2	5	30.0	+20.10
Totals	6	13	3	0	2	8	23.1	+17.10
11-12	1	1	0	1	0	0	0.0	-1.00
10-11	2	2	0	0	0	2	0.0	-2.00

JOCKEYS

	W-R	Per cent	£1 Level Stake
Mr T Davidson	3-5	60.0	+25.10

COURSE RECORD

	Total W-R	Non-Hndcps Hurdles Chases	Hndcps Hurdles Chases	NH Flat	Per cent	£1 Level Stake
Kelso	1-2	0-0 1-2	0-0 0-0	0-0	50.0	+19.00
Sedgefield	1-2	0-0 1-1	0-0 0-1	0-0	50.0	+5.00
Perth	1-3	0-1 1-2	0-0 0-0	0-0	33.3	-0.90

WINNING HORSES

Horse	Races Run	1st	2nd	3rd	£
Tommysteel	5	2	0	0	3808
*Gin Cobbler	4	1	0	1	936
Total winning prize-money					£4744
Favourites	1-2		50.0%		0.10

SANDY THOMSON

LAMBDEN, BERWICKS

	No. of Hrs	Races Run	1st	2nd	3rd	Unpl	Per cent	£1 Level Stake
NH Flat	1	1	0	0	0	1	0.0	-1.00
Hurdles	7	15	1	0	0	14	6.7	-8.00
Chases	3	15	1	3	0	11	6.7	-2.00
Totals	10	31	2	3	0	26	6.5	-11.00
11-12	6	27	2	3	2	20	7.4	-21.09
10-11	6	28	2	3	2	21	7.1	-9.50

JOCKEYS

	W-R	Per cent	£1 Level Stake
Peter Buchanan	1-7	14.3	+6.00
Ryan Mania	1-14	7.1	-7.00

COURSE RECORD

	Total W-R	Non-Hndcps Hurdles	Chases	Hndcps Hurdles	Chases	NH Flat	Per cent	£1 Level Stake
Musselbgh	1-4	0-1	0-0	1-2	0-0	0-1	25.0	+3.00
Ayr	1-7	0-1	0-1	0-2	1-3	0-0	14.3	+6.00

WINNING HORSES

Horse	Races Run	1st	2nd	3rd	£
Netminder	7	1	1	0	38988
Any Given Moment	1	1	0	0	3249
Total winning prize-money					£42237
Favourites	0-0		0.0%		0.00

ALISON THORPE

BRONWYDD ARMS, CARMARTHENS

	No. of Hrs	Races Run	1st	2nd	3rd	Unpl	Per cent	£1 Level Stake
NH Flat	0	0	0	0	0	0	0.0	0.00
Hurdles	7	10	0	1	1	8	0.0	-10.00
Chases	1	1	1	0	0	0	100.0	+8.00
Totals	8	11	1	1	1	8	9.1	-2.00
11-12	39	148	11	16	11	110	7.4	-81.59
10-11	43	178	20	21	17	120	11.2	-49.17

JOCKEYS

	W-R	Per cent	£1 Level Stake
Wayne Hutchinson	1-3	33.3	+6.00

COURSE RECORD

	Total W-R	Non-Hndcps Hurdles	Chases	Hndcps Hurdles	Chases	NH Flat	Per cent	£1 Level Stake
Ffos Las	1-1	0-0	0-0	0-0	1-1	0-0	100.0	+8.00

WINNING HORSES

Horse	Races Run	1st	2nd	3rd	£
Romanesco	1	1	0	0	3329
Total winning prize-money					£3329
Favourites	0-0		0.0%		0.00

COLIN TIZZARD

MILBORNE PORT, DORSET

	No. of Hrs	Races Run	1st	2nd	3rd	Unpl	Per cent	£1 Level Stake
NH Flat	13	21	2	0	3	16	9.5	-6.75
Hurdles	32	120	14	12	13	81	11.7	-17.50
Chases	36	171	27	17	29	98	15.8	+16.31
Totals	64	312	43	29	45	195	13.8	-7.94
11-12	68	318	45	38	45	189	14.2	-82.42
10-11	74	328	42	50	36	200	12.8	-35.38

BY MONTH

NH Flat	W-R	Per cent	£1 Level Stake	Hurdles	W-R	Per cent	£1 Level Stake
May	0-1	0.0	-1.00	May	0-3	0.0	-3.00
June	0-2	0.0	-2.00	June	0-0	0.0	0.00
July	0-1	0.0	-1.00	July	0-2	0.0	-2.00
August	0-0	0.0	0.00	August	1-2	50.0	+15.00
September	0-0	0.0	0.00	September	0-1	0.0	-1.00
October	0-0	0.0	0.00	October	3-16	18.8	+8.75
November	0-2	0.0	-2.00	November	2-18	11.1	-7.50
December	0-2	0.0	-2.00	December	0-13	0.0	-13.00
January	0-1	0.0	-1.00	January	3-13	23.1	+11.00
February	1-2	50.0	+1.25	February	3-18	16.7	-4.75
March	0-3	0.0	-3.00	March	2-17	11.8	-4.00
April	1-7	14.3	+4.00	April	0-17	0.0	-17.00

Chases	W-R	Per cent	£1 Level Stake	Totals	W-R	Per cent	£1 Level Stake
May	4-9	44.4	+13.75	May	4-13	30.8	+9.75
June	1-8	12.5	+5.00	June	1-10	10.0	+3.00
July	0-8	0.0	-8.00	July	0-11	0.0	-11.00
August	1-5	20.0	-1.50	August	2-7	28.6	+13.50
September	1-3	33.3	+5.00	September	1-4	25.0	+4.00
October	4-13	30.8	+16.50	October	7-29	24.1	+25.25
November	3-23	13.0	-6.17	November	5-43	11.6	-15.67
December	2-27	7.4	-18.25	December	2-42	4.8	-33.25
January	1-19	5.3	-13.50	January	4-33	12.1	-3.50
February	2-15	13.3	-7.63	February	6-35	17.1	-11.13
March	2-16	12.5	+17.50	March	4-36	11.1	+10.50
April	6-25	24.0	+13.60	April	7-49	14.3	+0.60

DISTANCE

Hurdles	W-R	Per cent	£1 Level Stake	Chases	W-R	Per cent	£1 Level Stake
2m-2m3f	10-72	13.9	+1.00	2m-2m3f	13-58	22.4	+34.08
2m4f-2m7f	3-39	7.7	-14.00	2m4f-2m7f	6-63	9.5	-42.02
3m+	1-9	11.1	-4.50	3m+	8-50	16.0	+24.25

TYPE OF RACE

Non-Handicaps	W-R	Per cent	£1 Level Stake	Handicaps	W-R	Per cent	£1 Level Stake
Nov Hrdls	1-32	3.1	-26.00	Nov Hrdls	3-15	20.0	+6.75
Hrdls	0-9	0.0	-9.00	Hrdls	10-61	16.4	+13.75
Nov Chs	7-39	17.9	+1.35	Nov Chs	2-18	11.1	-11.00
Chases	2-9	22.2	-1.63	Chases	16-105	15.2	+27.58
Sell/Claim	0-1	0.0	-1.00	Sell/Claim	0-2	0.0	-2.00

RACE CLASS

	W-R	Per cent	£1 Level Stake	FIRST TIME OUT	W-R	Per cent	£1 Level Stake
Class 1	5-39	12.8	+20.21	Bumpers	2-13	15.4	+1.25
Class 2	3-42	7.1	-20.50	Hurdles	0-22	0.0	-22.00
Class 3	11-79	13.9	-17.50	Chases	8-29	27.6	+23.58
Class 4	21-101	20.8	+43.10				
Class 5	2-33	6.1	-26.25	Totals	10-64	15.6	+2.83
Class 6	1-18	5.6	-7.00				

JOCKEYS

	W-R	Per cent	£1 Level Stake
Joe Tizzard	27-195	13.8	-33.69
Brendan Powell	11-63	17.5	+57.00
Mr M Legg	2-20	10.0	-11.75
Ryan Mahon	1-3	33.3	+1.50
Dave Crosse	1-8	12.5	-3.50
Tom O'Brien	1-10	10.0	-4.50

COURSE RECORD

	Total W-R	Non-Hndcps Hurdles	Chases	Hndcps Hurdles	Chases	NH Flat	Per cent	£1 Level Stake
Exeter	9-29	0-7	4-6	3-10	2-6	0-0	31.0	+14.08
Wincanton	9-52	1-7	0-5	4-19	3-14	1-7	17.3	-2.50
Chepstow	4-21	0-4	1-1	0-5	3-10	0-1	19.0	+10.50
Nton Abbot	4-22	0-2	1-1	1-4	2-12	0-3	18.2	+14.00
Aintree	2-9	0-0	0-2	0-2	2-5	0-0	22.2	+16.50
Ascot	2-13	0-2	1-3	1-2	0-6	0-0	15.4	-5.63
Taunton	2-22	0-3	0-2	1-6	0-9	1-2	9.1	-14.25
Cheltenham	2-28	0-1	1-8	0-7	1-12	0-0	7.1	+5.50
Hereford	1-2	0-0	0-0	0-1	1-1	0-0	50.0	+1.50
Ludlow	1-5	0-0	0-1	1-1	0-2	0-1	20.0	+14.00
Fontwell	1-7	0-2	1-2	0-1	0-0	0-2	14.3	-4.90
Plumpton	1-7	0-4	0-0	1-1	0-1	0-1	14.3	-2.50
Warwick	1-7	0-0	0-1	1-3	0-3	0-0	14.3	+8.00
Haydock	1-8	0-0	0-2	0-1	1-5	0-0	12.5	-2.50
Worcester	1-8	0-0	0-1	0-1	1-6	0-0	12.5	-4.00
Stratford	1-14	0-0	0-2	0-1	1-10	0-1	7.1	-1.00
Newbury	1-22	0-5	0-3	0-3	1-9	0-2	4.5	-18.75

WINNING HORSES

Horse	Races Run	1st	2nd	3rd	£
Cue Card	5	3	1	0	276611
Golden Chieftain	8	2	0	3	56908
Oiseau De Nuit	7	2	0	1	61805
Cannington Brook	7	1	1	0	21119
Theatre Guide	6	2	0	1	18480
Pasco	2	1	0	0	7027
Inside Dealer	7	2	0	0	10862
Theatrical Star	9	3	2	1	16765
Jumps Road	7	2	0	1	12828
Dimpsy Time	5	1	1	1	6498
Rateable Value	2	1	0	1	5991
Kings Lad	9	1	2	3	5848
Handy Andy	7	1	0	2	5653
Ivor's King	8	3	1	1	10179
Beside The Fire	7	2	0	1	7473
Xaarcet	9	3	1	1	10722
Masters Hill	2	1	0	0	3899
Sew On Target	9	2	1	0	7538
Mibleu	8	1	0	3	3574
Intac	6	1	0	0	3574
Dean's Grange	3	1	1	0	3574
Milarrow	7	1	3	2	3574
Virginia Ash	8	1	0	0	3422
Buckhorn Tom	7	1	1	0	3249
Flaming Charmer	7	1	1	2	3119
No Woman No Cry	8	1	0	1	3080
Dark Desire	1	1	0	0	2395
Robinsfirth	1	1	0	0	1625
Total winning prize-money					**£577392**
Favourites	11-34		32.4%		1.56

MISS C A TIZZARD

SHERBORNE, DORSET

	No. of Hrs	Races Run	1st	2nd	3rd	Unpl	Per cent	£1 Level Stake
NH Flat	0	0	0	0	0	0	0.0	0.00
Hurdles	0	0	0	0	0	0	0.0	0.00
Chases	1	6	2	2	0	2	33.3	+3.25
Totals	1	6	2	2	0	2	33.3	+3.25
11-12	1	4	1	2	0	1	25.0	-1.63

JOCKEYS

	W-R	Per cent	£1 Level Stake
Mr D Edwards	2-6	33.3	+3.25

COURSE RECORD

	Total W-R	Non-Hndcps Hurdles	Chases	Hndcps Hurdles	Chases	NH Flat	Per cent	£1 Level Stake
Cheltenham	1-2	0-0	1-2	0-0	0-0	0-0	50.0	+3.50
Wincanton	1-2	0-0	1-2	0-0	0-0	0-0	50.0	+1.75

WINNING HORSES

Horse	Races Run	1st	2nd	3rd	£
Coombe Hill	6	2	2	0	4419
Total winning prize-money					**£4419**
Favourites	0-0		0.0%		0.00

MARTIN TODHUNTER

ORTON, CUMBRIA

	No. of Hrs	Races Run	1st	2nd	3rd	Unpl	Per cent	£1 Level Stake
NH Flat	3	3	0	0	0	3	0.0	-3.00
Hurdles	17	45	2	2	3	38	4.4	-25.00
Chases	12	34	1	4	2	27	2.9	-29.00
Totals	**28**	**82**	**3**	**6**	**5**	**68**	**3.7**	**-57.00**
11-12	27	129	14	8	11	96	10.9	-15.00
10-11	38	175	16	21	20	118	9.1	-32.17

JOCKEYS

	W-R	Per cent	£1 Level Stake
Henry Brooke	2-24	8.3	-4.00
Lucy Alexander	1-22	4.5	-17.00

COURSE RECORD

	Total W-R	Non-Hndcps Hurdles	Chases	Hndcps Hurdles	Chases	NH Flat	Per cent	£1 Level Stake
Hexham	1-6	0-2	0-0	1-4	0-0	0-0	16.7	+9.00
Newcastle	1-8	0-2	0-1	1-2	0-3	0-0	12.5	-3.00
Wetherby	1-15	0-5	0-1	0-4	1-5	0-0	6.7	-10.00

WINNING HORSES

Horse	Races Run	1st	2nd	3rd	£
Allanard	8	1	1	2	3899
Acordingtoscript	5	1	0	0	2924
Almutaham	6	1	1	0	1819
Total winning prize-money					**£8642**
Favourites	1-4		25.0%		1.00

KEVIN TORK

LEIGH, SURREY

	No. of Hrs	Races Run	1st	2nd	3rd	Unpl	Per cent	£1 Level Stake
NH Flat	0	0	0	0	0	0	0.0	0.00
Hurdles	0	0	0	0	0	0	0.0	0.00
Chases	3	14	5	3	2	4	35.7	+55.38
Totals	**3**	**14**	**5**	**3**	**2**	**4**	**35.7**	**+55.38**
11-12	7	23	4	2	2	15	17.4	-2.50
10-11	3	20	0	1	1	18	0.0	-19.00

JOCKEYS

	W-R	Per cent	£1 Level Stake
Conor Shoemark	4-6	66.7	+53.88
Mne Kevin Jones	1-3	33.3	+6.50

COURSE RECORD

	Total W-R	Non-Hndcps Hurdles	Chases	Hndcps Hurdles	Chases	NH Flat	Per cent	£1 Level Stake
Plumpton	2-3	0-0	0-0	0-0	2-3	0-0	66.7	+40.38
Fontwell	2-6	0-0	0-0	0-0	2-6	0-0	33.3	+12.00
Kempton	1-1	0-0	0-0	0-0	1-1	0-0	100.0	+7.00

WINNING HORSES

Horse	Races Run	1st	2nd	3rd	£
*Upton Mead	6	4	1	0	11021
Zhukov	6	1	1	1	1819
Total winning prize-money					**£12840**
Favourites	1-2		50.0%		0.38

MRS H M TORY

BLANDFORD FORUM, DORSET

	No. of Hrs	Races Run	1st	2nd	3rd	Unpl	Per cent	£1 Level Stake
NH Flat	0	0	0	0	0	0	0.0	0.00
Hurdles	0	0	0	0	0	0	0.0	0.00
Chases	3	4	1	1	1	1	25.0	+1.00
Totals	**3**	**4**	**1**	**1**	**1**	**1**	**25.0**	**+1.00**
11-12	2	3	0	0	0	3	0.0	-3.00

JOCKEYS

	W-R	Per cent	£1 Level Stake
Miss E E MacMahon	1-2	50.0	+3.00

COURSE RECORD

	Total W-R	Non-Hndcps Hurdles	Chases	Hndcps Hurdles	Chases	NH Flat	Per cent	£1 Level Stake
Wincanton	1-1	0-0	1-1	0-0	0-0	0-0	100.0	+4.00

WINNING HORSES

Horse	Races Run	1st	2nd	3rd	£
Miss Midnight	2	1	0	1	1872
Total winning prize-money					**£1872**
Favourites	0-0		0.0%		0.00

ANDY TURNELL

BROAD HINTON, WILTS

	No. of Hrs	Races Run	1st	2nd	3rd	Unpl	Per cent	£1 Level Stake
NH Flat	4	5	1	0	0	4	20.0	+10.00
Hurdles	13	23	1	0	1	21	4.3	-2.00
Chases	6	36	3	7	6	20	8.3	-25.00
Totals	**17**	**64**	**5**	**7**	**7**	**45**	**7.8**	**-17.00**
11-12	24	97	9	9	11	67	9.3	-44.93
10-11	26	120	15	16	11	78	12.5	-32.88

JOCKEYS

	W-R	Per cent	£1 Level Stake
James Banks	3-20	15.0	-9.00
Gerard Tumelty	1-10	10.0	+5.00
Nick Scholfield	1-21	4.8	0.00

COURSE RECORD

	Total W-R	Non-Hndcps Hurdles	Chases	Hndcps Hurdles	Chases	NH Flat	Per cent	£1 Level Stake
Wincanton	2-10	0-5	1-1	0-2	0-1	1-1	20.0	+8.00
Southwell	1-1	0-0	0-0	0-0	1-1	0-0	100.0	+2.00
Ludlow	1-3	0-0	0-1	0-0	1-1	0-1	33.3	+2.00
Worcester	1-3	1-1	0-0	0-2	0-0	0-0	33.3	+18.00

WINNING HORSES

Horse	Races Run	1st	2nd	3rd	£
Micheal Flips	8	1	1	0	7596
The Druids Nephew	6	1	1	1	6975
Haar	5	1	1	1	3769
Faha	4	1	0	0	1949
Orchard Road	1	1	0	0	1711
Total winning prize-money					£22000
Favourites	1-6		16.7%		-3.00

BILL TURNER

SIGWELLS, SOMERSET

	No. of Hrs	Races Run	1st	2nd	3rd	Unpl	Per cent	£1 Level Stake
NH Flat	4	8	2	0	1	5	25.0	+6.50
Hurdles	10	26	1	5	3	17	3.8	-9.00
Chases	5	9	0	1	2	6	0.0	-9.00
Totals	13	43	3	6	6	28	7.0	-11.50
11-12	26	86	6	8	12	60	7.0	-49.00
10-11	22	54	3	4	4	43	5.6	+48.50

JOCKEYS

	W-R	Per cent	£1 Level Stake
Charlie Huxley	1-3	33.3	+4.00
Tom O'Connor	1-11	9.1	+6.00
Chris Davies	1-13	7.7	-5.50

COURSE RECORD

	Total W-R	Non-Hndcps Hurdles	Chases	Hndcps Hurdles	Chases	NH Flat	Per cent	£1 Level Stake
Worcester	2-3	1-2	0-0	0-0	0-0	1-1	66.7	+21.00
Hereford	1-2	0-0	0-0	0-0	0-0	1-2	50.0	+5.50

WINNING HORSES

Horse	Races Run	1st	2nd	3rd	£
Edlomond	2	1	0	0	1689
Floral Spinner	11	2	4	3	2874
Total winning prize-money					£4563
Favourites	0-1		0.0%		-1.00

KAREN TUTTY

OSMOTHERLEY, N YORKS

	No. of Hrs	Races Run	1st	2nd	3rd	Unpl	Per cent	£1 Level Stake
NH Flat	1	2	0	0	0	2	0.0	-2.00
Hurdles	4	19	2	2	2	13	10.5	-7.00
Chases	1	1	0	1	0	0	0.0	-1.00
Totals	6	22	2	3	2	15	9.1	-10.00
11-12	10	30	1	3	3	23	3.3	-25.67
10-11	8	32	2	4	2	24	6.3	-3.00

JOCKEYS

	W-R	Per cent	£1 Level Stake
Brian Toomey	1-4	25.0	0.00
Gemma Tutty	1-11	9.1	-3.00

COURSE RECORD

	Total W-R	Non-Hndcps Hurdles	Chases	Hndcps Hurdles	Chases	NH Flat	Per cent	£1 Level Stake
Southwell	1-2	0-0	0-0	1-2	0-0	0-0	50.0	+6.00
Hexham	1-5	1-2	0-0	0-3	0-0	0-0	20.0	-1.00

WINNING HORSES

Horse	Races Run	1st	2nd	3rd	£
Saddlers Mot	9	1	2	1	2053
Graceful Descent	2	1	0	0	1916
Total winning prize-money					£3969
Favourites	1-1		100.0%		3.00

NIGEL TWISTON-DAVIES

NAUNTON, GLOUCS

	No. of Hrs	Races Run	1st	2nd	3rd	Unpl	Per cent	£1 Level Stake
NH Flat	19	38	4	4	4	26	10.5	-16.25
Hurdles	62	228	34	29	24	141	14.9	-64.09
Chases	60	276	36	37	40	163	13.0	-73.90
Totals	117	542	74	70	68	330	13.7	-154.24
11-12	133	574	70	96	67	341	12.2	-180.65
10-11	174	708	98	73	80	457	13.8	+25.90

				Totals			
Class 5	11-81	13.6	-27.88	Totals	18-117	15.4	-28.59
Class 6	2-24	8.3	-9.00				

BY MONTH

NH Flat	W-R	Per cent	£1 Level Stake	Hurdles	W-R	Per cent	£1 Level Stake
May	1-2	50.0	+1.50	May	1-20	5.0	-16.75
June	1-4	25.0	+5.00	June	6-16	37.5	+15.88
July	0-0	0.0	0.00	July	4-15	26.7	-3.00
August	0-0	0.0	0.00	August	0-12	0.0	-12.00
September	0-0	0.0	0.00	September	0-5	0.0	-5.00
October	0-4	0.0	-4.00	October	5-25	20.0	-3.21
November	0-3	0.0	-3.00	November	4-28	14.3	+4.50
December	1-2	50.0	+1.25	December	3-25	12.0	-12.13
January	1-5	20.0	+1.00	January	2-12	16.7	-6.75
February	0-6	0.0	-6.00	February	4-30	13.3	-4.88
March	0-6	0.0	-6.00	March	4-18	22.2	-0.75
April	0-6	0.0	-6.00	April	1-22	4.5	-20.00

Chases	W-R	Per cent	£1 Level Stake	Totals	W-R	Per cent	£1 Level Stake
May	1-21	4.8	-16.50	May	3-43	7.0	-31.75
June	0-9	0.0	-9.00	June	7-29	24.1	+11.88
July	1-8	12.5	-5.00	July	5-23	21.7	-8.00
August	3-8	37.5	+11.00	August	3-20	15.0	-1.00
September	3-7	42.9	+10.50	September	3-12	25.0	+5.50
October	4-33	12.1	-14.09	October	9-62	14.5	-21.30
November	4-34	11.8	-16.21	November	8-65	12.3	-14.71
December	7-36	19.4	+0.94	December	11-63	17.5	-9.94
January	2-21	9.5	-4.75	January	5-38	13.2	-10.50
February	2-35	5.7	-29.00	February	6-71	8.5	-39.88
March	5-32	15.6	+3.96	March	9-56	16.1	-2.79
April	4-32	12.5	-5.75	April	5-60	8.3	-31.75

DISTANCE

Hurdles	W-R	Per cent	£1 Level Stake	Chases	W-R	Per cent	£1 Level Stake
2m-2m3f	8-71	11.3	-39.71	2m-2m3f	9-38	23.7	-4.22
2m4f-2m7f	20-101	19.8	-10.38	2m4f-2m7f	17-99	17.2	-17.56
3m+	6-56	10.7	-14.00	3m+	10-139	7.2	-52.13

TYPE OF RACE

Non-Handicaps	W-R	Per cent	£1 Level Stake	Handicaps	W-R	Per cent	£1 Level Stake
Nov Hrdls	11-53	20.8	-18.71	Nov Hrdls	5-21	23.8	+7.13
Hrdls	3-31	9.7	-20.50	Hrdls	14-116	12.1	-28.75
Nov Chs	8-46	17.4	-15.56	Nov Chs	4-16	25.0	-2.13
Chases	0-10	0.0	-10.00	Chases	24-204	11.8	-46.22
Sell/Claim	1-5	20.0	-1.25	Sell/Claim	0-2	0.0	-2.00

RACE CLASS

	W-R	Per cent	£1 Level Stake
Class 1	4-70	5.7	-45.75
Class 2	8-56	14.3	+6.00
Class 3	22-136	16.2	-17.79
Class 4	27-175	15.4	-59.82

FIRST TIME OUT

	W-R	Per cent	£1 Level Stake
Bumpers	3-19	15.8	-0.50
Hurdles	7-45	15.6	-14.09
Chases	8-53	15.1	-14.00

JOCKEYS

	W-R	Per cent	£1 Level Stake
Sam Twiston-Davies	70-430	16.3	-71.99
Ryan Hatch	2-26	7.7	-4.50
William Twiston-Davies	1-7	14.3	-2.50
David England	1-19	5.3	-15.25

COURSE RECORD

	Total W-R	Non-Hndcps Hurdles	Chases	Hndcps Hurdles	Chases	NH Flat	Per cent	£1 Level Stake
Cheltenham	8-54	3-10	1-12	1-10	3-20	0-2	14.8	+6.75
Uttoxeter	6-20	0-0	1-3	2-7	3-9	0-1	30.0	+6.88
Ludlow	5-35	0-9	1-4	0-3	3-15	1-4	14.3	-9.42
Stratford	4-19	0-2	0-2	0-6	2-7	2-2	21.1	+8.50
Newbury	4-20	0-1	0-3	3-6	1-8	0-2	20.0	+8.00
Ffos Las	4-24	0-1	1-2	2-8	1-12	0-1	16.7	-7.50
Worcester	4-26	3-8	0-0	0-8	1-9	0-1	15.4	-13.75
Mrket Rsn	3-9	0-0	1-1	1-5	1-2	0-1	33.3	+5.67
Fontwell	3-11	0-1	0-0	1-2	2-8	0-0	27.3	+5.00
Bangor	3-12	0-4	1-2	1-1	1-3	0-2	25.0	+8.25
Leicester	3-17	0-3	2-6	0-1	1-7	0-0	17.6	-7.81
Aintree	3-23	0-6	0-2	1-5	2-10	0-0	13.0	-0.63
Wincanton	2-5	0-0	0-0	1-2	1-3	0-0	40.0	+11.75
Hexham	2-8	1-4	0-1	1-2	0-1	0-0	25.0	+1.88
Cartmel	2-9	1-2	0-0	1-2	0-5	0-0	22.2	-1.75
Hereford	2-10	0-1	0-0	2-7	0-2	0-0	20.0	-1.00
Ascot	2-12	0-0	0-2	0-3	2-5	0-0	16.7	+8.00
Nton Abbot	2-15	1-2	0-1	0-8	1-3	0-1	13.3	-11.81
Perth	2-17	1-1	0-0	1-7	0-8	0-1	11.8	-11.75
Towcester	2-21	1-5	0-4	0-4	1-5	0-3	9.5	-13.38
Warwick	2-27	1-4	0-2	0-8	0-7	1-6	7.4	-19.50
Folkestone	1-3	0-0	0-1	0-0	1-2	0-0	33.3	-1.00
Doncaster	1-10	1-3	0-0	0-2	0-5	0-0	10.0	-7.38
Taunton	1-10	0-1	0-1	0-5	1-2	0-1	10.0	-6.25
Wetherby	1-10	1-1	0-0	0-2	0-6	0-1	10.0	-7.00
Haydock	1-14	0-1	0-0	1-6	0-6	0-1	7.1	-9.50
Southwell	1-14	1-4	0-0	0-1	0-8	0-1	7.1	-8.50

WINNING HORSES

Horse	Races Run	1st	2nd	3rd	£
The New One	6	4	2	0	97634
Hello Bud	3	1	0	1	61950
Little Josh	5	1	0	0	38057
Same Difference	8	2	2	2	42474
Tara Rose	6	2	3	0	17864
African Gold	8	5	2	0	26414
Ackertac	7	2	2	1	25024
Double Ross	9	1	1	2	12512
Pigeon Island	10	2	1	2	16638
Master Of The Sea	9	4	0	0	11574
Tour Des Champs	10	3	0	1	20045
Cootehill	10	2	0	3	17091

Hunters Lodge	7	3	0	2	19203
Oscar Magic	4	1	3	0	8123
Royal Riviera	9	2	1	2	9812
Kaylif Aramis	7	2	0	3	14005
Frontier Spirit	8	2	1	2	12380
What A Warrior	7	2	1	0	9384
According To Trev	7	2	0	1	8368
Changing Times	8	2	2	2	9045
Tullyraine	3	1	0	1	5393
Kruzhlinin	1	1	0	0	4791
Mavalenta	9	1	2	0	4549
Desolait	5	2	1	0	6602
Listen Boy	3	1	0	0	4549
Stormhoek	3	2	0	0	6874
Rhum	5	1	0	2	3899
Moulin De La Croix	8	3	1	2	9056
Red Rouble	9	1	3	1	3249
What An Oscar	5	1	0	0	3249
The Cockney Mackem	2	1	0	0	3249
*Foundry Square	3	1	1	0	3249
Papradon	8	2	2	1	4549
Imperial Leader	4	1	0	1	2599
Little Pop	4	1	0	0	2599
Nudge And Nurdle	4	1	0	1	2469
Brousse En Feux	5	1	0	0	2339
Quapriland	3	1	0	1	2053
*Miss Tilly Oscar	5	1	1	1	1949
Count Guido Deiro	3	1	1	0	1949
Samenerve	5	1	0	0	1819
Ricardo's Chance	5	1	1	0	1779
Red Riverman	11	1	2	2	1689
Pure Science	4	1	0	0	1560
Total winning prize-money					**£563659**
Favourites	**25-73**		**34.2%**		**0.39**

TIM VAUGHAN

ABERTHIN, VALE OF GLAMORGAN

	No. of Hrs	Races Run	1st	2nd	3rd	Unpl	Per cent	£1 Level Stake
NH Flat	26	39	4	7	4	24	10.3	-12.88
Hurdles	135	423	55	67	63	238	13.0	-138.31
Chases	58	171	24	29	25	93	14.0	-55.54
Totals	178	633	83	103	92	355	13.1	-206.73
11-12	170	578	98	101	71	308	17.0	-97.13
10-11	162	560	93	83	60	324	16.6	-124.58

BY MONTH

NH Flat	W-R	Per cent	£1 Level Stake	Hurdles	W-R	Per cent	£1 Level Stake
May	0-3	0.0	-3.00	May	6-34	17.6	+1.50
June	0-2	0.0	-2.00	June	6-29	20.7	+3.38
July	0-2	0.0	-2.00	July	6-38	15.8	+6.75
August	0-4	0.0	-4.00	August	12-36	33.3	+12.22
September	0-1	0.0	-1.00	September	4-27	14.8	-13.63
October	0-5	0.0	-5.00	October	5-54	9.3	-10.25
November				November	1-5	20.0	-1.75
December				December	0-1	0.0	-1.00
January				January	1-3	33.3	+2.00
February				February	0-2	0.0	-2.00
March				March	1-6	16.7	-3.13
April				April	1-5	20.0	+10.00

Chases	W-R	Per cent	£1 Level Stake	Totals	W-R	Per cent	£1 Level Stake
May	6-12	50.0	+22.82	May	12-49	24.5	+21.32
June	2-14	14.3	-5.75	June	8-45	17.8	-4.37
July	0-10	0.0	-10.00	July	6-50	12.0	-5.25
August	3-16	18.8	+4.09	August	15-56	26.8	+12.31
September	0-9	0.0	-9.00	September	4-37	10.8	-23.63
October	2-14	14.3	-4.50	October	7-73	9.6	-19.75
November	3-16	18.8	+0.73	November	10-81	12.3	-36.36
December	3-21	14.3	-11.68	December	9-62	14.5	-35.10
January	2-12	16.7	-4.80	January	3-28	10.7	-15.80
February	1-8	12.5	-5.25	February	4-50	8.0	-25.52
March	2-25	8.0	-18.20	March	4-60	6.7	-47.58
April	0-14	0.0	-14.00	April	1-42	2.4	-27.00

DISTANCE

Hurdles	W-R	Per cent	£1 Level Stake	Chases	W-R	Per cent	£1 Level Stake
2m-2m3f	40-226	17.7	-38.31	2m-2m3f	10-58	17.2	-3.76
2m4f-2m7f	12-139	8.6	-66.63	2m4f-2m7f	9-60	15.0	-9.55
3m+	3-58	5.2	-33.38	3m+	5-53	9.4	-42.23

TYPE OF RACE

Non-Handicaps	W-R	Per cent	£1 Level Stake	Handicaps	W-R	Per cent	£1 Level Stake
Nov Hrdls	16-93	17.2	+11.19	Nov Hrdls	3-44	6.8	-32.00
Hrdls	12-82	14.6	-37.17	Hrdls	16-178	9.0	-78.50
Nov Chs	6-50	12.0	-33.94	Nov Chs	4-19	21.1	-3.39
Chases	2-6	33.3	-1.80	Chases	12-96	12.5	-16.41
Sell/Claim	6-20	30.0	-4.59	Sell/Claim	2-5	40.0	+3.75

RACE CLASS

	W-R	Per cent	£1 Level Stake
Class 1	1-34	2.9	-21.00
Class 2	1-23	4.3	-19.75
Class 3	6-84	7.1	-44.27
Class 4	46-302	15.2	-69.11
Class 5	26-156	16.7	-38.47
Class 6	3-34	8.8	-14.13

FIRST TIME OUT

	W-R	Per cent	£1 Level Stake
Bumpers	3-26	11.5	-3.13
Hurdles	18-118	15.3	-4.71
Chases	10-34	29.4	+9.76
Totals	31-178	17.4	+1.92

JOCKEYS

	W-R	Per cent	£1 Level Stake
Richard Johnson	47-280	16.8	-65.80
Michael Byrne	13-144	9.0	-54.66
Dougie Costello	5-40	12.5	-22.63
Aidan Coleman	5-51	9.8	-27.16
J P Kiely	4-31	12.9	-2.65
Richard Killoran	4-38	10.5	-17.75

Mr Matthew Barber	2-6	33.3	0.00
Sam Twiston-Davies	1-1	100.0	+3.00
Robert Kirk	1-7	14.3	+14.00
Mr B Gibbs	1-14	7.1	-12.09

COURSE RECORD

	Total W-R	Non-Hndcps Hurdles	Non-Hndcps Chases	Hndcps Hurdles	Chases	NH Flat	Per cent	£1 Level Stake
Perth	8-19	3-7	0-0	3-6	2-6	0-0	42.1	+6.66
Ffos Las	8-60	2-18	0-2	3-22	3-11	0-7	13.3	-25.71
Stratford	7-34	5-15	0-3	2-9	0-4	0-3	20.6	+20.25
Uttoxeter	5-41	4-19	1-5	0-13	0-3	0-1	12.2	-15.63
Sedgefield	4-18	0-5	0-1	1-5	3-5	0-2	22.2	-6.27
Mrket Rsn	4-31	3-11	1-4	0-10	0-5	0-1	12.9	-20.59
Exeter	3-14	0-1	0-2	2-8	1-3	0-0	21.4	+4.50
Southwell	3-14	1-7	0-1	1-5	0-0	1-1	21.4	+9.75
Plumpton	3-15	1-5	0-0	1-4	1-5	0-1	20.0	-1.00
Fakenham	3-16	0-3	2-4	1-8	0-1	0-0	18.8	-8.07
Towcester	3-16	0-2	0-2	2-8	1-4	0-0	18.8	-6.80
Worcester	3-26	2-9	0-2	1-10	0-5	0-0	11.5	-9.50
Folkestone	2-8	1-4	1-1	0-1	0-1	0-1	25.0	-1.50
Musselbgh	2-9	1-4	0-1	0-2	0-1	1-1	22.2	-1.50
Ludlow	2-10	0-3	0-1	1-4	0-0	1-2	20.0	+8.25
Wetherby	2-15	0-6	1-4	0-4	0-0	1-1	13.3	-7.79
Bangor	2-16	1-7	0-0	0-7	1-2	0-0	12.5	+11.00
Newbury	2-16	1-4	0-0	0-7	1-5	0-0	12.5	-1.33
Fontwell	2-21	1-5	0-3	1-8	0-3	0-2	9.5	-12.50
Nton Abbot	2-23	2-8	0-1	0-8	0-4	0-2	8.7	-11.13
Kelso	1-1	0-0	1-1	0-0	0-0	0-0	100.0	+1.50
Carlisle	1-2	1-1	0-0	0-1	0-0	0-0	50.0	-0.27
Leicester	1-3	1-2	0-0	0-0	0-1	0-0	33.3	-1.00
Newcastle	1-3	0-0	1-1	0-1	0-0	0-1	33.3	-1.00
Catterick	1-4	0-1	0-0	1-3	0-0	0-0	25.0	-0.25
Lingfield	1-5	1-4	0-1	0-0	0-0	0-0	20.0	-3.09
Warwick	1-5	1-4	0-0	0-0	0-0	0-1	20.0	-1.25
Kempton	1-7	1-2	0-1	0-3	0-1	0-0	14.3	+6.00
Cartmel	1-9	0-1	0-1	1-5	0-2	0-0	11.1	+2.00
Huntingdon	1-9	0-4	0-0	0-2	1-2	0-1	11.1	-7.20
Taunton	1-11	1-2	0-1	0-5	0-1	0-2	9.1	-7.25
Wincanton	1-13	0-1	0-1	0-6	1-4	0-1	7.7	-8.00
Hereford	1-14	0-2	0-2	0-7	1-3	0-0	7.1	+7.00

WINNING HORSES

Horse	Races Run	1st	2nd	3rd	£
Solaras Exhibition	5	2	0	0	12544
Saved By John	6	2	1	1	12744
Hawkhill	10	4	3	1	16098
Gallox Bridge	5	1	1	1	6498
*Trop Fort	4	2	0	0	9032
Wings Of Smoke	7	2	0	3	9422
First Fandango	7	1	2	3	5991
Stonethrower	7	2	2	1	8902
Scorched Son	6	1	0	0	4549
Hidden Identity	6	3	1	0	10895
Qualviro	7	1	2	1	3899
Our Island	5	1	0	1	3899
*Bucking The Trend	6	2	1	0	6498
Groomed	5	2	0	1	3769
The Big Freeze	9	1	2	2	3574
Next Exit	5	1	2	2	3482
Aland Islands	3	1	1	0	3444
Skylancer	3	2	0	0	6587
Geminus	5	3	0	1	9920
*Juno The Muffinman	5	2	0	2	5956
Makhzoon	1	1	0	0	3249
*Chilbury Hill	4	3	0	1	7343
Grand Lahou	6	3	1	0	5198
Piment D'Estruval	5	1	2	2	3249
Amok	5	1	1	0	3249
Kack Handed	6	1	3	1	3054
Tout Regulier	5	1	0	1	3054
Swampfire	3	1	0	0	2738
*Ruttan Lake	4	2	1	1	4482
True Blue	6	1	1	0	2663
*Bingo Des Mottes	5	1	1	0	2599
Miracle House	4	1	1	0	2599
Rathnaroughy	3	1	0	0	2599
Spanish Optimist	1	1	0	0	2599
*Dovils Date	3	1	0	1	2599
*Swnymor	4	1	0	1	2599
Alborz	5	2	0	2	5133
Paddy Partridge	2	2	0	0	4679
Ivan Vasilevich	8	2	2	2	5068
*Third Half	3	1	1	0	2534
Dingat	1	1	0	0	2112
Billybo	5	1	3	0	2053
Coverholder	2	1	0	0	2053
Explained	5	1	0	1	2053
Truckers Benefit	6	1	0	1	1949
*Landenstown Star	9	1	3	0	1949
Alphabetical Order	2	1	0	0	1949
Be Bop Boru	4	1	3	0	1949
Got The Urge	3	1	0	0	1819
Sieglinde	3	1	0	1	1819
Whatshallwedo	7	2	1	2	3639
Latest Trend	6	1	2	1	1779
Peaks Of Fire	7	1	4	2	1689
Four Shuck Men	1	1	0	0	1643
*Silentplan	1	1	0	0	1643
Louis Ludwig	7	1	0	0	1622
Duneen Point	7	1	0	2	1560
Postmaster	5	1	0	0	1153
Total winning prize-money					**£253423**
Favourites	35-97		36.1%		-12.81

WILLIAM VAUGHAN

BRIDGEND, BRIDGEND

	No. of Hrs	Races Run	1st	2nd	3rd	Unpl	Per cent	£1 Level Stake
NH Flat	0	0	0	0	0	0	0.0	0.00
Hurdles	0	0	0	0	0	0	0.0	0.00

Chases	*1*	*4*	*2*	*0*	*1*	*1*	*50.0*	*+8.00*
Totals	*1*	*4*	*2*	*0*	*1*	*1*	*50.0*	*+8.00*

JOCKEYS

	W-R	Per cent	£1 Level Stake
Mr J F Mathias	1-1	100.0	+3.00
Mr B Gibbs	1-3	33.3	+5.00

COURSE RECORD

	Total W-R	Non-Hndcps Hurdles	Chases	Hndcps Hurdles	Chases	NH Flat	Per cent	£1 Level Stake
Cheltenham	1-1	0-0	1-1	0-0	0-0	0-0	100.0	+7.00
Aintree	1-2	0-0	1-2	0-0	0-0	0-0	50.0	+2.00

WINNING HORSES

Horse	Races Run	1st	2nd	3rd	£
Silver Story	4	2	0	1	4076
Total winning prize-money					£4076
Favourites	0-0		0.0%		0.00

JOHN WADE

MORDON, CO DURHAM

	No. of Hrs	Races Run	1st	2nd	3rd	Unpl	Per cent	£1 Level Stake
NH Flat	*12*	*23*	*0*	*1*	*3*	*19*	*0.0*	*-23.00*
Hurdles	*34*	*86*	*5*	*7*	*9*	*65*	*5.8*	*-53.17*
Chases	*32*	*117*	*19*	*12*	*14*	*72*	*16.2*	*-26.67*
Totals	*62*	*226*	*24*	*20*	*26*	*156*	*10.6*	*-102.84*
11-12	*57*	*163*	*13*	*22*	*24*	*104*	*8.0*	*-57.54*
10-11	*38*	*124*	*13*	*14*	*12*	*85*	*10.5*	*-9.85*

BY MONTH

NH Flat	W-R	Per cent	£1 Level Stake	Hurdles	W-R	Per cent	£1 Level Stake
May	0-6	0.0	-6.00	May	0-10	0.0	-10.00
June	0-1	0.0	-1.00	June	1-2	50.0	+2.33
July	0-0	0.0	0.00	July	0-2	0.0	-2.00
August	0-0	0.0	0.00	August	0-1	0.0	-1.00
September	0-0	0.0	0.00	September	0-0	0.0	0.00
October	0-0	0.0	0.00	October	0-1	0.0	-1.00
November	0-0	0.0	0.00	November	0-5	0.0	-5.00
December	0-4	0.0	-4.00	December	1-13	7.7	-9.50
January	0-3	0.0	-3.00	January	0-9	0.0	-9.00
February	0-2	0.0	-2.00	February	1-15	6.7	-12.00
March	0-4	0.0	-4.00	March	0-10	0.0	-10.00
April	0-3	0.0	-3.00	April	2-18	11.1	+4.00

Chases	W-R	Per cent	£1 Level Stake	Totals	W-R	Per cent	£1 Level Stake
May	1-11	9.1	-7.00	May	1-27	3.7	-23.00
June	2-4	50.0	+2.88	June	3-7	42.9	+4.21
July	0-5	0.0	-5.00	July	0-7	0.0	-7.00
August	0-4	0.0	-4.00	August	0-5	0.0	-5.00

September	0-2	0.0	-2.00	September	0-2	0.0	-2.00
October	0-2	0.0	-2.00	October	0-3	0.0	-3.00
November	1-8	12.5	-3.00	November	1-13	7.7	-8.00
December	3-20	15.0	-6.50	December	4-37	10.8	-20.00
January	2-8	25.0	-4.13	January	2-20	10.0	-16.13
February	3-18	16.7	-8.63	February	4-35	11.4	-22.63
March	4-14	28.6	+22.38	March	4-28	14.3	+8.38
April	3-21	14.3	-9.67	April	5-42	11.9	-8.67

DISTANCE

Hurdles	W-R	Per cent	£1 Level Stake	Chases	W-R	Per cent	£1 Level Stake
2m-2m3f	1-34	2.9	-29.67	2m-2m3f	5-29	17.2	-9.71
2m4f-2m7f	4-41	9.8	-12.50	2m4f-2m7f	7-43	16.3	+1.03
3m+	0-11	0.0	-11.00	3m+	7-45	15.6	-18.00

TYPE OF RACE

Non-Handicaps	W-R	Per cent	£1 Level Stake	Handicaps	W-R	Per cent	£1 Level Stake
Nov Hrdls	0-32	0.0	-32.00	Nov Hrdls	0-6	0.0	-6.00
Hrdls	1-5	20.0	-1.50	Hrdls	4-43	9.3	-13.67
Nov Chs	1-17	5.9	-14.00	Nov Chs	3-10	30.0	+0.13
Chases	2-5	40.0	+20.00	Chases	13-85	15.3	-32.80
Sell/Claim	0-0	0.0	0.00	Sell/Claim	0-0	0.0	0.00

RACE CLASS / FIRST TIME OUT

RACE CLASS	W-R	Per cent	£1 Level Stake	FIRST TIME OUT	W-R	Per cent	£1 Level Stake
Class 1	1-3	33.3	+18.00	Bumpers	0-12	0.0	-12.00
Class 2	0-6	0.0	-6.00	Hurdles	0-23	0.0	-23.00
Class 3	1-42	2.4	-35.50	Chases	2-27	7.4	-19.00
Class 4	13-115	11.3	-48.67				
Class 5	8-31	25.8	-5.68	Totals	2-62	3.2	-54.00
Class 6	1-29	3.4	-25.00				

JOCKEYS

	W-R	Per cent	£1 Level Stake
Wilson Renwick	9-79	11.4	-30.25
John Dawson	8-72	11.1	-34.54
Brian Hughes	5-52	9.6	-37.05
Samantha Drake	1-1	100.0	+4.00
Adrian Lane	1-2	50.0	+15.00

COURSE RECORD

	Total W-R	Non-Hndcps Hurdles	Chases	Hndcps Hurdles	Chases	NH Flat	Per cent	£1 Level Stake
Newcastle	4-21	0-3	1-1	0-5	3-12	0-0	19.0	-9.43
Catterick	4-23	0-3	0-4	0-6	4-7	0-3	17.4	-8.21
Wetherby	4-36	0-7	0-5	1-7	3-15	0-2	11.1	-21.25
Kelso	3-7	1-2	1-2	1-3	0-0	0-0	42.9	+34.50
Sedgefield	3-42	0-7	0-1	1-7	2-17	0-10	7.1	-30.00
Cartmel	2-7	0-0	1-1	1-2	0-4	0-0	28.6	+1.63
Carlisle	2-16	0-2	0-0	0-5	2-8	0-1	12.5	-3.00
Mrket Rsn	1-7	0-1	0-0	0-0	1-6	0-0	14.3	-2.67
Hexham	1-14	0-4	0-3	0-2	1-2	0-3	7.1	-11.13

WINNING HORSES

Horse	Races Run	1st	2nd	3rd	£
Always Right	4	1	0	0	11390
Harris Hawk	4	1	0	1	7148
Diamond Frontier	9	2	1	1	8642
Riskier	7	3	1	2	8740
Blazing Bull	8	3	0	1	12086
Pudsey House	7	1	0	0	3899
Beau Dandy	7	1	0	2	3769
Mannered	4	1	0	0	3488
Forty Crown	7	2	0	1	5884
Takaatuf	7	1	2	0	3119
Whats Up Woody	7	1	2	1	3054
*No Way Hozay	6	3	0	1	7545
Letterpress	3	1	1	1	2599
Dingo Bay	6	2	0	1	4341
*Call Me Mulligan	4	1	0	0	1248
Total winning prize-money					**£86952**
Favourites	13-25		52.0%		15.82

LUCY WADHAM

NEWMARKET, SUFFOLK

	No. of Hrs	Races Run	1st	2nd	3rd	Unpl	Per cent	£1 Level Stake
NH Flat	4	9	0	2	1	6	0.0	-9.00
Hurdles	21	77	12	10	8	47	15.6	-8.38
Chases	6	30	6	3	6	15	20.0	+31.85
Totals	25	116	18	15	15	68	15.5	+14.47
11-12	23	99	15	10	6	68	15.2	+28.48
10-11	27	103	13	14	14	62	12.6	-21.74

BY MONTH

NH Flat	W-R	Per cent	£1 Level Stake	Hurdles	W-R	Per cent	£1 Level Stake
May	0-0	0.0	0.00	May	0-7	0.0	-7.00
June	0-0	0.0	0.00	June	0-2	0.0	-2.00
July	0-0	0.0	0.00	July	0-0	0.0	0.00
August	0-0	0.0	0.00	August	0-0	0.0	0.00
September	0-0	0.0	0.00	September	0-0	0.0	0.00
October	0-0	0.0	0.00	October	1-2	50.0	+9.00
November	0-1	0.0	-1.00	November	4-13	30.8	+3.25
December	0-3	0.0	-3.00	December	0-7	0.0	-7.00
January	0-3	0.0	-3.00	January	0-5	0.0	-5.00
February	0-1	0.0	-1.00	February	2-14	14.3	+2.25
March	0-0	0.0	0.00	March	1-14	7.1	-11.50
April	0-1	0.0	-1.00	April	4-13	30.8	+9.63

Chases	W-R	Per cent	£1 Level Stake	Totals	W-R	Per cent	£1 Level Stake
May	1-1	100.0	+1.10	May	1-8	12.5	-5.90
June	0-1	0.0	-1.00	June	0-3	0.0	-3.00
July	0-0	0.0	0.00	July	0-0	0.0	0.00
August	0-0	0.0	0.00	August	0-0	0.0	0.00

(continued from previous page — BY MONTH, Hurdles / Chases)

Month	W-R	Per cent	£1 Level Stake	Month	W-R	Per cent	£1 Level Stake
September	0-0	0.0	0.00	September	0-0	0.0	0.00
October	0-0	0.0	0.00	October	1-2	50.0	+9.00
November	0-3	0.0	-3.00	November	4-17	23.5	-0.75
December	2-5	40.0	+38.38	December	2-15	13.3	+28.38
January	0-4	0.0	-4.00	January	0-12	0.0	-12.00
February	1-3	33.3	+7.00	February	3-18	16.7	+8.25
March	2-7	28.6	-0.63	March	3-21	14.3	-12.13
April	0-6	0.0	-6.00	April	4-20	20.0	+2.63

DISTANCE

Hurdles	W-R	Per cent	£1 Level Stake	Chases	W-R	Per cent	£1 Level Stake
2m-2m3f	8-43	18.6	-6.63	2m-2m3f	1-1	100.0	+40.00
2m4f-2m7f	4-27	14.8	+5.25	2m4f-2m7f	3-14	21.4	+1.00
3m+	0-7	0.0	-7.00	3m+	2-15	13.3	-9.15

TYPE OF RACE

Non-Handicaps	W-R	Per cent	£1 Level Stake	Handicaps	W-R	Per cent	£1 Level Stake
Nov Hrdls	5-22	22.7	-0.13	Nov Hrdls	0-3	0.0	-3.00
Hrdls	1-12	8.3	-9.25	Hrdls	6-40	15.0	+4.00
Nov Chs	3-4	75.0	+43.38	Nov Chs	0-1	0.0	-1.00
Chases	1-2	50.0	+0.10	Chases	2-23	8.7	-10.63
Sell/Claim	0-0	0.0	0.00	Sell/Claim	0-0	0.0	0.00

RACE CLASS / FIRST TIME OUT

	W-R	Per cent	£1 Level Stake		W-R	Per cent	£1 Level Stake
Class 1	0-7	0.0	-7.00	Bumpers	0-4	0.0	-4.00
Class 2	0-9	0.0	-9.00	Hurdles	1-18	5.6	-14.00
Class 3	7-28	25.0	+57.50	Chases	1-3	33.3	-0.90
Class 4	10-55	18.2	-12.13				
Class 5	0-7	0.0	-7.00	Totals	2-25	8.0	-18.90
Class 6	1-10	10.0	-7.90				

JOCKEYS

	W-R	Per cent	£1 Level Stake
Leighton Aspell	11-64	17.2	-13.25
Micheal Nolan	2-3	66.7	+3.10
Denis O'Regan	1-1	100.0	+10.00
Dave Crosse	1-4	25.0	+2.00
Aidan Coleman	1-5	20.0	-2.38
Richard Johnson	1-6	16.7	+7.00
Dominic Elsworth	1-8	12.5	+33.00

COURSE RECORD

	Total W-R	Non-Hndcps Hurdles	Non-Hndcps Chases	Hndcps Hurdles	Hndcps Chases	NH Flat	Per cent	£1 Level Stake
Mrket Rsn	4-9	3-5	0-0	1-2	0-2	0-0	44.4	+11.38
Fakenham	4-13	0-2	2-2	1-5	1-3	0-1	30.8	+13.85
Kempton	3-9	1-3	0-0	2-5	0-1	0-0	33.3	+13.50
Leicester	2-7	1-2	1-2	0-0	0-3	0-0	28.6	+1.63
Bangor	1-1	0-0	0-0	0-0	1-1	0-0	100.0	+1.38
Doncaster	1-5	0-1	1-1	0-1	0-2	0-0	20.0	+36.00
Fontwell	1-6	1-4	0-0	0-1	0-1	0-0	16.7	-3.25

Sandown	1-7	0-1	0-0	1-5	0-0	0-1	14.3	-3.50
Towcester	1-7	0-1	0-0	1-3	0-0	0-3	14.3	-4.50

WINNING HORSES

Horse	Races Run	1st	2nd	3rd	£
Wiesentraum	3	1	2	0	7148
El Dancer	10	3	3	0	16499
The Black Baron	7	1	0	2	6498
General Ting	4	2	1	0	8855
Baby Shine	7	1	1	0	5848
Le Reve	6	2	0	1	9747
Tealissio	9	1	1	0	3899
Brunton Blue	2	1	0	0	3285
*Watered Silk	4	2	0	0	6368
Dawn Twister	9	1	0	3	3249
Midnight Macarena	9	1	3	2	3129
All Annalena	6	1	0	1	3119
Eleazar	4	1	0	0	1021
Total winning prize-money					£78665
Favourites	5-11		45.5%		2.10

TRACY WAGGOTT

SPENNYMOOR, CO DURHAM

	No. of Hrs	Races Run	1st	2nd	3rd	Unpl	Per cent	£1 Level Stake
NH Flat	1	1	0	0	0	1	0.0	-1.00
Hurdles	5	13	1	0	0	12	7.7	+13.00
Chases	0	0	0	0	0	0	0.0	0.00
Totals	5	14	1	0	0	13	7.1	+12.00
11-12	6	12	0	0	0	12	0.0	-12.00
10-11	9	19	1	0	0	18	5.3	+48.00

JOCKEYS

	W-R	Per cent	£1 Level Stake
Alexander Voy	1-7	14.3	+19.00

COURSE RECORD

	Total W-R	Non-Hndcps Hurdles	Chases	Hndcps Hurdles	Chases	NH Flat	Per cent	£1 Level Stake
Sedgefield	1-5	0-2	0-0	1-3	0-0	0-0	20.0	+21.00

WINNING HORSES

Horse	Races Run	1st	2nd	3rd	£
Copt Hill	5	1	0	0	1949
Total winning prize-money					£1949
Favourites	0-0		0.0%		0.00

TIM WALFORD

SHERIFF HUTTON, N YORKS

	No. of Hrs	Races Run	1st	2nd	3rd	Unpl	Per cent	£1 Level Stake
NH Flat	8	10	1	0	0	9	10.0	+57.00
Hurdles	18	54	1	0	8	45	1.9	-51.13
Chases	5	10	1	3	3	3	10.0	-8.27
Totals	21	74	3	3	11	57	4.1	-2.40
11-12	24	82	12	11	8	51	14.6	+41.00
10-11	24	74	6	4	6	58	8.1	+0.50

JOCKEYS

	W-R	Per cent	£1 Level Stake
Mr M Walford	1-1	100.0	+1.88
Dougie Costello	1-1	100.0	+66.00
Daryl Jacob	1-5	20.0	-3.27

COURSE RECORD

	Total W-R	Non-Hndcps Hurdles	Chases	Hndcps Hurdles	Chases	NH Flat	Per cent	£1 Level Stake
Kelso	1-1	0-0	1-1	0-0	0-0	0-0	100.0	+0.73
Hexham	1-6	0-3	0-0	1-3	0-0	0-0	16.7	-3.13
Mrket Rsn	1-7	0-3	0-0	0-2	0-0	1-2	14.3	+60.00

WINNING HORSES

Horse	Races Run	1st	2nd	3rd	£
Fentara	7	2	2	2	3994
King Of Strings	1	1	0	0	1560
Total winning prize-money					£5554
Favourites	1-3		33.3%		-1.27

ROBERT WALFORD

CHILD OKEFORD, DORSET

	No. of Hrs	Races Run	1st	2nd	3rd	Unpl	Per cent	£1 Level Stake
NH Flat	4	9	1	1	1	6	11.1	-2.00
Hurdles	7	21	1	3	5	12	4.8	-17.00
Chases	3	3	0	0	1	2	0.0	-3.00
Totals	12	33	2	4	7	20	6.1	-22.00

JOCKEYS

	W-R	Per cent	£1 Level Stake
Daryl Jacob	2-17	11.8	-6.00

COURSE RECORD

	Total W-R	Non-Hndcps Hurdles	Chases	Hndcps Hurdles	Chases	NH Flat	Per cent	£1 Level Stake
Warwick	1-1	0-0	0-0	0-0	0-0	1-1	100.0	+6.00
Plumpton	1-3	1-1	0-0	0-1	0-1	0-0	33.3	+1.00

WINNING HORSES

Horse	Races Run	1st	2nd	3rd	£
Carole's Destiny	3	1	0	1	2738
Carole's Spirit	3	1	1	1	1884
Total winning prize-money					£4622
Favourites	0-3		0.0%		-3.00

SARAH WALL

DALLINGTON, E SUSSEX

	No. of Hrs	Races Run	1st	2nd	3rd	Unpl	Per cent	£1 Level Stake
NH Flat	1	2	0	0	0	2	0.0	-2.00
Hurdles	1	3	0	0	0	3	0.0	-3.00
Chases	1	5	1	0	1	3	20.0	+2.00
Totals	3	10	1	0	1	8	10.0	-3.00
11-12	2	9	1	1	1	6	11.1	-5.75
10-11	2	8	1	0	0	7	12.5	+5.00

JOCKEYS

	W-R	Per cent	£1 Level Stake
Marc Goldstein	1-9	11.1	-2.00

COURSE RECORD

	Total W-R	Non-Hndcps Hurdles	Chases	Hndcps Hurdles	Chases	NH Flat	Per cent	£1 Level Stake
Plumpton	1-5	0-0	0-0	0-1	1-3	0-1	20.0	+2.00

WINNING HORSES

Horse	Races Run	1st	2nd	3rd	£
Ballinhassig	5	1	0	1	3390
Total winning prize-money					£3390
Favourites	0-1		0.0%		-1.00

KATE WALTON

MIDDLEHAM MOOR, N YORKS

	No. of Hrs	Races Run	1st	2nd	3rd	Unpl	Per cent	£1 Level Stake
NH Flat	5	10	1	1	2	6	10.0	+5.00
Hurdles	16	39	1	0	5	33	2.6	-34.00
Chases	2	6	0	1	1	4	0.0	-6.00
Totals	21	55	2	2	8	43	3.6	-35.00
11-12	25	107	13	13	8	73	12.1	+20.75
10-11	27	105	14	10	16	65	13.3	+17.50

JOCKEYS

	W-R	Per cent	£1 Level Stake
Richie McGrath	2-33	6.1	-13.00

COURSE RECORD

	Total W-R	Non-Hndcps Hurdles	Chases	Hndcps Hurdles	Chases	NH Flat	Per cent	£1 Level Stake
Newcastle	1-2	0-0	0-0	0-1	0-0	1-1	50.0	+13.00
Cartmel	1-4	1-2	0-0	0-2	0-0	0-0	25.0	+1.00

WINNING HORSES

Horse	Races Run	1st	2nd	3rd	£
Jasper Massini	4	1	0	0	2599
Just Cameron	2	1	0	0	1560
Total winning prize-money					£4159
Favourites	0-0		0.0%		0.00

JAMES WALTON

THROPTON, NORTHUMBERLAND

	No. of Hrs	Races Run	1st	2nd	3rd	Unpl	Per cent	£1 Level Stake
NH Flat	2	3	0	0	0	3	0.0	-3.00
Hurdles	6	18	3	2	1	12	16.7	-3.75
Chases	5	17	2	2	0	13	11.8	-4.09
Totals	11	38	5	4	1	28	13.2	-10.84
11-12	5	23	3	3	3	14	13.0	-14.25
10-11	5	8	0	0	0	8	0.0	-8.00

JOCKEYS

	W-R	Per cent	£1 Level Stake
Miss C Walton	5-36	13.9	-8.84

COURSE RECORD

	Total W-R	Non-Hndcps Hurdles	Chases	Hndcps Hurdles	Chases	NH Flat	Per cent	£1 Level Stake
Hexham	2-8	1-2	0-2	1-1	0-2	0-1	25.0	+3.50
Kelso	2-12	0-3	1-4	0-2	1-3	0-0	16.7	+0.91
Carlisle	1-7	0-0	0-1	1-3	0-3	0-0	14.3	-4.25

WINNING HORSES

Horse	Races Run	1st	2nd	3rd	£
Saddle Pack	9	1	0	0	3899
Rupert Bear	8	3	1	1	9236
Sacred Mountain	3	1	1	0	1872
Total winning prize-money					£15007
Favourites	3-5		60.0%		3.66

MRS SARAH WARD

EAST WOODHAY, HAMPSHIRE

	No. of Hrs	Races Run	1st	2nd	3rd	Unpl	Per cent	£1 Level Stake
NH Flat	0	0	0	0	0	0	0.0	0.00
Hurdles	0	0	0	0	0	0	0.0	0.00

Chases	2	6	2	2	0	2	33.3	+0.25
Totals	2	6	2	2	0	2	33.3	+0.25
11-12	1	1	0	0	0	1	0.0	-1.00

JOCKEYS

	W-R	Per cent	£1 Level Stake
Mr T D Ward	2-6	33.3	+0.25

COURSE RECORD

	Total W-R	Non-Hndcps Hurdles	Chases	Hndcps Hurdles	Chases	NH Flat	Per cent	£1 Level Stake
Towcester	1-1	0-0	1-1	0-0	0-0	0-0	100.0	+1.75
Leicester	1-2	0-0	1-2	0-0	0-0	0-0	50.0	+1.50

WINNING HORSES

Horse	Races Run	1st	2nd	3rd	£
What Of It	4	2	2	0	2548
Total winning prize-money					£2548
Favourites	1-1		100.0%		1.75

SHARON WATT

BROMPTON-ON-SWALE, N YORKS

	No. of Hrs	Races Run	1st	2nd	3rd	Unpl	Per cent	£1 Level Stake
NH Flat	2	4	0	0	0	4	0.0	-4.00
Hurdles	2	6	1	2	1	2	16.7	-4.00
Chases	0	0	0	0	0	0	0.0	0.00
Totals	3	10	1	2	1	6	10.0	-8.00
11-12	3	12	0	0	1	11	0.0	-12.00
10-11	4	16	1	3	0	12	6.3	-9.50

JOCKEYS

	W-R	Per cent	£1 Level Stake
Joseph Palmowski	1-5	20.0	-3.00

COURSE RECORD

	Total W-R	Non-Hndcps Hurdles	Chases	Hndcps Hurdles	Chases	NH Flat	Per cent	£1 Level Stake
Newcastle	1-1	1-1	0-0	0-0	0-0	0-0	100.0	+1.00

WINNING HORSES

Horse	Races Run	1st	2nd	3rd	£
Madam Lilibet	5	1	2	1	4328
Total winning prize-money					£4328
Favourites	1-1		100.0%		1.00

PAUL WEBBER

MOLLINGTON, OXON

	No. of Hrs	Races Run	1st	2nd	3rd	Unpl	Per cent	£1 Level Stake
NH Flat	18	28	2	2	4	20	7.1	-15.67
Hurdles	35	96	7	12	7	70	7.3	-42.05
Chases	25	69	9	7	6	47	13.0	-21.64
Totals	64	193	18	21	17	137	9.3	-79.36
11-12	59	207	31	19	19	138	15.0	-65.35
10-11	62	203	28	22	19	132	13.8	-14.92

BY MONTH

NH Flat	W-R	Per cent	£1 Level Stake	Hurdles	W-R	Per cent	£1 Level Stake
May	0-1	0.0	-1.00	May	0-6	0.0	-6.00
June	0-2	0.0	-2.00	June	1-6	16.7	+9.00
July	1-2	50.0	+6.00	July	0-4	0.0	-4.00
August	0-1	0.0	-1.00	August	1-4	25.0	-0.25
September	0-0	0.0	0.00	September	0-3	0.0	-3.00
October	0-1	0.0	-1.00	October	1-14	7.1	-3.00
November	0-2	0.0	-2.00	November	1-14	7.1	-6.50
December	0-2	0.0	-2.00	December	1-16	6.3	-9.00
January	0-0	0.0	0.00	January	0-3	0.0	-3.00
February	0-5	0.0	-5.00	February	0-6	0.0	-6.00
March	0-3	0.0	-3.00	March	2-9	22.2	+0.70
April	1-9	11.1	-4.67	April	0-11	0.0	-11.00

Chases	W-R	Per cent	£1 Level Stake	Totals	W-R	Per cent	£1 Level Stake
May	0-7	0.0	-7.00	May	0-14	0.0	-14.00
June	1-8	12.5	-3.50	June	2-16	12.5	+3.50
July	1-4	25.0	+3.00	July	2-10	20.0	+5.00
August	3-4	75.0	+5.17	August	4-9	44.4	+3.92
September	0-2	0.0	-2.00	September	0-5	0.0	-5.00
October	0-7	0.0	-7.00	October	1-22	4.5	-11.00
November	0-12	0.0	-12.00	November	1-28	3.6	-20.50
December	2-4	50.0	+11.25	December	3-22	13.6	+0.25
January	1-3	33.3	-1.56	January	1-6	16.7	-4.56
February	1-7	14.3	+3.00	February	1-18	5.6	-8.00
March	0-4	0.0	-4.00	March	2-16	12.5	-6.30
April	0-7	0.0	-7.00	April	1-27	3.7	-22.67

DISTANCE

Hurdles	W-R	Per cent	£1 Level Stake	Chases	W-R	Per cent	£1 Level Stake
2m-2m3f	2-40	5.0	-17.50	2m-2m3f	7-25	28.0	-0.64
2m4f-2m7f	1-36	2.8	-32.25	2m4f-2m7f	2-26	7.7	-3.00
3m+	4-20	20.0	+7.70	3m+	0-18	0.0	-18.00

TYPE OF RACE

Non-Handicaps	W-R	Per cent	£1 Level Stake	Handicaps	W-R	Per cent	£1 Level Stake
Nov Hrdls	3-39	7.7	-25.55	Nov Hrdls	1-6	16.7	+5.00
Hrdls	0-15	0.0	-15.00	Hrdls	3-36	8.3	-6.50
Nov Chs	4-23	17.4	-12.14	Nov Chs	0-8	0.0	-8.00

Chases	1-5	20.0	+5.00	Chases	4-33	12.1	-6.50
Sell/Claim	0-0	0.0	0.00	Sell/Claim	0-0	0.0	0.00

RACE CLASS / FIRST TIME OUT

	W-R	Per cent	£1 Level Stake		W-R	Per cent	£1 Level Stake
Class 1	0-13	0.0	-13.00	Bumpers	0-18	0.0	-18.00
Class 2	1-19	5.3	-9.00	Hurdles	2-29	6.9	-3.00
Class 3	6-36	16.7	+1.69	Chases	1-17	5.9	-10.00
Class 4	8-86	9.3	-39.38				
Class 5	1-17	5.9	-10.00	Totals	3-64	4.7	-31.00
Class 6	2-22	9.1	-9.67				

JOCKEYS

	W-R	Per cent	£1 Level Stake
Dominic Elsworth	11-86	12.8	-8.58
A P McCoy	3-8	37.5	+0.03
Denis O'Regan	3-43	7.0	-27.80
Liam Treadwell	1-11	9.1	+2.00

COURSE RECORD

	Total W-R	Non-Hndcps Hurdles	Chases	Hndcps Hurdles	Chases	NH Flat	Per cent	£1 Level Stake
Fontwell	2-4	0-1	1-2	0-0	1-1	0-0	50.0	+3.50
Southwell	2-8	0-2	1-1	0-2	0-1	1-2	25.0	+1.67
Worcester	2-11	0-3	0-3	0-0	2-4	0-1	18.2	+0.50
Bangor	2-15	1-5	0-2	1-4	0-0	0-4	13.3	-4.25
Plumpton	1-1	0-0	1-1	0-0	0-0	0-0	100.0	+1.25
Lingfield	1-3	1-1	0-2	0-0	0-0	0-0	33.3	+4.50
Aintree	1-4	0-0	0-0	1-2	0-1	0-1	25.0	+7.00
Taunton	1-4	0-0	1-1	0-1	0-2	0-0	25.0	-2.56
Wetherby	1-5	0-2	0-1	0-1	0-0	1-1	20.0	-0.67
Leicester	1-9	0-1	0-1	0-1	1-6	0-0	11.1	+4.00
Stratford	1-12	0-3	0-1	1-2	0-6	0-0	8.3	+3.00
Mrket Rsn	1-13	0-2	0-0	1-6	0-2	0-3	7.7	-5.50
Ludlow	1-17	1-9	0-0	0-3	0-4	0-1	5.9	-14.80
Kempton	1-18	0-7	1-4	0-3	0-3	0-1	5.6	-8.00

WINNING HORSES

Horse	Races Run	1st	2nd	3rd	£
Alasi	5	1	2	0	12512
Sixty Something	7	3	0	0	16245
Cantlow	6	2	2	0	12346
Tafika	5	1	1	1	6330
Rajnagan	6	3	0	0	12862
Dunlough Bay	6	2	1	1	7408
Tindaro	8	1	2	2	3129
Danvilla	5	1	1	1	2534
Citrus Mark	4	2	0	0	4321
Couldhaveditall	2	1	1	0	1643
Antonius Lad	5	1	0	0	1506
Total winning prize-money					£80836
Favourites	3-10		30.0%		-4.89

SIMON WEST

MIDDLEHAM MOOR, N YORKS

	No. of Hrs	Races Run	1st	2nd	3rd	Unpl	Per cent	£1 Level Stake
NH Flat	5	12	0	1	0	11	0.0	-12.00
Hurdles	7	28	1	1	2	24	3.6	-15.00
Chases	1	1	0	0	0	1	0.0	-1.00
Totals	12	41	1	2	2	36	2.4	-28.00
11-12	15	38	4	2	5	27	10.5	-4.75
10-11	15	54	4	9	4	37	7.4	+34.33

JOCKEYS

	W-R	Per cent	£1 Level Stake
Barry Keniry	1-19	5.3	-6.00

COURSE RECORD

	Total W-R	Non-Hndcps Hurdles	Chases	Hndcps Hurdles	Chases	NH Flat	Per cent	£1 Level Stake
Hereford	1-2	0-0	0-0	1-2	0-0	0-0	50.0	+11.00

WINNING HORSES

Horse	Races Run	1st	2nd	3rd	£
The Tiddly Tadpole	9	1	1	1	2599
Total winning prize-money					£2599
Favourites	0-0		0.0%		0.00

SHEENA WEST

FALMER, E SUSSEX

	No. of Hrs	Races Run	1st	2nd	3rd	Unpl	Per cent	£1 Level Stake
NH Flat	1	3	0	2	0	1	0.0	-3.00
Hurdles	19	59	8	13	7	31	13.6	-24.97
Chases	6	12	2	3	2	5	16.7	-6.00
Totals	23	74	10	18	9	37	13.5	-33.97
11-12	21	80	14	16	12	38	17.5	+29.13
10-11	19	64	6	12	8	38	9.4	-29.72

BY MONTH

NH Flat	W-R	Per cent	£1 Level Stake	Hurdles	W-R	Per cent	£1 Level Stake
May	0-0	0.0	0.00	May	0-0	0.0	0.00
June	0-0	0.0	0.00	June	1-5	20.0	+0.50
July	0-0	0.0	0.00	July	1-2	50.0	+0.25
August	0-0	0.0	0.00	August	1-7	14.3	-4.80
September	0-0	0.0	0.00	September	1-9	11.1	-4.67
October	0-0	0.0	0.00	October	2-5	40.0	+1.75
November	0-0	0.0	0.00	November	1-6	16.7	-1.00
December	0-0	0.0	0.00	December	1-4	25.0	+4.00
January	0-0	0.0	0.00	January	0-3	0.0	-3.00
February	0-1	0.0	-1.00	February	0-3	0.0	-3.00
March	0-1	0.0	-1.00	March	0-4	0.0	-4.00
April	0-1	0.0	-1.00	April	0-11	0.0	-11.00

Chases	W-R	Per cent	£1 Level Stake	Totals	W-R	Per cent	£1 Level Stake
May	0-0	0.0	0.00	May	0-0	0.0	0.00
June	0-0	0.0	0.00	June	1-5	20.0	+0.50
July	0-0	0.0	0.00	July	1-2	50.0	+0.25
August	0-2	0.0	-2.00	August	1-9	11.1	-6.80
September	0-1	0.0	-1.00	September	1-10	10.0	-5.67
October	1-1	100.0	+1.75	October	3-6	50.0	+3.50
November	0-1	0.0	-1.00	November	1-7	14.3	-2.00
December	0-2	0.0	-2.00	December	1-6	16.7	+2.00
January	0-1	0.0	-1.00	January	0-4	0.0	-4.00
February	0-1	0.0	-1.00	February	0-5	0.0	-5.00
March	1-1	100.0	+2.25	March	1-6	16.7	-2.75
April	0-2	0.0	-2.00	April	0-14	0.0	-14.00

DISTANCE

Hurdles	W-R	Per cent	£1 Level Stake	Chases	W-R	Per cent	£1 Level Stake
2m-2m3f	8-46	17.4	-11.97	2m-2m3f	2-5	40.0	+1.00
2m4f-2m7f	0-12	0.0	-12.00	2m4f-2m7f	0-2	0.0	-2.00
3m+	0-1	0.0	-1.00	3m+	0-5	0.0	-5.00

TYPE OF RACE

Non-Handicaps	W-R	Per cent	£1 Level Stake	Handicaps	W-R	Per cent	£1 Level Stake
Nov Hrdls	1-4	25.0	0.00	Nov Hrdls	0-3	0.0	-3.00
Hrdls	3-17	17.6	-1.25	Hrdls	2-29	6.9	-19.17
Nov Chs	1-4	25.0	-1.25	Nov Chs	0-0	0.0	0.00
Chases	0-0	0.0	0.00	Chases	1-8	12.5	-4.75
Sell/Claim	2-5	40.0	-0.55	Sell/Claim	0-1	0.0	-1.00

RACE CLASS / FIRST TIME OUT

	W-R	Per cent	£1 Level Stake		W-R	Per cent	£1 Level Stake
Class 1	0-3	0.0	-3.00	Bumpers	0-1	0.0	-1.00
Class 2	0-4	0.0	-4.00	Hurdles	3-19	15.8	-3.25
Class 3	2-16	12.5	-8.92	Chases	0-3	0.0	-3.00
Class 4	6-35	17.1	-6.50				
Class 5	2-14	14.3	-9.55	Totals	3-23	13.0	-7.25
Class 6	0-2	0.0	-2.00				

JOCKEYS

	W-R	Per cent	£1 Level Stake
Marc Goldstein	10-64	15.6	-23.97

COURSE RECORD

	Total W-R	Non-Hndcps Hurdles	Chases	Hndcps Hurdles	Chases	NH Flat	Per cent	£1 Level Stake
Stratford	3-7	2-3	0-1	1-3	0-0	0-0	42.9	+1.78
Sandown	2-5	2-3	0-0	0-1	0-1	0-0	40.0	+8.00
Huntingdon	2-6	1-1	1-2	0-1	0-2	0-0	33.3	+0.75
Fontwell	2-17	1-7	0-1	1-7	0-1	0-1	11.8	-8.75
Plumpton	1-12	0-2	0-0	0-8	1-1	0-1	8.3	-8.75

WINNING HORSES

Horse	Races Run	1st	2nd	3rd	£
Hi Note	8	1	3	0	7596
Alfraamsey	4	1	2	0	7148
*Captain Cardington	5	1	0	1	4549
Mr Muddle	4	1	0	0	3899
Dubai Glory	3	1	2	0	3249
Feb Thirtyfirst	6	2	2	0	5783
Screaming Brave	1	1	0	0	2534
Forty Thirty	2	2	0	0	3834
Total winning prize-money					£38592
Favourites	4-5		80.0%		4.95

MISS JANE WESTERN

CHARD, SOMERSET

	No. of Hrs	Races Run	1st	2nd	3rd	Unpl	Per cent	£1 Level Stake
NH Flat	0	0	0	0	0	0	0.0	0.00
Hurdles	0	0	0	0	0	0	0.0	0.00
Chases	3	13	3	0	0	10	23.1	+5.75
Totals	3	13	3	0	0	10	23.1	+5.75
11-12	3	3	0	1	0	2	0.0	-3.00
10-11	4	11	1	1	0	9	9.1	-7.50

JOCKEYS

	W-R	Per cent	£1 Level Stake
Mr J Barber	3-7	42.9	+11.75

COURSE RECORD

	Total W-R	Non-Hndcps Hurdles	Chases	Hndcps Hurdles	Chases	NH Flat	Per cent	£1 Level Stake
Taunton	2-2	0-0	2-2	0-0	0-0	0-0	100.0	+13.00
Kempton	1-1	0-0	1-1	0-0	0-0	0-0	100.0	+2.75

WINNING HORSES

Horse	Races Run	1st	2nd	3rd	£
Benedictus	7	3	0	0	6644
Total winning prize-money					£6644
Favourites	1-1		100.0%		2.75

MISS JESSICA WESTWOOD

MINEHEAD, SOMERSET

	No. of Hrs	Races Run	1st	2nd	3rd	Unpl	Per cent	£1 Level Stake
NH Flat	1	1	0	0	0	1	0.0	-1.00
Hurdles	0	0	0	0	0	0	0.0	0.00
Chases	1	7	2	1	0	4	28.6	0.00
Totals	2	8	2	1	0	5	25.0	-1.00
11-12	1	1	1	0	0	0	100.0	+2.25

JOCKEYS

	W-R	Per cent	£1 Level Stake
Will Kennedy	2-7	28.6	0.00

COURSE RECORD

	Total W-R	Non-Hndcps Hurdles	Chases	Hndcps Hurdles	Chases	NH Flat	Per cent	£1 Level Stake
Doncaster	1-1	0-0	0-0	0-0	1-1	0-0	100.0	+2.75
Wincanton	1-2	0-0	0-0	0-0	1-1	0-1	50.0	+1.25

WINNING HORSES

Horse	Races Run	1st	2nd	3rd	£
Monkerty Tunkerty	7	2	1	0	17813
Total winning prize-money					£17813
Favourites	1-2		50.0%		1.75

JOHN WEYMES

MIDDLEHAM MOOR, N YORKS

	No. of Hrs	Races Run	1st	2nd	3rd	Unpl	Per cent	£1 Level Stake
NH Flat	0	0	0	0	0	0	0.0	0.00
Hurdles	3	9	1	1	1	6	11.1	+42.00
Chases	0	0	0	0	0	0	0.0	0.00
Totals	3	9	1	1	1	6	11.1	+42.00
11-12	3	13	0	0	2	11	0.0	-13.00
10-11	4	10	0	0	1	9	0.0	-10.00

JOCKEYS

	W-R	Per cent	£1 Level Stake
Richie McGrath	1-8	12.5	+43.00

COURSE RECORD

	Total W-R	Non-Hndcps Hurdles	Chases	Hndcps Hurdles	Chases	NH Flat	Per cent	£1 Level Stake
Wetherby	1-1	1-1	0-0	0-0	0-0	0-0	100.0	+50.00

WINNING HORSES

Horse	Races Run	1st	2nd	3rd	£
Harrys Whim	7	1	1	1	2534
Total winning prize-money					£2534
Favourites	0-1		0.0%		-1.00

DONALD WHILLANS

HAWICK, BORDERS

	No. of Hrs	Races Run	1st	2nd	3rd	Unpl	Per cent	£1 Level Stake
NH Flat	4	6	0	0	1	5	0.0	-6.00
Hurdles	14	45	2	3	4	36	4.4	-32.50

Chases	8	26	2	5	3	16	7.7	-18.50
Totals	19	77	4	8	8	57	5.2	-57.00
11-12	19	74	4	8	12	50	5.4	+26.63
10-11	21	78	4	11	9	54	5.1	-48.50

JOCKEYS

	W-R	Per cent	£1 Level Stake
Callum Whillans	3-56	5.4	-39.75
Wilson Renwick	1-15	6.7	-11.25

COURSE RECORD

	Total W-R	Non-Hndcps Hurdles	Chases	Hndcps Hurdles	Chases	NH Flat	Per cent	£1 Level Stake
Ayr	2-7	0-0	0-0	1-5	1-2	0-0	28.6	+4.25
Hexham	2-18	0-3	0-1	1-8	1-5	0-1	11.1	-9.25

WINNING HORSES

Horse	Races Run	1st	2nd	3rd	£
Harry Flashman	2	1	0	0	3087
Bollin Fiona	5	1	1	2	2177
Shadow Boxer	2	1	1	0	2144
King Kalium	7	1	0	0	2053
Total winning prize-money					£9461
Favourites	2-5		40.0%		2.50

ALISTAIR WHILLANS

NEWMILL-ON-SLITRIG, BORDERS

	No. of Hrs	Races Run	1st	2nd	3rd	Unpl	Per cent	£1 Level Stake
NH Flat	6	7	2	0	1	4	28.6	+12.50
Hurdles	18	78	10	9	4	55	12.8	+3.50
Chases	6	21	1	2	1	17	4.8	-9.00
Totals	26	106	13	11	6	76	12.3	+7.00
11-12	26	121	10	21	11	79	8.3	-66.42
10-11	34	112	13	5	15	79	11.6	-43.25

BY MONTH

NH Flat	W-R	Per cent	£1 Level Stake	Hurdles	W-R	Per cent	£1 Level Stake
May	0-0	0.0	0.00	May	3-11	27.3	+4.25
June	0-0	0.0	0.00	June	0-4	0.0	-4.00
July	0-0	0.0	0.00	July	1-5	20.0	+10.00
August	0-1	0.0	-1.00	August	3-8	37.5	+7.75
September	0-0	0.0	0.00	September	1-2	50.0	+8.00
October	0-0	0.0	0.00	October	0-4	0.0	-4.00
November	0-0	0.0	0.00	November	0-12	0.0	-12.00
December	0-0	0.0	0.00	December	0-6	0.0	-6.00
January	0-0	0.0	0.00	January	1-6	16.7	+2.50
February	0-2	0.0	-2.00	February	0-3	0.0	-3.00
March	1-1	100.0	+5.50	March	0-8	0.0	-8.00
April	1-3	33.3	+10.00	April	1-9	11.1	+8.00

Chases	W-R	Per cent	£1 Level Stake		Totals	W-R	Per cent	£1 Level Stake
May	0-1	0.0	-1.00		May	3-12	25.0	+3.25
June	0-1	0.0	-1.00		June	0-5	0.0	-5.00
July	1-3	33.3	+9.00		July	2-8	25.0	+19.00
August	0-0	0.0	0.00		August	3-9	33.3	+6.75
September	0-0	0.0	0.00		September	1-2	50.0	+8.00
October	0-3	0.0	-3.00		October	0-7	0.0	-7.00
November	0-3	0.0	-3.00		November	0-15	0.0	-15.00
December	0-2	0.0	-2.00		December	0-8	0.0	-8.00
January	0-4	0.0	-4.00		January	1-10	10.0	-1.50
February	0-2	0.0	-2.00		February	0-7	0.0	-7.00
March	0-2	0.0	-2.00		March	1-11	9.1	-4.50
April	0-0	0.0	0.00		April	2-12	16.7	+18.00

DISTANCE

Hurdles	W-R	Per cent	£1 Level Stake		Chases	W-R	Per cent	£1 Level Stake
2m-2m3f	5-39	12.8	-2.75		2m-2m3f	0-7	0.0	-7.00
2m4f-2m7f	2-24	8.3	-5.25		2m4f-2m7f	0-8	0.0	-8.00
3m+	3-15	20.0	+11.50		3m+	1-6	16.7	+6.00

TYPE OF RACE

Non-Handicaps	W-R	Per cent	£1 Level Stake		Handicaps	W-R	Per cent	£1 Level Stake
Nov Hrdls	0-2	0.0	-2.00		Nov Hrdls	1-6	16.7	+0.50
Hrdls	0-3	0.0	-3.00		Hrdls	9-66	13.6	+9.00
Nov Chs	0-1	0.0	-1.00		Nov Chs	0-0	0.0	0.00
Chases	0-0	0.0	0.00		Chases	1-20	5.0	-8.00
Sell/Claim	0-1	0.0	-1.00		Sell/Claim	0-0	0.0	0.00

RACE CLASS

	W-R	Per cent	£1 Level Stake		FIRST TIME OUT	W-R	Per cent	£1 Level Stake
Class 1	0-0	0.0	0.00		Bumpers	1-6	16.7	+0.50
Class 2	1-4	25.0	+9.00		Hurdles	3-17	17.6	-1.75
Class 3	3-23	13.0	+7.25		Chases	0-3	0.0	-3.00
Class 4	6-43	14.0	+10.00					
Class 5	2-32	6.3	-21.75		Totals	4-26	15.4	-4.25
Class 6	1-4	25.0	+2.50					

JOCKEYS

	W-R	Per cent	£1 Level Stake
Ewan Whillans	9-77	11.7	-1.25
Callum Whillans	2-13	15.4	+0.75
Mr C Bewley	1-1	100.0	+16.00
Mr B Campbell	1-2	50.0	+4.50

COURSE RECORD

	Total W-R	Non-Hndcps Hurdles	Chases	Hndcps Hurdles	Chases	NH Flat	Per cent	£1 Level Stake
Perth	3-19	0-0	0-0	2-15	1-3	0-1	15.8	+15.50
Mrket Rsn	2-2	0-0	0-0	2-2	0-0	0-0	100.0	+16.00
Hexham	2-8	0-1	0-0	2-6	0-1	0-0	25.0	+1.75
Cartmel	2-9	0-1	0-0	2-6	0-2	0-0	22.2	+10.00

Catterick	1-3	0-0	0-0	1-3	0-0	0-0	33.3	+5.50
Sedgefield	1-4	0-0	0-0	1-4	0-0	0-0	25.0	-0.25
Newcastle	1-8	0-1	0-0	0-3	0-2	1-2	12.5	-1.50
Ayr	1-13	0-2	0-0	0-6	0-3	1-2	7.7	0.00

WINNING HORSES

Horse	Races Run	1st	2nd	3rd	£
What A Steel	6	2	1	0	22743
Meadowcroft Boy	2	2	0	0	18087
Lady Bluesky	4	1	1	0	5848
Sotovik	4	1	0	0	5064
Ahhdehken	4	1	1	0	3743
Funky Munky	8	1	1	1	3249
Flying Doctor	10	2	0	0	5133
Claude Carter	7	2	0	0	5068
Benluna	3	1	0	0	1647
Total winning prize-money					£70582
Favourites	1-8		12.5%		-4.25

RICHARD WHITAKER

SCARCROFT, W YORKS

	No. of Hrs	Races Run	1st	2nd	3rd	Unpl	Per cent	£1 Level Stake
NH Flat	1	3	1	2	0	0	33.3	+0.75
Hurdles	0	0	0	0	0	0	0.0	0.00
Chases	0	0	0	0	0	0	0.0	0.00
Totals	1	3	1	2	0	0	33.3	+0.75
11-12	2	2	0	1	0	1	0.0	-2.00
10-11	1	1	0	0	0	1	0.0	-1.00

JOCKEYS

	W-R	Per cent	£1 Level Stake
Kyle James	1-1	100.0	+2.75

COURSE RECORD

	Total W-R	Non-Hndcps Hurdles	Chases	Hndcps Hurdles	Chases	NH Flat	Per cent	£1 Level Stake
Hereford	1-1	0-0	0-0	0-0	0-0	1-1	100.0	+2.75

WINNING HORSES

Horse	Races Run	1st	2nd	3rd	£
Woodacre	3	1	2	0	1365
Total winning prize-money					£1365
Favourites	0-138		0.0%		-138.00

ARTHUR WHITEHEAD

ASTON ON CLUN, SHROPSHIRE

	No. of Hrs	Races Run	1st	2nd	3rd	Unpl	Per cent	£1 Level Stake
NH Flat	0	0	0	0	0	0	0.0	0.00
Hurdles	5	22	1	1	2	18	4.5	-1.00

Chases	0	0	0	0	0	0	0.0	0.00
Totals	5	22	1	1	2	18	4.5	-1.00
11-12	5	18	2	2	2	12	11.1	0.00
10-11	3	19	3	3	3	10	15.8	+31.75

JOCKEYS

	W-R	Per cent	£1 Level Stake
Josh Wall	1-7	14.3	+14.00

COURSE RECORD

	Total W-R	Non-Hndcps Hurdles	Chases	Hndcps Hurdles	Chases	NH Flat	Per cent	£1 Level Stake
Chepstow	1-3	0-0	0-0	1-3	0-0	0-0	33.3	+18.00

WINNING HORSES

Horse	Races Run	1st	2nd	3rd	£
Della Sun	6	1	0	1	3119
Total winning prize-money					£3119
Favourites	0-0		0.0%		0.00

ARTHUR WHITING

NORTH NIBLEY, GLOUCS

	No. of Hrs	Races Run	1st	2nd	3rd	Unpl	Per cent	£1 Level Stake
NH Flat	3	4	0	0	0	4	0.0	-4.00
Hurdles	4	20	1	0	2	17	5.0	-15.50
Chases	2	2	0	0	1	1	0.0	-2.00
Totals	6	26	1	0	3	22	3.8	-21.50
11-12	9	35	1	2	4	28	2.9	+32.00
10-11	6	39	2	2	2	33	5.1	-23.25

JOCKEYS

	W-R	Per cent	£1 Level Stake
Micheal Nolan	1-13	7.7	-8.50

COURSE RECORD

	Total W-R	Non-Hndcps Hurdles	Chases	Hndcps Hurdles	Chases	NH Flat	Per cent	£1 Level Stake
Bangor	1-1	0-0	0-0	1-1	0-0	0-0	100.0	+3.50

WINNING HORSES

Horse	Races Run	1st	2nd	3rd	£
The Wee Midget	7	1	0	1	1779
Total winning prize-money					£1779
Favourites	1-1		100.0%		3.50

HARRY WHITTINGTON

SPARSHOLT, OXFORSHIRE

	No. of Hrs	Races Run	1st	2nd	3rd	Unpl	Per cent	£1 Level Stake
NH Flat	2	3	1	0	0	2	33.3	+48.00
Hurdles	4	10	2	1	1	6	20.0	-3.00
Chases	1	1	0	0	0	1	0.0	-1.00
Totals	6	14	3	1	1	9	21.4	+44.00
11-12	1	1	0	0	0	1	0.0	-1.00
10-11	1	4	1	1	0	2	25.0	+3.50

JOCKEYS

	W-R	Per cent	£1 Level Stake
Aidan Coleman	1-2	50.0	+49.00
Jeremiah McGrath	1-3	33.3	+2.00
James Banks	1-5	20.0	-3.00

COURSE RECORD

	Total W-R	Non-Hndcps Hurdles	Chases	Hndcps Hurdles	Chases	NH Flat	Per cent	£1 Level Stake
Uttoxeter	1-1	1-1	0-0	0-0	0-0	0-0	100.0	+1.00
Chepstow	1-2	0-1	0-0	1-1	0-0	0-0	50.0	+3.00
Newbury	1-2	0-0	0-0	0-1	0-0	1-1	50.0	+49.00

WINNING HORSES

Horse	Races Run	1st	2nd	3rd	£
Fourovakind	4	2	1	1	5328
Dubai Kiss	2	1	0	0	1711
Total winning prize-money					£7039
Favourites	2-3		66.7%		4.00

DAI WILLIAMS

GREAT SHEFFORD, BERKS

	No. of Hrs	Races Run	1st	2nd	3rd	Unpl	Per cent	£1 Level Stake
NH Flat	1	1	0	0	0	1	0.0	-1.00
Hurdles	6	24	0	0	2	22	0.0	-24.00
Chases	6	24	1	2	4	17	4.2	-14.00
Totals	10	49	1	2	6	40	2.0	-39.00
11-12	7	20	0	0	1	19	0.0	-20.00
10-11	1	1	0	0	0	1	0.0	-1.00

JOCKEYS

	W-R	Per cent	£1 Level Stake
Dave Crosse	1-14	7.1	-4.00

COURSE RECORD

	Total W-R	Non-Hndcps Hurdles	Chases	Hndcps Hurdles	Chases	NH Flat	Per cent	£1 Level Stake
Uttoxeter	1-8	0-2	0-1	0-1	1-3	0-1	12.5	+2.00

WINNING HORSES

Horse	Races Run	1st	2nd	3rd	£
Cherokee Star	5	1	0	1	3054
Total winning prize-money					£3054
Favourites	0-1		0.0%		-1.00

IAN WILLIAMS

PORTWAY, WORCS

	No. of Hrs	Races Run	1st	2nd	3rd	Unpl	Per cent	£1 Level Stake
NH Flat	10	14	1	0	2	11	7.1	-8.00
Hurdles	37	75	5	7	8	55	6.7	-27.25
Chases	12	23	3	0	5	15	13.0	-9.75
Totals	51	112	9	7	15	81	8.0	-45.00
11-12	69	228	29	26	25	148	12.7	-93.48
10-11	61	195	25	33	17	120	12.8	-71.18

JOCKEYS

	W-R	Per cent	£1 Level Stake
Paddy Brennan	6-30	20.0	+9.75
Dougie Costello	2-15	13.3	-6.75
Harry Skelton	1-26	3.8	-7.00

COURSE RECORD

	Total W-R	Non-Hndcps Hurdles	Chases	Hndcps Hurdles	Chases	NH Flat	Per cent	£1 Level Stake
Stratford	3-9	1-3	0-0	1-4	0-0	1-2	33.3	+9.88
Worcester	2-6	0-1	0-1	1-3	1-1	0-0	33.3	+9.50
Kelso	1-2	0-0	0-0	0-0	1-2	0-0	50.0	+0.25
Mrket Rsn	1-5	0-0	0-1	0-0	1-2	0-2	20.0	+3.50
Huntingdon	1-7	0-3	0-0	1-3	0-0	0-1	14.3	+12.00
Uttoxeter	1-11	1-5	0-0	0-4	0-1	0-1	9.1	-8.13

WINNING HORSES

Horse	Races Run	1st	2nd	3rd	£
Upthemsteps	3	1	0	0	4660
Rebel Dancer	7	1	1	2	3249
Tyrana	3	1	0	0	2924
Western Approaches	4	2	0	1	5198
Drumlang	2	1	0	1	2534
Bittersweetheart	2	1	0	0	2053
Aqualung	2	1	0	1	1949
Fearless Leader	3	1	0	0	1949
Total winning prize-money					£24516
Favourites	1-10		10.0%		-7.75

NICK WILLIAMS

GEORGE NYMPTON, DEVON

	No. of Hrs	Races Run	1st	2nd	3rd	Unpl	Per cent	£1 Level Stake
NH Flat	4	8	3	1	1	3	37.5	+23.50
Hurdles	15	38	5	5	6	22	13.2	-21.02
Chases	22	75	12	7	10	46	16.0	-22.00
Totals	39	121	20	13	17	71	16.5	-19.52
11-12	37	131	20	20	21	70	15.3	-52.54
10-11	31	113	17	14	13	69	15.0	+20.71

BY MONTH

NH Flat	W-R	Per cent	£1 Level Stake	Hurdles	W-R	Per cent	£1 Level Stake
May	0-0	0.0	0.00	May	1-1	100.0	+1.75
June	0-0	0.0	0.00	June	0-0	0.0	0.00
July	0-0	0.0	0.00	July	0-1	0.0	-1.00
August	0-0	0.0	0.00	August	0-0	0.0	0.00
September	0-0	0.0	0.00	September	0-0	0.0	0.00
October	0-0	0.0	0.00	October	1-7	14.3	-3.25
November	0-0	0.0	0.00	November	0-3	0.0	-3.00
December	1-2	50.0	+3.50	December	2-10	20.0	-2.40
January	0-0	0.0	0.00	January	1-6	16.7	-3.13
February	0-1	0.0	-1.00	February	0-6	0.0	-6.00
March	0-2	0.0	-2.00	March	0-4	0.0	-4.00
April	2-3	66.7	+23.00	April	0-0	0.0	0.00

Chases	W-R	Per cent	£1 Level Stake	Totals	W-R	Per cent	£1 Level Stake
May	0-1	0.0	-1.00	May	1-2	50.0	+0.75
June	0-4	0.0	-4.00	June	0-4	0.0	-4.00
July	0-3	0.0	-3.00	July	0-4	0.0	-4.00
August	1-2	50.0	+0.25	August	1-2	50.0	+0.25
September	0-4	0.0	-4.00	September	0-4	0.0	-4.00
October	2-9	22.2	-0.50	October	3-16	18.8	-3.75
November	2-12	16.7	-5.00	November	2-15	13.3	-8.00
December	2-15	13.3	-7.50	December	5-27	18.5	-6.40
January	1-7	14.3	-0.50	January	2-13	15.4	-3.63
February	2-9	22.2	-0.25	February	2-16	12.5	-7.25
March	2-5	40.0	+7.50	March	2-11	18.2	+1.50
April	0-4	0.0	-4.00	April	2-7	28.6	+19.00

DISTANCE

Hurdles	W-R	Per cent	£1 Level Stake	Chases	W-R	Per cent	£1 Level Stake
2m-2m3f	3-18	16.7	-9.40	2m-2m3f	5-22	22.7	-4.50
2m4f-2m7f	0-15	0.0	-15.00	2m4f-2m7f	4-30	13.3	-11.50
3m+	2-5	40.0	+3.38	3m+	3-23	13.0	-6.00

TYPE OF RACE

Non-Handicaps	W-R	Per cent	£1 Level Stake	Handicaps	W-R	Per cent	£1 Level Stake
Nov Hrdls	2-9	22.2	-3.15	Nov Hrdls	0-3	0.0	-3.00
Hrdls	3-14	21.4	-2.88	Hrdls	0-12	0.0	-12.00
Nov Chs	1-16	6.3	-13.75	Nov Chs	3-6	50.0	+11.00

	W-R	Per cent	£1 Level Stake		W-R	Per cent	£1 Level Stake
Chases	0-5	0.0	-5.00	Chases	8-48	16.7	-14.25
Sell/Claim	0-0	0.0	0.00	Sell/Claim	0-0	0.0	0.00

RACE CLASS

	W-R	Per cent	£1 Level Stake
Class 1	3-23	13.0	-9.63
Class 2	0-13	0.0	-13.00
Class 3	3-25	12.0	-11.00
Class 4	10-47	21.3	-7.15
Class 5	1-5	20.0	-2.25
Class 6	3-8	37.5	+23.50

FIRST TIME OUT

	W-R	Per cent	£1 Level Stake
Bumpers	2-4	50.0	+20.50
Hurdles	1-13	7.7	-10.25
Chases	3-22	13.6	-11.25
Totals	6-39	15.4	-1.00

JOCKEYS

	W-R	Per cent	£1 Level Stake
Nick Scholfield	5-30	16.7	-14.50
Richard Johnson	3-6	50.0	+7.88
Daryl Jacob	3-25	12.0	-10.00
David Bass	2-5	40.0	+2.75
Miss E Kelly	2-5	40.0	+22.50
Noel Fehily	2-10	20.0	-1.00
Mark Quinlan	2-17	11.8	-7.90
James Reveley	1-6	16.7	-2.25

COURSE RECORD

	Total W-R	Non-Hndcps Hurdles	Chases	Hndcps Hurdles	Chases	NH Flat	Per cent	£1 Level Stake
Uttoxeter	3-7	2-2	0-2	0-0	1-3	0-0	42.9	+3.25
Exeter	3-10	1-3	0-2	0-1	1-3	1-1	30.0	+6.10
Wincanton	2-8	0-1	0-0	0-2	1-4	1-1	25.0	+17.50
Fakenham	1-1	0-0	0-0	0-0	1-1	0-0	100.0	+2.50
Hereford	1-1	0-0	0-0	0-0	1-1	0-0	100.0	+2.50
Fontwell	1-2	0-0	0-0	0-0	1-2	0-0	50.0	+1.50
Taunton	1-2	0-0	0-0	0-1	1-1	0-0	50.0	+1.50
Aintree	1-3	0-0	0-1	0-0	1-2	0-0	33.3	+2.00
Warwick	1-4	0-1	0-1	0-0	1-2	0-0	25.0	0.00
Cheltenham	1-6	1-3	0-1	0-1	0-1	0-0	16.7	-3.13
Chepstow	1-7	0-3	0-0	0-1	0-1	1-2	14.3	0.00
Worcester	1-7	0-1	1-2	0-1	0-3	0-0	14.3	-4.75
Ascot	1-8	1-1	0-2	0-1	0-4	0-0	12.5	-2.50
Sandown	1-9	0-2	0-1	0-2	1-4	0-0	11.1	-5.00
Ffos Las	1-10	0-2	0-1	0-1	1-4	0-2	10.0	-5.00

WINNING HORSES

Horse	Races Run	1st	2nd	3rd	£
Reve De Sivola	4	2	1	0	76373
For Non Stop	5	1	1	1	37018
Politeo	6	1	0	3	16245
Greywell Boy	5	2	2	0	11849
Royale's Charter	4	2	0	0	8447
Misstree Dancer	4	2	0	1	7456
Wayward Frolic	6	1	0	0	3994
George Nympton	5	1	1	0	3899
Material Boy	6	1	1	0	3861
The Italian Yob	5	1	1	1	3249

Father Probus	3	1	0	2	3054
Un Bon P'Tit Gars	3	2	0	0	4679
Comte D'Anjou	1	1	0	0	1625
Tea For Two	1	1	0	0	1625
Amore Alato	2	1	0	0	1560
Total winning prize-money					£184934
Favourites	4-16		25.0%		-3.53

EVAN WILLIAMS

LLANCARFAN, VALE OF GLAMORGAN

	No. of Hrs	Races Run	1st	2nd	3rd	Unpl	Per cent	£1 Level Stake
NH Flat	9	15	1	2	2	10	6.7	-4.00
Hurdles	96	302	33	41	36	192	10.9	-87.26
Chases	50	192	23	20	27	121	12.0	-73.07
Totals	120	509	57	63	65	323	11.2	-164.33
11-12	136	567	86	70	76	334	15.2	-102.45
10-11	149	593	89	84	86	334	15.0	-86.37

BY MONTH

NH Flat	W-R	Per cent	£1 Level Stake	Hurdles	W-R	Per cent	£1 Level Stake
May	0-0	0.0	0.00	May	5-26	19.2	-12.43
June	0-0	0.0	0.00	June	3-22	13.6	-8.50
July	0-2	0.0	-2.00	July	3-28	10.7	+6.00
August	0-1	0.0	-1.00	August	3-19	15.8	+1.33
September	0-1	0.0	-1.00	September	2-16	12.5	+3.25
October	0-2	0.0	-2.00	October	2-32	6.3	-22.38
November	0-1	0.0	-1.00	November	3-27	11.1	-18.25
December	0-0	0.0	0.00	December	1-25	4.0	-20.67
January	0-1	0.0	-1.00	January	0-12	0.0	-12.00
February	1-2	50.0	+9.00	February	6-36	16.7	+20.63
March	0-2	0.0	-2.00	March	4-33	12.1	-3.25
April	0-3	0.0	-3.00	April	1-26	3.8	-21.00

Chases	W-R	Per cent	£1 Level Stake	Totals	W-R	Per cent	£1 Level Stake
May	5-20	25.0	+19.00	May	10-46	21.7	+6.57
June	2-16	12.5	-8.50	June	5-38	13.2	-17.00
July	2-12	16.7	-4.00	July	5-42	11.9	0.00
August	0-12	0.0	-12.00	August	3-32	9.4	-11.67
September	0-8	0.0	-8.00	September	2-25	8.0	-5.28
October	1-23	4.3	-20.90	October	3-57	5.3	-45.28
November	5-21	23.8	+9.00	November	8-49	16.3	-10.25
December	1-10	10.0	-6.50	December	2-35	5.7	-27.17
January	3-11	27.3	+3.50	January	3-24	12.5	-9.50
February	1-17	5.9	-12.67	February	8-55	14.5	+16.96
March	2-19	10.5	-12.25	March	6-54	11.1	-17.50
April	1-23	4.3	-19.75	April	2-52	3.8	-43.75

DISTANCE

Hurdles	W-R	Per cent	£1 Level Stake	Chases	W-R	Per cent	£1 Level Stake
2m-2m3f	23-189	12.2	-49.05	2m-2m3f	10-80	12.5	-29.92
2m4f-2m7f	8-85	9.4	-27.54	2m4f-2m7f	7-57	12.3	-21.75
3m+	2-28	7.1	-10.67	3m+	6-55	10.9	-21.40

TYPE OF RACE

Non-Handicaps

	W-R	Per cent	£1 Level Stake
Nov Hrdls	6-76	7.9	-56.17
Hrdls	8-47	17.0	-4.47
Nov Chs	5-32	15.6	-13.90
Chases	0-7	0.0	-7.00
Sell/Claim	0-15	0.0	-15.00

Handicaps

	W-R	Per cent	£1 Level Stake
Nov Hrdls	3-16	18.8	-2.42
Hrdls	15-148	10.1	-16.21
Nov Chs	4-14	28.6	+6.58
Chases	14-137	10.2	-56.75
Sell/Claim	1-3	33.3	+4.00

RACE CLASS

	W-R	Per cent	£1 Level Stake
Class 1	1-31	3.2	-26.00
Class 2	4-42	9.5	-2.00
Class 3	12-118	10.2	-19.33
Class 4	28-215	13.0	-66.95
Class 5	12-90	13.3	-37.04
Class 6	0-13	0.0	-13.00

FIRST TIME OUT

	W-R	Per cent	£1 Level Stake
Bumpers	1-9	11.1	+2.00
Hurdles	8-79	10.1	-36.29
Chases	7-32	21.9	+10.60
Totals	16-120	13.3	-23.69

JOCKEYS

	W-R	Per cent	£1 Level Stake
Paul Moloney	37-309	12.0	-82.44
Adam Wedge	14-115	12.2	-42.26
Conor Ring	3-49	6.1	-13.25
A P McCoy	2-8	25.0	-1.63
Lucy Alexander	1-1	100.0	+2.25

COURSE RECORD

	Total W-R	Non-Hndcps Hurdles	Chases	Hndcps Hurdles	Chases	NH Flat	Per cent	£1 Level Stake
Ffos Las	10-96	1-11	2-5	2-41	5-35	0-4	10.4	-29.32
Ludlow	6-62	3-18	0-4	1-16	2-20	0-4	9.7	-29.63
Nton Abbot	5-29	1-11	1-4	3-9	0-4	0-1	17.2	-11.09
Plumpton	4-12	0-4	0-0	3-5	1-3	0-0	33.3	+15.75
Uttoxeter	4-26	1-9	0-1	1-9	2-6	0-1	15.4	+0.88
Fakenham	3-7	0-2	1-1	0-1	2-3	0-0	42.9	+15.00
Fontwell	3-11	2-3	0-1	1-4	0-3	0-0	27.3	+3.75
Taunton	3-25	0-5	0-2	1-12	1-5	1-1	12.0	+16.33
Worcester	3-25	1-15	0-1	2-3	0-6	0-0	12.0	-12.83
Huntingdon	2-5	1-1	0-1	1-2	0-1	0-0	40.0	+1.38
Sedgefield	2-8	1-4	0-0	0-1	1-3	0-0	25.0	-1.88
Ayr	1-1	0-0	0-0	1-1	0-0	0-0	100.0	+4.00
Perth	1-4	0-0	1-1	0-0	0-3	0-0	25.0	+1.00
Kempton	1-6	0-2	0-0	1-2	0-2	0-0	16.7	-1.50
Ascot	1-7	0-2	0-0	0-1	1-4	0-0	14.3	+1.00
Warwick	1-8	0-2	0-1	1-5	0-0	0-0	12.5	-3.67
Sandown	1-9	0-1	0-1	0-3	1-4	0-0	11.1	-7.00
Bangor	1-13	1-6	0-2	0-3	0-2	0-0	7.7	-10.00
Mrket Rsn	1-14	1-4	0-0	0-6	0-4	0-0	7.1	-11.00
Southwell	1-14	0-6	0-0	1-5	0-3	0-0	7.1	+7.00
Cheltenham	1-16	1-4	0-1	0-7	0-3	0-1	6.3	-9.00
Chepstow	1-23	0-4	0-3	0-6	1-9	0-1	4.3	-19.50
Stratford	1-23	0-8	0-1	0-4	1-9	0-1	4.3	-19.00

WINNING HORSES

Horse	Races Run	1st	2nd	3rd	£
Court Minstrel	5	3	0	1	56671
William's Wishes	2	2	0	0	49766
Barizan	4	1	0	0	12660
Sublime Talent	10	3	2	0	16898
Plunkett	3	2	0	0	10202
Triptico	5	1	2	0	7148
Prima Porta	4	1	1	0	6647
Tiger O'Toole	7	1	2	0	6498
Firebird Flyer	9	3	2	0	13348
Ugo	6	1	2	1	5848
Buck Mulligan	9	1	0	2	5507
Simarian	5	2	0	0	8123
Hold Court	6	2	1	1	7473
Tarkari	11	1	0	0	4431
Bonoman	10	1	1	2	3899
Gambo	6	1	0	2	3899
Tin Pot Man	10	2	1	1	6043
Makethe Mostofnow	8	1	2	1	3899
The Rockies	6	1	0	3	3899
Milo Man	2	1	0	0	3798
Di Kaprio	3	1	0	0	3769
Stormyisland Ahead	3	1	0	1	3769
One In A Milan	4	1	1	2	3769
Tornado In Milan	7	1	2	1	3422
Tempting Paradise	6	1	0	0	3418
Barrakilla	4	2	1	0	5913
Battlecat	8	2	3	0	6329
De Faoithesdream	6	2	0	1	4938
Lava Lamp	11	1	0	1	3119
Islandmagee	4	1	0	1	3119
Still Believing	2	1	0	0	3119
Bay Central	9	1	0	2	2975
Thegaygardener	6	1	1	2	2859
Captain Brown	3	1	1	0	2534
Zarzal	5	1	1	1	2274
Oran Flyer	4	1	0	0	2259
Behtarini	4	2	0	0	4106
Billy Blade	9	2	0	0	3833
Lauberhorn	10	1	4	0	1949
*Lienosus	4	1	1	1	1949
Clarion Call	14	1	4	2	1779
Total winning prize-money					**£307858**
Favourites	18-51		35.3%		-1.20

VENETIA WILLIAMS

KINGS CAPLE, H'FORDS

	No. of Hrs	Races Run	1st	2nd	3rd	Unpl	Per cent	£1 Level Stake
NH Flat	19	28	2	2	4	20	7.1	-12.75
Hurdles	62	220	29	22	23	146	13.2	-64.63
Chases	55	290	61	51	38	138	21.0	+47.55

Class 3	27-118	22.9	+27.28		Chases	9-40	22.5	+0.35
Class 4	36-196	18.4	-30.15					
Class 5	12-60	20.0	-22.08		Totals	17-110	15.5	-24.92
Class 6	2-23	8.7	-6.75					

Totals	110	538	92	75	65	304	17.1	-29.83
11-12	*98*	*397*	*51*	*46*	*29*	*271*	*12.8*	*-71.44*
10-11	*108*	*369*	*38*	*27*	*42*	*262*	*10.3*	*-80.62*

BY MONTH

NH Flat	W-R	Per cent	£1 Level Stake	Hurdles	W-R	Per cent	£1 Level Stake
May	1-2	50.0	+1.25	May	5-22	22.7	-5.35
June	0-0	0.0	0.00	June	0-5	0.0	-5.00
July	0-0	0.0	0.00	July	1-3	33.3	+5.00
August	0-0	0.0	0.00	August	1-2	50.0	+7.00
September	0-1	0.0	-1.00	September	0-6	0.0	-6.00
October	0-2	0.0	-2.00	October	2-19	10.5	+2.00
November	0-3	0.0	-3.00	November	2-21	9.5	-11.00
December	0-4	0.0	-4.00	December	3-25	12.0	+0.50
January	0-1	0.0	-1.00	January	4-22	18.2	-11.33
February	0-5	0.0	-5.00	February	5-32	15.6	-11.08
March	1-5	20.0	+7.00	March	3-31	9.7	-21.59
April	0-5	0.0	-5.00	April	3-32	9.4	-7.77

Chases	W-R	Per cent	£1 Level Stake	Totals	W-R	Per cent	£1 Level Stake
May	4-10	40.0	-0.67	May	10-34	29.4	-4.77
June	3-6	50.0	+8.25	June	3-11	27.3	+3.25
July	1-4	25.0	-0.75	July	2-7	28.6	+4.25
August	1-2	50.0	+15.00	August	2-4	50.0	+22.00
September	0-6	0.0	-6.00	September	0-13	0.0	-13.00
October	3-17	17.6	-3.63	October	5-38	13.2	-3.63
November	8-42	19.0	+22.00	November	10-66	15.2	+8.00
December	8-47	17.0	-2.52	December	11-76	14.5	-6.02
January	11-40	27.5	+13.00	January	15-63	23.8	+0.67
February	12-45	26.7	-3.89	February	17-82	20.7	-19.97
March	8-40	20.0	+30.27	March	12-76	15.8	+15.68
April	2-31	6.5	-23.50	April	5-68	7.4	-36.27

DISTANCE

Hurdles	W-R	Per cent	£1 Level Stake	Chases	W-R	Per cent	£1 Level Stake
2m-2m3f	13-103	12.6	-27.95	2m-2m3f	22-91	24.2	+16.48
2m4f-2m7f	7-76	9.2	-42.02	2m4f-2m7f	20-106	18.9	+27.30
3m+	9-41	22.0	+5.34	3m+	19-93	20.4	+3.77

TYPE OF RACE

Non-Handicaps	W-R	Per cent	£1 Level Stake	Handicaps	W-R	Per cent	£1 Level Stake
Nov Hrdls	4-45	8.9	-23.77	Nov Hrdls	5-23	21.7	+10.27
Hrdls	3-42	7.1	-34.95	Hrdls	17-111	15.3	-17.17
Nov Chs	15-66	22.7	+8.52	Nov Chs	8-32	25.0	-7.52
Chases	0-6	0.0	-6.00	Chases	38-184	20.7	+54.55
Sell/Claim	0-0	0.0	0.00	Sell/Claim	0-0	0.0	0.00

RACE CLASS / FIRST TIME OUT

	W-R	Per cent	£1 Level Stake		W-R	Per cent	£1 Level Stake
Class 1	4-66	6.1	+6.00	Bumpers	2-19	10.5	-3.75
Class 2	11-75	14.7	-2.13	Hurdles	6-51	11.8	-21.52

JOCKEYS

	W-R	Per cent	£1 Level Stake
Aidan Coleman	60-342	17.5	-71.76
Liam Treadwell	18-70	25.7	+82.62
Robert Dunne	5-34	14.7	-4.50
Harry Challoner	4-34	11.8	-1.50
Mr W Biddick	2-7	28.6	+3.91
Micheal Nolan	1-1	100.0	+0.91
A P McCoy	1-2	50.0	+2.50
Sam Thomas	1-43	2.3	-37.00

COURSE RECORD

	Total W-R	Non-Hndcps Hurdles	Chases	Hndcps Hurdles	Chases	NH Flat	Per cent	£1 Level Stake
Ludlow	9-35	0-7	1-5	2-8	6-15	0-0	25.7	+5.60
Taunton	7-20	0-4	1-4	5-7	1-3	0-2	35.0	+15.08
Towcester	7-21	0-6	2-3	1-4	3-5	1-3	33.3	+6.98
Plumpton	5-24	3-10	0-0	0-6	2-7	0-1	20.8	-11.11
Wincanton	5-41	0-7	1-4	1-9	2-19	1-2	12.2	-7.88
Musselbgh	4-10	0-0	0-1	3-5	1-4	0-0	40.0	+5.75
Bangor	4-12	0-2	2-3	0-2	2-2	0-3	33.3	+11.63
Exeter	4-15	1-3	1-5	2-6	0-1	0-0	26.7	+1.88
Sandown	4-28	0-2	1-4	0-7	3-14	0-1	14.3	-12.93
Cheltenham	4-44	0-2	0-4	1-15	3-21	0-2	9.1	+42.00
Ffos Las	3-7	0-1	1-1	1-2	1-3	0-0	42.9	+35.00
Leicester	3-8	0-0	1-2	0-0	2-6	0-0	37.5	+2.00
Fontwell	3-19	0-1	2-6	1-7	0-4	0-1	15.8	-5.89
Uttoxeter	3-19	1-5	0-3	1-4	1-5	0-2	15.8	-9.10
Newbury	3-22	0-1	0-2	0-4	3-15	0-0	13.6	-6.25
Wetherby	2-4	0-0	0-0	1-1	1-2	0-1	50.0	+2.50
Worcester	2-4	0-0	0-0	1-1	1-1	0-1	50.0	+7.25
Doncaster	2-5	0-0	0-2	1-1	1-2	0-0	40.0	+5.50
Southwell	2-7	0-1	0-0	0-1	2-4	0-1	28.6	-2.90
Stratford	2-11	1-2	0-0	0-4	1-3	0-1	18.2	-2.25
Haydock	2-14	0-2	1-2	0-4	1-6	0-0	14.3	-5.80
Nton Abbot	2-19	1-6	0-1	0-4	1-7	0-1	10.5	-8.38
Carlisle	1-1	0-0	0-0	0-0	1-1	0-0	100.0	+1.88
Cartmel	1-1	0-0	0-0	0-0	1-1	0-0	100.0	+2.25
Kelso	1-2	0-1	0-0	0-0	1-1	0-0	50.0	+10.00
Mrket Rsn	1-5	0-0	0-1	0-0	1-4	0-0	20.0	-0.50
Hereford	1-6	0-1	0-0	0-1	1-3	0-1	16.7	-3.63
Catterick	1-7	0-0	0-1	0-1	1-3	0-0	14.3	-4.25
Lingfield	1-10	0-0	0-4	0-1	1-5	0-0	10.0	-6.75
Huntingdon	1-15	0-4	0-2	1-5	0-3	0-1	6.7	-9.50
Warwick	1-20	0-5	0-3	0-4	1-6	0-2	5.0	-14.00
Chepstow	1-23	0-7	0-1	0-4	1-10	0-1	4.3	-15.00

WINNING HORSES

Horse	Races Run	1st	2nd	3rd	£
Carrickboy	7	2	0	0	67500
Rigadin De Beauchene	7	1	3	1	34170
Katenko	4	2	1	0	59755
Quartz De Thaix	6	2	1	0	30758
Emperor's Choice	9	3	3	0	30098
Houblon Des Obeaux	8	2	2	1	17292
Monetary Fund	12	2	3	2	19494
Idarah	12	2	0	1	22407
Brick Red	11	4	2	1	27003
Art Professor	6	1	0	0	12021
Kapga De Cerisy	8	2	0	1	20958
Drumshambo	11	4	1	2	25192
Stars Du Granits	3	2	1	0	12470
Ballyoliver	9	3	2	1	21939
Shangani	7	2	1	3	14296
Pentiffic	8	1	0	0	7798
Mentalist	6	2	1	2	11365
Plein Pouvoir	9	2	3	1	10672
Dare Me	6	1	3	1	7148
Howard's Legacy	8	2	1	1	13646
Nobunaga	11	3	2	2	20424
Relax	8	2	2	0	12151
Bennys Mist	11	5	0	1	15057
Lower Hope Dandy	5	2	0	1	7621
Adelar	6	2	0	1	8928
Hada Men	7	1	0	1	5393
Jupiter Rex	10	7	0	0	24964
Last Shot	11	1	3	1	4874
Duaiseoir	9	1	2	1	4243
Market Option	7	1	1	1	4224
Reginaldinho	9	2	0	2	6498
Sustainability	7	2	3	0	7110
Opera Og	5	3	1	0	7538
Gorgehous Lliege	7	2	1	0	5633
Ciceron	9	1	3	2	3671
Aachen	1	1	0	0	3390
Tuskar Rock	5	1	0	1	3249
Red Courtier	2	1	1	0	3249
Rydalis	9	3	1	0	5653
Tenor Nivernais	6	1	0	1	3054
Nagpur	5	1	1	0	2864
*Looking On	3	1	1	1	2738
Saroque	7	1	1	0	2599
Santo Thomas	1	1	0	0	2534
Guydus	3	1	2	0	2339
*Leviathan	5	1	1	1	2053
Cool Cascade	2	1	0	0	1949
Call Carlo	2	1	0	0	0
Total winning prize-money					**£639982**
Favourites	46-95		48.4%		29.92

H WILSON

HANBURY, WORCS

	No. of Hrs	Races Run	1st	2nd	3rd	Unpl	Per cent	£1 Level Stake
NH Flat	0	0	0	0	0	0	0.0	0.00
Hurdles	0	0	0	0	0	0	0.0	0.00
Chases	2	3	1	1	0	1	33.3	-1.75
Totals	2	3	1	1	0	1	33.3	-1.75
11-12	3	9	4	1	1	3	44.4	+4.00

JOCKEYS

	W-R	Per cent	£1 Level Stake
Mr M Wall	1-3	33.3	-1.75

COURSE RECORD

	Total W-R	Non-Hndcps Hurdles	Chases	Hndcps Hurdles	Chases	NH Flat	Per cent	£1 Level Stake
Folkestone	1-2	0-0	1-2	0-0	0-0	0-0	50.0	-0.75

WINNING HORSES

Horse	Races Run	1st	2nd	3rd	£
Divine Intavention	2	1	0	0	1153
Total winning prize-money					**£1153**
Favourites	1-1		100.0%		0.25

CHRISTOPHER WILSON

MANFIELD, N YORKS

	No. of Hrs	Races Run	1st	2nd	3rd	Unpl	Per cent	£1 Level Stake
NH Flat	0	0	0	0	0	0	0.0	0.00
Hurdles	3	3	0	1	0	2	0.0	-3.00
Chases	2	8	1	1	0	6	12.5	-3.50
Totals	4	11	1	2	0	8	9.1	-6.50
11-12	5	16	0	3	3	10	0.0	-16.00
10-11	5	17	3	1	3	10	17.6	+4.38

JOCKEYS

	W-R	Per cent	£1 Level Stake
Will Kennedy	1-2	50.0	+2.50

COURSE RECORD

	Total W-R	Non-Hndcps Hurdles	Chases	Hndcps Hurdles	Chases	NH Flat	Per cent	£1 Level Stake
Hexham	1-4	0-1	0-0	0-0	1-3	0-0	25.0	+0.50

WINNING HORSES

Horse	Races Run	1st	2nd	3rd	£
Ormus	4	1	0	0	3249
Total winning prize-money					**£3249**
Favourites	0-0		0.0%		0.00

ADRIAN WINTLE

WESTBURY-ON-SEVERN, GLOUCS

	No. of Hrs	Races Run	1st	2nd	3rd	Unpl	Per cent	£1 Level Stake
NH Flat	1	1	0	0	0	1	0.0	-1.00
Hurdles	4	11	1	0	1	9	9.1	+15.00
Chases	2	5	1	1	0	3	20.0	0.00
Totals	5	17	2	1	1	13	11.8	+14.00
11-12	7	22	0	1	4	17	0.0	-22.00
10-11	5	7	0	1	0	6	0.0	-7.00

JOCKEYS

	W-R	Per cent	£1 Level Stake
Gerard Tumelty	1-3	33.3	+23.00
Richard Johnson	1-6	16.7	-1.00

COURSE RECORD

	Total W-R	Non-Hndcps Hurdles Chases		Hndcps Hurdles Chases		NH Flat	Per cent	£1 Level Stake
Uttoxeter	1-1	0-0	0-0	1-1	0-0	0-0	100.0	+25.00
Stratford	1-3	0-0	0-0	0-1	1-2	0-0	33.3	+2.00

WINNING HORSES

Horse	Races Run	1st	2nd	3rd	£
Shalone	4	1	0	0	3671
Silver Coaster	7	1	1	1	2599
Total winning prize-money					**£6270**
Favourites	0-1		0.0%		-1.00

RICHARD WOOLLACOTT

SOUTH MOLTON, DEVON

	No. of Hrs	Races Run	1st	2nd	3rd	Unpl	Per cent	£1 Level Stake
NH Flat	6	7	0	1	0	6	0.0	-7.00
Hurdles	23	60	6	4	6	44	10.0	-28.25
Chases	18	48	10	4	4	30	20.8	-4.34
Totals	37	115	16	9	10	80	13.9	-39.59
11-12	2	3	0	2	1	0	0.0	-3.00
10-11	4	7	1	2	1	3	14.3	-4.80

BY MONTH

NH Flat	W-R	Per cent	£1 Level Stake	Hurdles	W-R	Per cent	£1 Level Stake
May	0-0	0.0	0.00	May	0-0	0.0	0.00
June	0-3	0.0	-3.00	June	1-4	25.0	+3.00
July	0-1	0.0	-1.00	July	1-7	14.3	-3.00
August	0-0	0.0	0.00	August	1-5	20.0	+0.50
September	0-0	0.0	0.00	September	0-0	0.0	0.00
October	0-0	0.0	0.00	October	0-6	0.0	-6.00
November	0-1	0.0	-1.00	November	0-3	0.0	-3.00
December	0-0	0.0	0.00	December	1-6	16.7	-0.50
January	0-0	0.0	0.00	January	1-5	20.0	-1.25
February	0-0	0.0	0.00	February	0-11	0.0	-11.00
March	0-2	0.0	-2.00	March	0-6	0.0	-6.00
April	0-0	0.0	0.00	April	1-7	14.3	-1.00

Chases	W-R	Per cent	£1 Level Stake	Totals	W-R	Per cent	£1 Level Stake
May	0-2	0.0	-2.00	May	0-2	0.0	-2.00
June	0-1	0.0	-1.00	June	1-8	12.5	-1.00
July	4-6	66.7	+9.96	July	5-14	35.7	+5.96
August	3-7	42.9	+11.83	August	4-12	33.3	+12.33
September	1-4	25.0	-1.13	September	1-4	25.0	-1.13
October	0-3	0.0	-3.00	October	0-9	0.0	-9.00
November	0-2	0.0	-2.00	November	0-6	0.0	-6.00
December	0-1	0.0	-1.00	December	1-7	14.3	-1.50
January	0-7	0.0	-7.00	January	1-12	8.3	-8.25
February	0-3	0.0	-3.00	February	0-14	0.0	-14.00
March	2-7	28.6	-1.00	March	2-15	13.3	-9.00
April	0-5	0.0	-5.00	April	1-12	8.3	-6.00

DISTANCE

Hurdles	W-R	Per cent	£1 Level Stake	Chases	W-R	Per cent	£1 Level Stake
2m-2m3f	3-32	9.4	-17.25	2m-2m3f	1-8	12.5	+7.00
2m4f-2m7f	2-22	9.1	-11.00	2m4f-2m7f	5-19	26.3	-0.01
3m+	1-6	16.7	0.00	3m+	4-21	19.0	-11.33

TYPE OF RACE

Non-Handicaps	W-R	Per cent	£1 Level Stake	Handicaps	W-R	Per cent	£1 Level Stake
Nov Hrdls	0-15	0.0	-15.00	Nov Hrdls	2-6	33.3	+3.75
Hrdls	2-10	20.0	+1.00	Hrdls	2-29	6.9	-18.00
Nov Chs	1-12	8.3	+3.00	Nov Chs	1-2	50.0	+0.25
Chases	1-4	25.0	-2.33	Chases	7-30	23.3	-5.26
Sell/Claim	0-0	0.0	0.00	Sell/Claim	0-0	0.0	0.00

RACE CLASS

	W-R	Per cent	£1 Level Stake
Class 1	0-0	0.0	0.00
Class 2	0-1	0.0	-1.00
Class 3	0-12	0.0	-12.00
Class 4	8-54	14.8	-13.57
Class 5	7-42	16.7	-8.69
Class 6	1-6	16.7	-4.33

FIRST TIME OUT

	W-R	Per cent	£1 Level Stake
Bumpers	0-6	0.0	-6.00
Hurdles	1-16	6.3	-12.25
Chases	4-15	26.7	-0.25
Totals	5-37	13.5	-18.50

JOCKEYS

	W-R	Per cent	£1 Level Stake
Micheal Nolan	6-34	17.6	-10.34
Andrew Glassonbury	5-22	22.7	+13.71
Mr Joshua Guerriero	1-2	50.0	-0.33
Tom O'Brien	1-4	25.0	-0.25
Paddy Brennan	1-5	20.0	-2.13
Daryl Jacob	1-9	11.1	-6.75
Matt Griffiths	1-14	7.1	-8.50

COURSE RECORD

	Total W-R	Non-Hndcps Hurdles	Chases	Hndcps Hurdles	Chases	NH Flat	Per cent	£1 Level Stake
Uttoxeter	4-9	1-2	0-1	1-2	2-4	0-0	44.4	+5.63
Worcester	4-16	1-7	0-1	0-2	3-4	0-2	25.0	+3.93
Stratford	2-6	0-0	1-1	0-0	1-5	0-0	33.3	+10.73
Hereford	1-3	0-1	0-0	1-2	0-0	0-0	33.3	+2.50
Ffos Las	1-4	0-1	0-0	0-0	1-3	0-0	25.0	+0.33
Exeter	1-5	0-0	1-4	0-1	0-0	0-0	20.0	-3.33
Nton Abbot	1-11	0-1	0-1	0-3	1-4	0-2	9.1	-8.13
Wincanton	1-13	0-5	0-2	1-5	0-1	0-0	7.7	-9.25
Taunton	1-16	0-4	0-0	1-9	0-2	0-1	6.3	-10.00

WINNING HORSES

Horse	Races Run	1st	2nd	3rd	£
*Come What Augustus	4	1	0	1	3899
Valoroso	4	1	0	1	3769
Deb's Dasher	4	1	0	1	3278
*Cridda Boy	1	1	0	0	3249
*Allerford Jack	6	4	0	1	10313
Midnight Whisper	5	1	0	0	3080
*Gay Sloane	7	1	0	1	2599
Vintage Tea	4	1	0	0	2534
Carriglea Wood	3	1	0	0	1864
Qualypso D'Allier	2	1	0	0	1819
Parkam Jack	3	1	1	0	1779
Prickles	6	1	2	1	1689
*Robin Will	2	1	0	1	960
Total winning prize-money					£40832
Favourites	8-19		42.1%		2.58

N R W WRIGHT

CHIPPENHAM, WILTSHIRE

	No. of Hrs	Races Run	1st	2nd	3rd	Unpl	Per cent	£1 Level Stake
NH Flat	0	0	0	0	0	0	0.0	0.00
Hurdles	0	0	0	0	0	0	0.0	0.00
Chases	2	2	1	0	1	0	50.0	-0.56
Totals	2	2	1	0	1	0	50.0	-0.56
11-12	1	1	1	0	0	0	100.0	+6.00

JOCKEYS

	W-R	Per cent	£1 Level Stake
Miss Carey Williamson	1-2	50.0	-0.56

COURSE RECORD

	Total W-R	Non-Hndcps Hurdles	Chases	Hndcps Hurdles	Chases	NH Flat	Per cent	£1 Level Stake
Folkestone	1-1	0-0	1-1	0-0	0-0	0-0	100.0	+0.44

WINNING HORSES

Horse	Races Run	1st	2nd	3rd	£
It Was Me	1	1	0	0	1317
Total winning prize-money					£1317
Favourites	1-2		50.0%		-0.56

P YORK

COBHAM, SURREY

	No. of Hrs	Races Run	1st	2nd	3rd	Unpl	Per cent	£1 Level Stake
NH Flat	0	0	0	0	0	0	0.0	0.00
Hurdles	0	0	0	0	0	0	0.0	0.00
Chases	5	6	1	3	0	2	16.7	-3.63
Totals	5	6	1	3	0	2	16.7	-3.63
11-12	3	6	1	1	2	2	16.7	-1.00
10-11	3	3	0	0	1	2	0.0	-3.00

JOCKEYS

	W-R	Per cent	£1 Level Stake
Mr P York	1-5	20.0	-2.63

COURSE RECORD

	Total W-R	Non-Hndcps Hurdles	Chases	Hndcps Hurdles	Chases	NH Flat	Per cent	£1 Level Stake
Huntingdon	1-1	0-0	1-1	0-0	0-0	0-0	100.0	+1.38

WINNING HORSES

Horse	Races Run	1st	2nd	3rd	£
*Freddies Return	2	1	1	0	988
Total winning prize-money					£988
Favourites	1-2		50.0%		-0.38

RAYMOND YORK

MARTYR'S GREEN, SURREY

	No. of Hrs	Races Run	1st	2nd	3rd	Unpl	Per cent	£1 Level Stake
NH Flat	3	3	0	0	0	3	0.0	-3.00
Hurdles	8	20	1	1	1	17	5.0	-16.50
Chases	1	8	1	0	2	5	12.5	0.00
Totals	11	31	2	1	3	25	6.5	-19.50
11-12	12	21	1	0	1	19	4.8	-19.39
10-11	9	21	0	0	3	18	0.0	-21.00

JOCKEYS

	W-R	Per cent	£1 Level Stake
Tom Cannon	1-3	33.3	+0.50
Mr P York	1-16	6.3	-8.00

COURSE RECORD

	Total W-R	Non-Hndcps Hurdles	Chases	Hndcps Hurdles	Chases	NH Flat	Per cent	£1 Level Stake
Lingfield	1-3	0-0	0-0	0-0	1-3	0-0	33.3	+5.00
Uttoxeter	1-7	0-2	0-0	1-3	0-0	0-2	14.3	-3.50

WINNING HORSES

Horse	Races Run	1st	2nd	3rd	£
Ringa Bay	8	1	0	2	3769
*Murfreesboro	4	1	0	0	1689
Total winning prize-money					£5458
Favourites	0-2		0.0%		-2.00

LAURA YOUNG

BROOMFIELD, SOMERSET

	No. of Hrs	Races Run	1st	2nd	3rd	Unpl	Per cent	£1 Level Stake
NH Flat	5	5	0	0	0	5	0.0	-5.00
Hurdles	10	36	2	3	2	29	5.6	-22.75
Chases	4	13	1	3	2	7	7.7	-9.75
Totals	16	54	3	6	4	41	5.6	-37.50
11-12	17	50	2	3	4	41	4.0	-30.00
10-11	14	35	1	3	2	29	2.9	-30.00

JOCKEYS

	W-R	Per cent	£1 Level Stake
Andrew Glassonbury	2-21	9.5	-7.75
Dougie Costello	1-5	20.0	-1.75

COURSE RECORD

	Total W-R	Non-Hndcps Hurdles	Chases	Hndcps Hurdles	Chases	NH Flat	Per cent	£1 Level Stake
Worcester	1-3	0-1	0-0	1-1	0-0	0-1	33.3	+7.00
Towcester	1-4	0-0	0-0	0-1	1-3	0-0	25.0	-0.75
Taunton	1-6	0-2	0-0	1-4	0-0	0-0	16.7	-2.75

WINNING HORSES

Horse	Races Run	1st	2nd	3rd	£
Admiral Blake	5	1	3	0	2395
Kap West	6	1	2	1	2144
Courting Whitney	13	1	0	1	2053
Total winning prize-money					£6592
Favourites	2-5		40.0%		1.50

LEADING JUMP TRAINERS IN JANUARY
(SINCE 2009)

	Total W-R	Nov Hdle	H'cap Hdle	Other Hdle	Nov Chase	H'cap Chase	Other Chase	Hunter Chase	N.H. Flat	Per cent	£1 Level stake
Nicky Henderson	90-318	29-83	4-44	17-66	22-50	2-28	7-19	0-0	10-30	28.3	-48.42
Paul Nicholls	62-288	17-61	4-44	13-51	10-33	5-58	12-27	0-0	1-15	21.5	-101.31
David Pipe	56-307	10-61	14-83	12-37	3-11	12-78	2-20	0-0	3-17	18.2	-3.92
Donald McCain	56-305	24-82	4-56	7-53	6-32	6-42	5-22	0-0	4-19	18.4	-119.75
Venetia Williams	51-305	6-48	16-78	1-36	6-28	18-100	2-8	0-0	2-7	16.7	+118.90
Alan King	47-334	14-94	8-71	13-50	5-38	5-40	1-11	0-0	1-32	14.1	-56.33
Philip Hobbs	37-280	6-75	7-59	8-25	5-38	7-53	1-15	0-0	3-17	13.2	-112.28
Jonjo O'Neill	32-315	5-75	9-74	1-34	3-23	11-84	3-12	0-1	0-12	10.2	-160.77
Howard Johnson	28-161	11-44	0-28	3-14	5-14	2-32	4-18	0-0	3-11	17.4	-27.32
Gary Moore	24-187	3-37	4-48	4-28	4-23	7-41	1-7	0-0	1-4	12.8	+54.59
Keith Reveley	24-107	3-16	5-15	1-13	3-7	8-30	0-3	0-0	4-23	22.4	+15.11
Evan Williams	23-199	2-28	5-68	4-34	4-16	5-38	1-6	0-1	2-8	11.6	-23.04
Nigel Twiston-Davies	21-251	5-39	5-46	1-25	2-30	6-80	0-16	0-0	2-15	8.4	-17.69
Lucinda Russell	21-192	3-31	6-46	4-19	1-11	6-64	1-8	0-0	0-13	10.9	-94.61
Tom George	20-135	2-28	1-18	0-11	5-22	10-43	0-6	0-0	2-7	14.8	-29.73
Henry Daly	18-109	0-21	4-12	4-22	3-15	5-28	2-4	0-0	0-7	16.5	-2.98
Charlie Longsdon	17-134	3-34	3-27	2-10	1-10	3-37	1-3	0-0	4-14	12.7	+2.50
Ferdy Murphy	15-173	1-30	3-28	1-14	2-23	5-58	3-15	0-0	0-5	8.7	-85.84
Colin Tizzard	15-165	1-23	4-29	0-7	2-14	5-56	2-13	0-0	1-23	9.1	-49.88
Charlie Mann	14-123	2-24	6-25	1-18	2-10	2-37	1-6	0-0	0-4	11.4	-24.47
Victor Dartnall	14-76	2-19	3-13	0-4	4-12	3-22	1-2	0-1	1-3	18.4	+10.65
Tony Carroll	14-86	1-13	6-26	1-12	1-4	4-25	1-5	0-0	0-1	16.3	+47.33
James Ewart	14-89	0-15	1-12	1-11	1-7	4-20	5-8	0-0	2-16	15.7	-1.64
Jim Goldie	13-103	2-18	5-40	1-12	2-2	2-18	0-3	0-0	1-10	12.6	+8.75
Nick Williams	13-71	2-6	3-12	1-9	2-13	3-22	2-7	0-0	0-2	18.3	-1.62
Neil Mulholland	13-102	1-32	4-26	1-6	1-4	5-25	1-3	0-0	0-7	12.7	+19.63
Martin Keighley	12-80	1-13	4-22	1-7	1-8	2-21	0-4	0-0	3-5	15.0	-12.42
Rebecca Curtis	12-59	1-8	1-14	4-15	3-7	0-6	0-2	0-0	3-7	20.3	-1.77
Malcolm Jefferson	11-90	2-22	3-18	0-5	0-5	3-19	1-6	0-0	2-15	12.2	+20.00
Bob Buckler	11-74	1-12	0-3	0-4	1-4	7-33	1-5	0-0	1-13	14.9	+2.96
Sue Smith	11-154	0-33	6-36	0-5	1-14	4-57	0-1	0-0	0-8	7.1	-80.83
Nicky Richards	11-91	4-30	2-23	1-12	2-9	0-10	1-4	0-0	1-3	12.1	-22.22
Richard Lee	10-73	1-11	1-19	0-5	1-7	4-25	1-3	0-0	2-3	13.7	+23.33
Henrietta Knight	10-88	1-25	0-7	0-9	1-9	5-21	2-7	0-0	1-10	11.4	-27.17
Brian Ellison	10-64	1-10	4-31	2-11	0-0	1-7	2-2	0-0	0-3	15.6	-10.50
Neil King	10-100	1-16	1-24	2-17	1-2	4-28	1-5	0-0	0-8	10.0	-44.38
Lucy Wadham	10-83	0-17	4-29	3-13	1-5	0-7	1-5	0-0	1-7	12.0	-18.50
Tim Vaughan	10-157	1-26	3-42	1-28	1-11	1-23	2-9	0-0	1-19	6.4	-100.61
Seamus Mullins	9-102	1-17	1-19	0-10	0-11	4-20	0-8	0-0	3-18	8.8	+38.88
Paul Webber	9-81	4-20	0-5	1-17	2-11	1-13	1-4	0-0	0-11	11.1	-15.02
Emma Lavelle	9-115	4-39	2-20	0-16	2-10	1-9	0-6	0-0	0-16	7.8	-70.13
Dr Richard Newland	9-53	0-5	4-14	1-5	0-1	4-27	0-0	0-0	0-1	17.0	+8.25
John Ferguson	9-26	3-9	0-1	5-11	0-1	0-1	0-0	0-0	1-3	34.6	+10.50
Oliver Sherwood	8-88	1-22	1-13	3-17	1-7	1-19	1-5	0-0	0-5	9.1	+42.37
Robin Dickin	8-68	3-21	1-12	1-9	0-2	3-19	0-2	0-0	0-3	11.8	-22.25
Ian Williams	8-88	3-19	2-31	0-11	1-8	1-9	0-1	0-0	1-9	9.1	-53.01
Jeremy Scott	7-66	3-16	0-18	2-10	2-5	0-10	0-2	0-0	0-5	10.6	-0.25
Richard Rowe	7-61	2-11	1-10	1-6	1-6	2-22	0-0	0-0	0-6	11.5	-3.80
Lawney Hill	7-36	0-5	4-13	2-8	0-0	0-5	0-0	0-0	1-5	19.4	-0.72
Chris Grant	7-95	0-21	4-21	0-4	0-2	2-30	0-6	0-0	1-11	7.4	-45.92
Alex Hales	7-62	2-12	1-20	0-10	2-5	2-12	0-2	0-0	0-1	11.3	-5.00

LEADING JUMP TRAINERS IN FEBRUARY
(SINCE 2009)

	Total W-R	Nov Hdle	H'cap Hdle	Other Hdle	Nov Chase	H'cap Chase	Other Chase	Hunter Chase	N.H. Flat	Per cent	£1 Level stake
Nicky Henderson	99-375	31-106	3-57	24-75	13-44	6-30	11-30	2-2	9-31	26.4	-105.65
Paul Nicholls	79-328	19-68	7-54	14-51	11-38	5-47	11-37	7-10	5-23	24.1	-52.14
Venetia Williams	66-345	7-49	14-72	13-49	10-34	13-107	6-14	2-3	1-17	19.1	-64.07
Alan King	61-392	17-101	9-79	7-53	11-37	6-44	6-24	0-2	5-52	15.6	-95.20
Donald McCain	58-325	20-97	6-61	7-45	8-35	5-39	7-20	0-2	5-26	17.8	-55.01
David Pipe	54-303	9-57	9-83	10-54	4-13	12-58	1-10	0-0	9-28	17.8	-67.31
Jonjo O'Neill	39-295	10-64	12-65	3-45	2-15	7-63	1-5	3-19	1-19	13.2	-72.51
Philip Hobbs	36-272	7-52	9-61	3-32	5-24	5-55	3-18	0-2	4-28	13.2	-82.67
Gary Moore	32-217	5-43	7-69	6-38	5-15	8-36	0-6	0-0	1-10	14.7	-57.89
Nigel Twiston-Davies	29-314	6-47	6-54	1-34	3-24	5-100	1-16	4-10	3-29	9.2	-60.04
Colin Tizzard	28-173	3-20	5-30	4-16	2-19	7-57	2-8	0-1	5-22	16.2	-29.25
Evan Williams	24-232	3-33	6-63	6-53	1-17	4-53	2-6	1-2	1-5	10.3	+ 49.91
Lucinda Russell	22-176	5-26	3-42	0-14	5-12	6-64	2-6	0-1	1-11	12.5	-32.11
Tim Vaughan	21-178	4-36	5-55	4-33	2-15	1-17	1-1	0-1	4-20	11.8	-1.35
Sue Smith	20-188	1-25	7-51	0-8	5-24	7-60	0-7	0-0	0-13	10.6	-53.74
Tom George	20-147	2-12	1-20	1-28	4-13	9-55	2-12	0-1	1-6	13.6	-34.92
Charlie Longsdon	19-146	5-27	3-34	4-15	0-12	6-34	0-3	1-1	0-20	13.0	-1.11
Nicky Richards	18-96	4-21	3-26	2-9	3-5	1-17	2-7	0-0	3-11	18.8	-1.89
Charlie Mann	17-125	5-21	0-19	2-20	1-16	4-28	4-15	0-0	1-6	13.6	+ 25.78
Nick Gifford	16-87	0-16	3-20	2-10	1-4	3-20	2-5	0-1	5-11	18.4	+ 31.08
Richard Lee	15-106	1-14	3-19	2-15	3-9	4-42	1-2	0-0	1-5	14.2	-16.45
Keith Reveley	15-129	2-21	5-27	0-10	2-8	4-32	0-3	0-0	2-28	11.6	-39.92
Howard Johnson	13-156	5-45	4-37	1-10	0-16	1-23	1-8	0-2	1-15	8.3	-36.13
Victor Dartnall	12-90	3-21	2-17	0-6	1-4	4-23	0-2	0-3	2-14	13.3	+ 3.38
Lucy Wadham	12-85	2-19	4-33	0-4	0-5	3-13	1-3	0-1	2-7	14.1	+ 5.50
James Ewart	12-93	2-14	0-20	3-11	1-6	4-22	1-4	0-0	1-16	12.9	-23.73
Rebecca Curtis	12-79	2-12	2-19	2-14	1-8	0-9	0-1	1-4	4-12	15.2	-25.63
Oliver Sherwood	11-101	1-20	0-23	1-14	2-5	5-27	0-1	0-0	2-11	10.9	-26.50
Malcolm Jefferson	11-101	3-21	1-22	0-9	1-7	4-22	0-4	0-0	2-16	10.9	+ 1.60
Brian Ellison	11-89	1-18	6-43	1-11	1-2	1-9	1-1	0-0	0-5	12.4	-39.05
Alan Swinbank	11-57	2-15	2-7	0-1	1-3	1-5	0-2	0-0	5-24	19.3	+ 13.38
Emma Lavelle	11-106	6-35	0-17	0-11	2-6	0-13	1-5	0-0	2-19	10.4	-52.77
Ferdy Murphy	10-143	0-21	0-26	0-5	3-14	5-63	2-10	0-0	0-4	7.0	-92.11
Ian Williams	10-92	2-24	3-26	1-11	2-6	0-12	1-3	0-2	1-8	10.9	-43.95
Henry Daly	10-118	3-23	0-10	1-18	2-9	0-33	2-8	0-0	2-17	8.5	-46.41
Nick Williams	10-65	2-10	0-10	0-6	3-7	4-21	0-5	0-0	1-6	15.4	-9.15
John Ferguson	10-35	3-11	2-7	2-12	0-1	1-1	0-0	0-1	2-2	28.6	-6.91
David Arbuthnot	9-37	3-6	1-4	0-5	2-5	1-10	0-0	0-0	2-7	24.3	+ 15.19
Chris Grant	9-94	1-17	2-22	1-6	0-8	2-22	1-5	0-0	2-14	9.6	-49.05
Brendan Powell	9-122	1-21	1-35	0-16	2-9	3-25	1-6	1-2	0-8	7.4	-72.40
Anthony Honeyball	9-44	0-9	2-6	0-3	0-2	2-5	1-3	0-0	4-16	20.5	+ 17.75
Warren Greatrex	9-68	2-18	3-20	3-11	0-3	0-6	0-0	0-0	1-10	13.2	+ 23.00
Kim Bailey	8-69	0-14	1-18	1-7	0-3	3-17	1-3	0-0	2-7	11.6	+ 23.25
Jim Goldie	8-69	1-7	5-34	0-4	0-1	2-14	0-0	0-0	0-9	11.6	+ 3.62
Richard Phillips	8-81	0-11	2-36	1-11	2-5	3-14	0-0	0-0	0-4	9.9	-11.08
John Quinn	8-50	1-13	2-18	2-9	1-1	1-7	0-0	0-0	1-2	16.0	+ 9.96
Paul Webber	8-76	3-20	0-7	2-8	0-9	1-10	2-4	0-0	0-18	10.5	-13.83
Caroline Bailey	8-58	1-14	3-11	0-3	1-5	3-22	0-2	0-0	0-1	13.8	+ 44.00
Martin Keighley	8-52	0-10	3-15	2-4	0-1	1-13	1-2	0-1	1-6	15.4	-9.93
Seamus Mullins	7-88	0-11	2-23	2-14	0-6	3-14	0-5	0-0	0-15	8.0	-42.25
Neil King	7-70	1-7	2-26	0-6	0-0	3-22	0-1	0-0	1-8	10.0	-6.25

LEADING JUMP TRAINERS IN MARCH
(SINCE 2009)

	Total W-R	Nov Hdle	H'cap Hdle	Other Hdle	Nov Chase	H'cap Chase	Other Chase	Hunter Chase	N.H. Flat	Per cent	£1 Level stake
Nicky Henderson	87-480	19-95	17-119	21-95	4-40	2-51	10-38	0-1	15-57	18.1	+ 15.66
Paul Nicholls	72-380	17-63	8-71	13-63	13-42	8-60	6-55	2-11	5-27	18.9	-55.48
Philip Hobbs	61-382	14-61	10-116	6-51	8-29	11-77	5-19	1-4	7-36	16.0	-79.41
Donald McCain	61-390	24-110	8-87	11-58	2-29	5-43	3-25	0-1	8-40	15.6	-123.66
Alan King	58-431	13-92	5-113	12-69	7-22	8-72	4-20	0-1	10-53	13.5	-185.82
Evan Williams	51-329	12-61	14-93	7-49	8-25	6-72	1-9	1-2	2-22	15.5	-49.10
Venetia Williams	45-356	7-44	10-95	4-45	9-37	14-111	1-12	0-1	1-19	12.6	-126.82
David Pipe	42-375	5-51	20-148	6-56	1-18	11-90	1-17	0-0	0-14	11.2	-63.98
Jonjo O'Neill	40-315	2-37	8-90	3-67	4-19	16-78	4-14	1-10	3-14	12.7	-7.45
Sue Smith	40-267	4-36	10-54	1-11	5-32	15-104	2-15	0-0	3-16	15.0	+ 82.95
Nigel Twiston-Davies	35-360	3-41	6-74	5-44	3-27	12-125	4-17	1-7	1-33	9.7	-87.61
Howard Johnson	33-228	9-59	1-47	3-15	8-26	3-33	5-25	1-1	3-25	14.5	-86.31
Lucinda Russell	31-222	3-47	3-56	1-9	4-18	16-71	1-6	0-1	3-14	14.0	-42.48
Tim Vaughan	31-263	6-41	5-73	2-34	1-21	9-51	1-10	2-3	5-31	11.8	-144.15
Ferdy Murphy	28-216	6-31	4-34	1-13	5-18	7-91	3-21	0-0	2-8	13.0	-28.20
Tom George	27-164	3-22	2-21	3-27	6-24	11-56	0-7	0-3	2-5	16.5	-4.97
Charlie Longsdon	27-200	4-32	5-47	2-16	1-10	8-54	0-7	0-2	8-35	13.5	+ 8.82
Gary Moore	26-263	3-41	8-97	9-46	3-24	3-53	0-5	0-0	0-5	9.9	-67.69
Keith Reveley	22-159	3-20	3-37	3-21	4-9	7-43	0-2	0-0	2-28	13.8	-48.19
Colin Tizzard	22-169	3-22	4-32	3-13	2-15	7-59	1-6	0-2	2-22	13.0	+ 56.64
Victor Dartnall	21-129	3-21	5-30	2-11	0-12	4-29	2-5	2-4	3-18	16.3	-10.89
Charlie Mann	20-140	3-25	5-36	2-19	3-8	4-31	3-15	0-4	0-5	14.3	-7.54
Tony Carroll	20-133	4-21	13-66	1-15	0-11	2-14	0-2	0-0	0-6	15.0	+ 91.62
Chris Grant	19-110	2-25	9-31	2-8	0-10	3-20	3-5	0-1	0-10	17.3	+ 19.71
Nicky Richards	18-120	5-35	4-38	0-5	3-10	1-14	2-4	0-0	3-15	15.0	-10.60
Malcolm Jefferson	17-142	3-36	6-35	1-11	0-6	5-27	0-6	0-0	3-22	12.0	+ 15.08
Brian Ellison	17-91	3-16	8-43	1-21	1-1	4-13	0-0	0-0	0-1	18.7	+ 4.79
Henry Daly	17-156	0-24	3-22	4-20	3-17	6-49	0-4	0-2	1-18	10.9	-69.01
James Ewart	17-112	3-19	0-20	1-10	3-13	5-30	2-4	0-0	3-17	15.2	-46.66
Oliver Sherwood	16-125	1-20	1-25	3-16	1-7	4-31	2-4	0-0	4-22	12.8	-18.77
Alan Swinbank	16-91	4-21	3-11	0-8	0-6	0-2	1-5	0-0	8-38	17.6	-26.18
Richard Lee	15-81	4-7	1-11	0-10	3-9	7-40	0-3	0-0	0-2	18.5	-9.63
Rebecca Curtis	15-68	3-16	3-16	3-11	1-2	1-5	2-4	0-3	2-11	22.1	-8.47
Caroline Bailey	14-70	0-7	0-12	0-5	2-6	11-32	1-4	0-0	0-4	20.0	-4.11
Emma Lavelle	14-110	4-25	2-25	2-20	1-6	4-22	0-4	0-0	1-13	12.7	-43.57
Jennie Candlish	14-87	4-14	4-30	1-16	1-4	3-13	0-1	0-0	1-12	16.1	-5.17
David Arbuthnot	13-47	3-7	1-9	0-6	2-7	3-10	2-2	0-0	2-6	27.7	-3.58
Kim Bailey	13-125	1-21	1-33	1-16	2-9	4-28	1-6	0-0	3-13	10.4	-52.39
Jeremy Scott	13-72	0-10	7-32	2-8	0-3	3-12	0-1	0-0	1-8	18.1	-0.04
Jim Goldie	13-80	3-16	3-31	0-6	1-2	4-19	0-0	0-0	2-6	16.3	+ 0.74
John Quinn	13-54	3-13	3-17	5-12	0-1	2-8	0-0	0-0	0-3	24.1	+ 39.68
Dianne Sayer	13-75	3-16	8-40	0-2	0-3	2-18	0-1	0-0	0-0	17.3	+ 25.50
Dr Richard Newland	13-70	1-4	3-21	2-8	2-4	5-28	0-3	0-5	0-1	18.6	-11.84
Chris Down	12-98	1-21	6-41	2-19	1-2	2-5	0-0	0-0	0-10	12.2	+ 5.13
Ian Williams	12-86	1-11	3-32	3-10	0-1	3-16	0-4	1-3	1-11	14.0	-9.93
Brendan Powell	12-150	1-22	4-51	1-15	4-9	0-31	0-0	1-4	1-19	8.0	-50.42
Martin Keighley	12-101	2-11	4-41	1-11	0-6	4-19	0-2	0-1	1-10	11.9	-29.00
Anthony Honeyball	12-55	1-3	2-9	0-10	4-6	1-10	2-5	0-0	2-13	21.8	+ 14.42
Neil King	11-120	1-9	4-42	0-19	1-3	4-37	0-2	0-0	1-11	9.2	-60.06
Lucy Wadham	11-94	1-9	5-37	3-22	1-5	1-18	1-1	0-1	0-5	11.7	-22.07
Warren Greatrex	11-68	2-18	3-20	1-9	1-3	3-9	0-1	0-0	1-10	16.2	+ 5.50

LEADING JUMP TRAINERS IN APRIL

(SINCE 2009)

	Total W-R	Nov Hdle	H'cap Hdle	Other Hdle	Nov Chase	H'cap Chase	Other Chase	Hunter Chase	N.H. Flat	Per cent	£1 Level stake
Nicky Henderson	92-420	22-65	15-107	14-77	10-36	3-45	6-27	0-0	26-86	21.9	-4.31
Paul Nicholls	74-408	15-66	6-73	11-48	16-56	9-94	7-31	1-10	9-39	18.1	-129.02
Philip Hobbs	57-337	11-49	13-100	6-32	8-26	12-92	2-8	1-3	4-35	16.9	+ 9.50
Alan King	57-380	16-70	8-83	12-67	9-34	6-55	1-6	0-2	6-73	15.0	-58.04
Donald McCain	54-335	13-76	6-92	8-45	6-28	6-51	3-5	2-4	10-40	16.1	-82.69
David Pipe	49-296	7-36	20-114	5-48	5-13	8-82	2-6	0-0	2-10	16.6	-34.61
Nigel Twiston-Davies	37-317	3-36	7-60	7-33	5-18	11-131	1-12	2-6	2-27	11.7	-55.27
Tim Vaughan	35-223	5-37	5-58	3-20	1-13	11-56	3-7	1-6	6-27	15.7	+ 19.50
Jonjo O'Neill	33-252	4-28	6-67	6-35	2-13	8-56	2-12	4-15	2-32	13.1	-45.82
Howard Johnson	30-177	6-39	4-35	0-15	9-23	7-41	1-5	0-0	3-22	16.9	+ 14.08
Charlie Longsdon	27-160	4-30	7-43	1-20	3-8	7-38	0-0	1-1	4-26	16.9	+ 22.64
Evan Williams	26-252	8-46	2-60	6-46	6-31	4-50	0-6	0-4	0-11	10.3	-110.39
Rebecca Curtis	26-98	5-13	1-26	5-16	3-9	3-10	0-0	0-2	9-24	26.5	+ 3.72
Gary Moore	24-197	5-33	6-68	3-28	4-19	3-38	1-4	0-1	2-8	12.2	-26.24
Ferdy Murphy	22-181	2-19	4-32	3-14	4-21	9-80	0-7	0-0	0-9	12.2	-29.50
Lucinda Russell	20-200	1-28	4-52	2-17	2-19	8-64	1-3	0-1	2-17	10.0	-6.78
Venetia Williams	20-220	5-26	5-54	1-29	3-26	6-79	0-4	0-0	0-9	9.1	-7.84
Sue Smith	19-197	2-22	3-42	0-6	3-24	11-88	0-2	0-0	0-14	9.6	+ 0.25
Colin Tizzard	19-150	2-24	0-20	1-10	6-17	7-56	0-3	0-0	3-20	12.7	-44.52
Kim Bailey	18-118	2-25	6-38	0-8	3-6	4-23	0-2	0-0	3-17	15.3	+ 31.70
Peter Bowen	18-134	0-14	5-40	2-12	2-10	6-35	0-3	0-5	4-19	13.4	+ 15.45
Emma Lavelle	17-107	5-20	1-23	1-10	2-9	5-30	0-2	0-0	3-14	15.9	+ 4.90
Tom George	16-119	0-18	1-11	5-22	3-12	6-36	1-8	0-5	0-11	13.4	-20.80
Victor Dartnall	16-90	5-12	8-31	0-6	1-10	0-19	0-0	0-0	2-14	17.8	+ 12.91
Charlie Mann	15-105	4-19	1-26	4-14	4-14	2-24	1-3	0-0	0-6	14.3	-24.48
Henry Daly	14-141	2-26	4-28	0-13	2-13	3-39	1-1	0-1	2-23	9.9	-56.06
Malcolm Jefferson	13-134	2-22	3-39	1-6	4-15	1-31	1-2	0-0	2-21	9.7	-49.15
Jeremy Scott	13-77	5-13	5-19	0-9	0-5	1-15	0-2	0-1	2-14	16.9	+ 52.38
David Arbuthnot	12-39	2-6	2-6	1-1	3-4	2-13	0-0	0-0	2-9	30.8	+ 31.45
Brian Ellison	12-64	1-11	5-30	4-7	0-2	2-14	0-0	0-0	0-1	18.8	+ 5.39
Nicky Richards	12-105	2-24	6-35	0-10	1-9	2-16	0-3	1-3	0-7	11.4	-11.65
Brendan Powell	12-152	2-23	2-49	0-21	1-6	6-39	0-3	0-2	1-11	7.9	-98.43
Philip Kirby	12-68	4-13	4-29	0-0	0-3	3-13	0-1	0-1	1-8	17.6	-3.63
Bernard Llewellyn	11-64	2-10	6-31	0-8	1-2	2-9	0-1	0-0	0-4	17.2	+ 40.00
Seamus Mullins	11-124	3-22	3-34	2-13	0-12	1-28	0-0	0-0	2-17	8.9	+ 7.05
Keith Reveley	11-80	3-9	1-20	1-5	2-8	3-26	0-1	0-0	1-12	13.8	-9.50
Dianne Sayer	11-67	1-9	8-36	0-1	0-3	2-16	0-0	0-0	0-2	16.4	+ 10.92
Alan Swinbank	11-51	3-13	0-6	1-5	1-1	0-1	0-0	0-0	6-26	21.6	-11.13
Jennie Candlish	11-61	2-6	5-21	0-4	2-3	0-9	0-0	0-0	2-19	18.0	+ 46.75
Chris Gordon	11-91	1-13	6-30	0-11	1-5	3-25	0-0	0-3	0-4	12.1	+ 17.50
Oliver Sherwood	10-112	2-22	3-31	0-7	2-10	1-15	0-3	0-1	2-25	8.9	-58.67
Andy Turnell	10-87	3-16	1-21	0-9	0-10	5-29	0-0	0-0	1-5	11.5	-21.47
Susan Gardner	10-45	3-15	4-19	0-2	0-1	2-3	0-0	0-0	1-5	22.2	+ 80.50
Neil King	10-103	1-9	2-41	1-10	1-3	4-30	0-3	0-0	1-9	9.7	+ 1.76
Nick Williams	10-68	0-13	1-6	3-8	1-3	1-18	2-15	0-0	2-5	14.7	+ 37.35
Alison Thorpe	10-72	1-15	3-29	3-14	1-4	0-5	0-1	0-0	2-4	13.9	-10.37
John Wade	9-73	0-19	3-21	0-2	1-11	4-38	0-1	0-3	1-9	8.7	-6.25
Bob Buckler	9-63	0-8	0-10	0-1	0-2	7-29	1-6	0-0	1-8	14.3	+ 32.33
Lucy Wadham	9-74	6-17	0-21	1-12	0-6	1-10	0-1	1-2	0-8	12.2	-15.04
Nick Gifford	9-73	0-13	1-16	2-9	2-9	3-21	0-0	0-0	1-6	12.3	-16.34
George Charlton	9-90	5-11	1-30	1-6	0-6	1-13	1-1	0-0	0-23	10.0	-23.23

LEADING JUMP TRAINERS IN MAY
(SINCE 2009)

	Total W-R	Nov Hdle	H'cap Hdle	Other Hdle	Nov Chase	H'cap Chase	Other Chase	Hunter Chase	N.H. Flat	Per cent	£1 Level stake
Tim Vaughan	47-170	7-36	6-44	10-26	6-13	13-31	1-4	2-3	2-13	27.6	+ 77.61
Donald McCain	43-223	12-42	4-48	11-52	7-17	4-29	1-5	0-3	4-27	19.3	-78.12
Paul Nicholls	37-117	4-18	5-19	3-13	4-14	3-13	6-15	3-7	9-18	31.6	+ 15.50
Nicky Henderson	36-154	9-24	7-45	6-21	1-3	1-18	2-5	0-0	10-38	23.4	+ 20.97
Jonjo O'Neill	35-201	5-29	10-55	1-15	3-11	8-54	1-5	5-17	2-15	17.4	-50.98
Peter Bowen	35-169	4-24	8-48	4-11	6-12	5-37	1-6	3-9	4-22	20.7	+ 69.08
Evan Williams	34-203	5-40	5-44	9-34	2-24	9-45	3-10	0-1	1-5	16.7	-13.47
David Pipe	25-148	3-19	9-65	3-16	2-5	2-25	3-11	0-0	3-7	16.9	-27.79
Philip Hobbs	23-143	3-6	5-58	4-14	2-4	5-28	3-9	1-10	0-14	16.1	-37.12
Lucinda Russell	18-117	6-21	3-35	1-10	1-8	5-34	1-2	0-2	1-5	15.4	-30.73
Gary Moore	15-132	3-14	3-50	3-20	1-6	2-28	1-5	1-5	1-4	11.4	-67.55
Venetia Williams	14-77	2-11	2-30	3-6	2-4	4-23	0-0	0-1	1-2	18.2	-26.45
Ian Williams	14-65	5-15	3-20	1-6	1-2	1-8	2-3	0-3	1-8	21.5	-1.62
Martin Keighley	14-71	1-8	2-24	2-7	1-2	6-23	1-2	0-0	1-5	19.7	+ 7.71
Rebecca Curtis	14-54	5-9	4-18	1-5	2-3	0-6	0-2	0-2	2-9	25.9	-3.34
Milton Harris	13-69	1-4	6-30	1-10	1-5	4-12	0-5	0-2	0-1	18.8	+ 42.50
Seamus Mullins	13-102	0-12	3-33	0-7	1-8	5-26	2-5	0-0	2-11	12.7	-6.50
Charlie Mann	13-64	5-14	4-16	2-10	0-3	0-13	2-7	0-0	0-1	20.3	+ 20.31
Alison Thorpe	13-75	2-10	4-39	4-17	1-2	1-3	1-2	0-0	0-2	17.3	-22.11
Nigel Twiston-Davies	12-149	2-17	2-46	2-9	1-9	3-50	0-3	1-5	1-10	8.1	-82.07
Kim Bailey	11-84	1-12	3-21	1-9	0-4	3-20	0-7	0-0	3-11	13.1	+ 22.17
Maurice Barnes	11-81	1-15	5-38	2-14	1-5	2-7	0-0	0-0	0-2	13.6	+ 12.49
Tom George	11-83	1-16	2-12	2-11	1-5	3-23	0-4	1-6	1-6	13.3	-31.25
Tony Carroll	11-68	2-15	4-30	2-9	1-1	2-7	0-0	0-0	0-6	16.2	+ 39.29
Chris Grant	11-65	3-12	4-25	0-5	1-7	3-14	0-0	0-0	0-2	16.9	-4.02
Dr Richard Newland	10-34	0-2	3-13	1-2	1-1	5-9	0-0	0-7	0-0	29.4	+ 15.25
Michael Scudamore	10-63	2-8	2-18	1-3	1-2	2-22	1-1	1-5	0-4	15.9	+ 25.00
Malcolm Jefferson	9-58	1-12	0-10	2-5	1-5	4-17	0-1	0-0	1-8	15.5	-10.75
Howard Johnson	9-47	2-6	0-14	2-7	2-7	3-10	0-1	0-0	0-2	19.1	-6.75
Alistair Whillans	9-46	2-9	4-21	0-2	1-2	2-7	0-1	0-0	0-4	19.6	+ 9.08
Lawney Hill	9-44	0-4	3-11	1-9	0-0	1-10	0-0	2-6	2-4	20.5	+ 20.10
Neil King	9-95	1-13	2-32	0-8	0-3	6-31	0-1	0-0	0-7	9.5	-34.00
Alan King	9-123	1-28	0-32	4-20	1-7	2-15	0-4	0-0	1-17	7.3	-79.48
Charlie Longsdon	9-69	0-12	0-16	0-3	4-12	1-14	1-2	0-1	3-9	13.0	-17.35
Sue Smith	8-85	1-8	2-16	0-8	0-7	3-36	1-4	0-0	1-6	9.4	-31.60
Chris Bealby	8-49	0-6	3-13	2-4	0-2	2-18	0-1	1-1	0-4	16.3	-12.01
Paul Webber	8-66	2-15	2-12	0-5	0-4	1-17	1-2	0-0	2-11	12.1	-18.38
Fergal O'Brien	8-34	1-5	0-5	1-6	0-0	1-3	0-0	5-15	0-0	23.5	+ 21.58
Brendan Powell	8-98	1-15	2-31	1-11	0-6	1-18	1-6	1-2	1-9	8.2	-35.75
George Moore	7-32	1-5	2-11	2-3	1-5	0-4	1-1	0-0	0-3	21.9	-3.80
Ferdy Murphy	7-78	1-11	2-20	1-5	0-4	2-32	1-2	0-0	0-4	9.0	-38.64
Keith Reveley	7-50	3-8	0-11	1-11	1-1	2-13	0-2	0-0	0-4	14.0	-14.09
Martin Todhunter	7-77	1-13	4-29	0-6	1-3	1-23	0-0	0-0	0-3	9.1	-18.67
Colin Tizzard	7-68	0-10	2-14	0-5	0-3	5-33	0-0	0-0	0-3	10.3	-25.38
Andrew Haynes	7-21	1-4	0-8	4-5	2-2	0-1	0-0	0-0	0-1	33.3	+ 4.16
Neil Mulholland	7-62	4-15	1-18	0-6	2-7	0-12	0-1	0-0	0-3	11.3	-5.61
Brian Ellison	6-22	2-5	0-6	2-6	1-3	1-1	0-1	0-0	0-0	27.3	-7.92
Micky Hammond	6-47	0-8	2-16	0-4	1-3	2-12	0-1	0-0	1-3	12.8	+ 2.25
Barry Murtagh	6-49	1-8	2-18	0-4	0-2	3-13	0-1	0-0	0-3	12.2	+ 27.62
Dianne Sayer	6-55	2-10	3-26	0-1	0-5	1-13	0-0	0-0	0-0	10.9	-4.25
Pauline Robson	6-18	2-7	2-4	0-2	0-0	0-2	0-0	0-0	2-3	33.3	+ 9.10

LEADING JUMP TRAINERS IN JUNE
(SINCE 2009)

	Total W-R	Nov Hdle	H'cap Hdle	Other Hdle	Nov Chase	H'cap Chase	Other Chase	Hunter Chase	N.H. Flat	Per cent	£1 Level stake
Jonjo O'Neill	39-182	5-22	10-43	5-23	2-13	13-66	3-6	0-0	1-9	21.4	+ 0.24
Evan Williams	37-182	7-35	11-45	4-29	7-17	4-46	4-8	0-1	0-1	20.3	+ 1.48
Tim Vaughan	35-195	8-43	7-48	7-34	3-13	4-37	2-3	0-1	4-16	17.9	-73.14
Peter Bowen	34-150	4-23	7-28	3-15	3-15	10-40	1-3	1-2	5-24	22.7	-3.93
Donald McCain	23-100	7-22	7-18	5-27	1-7	1-13	0-0	0-1	2-12	23.0	-10.88
Nicky Henderson	19-65	3-8	3-22	4-10	0-2	2-7	0-0	0-0	7-16	29.2	+ 2.53
Nigel Twiston-Davies	18-118	5-20	5-29	1-11	1-2	5-46	0-2	0-0	1-8	15.3	-20.01
Paul Nicholls	14-67	3-6	1-11	2-14	3-11	2-9	2-10	0-1	1-5	20.9	-20.77
David Pipe	14-138	0-13	7-61	2-26	1-6	3-25	1-2	0-0	0-5	10.1	-56.73
Seamus Mullins	11-43	0-3	5-11	1-4	1-3	3-13	0-4	0-0	1-5	25.6	+ 17.38
Lucinda Russell	10-90	2-17	2-24	2-6	1-7	2-28	0-2	0-0	1-6	11.1	-40.42
Tony Carroll	10-69	2-11	7-35	0-8	0-4	1-5	0-0	0-0	0-6	14.5	-17.50
Rebecca Curtis	10-35	3-6	0-7	0-2	2-4	2-7	0-1	0-1	3-7	28.6	-7.44
Alan Swinbank	9-22	1-4	0-2	2-4	0-2	0-0	0-0	0-0	6-10	40.9	+ 3.75
Keith Goldsworthy	9-51	0-5	1-15	0-5	1-2	3-7	0-1	0-1	4-15	17.6	+ 11.68
Dr Richard Newland	9-44	0-2	3-16	3-7	2-4	1-9	0-5	0-0	0-1	20.5	+ 4.25
Paul Webber	7-37	1-6	2-8	0-4	0-4	1-9	1-2	0-0	2-4	18.9	+ 2.40
Ian Williams	7-50	3-11	1-17	0-10	1-1	2-6	0-0	0-0	0-5	14.0	+ 2.74
Michael Blake	7-28	2-4	2-14	2-6	0-1	1-3	0-0	0-0	0-0	25.0	+ 8.71
Milton Harris	6-42	0-3	1-15	2-9	1-3	2-8	0-3	0-0	0-1	14.3	+ 4.00
Susan Gardner	6-22	1-1	3-11	0-4	1-1	1-2	0-1	0-0	0-2	27.3	+ 15.75
Lawney Hill	6-35	0-4	2-15	4-8	0-2	0-5	0-1	0-0	0-0	17.1	+ 30.53
Gary Moore	6-47	1-9	2-11	1-8	0-4	1-11	1-4	0-0	0-0	12.8	-20.08
Charlie Mann	6-40	2-6	1-11	1-8	1-4	1-10	0-1	0-0	0-0	15.0	-3.96
Venetia Williams	6-28	0-3	1-9	1-2	1-2	2-11	0-0	0-0	1-1	21.4	-1.87
Nicky Richards	6-34	2-3	1-11	1-6	1-3	0-7	1-2	0-0	0-2	17.6	+ 5.12
David Bridgwater	6-23	1-5	0-1	0-5	0-2	5-9	0-0	0-0	0-1	26.1	+ 9.00
Alan King	6-36	2-7	1-16	3-6	0-1	0-3	0-1	0-0	0-2	16.7	-11.75
Jim Best	6-34	2-6	2-13	0-12	0-0	2-2	0-0	0-0	0-1	17.6	-17.26
Chris Gordon	6-42	1-7	3-17	0-2	0-1	2-14	0-0	0-0	0-1	14.3	-7.70
Jamie Snowden	6-29	0-4	1-7	1-3	1-1	2-9	1-2	0-0	0-3	20.7	+ 32.38
Kim Bailey	5-41	1-5	0-9	0-5	1-5	2-10	1-5	0-0	0-2	12.2	-17.31
Brian Ellison	5-30	1-6	0-7	1-9	2-2	1-1	0-0	0-0	0-5	16.7	-7.40
Richard Phillips	5-40	0-5	3-14	1-2	0-2	1-10	0-1	0-0	0-6	12.5	+ 3.50
Emma Lavelle	5-28	0-4	1-7	1-2	0-1	3-13	0-1	0-0	0-0	17.9	+ 55.00
Alison Thorpe	5-54	1-17	3-18	1-13	0-2	0-2	0-1	0-0	0-1	9.3	-29.25
Sarah Humphrey	5-29	2-3	0-4	0-5	1-3	2-9	0-3	0-0	0-2	17.2	+ 3.33
Andrew Haynes	5-25	2-3	2-7	1-10	0-0	0-2	0-2	0-0	0-1	20.0	+ 6.55
George Moore	4-14	2-6	1-3	0-0	1-3	0-1	0-0	0-0	0-1	28.6	-1.08
Philip Hobbs	4-59	0-7	0-12	1-8	0-4	1-19	1-4	0-1	1-4	6.8	-46.92
Ron Hodges	4-20	0-1	0-7	2-2	1-1	1-7	0-0	0-0	0-2	20.0	+ 96.50
Malcolm Jefferson	4-31	2-6	0-5	0-1	1-3	1-12	0-0	0-0	0-4	12.9	+ 6.00
Bill Turner	4-23	1-4	0-1	2-11	0-0	0-3	0-2	0-0	1-2	17.4	+ 115.00
Chris Down	4-24	0-5	0-7	1-5	1-1	2-5	0-0	0-0	0-1	16.7	+ 2.75
Micky Hammond	4-24	0-6	2-5	1-4	0-0	1-6	0-0	0-0	0-3	16.7	-1.50
Debra Hamer	4-22	1-3	2-9	0-3	1-2	0-2	0-0	0-0	0-3	18.2	+ 11.50
Martin Todhunter	4-44	0-7	2-20	0-5	0-1	2-11	0-0	0-0	0-0	9.1	-12.00
John Flint	4-41	1-8	0-16	2-6	0-1	1-6	0-0	0-0	0-4	9.8	-16.38
Colin Tizzard	4-42	0-2	0-5	1-3	0-3	3-27	0-0	0-0	0-2	9.5	-5.00
Sophie Leech	4-43	0-2	1-19	1-7	1-4	1-7	0-1	0-0	0-3	9.3	-14.25
R H & Mrs S Alner	4-9	0-0	0-0	0-0	0-0	4-9	0-0	0-0	0-0	44.4	+ 26.00

LEADING JUMP TRAINERS IN JULY
(SINCE 2009)

	Total W-R	Nov Hdle	H'cap Hdle	Other Hdle	Nov Chase	H'cap Chase	Other Chase	Hunter Chase	N.H. Flat	Per cent	£1 Level stake
Tim Vaughan	38-199	10-44	6-46	9-41	7-20	2-29	3-9	0-0	1-12	19.1	-18.99
Peter Bowen	34-154	2-13	10-44	4-18	3-14	10-50	1-6	0-0	4-14	22.1	+ 71.05
Jonjo O'Neill	27-166	3-17	12-58	2-13	5-17	5-49	0-8	0-0	0-4	16.3	+ 2.38
Evan Williams	19-160	7-37	1-37	3-28	4-12	4-37	0-10	0-0	0-2	11.9	-51.51
David Pipe	18-119	0-9	8-54	2-23	1-3	4-21	2-7	0-0	1-7	15.1	-29.65
Donald McCain	18-94	5-17	3-24	7-31	0-5	1-10	1-3	0-0	1-6	19.1	+ 11.72
Nigel Twiston-Davies	16-92	6-17	3-25	3-11	3-12	2-24	0-2	0-0	0-2	17.4	-26.98
Lawney Hill	11-60	1-8	4-24	0-3	4-8	2-15	0-1	0-0	0-1	18.3	-13.18
Dr Richard Newland	11-49	3-4	5-22	1-6	0-1	1-11	1-6	0-0	0-1	22.4	+ 0.56
Paul Nicholls	10-41	1-3	1-4	1-6	1-5	0-7	6-16	0-0	0-0	24.4	+ 20.54
Lucinda Russell	9-69	1-10	1-28	1-3	3-8	2-16	0-0	0-0	1-4	13.0	-18.50
Martin Keighley	9-47	3-5	3-18	0-6	1-5	2-9	0-0	0-0	0-4	19.1	+ 55.75
Alison Thorpe	7-51	1-3	3-30	2-13	1-1	0-5	0-1	0-0	0-0	13.7	+ 1.67
Brendan Powell	7-53	3-7	0-12	3-12	0-7	0-10	1-3	0-0	0-2	13.2	+ 2.44
Nicky Henderson	6-33	4-11	0-12	0-3	0-0	0-1	1-2	0-0	1-4	18.2	-22.94
Sue Smith	6-48	0-6	1-8	0-3	0-3	3-22	1-3	0-0	1-3	12.5	+ 3.23
Jim Goldie	6-27	1-2	3-14	2-8	0-2	0-2	0-0	0-0	0-0	22.2	-2.87
Paul Webber	6-30	0-5	3-10	1-8	0-2	1-5	0-1	0-0	2-3	20.0	+ 24.75
Tony Carroll	6-61	1-13	3-25	0-7	2-6	0-7	0-0	0-0	0-3	9.8	-8.00
Ian Williams	6-31	2-4	1-10	1-5	0-3	1-5	1-3	0-0	0-1	19.4	-9.96
Michael Easterby	5-29	1-6	1-6	0-0	0-1	1-12	0-1	0-0	2-3	17.2	-3.59
Neil King	5-34	0-5	2-12	0-5	2-3	1-7	0-2	0-0	0-1	14.7	+ 17.66
Dianne Sayer	5-45	1-5	3-28	0-3	0-0	1-8	0-0	0-0	0-1	11.1	-8.50
David Rees	5-32	0-2	3-14	1-5	0-0	1-10	0-1	0-0	0-0	15.6	+ 1.75
Philip Kirby	5-28	1-8	2-13	0-1	0-2	1-3	1-1	0-0	0-0	17.9	-2.42
Richard Woollacott	5-14	0-4	0-1	1-2	0-0	4-4	0-2	0-0	0-1	35.7	+ 5.96
Jim Best	4-26	1-7	1-8	2-8	0-1	0-1	0-0	0-0	0-1	15.4	-12.34
Philip Hobbs	4-48	1-4	1-16	0-10	0-1	2-18	0-2	0-0	0-0	8.3	-15.00
Pam Sly	4-17	3-7	0-6	0-2	0-1	1-2	0-0	0-0	0-0	23.5	+ 7.88
Kim Bailey	4-29	1-5	1-8	1-3	0-1	1-10	0-2	0-0	0-0	13.8	+ 7.75
Bob Buckler	4-14	0-3	0-0	0-0	0-0	4-11	0-0	0-0	0-0	28.6	-0.67
David Evans	4-26	0-3	0-6	2-8	1-2	1-7	0-0	0-0	0-0	15.4	-1.17
Don Cantillon	4-8	0-1	0-1	0-1	0-1	2-2	0-0	0-0	2-2	50.0	+ 27.00
Venetia Williams	4-18	0-1	3-7	0-2	0-0	1-8	0-0	0-0	0-0	22.2	+ 2.00
Alan Swinbank	4-12	2-2	0-2	0-1	0-0	0-1	1-1	0-0	1-5	33.3	-1.63
Lucy Normile	4-25	0-1	2-16	0-2	1-2	1-4	0-0	0-0	0-0	16.0	+ 24.50
Keith Goldsworthy	4-31	1-7	0-2	2-10	0-1	0-5	0-0	0-0	1-6	12.9	-1.13
Sophie Leech	4-45	1-7	2-13	0-6	1-7	0-11	0-2	0-0	0-0	8.9	-21.50
Rebecca Curtis	4-26	0-2	0-2	2-6	1-3	0-5	1-4	0-0	0-4	15.4	-15.38
Milton Harris	3-24	1-6	0-9	1-4	1-1	0-3	0-0	0-0	0-1	12.5	-7.00
Brian Ellison	3-23	2-8	1-5	0-4	0-4	0-2	0-1	0-0	0-0	13.0	+ 22.50
Gary Moore	3-20	0-8	1-6	2-4	0-1	0-0	0-1	0-0	0-0	15.0	+ 0.50
Tom George	3-28	1-3	0-4	0-2	1-2	1-14	0-3	0-0	0-1	10.7	-4.12
Keith Reveley	3-12	2-5	1-5	0-0	0-1	0-1	0-0	0-0	0-0	25.0	-2.43
John Berry	3-4	1-1	1-1	1-2	0-0	0-0	0-0	0-0	0-0	75.0	+ 7.16
Martin Todhunter	3-38	0-5	2-18	0-2	0-4	1-7	0-1	0-0	0-1	7.9	+ 4.00
John Flint	3-27	0-4	2-14	1-6	0-1	0-3	0-0	0-0	0-0	11.1	-9.90
Colin Tizzard	3-46	0-2	0-5	0-1	0-4	2-29	1-4	0-0	0-1	6.5	-35.88
Henry Daly	3-15	0-2	0-1	0-1	1-3	1-4	1-2	0-0	0-2	20.0	-4.00
Nicky Richards	3-31	0-4	2-18	0-1	0-0	1-7	0-0	0-0	0-1	9.7	-1.50
Barry Leavy	3-16	0-0	0-8	1-2	1-1	1-5	0-0	0-0	0-0	18.8	+ 5.50

LEADING JUMP TRAINERS IN AUGUST
(SINCE 2009)

	Total W-R	Nov Hdle	H'cap Hdle	Other Hdle	Nov Chase	H'cap Chase	Other Chase	Hunter Chase	N.H. Flat	Per cent	£1 Level stake
Tim Vaughan	59-266	20-63	9-60	13-47	4-24	11-51	2-6	0-0	0-15	22.2	-30.78
Jonjo O'Neill	25-153	2-15	5-42	1-12	2-12	13-64	0-0	0-0	2-8	16.3	-32.31
Donald McCain	23-94	9-24	7-21	3-30	2-4	0-9	1-1	0-0	1-5	24.5	+ 5.50
Nigel Twiston-Davies	20-93	1-10	8-24	1-9	2-10	8-36	0-0	0-0	0-4	21.5	+ 39.23
David Pipe	19-119	2-11	8-56	2-13	3-11	3-24	0-1	0-0	1-3	16.0	-11.62
Peter Bowen	18-159	4-35	5-42	0-12	0-10	4-45	1-1	0-0	4-14	11.3	-76.67
Evan Williams	18-165	4-29	2-36	7-24	2-18	3-53	0-3	0-0	0-2	10.9	-76.10
Paul Nicholls	14-47	5-9	0-4	0-2	5-12	2-17	0-1	0-0	2-2	29.8	+ 0.18
Lawney Hill	12-49	2-6	1-12	0-5	3-9	4-15	1-1	0-0	1-1	24.5	+ 27.79
Paul Webber	11-28	2-5	0-2	1-4	2-5	4-8	1-1	0-0	1-3	39.3	+ 29.92
Brian Ellison	10-31	6-10	2-8	1-7	0-1	1-3	0-1	0-0	0-1	32.3	+ 11.53
John Flint	10-43	2-5	5-22	1-6	0-1	2-8	0-0	0-0	0-1	23.3	+ 5.05
Colin Tizzard	10-45	0-0	1-7	0-1	2-6	7-30	0-0	0-0	0-1	22.2	+ 21.50
Philip Hobbs	9-46	0-2	2-12	0-4	2-7	5-21	0-0	0-0	0-0	19.6	+ 21.58
Lucinda Russell	9-62	2-12	2-17	0-6	1-4	4-20	0-1	0-0	0-2	14.5	-26.13
Rebecca Curtis	9-28	4-8	0-3	1-5	2-2	1-5	0-0	0-0	1-5	32.1	+ 9.43
Brendan Powell	8-62	1-10	2-19	2-10	2-9	0-13	0-0	0-0	1-1	12.9	-26.25
Sophie Leech	8-49	2-11	2-17	0-4	1-3	1-12	2-2	0-0	0-0	16.3	-6.82
John Quinn	7-16	0-2	2-5	3-6	1-1	1-2	0-0	0-0	0-0	43.8	+ 11.13
Dianne Sayer	7-35	0-5	4-19	0-2	0-3	3-6	0-0	0-0	0-0	20.0	+ 30.85
Alan Swinbank	7-19	2-4	1-3	1-2	0-1	0-1	1-1	0-0	2-7	36.8	-1.27
Alison Thorpe	7-46	2-7	2-19	2-13	0-0	1-6	0-0	0-0	0-1	15.2	-8.56
Keith Goldsworthy	7-40	2-12	1-6	2-8	0-3	0-2	0-0	0-0	2-9	17.5	+ 27.58
Ian Williams	6-28	3-6	2-8	0-7	0-2	0-2	0-1	0-0	1-2	21.4	+ 7.88
Nicky Richards	6-27	2-6	3-16	0-2	0-0	1-2	0-0	0-0	0-1	22.2	+ 12.75
Anthony Honeyball	6-19	0-4	1-3	0-2	4-5	0-1	1-1	0-0	0-3	31.6	+ 5.75
Chris Gordon	6-32	1-6	4-12	0-2	0-3	1-7	0-1	0-0	0-1	18.8	+ 24.50
Nicky Henderson	5-18	3-7	2-7	0-1	0-1	0-0	0-0	0-0	0-2	27.8	-0.46
Kim Bailey	5-19	2-4	1-7	2-3	0-1	0-3	0-1	0-0	0-0	26.3	+ 1.62
Harriet Graham	5-10	0-2	2-5	0-0	0-0	3-3	0-0	0-0	0-0	50.0	+ 4.74
Jim Goldie	5-20	0-5	3-7	1-3	0-1	0-3	0-0	0-0	1-1	25.0	+ 12.75
Alan Jones	5-17	1-2	1-6	0-1	0-2	2-4	0-0	0-0	1-2	29.4	+ 16.00
Martin Keighley	5-43	0-1	1-16	0-3	0-4	3-14	0-1	0-0	1-4	11.6	-12.59
Sarah Humphrey	5-18	0-3	1-3	1-4	0-2	3-6	0-0	0-0	0-0	27.8	+ 13.54
Dr Richard Newland	5-34	0-5	1-4	2-8	0-3	2-12	0-2	0-0	0-0	14.7	-2.63
George Moore	4-15	3-6	0-3	1-4	0-0	0-1	0-0	0-0	0-1	26.7	+ 37.50
Sue Smith	4-46	0-7	1-10	0-5	0-3	3-18	0-0	0-0	0-3	8.7	+ 0.50
Bernard Llewellyn	4-32	1-4	1-19	2-6	0-2	0-1	0-0	0-0	0-0	12.5	-5.63
Richard Ford	4-14	0-2	0-4	0-0	0-1	4-6	0-0	0-0	0-1	28.6	+ 1.75
Martin Todhunter	4-27	2-7	0-13	1-1	0-1	1-5	0-0	0-0	0-0	14.8	-1.12
Richard Woollacott	4-12	0-2	1-2	0-1	1-1	2-6	0-0	0-0	0-0	33.3	+ 12.33
Tim Walford	3-10	0-3	2-4	0-1	0-1	1-1	0-0	0-0	0-0	30.0	+ 18.50
Michael Chapman	3-49	1-7	1-17	0-7	0-2	1-14	0-1	0-0	0-1	6.1	-30.75
Milton Harris	3-26	0-3	1-7	1-5	1-4	0-7	0-0	0-0	0-0	11.5	-2.00
David Evans	3-20	0-2	0-4	2-6	1-2	0-2	0-0	0-0	0-4	15.0	+ 24.41
Alistair Whillans	3-14	0-2	3-7	0-1	0-0	0-2	0-0	0-0	0-2	21.4	+ 1.75
Micky Hammond	3-20	0-4	0-1	1-2	1-2	1-11	0-0	0-0	0-0	15.0	+ 14.63
Don Cantillon	3-4	0-1	0-0	0-0	1-1	1-1	1-1	0-0	0-0	75.0	+ 5.82
Susan Gardner	3-28	0-8	2-13	0-1	0-0	0-2	0-0	0-0	1-4	10.7	-2.50
Sheena West	3-21	1-3	0-5	2-11	0-0	0-0	0-2	0-0	0-0	14.3	+ 3.70
Neil King	3-35	1-3	0-15	1-8	0-3	1-6	0-0	0-0	0-0	8.6	-22.13

LEADING JUMP TRAINERS IN SEPTEMBER
(SINCE 2009)

	Total W-R	Nov Hdle	H'cap Hdle	Other Hdle	Nov Chase	H'cap Chase	Other Chase	Hunter Chase	N.H. Flat	Per cent	£1 Level stake
Nigel Twiston-Davies	23-109	4-22	2-22	2-12	5-9	8-33	0-2	0-0	2-9	21.1	-11.04
Jonjo O'Neill	20-131	2-16	7-44	2-13	2-9	5-45	0-0	0-0	2-4	15.3	-26.25
Evan Williams	17-141	5-24	2-42	3-22	2-16	3-34	2-6	0-0	0-1	12.1	-57.30
Tim Vaughan	17-135	1-26	5-35	6-29	2-11	2-24	0-5	0-0	1-6	12.6	-58.63
Peter Bowen	14-110	3-20	1-29	0-9	0-5	6-33	0-2	0-0	4-13	12.7	-28.03
David Pipe	12-96	2-9	1-37	1-13	1-5	4-24	1-5	0-0	2-3	12.5	-45.84
Philip Hobbs	11-71	3-7	1-18	1-9	1-6	2-26	2-4	0-0	1-1	15.5	-22.64
Donald McCain	11-64	1-12	2-16	7-25	0-3	0-7	1-3	0-0	0-2	17.2	-11.97
Charlie Longsdon	11-43	2-5	0-5	0-6	0-1	4-12	1-5	0-0	4-10	25.6	+ 22.00
Brian Ellison	8-37	2-9	2-8	1-11	0-2	3-8	0-0	0-0	0-0	21.6	+ 17.23
Lawney Hill	8-37	0-1	0-10	0-2	0-4	7-15	0-1	0-0	1-4	21.6	+ 7.50
Bernard Llewellyn	7-35	1-3	5-24	1-6	0-0	0-1	0-0	0-0	0-1	20.0	+ 41.12
Paul Nicholls	7-24	1-3	0-1	1-2	3-8	1-7	0-2	0-0	1-1	29.2	-3.19
Brendan Powell	7-42	1-4	2-12	1-10	1-1	2-10	0-1	0-0	0-4	16.7	+ 13.25
Sheena West	6-28	0-6	2-11	4-9	0-1	0-1	0-0	0-0	0-0	21.4	+ 17.53
Jim Goldie	6-35	3-7	2-11	0-10	0-3	0-2	1-1	0-0	0-1	17.1	+ 19.00
Gary Moore	6-29	1-7	3-9	1-7	0-0	0-5	1-1	0-0	0-0	20.7	+ 17.75
Alison Thorpe	6-33	1-7	4-21	1-4	0-0	0-2	0-0	0-0	0-0	18.2	+ 11.75
Dr Richard Newland	6-29	0-3	2-14	2-5	0-1	2-8	0-0	0-0	0-0	20.7	+ 0.63
Chris Gordon	6-35	1-5	4-15	0-1	0-0	1-11	0-2	0-0	0-1	17.1	+ 22.50
Rebecca Curtis	6-23	1-4	0-4	2-5	0-0	0-2	1-1	0-0	2-7	26.1	-12.14
Malcolm Jefferson	5-42	1-4	0-12	0-3	2-4	2-10	0-2	0-0	0-7	11.9	+ 18.50
Kim Bailey	4-13	1-4	0-3	0-0	0-0	3-6	0-0	0-0	0-0	30.8	+ 11.50
Jeremy Scott	4-11	1-1	1-4	0-0	1-1	1-4	0-0	0-0	0-1	36.4	+ 6.85
David Evans	4-31	0-4	0-6	1-10	1-1	1-4	0-0	0-0	1-6	12.9	-8.50
Maurice Barnes	4-28	1-8	2-10	0-6	0-0	1-3	0-0	0-0	0-1	14.3	+ 26.00
Neil King	4-28	1-4	0-7	1-6	0-0	2-10	0-0	0-0	0-1	14.3	-2.25
Sophie Leech	4-31	1-8	1-14	0-0	1-3	1-6	0-0	0-0	0-0	12.9	+ 15.50
Nicky Henderson	3-14	2-3	1-9	0-3	0-0	0-0	0-0	0-0	0-1	21.4	-0.67
Evelyn Slack	3-13	0-0	3-9	0-2	0-0	0-1	0-1	0-0	0-0	23.1	+ 19.50
John O'Shea	3-18	0-5	1-4	0-3	1-1	0-1	0-0	0-0	1-4	16.7	+ 10.00
Sue Smith	3-37	1-6	0-8	1-3	1-2	0-13	0-0	0-0	0-5	8.1	-27.65
Lucinda Russell	3-61	1-11	2-12	0-7	0-8	0-18	0-0	0-0	0-5	4.9	-43.50
C Roberts	3-9	0-1	1-2	0-2	0-1	0-1	1-1	0-0	1-1	33.3	+ 11.00
John Quinn	3-10	0-2	0-3	3-3	0-1	0-1	0-0	0-0	0-0	30.0	-0.01
Paul Webber	3-24	1-5	0-4	1-6	1-4	0-4	0-0	0-0	0-2	12.5	-9.83
Martin Todhunter	3-25	1-5	0-12	0-1	0-0	2-6	0-1	0-0	0-0	12.0	-6.25
John Flint	3-25	0-4	2-14	1-2	0-0	0-4	0-0	0-0	0-1	12.0	-3.00
Chris Grant	3-27	0-4	2-9	0-6	0-0	0-5	0-0	0-0	1-3	11.1	-2.75
Ian Williams	3-30	1-4	1-14	0-5	0-1	1-2	0-1	0-0	0-3	10.0	-14.33
Emma Lavelle	3-20	0-0	0-4	0-3	1-6	2-6	0-1	0-0	0-0	15.0	-2.93
Alan King	3-19	0-9	0-1	0-5	2-3	1-1	0-0	0-0	0-0	15.8	-8.33
Fergal O'Brien	3-13	1-4	0-2	0-1	1-2	1-4	0-0	0-0	0-0	23.1	+ 13.00
Laura Mongan	3-9	2-4	1-3	0-1	0-1	0-0	0-0	0-0	0-0	33.3	+ 1.79
Michael Scudamore	3-32	0-5	1-9	1-3	0-1	1-14	0-0	0-0	0-0	9.4	-6.50
George Moore	2-20	0-6	2-5	0-3	0-1	0-3	0-2	0-0	0-0	10.0	-11.75
Barney Curley	2-5	0-2	2-3	0-0	0-0	0-0	0-0	0-0	0-0	40.0	+ 4.25
Milton Harris	2-23	0-3	2-7	0-4	0-6	0-3	0-0	0-0	0-0	8.7	-5.00
Mike Sowersby	2-21	0-9	0-7	0-2	0-0	2-3	0-0	0-0	0-0	9.5	+ 11.00
Micky Hammond	2-22	0-4	0-4	0-2	0-3	2-7	0-0	0-0	0-2	9.1	-14.50
Anabel K Murphy	2-12	0-1	2-7	0-0	0-0	0-3	0-0	0-0	0-1	16.7	+ 24.00

LEADING JUMP TRAINERS IN OCTOBER
(SINCE 2009)

	Total W-R	Nov Hdle	H'cap Hdle	Other Hdle	Nov Chase	H'cap Chase	Other Chase	Hunter Chase	N.H. Flat	Per cent	£1 Level stake
Paul Nicholls	56-212	14-43	7-30	12-40	13-31	5-41	3-14	0-0	3-18	26.4	-17.77
Philip Hobbs	47-231	9-38	10-62	10-36	8-19	4-52	1-14	0-0	5-17	20.3	-10.69
Nigel Twiston-Davies	46-279	9-45	6-40	9-35	4-33	14-93	4-15	0-0	0-20	16.5	+ 48.67
Tim Vaughan	37-227	13-50	5-59	8-42	2-12	7-38	0-7	0-0	2-20	16.3	-52.10
Jonjo O'Neill	35-297	4-48	15-77	4-37	1-17	8-87	1-10	0-0	2-22	11.8	-107.60
Donald McCain	33-224	8-47	5-46	8-47	2-18	6-32	1-9	0-0	4-27	14.7	-34.43
Charlie Longsdon	33-174	1-30	7-37	5-26	3-8	11-43	2-10	0-0	4-20	19.0	-45.58
David Pipe	28-172	3-25	7-73	8-27	3-5	4-30	3-7	0-0	1-6	16.3	-41.38
Evan Williams	27-223	5-39	6-52	3-39	3-20	2-46	6-19	0-0	2-11	12.1	-85.77
Howard Johnson	22-91	2-14	2-14	5-25	3-8	6-18	3-7	0-0	1-5	24.2	+ 15.99
Nicky Henderson	20-97	8-25	2-13	0-16	3-12	2-9	2-5	0-0	4-10	20.6	-27.99
Colin Tizzard	20-116	3-24	2-13	1-6	3-10	10-47	1-8	0-0	0-9	17.2	+ 13.79
Sue Smith	18-137	2-19	3-25	2-16	1-6	7-49	1-8	0-0	2-14	13.1	+ 1.96
Lucinda Russell	18-150	0-22	2-24	2-13	1-9	11-66	0-6	0-0	2-10	12.0	-47.64
Alan King	18-100	3-18	3-27	8-34	2-7	0-13	1-3	0-0	1-4	18.0	-12.77
Ian Williams	14-72	2-10	6-27	1-15	2-4	2-6	1-5	0-0	0-6	19.4	+ 21.51
Martin Keighley	14-86	2-14	2-24	3-10	4-9	2-19	0-4	0-0	1-7	16.3	-14.60
Peter Bowen	13-157	3-16	2-39	0-24	1-11	5-52	1-3	0-0	1-13	8.3	-45.37
Emma Lavelle	13-83	7-19	2-18	1-7	1-4	2-22	0-7	0-0	1-7	15.7	+ 11.71
Jeremy Scott	12-51	3-16	2-12	0-6	1-1	2-7	2-2	0-0	2-7	23.5	+ 19.53
Tom George	12-87	2-7	0-13	2-13	1-7	4-30	3-11	0-0	0-6	13.8	-22.25
Oliver Sherwood	11-63	1-12	2-12	2-12	0-5	1-10	3-5	0-0	2-7	17.5	+ 16.63
Kim Bailey	11-84	2-19	1-20	3-15	0-5	4-16	1-6	0-0	0-3	13.1	-19.13
Gary Moore	11-102	2-16	2-30	2-25	0-4	1-18	3-8	0-0	1-4	10.8	-36.51
David Bridgwater	11-43	0-7	0-5	1-9	2-2	6-16	1-2	0-0	1-2	25.6	+ 4.73
Neil Mulholland	11-96	3-19	1-20	2-13	0-5	5-28	0-3	0-0	0-8	11.5	-14.25
Robin Dickin	9-52	0-16	1-10	2-7	1-4	3-11	0-0	0-0	2-5	17.3	+ 22.75
Sheena West	9-31	1-7	1-9	5-16	0-0	0-0	2-2	0-0	0-0	29.0	+ 7.09
John Quinn	9-43	1-7	1-10	6-17	0-2	0-6	1-1	0-0	0-0	20.9	-2.09
Paul Webber	9-92	3-24	1-9	2-17	1-11	1-21	1-8	0-0	0-2	9.8	-40.54
Nicky Richards	9-69	3-12	1-17	1-10	1-8	2-10	1-6	0-0	0-6	13.0	-13.06
Nick Williams	9-60	2-18	2-8	1-5	0-3	2-15	2-10	0-0	0-1	15.0	-10.17
Brendan Powell	9-107	2-16	4-32	1-12	0-6	0-31	0-4	0-0	2-6	8.4	-32.68
Rebecca Curtis	9-64	0-12	2-13	4-13	0-7	1-4	0-2	0-0	2-13	14.1	-28.41
Malcolm Jefferson	8-79	2-16	1-16	0-5	3-10	2-15	0-4	0-0	0-13	10.1	-41.43
Brian Ellison	8-55	0-9	1-18	3-16	2-3	2-7	0-0	0-0	0-2	14.5	+ 7.98
John Ferguson	8-38	3-15	0-1	2-10	0-1	0-2	1-2	0-0	2-7	21.1	+ 17.46
Maurice Barnes	7-74	3-19	3-27	1-11	0-1	0-9	0-1	0-0	0-6	9.5	+ 99.00
Sarah Humphrey	7-30	0-3	0-7	0-1	1-4	6-13	0-0	0-0	0-2	23.3	-3.42
Dr Richard Newland	7-38	2-6	2-16	0-2	0-0	3-13	0-0	0-0	0-1	18.4	-14.06
Andy Turnell	6-52	1-13	1-11	0-5	0-6	3-13	1-5	0-0	0-0	11.5	-12.75
Renee Robeson	6-33	0-7	2-8	2-6	2-2	0-8	0-0	0-0	0-2	18.2	+ 73.40
Venetia Williams	6-77	0-11	2-23	0-14	1-4	2-20	1-4	0-0	0-4	7.8	-33.63
Alan Swinbank	6-34	2-9	0-5	1-5	0-1	0-1	1-1	0-0	2-12	17.6	+ 8.51
David Rees	6-30	1-3	1-11	1-8	1-1	2-7	0-0	0-0	0-0	20.0	-1.25
Barry Leavy	6-31	0-3	2-10	2-7	0-1	2-8	0-1	0-0	0-1	19.4	+ 15.00
Alison Thorpe	6-44	1-7	3-16	2-14	0-0	0-4	0-1	0-0	0-2	13.6	-16.83
Michael Blake	6-27	0-1	4-14	0-3	0-1	2-6	0-1	0-0	0-1	22.2	+ 28.00
Anthony Honeyball	6-29	0-7	1-3	2-6	0-0	0-2	0-0	0-0	3-11	20.7	+ 19.96
Michael Scudamore	6-57	0-7	3-23	0-5	0-2	3-17	0-0	0-0	0-4	10.5	+ 2.25
Jamie Snowden	6-46	1-8	2-9	1-10	1-5	1-11	0-1	0-0	0-2	13.0	-15.35

LEADING JUMP TRAINERS IN NOVEMBER

(SINCE 2009)

	Total W-R	Nov Hdle	H'cap Hdle	Other Hdle	Nov Chase	H'cap Chase	Other Chase	Hunter Chase	N.H. Flat	Per cent	£1 Level stake
Paul Nicholls	94-369	17-60	12-60	15-68	16-47	10-79	20-45	0-0	5-22	25.5	-40.88
Nicky Henderson	91-290	17-49	8-48	27-70	11-31	7-45	16-31	0-0	7-25	31.4	-31.94
Donald McCain	69-318	20-77	6-57	16-57	5-25	4-38	11-32	0-0	7-36	21.7	-29.93
Alan King	54-342	12-74	7-73	14-66	6-28	10-59	3-18	0-0	3-32	15.8	-57.29
Jonjo O'Neill	51-400	7-72	17-93	3-51	3-24	12-114	7-25	0-0	2-24	12.8	-124.13
Nigel Twiston-Davies	44-331	9-59	5-55	2-35	7-37	13-111	3-19	0-0	5-24	13.3	-87.96
David Pipe	40-259	2-28	8-86	6-43	7-16	13-75	2-8	0-0	4-14	15.4	-42.50
Philip Hobbs	38-299	9-61	9-59	6-49	2-20	6-68	5-25	0-0	1-21	12.7	-52.92
Evan Williams	38-212	6-35	3-47	9-30	6-29	10-54	2-9	0-0	2-8	17.9	-2.80
Emma Lavelle	33-125	10-38	4-22	5-22	1-8	5-16	6-10	0-0	3-13	26.4	+ 63.61
Colin Tizzard	29-177	6-29	3-17	2-18	3-30	8-51	6-17	0-0	1-16	16.4	+ 1.40
Sue Smith	27-186	4-30	0-22	1-14	3-12	15-76	3-18	0-0	1-16	14.5	-32.29
Venetia Williams	27-237	0-38	5-58	3-25	4-22	12-70	3-20	0-0	0-9	11.4	-40.22
Tim Vaughan	27-222	6-53	2-48	9-53	2-13	3-31	1-7	0-0	4-18	12.2	-101.10
Ferdy Murphy	24-228	1-38	2-30	4-25	3-22	10-85	4-21	0-0	0-8	10.5	-61.59
Charlie Longsdon	24-159	4-25	3-34	3-24	2-10	8-49	2-7	0-0	2-13	15.1	-27.74
Lucinda Russell	23-200	3-31	3-41	3-18	3-20	6-74	2-7	0-0	3-9	11.5	-29.93
Kim Bailey	22-121	4-34	3-24	0-7	4-8	8-29	1-10	0-0	2-9	18.2	+ 27.79
Oliver Sherwood	20-106	4-26	3-19	4-18	0-5	3-19	1-7	0-0	5-12	18.9	-1.42
Howard Johnson	20-116	5-26	5-19	4-16	0-7	4-31	1-11	0-0	1-7	17.2	-14.66
Tom George	20-155	5-35	3-19	2-25	2-20	5-36	2-11	0-0	1-11	12.9	-37.15
Rebecca Curtis	19-89	8-21	1-14	2-19	2-10	1-8	2-3	0-0	3-17	21.3	-7.88
Charlie Mann	18-124	0-16	2-25	2-16	3-14	9-41	2-10	0-0	0-2	14.5	-32.05
Gary Moore	16-207	1-34	5-55	1-28	3-23	4-51	0-9	0-0	2-9	7.7	-109.28
Nick Williams	16-88	1-12	2-14	3-12	2-12	5-27	4-11	0-0	0-2	18.2	+ 25.62
Martin Keighley	16-101	2-15	6-28	1-10	2-10	5-31	0-5	0-0	0-4	15.8	-9.75
Jim Best	16-58	3-15	9-27	3-11	0-1	0-1	0-1	0-0	1-2	27.6	+ 9.49
Neil Mulholland	16-100	0-22	5-25	3-9	3-10	4-23	1-4	0-0	0-7	16.0	+ 13.72
Peter Bowen	15-127	3-21	6-37	0-10	1-11	4-33	1-7	0-0	0-10	11.8	-20.95
Victor Dartnall	15-87	0-15	5-20	1-9	2-6	7-27	0-2	0-0	0-8	17.2	+ 19.00
James Ewart	15-72	2-12	2-11	1-8	3-10	6-21	1-3	0-0	0-8	20.8	+ 23.99
Richard Lee	14-91	0-9	3-13	2-12	0-7	8-43	1-5	0-0	0-3	15.4	+ 16.75
Dr Richard Newland	14-48	3-7	5-18	1-4	2-2	3-17	0-1	0-0	0-0	29.2	+ 16.61
Warren Greatrex	14-87	2-20	1-10	3-16	0-5	1-8	1-7	0-0	6-21	16.1	-31.57
Keith Reveley	13-105	1-14	2-20	3-12	1-9	4-28	1-6	0-0	1-16	12.4	-35.92
Brendan Powell	13-122	1-20	2-35	2-22	0-8	6-27	0-4	0-0	2-8	10.7	-10.37
Malcolm Jefferson	12-96	4-16	2-24	0-7	0-5	4-25	1-7	0-0	1-14	12.5	-16.25
Brian Ellison	11-85	1-18	6-33	2-18	1-4	1-10	0-1	0-0	0-2	12.9	-14.91
Steve Gollings	11-41	2-5	2-11	1-5	2-4	2-2	0-4	0-0	2-10	26.8	+ 24.83
Tim Easterby	11-70	3-15	2-11	0-17	0-1	3-15	2-3	0-0	1-8	15.7	+ 17.06
Alan Swinbank	11-51	4-9	2-11	1-7	0-0	0-4	1-1	0-0	3-19	21.6	+ 7.84
Nick Gifford	11-77	2-16	0-12	2-10	2-10	4-24	1-5	0-0	0-1	14.3	-16.56
Ian Williams	10-112	0-22	3-35	4-30	2-4	0-12	0-3	0-0	1-10	8.9	-54.42
Robin Dickin	9-58	1-14	2-17	2-6	0-2	2-9	1-2	0-0	1-8	15.5	+ 31.62
Paul Webber	9-112	1-24	0-15	2-19	3-14	1-20	2-12	0-0	0-9	8.0	-43.75
Lucy Wadham	9-64	2-16	5-23	1-14	0-1	0-8	1-4	0-0	0-2	14.1	-18.52
Henry Daly	9-106	3-26	0-11	0-14	1-12	3-28	1-9	0-0	1-6	8.5	-42.63
N W Alexander	9-50	0-9	4-16	2-5	1-2	1-11	1-3	0-0	0-4	18.0	+ 17.95
Jeremy Scott	8-76	2-18	3-23	0-8	0-5	1-10	0-5	0-0	2-8	10.5	-32.82
Seamus Mullins	8-94	2-20	3-17	1-12	1-9	1-17	0-5	0-0	0-14	8.5	+ 8.24
Martin Todhunter	8-64	0-9	2-19	1-4	0-3	5-28	0-1	0-0	0-0	12.5	-3.50

LEADING JUMP TRAINERS IN DECEMBER

(SINCE 2009)

	Total W-R	Nov Hdle	H'cap Hdle	Other Hdle	Nov Chase	H'cap Chase	Other Chase	Hunter Chase	N.H. Flat	Per cent	£1 Level stake
Nicky Henderson	83-283	19-52	9-53	22-67	16-50	5-28	9-26	0-0	5-17	29.3	+ 3.48
Paul Nicholls	65-281	10-42	8-40	12-47	12-45	8-56	13-43	0-0	2-14	23.1	-32.92
Donald McCain	62-270	17-66	5-44	13-62	6-25	6-29	8-21	0-0	7-24	23.0	+ 10.52
David Pipe	48-293	9-52	10-82	4-35	3-9	11-69	3-23	0-0	8-27	16.4	-22.80
Jonjo O'Neill	43-319	6-64	10-58	3-49	7-33	10-81	3-19	0-0	4-16	13.5	-63.19
Alan King	40-276	10-61	8-49	10-51	3-34	4-37	3-18	0-0	3-28	14.5	-40.40
Philip Hobbs	39-251	10-50	4-46	7-38	7-31	3-49	4-24	0-0	4-14	15.5	-73.51
Nigel Twiston-Davies	28-293	4-41	6-44	3-40	4-32	10-102	0-14	0-0	1-21	9.6	-121.69
Venetia Williams	24-252	1-34	6-58	0-34	3-27	12-77	2-13	0-0	0-11	9.5	-102.75
Tim Vaughan	23-174	1-24	8-61	5-31	2-12	5-36	0-3	0-0	2-10	13.2	-42.00
Nick Williams	21-79	3-8	0-10	5-15	5-12	3-23	4-10	0-0	1-2	26.6	+ 19.78
Charlie Longsdon	21-130	3-20	3-30	1-15	4-11	8-40	0-6	0-0	2-8	16.2	+ 42.45
Kim Bailey	16-96	3-10	3-18	2-19	1-8	4-31	2-3	0-0	1-7	16.7	-16.51
Richard Lee	15-63	2-6	1-7	1-4	0-4	8-36	2-3	0-0	1-3	23.8	+ 75.20
Keith Reveley	15-81	1-12	4-12	1-7	1-6	5-30	1-3	0-0	2-11	18.5	+ 82.13
Sue Smith	14-139	1-22	1-22	0-6	3-16	9-53	0-5	0-0	0-15	10.1	-48.65
Tom George	14-118	3-15	1-16	1-15	4-23	4-30	1-15	0-0	0-5	11.9	-35.37
Evan Williams	14-136	1-14	1-47	2-17	2-19	6-31	1-3	0-0	1-5	10.3	-46.36
Lucinda Russell	13-127	2-21	1-29	1-12	1-11	4-41	3-6	0-0	1-7	10.2	-51.92
Brendan Powell	13-100	1-12	3-31	2-16	0-14	3-17	1-3	0-0	3-8	13.0	+ 19.21
Neil King	12-82	1-10	4-27	2-13	0-1	2-22	1-1	0-0	2-8	14.6	+ 31.50
Paul Webber	12-88	2-24	2-16	1-12	2-8	2-16	3-3	0-0	0-9	13.6	+ 5.39
Colin Tizzard	12-140	2-23	1-15	1-8	3-28	4-48	0-8	0-0	1-10	8.6	-51.81
Henry Daly	12-90	3-20	1-9	3-12	2-10	1-23	2-6	0-0	0-10	13.3	+ 3.40
Emma Lavelle	12-97	0-24	3-17	2-18	4-12	3-7	0-7	0-0	0-12	12.4	-41.37
Brian Ellison	11-83	2-12	4-31	3-24	1-5	1-6	0-2	0-0	0-6	13.3	-29.80
Nicky Richards	11-60	2-10	5-19	1-6	1-5	2-13	0-4	0-0	0-3	18.3	+ 8.86
Martin Keighley	11-86	1-4	5-34	0-6	1-7	4-25	0-4	0-0	0-6	12.8	-12.63
Rebecca Curtis	11-69	2-19	3-15	1-10	1-7	1-8	0-1	0-0	3-10	15.9	-20.72
John Wade	10-76	1-12	0-6	1-5	2-8	6-31	0-2	0-0	0-12	13.2	-28.38
Malcolm Jefferson	10-60	2-10	0-8	1-7	0-5	4-19	1-2	0-0	2-9	16.7	+ 25.97
Oliver Sherwood	9-78	2-19	0-15	2-15	0-8	3-13	0-3	0-0	2-6	11.5	-8.23
Howard Johnson	9-49	0-8	2-8	2-8	2-5	1-6	1-8	0-0	1-6	18.4	+ 0.40
Steve Gollings	9-36	2-13	1-9	1-5	1-2	1-5	2-2	0-0	1-3	25.0	+ 9.16
Ferdy Murphy	8-135	0-13	1-18	1-9	2-16	4-67	0-9	0-0	0-3	5.9	-80.48
Gary Moore	8-139	2-24	0-34	2-25	0-15	4-29	0-5	0-0	0-10	5.8	-72.25
John Ferguson	8-30	3-8	0-2	3-10	0-3	1-2	0-1	0-0	1-4	26.7	-3.77
Jeremy Scott	7-58	3-11	1-14	2-10	0-7	1-9	0-5	0-0	0-2	12.1	-19.38
Charlie Mann	7-90	1-15	2-16	0-10	1-10	3-30	0-6	0-0	0-3	7.8	-42.50
Caroline Bailey	7-44	1-7	1-8	0-1	1-4	3-17	1-4	0-0	0-3	15.9	+ 39.83
Dr Richard Newland	7-48	1-12	3-15	1-10	0-3	2-11	0-0	0-0	0-1	14.6	-5.50
Kevin Bishop	6-29	0-5	3-10	0-3	0-2	3-6	0-0	0-0	0-3	20.7	+ 22.42
Sheena West	6-22	0-0	1-4	2-10	0-0	1-3	1-2	0-0	1-3	27.3	+ 53.63
Victor Dartnall	6-57	0-6	2-12	1-4	0-6	1-24	1-3	0-0	1-2	10.5	-23.75
Chris Grant	6-79	3-13	1-20	0-17	0-5	1-15	1-3	0-0	0-6	7.6	-2.63
James Ewart	6-63	0-8	1-6	2-9	0-4	2-21	1-8	0-0	0-7	9.5	-37.79
Chris Gordon	6-52	0-4	2-21	0-5	2-5	2-16	0-1	0-0	0-0	11.5	+ 15.00
Warren Greatrex	6-63	2-14	2-14	1-13	0-4	1-6	0-4	0-0	0-9	9.5	-32.92
Tim Walford	5-41	1-9	3-14	1-7	1-3	0-3	0-1	0-0	0-5	12.2	-11.50
Mike Sowersby	5-29	0-4	3-16	0-3	0-0	2-3	0-1	0-0	0-2	17.2	+ 46.50
Kate Walton	5-37	1-8	1-11	1-6	0-0	1-6	0-2	0-0	1-4	13.5	+ 13.00

LEADING JUMP TRAINERS AT AINTREE (SINCE 2009)

	Total W-R	Nov Hdle	H'cap Hdle	Other Hdle	Nov Chase	H'cap Chase	Other Chase	Hunter Chase	N.H. Flat	Per cent	£1 Level stake
Nicky Henderson	23-152	6-21	4-43	3-32	6-11	1-29	3-13	0-0	1-17	15.1	- 25.62
Peter Bowen	18-115	2-16	2-29	2-9	2-3	5-43	0-2	1-2	4-14	15.7	+ 51.50
Paul Nicholls	17-162	0-19	0-22	6-32	5-19	3-55	2-12	0-4	1-7	10.5	- 68.03
Nigel Twiston-Davies	12-117	1-9	2-19	1-13	0-5	6-64	0-3	1-3	1-4	10.3	- 32.63
Alan King	11-80	2-14	1-17	5-18	1-4	2-14	1-3	0-0	0-14	13.8	- 6.80
Donald McCain	11-130	4-24	1-40	2-19	0-5	3-26	0-1	1-2	0-17	8.5	- 63.15
Philip Hobbs	10-89	1-8	3-31	0-12	2-5	2-27	0-2	0-2	2-10	11.2	- 32.75
Jonjo O'Neill	8-83	0-8	2-21	2-15	0-1	4-27	1-5	0-2	0-8	9.6	- 17.25
Howard Johnson	8-60	0-10	0-9	2-9	2-4	4-26	0-1	0-0	0-4	13.3	+ 3.12
Ian Williams	7-46	3-8	2-11	0-10	0-2	2-6	0-0	0-2	0-8	15.2	+ 3.58
Rebecca Curtis	7-38	4-8	1-12	0-5	0-2	2-5	0-0	0-2	0-6	18.4	- 11.88
John Quinn	5-29	0-2	2-7	1-6	0-2	2-11	0-0	0-0	0-1	17.2	+ 6.88
David Pipe	5-84	0-4	1-31	1-17	1-3	0-33	1-3	0-0	1-5	6.0	- 44.25
Tim Vaughan	5-40	2-9	0-8	0-3	0-1	2-13	0-1	1-4	0-2	12.5	+ 21.50
Robin Dickin	3-5	0-0	3-4	0-1	0-0	0-0	0-0	0-0	0-0	60.0	+ 46.00
Alistair Whillans	3-19	0-5	2-6	0-1	0-0	1-3	0-0	0-0	0-4	15.8	+ 1.00
Kate Walton	3-10	1-1	1-6	0-0	0-0	0-0	0-0	0-0	1-3	30.0	+ 64.25
Lucinda Russell	3-42	0-10	1-10	0-4	0-1	2-13	0-0	0-0	0-5	7.1	+ 31.75
Tom George	3-39	0-4	0-4	0-3	1-2	0-14	2-8	0-2	0-3	7.7	- 25.63
Venetia Williams	3-62	0-7	1-22	0-9	0-1	2-28	0-0	0-0	0-0	4.8	+ 63.00
Colin Tizzard	3-37	0-8	0-3	1-2	0-4	2-18	0-1	0-0	0-1	8.1	- 10.00
George Moore	2-7	0-2	2-3	0-1	0-1	0-0	0-0	0-0	0-1	28.6	+ 23.00
James Bethell	2-4	0-0	1-2	1-2	0-0	0-0	0-0	0-0	0-0	50.0	+ 22.00
Malcolm Jefferson	2-25	0-5	2-7	1-3	0-1	0-8	0-1	0-0	0-2	8.0	+ 5.00
Kevin Bishop	2-4	0-1	1-1	0-0	0-0	1-2	0-0	0-0	0-0	50.0	+ 9.50
Milton Harris	2-18	0-0	0-4	0-0	0-0	2-8	0-1	0-2	0-3	11.1	+ 18.00
Brian Ellison	2-22	0-4	2-7	0-8	0-1	0-2	0-0	0-0	0-1	9.1	+ 33.00
Sue Smith	2-38	0-7	0-8	0-3	0-0	2-19	0-1	0-0	0-1	5.3	+ 33.33
Ferdy Murphy	2-50	0-2	0-9	0-11	1-4	1-18	0-3	0-0	0-4	4.0	- 41.75
Charles Egerton	2-6	0-0	0-2	0-0	0-0	0-1	0-0	0-0	2-3	33.3	+ 16.50
Gary Moore	2-32	1-5	0-14	0-2	0-4	0-7	0-0	0-0	1-2	6.3	+ 1.00

LEADING JUMP TRAINERS AT ASCOT (SINCE 2009)

	Total W-R	Nov Hdle	H'cap Hdle	Other Hdle	Nov Chase	H'cap Chase	Other Chase	Hunter Chase	N.H. Flat	Per cent	£1 Level stake
Nicky Henderson	35-137	9-35	2-31	7-31	4-11	2-12	8-17	0-0	3-8	25.5	- 42.30
Paul Nicholls	23-110	5-15	2-20	5-20	1-11	3-25	7-18	1-2	0-6	20.9	- 38.70
Alan King	16-96	5-19	3-26	6-25	2-8	0-9	2-7	0-0	0-9	16.7	+ 55.12
Philip Hobbs	10-88	2-15	1-17	1-10	1-5	2-22	1-11	0-1	2-11	11.4	- 29.25
David Pipe	10-64	1-3	3-23	0-10	0-1	5-22	0-7	0-0	1-2	15.6	+ 4.64
Gary Moore	8-72	1-12	0-19	1-11	2-6	3-20	0-3	0-1	1-4	11.1	- 11.50
Donald McCain	6-29	2-4	2-11	2-8	0-3	0-5	0-0	0-0	0-1	20.7	+ 19.38
Oliver Sherwood	4-22	1-4	1-5	1-2	0-1	0-5	0-1	0-0	1-4	18.2	- 3.44
Jonjo O'Neill	4-36	0-3	0-7	0-5	1-4	0-7	1-4	1-2	1-7	11.1	- 9.00
Kim Bailey	4-15	0-4	1-2	0-1	2-4	1-3	0-0	0-0	0-1	26.7	+ 22.37
Henry Daly	4-22	1-1	0-3	1-3	0-2	2-14	0-0	0-0	0-0	18.2	- 6.13
Nigel Twiston-Davies	3-58	1-10	0-8	0-10	0-9	2-17	0-4	0-0	0-1	5.2	- 33.67
Henrietta Knight	3-32	0-7	0-1	0-6	2-6	0-4	1-5	0-0	0-3	9.4	- 6.00
Colin Tizzard	3-29	1-2	0-2	0-4	0-4	0-10	1-5	0-0	1-4	10.3	- 16.63
Emma Lavelle	3-45	0-15	2-7	1-12	0-3	1-4	0-4	0-0	0-2	6.7	- 30.50
Evan Williams	3-29	0-4	1-6	1-4	0-1	1-13	0-1	0-0	0-1	10.3	+ 37.00
Fergal O'Brien	3-7	0-0	1-2	0-1	0-1	0-0	0-0	1-1	1-2	42.9	+ 5.16
Martin Keighley	3-9	1-2	0-0	0-0	1-1	1-5	0-0	0-0	0-1	33.3	+ 1.12
Jamie Snowden	3-6	0-0	0-1	0-0	2-2	1-3	0-0	0-0	0-0	50.0	+ 28.00
Barney Curley	2-4	1-2	1-2	0-0	0-0	0-0	0-0	0-0	0-0	50.0	+ 3.25
Richard Rowe	2-12	0-1	0-2	0-0	0-1	2-7	0-1	0-0	0-0	16.7	+ 20.00
Charlie Mann	2-28	1-12	0-6	0-6	1-1	0-4	0-0	0-0	0-0	7.1	- 8.62
Victor Dartnall	2-10	0-0	1-2	0-0	0-0	1-6	0-0	0-0	0-2	20.0	+ 37.00
Nick Williams	2-27	0-2	0-2	1-5	1-4	0-8	0-7	0-0	0-0	7.4	- 17.00
Nick Gifford	2-32	0-6	1-10	0-4	1-2	0-8	0-2	0-0	0-2	6.3	+ 14.00
Dr Richard Newland	2-12	0-1	2-5	0-3	0-1	0-3	0-1	0-0	0-0	16.7	+ 25.00
Chris Gordon	2-20	0-1	0-6	0-1	1-5	1-6	0-0	0-0	0-1	10.0	- 9.25
R H & Mrs S Alner	2-7	0-1	0-0	0-0	0-0	2-6	0-0	0-0	0-0	28.6	+ 7.50
John Ferguson	2-3	0-0	0-1	0-0	0-0	0-0	0-0	0-0	2-2	66.7	+ 6.38
Patrick Rodford	1-1	0-0	0-0	1-1	0-0	0-0	0-0	0-0	0-0	100.0	+ 7.00
David Arbuthnot	1-13	0-1	0-5	0-3	0-1	1-3	0-1	0-0	0-1	7.7	- 7.50

LEADING JUMP TRAINERS AT AYR (SINCE 2009)

	Total W-R	Nov Hdle	H'cap Hdle	Other Hdle	Nov Chase	H'cap Chase	Other Chase	Hunter Chase	N.H. Flat	Per cent	£1 Level stake
Lucinda Russell	34-235	3-40	4-67	4-21	6-15	9-62	3-9	0-1	5-20	14.5	- 55.04
Donald McCain	34-112	12-28	3-25	5-13	3-10	7-20	3-8	0-0	1-8	30.4	+ 11.10
Jim Goldie	21-170	2-29	10-72	0-14	1-3	6-35	0-1	0-0	2-16	12.4	+ 19.88
Nicky Richards	17-123	3-31	6-36	2-16	3-10	2-19	1-3	0-0	0-8	13.8	- 20.63
Nicky Henderson	11-44	0-1	5-18	0-1	1-9	1-9	1-1	0-0	3-5	25.0	+ 8.29
J J Lambe	10-52	3-16	4-15	1-8	0-2	1-8	1-3	0-0	0-0	19.2	+ 66.25
Ferdy Murphy	9-77	0-7	2-14	0-5	1-5	5-42	1-3	0-0	0-1	11.7	- 0.31
James Ewart	9-75	1-11	0-15	1-12	0-5	3-16	1-2	0-0	3-14	12.0	- 38.84
Howard Johnson	8-51	3-10	0-11	1-5	3-8	0-10	1-4	0-0	0-3	15.7	- 25.59
Paul Nicholls	6-35	0-3	2-11	1-2	0-5	2-12	1-2	0-0	0-0	17.1	- 8.32
William Amos	6-50	2-7	1-19	1-8	0-3	0-3	0-1	0-0	2-9	12.0	+ 35.67
Andrew Parker	5-25	0-3	2-7	0-4	0-1	3-7	0-1	0-0	0-2	20.0	+ 51.50
Maurice Barnes	5-35	0-5	2-15	0-3	0-1	2-5	1-1	0-0	0-5	14.3	+ 16.41
Alistair Whillans	5-69	0-7	0-25	0-4	0-0	4-25	0-0	0-0	1-8	7.2	- 44.29
David Pipe	5-26	1-2	1-8	1-1	1-1	1-12	0-1	0-0	0-1	19.2	- 4.95
Chris Grant	5-29	0-1	2-12	0-1	1-2	1-5	0-1	0-0	1-7	17.2	+ 33.37
Ann Hamilton	4-8	1-1	0-0	0-0	0-0	3-7	0-0	0-0	0-0	50.0	+ 14.75
Sue Smith	4-57	1-5	0-14	0-1	2-9	1-25	0-2	0-0	0-1	7.0	- 32.25
Donald Whillans	4-29	0-1	3-21	0-1	0-0	1-5	0-0	0-0	0-1	13.8	- 0.75
Keith Reveley	4-30	0-4	1-8	0-3	0-4	3-7	0-2	0-0	0-2	13.3	- 13.42
C A McBratney	4-16	1-4	0-1	0-1	0-1	2-4	1-2	0-0	0-3	25.0	+ 4.79
Alan Swinbank	4-23	0-5	2-2	0-2	0-2	0-2	0-0	0-0	2-10	17.4	+ 7.00
N W Alexander	4-59	0-11	2-17	0-5	0-1	1-14	0-0	0-1	1-10	6.8	- 33.25
R T J Wilson	4-19	1-5	2-3	0-2	1-2	0-2	0-1	0-0	0-4	21.1	+ 6.87
S R B Crawford	4-34	1-6	1-10	0-7	0-0	0-4	0-1	0-0	2-6	11.8	+ 8.00
Nigel Twiston-Davies	3-14	0-0	1-2	0-0	0-0	1-8	1-2	0-0	0-2	21.4	+ 4.38
Rayson Nixon	3-11	0-0	3-11	0-0	0-0	0-0	0-0	0-0	0-0	27.3	+ 17.50
I R Ferguson	3-7	0-1	0-2	1-1	1-2	0-0	0-0	0-0	1-1	42.9	+ 6.50
Brian Ellison	3-18	0-1	2-7	0-1	0-0	1-8	0-0	0-0	0-1	16.7	+ 0.50
Martin Todhunter	3-56	0-4	0-15	0-3	1-5	2-28	0-1	0-0	0-0	5.4	- 41.88
Dianne Sayer	3-25	0-3	2-16	0-1	0-0	1-4	0-1	0-0	0-0	12.0	- 8.00

LEADING JUMP TRAINERS AT BANGOR-ON-DEE (SINCE 2009)

	Total W-R	Nov Hdle	H'cap Hdle	Other Hdle	Nov Chase	H'cap Chase	Other Chase	Hunter Chase	N.H. Flat	Per cent	£1 Level stake
Donald McCain	62-308	21-92	9-55	10-50	4-27	4-34	5-8	0-2	9-40	20.1	- 16.21
Nicky Henderson	18-56	8-14	1-5	2-10	1-7	0-2	1-3	0-0	5-15	32.1	- 4.76
Tim Vaughan	15-83	5-19	3-20	2-15	0-4	4-17	0-0	0-0	1-8	18.1	+ 5.87
Rebecca Curtis	15-51	6-13	2-11	0-4	2-8	0-3	1-1	0-0	4-11	29.4	+ 4.86
Jonjo O'Neill	14-155	2-45	4-36	0-9	2-8	4-37	0-4	0-5	2-11	9.0	- 98.51
Venetia Williams	14-89	2-20	1-18	2-9	3-9	4-19	1-4	1-1	0-9	15.7	- 8.47
Philip Hobbs	13-52	3-7	5-16	0-1	3-6	2-13	0-2	0-0	0-7	25.0	+ 19.45
Charlie Longsdon	13-57	2-6	3-10	1-4	4-8	2-15	0-5	0-0	1-9	22.8	+ 34.75
Alan King	12-78	2-20	0-17	3-12	3-8	3-8	0-2	0-0	1-11	15.4	- 36.86
Nigel Twiston-Davies	8-63	1-16	2-9	0-8	2-5	2-15	1-1	0-1	0-8	12.7	- 26.33
Richard Lee	7-44	0-4	2-5	1-5	0-4	4-22	0-2	0-0	0-2	15.9	- 9.15
Henry Daly	7-49	2-12	2-4	0-3	0-5	2-13	0-2	0-1	1-9	14.3	+ 40.50
Sue Smith	6-49	0-5	1-12	0-2	0-5	4-17	0-2	0-0	1-6	12.2	- 29.72
Evan Williams	6-63	2-18	0-20	3-9	1-7	0-7	0-1	0-0	0-1	9.5	- 48.12
Paul Webber	5-37	1-9	2-9	0-2	0-3	2-7	0-0	0-0	0-7	13.5	- 6.00
David Pipe	5-33	0-9	0-10	0-2	2-3	2-5	0-0	0-0	1-4	15.2	- 1.50
Barry Leavy	5-28	0-7	1-12	0-2	1-1	3-6	0-0	0-0	0-0	17.9	+ 10.50
Peter Bowen	4-56	1-4	2-21	0-5	0-4	0-14	0-0	0-1	1-7	7.1	- 23.05
Brian Ellison	4-23	0-8	1-6	2-5	0-3	1-1	0-0	0-0	0-0	17.4	- 11.96
Martin Todhunter	4-20	0-4	0-5	1-2	0-1	2-6	1-2	0-0	0-0	20.0	+ 6.00
Tony Carroll	4-27	0-7	1-9	0-4	1-3	2-2	0-0	0-0	0-2	14.8	+ 9.62
Alison Thorpe	4-23	1-3	3-13	0-6	0-0	0-1	0-0	0-0	0-0	17.4	+ 4.00
Jennie Candlish	4-44	0-9	0-12	0-8	1-2	1-3	0-3	0-0	2-7	9.1	- 6.25
Robin Dickin	3-18	1-7	1-4	0-1	0-0	0-3	1-1	0-0	0-2	16.7	- 5.13
Reg Hollinshead	3-26	0-11	2-7	1-4	0-0	0-0	0-0	0-0	0-4	11.5	+ 20.00
Kim Bailey	3-28	1-9	1-1	0-4	0-1	0-7	0-1	0-0	1-5	10.7	- 12.88
Milton Harris	3-20	1-3	1-8	0-2	1-2	0-3	0-0	0-0	0-2	15.0	+ 9.00
Michael Easterby	3-37	0-5	1-10	0-4	1-2	1-6	0-2	0-0	0-8	8.1	+ 8.50
John O'Shea	3-25	0-7	2-9	0-3	0-1	1-4	0-0	0-0	0-1	12.0	+ 3.57
Paul Nicholls	3-18	2-5	0-4	0-0	1-5	0-0	0-2	0-0	0-2	16.7	- 8.25
Lawney Hill	3-13	0-2	1-5	0-1	0-0	1-3	0-0	0-0	1-2	23.1	+ 11.50

LEADING JUMP TRAINERS AT CARLISLE (SINCE 2009)

	Total W-R	Nov Hdle	H'cap Hdle	Other Hdle	Nov Chase	H'cap Chase	Other Chase	Hunter Chase	N.H. Flat	Per cent	£1 Level stake
Donald McCain	26-145	11-50	2-24	1-8	3-19	0-12	4-12	1-1	4-19	17.9	- 56.65
Sue Smith	24-136	5-15	1-16	0-1	2-23	14-53	2-19	0-0	0-9	17.6	+ 30.68
Lucinda Russell	21-156	2-33	0-21	1-3	3-18	12-68	1-3	0-0	2-10	13.5	- 11.50
Howard Johnson	20-90	6-16	2-12	1-1	7-21	2-19	2-12	0-0	0-9	22.2	- 9.05
Alan Swinbank	10-47	3-19	2-6	0-3	0-1	0-0	0-1	0-0	5-17	21.3	+ 28.98
Nicky Richards	9-46	4-11	3-8	0-1	0-9	0-6	2-2	0-0	0-9	19.6	+ 15.46
Micky Hammond	8-40	1-6	3-13	0-1	1-9	1-6	1-3	0-0	1-2	20.0	+ 30.88
Ferdy Murphy	8-76	2-15	0-7	0-2	2-13	2-27	2-10	0-0	0-2	10.5	- 12.00
James Ewart	7-59	0-7	1-10	0-1	0-9	5-18	0-2	0-0	1-12	11.9	- 5.60
Malcolm Jefferson	6-55	0-10	1-8	0-3	1-5	3-13	0-5	0-0	1-11	10.9	- 5.54
Jonjo O'Neill	6-45	0-2	3-8	0-0	2-7	0-24	1-4	0-0	0-0	13.3	- 24.81
William Amos	6-42	0-10	1-4	0-1	2-3	2-15	0-1	0-0	1-8	14.3	+ 1.75
Dianne Sayer	6-58	2-18	2-19	0-0	1-3	1-17	0-1	0-0	0-0	10.3	+ 8.50
Nigel Twiston-Davies	5-33	0-5	0-3	0-1	1-3	3-17	1-4	0-0	0-0	15.2	- 5.83
Keith Reveley	5-32	1-6	0-2	1-2	1-3	0-9	0-2	0-0	2-8	15.6	+ 6.91
James Moffatt	5-30	3-9	1-11	1-1	0-4	0-2	0-1	0-0	0-2	16.7	- 4.34
Maurice Barnes	4-52	2-12	1-17	0-2	1-7	0-4	0-3	0-0	0-7	7.7	- 23.75
Brian Ellison	4-24	1-9	2-8	0-1	0-0	1-3	0-0	0-0	0-3	16.7	- 6.25
George Bewley	4-19	1-3	1-4	1-1	1-2	0-4	0-1	0-1	0-3	21.1	+ 20.54
Martin Todhunter	4-54	0-11	0-8	1-1	0-4	3-29	0-0	0-0	0-1	7.4	+ 1.00
Venetia Williams	4-15	1-2	2-4	0-0	0-1	1-6	0-1	0-0	0-1	26.7	- 3.63
Pauline Robson	4-13	0-1	0-1	0-0	2-6	2-4	0-1	0-0	0-0	30.8	+ 8.00
N W Alexander	4-34	0-9	0-4	0-1	0-2	3-12	0-4	0-0	1-2	11.8	- 10.00
Richard Lee	3-14	0-2	0-1	0-0	3-5	0-6	0-0	0-0	0-0	21.4	- 5.59
John Wade	3-33	0-11	1-6	0-1	0-2	2-9	0-0	0-0	0-4	9.1	+ 3.00
P Monteith	3-23	0-1	0-2	0-0	1-6	2-11	0-3	0-0	0-0	13.0	+ 9.50
Peter Bowen	3-8	1-1	0-2	0-0	0-0	2-3	0-0	0-0	0-2	37.5	+ 34.50
Barry Murtagh	3-56	0-16	1-10	0-1	1-6	1-18	0-1	0-0	0-4	5.4	- 37.25
Tim Easterby	3-26	2-6	0-6	0-1	0-2	0-5	0-1	0-0	1-5	11.5	- 10.13
Philip Kirby	3-25	1-10	0-3	0-0	0-2	2-5	0-0	0-0	0-5	12.0	+ 14.50
George Charlton	3-20	0-0	1-2	0-0	0-0	0-11	2-2	0-0	0-5	15.0	- 8.17

LEADING JUMP TRAINERS AT CARTMEL (SINCE 2009)

	Total W-R	Nov Hdle	H'cap Hdle	Other Hdle	Nov Chase	H'cap Chase	Other Chase	Hunter Chase	N.H. Flat	Per cent	£1 Level stake
Donald McCain	18-66	5-16	4-16	4-17	3-4	0-7	2-5	0-1	0-0	27.3	- 3.96
Dianne Sayer	9-44	3-9	4-21	0-3	0-0	2-11	0-0	0-0	0-0	20.5	+ 14.25
Harriet Graham	7-19	0-3	2-5	0-2	0-0	5-9	0-0	0-0	0-0	36.8	+ 9.24
Nigel Twiston-Davies	5-21	2-2	2-6	0-1	0-0	1-11	0-1	0-0	0-0	23.8	- 3.92
Richard Ford	5-22	1-7	0-3	1-1	0-1	3-10	0-0	0-0	0-0	22.7	+ 12.50
Tim Vaughan	5-36	1-12	1-8	1-3	0-0	0-9	2-4	0-0	0-0	13.9	- 13.27
George Moore	4-13	2-5	0-4	2-4	0-0	0-0	0-0	0-0	0-0	30.8	+ 23.83
Lucinda Russell	4-40	1-8	1-13	1-5	0-1	1-12	0-1	0-0	0-0	10.0	- 27.60
John Quinn	4-10	0-1	2-3	2-6	0-0	0-0	0-0	0-0	0-0	40.0	+ 5.75
Sophie Leech	4-17	0-3	0-6	0-0	1-1	1-5	2-2	0-0	0-0	23.5	- 2.70
Michael Chapman	3-55	0-7	1-15	0-3	0-2	2-25	0-3	0-0	0-0	5.5	- 35.25
Jonjo O'Neill	3-6	0-0	2-2	0-0	0-0	1-4	0-0	0-0	0-0	50.0	+ 9.00
Peter Bowen	3-32	0-6	0-7	0-2	0-2	3-12	0-3	0-0	0-0	9.4	- 15.00
Alistair Whillans	3-21	0-3	2-10	0-1	0-0	1-6	0-1	0-0	0-0	14.3	+ 2.00
Brian Ellison	3-8	2-2	0-2	1-2	0-0	0-1	0-1	0-0	0-0	37.5	+ 15.91
Sue Smith	3-20	0-3	0-5	0-1	0-0	2-9	1-2	0-0	0-0	15.0	- 2.50
Tina Jackson	3-5	0-0	3-5	0-0	0-0	0-0	0-0	0-0	0-0	60.0	+ 9.50
Martin Todhunter	3-27	2-4	0-9	0-4	0-1	1-9	0-0	0-0	0-0	11.1	+ 3.00
George Charlton	3-14	0-2	1-1	0-0	0-1	1-9	1-1	0-0	0-0	21.4	- 4.08
John Wade	2-8	0-0	1-2	0-0	0-0	0-4	0-0	1-1	0-0	25.0	+ 0.33
Roger Fisher	2-11	0-3	2-7	0-1	0-0	0-0	0-0	0-0	0-0	18.2	+ 15.00
Maurice Barnes	2-15	0-4	1-7	1-3	0-0	0-0	0-1	0-0	0-0	13.3	+ 17.50
Kate Walton	2-12	1-3	0-5	1-1	0-0	0-3	0-0	0-0	0-0	16.7	- 4.00
Tom George	2-13	0-2	0-1	1-1	0-2	1-3	0-2	0-2	0-0	15.4	- 7.00
Keith Reveley	2-6	1-1	0-2	0-0	0-0	0-3	0-0	0-0	0-0	33.3	+ 6.50
Barry Murtagh	2-20	0-2	0-7	0-3	0-1	2-7	0-0	0-0	0-0	10.0	+ 8.50
Tony Carroll	2-7	1-3	1-3	0-0	0-0	0-1	0-0	0-0	0-0	28.6	+ 2.50
Venetia Williams	2-3	1-1	0-1	0-0	0-0	1-1	0-0	0-0	0-0	66.7	+ 5.25
Pauline Robson	2-5	2-3	0-0	0-1	0-0	0-1	0-0	0-0	0-0	40.0	+ 0.85
Alan Swinbank	2-6	0-1	0-2	1-2	0-0	0-0	1-1	0-0	0-0	33.3	+ 1.80
Nicky Richards	2-16	0-6	0-2	1-4	0-0	1-4	0-0	0-0	0-0	12.5	- 7.67

LEADING JUMP TRAINERS AT CATTERICK (SINCE 2009)

	Total W-R	Nov Hdle	H'cap Hdle	Other Hdle	Nov Chase	H'cap Chase	Other Chase	Hunter Chase	N.H. Flat	Per cent	£1 Level stake
Keith Reveley	20-96	3-19	4-12	1-7	4-8	5-21	1-6	0-0	2-23	20.8	+ 61.80
Donald McCain	18-94	7-29	2-17	1-7	0-8	3-9	2-9	0-0	3-15	19.1	- 13.43
Micky Hammond	9-63	2-10	5-19	0-6	0-5	0-9	1-5	0-0	1-9	14.3	+ 20.50
Sue Smith	8-103	0-14	3-27	0-4	4-9	0-24	1-4	0-0	0-21	7.8	- 54.08
James Ewart	8-37	0-4	1-4	0-1	2-4	1-9	3-6	0-0	1-9	21.6	+ 14.10
John Wade	7-55	0-9	0-9	0-1	1-4	6-15	0-2	0-5	0-10	12.7	- 6.70
Howard Johnson	7-65	1-15	1-10	0-2	0-5	2-10	1-12	1-1	1-10	10.8	- 23.52
Ferdy Murphy	6-75	1-11	0-12	0-2	1-8	2-27	1-9	0-0	1-6	8.0	- 46.21
Chris Grant	6-82	0-13	2-26	0-8	0-3	2-17	2-10	0-0	0-5	7.3	- 22.17
Brian Ellison	5-23	2-8	2-3	0-9	0-0	0-1	1-1	0-0	0-1	21.7	+ 12.50
Alan Swinbank	5-32	1-9	0-0	0-4	0-1	0-3	0-3	0-0	4-12	15.6	- 3.25
Michael Easterby	4-42	1-11	1-11	0-3	0-1	0-2	0-3	0-0	2-11	9.5	- 5.50
Mike Sowersby	4-39	0-2	3-25	0-3	0-2	1-3	0-2	0-0	0-2	10.3	- 4.50
John Ferguson	4-6	1-3	0-0	3-3	0-0	0-0	0-0	0-0	0-0	66.7	+ 6.78
Malcolm Jefferson	3-39	1-11	0-5	0-3	0-1	1-5	0-4	0-0	1-10	7.7	- 25.40
Chris Bealby	3-16	2-6	0-2	0-2	0-1	1-2	0-0	0-0	0-3	18.8	+ 25.50
Simon Shirley-Beavan	3-8	0-2	0-1	0-0	2-2	0-0	1-1	0-0	0-2	37.5	+ 10.08
Andrew Crook	3-25	1-6	0-8	0-3	0-2	2-4	0-0	0-0	0-2	12.0	+ 3.00
Tim Easterby	3-34	0-5	0-3	0-5	0-1	3-9	0-2	0-0	0-9	8.8	- 8.50
Dianne Sayer	3-35	0-3	3-22	0-0	0-3	0-5	0-0	0-0	0-2	8.6	- 0.50
Martin Keighley	3-9	0-1	0-2	0-1	0-1	1-2	1-1	0-0	1-1	33.3	+ 0.50
S R B Crawford	3-12	0-1	0-2	0-0	0-0	0-0	1-3	0-0	2-6	25.0	+ 7.63
David O'Meara	3-14	0-3	1-4	1-4	0-0	0-1	1-1	0-0	0-1	21.4	+ 12.50
Tim Walford	2-29	0-7	1-11	1-1	0-0	0-6	0-0	0-0	0-4	6.9	- 22.50
George Moore	2-40	0-8	1-11	1-3	0-3	0-2	0-9	0-0	0-4	5.0	- 23.47
Jonjo O'Neill	2-8	1-1	0-2	0-0	0-0	1-3	0-2	0-0	0-0	25.0	- 1.25
Tom Tate	2-6	2-2	0-0	0-3	0-0	0-0	0-0	0-0	0-1	33.3	- 1.12
Kate Walton	2-24	0-4	0-8	0-1	0-0	1-4	0-2	0-0	1-5	8.3	- 8.00
Steve Gollings	2-12	0-4	0-1	0-0	0-0	0-2	1-2	0-0	1-3	16.7	+ 6.75
John Quinn	2-19	0-4	0-4	2-6	0-1	0-3	0-0	0-0	0-1	10.5	- 15.29
Stuart Coltherd	2-9	2-2	0-1	0-0	0-1	0-3	0-0	0-0	0-2	22.2	+ 52.00

LEADING JUMP TRAINERS AT CHELTENHAM (SINCE 2009)

	Total W-R	Nov Hdle	H'cap Hdle	Other Hdle	Nov Chase	H'cap Chase	Other Chase	Hunter Chase	N.H. Flat	Per cent	£1 Level stake
Paul Nicholls	66-421	9-51	10-85	17-75	13-46	9-99	5-56	0-8	3-13	15.7	- 70.25
Nicky Henderson	59-370	10-49	11-104	15-69	3-33	9-76	9-35	0-1	4-16	15.9	+ 12.14
Philip Hobbs	29-262	3-22	7-83	1-24	4-27	8-80	3-15	1-7	2-11	11.1	- 70.56
Nigel Twiston-Davies	28-323	4-34	7-60	2-38	3-47	8-112	3-25	1-5	1-18	8.7	+ 33.98
David Pipe	26-288	0-24	8-105	5-38	5-19	10-98	1-19	0-0	0-5	9.0	- 50.48
W P Mullins	20-161	2-29	4-31	8-31	1-5	0-15	4-32	0-1	2-20	12.4	- 24.00
Jonjo O'Neill	14-161	1-10	2-51	1-21	0-13	7-56	3-11	1-7	0-6	8.7	- 16.13
Venetia Williams	13-158	1-10	4-52	1-16	1-11	7-66	0-7	0-2	0-2	8.2	+ 56.75
Alan King	13-239	3-36	2-65	2-52	1-10	4-53	0-16	0-0	1-18	5.4	- 97.86
Colin Tizzard	10-103	2-15	0-13	0-3	3-22	2-29	2-13	0-0	1-8	9.7	+ 57.37
Gordon Elliott	9-79	1-8	4-32	0-12	3-10	0-15	1-4	0-2	0-0	11.4	+ 13.37
Tom George	7-76	3-13	2-17	1-15	0-11	1-14	0-5	0-1	0-1	9.2	- 22.37
Martin Keighley	7-66	2-16	2-18	1-4	1-7	1-16	0-4	0-0	0-3	10.6	- 12.80
Donald McCain	7-106	3-9	1-39	0-23	2-9	1-14	0-9	0-2	0-5	6.6	- 32.25
Neil Mulholland	7-20	0-1	1-3	0-0	1-2	4-9	1-4	0-0	0-1	35.0	+ 34.25
Nick Williams	6-71	2-13	0-12	1-10	1-9	0-15	2-12	0-0	0-1	8.5	- 38.09
Rebecca Curtis	6-63	2-17	1-16	1-5	0-7	0-3	1-2	0-3	1-10	9.5	- 24.70
Henry De Bromhead	5-31	2-5	0-3	0-2	0-6	1-7	2-9	0-0	0-1	16.1	+ 0.25
Ian Williams	5-51	1-7	0-18	0-2	3-6	1-14	0-3	0-1	0-1	9.8	- 15.50
Emma Lavelle	5-64	1-15	1-21	0-13	2-5	1-12	0-2	0-0	0-1	7.8	- 27.00
Fergal O'Brien	5-33	0-1	0-3	0-1	0-2	0-8	0-0	4-14	1-4	15.2	+ 21.00
Peter Bowen	4-40	0-1	1-13	1-3	0-2	1-11	0-2	2-7	0-3	10.0	+ 10.50
Ferdy Murphy	4-64	0-2	0-7	0-0	1-6	2-40	1-9	0-0	0-0	6.3	- 28.50
E Bolger	4-31	0-0	0-0	0-0	0-0	3-22	1-8	0-1	0-0	12.9	- 14.58
Paul Webber	4-44	0-4	1-11	0-13	2-7	1-7	0-4	0-0	0-2	9.1	- 5.59
Malcolm Jefferson	3-25	0-1	2-8	1-4	0-2	0-9	1-2	0-0	0-0	12.0	+ 19.00
Charlie Mann	3-46	0-6	1-10	1-3	0-1	1-18	1-8	0-1	0-0	6.5	- 24.75
C Byrnes	3-19	1-6	0-3	1-4	0-3	0-1	1-2	0-0	0-0	15.8	+ 10.50
Evan Williams	3-84	1-15	0-32	1-14	1-6	0-10	0-5	0-0	0-3	3.6	- 71.25
Jennie Candlish	3-23	0-0	2-10	1-12	0-0	0-2	0-0	0-0	1-4	13.0	+ 14.50
Robin Dickin	2-18	2-7	0-3	0-5	0-2	0-1	0-0	0-0	0-1	11.1	- 11.83

LEADING JUMP TRAINERS AT CHEPSTOW (SINCE 2009)

	Total W-R	Nov Hdle	H'cap Hdle	Other Hdle	Nov Chase	H'cap Chase	Other Chase	Hunter Chase	N.H. Flat	Per cent	£1 Level stake
Philip Hobbs	30-147	3-23	7-35	3-23	4-8	6-36	2-9	0-0	5-16	20.4	+ 41.58
Paul Nicholls	27-160	7-23	3-31	6-40	3-15	2-24	3-11	0-0	3-19	16.9	- 77.21
David Pipe	21-89	5-13	8-27	5-17	0-0	4-26	0-3	0-0	0-4	23.6	+ 40.75
Colin Tizzard	14-105	3-10	0-8	2-15	2-11	6-44	0-4	0-1	1-12	13.3	- 24.47
Victor Dartnall	12-67	0-8	3-13	2-8	1-4	2-20	1-2	0-0	3-12	17.9	- 10.12
Nigel Twiston-Davies	11-103	2-12	2-26	0-13	2-4	3-32	2-6	0-0	0-12	10.7	- 20.65
Richard Lee	10-70	1-8	0-12	1-6	0-5	7-34	1-2	0-0	0-3	14.3	+ 20.00
Jonjo O'Neill	10-109	0-17	1-24	1-13	1-7	5-34	1-3	0-0	1-11	9.2	- 33.75
Evan Williams	10-117	2-16	6-34	0-25	0-11	2-29	0-2	0-0	0-2	8.5	- 19.00
Nick Williams	9-31	1-6	3-7	2-5	1-2	0-6	1-1	0-0	1-4	29.0	+ 34.37
Venetia Williams	8-98	1-13	1-17	1-24	0-5	5-35	0-1	0-0	0-5	8.2	- 44.50
Rebecca Curtis	8-47	0-8	0-9	2-7	2-3	2-9	0-2	0-0	2-9	17.0	- 17.63
Bernard Llewellyn	7-74	2-9	2-39	1-11	0-0	2-10	0-2	0-0	0-3	9.5	+ 32.50
Tom George	7-57	2-10	0-10	3-13	0-6	2-11	0-2	0-0	0-5	12.3	- 18.38
Donald McCain	7-44	1-6	1-11	2-14	2-3	0-5	0-1	0-0	2-5	15.9	- 17.98
Tim Vaughan	7-117	0-12	1-30	1-27	0-4	3-25	0-3	1-2	1-14	6.0	- 56.40
Mark Gillard	6-27	1-4	3-8	0-3	0-1	2-9	0-1	0-0	0-1	22.2	- 0.00
David Rees	6-19	0-0	2-6	0-2	1-1	3-8	0-0	0-2	0-0	31.6	+ 23.83
Alan King	6-89	1-18	1-22	3-24	0-3	1-15	0-2	0-0	0-7	6.7	- 66.52
Jeremy Scott	5-34	2-7	0-7	2-7	0-1	0-6	0-0	0-0	1-6	14.7	- 2.00
Peter Bowen	5-59	1-4	2-19	0-9	0-3	0-18	0-1	0-0	2-6	8.5	- 14.70
C Roberts	5-25	0-2	0-5	0-5	0-1	5-9	0-0	0-0	0-3	20.0	+ 16.75
Keith Goldsworthy	5-28	2-10	0-9	1-6	0-0	0-0	0-1	1-2	1-1	17.9	- 9.87
Dai Burchell	4-39	1-9	3-16	0-3	0-0	0-9	0-0	0-0	0-2	10.3	- 8.50
Seamus Mullins	4-24	1-8	0-4	1-3	0-0	1-7	0-0	0-0	1-2	16.7	+ 44.50
Emma Lavelle	4-30	2-6	0-9	1-3	0-1	1-7	0-0	0-0	0-4	13.3	- 8.92
Jennie Candlish	4-18	1-3	2-7	0-1	0-0	0-3	0-1	0-0	1-3	22.2	+ 30.00
Martin Keighley	4-40	0-5	3-18	1-5	0-1	0-7	0-0	0-0	0-5	10.0	+ 1.00
Michael Scudamore	4-31	1-5	0-5	0-2	0-2	2-13	0-0	0-0	1-4	12.9	+ 20.00
Kim Bailey	3-32	1-4	0-14	0-4	0-1	1-5	0-1	0-0	1-3	9.4	- 18.50
Jim Old	3-37	0-6	1-12	2-10	0-2	0-4	0-2	0-0	0-1	8.1	- 6.00

LEADING JUMP TRAINERS AT DONCASTER (SINCE 2009)

	Total W-R	Nov Hdle	H'cap Hdle	Other Hdle	Nov Chase	H'cap Chase	Other Chase	Hunter Chase	N.H. Flat	Per cent	£1 Level stake
Nicky Henderson	23-91	5-22	3-12	5-20	5-10	1-11	2-7	0-0	2-9	25.3	- 10.38
Alan King	17-120	5-35	4-23	3-18	1-10	0-15	2-5	0-0	2-14	14.2	- 59.38
Paul Nicholls	14-45	1-6	1-3	2-8	7-10	3-17	0-0	0-0	0-1	31.1	+ 0.90
Keith Reveley	12-81	1-8	5-17	0-9	1-7	4-24	0-1	0-0	1-15	14.8	+ 0.37
John Quinn	10-39	4-13	1-7	4-9	0-0	1-7	0-0	0-0	0-3	25.6	+ 39.08
Howard Johnson	8-49	5-13	0-6	1-5	1-5	1-15	0-2	0-0	0-3	16.3	+ 5.85
Donald McCain	7-68	2-23	0-9	2-15	1-6	1-8	0-3	0-0	1-4	10.3	- 15.53
James Ewart	7-27	0-3	0-3	0-2	3-5	4-11	0-2	0-0	0-1	25.9	+ 13.75
Philip Hobbs	6-38	0-7	3-9	1-4	1-7	1-9	0-2	0-0	0-0	15.8	+ 11.75
Henry Daly	6-43	1-9	1-4	0-3	1-4	1-17	2-2	0-0	0-4	14.0	- 12.11
Malcolm Jefferson	5-54	2-13	0-9	0-6	0-5	1-17	0-0	0-0	2-4	9.3	- 16.50
Tony Carroll	5-28	1-9	3-11	1-7	0-0	0-1	0-0	0-0	0-0	17.9	+ 22.50
John Ferguson	5-13	2-3	0-0	0-3	0-2	1-1	0-0	0-0	2-4	38.5	+ 1.79
Jonjo O'Neill	4-42	0-9	3-12	0-10	0-2	0-6	0-0	1-2	0-1	9.5	+ 15.00
Brian Ellison	4-16	0-2	1-5	0-2	1-2	2-3	0-1	0-0	0-1	25.0	+ 8.63
Sue Smith	4-73	1-14	2-9	0-4	0-10	1-31	0-1	0-0	0-4	5.5	- 44.00
Ferdy Murphy	4-52	0-7	0-5	0-4	1-8	3-28	0-0	0-0	0-0	7.7	- 25.75
Tom George	4-30	2-12	0-4	0-3	0-2	2-9	0-0	0-0	0-0	13.3	- 8.25
Paul Webber	4-35	2-14	0-3	1-5	0-1	0-3	1-1	0-0	0-8	11.4	- 9.63
Venetia Williams	4-25	0-2	1-4	0-0	2-3	1-14	0-2	0-0	0-0	16.0	- 10.02
David Pipe	4-28	2-5	0-5	0-0	0-0	2-11	0-1	0-0	0-6	14.3	- 4.50
Emma Lavelle	4-15	0-3	0-3	0-0	0-1	4-7	0-0	0-0	0-1	26.7	+ 6.50
George Moore	3-32	1-10	0-4	2-7	0-1	0-4	0-2	0-0	0-6	9.4	+ 50.00
Nigel Twiston-Davies	3-39	1-7	0-6	2-7	0-0	0-15	0-2	0-0	0-2	7.7	- 22.38
John Mackie	3-28	1-9	1-8	0-3	0-0	1-4	0-2	0-0	0-2	10.7	+ 34.00
Michael Easterby	3-25	0-7	1-6	1-7	0-1	0-0	0-0	0-0	1-4	12.0	+ 18.25
Steve Gollings	3-26	0-10	0-3	1-2	2-5	0-2	0-0	0-0	0-4	11.5	- 16.00
Tim Vaughan	3-19	1-6	1-3	0-2	0-3	0-3	1-1	0-1	0-0	15.8	- 9.70
Richard Lee	2-4	0-1	0-0	0-0	0-1	2-2	0-0	0-0	0-0	50.0	+ 27.50
John Wade	2-20	1-4	0-2	0-1	0-3	1-8	0-0	0-0	0-2	10.0	- 11.00
Mrs John Harrington	2-4	1-1	0-0	1-3	0-0	0-0	0-0	0-0	0-0	50.0	+ 11.00

LEADING JUMP TRAINERS AT EXETER (SINCE 2009)

	Total W-R	Nov Hdle	H'cap Hdle	Other Hdle	Nov Chase	H'cap Chase	Other Chase	Hunter Chase	N.H. Flat	Per cent	£1 Level stake
Paul Nicholls	34-115	14-42	3-14	2-8	8-18	1-7	6-14	0-1	0-11	29.6	- 19.97
Philip Hobbs	32-186	9-53	6-39	3-16	2-15	4-24	3-19	1-2	4-18	17.2	- 54.59
David Pipe	19-158	1-37	11-64	1-9	0-8	2-26	2-6	0-0	2-8	12.0	- 64.89
Victor Dartnall	18-90	2-26	7-20	1-5	2-11	2-12	2-6	1-1	1-9	20.0	+ 38.52
Jeremy Scott	15-80	3-26	7-24	1-7	0-4	3-8	0-6	0-0	1-5	18.8	+ 8.66
Jonjo O'Neill	14-97	4-28	2-21	0-5	2-5	4-27	1-8	0-0	1-3	14.4	+ 5.07
Colin Tizzard	13-90	1-22	3-19	0-3	3-12	4-20	2-9	0-0	0-5	14.4	- 31.17
Susan Gardner	11-74	5-27	3-29	0-6	0-1	3-6	0-1	0-0	0-4	14.9	+ 27.75
Nick Williams	11-47	2-12	0-5	2-4	3-8	1-13	2-4	0-0	1-1	23.4	+ 7.73
Chris Down	9-98	3-32	4-30	1-11	0-4	1-10	0-1	0-0	0-10	9.2	+ 16.25
Emma Lavelle	9-68	4-26	0-8	1-4	2-6	1-8	1-9	0-0	0-7	13.2	- 39.93
Evan Williams	9-41	5-12	2-15	0-2	1-4	0-2	0-1	0-0	1-5	22.0	+ 17.94
Tim Vaughan	9-45	2-11	2-14	0-1	2-6	1-5	0-3	0-1	2-4	20.0	+ 2.79
Kim Bailey	8-29	3-10	0-9	1-3	1-1	1-4	2-2	0-0	0-0	27.6	+ 9.75
Alan King	8-59	0-20	2-9	0-5	2-6	1-5	2-7	0-0	1-7	13.6	- 15.29
Nigel Twiston-Davies	6-63	1-12	2-11	0-1	0-4	3-27	0-6	0-0	0-2	9.5	+ 12.50
Seamus Mullins	6-64	3-16	0-17	0-6	0-4	3-12	0-4	0-0	0-5	9.4	- 4.25
Venetia Williams	6-56	0-14	3-16	1-4	0-6	1-9	1-5	0-0	0-2	10.7	- 29.13
Charlie Longsdon	6-37	2-11	0-8	0-2	2-4	2-10	0-0	0-0	0-2	16.2	- 6.53
Oliver Sherwood	5-28	1-11	1-6	1-3	0-0	1-6	0-0	0-0	1-2	17.9	- 10.42
Nicky Henderson	5-17	1-4	0-2	1-3	0-2	0-1	2-2	0-0	1-3	29.4	- 1.93
Tom George	5-42	3-11	0-3	1-6	1-6	0-7	0-5	0-1	0-3	11.9	- 12.55
Brendan Powell	5-50	0-13	0-13	0-2	1-5	1-5	0-5	0-1	3-6	10.0	- 28.77
James Frost	5-84	3-32	1-26	0-6	0-3	1-10	0-5	0-0	0-2	6.0	- 55.30
R H & Mrs S Alner	5-45	1-9	1-8	0-2	1-5	2-16	0-5	0-0	0-0	11.1	- 7.40
Richard Lee	4-29	0-3	1-4	1-4	0-3	1-11	0-2	0-0	1-2	13.8	+ 3.75
Kevin Bishop	4-49	0-9	2-14	0-7	2-4	0-9	0-0	0-0	0-6	8.2	+ 9.00
Peter Bowen	4-26	1-6	0-8	0-2	0-2	0-2	1-2	1-1	1-3	15.4	- 9.42
Alex Hales	4-13	0-1	2-3	0-0	1-4	1-4	0-1	0-0	0-0	30.8	+ 36.50
Donald McCain	4-18	1-5	0-3	0-2	1-2	0-0	0-3	0-0	2-3	22.2	+ 1.37
Anthony Honeyball	4-21	0-4	1-8	0-2	1-1	1-3	1-3	0-0	0-0	19.0	+ 13.25

LEADING JUMP TRAINERS AT FAKENHAM (SINCE 2009)

	Total W-R	Nov Hdle	H'cap Hdle	Other Hdle	Nov Chase	H'cap Chase	Other Chase	Hunter Chase	N.H. Flat	Per cent	£1 Level stake
Nicky Henderson	19-41	5-10	0-4	3-8	3-8	2-2	1-2	1-1	4-6	46.3	+ 5.56
Evan Williams	14-45	2-9	1-9	2-8	1-4	5-10	3-4	0-0	0-1	31.1	+ 34.44
Tim Vaughan	14-61	2-12	3-14	2-10	1-3	4-12	2-6	0-0	0-4	23.0	- 24.69
Lucy Wadham	9-47	0-7	2-9	0-6	2-4	3-10	0-4	2-3	0-4	19.1	+ 9.06
Pam Sly	8-41	2-6	1-15	1-5	2-4	0-5	1-2	0-0	1-4	19.5	+ 30.08
Milton Harris	7-37	1-4	3-10	1-7	0-0	2-12	0-3	0-0	0-1	18.9	- 3.58
Renee Robeson	7-23	0-4	2-5	1-3	2-2	2-4	0-0	0-0	0-5	30.4	+ 27.88
Peter Bowen	6-26	0-4	1-2	2-3	1-4	1-11	1-2	0-0	0-0	23.1	+ 0.78
Neil King	6-102	0-13	3-32	0-13	0-2	2-26	1-6	0-0	0-10	5.9	- 56.50
Caroline Bailey	6-36	1-7	1-9	0-3	0-0	4-16	0-1	0-0	0-0	16.7	- 9.75
Alex Hales	6-28	1-6	2-8	1-4	0-0	2-8	0-0	0-0	0-2	21.4	+ 13.37
Steve Gollings	5-20	1-2	1-4	1-2	0-0	0-6	1-3	0-0	1-3	25.0	- 3.56
Charlie Mann	5-32	1-3	1-5	2-6	0-4	0-8	1-6	0-0	0-0	15.6	- 14.34
Sarah Humphrey	5-33	0-3	1-9	2-7	0-0	2-11	0-2	0-0	0-1	15.2	- 15.20
Jonjo O'Neill	4-34	1-14	1-6	0-7	1-1	0-4	0-0	1-2	0-0	11.8	- 22.96
Paul Nicholls	4-18	0-5	0-0	0-1	1-3	0-3	3-6	0-0	0-0	22.2	- 8.91
Lawney Hill	4-15	0-2	0-4	2-4	0-0	2-5	0-0	0-0	0-0	26.7	- 2.15
Michael Quinlan	4-10	1-3	1-4	2-2	0-1	0-0	0-0	0-0	0-0	40.0	+ 11.26
Jim Best	4-32	0-4	2-17	2-9	0-0	0-1	0-0	0-0	0-1	12.5	- 20.01
Neil Mulholland	4-14	0-2	1-2	1-3	0-1	2-6	0-0	0-0	0-0	28.6	+ 13.88
John Ferguson	4-18	1-5	0-1	0-5	0-0	0-1	0-0	2-3	1-3	22.2	+ 5.85
Oliver Sherwood	3-19	0-3	0-2	3-6	0-1	0-6	0-0	0-0	0-1	15.8	+ 5.50
David Arbuthnot	3-5	0-0	0-0	1-1	0-2	1-1	1-1	0-0	0-0	60.0	+ 12.36
John Cornwall	3-41	0-2	0-4	0-0	0-10	3-22	0-3	0-0	0-0	7.3	- 15.00
Gary Moore	3-20	1-4	0-1	1-4	0-1	1-8	0-1	0-0	0-1	15.0	- 10.06
David Pipe	3-5	2-4	0-0	0-0	1-1	0-0	0-0	0-0	0-0	60.0	+ 9.64
J M Turner	2-15	0-0	0-0	0-0	0-0	0-0	0-0	2-15	0-0	13.3	- 8.88
Jeff Pearce	2-8	0-2	1-4	1-2	0-0	0-0	0-0	0-0	0-0	25.0	+ 12.50
Michael Chapman	2-84	0-7	0-22	0-13	0-5	2-26	0-11	0-0	0-0	2.4	- 64.50
Charles Pogson	2-17	1-3	0-4	0-2	1-4	0-2	0-1	0-0	0-1	11.8	- 14.00
Noel Chance	2-11	1-2	0-1	0-2	1-1	0-2	0-0	0-0	0-3	18.2	- 4.13

LEADING JUMP TRAINERS AT FFOS LAS (SINCE 2009)

	Total W-R	Nov Hdle	H'cap Hdle	Other Hdle	Nov Chase	H'cap Chase	Other Chase	Hunter Chase	N.H. Flat	Per cent	£1 Level stake
Evan Williams	46-339	3-39	9-99	8-41	9-45	15-94	1-4	0-0	1-17	13.6	- 28.54
Rebecca Curtis	40-160	11-35	5-33	7-33	4-13	3-14	0-2	0-2	10-28	25.0	- 13.62
Jonjo O'Neill	30-137	5-11	9-36	1-20	2-10	9-45	0-2	0-2	2-11	21.9	+ 21.17
Peter Bowen	30-258	4-44	9-57	1-37	3-17	8-60	1-5	0-2	4-36	11.6	- 114.26
Tim Vaughan	30-245	2-44	6-59	4-45	3-18	9-43	0-2	0-0	6-34	12.2	- 108.61
Nicky Henderson	22-57	6-15	3-9	3-9	4-8	0-3	0-2	0-0	6-11	38.6	+ 12.12
Nigel Twiston-Davies	21-123	3-10	6-27	1-12	4-11	7-48	0-3	0-1	0-11	17.1	- 23.45
David Pipe	16-101	1-12	4-32	4-16	0-4	2-24	1-1	0-0	4-12	15.8	- 15.21
Philip Hobbs	15-87	0-10	3-22	3-16	3-7	3-20	0-2	0-0	3-10	17.2	- 19.03
Keith Goldsworthy	12-132	1-21	2-34	2-18	0-9	2-20	0-1	1-1	4-28	9.1	- 5.25
Richard Lee	8-33	0-3	1-8	0-3	1-1	5-15	0-1	0-0	1-2	24.2	+ 33.95
David Rees	8-57	1-8	2-20	2-8	1-7	2-14	0-0	0-0	0-0	14.0	+ 29.50
Charlie Mann	7-40	2-5	0-11	2-8	1-7	2-6	0-0	0-0	0-3	17.5	+ 24.78
John Flint	7-58	1-11	3-18	1-4	0-1	1-9	0-1	0-0	1-14	12.1	+ 76.38
Anthony Honeyball	6-13	0-1	0-0	0-2	1-1	3-3	0-0	0-0	2-6	46.2	+ 21.25
Bernard Llewellyn	5-82	2-11	1-34	1-14	1-4	0-15	0-0	0-0	0-4	6.1	+ 25.50
Paul Nicholls	5-24	1-3	1-3	2-8	1-3	0-2	0-1	0-1	0-3	20.8	- 10.38
Debra Hamer	5-49	1-13	1-8	0-10	1-2	1-7	1-1	0-0	0-8	10.2	- 17.29
Donald McCain	5-28	1-4	1-5	2-7	0-3	1-7	0-1	0-0	0-1	17.9	- 10.98
Dr Richard Newland	5-14	0-1	2-7	1-1	0-1	2-4	0-0	0-0	0-0	35.7	+ 14.00
Mark Bradstock	4-8	0-0	2-3	0-0	0-0	2-3	0-0	0-0	0-2	50.0	+ 16.38
Bob Buckler	4-17	0-3	1-4	0-1	0-0	3-8	0-0	0-0	0-1	23.5	+ 21.25
Tom George	4-32	0-3	0-5	0-1	1-7	2-10	0-2	0-1	1-3	12.5	- 13.00
Venetia Williams	4-17	0-2	1-2	0-5	1-2	1-5	1-1	0-0	0-0	23.5	+ 28.75
Alan King	4-37	0-6	1-7	0-4	1-5	1-5	0-2	0-0	1-8	10.8	- 5.13
Alison Thorpe	4-65	0-18	3-24	0-15	0-1	1-1	0-0	0-0	0-6	6.2	- 32.62
Kim Bailey	3-22	0-0	1-5	0-3	0-6	0-4	0-0	0-0	2-4	13.6	- 3.67
David Evans	3-35	0-3	1-9	0-7	1-3	0-4	0-1	0-0	1-8	8.6	- 11.50
Lawney Hill	3-5	0-0	1-3	0-0	2-2	0-0	0-0	0-0	0-0	60.0	+ 6.31
Henry Daly	3-15	1-2	1-2	0-0	0-5	0-1	1-2	0-0	0-3	20.0	- 6.00
Gordon Elliott	3-14	1-1	0-3	1-4	0-0	1-4	0-1	0-0	0-1	21.4	+ 1.00

LEADING JUMP TRAINERS AT FOLKESTONE (SINCE 2009)

	Total W-R	Nov Hdle	H'cap Hdle	Other Hdle	Nov Chase	H'cap Chase	Other Chase	Hunter Chase	N.H. Flat	Per cent	£1 Level stake
Jonjo O'Neill	9-41	1-6	1-5	2-10	0-0	3-11	1-5	0-1	1-3	22.0	- 2.62
Gary Moore	9-56	0-6	4-16	1-10	0-3	3-12	1-7	0-1	0-1	16.1	+ 6.55
Warren Greatrex	8-24	2-6	0-1	3-7	0-0	0-1	1-4	0-0	2-5	33.3	+ 2.92
Tim Vaughan	6-23	0-3	2-9	1-2	1-1	0-4	0-0	1-1	1-3	26.1	- 6.06
Nicky Henderson	5-13	2-2	0-0	2-5	0-0	0-0	1-5	0-0	0-1	38.5	- 1.61
Alan King	5-16	0-4	1-2	0-2	1-1	1-3	2-3	0-0	0-1	31.3	+ 0.61
Nick Gifford	5-30	0-4	0-1	1-7	1-2	1-7	2-6	0-0	0-3	16.7	+ 7.05
Jim Best	5-29	1-8	3-12	0-2	1-2	0-4	0-0	0-0	0-1	17.2	- 10.38
Oliver Sherwood	4-24	0-6	0-2	1-5	0-2	2-6	0-1	0-0	1-2	16.7	+ 10.33
Nigel Twiston-Davies	4-22	1-4	0-2	0-3	0-1	2-9	0-2	0-0	1-1	18.2	- 10.75
Alan Hill	4-5	0-0	0-0	0-0	0-0	0-0	0-0	4-5	0-0	80.0	+ 9.34
Peter Bowen	4-11	0-0	2-4	0-0	0-1	2-5	0-1	0-0	0-0	36.4	+ 10.18
Richard Rowe	4-39	0-5	2-5	0-5	2-7	0-12	0-0	0-0	0-5	10.3	- 23.80
P York	3-13	0-0	0-0	0-0	0-0	0-0	0-0	3-13	0-0	23.1	- 6.35
Neil King	4-27	1-2	0-11	1-3	0-0	2-10	0-0	0-0	0-1	14.8	+ 20.50
Charlie Mann	4-20	1-3	2-2	0-4	0-1	1-6	0-3	0-0	0-1	20.0	+ 2.75
Anna Newton-Smith	4-34	0-2	0-6	0-2	0-1	4-14	0-5	0-0	0-4	11.8	- 14.50
Paul Henderson	4-11	0-0	1-2	0-1	0-0	2-6	0-0	0-0	1-2	36.4	+ 41.50
Roger Curtis	3-26	0-3	0-5	0-2	1-3	2-10	0-0	0-0	0-3	11.5	- 12.25
Diana Grissell	3-21	0-3	0-5	1-4	0-1	1-3	0-1	0-1	1-3	14.3	+ 29.44
Sheena West	3-12	1-4	0-1	0-4	0-0	2-3	0-0	0-0	0-0	25.0	+ 26.63
Seamus Mullins	3-26	1-4	0-4	1-3	0-4	0-5	0-2	0-0	1-4	11.5	- 16.34
Venetia Williams	3-26	1-6	0-3	2-5	0-0	0-9	0-2	0-0	0-1	11.5	- 18.25
Lucy Wadham	3-13	0-4	1-1	1-3	0-2	0-1	1-1	0-0	0-1	23.1	+ 3.88
David Pipe	3-12	0-2	0-2	2-4	1-1	0-3	0-0	0-0	0-0	25.0	+ 1.75
Colin Tizzard	3-21	0-0	0-1	1-3	0-2	2-9	0-2	0-0	0-4	14.3	- 12.21
Suzy Smith	3-16	0-2	1-5	0-2	0-0	0-3	1-2	1-2	0-0	18.8	+ 7.00
Sarah Humphrey	3-9	2-3	1-2	0-1	0-0	0-2	0-1	0-0	0-0	33.3	+ 2.38
Chris Gordon	3-36	0-4	1-9	0-2	0-3	1-15	0-1	1-2	0-0	8.3	- 24.42
Kim Bailey	2-9	1-2	0-3	0-1	0-0	0-2	0-0	0-0	1-1	22.2	+ 3.75
Bob Buckler	2-11	0-0	0-1	0-1	0-0	2-6	0-1	0-0	0-2	18.2	- 4.25

LEADING JUMP TRAINERS AT FONTWELL (SINCE 2009)

	Total W-R	Nov Hdle	H'cap Hdle	Other Hdle	Nov Chase	H'cap Chase	Other Chase	Hunter Chase	N.H. Flat	Per cent	£1 Level stake
Gary Moore	36-228	5-20	7-65	10-43	4-11	7-64	3-10	0-0	0-15	15.8	- 49.78
Paul Nicholls	30-88	4-13	0-7	3-15	6-15	1-8	9-15	2-2	5-13	34.1	- 6.47
Chris Gordon	24-231	3-30	13-88	0-23	0-8	6-70	0-0	0-0	2-12	10.4	+ 39.38
Alan King	21-78	6-17	1-9	7-26	3-7	1-4	2-9	0-0	1-6	26.9	- 4.57
Tim Vaughan	21-111	7-20	4-25	1-13	1-9	7-26	0-5	0-0	1-13	18.9	- 36.10
Oliver Sherwood	15-63	2-13	3-15	2-10	2-6	1-6	1-2	0-0	4-11	23.8	+ 56.92
Nicky Henderson	15-36	3-4	1-4	1-6	3-6	1-1	1-2	1-1	4-12	41.7	+ 2.55
Jonjo O'Neill	15-76	2-8	4-21	0-4	2-4	4-29	0-3	1-2	2-5	19.7	+ 12.28
David Pipe	15-82	4-11	1-33	2-16	1-4	3-7	1-1	0-0	3-10	18.3	- 25.37
Seamus Mullins	13-121	0-8	3-21	2-13	1-5	6-45	0-5	0-0	1-24	10.7	+ 18.24
Brendan Powell	13-159	2-18	7-53	0-17	0-6	3-49	0-3	0-0	1-13	8.2	- 78.93
Lawney Hill	12-51	0-6	7-25	1-3	0-2	3-10	0-3	0-0	1-2	23.5	+ 17.57
Colin Tizzard	12-55	1-3	3-11	1-8	1-2	1-19	2-2	0-0	3-10	21.8	+ 25.20
Evan Williams	12-77	1-14	2-18	2-11	1-2	3-22	2-6	0-0	1-4	15.6	- 32.00
Venetia Williams	11-64	1-10	5-20	2-5	1-5	0-12	2-5	0-1	0-6	17.2	- 20.10
Emma Lavelle	11-46	2-8	1-8	3-6	1-2	2-11	1-6	0-0	1-5	23.9	+ 36.13
Nick Gifford	11-83	0-13	0-12	2-17	0-3	4-17	1-8	0-0	4-13	13.3	- 32.39
Neil Mulholland	11-103	3-16	6-38	0-7	0-4	1-30	1-4	0-0	0-4	10.7	- 20.58
Philip Hobbs	10-38	3-5	1-12	2-8	1-1	1-8	0-1	0-0	2-3	26.3	+ 4.22
Nigel Twiston-Davies	8-44	1-4	2-6	0-2	0-2	5-26	0-0	0-0	0-4	18.2	+ 10.75
Charlie Mann	8-64	2-10	0-10	1-13	1-2	3-23	0-2	0-0	1-4	12.5	- 10.75
David Bridgwater	7-29	1-4	0-3	1-6	0-1	5-13	0-2	0-0	0-0	24.1	- 1.40
Charlie Longsdon	7-61	2-13	0-13	1-7	0-0	2-19	1-2	0-0	1-7	11.5	- 31.46
Bob Buckler	6-45	0-8	0-7	0-1	0-2	6-20	0-1	0-0	0-6	13.3	+ 2.33
Richard Rowe	6-87	1-15	0-21	1-5	0-2	4-26	0-3	0-0	0-15	6.9	- 45.42
Helen Nelmes	6-59	0-5	3-19	0-8	0-4	2-11	0-5	0-0	1-7	10.2	+ 27.00
Lydia Richards	6-39	0-1	0-6	0-4	0-2	6-21	0-0	0-0	0-5	15.4	- 13.50
Victor Dartnall	6-38	1-6	2-9	0-7	0-0	3-11	0-1	0-0	0-4	15.8	- 4.09
Sarah Humphrey	6-29	1-4	1-5	1-3	1-1	2-11	0-2	0-1	0-2	20.7	+ 9.23
Anthony Honeyball	6-21	0-3	2-2	0-2	1-1	1-5	0-0	0-0	2-8	28.6	+ 3.13
Sophie Leech	6-28	0-4	2-13	0-0	1-3	3-7	0-0	0-0	0-1	21.4	+ 16.50

LEADING JUMP TRAINERS AT HAYDOCK (SINCE 2009)

	Total W-R	Nov Hdle	H'cap Hdle	Other Hdle	Nov Chase	H'cap Chase	Other Chase	Hunter Chase	N.H. Flat	Per cent	£1 Level stake
Donald McCain	37-147	13-30	8-45	5-20	3-11	3-20	2-5	0-1	3-16	25.2	+ 4.00
Nicky Henderson	10-59	2-11	2-26	2-11	0-3	0-2	2-4	0-0	2-5	16.9	- 12.37
Sue Smith	10-106	0-15	0-22	0-5	3-12	6-47	1-2	0-0	0-5	9.4	- 15.84
Paul Nicholls	10-46	2-6	1-11	1-6	1-4	1-10	4-8	0-1	0-1	21.7	- 0.47
Alan King	10-49	1-3	1-11	2-8	1-6	2-14	1-2	0-1	2-5	20.4	- 6.53
Philip Hobbs	9-59	4-8	3-30	0-3	0-2	1-11	0-2	0-0	1-4	15.3	- 13.26
David Pipe	9-52	0-0	3-29	3-5	0-1	3-16	0-1	0-0	1-2	17.3	- 1.26
Brian Ellison	7-41	0-1	4-24	0-6	1-1	2-9	0-0	0-0	0-0	17.1	+ 17.50
Lucinda Russell	7-36	1-2	0-7	0-1	1-3	4-21	0-1	0-0	1-1	19.4	+ 13.00
Venetia Williams	7-61	1-4	1-18	1-6	2-8	2-24	0-1	0-0	0-1	11.5	- 32.43
Nigel Twiston-Davies	5-70	0-6	2-18	0-7	1-5	0-28	1-2	1-1	0-6	7.1	- 41.97
Malcolm Jefferson	5-48	1-7	0-14	0-5	0-0	4-19	0-0	0-0	0-5	10.4	- 2.00
Tom George	5-25	0-1	1-6	0-1	1-7	3-9	0-2	0-0	0-0	20.0	+ 8.75
Keith Reveley	4-41	0-2	2-13	0-2	0-4	2-14	0-1	0-0	0-5	9.8	- 10.79
Tim Easterby	4-28	1-9	1-4	0-6	0-0	1-6	0-0	0-0	1-3	14.3	+ 8.50
Colin Tizzard	4-16	0-0	1-3	0-1	1-4	2-7	0-1	0-0	0-0	25.0	+ 3.83
Henry Daly	4-28	0-3	1-4	0-1	2-4	0-11	0-0	0-0	1-5	14.3	- 9.17
Nick Williams	4-16	1-2	1-5	1-3	1-1	1-5	0-1	0-0	0-1	25.0	+ 1.33
Charlie Longsdon	4-36	0-4	2-11	1-1	0-1	1-17	0-1	0-0	0-1	11.1	- 10.00
Jonjo O'Neill	3-52	0-6	1-16	0-2	1-4	0-20	0-0	0-1	1-3	5.8	- 6.67
Peter Bowen	3-28	0-3	1-6	1-2	0-2	1-12	0-2	0-0	0-2	10.7	- 4.00
Ferdy Murphy	3-35	0-3	1-6	0-2	1-3	0-16	0-3	0-0	1-3	8.6	- 20.67
Caroline Bailey	3-8	0-1	0-0	0-0	0-0	3-7	0-0	0-0	0-0	37.5	+ 13.75
Evan Williams	3-28	0-1	1-13	0-2	1-2	1-8	0-2	0-0	0-0	10.7	+ 0.50
John Wade	2-14	0-0	0-3	0-0	0-0	2-11	0-0	0-0	0-0	14.3	+ 5.00
David Arbuthnot	2-8	0-0	0-3	0-1	1-1	1-3	0-0	0-0	0-1	25.0	- 1.12
Alan Swinbank	2-14	1-1	1-4	0-0	0-2	0-1	0-0	0-0	0-6	14.3	- 1.00
Howard Johnson	2-20	1-4	0-7	0-2	0-2	1-4	0-1	0-0	0-0	10.0	+ 5.00
J J O'Shea	2-2	0-0	0-0	0-0	0-0	0-0	0-0	2-2	0-0	100.0	+ 24.25
John Quinn	2-10	0-1	0-3	2-2	0-1	0-2	0-0	0-0	0-1	20.0	+ 3.25
Emma Lavelle	2-13	0-2	0-4	1-5	0-2	0-0	0-0	0-0	1-1	15.4	- 5.77

LEADING JUMP TRAINERS AT **HEREFORD** (SINCE 2009)

	Total W-R	Nov Hdle	H'cap Hdle	Other Hdle	Nov Chase	H'cap Chase	Other Chase	Hunter Chase	N.H. Flat	Per cent	£1 Level stake
Venetia Williams	16-95	0-15	5-28	3-18	2-9	4-20	1-1	0-0	1-4	16.8	+ 14.30
Evan Williams	16-152	5-29	2-39	1-25	3-18	4-30	1-4	0-0	0-7	10.5	+ 0.62
Rebecca Curtis	16-47	2-7	1-6	3-15	1-1	2-5	0-0	0-0	7-13	34.0	+ 11.03
Alan King	13-70	5-23	0-11	3-17	3-7	1-2	1-3	0-1	0-6	18.6	- 15.92
Tim Vaughan	13-102	3-19	1-26	4-17	0-6	4-21	0-3	0-0	1-10	12.7	+ 40.37
Jonjo O'Neill	12-91	3-18	2-22	3-18	1-6	3-20	0-2	0-0	0-5	13.2	- 30.50
Paul Nicholls	12-54	3-12	0-2	2-17	2-9	0-2	3-6	0-0	2-6	22.2	- 15.92
Nicky Henderson	11-36	3-9	1-4	4-11	0-0	0-1	0-0	0-0	3-11	30.6	- 7.52
Charlie Longsdon	11-36	1-5	1-4	0-4	2-3	4-13	0-1	0-0	3-6	30.6	+ 108.88
Philip Hobbs	10-44	1-10	0-6	4-8	1-4	2-8	0-1	0-0	2-7	22.7	- 4.94
Richard Lee	10-59	1-9	1-9	2-7	2-3	4-27	0-0	0-0	0-4	16.9	+ 5.96
Martin Keighley	9-41	0-7	4-15	1-4	1-2	3-7	0-1	0-0	0-5	22.0	+ 20.73
Donald McCain	8-51	2-12	1-9	4-19	0-4	0-2	0-1	0-0	1-4	15.7	- 12.15
Jim Best	8-21	1-2	6-14	1-2	0-0	0-1	0-0	0-0	0-2	38.1	+ 12.61
Nigel Twiston-Davies	7-74	1-13	3-17	2-14	0-2	1-15	0-1	0-0	0-12	9.5	- 26.50
David Pipe	7-48	2-10	2-15	0-6	0-3	2-10	1-2	0-0	0-2	14.6	- 24.01
Peter Bowen	6-39	0-9	0-9	0-2	0-0	1-9	1-1	0-3	4-6	15.4	+ 4.93
Colin Tizzard	6-25	0-1	1-5	0-0	1-3	4-12	0-0	0-0	0-4	24.0	- 0.00
Kim Bailey	5-47	0-10	1-12	0-7	0-1	2-10	0-1	0-0	2-6	10.6	+ 20.25
Tom George	5-37	1-4	1-4	0-9	0-2	2-14	0-0	0-0	1-4	13.5	- 8.00
Tony Carroll	5-51	0-9	2-23	0-3	0-1	2-7	1-1	0-0	0-7	9.8	- 19.82
Henry Daly	5-30	0-6	0-4	2-9	2-4	0-4	1-1	0-0	0-2	16.7	- 15.85
Jennie Candlish	5-21	1-3	4-13	0-2	0-1	0-2	0-0	0-0	0-0	23.8	+ 8.55
Kevin Bishop	4-28	0-4	4-13	0-2	0-0	0-5	0-0	0-0	0-4	14.3	+ 13.50
Matt Sheppard	4-46	1-13	2-15	0-2	0-5	1-10	0-0	0-0	0-1	8.7	+ 4.00
David Richards	4-7	0-0	3-4	0-1	0-0	0-0	0-0	0-0	1-2	57.1	+ 14.33
Warren Greatrex	4-14	1-3	2-5	0-1	0-0	0-2	0-0	0-0	1-3	28.6	+ 10.75
Dai Burchell	3-31	1-6	2-14	0-5	0-0	0-2	0-2	0-0	0-2	9.7	- 9.00
David Evans	3-33	0-7	1-14	0-1	1-4	0-2	0-0	0-0	1-5	9.1	- 20.50
Henrietta Knight	3-31	0-6	0-1	0-6	2-6	1-6	0-0	0-0	0-6	9.7	- 20.63
Gary Moore	3-15	2-7	1-3	0-3	0-1	0-1	0-0	0-0	0-0	20.0	+ 17.50

LEADING JUMP TRAINERS AT **HEXHAM** (SINCE 2009)

	Total W-R	Nov Hdle	H'cap Hdle	Other Hdle	Nov Chase	H'cap Chase	Other Chase	Hunter Chase	N.H. Flat	Per cent	£1 Level stake
Lucinda Russell	27-156	1-21	4-36	4-12	2-13	9-60	2-3	0-0	5-11	17.3	- 41.12
Howard Johnson	20-75	5-25	1-9	3-8	4-10	4-9	0-4	0-0	3-10	26.7	+ 7.19
Sue Smith	19-119	0-17	3-16	1-11	3-7	7-53	2-3	0-0	3-12	16.0	- 24.50
Ferdy Murphy	17-118	5-20	2-12	2-17	3-15	4-42	0-7	0-0	1-5	14.4	- 0.13
Donald McCain	13-80	5-28	2-16	3-13	1-6	0-8	1-3	0-0	1-6	16.3	- 46.17
J J Lambe	11-53	6-13	1-16	2-7	0-5	1-7	1-2	0-0	0-3	20.8	- 3.90
Maurice Barnes	9-83	3-22	3-24	2-14	1-7	0-8	0-1	0-0	0-7	10.8	+ 102.99
Micky Hammond	8-44	0-11	5-10	1-2	0-2	2-15	0-0	0-0	0-4	18.2	- 4.55
Ann Hamilton	7-36	0-5	2-6	0-5	1-1	4-16	0-1	0-1	0-1	19.4	+ 9.88
Alistair Whillans	7-42	1-9	4-18	0-1	0-0	1-9	1-2	0-0	0-3	16.7	+ 1.75
John Quinn	7-17	0-1	1-7	4-4	0-1	1-1	0-0	0-0	1-3	41.2	+ 13.47
Martin Todhunter	7-75	0-7	3-28	0-5	1-3	3-30	0-0	0-0	0-2	9.3	- 19.00
N W Alexander	7-32	0-7	2-10	1-1	0-2	2-9	1-2	1-1	0-0	21.9	+ 21.70
James Ewart	7-38	1-6	1-2	0-4	2-5	3-14	0-3	0-0	0-4	18.4	+ 9.70
George Moore	6-31	2-12	2-5	1-3	1-6	0-2	0-0	0-0	0-3	19.4	- 6.83
Malcolm Jefferson	6-47	2-15	2-10	0-2	1-5	1-8	0-1	0-0	0-6	12.8	- 22.06
Donald Whillans	6-63	0-10	2-24	0-5	1-5	3-13	0-1	0-0	0-5	9.5	- 32.75
Brian Ellison	5-26	2-6	1-7	2-9	0-1	0-0	0-0	0-0	0-3	19.2	- 7.46
Keith Reveley	5-28	2-8	1-2	2-4	0-4	0-7	0-0	0-0	0-3	17.9	- 4.44
Evan Williams	5-12	3-4	0-1	2-3	0-2	0-2	0-0	0-0	0-0	41.7	+ 9.61
Tim Vaughan	5-32	2-10	1-7	1-5	1-4	0-4	0-1	0-0	0-1	15.6	- 22.37
Nigel Twiston-Davies	4-11	2-4	2-3	0-1	0-0	0-2	0-1	0-0	0-0	36.4	+ 11.38
Kate Walton	4-41	3-13	0-8	0-3	0-2	1-8	0-1	0-2	0-4	9.8	+ 11.00
Stuart Coltherd	4-30	1-5	0-7	0-1	0-1	3-15	0-1	0-0	0-0	13.3	+ 25.00
Chris Grant	4-47	1-15	1-8	0-4	0-4	1-9	1-1	0-0	0-6	8.5	- 12.25
Alan Swinbank	4-23	2-8	0-3	0-2	0-0	0-0	1-2	0-0	1-8	17.4	- 9.46
Nicky Richards	4-27	1-4	0-9	0-5	1-4	0-2	2-3	0-0	0-0	14.8	- 20.78
Elliott Cooper	4-19	0-4	2-5	0-2	1-4	1-1	0-0	0-0	0-3	21.1	+ 11.75
Tim Walford	3-23	0-6	3-10	0-1	0-1	0-4	0-0	0-0	0-1	13.0	- 9.13
Jonathan Haynes	3-27	0-4	0-2	0-1	0-0	3-16	0-1	0-0	0-3	11.1	+ 12.00
Evelyn Slack	3-29	0-2	1-12	0-1	0-0	2-13	0-0	0-0	0-1	10.3	+ 11.50

LEADING JUMP TRAINERS AT **HUNTINGDON** (SINCE 2009)

	Total W-R	Nov Hdle	H'cap Hdle	Other Hdle	Nov Chase	H'cap Chase	Other Chase	Hunter Chase	N.H. Flat	Per cent	£1 Level stake
Nicky Henderson	39-97	16-34	0-6	7-16	6-12	0-3	2-6	0-0	8-20	40.2	- 2.74
Alan King	22-126	5-32	5-35	4-16	3-11	3-13	0-1	0-0	2-18	17.5	- 4.27
Neil King	15-142	3-22	5-62	1-13	0-6	4-22	0-3	0-0	2-14	10.6	- 29.38
Jonjo O'Neill	14-123	0-29	8-42	1-17	1-4	4-21	0-1	0-1	0-8	11.4	- 54.02
Charlie Longsdon	13-76	3-14	3-21	0-1	2-8	2-17	1-3	1-1	1-11	17.1	- 9.21
Gary Moore	11-99	1-20	3-28	2-11	1-12	1-18	1-3	1-2	1-5	11.1	- 18.52
Henry Daly	10-58	0-14	5-7	2-6	2-12	0-10	1-3	0-0	0-6	17.2	+ 14.37
Brendan Powell	8-70	1-5	1-23	1-10	0-6	3-20	0-0	1-2	1-4	11.4	- 21.50
Tim Vaughan	8-44	0-9	0-10	3-9	1-4	3-8	1-1	0-0	0-3	18.2	- 13.72
Philip Hobbs	7-50	1-15	0-7	2-6	3-8	0-7	0-1	0-1	1-5	14.0	- 25.40
Kim Bailey	7-39	1-10	0-9	2-2	0-4	2-8	0-0	0-0	2-6	17.9	+ 3.00
Jeremy Scott	7-20	5-8	0-4	0-1	1-1	0-4	0-0	0-0	1-2	35.0	+ 5.06
Caroline Bailey	7-47	1-15	1-13	0-1	0-2	5-12	0-1	0-0	0-3	14.9	- 6.50
Ian Williams	7-36	1-6	4-13	1-6	1-2	0-4	0-1	0-0	0-4	19.4	+ 7.16
Oliver Sherwood	6-35	1-8	0-7	0-7	1-3	1-1	0-1	0-0	3-8	17.1	- 0.12
Nigel Twiston-Davies	6-75	0-9	1-14	1-7	2-10	2-23	0-1	0-0	0-11	8.0	- 45.14
Pam Sly	6-54	1-11	3-18	0-4	1-8	1-6	0-0	0-0	0-7	11.1	- 10.00
Paul Nicholls	6-19	3-5	0-1	0-1	0-3	0-1	2-5	1-2	0-1	31.6	- 7.71
Paul Webber	6-52	1-17	0-9	1-5	1-7	2-7	1-2	0-0	0-5	11.5	- 11.42
Venetia Williams	6-72	1-9	4-22	0-9	1-10	0-15	0-2	0-0	0-5	8.3	+ 35.00
Dr Richard Newland	6-23	0-1	6-10	0-4	0-2	0-3	0-2	0-1	0-0	26.1	+ 7.97
Robin Dickin	5-29	1-13	0-3	0-5	2-3	1-3	0-0	0-0	1-2	17.2	+ 14.00
Lawney Hill	5-33	0-4	1-15	2-6	0-1	1-3	1-1	0-1	0-2	15.2	+ 4.73
Sheena West	5-22	1-7	1-5	1-5	1-2	0-2	1-1	0-0	0-0	22.7	- 5.96
J R Jenkins	4-53	0-7	3-17	0-13	1-7	0-1	0-1	0-0	0-7	7.5	- 20.50
Don Cantillon	4-9	0-0	0-0	0-1	0-0	2-2	1-1	0-0	1-5	44.4	+ 2.82
Richard Phillips	4-56	0-12	2-32	0-3	0-1	2-6	0-1	0-0	0-1	7.1	- 0.00
Tony Carroll	4-34	0-4	3-18	0-3	0-2	1-6	0-0	0-0	0-1	11.8	+ 0.25
Lucy Wadham	4-52	2-10	1-15	0-6	0-0	0-9	0-2	0-0	1-10	7.7	- 27.25
Evan Williams	4-31	2-4	1-8	0-6	0-6	0-5	1-1	0-0	0-1	12.9	- 10.23
Ben Case	4-30	0-2	4-13	0-3	0-2	0-1	0-0	0-0	0-9	13.3	+ 24.00

LEADING JUMP TRAINERS AT **KELSO** (SINCE 2009)

	Total W-R	Nov Hdle	H'cap Hdle	Other Hdle	Nov Chase	H'cap Chase	Other Chase	Hunter Chase	N.H. Flat	Per cent	£1 Level stake
Nicky Richards	22-113	3-30	4-29	2-7	4-11	2-18	2-5	1-1	4-12	19.5	- 5.59
Lucinda Russell	21-200	8-51	3-42	2-17	3-21	4-53	1-3	0-2	0-11	10.5	- 37.03
Donald McCain	20-100	6-23	0-11	4-20	4-15	4-18	0-6	0-0	2-7	20.0	+ 4.23
Howard Johnson	18-92	4-31	4-15	2-9	2-9	3-16	1-2	0-0	2-10	19.6	+ 31.61
James Ewart	14-93	4-20	1-16	2-11	2-11	3-24	1-2	0-1	1-8	15.1	- 14.73
Sue Smith	10-52	1-10	3-12	0-0	3-7	3-21	0-1	0-0	0-1	19.2	+ 10.57
Chris Grant	10-73	2-19	4-19	0-5	0-7	3-12	0-2	0-0	1-9	13.7	+ 22.00
Ann Hamilton	9-36	0-5	3-4	0-3	2-4	3-16	0-0	1-2	0-2	25.0	+ 35.58
Jim Goldie	9-76	3-17	4-29	0-7	1-5	0-13	0-0	0-0	1-5	11.8	- 37.90
Alan Swinbank	9-43	6-17	0-7	2-7	0-2	0-0	1-1	0-0	0-9	20.9	- 1.05
George Charlton	9-87	3-27	1-21	1-6	1-9	2-11	0-0	0-0	1-13	10.3	- 41.23
Malcolm Jefferson	7-54	1-12	0-13	1-2	1-7	2-10	0-2	0-0	2-8	13.0	- 7.25
N W Alexander	7-74	1-19	1-12	0-5	1-5	3-13	0-1	1-12	0-7	9.5	+ 4.20
Rose Dobbin	7-76	4-28	0-15	0-9	0-2	1-8	1-2	0-2	1-10	9.2	- 35.84
John Wade	6-40	0-8	1-9	1-2	0-8	2-8	1-1	1-1	0-3	15.0	+ 9.50
Maurice Barnes	6-80	2-30	3-27	0-8	1-4	0-6	0-1	0-0	0-4	7.5	- 33.90
Alistair Whillans	6-73	1-18	2-31	0-3	0-1	0-11	0-0	0-0	3-9	8.2	- 30.67
Ferdy Murphy	6-78	0-7	1-16	2-6	1-10	1-32	1-7	0-0	0-0	7.7	- 56.73
Kate Walton	6-23	1-4	4-13	0-1	0-0	1-3	0-0	0-0	0-2	26.1	+ 23.00
Stuart Coltherd	6-70	0-19	3-13	0-7	0-8	2-15	0-3	1-3	0-2	8.6	+ 34.75
Dianne Sayer	6-63	3-15	1-26	0-4	0-2	2-15	0-0	0-0	0-1	9.5	- 4.00
George Moore	5-24	1-3	1-7	1-3	1-2	1-3	0-0	0-0	0-6	20.8	- 4.67
P Monteith	5-82	0-17	1-27	0-2	0-10	3-21	0-2	0-1	1-2	6.1	- 51.92
Andrew Parker	5-29	1-8	1-6	0-2	2-4	1-7	0-0	0-1	0-1	17.2	- 8.59
William Amos	5-46	0-10	1-13	1-2	2-7	1-11	0-0	0-0	0-3	10.9	- 23.88
Simon Shirley-Beavan	5-14	0-3	0-0	0-1	1-1	1-4	0-0	3-4	0-1	35.7	+ 3.41
Keith Reveley	5-32	1-5	0-4	0-0	1-2	3-13	0-0	0-0	0-8	15.6	- 9.60
Pauline Robson	5-26	1-4	2-11	0-3	1-1	1-7	0-0	0-0	0-0	19.2	+ 1.11
Nicky Henderson	4-6	1-2	0-0	1-2	1-1	0-0	1-1	0-0	0-0	66.7	+ 1.71
Sue Bradburne	4-45	0-11	0-7	0-6	1-5	3-14	0-1	0-0	0-1	8.9	- 13.00
George Bewley	4-30	0-4	2-14	1-4	0-0	1-5	0-1	0-1	0-1	13.3	+ 2.50

LEADING JUMP TRAINERS AT KEMPTON (SINCE 2009)

	Total W-R	Nov Hdle	H'cap Hdle	Other Hdle	Nov Chase	H'cap Chase	Other Chase	Hunter Chase	N.H. Flat	Per cent	£1 Level stake
Nicky Henderson	64-206	12-42	7-48	12-27	14-31	3-24	9-20	0-0	9-19	31.1	+ 47.40
Paul Nicholls	27-132	6-28	2-19	5-18	5-18	3-19	5-22	0-1	1-8	20.5	- 30.93
Philip Hobbs	21-120	6-24	4-30	2-14	2-11	3-22	3-10	0-0	1-11	17.5	- 16.38
Alan King	20-147	7-40	6-41	3-16	3-15	1-16	0-6	0-1	0-15	13.6	- 15.65
Gary Moore	14-131	3-26	3-29	0-15	4-22	2-20	2-7	0-0	1-3	10.7	- 34.91
Emma Lavelle	13-52	6-18	3-11	0-2	1-5	2-6	0-2	0-0	1-9	25.0	+ 27.10
Tom George	8-41	1-8	0-4	1-2	2-5	3-16	1-5	0-0	0-1	19.5	+ 9.00
David Pipe	8-57	0-4	1-22	2-5	2-2	2-13	1-10	0-0	0-1	14.0	- 22.43
Jonjo O'Neill	6-74	1-16	1-13	1-10	0-5	3-19	0-4	0-1	0-6	8.1	- 46.75
Andy Turnell	6-37	1-5	2-9	0-3	1-4	2-10	0-2	0-0	0-4	16.2	+ 5.83
David Arbuthnot	5-22	1-3	3-11	0-1	0-2	0-3	0-0	0-0	1-3	22.7	+ 13.96
Kim Bailey	5-36	0-11	1-10	0-2	1-3	2-8	0-0	0-0	1-2	13.9	+ 29.00
Paul Webber	4-63	0-22	0-9	1-8	0-1	0-9	3-7	0-0	0-7	6.3	- 45.20
Venetia Williams	4-65	0-9	1-23	0-5	0-2	2-23	1-4	0-0	0-0	6.2	- 38.00
Lucy Wadham	4-22	1-4	3-11	0-1	0-3	0-1	0-0	0-0	0-2	18.2	+ 23.50
Evan Williams	4-23	1-6	2-7	0-2	1-2	0-5	0-1	0-0	0-0	17.4	+ 4.25
Donald McCain	4-28	0-3	1-9	1-7	1-4	0-5	1-1	0-0	0-0	14.3	- 5.50
Jim Best	4-14	2-7	1-3	1-3	0-0	0-0	0-0	0-0	0-1	28.6	- 2.07
Charlie Longsdon	4-37	0-7	2-13	0-2	0-3	1-7	0-0	0-0	1-6	10.8	- 4.50
R H & Mrs S Alner	4-27	1-3	0-1	0-0	0-1	2-14	0-1	0-0	1-7	14.8	+ 8.50
Nigel Twiston-Davies	3-49	1-11	0-5	0-6	0-5	1-16	0-5	0-0	1-1	6.1	- 25.50
Henrietta Knight	3-41	0-7	0-4	0-5	1-6	1-10	1-3	0-0	0-6	7.3	- 31.58
Victor Dartnall	3-23	0-6	0-3	0-1	1-3	0-5	0-0	0-0	2-5	13.0	+ 11.50
Tony Carroll	3-22	1-6	2-11	0-1	0-2	0-0	0-1	0-0	0-1	13.6	+ 56.25
Colin Tizzard	3-44	0-3	0-6	1-1	0-5	1-17	0-6	0-0	1-6	6.8	- 31.40
Nick Gifford	3-53	0-15	1-14	0-3	1-8	1-10	0-1	0-0	0-2	5.7	- 31.50
Tim Vaughan	3-20	3-8	0-8	0-2	0-2	0-1	0-0	0-0	0-0	15.0	- 0.80
Warren Greatrex	3-33	0-8	2-10	0-3	0-1	0-6	1-3	0-0	0-3	9.1	- 13.75
Noel Chance	2-10	0-3	0-1	0-0	0-0	1-4	0-0	0-0	1-2	20.0	+ 2.00
Diana Grissell	2-16	0-7	0-1	0-1	1-3	1-2	0-2	0-0	0-0	12.5	+ 8.50
Sheena West	2-20	0-2	0-9	2-5	0-1	0-0	0-2	0-0	0-1	10.0	- 9.63

LEADING JUMP TRAINERS AT LEICESTER (SINCE 2009)

	Total W-R	Nov Hdle	H'cap Hdle	Other Hdle	Nov Chase	H'cap Chase	Other Chase	Hunter Chase	N.H. Flat	Per cent	£1 Level stake
Nicky Henderson	12-30	3-6	0-2	2-5	5-11	1-3	1-3	0-0	0-0	40.0	+ 16.78
Jonjo O'Neill	11-55	1-10	3-9	1-3	3-12	2-20	1-1	0-0	0-0	20.0	- 5.14
Caroline Bailey	10-55	0-9	1-6	0-3	4-10	4-22	1-5	0-0	0-0	18.2	+ 17.00
Venetia Williams	9-35	1-5	0-7	0-3	2-7	4-11	2-2	0-0	0-0	25.7	- 4.63
Tom George	8-38	0-0	1-2	0-3	3-11	4-21	0-0	0-1	0-0	21.1	+ 2.98
Nigel Twiston-Davies	7-51	1-9	0-6	0-3	2-10	4-19	0-3	0-1	0-0	13.7	- 9.78
Neil King	5-26	1-8	0-3	2-5	0-0	1-9	1-1	0-0	0-0	19.2	- 2.50
David Pipe	5-22	1-3	2-6	0-4	0-2	2-6	0-1	0-0	0-0	22.7	- 7.96
Evan Williams	5-27	0-4	0-5	2-5	2-6	0-4	0-2	1-1	0-0	18.5	- 7.53
Donald McCain	5-28	3-11	0-1	1-8	1-4	0-3	0-1	0-0	0-0	17.9	+ 5.85
Tim Vaughan	5-29	1-5	1-6	2-8	0-3	0-5	1-2	0-0	0-0	17.2	- 2.60
Philip Hobbs	4-21	0-3	2-4	0-1	1-6	0-4	1-3	0-0	0-0	19.0	- 0.98
Richard Lee	4-18	0-4	1-3	0-0	1-2	1-6	1-3	0-0	0-0	22.2	+ 5.83
Robin Dickin	4-27	0-4	0-2	1-4	2-5	1-11	0-1	0-0	0-0	14.8	- 0.50
Paul Webber	4-34	0-6	0-3	0-2	0-7	3-14	1-2	0-0	0-0	11.8	- 8.96
Tony Carroll	4-44	0-4	1-17	2-7	1-7	0-9	0-0	0-0	0-0	9.1	- 12.00
Lucy Wadham	4-21	2-6	0-2	1-3	0-3	0-6	1-1	0-0	0-0	19.0	- 4.63
Richard Guest	4-14	0-0	1-1	1-2	1-3	1-8	0-0	0-0	0-0	28.6	+ 14.00
Charlie Longsdon	4-22	0-5	0-2	0-1	1-4	3-8	0-2	0-0	0-0	18.2	+ 8.00
Oliver Sherwood	3-20	0-3	0-2	1-3	0-3	1-7	1-2	0-0	0-0	15.0	+ 0.08
Kim Bailey	3-21	0-2	2-7	0-1	0-1	1-9	0-1	0-0	0-0	14.3	- 4.00
S Flook	3-11	0-0	0-0	0-0	0-0	0-0	0-0	3-11	0-0	27.3	+ 32.00
John Flint	3-5	0-0	2-3	1-1	0-0	0-1	0-0	0-0	0-0	60.0	+ 3.50
Alan King	3-37	1-14	0-6	0-3	0-7	0-4	2-3	0-0	0-0	8.1	- 23.81
Jennie Candlish	3-10	0-3	1-2	0-1	1-1	1-3	0-0	0-0	0-0	30.0	+ 10.00
James Fanshawe	2-2	1-1	0-0	0-0	0-0	0-0	1-1	0-0	0-0	100.0	+ 1.21
Anabel K Murphy	2-4	1-1	1-2	0-0	0-1	0-0	0-0	0-0	0-0	50.0	+ 1.20
G D Hanmer	2-3	0-0	0-0	0-0	0-0	0-0	0-0	2-3	0-0	66.7	+ 9.00
Claire Dyson	2-13	0-2	0-0	0-2	0-0	2-9	0-0	0-0	0-0	15.4	- 3.00
Richard Harper	2-3	0-0	0-0	0-0	1-1	1-2	0-0	0-0	0-0	66.7	+ 10.25
Barry Brennan	2-5	0-0	1-3	1-1	0-0	0-1	0-0	0-0	0-0	40.0	+ 23.25

LEADING JUMP TRAINERS AT LINGFIELD (SINCE 2009)

	Total W-R	Nov Hdle	H'cap Hdle	Other Hdle	Nov Chase	H'cap Chase	Other Chase	Hunter Chase	N.H. Flat	Per cent	£1 Level stake
Gary Moore	11-76	1-7	3-21	2-14	1-5	4-23	0-6	0-0	0-0	14.5	+ 11.67
David Pipe	6-24	1-4	2-7	1-4	0-1	2-7	0-1	0-0	0-0	25.0	+ 1.35
Philip Hobbs	5-11	1-4	0-2	2-2	1-1	1-2	0-0	0-0	0-0	45.5	+ 1.55
Jonjo O'Neill	5-35	1-7	2-4	0-8	0-2	0-12	2-2	0-0	0-0	14.3	- 15.71
Venetia Williams	5-46	0-9	0-10	1-6	0-6	4-13	0-2	0-0	0-0	10.9	+ 10.00
Nick Gifford	5-18	1-5	0-1	1-4	1-2	1-4	1-2	0-0	0-0	27.8	+ 19.75
Seamus Mullins	4-20	1-4	2-3	0-3	0-2	1-6	0-2	0-0	0-0	20.0	+ 26.75
Charlie Mann	4-17	0-2	1-3	0-3	0-2	3-5	0-2	0-0	0-0	23.5	+ 0.87
Tom George	4-16	0-2	0-1	0-1	1-1	3-10	0-1	0-0	0-0	25.0	- 1.50
Emma Lavelle	4-12	1-3	0-1	1-5	1-2	1-1	0-0	0-0	0-0	33.3	+ 0.24
Alan King	4-27	2-10	1-7	0-3	1-1	0-5	0-1	0-0	0-0	14.8	- 3.20
Laura Mongan	4-20	0-5	3-8	0-2	0-1	1-4	0-0	0-0	0-0	20.0	+ 23.50
Tim Vaughan	4-14	0-2	2-4	1-4	0-2	1-2	0-0	0-0	0-0	28.6	+ 4.91
Nicky Henderson	3-13	0-3	0-1	2-6	1-2	0-0	0-1	0-0	0-0	23.1	- 3.05
Jamie Poulton	3-10	0-2	1-3	0-0	0-2	2-3	0-0	0-0	0-0	30.0	+ 20.50
Paul Webber	3-8	2-3	0-0	1-2	0-1	0-1	0-1	0-0	0-0	37.5	+ 18.00
Lucy Wadham	3-20	0-7	2-6	0-3	1-2	0-2	0-0	0-0	0-0	15.0	- 3.88
Charlie Longsdon	3-21	1-7	0-5	0-1	0-1	2-7	0-0	0-0	0-0	14.3	- 14.27
Anthony Middleton	3-7	1-1	1-3	0-1	0-0	0-1	1-1	0-0	0-0	42.9	+ 17.50
Nigel Twiston-Davies	2-21	2-6	0-3	0-3	0-1	0-7	0-1	0-0	0-0	9.5	- 15.21
Richard Phillips	2-19	0-3	0-5	0-1	0-1	1-8	1-1	0-0	0-0	10.5	- 9.13
Anna Newton-Smith	2-19	0-4	0-0	0-0	1-1	1-14	0-0	0-0	0-0	10.5	- 13.00
Brendan Powell	2-21	0-4	1-10	0-0	0-2	1-4	0-1	0-0	0-0	9.5	- 9.00
Chris Gordon	2-23	0-3	0-8	0-1	0-2	2-9	0-0	0-0	0-0	8.7	+ 1.00
George Baker	2-6	0-3	1-1	0-1	0-0	1-1	0-0	0-0	0-0	33.3	- 0.63
Tom Gretton	2-3	0-0	0-0	0-0	0-1	2-2	0-0	0-0	0-0	66.7	+ 3.00
J R Jenkins	1-2	1-2	0-0	0-0	0-0	0-0	0-0	0-0	0-0	50.0	+ 1.00
Roger Curtis	1-4	0-0	0-1	0-0	1-1	0-2	0-0	0-0	0-0	25.0	+ 2.00
Richard Lee	1-2	0-0	0-0	0-0	0-0	1-2	0-0	0-0	0-0	50.0	+ 4.50
Oliver Sherwood	1-12	0-3	0-1	0-1	1-2	0-4	0-1	0-0	0-0	8.3	- 8.00
Richard Mitchell	1-6	0-0	0-0	0-0	0-0	1-5	0-0	0-1	0-0	16.7	+ 0.50

LEADING JUMP TRAINERS AT LUDLOW (SINCE 2009)

	Total W-R	Nov Hdle	H'cap Hdle	Other Hdle	Nov Chase	H'cap Chase	Other Chase	Hunter Chase	N.H. Flat	Per cent	£1 Level stake
Evan Williams	40-243	3-30	1-41	13-60	6-22	9-61	3-8	0-3	5-18	16.5	- 75.44
Nicky Henderson	34-104	6-20	3-17	11-30	1-5	0-6	4-5	0-0	9-21	32.7	- 6.01
Nigel Twiston-Davies	16-147	0-17	1-21	4-29	1-10	5-50	1-5	2-6	2-9	10.9	- 46.98
Venetia Williams	14-79	0-3	2-17	0-11	4-14	6-31	2-3	0-0	0-0	17.7	- 19.70
Jonjo O'Neill	12-73	0-6	3-13	0-12	0-4	5-25	1-3	3-8	0-2	16.4	- 8.75
Henry Daly	12-121	2-19	2-16	3-23	1-10	3-31	0-5	0-2	1-15	9.9	- 50.29
Philip Hobbs	11-84	2-14	0-8	1-24	3-6	3-21	1-5	1-1	0-5	13.1	- 31.63
Rebecca Curtis	10-33	2-3	2-6	3-10	0-2	0-4	0-0	0-1	3-7	30.3	+ 5.72
Tim Vaughan	8-54	1-8	1-13	1-12	0-1	2-8	0-1	1-2	2-9	14.8	- 9.50
Richard Lee	7-77	0-2	0-9	1-16	2-10	3-34	1-3	0-0	0-3	9.1	- 30.20
Paul Webber	7-53	3-11	0-5	2-12	0-1	0-11	1-3	0-0	1-10	13.2	- 10.26
Keith Goldsworthy	7-40	3-10	1-9	1-8	0-3	0-3	0-1	1-2	1-4	17.5	+ 115.17
David Evans	6-66	0-10	3-16	1-20	1-4	1-8	0-2	0-0	0-6	9.1	- 21.67
Charlie Mann	6-32	1-6	2-6	1-7	1-4	0-4	0-1	1-2	0-0	18.8	+ 35.37
Neil Mulholland	6-19	1-2	1-5	2-3	1-2	1-5	0-0	0-0	0-2	31.6	+ 41.12
Robin Dickin	5-52	1-15	1-12	1-10	0-2	0-5	0-0	0-0	2-8	9.6	+ 1.50
Michael Chapman	5-61	1-8	2-12	1-15	0-7	1-13	0-4	0-0	0-2	8.2	+ 66.75
Paul Nicholls	5-29	1-4	0-2	1-8	2-4	1-6	0-1	0-0	0-4	17.2	- 13.20
Tom George	5-44	0-8	0-3	2-11	1-4	1-10	0-2	0-1	1-5	11.4	- 9.81
David Pipe	5-42	1-5	1-11	2-16	0-0	0-5	0-2	0-0	1-3	11.9	- 18.63
Martin Keighley	5-16	1-2	1-4	2-4	0-0	1-5	0-0	0-0	0-1	31.3	- 1.05
Oliver Sherwood	4-41	2-6	0-7	1-12	0-2	0-2	0-2	0-0	1-10	9.8	- 23.25
Kim Bailey	4-38	1-7	1-9	0-5	0-3	2-8	0-3	0-0	0-3	10.5	- 6.75
Ann Price	4-51	0-1	0-2	0-4	0-3	4-22	0-8	0-11	0-0	7.8	+ 3.00
Brian Ellison	4-17	0-4	2-5	2-7	0-0	0-0	0-1	0-0	0-0	23.5	+ 0.58
Jackie Du Plessis	4-8	0-1	0-0	0-1	0-0	1-2	0-0	3-4	0-0	50.0	+ 4.18
John Price	4-9	1-1	1-2	1-4	0-0	1-2	0-0	0-0	0-0	44.4	+ 22.50
S Flook	4-28	0-0	0-0	0-0	0-0	0-0	0-0	4-28	0-0	14.3	- 9.22
Martin Bosley	4-8	0-0	2-4	0-1	1-2	1-1	0-0	0-0	0-0	50.0	+ 25.33
Nick Williams	4-21	0-3	0-2	0-4	0-0	3-10	1-1	0-0	0-1	19.0	+ 10.33
Alan King	4-22	2-5	0-5	2-6	0-1	0-2	0-0	0-1	0-2	18.2	- 1.45

LEADING JUMP TRAINERS AT MARKET RASEN (SINCE 2009)

	Total W-R	Nov Hdle	H'cap Hdle	Other Hdle	Nov Chase	H'cap Chase	Other Chase	Hunter Chase	N.H. Flat	Per cent	£1 Level stake
Jonjo O'Neill	28-177	5-39	4-42	1-8	1-14	15-56	1-7	0-2	1-9	15.8	- 30.79
Tim Vaughan	19-122	9-33	1-33	4-14	3-11	0-20	2-6	0-0	0-8	15.6	- 43.80
Malcolm Jefferson	18-120	8-30	4-37	1-5	2-7	0-18	0-3	0-0	3-20	15.0	+ 4.60
Peter Bowen	18-89	2-9	4-26	0-10	2-7	7-30	0-1	0-0	3-12	20.2	+ 42.88
Nicky Henderson	15-38	7-12	1-9	1-3	2-4	1-4	0-1	0-0	3-7	39.5	+ 11.30
Steve Gollings	15-94	7-29	4-25	3-13	0-9	2-7	0-3	0-0	1-12	16.0	- 23.87
Charlie Longsdon	15-61	1-13	1-9	2-5	1-4	6-19	1-1	0-0	3-11	24.6	+ 14.43
Alan Swinbank	12-38	3-3	1-8	1-3	1-2	0-3	1-1	0-0	5-18	31.6	+ 1.39
Donald McCain	12-88	2-24	0-21	3-16	1-8	1-12	1-4	0-0	4-9	13.6	- 39.94
Brian Ellison	10-66	5-21	3-24	1-15	1-2	0-5	0-0	0-0	0-1	15.2	+ 25.73
Sue Smith	10-108	1-12	3-23	1-6	0-7	5-48	0-1	0-0	0-11	9.3	+ 29.00
Chris Bealby	10-78	2-21	3-17	0-2	0-6	4-19	0-2	0-0	1-11	12.8	- 4.88
Nigel Twiston-Davies	9-53	1-9	1-13	1-3	2-4	4-20	1-1	0-0	0-4	17.0	+ 0.17
Kim Bailey	8-32	1-4	0-5	0-1	2-4	3-12	2-5	0-0	0-1	25.0	- 7.20
David Pipe	8-45	1-3	3-21	1-8	1-2	1-14	0-1	0-0	1-1	17.8	- 3.50
Evan Williams	8-71	4-14	2-28	1-12	1-7	0-16	0-1	0-0	0-0	11.3	- 19.00
Philip Kirby	8-59	1-17	5-25	0-5	0-4	1-5	0-0	0-1	1-2	13.6	+ 0.25
John Quinn	7-39	0-12	0-9	5-9	1-1	1-5	0-1	0-0	0-2	17.9	- 10.84
Paul Webber	7-27	1-5	2-8	1-5	1-2	0-4	1-2	0-0	2-6	25.9	+ 25.00
Ian Williams	7-29	1-4	2-8	1-4	2-4	1-4	0-1	0-0	0-4	24.1	- 1.13
Nicky Richards	7-41	3-7	3-16	0-2	0-3	0-8	0-1	1-2	0-2	17.1	- 3.70
Alan King	7-72	1-18	0-17	3-11	2-7	0-9	1-3	0-0	0-7	9.7	- 34.25
Martin Keighley	7-31	0-1	3-13	1-2	1-3	2-11	0-2	0-0	0-0	22.6	+ 19.75
Sarah Humphrey	7-38	1-7	1-5	0-3	0-4	4-13	1-2	0-0	0-4	18.4	+ 15.63
Dr Richard Newland	7-51	0-4	1-16	0-4	1-1	5-27	0-2	0-1	0-0	13.7	- 6.50
Philip Hobbs	6-25	2-4	3-13	0-3	0-2	1-4	0-2	0-0	0-0	24.0	+ 4.04
Charlie Mann	6-47	2-8	2-15	0-4	1-11	1-9	0-0	0-0	0-1	12.8	- 13.25
Tim Easterby	6-53	3-17	1-12	0-12	1-2	1-4	0-0	0-0	0-6	11.3	- 31.89
Dianne Sayer	6-35	1-4	5-23	0-1	0-2	0-3	0-0	0-0	0-2	17.1	- 1.33
Alan Brown	5-18	0-5	0-0	0-2	1-3	4-7	0-1	0-0	0-0	27.8	+ 22.50
Pam Sly	5-48	3-18	1-16	0-5	0-3	1-3	0-1	0-0	0-4	10.4	- 16.50

LEADING JUMP TRAINERS AT MUSSELBURGH (SINCE 2009)

	Total W-R	Nov Hdle	H'cap Hdle	Other Hdle	Nov Chase	H'cap Chase	Other Chase	Hunter Chase	N.H. Flat	Per cent	£1 Level stake
Donald McCain	19-77	4-18	1-20	4-12	2-4	3-14	3-4	0-1	2-4	24.7	- 9.28
Howard Johnson	17-81	6-18	3-23	2-9	0-6	2-10	1-5	0-1	3-9	21.0	- 0.72
Lucinda Russell	14-143	1-17	3-38	1-17	2-8	7-43	0-8	0-0	0-12	9.8	- 75.02
Brian Ellison	13-61	0-4	5-32	2-10	1-2	3-8	2-2	0-0	0-3	21.3	- 3.81
Jim Goldie	10-100	3-12	3-46	1-14	2-4	0-13	0-1	0-0	1-10	10.0	- 4.75
Nicky Richards	8-55	2-8	4-24	0-3	1-3	0-8	0-1	0-0	1-8	14.5	+ 20.50
Ferdy Murphy	6-80	0-15	2-17	1-7	2-11	1-24	0-3	0-0	0-3	7.5	- 45.45
Keith Reveley	6-48	1-5	1-9	2-7	0-4	1-11	1-3	0-0	0-9	12.5	- 9.17
James Ewart	6-65	0-11	0-10	5-11	0-3	0-11	1-5	0-0	0-14	9.2	- 45.19
Gordon Elliott	6-13	2-5	0-2	1-2	0-0	1-1	0-0	0-0	2-3	46.2	+ 3.00
Kate Walton	5-22	0-1	4-17	0-1	0-1	1-2	0-0	0-0	0-0	22.7	+ 11.00
Peter Niven	5-28	0-2	1-7	0-6	0-0	0-3	0-0	0-0	4-10	17.9	+ 25.00
N W Alexander	5-36	0-0	1-16	1-3	0-1	3-10	0-0	0-0	0-6	13.9	- 1.50
Nicky Henderson	4-14	1-3	1-4	1-1	0-3	0-1	0-0	0-0	1-2	28.6	- 2.53
Bruce Mactaggart	4-11	0-0	0-2	0-0	2-2	2-7	0-0	0-0	0-0	36.4	+ 6.75
Richard Fahey	4-37	1-5	1-15	2-13	0-0	0-1	0-0	0-0	0-3	10.8	- 22.25
Venetia Williams	4-10	0-0	3-5	0-0	0-0	1-4	0-1	0-0	0-0	40.0	+ 5.75
David Pipe	4-6	0-0	3-3	0-1	0-0	0-1	0-0	0-0	1-1	66.7	+ 6.75
Alan Swinbank	4-22	1-5	1-3	0-2	0-0	0-0	0-0	0-0	2-12	18.2	- 9.15
Michael Smith	4-19	1-3	1-3	1-10	0-0	0-0	0-0	0-0	1-3	21.1	- 0.84
John Wade	3-34	0-3	1-7	0-2	1-3	1-12	0-1	0-0	0-6	8.8	- 13.10
Malcolm Jefferson	3-16	1-2	1-7	0-0	0-2	0-1	0-0	0-0	1-4	18.8	- 0.50
Chris Grant	3-64	0-5	1-17	1-13	0-5	1-19	0-1	0-0	0-4	4.7	- 46.75
Evan Williams	3-5	0-1	1-1	0-0	0-0	0-1	1-1	1-1	0-0	60.0	+ 5.10
Karen McLintock	3-22	1-2	0-7	0-0	0-0	0-2	0-1	0-0	2-10	13.6	- 4.17
Charlie Longsdon	3-11	2-2	0-4	1-3	0-0	0-2	0-0	0-0	0-0	27.3	+ 10.67
Philip Kirby	3-27	0-2	2-14	0-5	0-1	1-4	0-1	0-0	0-0	11.1	- 5.00
John Ferguson	3-12	0-1	1-4	1-4	0-1	1-2	0-0	0-0	0-0	25.0	+ 1.25
Ann Hamilton	2-15	0-1	0-3	0-1	0-0	2-7	0-1	0-0	0-2	13.3	+ 7.00
Patrick Griffin	2-11	1-2	0-1	0-2	0-2	0-2	1-2	0-0	0-0	18.2	+ 93.50
I R Ferguson	2-11	0-0	0-1	0-0	0-1	0-1	0-2	1-3	1-3	18.2	- 4.83

LEADING JUMP TRAINERS AT NEWBURY (SINCE 2009)

	Total W-R	Nov Hdle	H'cap Hdle	Other Hdle	Nov Chase	H'cap Chase	Other Chase	Hunter Chase	N.H. Flat	Per cent	£1 Level stake
Paul Nicholls	49-207	8-31	5-38	10-31	11-31	8-45	5-19	0-1	3-16	23.7	+ 6.23
Nicky Henderson	48-250	12-55	4-50	12-41	5-39	3-35	5-11	0-0	9-25	19.2	- 72.69
Alan King	19-181	5-38	1-37	6-29	3-22	2-34	0-4	0-0	3-23	10.5	- 60.03
Philip Hobbs	17-151	6-27	2-41	2-17	2-15	4-39	1-6	0-0	0-8	11.3	+ 12.50
David Pipe	13-107	1-15	4-26	1-13	3-10	2-35	0-3	0-0	2-5	12.1	+ 9.14
Tom George	12-72	0-14	3-12	0-4	4-19	3-19	1-3	0-0	1-2	16.7	- 10.04
Nigel Twiston-Davies	10-112	1-21	3-18	0-5	2-23	4-32	0-6	0-1	0-7	8.9	- 45.92
Venetia Williams	10-77	0-4	2-16	0-10	2-17	5-30	0-0	1-1	0-0	13.0	- 31.86
Colin Tizzard	10-81	3-11	1-8	1-8	3-16	2-24	0-2	0-0	0-13	12.3	+ 2.00
Jonjo O'Neill	9-94	3-17	2-18	1-15	2-17	0-16	0-3	0-2	1-6	9.6	- 47.67
Gary Moore	7-103	0-25	3-31	2-16	0-10	1-14	0-1	0-0	1-7	6.8	+ 11.00
Emma Lavelle	7-66	3-19	1-10	1-11	2-6	1-9	0-0	0-0	0-12	10.6	- 16.80
Nick Williams	7-37	1-3	1-3	1-6	2-6	1-13	1-3	0-0	0-3	18.9	- 7.96
Oliver Sherwood	6-32	1-7	0-5	2-3	0-2	2-10	1-1	0-0	0-4	18.8	+ 22.07
Charlie Longsdon	6-43	0-9	0-6	0-3	1-4	4-14	0-1	0-0	1-7	14.0	- 2.62
Donald McCain	5-42	2-11	0-9	2-11	0-6	1-4	0-3	0-0	0-0	11.9	- 5.92
Kim Bailey	4-37	0-14	0-3	0-6	2-6	2-8	0-0	0-0	0-0	10.8	- 11.50
Rebecca Curtis	4-29	1-3	2-10	1-6	0-3	0-3	0-1	0-0	0-5	13.8	- 3.25
Harry Fry	4-5	0-0	0-0	1-1	0-0	0-1	1-1	0-0	2-2	80.0	+ 9.25
Richard Lee	3-20	1-3	1-5	0-1	0-1	1-10	0-0	0-0	0-0	15.0	- 1.00
Paul Webber	3-37	0-7	0-3	0-8	1-7	0-7	1-1	0-0	1-5	8.1	- 18.97
Tony Carroll	3-31	1-6	2-13	0-6	0-1	0-2	0-2	0-0	0-1	9.7	- 7.00
Evan Williams	3-29	3-9	0-3	0-2	0-3	0-9	0-1	0-1	0-1	10.3	- 11.63
Tim Vaughan	3-36	1-4	0-13	1-7	0-3	1-7	0-0	0-0	0-3	8.3	- 15.33
Anthony Honeyball	3-15	0-2	1-3	0-3	2-2	0-2	0-1	0-0	0-2	20.0	- 2.00
Warren Greatrex	3-33	0-10	0-7	0-6	1-4	1-4	0-0	0-0	1-2	9.1	+ 1.00
Jim Old	2-17	0-3	2-7	0-4	0-2	0-0	0-0	0-0	0-1	11.8	+ 23.00
R Barber	2-2	0-0	0-0	0-0	0-0	0-0	0-0	2-2	0-0	100.0	+ 3.57
Mark Bradstock	2-13	0-5	0-0	0-0	0-0	1-6	1-1	0-0	0-1	15.4	+ 0.25
Bob Buckler	2-27	0-1	0-1	0-2	0-1	1-13	0-2	0-0	1-7	7.4	- 10.00
Peter Bowen	2-22	0-1	1-8	0-1	0-0	1-8	0-0	0-1	0-3	9.1	+ 1.00

LEADING JUMP TRAINERS AT NEWCASTLE (SINCE 2009)

	Total W-R	Nov Hdle	H'cap Hdle	Other Hdle	Nov Chase	H'cap Chase	Other Chase	Hunter Chase	N.H. Flat	Per cent	£1 Level stake
Lucinda Russell	20-146	4-21	4-37	1-11	0-10	10-57	1-3	0-0	0-7	13.7	- 24.17
Keith Reveley	18-90	2-20	1-18	3-10	2-4	8-26	0-0	0-0	2-12	20.0	- 12.76
Donald McCain	17-84	5-32	4-13	4-11	2-7	0-12	1-2	0-0	1-7	20.2	- 2.82
Chris Grant	14-96	3-30	5-25	0-3	0-5	4-23	0-1	0-0	2-9	14.6	- 27.55
Sue Smith	12-113	3-22	1-23	0-5	0-10	7-42	0-1	0-0	1-10	10.6	+ 1.63
Nicky Richards	11-71	6-25	2-21	0-3	0-0	1-13	0-3	0-0	2-6	15.5	- 4.02
Howard Johnson	9-72	3-26	0-13	0-2	2-7	2-11	1-5	0-0	1-8	12.5	- 14.82
N W Alexander	9-53	0-13	4-12	2-5	1-1	2-19	0-1	0-0	0-2	17.0	+ 14.25
James Ewart	9-78	2-22	0-6	1-11	0-3	2-19	3-4	0-0	1-13	11.5	- 37.25
Malcolm Jefferson	8-50	2-15	2-11	0-4	0-1	2-8	1-3	0-0	1-8	16.0	+ 48.25
John Wade	7-64	0-18	0-8	0-3	2-6	5-25	0-1	0-0	0-3	10.9	- 41.26
Martin Todhunter	7-50	1-5	2-17	0-2	2-4	2-20	0-1	0-0	0-1	14.0	+ 4.00
Alistair Whillans	6-43	2-11	2-15	0-3	0-0	1-11	0-0	0-0	1-3	14.0	- 14.75
Kate Walton	5-28	1-9	0-8	0-0	0-0	2-7	0-0	0-0	2-4	17.9	+ 11.25
John Quinn	5-17	1-5	3-9	1-3	0-0	0-0	0-0	0-0	0-0	29.4	+ 12.50
Tim Easterby	5-37	3-11	0-2	0-3	0-2	1-10	1-3	0-0	0-6	13.5	- 25.72
David O'Meara	5-20	2-7	1-4	0-1	0-1	1-4	0-0	0-0	1-3	25.0	+ 1.63
Ann Hamilton	4-21	1-4	0-2	0-0	2-3	1-11	0-0	0-0	0-1	19.0	- 5.00
Ferdy Murphy	4-65	1-19	0-8	0-3	1-6	1-26	1-3	0-0	0-0	6.2	- 44.97
Donald Whillans	4-46	1-13	2-23	0-2	0-0	1-5	0-0	0-0	0-3	8.7	- 22.38
Jim Goldie	4-35	0-7	2-15	0-5	0-0	2-8	0-0	0-0	1-2	11.4	- 12.50
David Pipe	4-13	1-2	0-3	1-1	0-0	1-5	0-0	0-0	1-2	30.8	+ 0.93
Philip Kirby	4-30	3-8	1-14	0-1	0-0	0-5	0-0	0-0	0-2	13.3	- 3.25
George Moore	3-34	1-12	0-8	1-3	0-0	0-2	0-2	0-0	1-7	8.8	- 14.38
Dianne Sayer	3-24	1-6	1-12	0-0	0-1	1-5	0-0	0-0	0-0	12.5	+ 7.50
Henry Hogarth	3-31	1-6	0-7	0-1	0-1	1-15	1-1	0-0	0-0	9.7	- 18.75
Nicky Henderson	2-5	0-0	0-0	2-4	0-0	0-1	0-0	0-0	0-0	40.0	- 1.83
Peter Bowen	2-6	0-2	0-0	0-0	1-2	0-1	1-1	0-0	0-0	33.3	+ 8.00
Sandy Thomson	2-16	0-4	0-2	0-1	0-3	2-5	0-0	0-0	0-1	12.5	+ 39.00
Micky Hammond	2-35	0-9	2-12	0-1	0-3	0-9	0-0	0-0	0-1	5.7	- 17.50
Michael Dods	2-8	0-1	2-3	0-0	0-0	0-0	0-0	0-0	0-4	25.0	- 0.12

LEADING JUMP TRAINERS AT NEWTON ABBOT (SINCE 2009)

	Total W-R	Nov Hdle	H'cap Hdle	Other Hdle	Nov Chase	H'cap Chase	Other Chase	Hunter Chase	N.H. Flat	Per cent	£1 Level stake
Paul Nicholls	45-135	4-16	3-17	7-20	10-28	5-27	6-13	2-4	8-10	33.3	+ 42.91
David Pipe	27-190	3-18	11-82	3-41	0-2	5-33	2-8	0-0	3-6	14.2	- 22.24
Evan Williams	25-133	6-30	5-28	7-23	4-14	3-35	0-2	0-0	0-1	18.8	- 28.17
Tim Vaughan	19-138	6-26	2-36	3-29	0-5	4-25	0-2	0-0	4-15	13.8	- 72.08
Jonjo O'Neill	17-104	2-18	6-34	2-13	2-4	4-29	0-2	0-0	1-4	16.3	+ 11.21
Philip Hobbs	16-107	3-12	0-26	2-16	1-6	10-43	0-2	0-0	0-2	15.0	- 30.42
Colin Tizzard	15-109	1-13	2-21	1-10	4-9	7-51	0-1	0-0	0-4	13.8	- 6.50
Nigel Twiston-Davies	11-52	1-7	4-18	1-5	0-2	5-16	0-0	0-1	0-3	21.2	+ 27.03
Nicky Henderson	10-27	6-7	2-12	1-4	0-0	0-1	0-0	0-0	1-3	37.0	+ 5.63
Peter Bowen	10-97	2-14	3-30	2-12	0-6	2-22	0-2	0-0	1-11	10.3	- 31.72
Bernard Llewellyn	10-69	2-11	5-43	2-12	0-0	1-2	0-0	0-0	0-1	14.5	+ 23.37
Alison Thorpe	9-47	3-10	2-17	3-13	0-0	1-4	0-0	0-0	0-3	19.1	+ 7.69
Sophie Leech	9-69	2-10	4-31	1-13	0-3	1-10	1-2	0-0	0-0	13.0	- 4.38
Susan Gardner	8-79	1-19	7-37	0-12	0-1	0-4	0-1	0-0	0-5	10.1	- 12.00
Brendan Powell	7-35	2-6	0-8	2-9	1-2	0-4	1-3	0-0	1-3	20.0	- 6.18
Martin Keighley	7-36	0-1	2-13	0-1	0-5	3-12	1-1	0-0	1-3	19.4	- 2.59
Gordon Elliott	7-18	3-4	1-3	1-4	0-2	1-4	1-1	0-0	0-0	38.9	+ 1.60
Paul Henderson	7-43	0-9	3-15	0-3	2-4	2-11	0-0	0-0	0-1	16.3	+ 15.75
Alan Jones	6-45	1-7	2-11	0-6	1-3	1-8	0-2	0-0	1-8	13.3	+ 8.50
Seamus Mullins	5-49	1-13	2-10	0-5	0-3	1-11	0-1	0-0	1-6	10.2	- 3.00
Victor Dartnall	5-38	1-8	1-10	2-7	1-4	0-5	0-0	0-0	0-4	13.2	- 16.28
John Flint	5-38	0-7	3-22	1-3	0-1	1-4	0-0	0-0	0-1	13.2	- 12.60
David Rees	5-28	1-3	2-12	0-1	0-0	2-12	0-0	0-0	0-0	17.9	+ 13.00
James Frost	5-120	0-27	2-36	2-30	0-5	1-15	0-1	0-1	0-5	4.2	- 91.13
Andrew Haynes	5-19	1-4	1-7	1-3	1-1	1-2	0-2	0-0	0-0	26.3	+ 39.05
David Arbuthnot	4-9	1-2	0-2	0-2	1-1	1-1	0-0	0-0	1-1	44.4	+ 10.38
Jeremy Scott	4-30	1-6	2-12	1-7	0-0	0-1	0-1	0-0	0-3	13.3	- 19.16
Charlie Mann	4-21	1-4	1-4	0-3	1-3	1-6	0-1	0-0	0-0	19.0	- 2.83
Venetia Williams	4-36	1-6	0-5	0-8	1-3	2-12	0-0	0-0	0-2	11.1	- 19.38
Keith Goldsworthy	4-33	2-11	1-4	0-6	0-2	0-1	0-0	0-1	1-8	12.1	+ 15.62
Donald McCain	4-6	1-2	0-1	2-2	1-1	0-0	0-0	0-0	0-0	66.7	+ 4.88

LEADING JUMP TRAINERS AT PERTH (SINCE 2009)

	Total W-R	Nov Hdle	H'cap Hdle	Other Hdle	Nov Chase	H'cap Chase	Other Chase	Hunter Chase	N.H. Flat	Per cent	£1 Level stake
Gordon Elliott	66-241	12-34	18-64	14-48	12-35	6-46	1-5	0-0	3-9	27.4	- 21.82
Lucinda Russell	30-273	5-45	10-74	3-28	4-32	6-71	1-3	0-2	1-18	11.0	- 99.00
Nigel Twiston-Davies	25-117	5-19	3-28	4-11	6-17	5-32	0-4	0-1	2-5	21.4	+ 5.09
Jim Goldie	19-108	2-13	10-51	4-20	0-8	1-12	1-2	0-0	1-2	17.6	- 2.50
Tim Vaughan	16-43	2-9	5-10	3-5	4-10	1-7	0-0	0-0	1-2	37.2	+ 12.22
Donald McCain	12-50	4-11	1-10	4-12	3-6	0-6	0-0	0-0	0-5	24.0	- 3.76
Peter Bowen	8-24	0-2	2-4	0-0	1-4	4-12	0-0	0-0	1-2	33.3	+ 15.73
Malcolm Jefferson	7-28	0-4	0-3	0-3	4-4	2-10	1-1	0-0	0-3	25.0	+ 44.25
Alistair Whillans	7-65	0-10	2-30	0-7	1-3	4-10	0-0	0-0	0-5	10.8	+ 1.50
S R B Crawford	7-63	1-8	0-16	1-12	1-5	0-9	0-0	0-0	4-13	11.1	- 31.50
P Monteith	6-46	1-9	1-11	0-5	0-7	4-11	0-1	0-0	0-2	13.0	+ 14.83
Nicky Richards	6-64	0-10	2-15	0-11	1-5	3-20	0-1	0-1	0-1	9.4	- 23.87
N W Alexander	6-68	1-11	1-15	1-11	0-3	2-13	0-2	0-6	1-7	8.8	+ 10.50
I R Ferguson	5-25	0-1	0-1	4-9	0-2	0-7	0-0	1-1	0-4	20.0	+ 12.25
A J Martin	5-39	1-8	1-11	1-4	1-7	1-9	0-0	0-0	0-0	12.8	- 2.09
Barry Murtagh	5-32	0-4	2-13	0-2	2-8	1-5	0-0	0-0	0-0	15.6	- 4.37
C A McBratney	5-53	4-13	0-13	1-10	0-4	0-7	0-2	0-0	0-4	9.4	- 32.35
Lisa Harrison	5-58	0-13	2-22	1-9	1-2	1-7	0-0	0-0	0-5	8.6	- 20.75
Nicky Henderson	4-15	0-4	0-1	1-3	0-2	0-0	0-0	0-0	1-1	26.7	- 2.87
Maurice Barnes	4-61	2-14	1-19	0-15	0-3	1-8	0-0	0-0	0-2	6.6	- 0.50
Ferdy Murphy	4-44	0-4	1-11	1-4	0-2	2-21	0-0	0-0	0-2	9.1	- 11.00
George Bewley	4-15	0-1	2-7	0-1	0-1	0-0	0-0	0-0	2-5	26.7	+ 5.75
Tom George	4-25	0-2	1-4	1-2	0-2	2-12	0-0	0-2	0-1	16.0	- 1.20
Victor Dartnall	4-14	3-3	1-4	0-1	0-3	0-3	0-0	0-0	0-0	28.6	+ 1.12
Venetia Williams	4-17	1-2	2-6	0-1	0-1	1-7	0-0	0-0	0-0	23.5	- 2.77
Michael Easterby	3-12	1-3	1-3	1-3	0-1	0-1	0-0	0-0	0-1	25.0	+ 0.91
David Pipe	3-17	0-1	2-8	0-0	1-2	0-5	0-0	0-0	0-1	17.6	- 8.57
Howard Johnson	3-54	0-8	0-13	0-11	1-5	1-12	1-1	0-0	0-4	5.6	- 41.50
Sue Smith	3-15	0-1	2-4	0-0	0-2	1-8	0-0	0-0	0-0	20.0	+ 12.00
R Mike Smith	3-25	0-3	0-1	0-5	0-2	2-6	0-1	1-4	0-3	12.0	- 1.50
Dianne Sayer	3-54	0-8	2-37	0-2	0-0	1-6	0-0	0-0	0-1	5.6	- 40.40

TRAINERS JUMPS STATISTICS 213

LEADING JUMP TRAINERS AT PERTH (SINCE 2009)

	Total W-R	Nov Hdle	H'cap Hdle	Other Hdle	Nov Chase	H'cap Chase	Other Chase	Hunter Chase	N.H. Flat	Per cent	£1 Level stake
Gordon Elliott	66-241	12-34	18-64	14-48	12-35	6-46	1-5	0-0	3-9	27.4	- 21.82
Lucinda Russell	30-273	5-45	10-74	3-28	4-32	6-71	1-3	0-2	1-18	11.0	- 99.00
Nigel Twiston-Davies	25-117	5-19	3-28	4-11	6-17	5-32	0-4	0-1	2-5	21.4	+ 5.09
Jim Goldie	19-108	2-13	10-51	4-20	0-8	1-12	1-2	0-0	1-2	17.6	- 2.50
Tim Vaughan	16-43	2-9	5-10	3-5	4-10	1-7	0-0	0-0	1-2	37.2	+ 12.22
Donald McCain	12-50	4-11	1-10	4-12	3-6	0-6	0-0	0-0	0-5	24.0	- 3.76
Peter Bowen	8-24	0-2	2-4	0-0	1-4	4-12	0-0	0-0	1-2	33.3	+ 15.73
Malcolm Jefferson	7-28	0-4	0-3	0-3	4-4	2-10	1-1	0-0	0-3	25.0	+ 44.25
Alistair Whillans	7-65	0-10	2-30	0-7	1-3	4-10	0-0	0-0	0-5	10.8	+ 1.50
S R B Crawford	7-63	1-8	0-16	1-12	1-5	0-9	0-0	0-0	4-13	11.1	- 31.50
P Monteith	6-46	1-9	1-11	0-5	0-7	4-11	0-1	0-0	0-2	13.0	+ 14.83
Nicky Richards	6-64	0-10	2-15	0-11	1-5	3-20	0-1	0-1	0-1	9.4	- 23.87
N W Alexander	6-68	1-11	1-15	1-11	0-3	2-13	0-2	0-6	1-7	8.8	+ 10.50
I R Ferguson	5-25	0-1	0-1	4-9	0-2	0-7	0-0	1-1	0-4	20.0	+ 12.25
A J Martin	5-39	1-8	1-11	1-4	1-7	1-9	0-0	0-0	0-0	12.8	- 2.09
Barry Murtagh	5-32	0-4	2-13	0-2	2-8	1-5	0-0	0-0	0-0	15.6	- 4.37
C A McBratney	5-53	4-13	0-13	1-10	0-4	0-7	0-2	0-0	0-4	9.4	- 32.35
Lisa Harrison	5-58	0-13	2-22	1-9	1-2	1-7	0-0	0-0	0-5	8.6	- 20.75
Nicky Henderson	4-15	2-4	0-4	0-1	1-3	0-2	0-0	0-0	1-1	26.7	- 2.87
Maurice Barnes	4-61	2-14	1-19	0-15	0-3	1-8	0-0	0-0	0-2	6.6	- 0.50
Ferdy Murphy	4-44	0-4	1-11	1-4	0-2	2-21	0-0	0-0	0-2	9.1	- 11.00
George Bewley	4-15	0-1	2-7	0-1	0-1	0-0	0-0	0-0	2-5	26.7	+ 5.75
Tom George	4-25	0-2	1-4	1-2	0-2	2-12	0-0	0-2	0-1	16.0	- 1.20
Victor Dartnall	4-14	3-3	1-4	0-1	0-3	0-3	0-0	0-0	0-0	28.6	+ 1.12
Venetia Williams	4-17	1-2	2-6	0-1	0-1	1-7	0-0	0-0	0-0	23.5	- 2.77
Michael Easterby	3-12	1-3	1-3	1-3	0-1	0-1	0-0	0-0	0-1	25.0	+ 0.91
David Pipe	3-17	0-1	2-8	0-0	1-2	0-5	0-0	0-0	0-1	17.6	- 8.57
Howard Johnson	3-54	0-8	0-13	0-11	1-5	1-12	1-1	0-0	0-4	5.6	- 41.50
Sue Smith	3-15	0-1	2-4	0-0	0-2	1-8	0-0	0-0	0-0	20.0	+ 12.00
R Mike Smith	3-25	0-3	0-1	0-5	0-2	2-6	0-1	1-4	0-3	12.0	- 1.50
Dianne Sayer	3-54	0-8	2-37	0-2	0-0	1-6	0-0	0-0	0-1	5.6	- 40.40

LEADING JUMP TRAINERS AT SANDOWN (SINCE 2009)

	Total W-R	Nov Hdle	H'cap Hdle	Other Hdle	Nov Chase	H'cap Chase	Other Chase	Hunter Chase	N.H. Flat	Per cent	£1 Level stake
Nicky Henderson	34-148	11-34	9-51	8-29	3-11	3-16	3-9	0-0	0-10	23.0	+ 19.02
Paul Nicholls	29-129	1-9	3-29	2-16	6-14	4-38	7-22	4-4	2-5	22.5	- 29.43
David Pipe	13-75	3-9	3-39	2-13	2-2	0-12	2-6	0-0	1-3	17.3	- 13.63
Alan King	11-80	1-14	3-27	1-13	1-3	4-16	0-3	0-0	1-9	13.8	- 8.42
Philip Hobbs	10-84	3-10	3-29	2-9	0-4	3-29	0-5	0-0	0-4	11.9	- 30.85
Gary Moore	9-120	1-27	4-42	1-22	0-5	2-24	0-4	0-0	1-5	7.5	- 35.33
Venetia Williams	9-82	0-8	2-27	1-9	2-6	4-33	0-1	0-0	0-3	11.0	- 26.18
Jonjo O'Neill	8-68	3-16	0-22	1-7	1-3	3-18	0-0	0-2	0-4	11.8	- 17.38
Charlie Longsdon	8-36	0-4	3-11	2-4	1-2	3-12	0-1	0-0	0-3	22.2	+ 34.00
Charlie Mann	7-40	0-2	3-13	0-8	1-1	1-6	2-11	0-0	0-2	17.5	+ 34.25
Victor Dartnall	5-29	0-4	2-7	0-2	0-0	3-13	0-0	0-1	0-3	17.2	+ 19.33
Emma Lavelle	5-33	3-11	1-10	0-4	0-1	0-5	1-1	0-0	0-3	15.2	- 12.05
David Arbuthnot	4-21	2-6	0-5	0-3	0-1	1-5	0-0	0-0	1-2	19.0	+ 6.36
Neil King	4-14	0-0	1-7	1-5	0-0	2-3	0-1	0-0	0-0	28.6	+ 16.50
Nick Williams	4-30	0-3	1-9	0-3	0-3	2-7	0-4	0-0	1-1	13.3	+ 10.00
Donald McCain	4-30	0-5	1-10	0-4	0-0	1-8	2-4	0-0	0-0	13.3	- 13.58
Nigel Twiston-Davies	3-50	0-6	1-10	1-1	0-2	1-24	0-4	0-1	0-2	6.0	- 34.50
Sheena West	3-9	0-0	0-4	2-4	0-0	0-1	1-1	0-0	0-0	33.3	+ 17.00
Lucy Wadham	3-25	0-2	3-18	1-4	0-0	0-0	0-0	0-0	0-5	12.0	+ 4.50
Nick Gifford	3-39	0-4	2-14	0-6	0-2	1-13	0-0	0-1	0-2	7.7	- 10.00
Oliver Sherwood	2-33	0-3	0-15	0-2	0-1	2-9	0-0	0-0	0-4	6.1	- 3.00
F Doumen	2-4	1-3	0-0	0-0	1-1	0-0	0-0	0-0	0-0	50.0	+ 7.23
Jeremy Scott	2-11	1-2	0-4	0-0	0-0	1-2	0-0	0-0	0-3	18.2	- 3.00
Paul Webber	2-35	1-10	0-6	0-2	0-2	1-11	0-2	0-0	0-2	5.7	- 16.00
Tony Carroll	2-38	1-5	1-24	0-6	0-2	0-0	0-2	0-0	0-1	5.3	- 15.50
Ian Williams	2-20	1-5	0-7	0-2	0-0	0-4	0-1	1-1	0-1	10.0	- 15.10
Evan Williams	2-40	0-1	0-19	0-7	0-3	2-10	0-3	0-0	0-1	5.0	- 27.00
Brendan Powell	2-27	0-2	0-11	1-6	0-1	1-7	0-0	0-0	0-2	7.4	- 4.50
Fiona Shaw	2-2	0-0	0-0	0-0	0-0	2-2	0-0	0-0	0-0	100.0	+ 12.75
Laura Mongan	2-11	0-1	1-6	2-6	0-1	0-0	0-0	0-0	0-0	18.2	+ 17.50
Dr Richard Newland	2-25	0-4	0-9	0-7	0-1	2-9	0-0	0-0	0-0	8.0	- 9.00

LEADING JUMP TRAINERS AT SEDGEFIELD (SINCE 2009)

	Total W-R	Nov Hdle	H'cap Hdle	Other Hdle	Nov Chase	H'cap Chase	Other Chase	Hunter Chase	N.H. Flat	Per cent	£1 Level stake
Donald McCain	34-125	14-43	3-19	8-20	0-7	1-6	2-11	0-0	6-19	27.2	- 37.93
Ferdy Murphy	25-169	1-27	3-30	4-10	3-12	8-61	6-19	0-0	0-10	14.8	- 1.49
Sue Smith	23-161	1-24	5-32	2-9	1-12	11-59	1-12	0-0	2-13	14.3	- 23.62
Howard Johnson	17-82	5-25	2-18	1-5	2-4	1-8	6-13	0-0	0-9	20.7	- 28.35
Malcolm Jefferson	12-76	1-14	1-13	0-2	0-7	9-28	0-6	0-0	1-6	15.8	+ 13.92
Chris Grant	12-82	1-16	8-30	0-3	0-2	2-18	1-6	0-2	0-5	14.6	+ 18.88
Martin Todhunter	11-95	3-14	4-40	1-3	1-3	2-29	0-2	0-0	0-4	11.6	- 28.13
Alan Swinbank	11-62	2-20	1-8	0-2	1-3	0-3	1-5	0-0	6-21	17.7	- 20.82
John Wade	10-160	0-39	2-23	0-8	1-10	6-50	0-7	0-2	1-21	6.3	- 82.75
Brian Ellison	10-64	3-19	3-18	2-10	1-4	1-7	0-1	0-0	0-5	15.6	- 23.19
Keith Reveley	10-60	4-13	0-12	0-6	3-8	1-14	0-3	0-0	2-4	16.7	+ 19.96
Dianne Sayer	10-80	1-10	7-38	0-4	0-8	2-20	0-0	0-0	0-0	12.5	+ 62.75
Tim Walford	9-57	1-14	3-18	0-4	0-1	4-12	1-4	0-0	0-4	15.8	- 8.12
George Moore	9-67	3-14	3-23	1-8	0-2	1-8	1-4	0-0	0-8	13.4	- 15.06
Nicky Richards	9-37	3-14	2-12	1-2	2-4	1-2	0-2	0-0	0-1	24.3	+ 9.82
Tim Vaughan	9-49	1-15	3-15	1-1	1-4	3-10	0-1	0-0	0-3	18.4	- 23.61
S R B Crawford	8-21	1-4	0-2	1-3	0-0	1-2	0-2	0-0	5-8	38.1	+ 25.90
Micky Hammond	7-66	0-9	0-18	1-8	1-4	3-14	0-4	0-0	2-9	10.6	- 14.75
Barry Murtagh	7-43	1-3	5-26	0-0	0-1	1-10	0-1	0-0	0-2	16.3	- 0.92
Evan Williams	7-35	3-10	0-6	1-4	0-2	1-9	2-3	0-0	0-1	20.0	- 9.17
Robert Johnson	6-78	0-13	1-20	0-7	0-7	5-21	0-5	0-0	0-5	7.7	+ 19.50
Andrew Crook	6-68	0-6	1-25	0-3	0-5	5-25	0-0	0-0	0-4	8.8	- 13.50
Tim Easterby	6-53	3-19	0-5	1-12	0-1	0-6	1-4	0-0	1-6	11.3	- 26.19
Gordon Elliott	6-24	2-6	0-2	2-6	1-5	0-2	1-2	0-0	0-1	25.0	- 5.05
Philip Kirby	6-71	1-16	2-34	0-3	0-1	2-11	0-0	1-2	0-4	8.5	- 34.55
Rose Dobbin	6-41	1-6	2-16	0-3	0-2	2-10	0-1	0-0	1-3	14.6	+ 1.00
Michael Easterby	5-56	2-17	0-10	0-6	2-3	0-9	0-4	0-0	1-7	8.9	- 26.75
Maurice Barnes	5-66	1-19	3-27	0-6	0-4	1-4	0-3	0-0	0-3	7.6	- 19.00
Sandy Forster	5-43	0-2	1-10	0-1	0-5	4-22	0-2	0-0	0-1	11.6	- 6.25
Evelyn Slack	4-55	0-4	2-19	1-5	0-1	1-25	0-1	0-0	0-0	7.3	- 21.50
Ann Hamilton	4-21	1-6	1-2	0-0	0-0	2-9	0-1	0-0	0-3	19.0	+ 8.33

LEADING JUMP TRAINERS AT SOUTHWELL (SINCE 2009)

	Total W-R	Nov Hdle	H'cap Hdle	Other Hdle	Nov Chase	H'cap Chase	Other Chase	Hunter Chase	N.H. Flat	Per cent	£1 Level stake
Jonjo O'Neill	21-120	2-13	6-36	3-26	1-6	7-25	0-1	1-3	1-10	17.5	- 43.58
Tim Vaughan	16-67	2-13	1-17	5-17	3-7	3-7	1-4	0-0	1-2	23.9	- 6.74
Keith Reveley	14-61	4-6	4-19	1-10	0-1	3-15	0-0	0-0	2-10	23.0	+ 11.95
Nicky Henderson	13-42	2-9	1-7	5-10	2-3	0-1	0-2	0-0	3-10	31.0	- 3.71
Peter Bowen	13-50	0-3	3-16	1-5	2-7	5-14	1-1	0-1	1-3	26.0	+ 43.25
Evan Williams	12-85	2-12	4-23	3-16	0-8	2-17	1-6	0-1	0-2	14.1	- 6.55
Alan King	12-72	3-13	0-13	3-15	1-7	1-9	1-2	0-0	3-13	16.7	- 27.02
Venetia Williams	8-30	0-2	3-8	0-3	0-4	4-10	1-2	0-0	0-1	26.7	+ 1.60
Nigel Twiston-Davies	7-54	4-10	1-12	0-8	0-1	2-17	0-2	0-0	0-4	13.0	- 13.92
John Cornwall	7-58	0-2	0-8	0-1	2-10	5-36	0-1	0-0	0-0	12.1	- 16.75
Charlie Mann	7-36	1-4	1-8	2-5	0-3	1-11	2-3	0-0	0-2	19.4	+ 6.78
Donald McCain	7-42	2-6	1-7	2-17	2-2	0-5	0-1	0-0	0-4	16.7	- 25.28
Charlie Longsdon	7-39	1-7	0-5	1-8	0-1	2-6	0-0	0-1	3-11	17.9	- 11.00
Sue Smith	6-68	0-11	3-13	0-6	0-3	3-25	0-2	0-0	0-8	8.8	- 1.00
Chris Bealby	6-54	1-8	0-13	1-9	1-3	2-12	0-1	1-1	0-7	11.1	- 29.25
Robin Dickin	5-45	0-12	3-13	0-5	0-1	1-5	0-0	0-0	1-9	11.1	+ 14.00
Kim Bailey	5-24	1-3	1-9	1-4	0-1	2-4	0-2	0-0	0-1	20.8	+ 1.25
Lawney Hill	5-24	0-1	2-11	1-5	1-2	1-3	0-1	0-0	0-1	20.8	- 7.18
Steve Gollings	5-11	1-2	1-1	0-0	1-2	2-2	0-1	0-0	0-3	45.5	+ 36.25
David Pipe	5-29	0-2	2-13	0-3	1-2	1-6	1-2	0-0	0-1	17.2	- 7.00
Heather Dalton	5-9	0-0	1-1	0-0	0-1	4-6	0-0	0-0	0-1	55.6	+ 25.25
Martin Keighley	5-36	0-1	2-11	0-8	0-0	2-11	0-0	0-0	1-5	13.9	+ 6.23
Michael Scudamore	5-28	0-1	0-4	0-3	0-1	4-15	1-2	0-0	0-2	17.9	- 9.50
Philip Hobbs	4-24	1-6	2-6	0-4	1-1	0-6	0-1	0-0	0-0	16.7	- 8.50
Renee Robeson	4-14	0-1	2-7	1-1	1-2	0-0	0-0	0-0	0-3	28.6	+ 16.75
Tom George	4-39	0-2	0-5	0-12	0-1	2-15	1-1	0-0	1-3	10.3	- 4.12
Alan Swinbank	4-12	0-1	0-3	0-0	0-0	0-0	0-0	0-0	4-8	33.3	- 3.09
Caroline Bailey	4-47	1-11	0-6	0-5	0-4	2-18	1-3	0-0	0-0	8.5	- 20.52
Dr Richard Newland	4-13	0-0	0-3	4-8	0-0	0-2	0-0	0-0	0-0	30.8	- 1.22
Sean Curran	4-15	0-2	2-8	1-2	0-0	1-2	0-0	0-0	0-1	26.7	+ 14.33
Sophie Leech	4-25	0-0	1-12	2-6	1-2	0-4	0-0	0-0	0-1	16.0	+ 7.62

LEADING JUMP TRAINERS AT STRATFORD (SINCE 2009)

	Total W-R	Nov Hdle	H'cap Hdle	Other Hdle	Nov Chase	H'cap Chase	Other Chase	Hunter Chase	N.H. Flat	Per cent	£1 Level stake
Tim Vaughan	20-115	6-23	4-26	6-23	1-12	2-22	0-0	0-1	1-8	17.4	+ 8.36
Nigel Twiston-Davies	17-117	3-17	2-19	4-13	3-13	3-38	0-5	0-2	2-10	14.5	+ 33.31
Paul Nicholls	15-53	2-12	0-2	0-6	5-9	1-8	0-2	1-4	6-10	28.3	+ 5.25
Jonjo O'Neill	14-100	0-9	2-19	1-7	1-12	9-42	1-3	0-4	0-4	14.0	- 16.21
Peter Bowen	14-72	5-13	4-12	0-4	0-4	3-19	0-2	0-3	2-15	19.4	- 3.59
David Pipe	13-64	2-12	4-23	2-8	2-4	2-12	1-2	0-0	0-3	20.3	+ 11.70
Evan Williams	13-106	2-27	1-16	3-22	5-11	1-23	0-2	0-0	1-5	12.3	- 44.14
Charlie Longsdon	13-65	2-8	2-12	1-9	0-3	5-20	0-3	1-1	2-9	20.0	+ 12.88
Ian Williams	12-55	7-16	3-19	1-4	0-2	0-2	0-3	0-2	1-7	21.8	+ 26.05
Nicky Henderson	9-41	4-12	3-12	1-4	0-1	0-5	0-1	0-0	1-6	22.0	- 10.97
Paul Webber	9-47	2-10	3-8	0-8	2-5	2-11	0-2	0-0	0-3	19.1	+ 16.50
Rebecca Curtis	8-41	1-7	1-10	2-3	1-1	0-7	1-2	0-2	2-9	19.5	- 17.78
David Evans	7-36	2-10	1-7	2-10	0-1	2-6	0-0	0-0	0-2	19.4	+ 13.74
Henry Daly	7-38	0-5	1-5	0-5	2-8	3-9	1-1	0-1	0-4	18.4	- 7.37
Keith Goldsworthy	7-37	2-9	0-7	2-5	1-3	1-6	0-1	0-2	1-4	18.9	+ 2.96
Dr Richard Newland	7-27	1-2	3-7	2-5	0-2	1-9	0-0	0-2	0-0	25.9	+ 0.27
Emma Lavelle	6-25	0-0	3-5	0-1	1-3	2-15	0-0	0-0	0-1	24.0	+ 22.25
Alison Thorpe	6-39	0-3	2-21	4-9	0-0	0-6	0-0	0-0	0-0	15.4	+ 4.00
Dai Burchell	5-38	1-8	3-10	0-12	0-1	1-7	0-0	0-0	0-0	13.2	+ 7.50
Jeremy Scott	5-31	0-5	1-4	0-3	0-0	0-10	1-1	1-2	2-6	16.1	+ 38.88
Milton Harris	5-54	1-8	0-13	1-10	2-6	1-12	0-2	0-1	0-2	9.3	- 18.00
Lawney Hill	5-32	2-2	0-5	0-3	2-6	1-14	0-1	0-0	0-1	15.6	- 5.46
Gary Moore	5-32	0-7	1-9	3-9	1-1	0-6	0-0	0-0	0-0	15.6	- 9.20
Venetia Williams	5-33	1-5	1-7	1-4	0-0	2-13	0-1	0-0	0-3	15.2	- 4.75
Alan King	5-31	2-4	0-8	1-4	0-3	2-8	0-1	0-0	0-3	16.1	- 10.93
Anthony Honeyball	5-14	1-4	1-2	0-1	1-2	0-1	1-1	0-0	1-3	35.7	+ 11.00
Phil Middleton	5-21	0-4	4-9	0-1	0-2	1-3	0-0	0-0	0-2	23.8	+ 28.00
Philip Hobbs	4-68	0-8	0-18	1-4	0-4	2-25	1-3	0-3	0-3	5.9	- 43.10
Sheena West	4-26	0-5	1-9	3-11	0-0	0-0	0-1	0-0	0-0	15.4	- 15.02
Neil King	4-56	1-5	2-23	0-5	0-4	1-16	0-1	0-0	0-2	7.1	- 24.00
Tom George	4-24	0-4	0-0	0-2	1-5	2-11	1-1	0-1	0-0	16.7	+ 2.73

LEADING JUMP TRAINERS AT TAUNTON (SINCE 2009)

	Total W-R	Nov Hdle	H'cap Hdle	Other Hdle	Nov Chase	H'cap Chase	Other Chase	Hunter Chase	N.H. Flat	Per cent	£1 Level stake
Paul Nicholls	53-160	22-52	8-35	9-19	5-15	0-14	2-8	1-2	6-15	33.1	- 4.42
David Pipe	23-186	4-61	10-70	2-28	0-2	6-16	0-3	0-0	1-6	12.4	- 67.63
Philip Hobbs	21-136	8-51	3-35	2-16	3-9	1-6	3-6	0-1	1-12	15.4	- 47.96
Venetia Williams	19-72	2-17	8-20	3-10	2-7	2-9	2-5	0-0	0-4	26.4	+ 33.89
Alan King	16-113	6-35	4-37	2-11	2-10	2-7	0-1	0-0	0-12	14.2	- 31.01
Evan Williams	14-111	3-22	3-41	3-14	2-7	1-18	0-5	0-0	2-4	12.6	+ 9.69
Nicky Henderson	10-48	3-16	1-12	3-7	2-6	0-0	0-0	0-0	1-7	20.8	- 11.98
Colin Tizzard	9-108	1-18	2-24	0-6	1-14	2-31	2-5	0-0	1-10	8.3	- 58.51
Victor Dartnall	8-45	4-11	2-16	0-5	0-1	1-7	0-3	1-1	0-1	17.8	+ 13.13
Emma Lavelle	8-30	1-8	2-7	1-2	0-2	2-7	1-2	0-0	1-2	26.7	+ 23.15
Charlie Mann	7-26	1-5	2-8	0-2	0-2	2-5	2-4	0-0	0-0	26.9	+ 19.75
Tim Vaughan	7-50	3-11	2-18	0-7	0-0	1-7	0-1	0-0	1-6	14.0	+ 14.25
Ron Hodges	6-96	1-11	2-40	0-9	1-11	2-20	0-1	0-0	0-4	6.3	- 67.42
Nick Williams	5-24	0-3	1-5	1-2	2-5	1-5	0-1	0-0	0-3	20.8	- 4.67
Neil Mulholland	5-62	0-16	2-21	0-4	1-2	1-11	1-3	0-0	0-5	8.1	- 16.88
Patrick Rodford	4-19	0-1	0-1	0-2	1-3	2-9	0-0	0-0	1-3	21.1	+ 2.35
Jeremy Scott	4-37	1-11	1-14	0-2	0-2	0-0	0-1	0-0	2-7	10.8	- 1.50
Chris Down	4-76	0-17	3-38	0-8	0-2	1-2	0-0	0-0	0-9	5.3	- 47.00
Lawney Hill	4-10	0-1	3-5	0-1	0-1	0-0	0-0	0-0	1-2	40.0	+ 4.63
Tom George	4-34	0-2	0-7	0-8	2-4	0-7	1-2	0-0	1-4	11.8	- 9.00
Caroline Keevil	4-48	0-18	1-13	0-6	1-4	2-4	0-0	0-0	0-3	8.3	- 29.50
Simon Burrough	4-49	0-9	1-10	0-3	0-5	3-19	0-0	0-0	0-3	8.2	- 18.87
Kevin Bishop	3-30	0-1	3-17	0-3	0-1	0-4	0-1	0-0	0-3	10.0	- 13.25
David Arbuthnot	3-11	1-1	1-2	0-2	0-1	1-1	0-1	0-0	0-3	27.3	+ 3.87
Susan Gardner	3-22	0-1	3-13	0-4	0-0	0-0	0-0	0-0	0-4	13.6	- 7.25
Barry Brennan	3-6	0-0	1-4	0-0	0-0	2-2	0-0	0-0	0-0	50.0	+ 41.00
Brendan Powell	3-33	0-6	1-15	1-4	1-4	0-1	0-0	0-0	0-3	9.1	- 23.00
Dr Richard Newland	3-13	0-1	2-6	1-2	0-0	0-4	0-0	0-0	0-0	23.1	+ 0.25
Anthony Honeyball	3-33	0-13	2-5	0-2	0-3	0-4	0-1	0-0	1-5	9.1	- 12.00
Miss Jane Western	3-4	0-0	0-0	0-0	0-0	0-0	0-0	3-4	0-0	75.0	+ 15.00
Jamie Snowden	3-27	0-7	1-6	0-3	0-3	2-7	0-1	0-0	0-0	11.1	+ 12.50

LEADING JUMP TRAINERS AT TOWCESTER (SINCE 2009)

	Total W-R	Nov Hdle	H'cap Hdle	Other Hdle	Nov Chase	H'cap Chase	Other Chase	Hunter Chase	N.H. Flat	Per cent	£1 Level stake
Venetia Williams	18-100	5-22	2-17	1-13	6-12	1-22	0-4	0-0	3-10	18.0	- 37.24
Jonjo O'Neill	16-108	2-26	6-21	0-13	1-6	6-32	1-2	0-2	0-6	14.8	- 30.65
Tim Vaughan	15-65	5-15	3-17	1-6	0-5	2-10	2-4	0-0	2-8	23.1	- 14.80
Robin Dickin	14-95	2-19	2-22	3-12	1-7	6-26	0-3	0-0	0-6	14.7	- 16.81
David Pipe	14-48	2-11	2-9	3-6	2-2	3-9	0-2	0-0	2-9	29.2	+ 7.00
Alan King	13-47	5-16	0-7	3-5	0-3	0-2	0-0	0-0	5-14	27.7	+ 12.02
Nicky Henderson	12-53	6-17	1-3	1-9	1-1	0-0	0-3	0-0	3-20	22.6	- 3.06
Kim Bailey	12-52	2-11	4-18	0-2	0-2	6-16	0-0	0-0	0-3	23.1	+ 16.63
Martin Keighley	11-70	3-20	2-17	1-7	0-4	3-14	0-2	0-0	2-6	15.7	- 13.92
Oliver Sherwood	10-55	1-14	1-10	1-8	0-5	5-11	1-3	0-0	1-4	18.2	- 0.93
Nigel Twiston-Davies	10-105	3-25	1-20	1-8	1-7	3-27	1-7	0-1	0-10	9.5	- 47.70
Jim Old	10-44	0-4	4-14	1-5	1-6	2-9	2-4	0-0	0-2	22.7	+ 21.00
Ian Williams	10-40	0-5	2-12	2-8	1-2	0-3	3-3	0-0	2-7	25.0	+ 18.10
Donald McCain	10-70	1-23	0-8	2-12	0-4	0-5	5-9	0-0	2-9	14.3	- 42.14
Charlie Longsdon	9-59	2-15	1-12	0-5	1-2	2-14	1-3	0-0	2-8	15.3	+ 17.55
Tony Carroll	8-78	1-11	1-23	2-13	0-4	4-21	0-2	0-0	0-4	10.3	- 9.01
Brendan Powell	8-66	2-10	1-16	0-11	0-2	1-11	1-5	1-2	2-9	12.1	- 8.37
Seamus Mullins	7-65	0-9	2-17	0-6	0-5	1-16	1-1	0-0	3-11	10.8	+ 1.00
Richard Lee	6-27	0-2	0-4	1-4	0-2	2-12	2-2	0-0	1-1	22.2	+ 40.00
Henry Daly	6-62	2-17	0-7	2-13	1-3	1-11	0-5	0-0	0-6	9.7	- 30.28
Philip Hobbs	5-21	2-5	1-3	1-5	1-2	0-1	0-4	0-0	0-1	23.8	- 4.33
Peter Pritchard	5-54	0-1	1-14	0-1	0-4	3-30	1-1	0-0	0-3	9.3	- 3.50
David Arbuthnot	5-10	3-4	0-1	0-0	0-0	0-1	0-0	0-0	2-4	50.0	+ 2.91
Chris Bealby	5-50	1-14	1-11	0-5	1-3	1-12	0-0	0-0	1-5	10.0	- 15.38
Lucy Wadham	5-25	2-5	3-13	0-1	0-0	0-1	0-2	0-0	0-3	20.0	- 4.67
Fergal O'Brien	5-23	1-7	0-4	2-4	2-2	0-3	0-0	0-0	0-3	21.7	- 4.75
Jim Best	5-23	1-2	0-8	0-0	0-0	2-6	0-0	0-0	2-7	21.7	+ 25.38
Anthony Middleton	5-29	2-4	0-10	1-5	0-0	2-8	0-0	0-0	0-2	17.2	+ 26.50
Jamie Snowden	5-23	1-7	2-5	2-6	0-1	0-1	0-1	0-0	0-2	21.7	+ 3.72
Bob Buckler	4-28	1-6	0-2	0-0	1-2	2-15	0-2	0-0	0-1	14.3	- 1.75
Milton Harris	4-18	0-1	3-9	0-4	0-0	1-2	0-1	0-0	0-1	22.2	+ 17.50

LEADING JUMP TRAINERS AT TOWCESTER (SINCE 2009)

	Total W-R	Nov Hdle	H'cap Hdle	Other Hdle	Nov Chase	H'cap Chase	Other Chase	Hunter Chase	N.H. Flat	Per cent	£1 Level stake
Venetia Williams	18-100	5-22	2-17	1-13	6-12	1-22	0-4	0-0	3-10	18.0	- 37.24
Jonjo O'Neill	16-108	2-26	6-21	0-13	1-6	6-32	1-2	0-2	0-6	14.8	- 30.65
Tim Vaughan	15-65	5-15	3-17	1-6	0-5	2-10	2-4	0-0	2-8	23.1	- 14.80
Robin Dickin	14-95	2-19	2-22	3-12	1-7	6-26	0-3	0-0	0-6	14.7	- 16.81
David Pipe	14-48	2-11	2-9	3-6	2-2	3-9	0-2	0-0	2-9	29.2	+ 7.00
Alan King	13-47	5-16	0-7	3-5	0-3	0-2	0-0	0-0	5-14	27.7	+ 12.02
Nicky Henderson	12-53	6-17	1-3	1-9	1-1	0-0	0-3	0-0	3-20	22.6	- 3.06
Kim Bailey	12-52	2-11	4-18	0-2	0-2	6-16	0-0	0-0	0-3	23.1	+ 16.63
Martin Keighley	11-70	3-20	2-17	1-7	0-4	3-14	0-2	0-0	2-6	15.7	- 13.92
Oliver Sherwood	10-55	1-14	1-10	1-8	0-5	5-11	1-3	0-0	1-4	18.2	- 0.93
Nigel Twiston-Davies	10-105	3-25	1-20	1-8	1-7	3-27	1-7	0-1	0-10	9.5	- 47.70
Jim Old	10-44	0-4	4-14	1-5	1-6	2-9	2-4	0-0	0-2	22.7	+ 21.00
Ian Williams	10-40	0-5	2-12	2-8	1-2	0-3	3-3	0-0	2-7	25.0	+ 18.10
Donald McCain	10-70	1-23	0-8	2-12	0-4	0-5	5-9	0-0	2-9	14.3	- 42.14
Charlie Longsdon	9-59	2-15	1-12	0-5	1-2	2-14	1-3	0-0	2-8	15.3	+ 17.55
Tony Carroll	8-78	1-11	1-23	2-13	0-4	4-21	0-2	0-0	0-4	10.3	- 9.01
Brendan Powell	8-66	2-10	1-16	0-11	0-2	1-11	1-5	1-2	2-9	12.1	- 8.37
Seamus Mullins	7-65	0-9	2-17	0-6	0-5	1-16	1-1	0-0	3-11	10.8	+ 1.00
Richard Lee	6-27	0-2	0-4	1-4	0-2	2-12	2-2	0-0	1-1	22.2	+ 40.00
Henry Daly	6-62	2-17	0-7	2-13	1-3	1-11	0-5	0-0	0-6	9.7	- 30.28
Philip Hobbs	5-21	2-5	1-3	1-5	1-2	0-1	0-4	0-0	0-1	23.8	- 4.33
Peter Pritchard	5-54	0-1	1-14	0-1	0-4	3-30	1-1	0-0	0-3	9.3	- 3.50
David Arbuthnot	5-10	3-4	0-1	0-0	0-0	0-1	0-0	0-0	2-4	50.0	+ 2.91
Chris Bealby	5-50	1-14	1-11	0-5	1-3	1-12	0-0	0-0	1-5	10.0	- 15.38
Lucy Wadham	5-25	2-5	3-13	0-1	0-0	0-1	0-2	0-0	0-3	20.0	- 4.67
Fergal O'Brien	5-23	1-7	0-4	2-4	2-2	0-3	0-0	0-0	0-3	21.7	- 4.75
Jim Best	5-23	1-2	0-8	0-0	0-0	2-6	0-0	0-0	2-7	21.7	+ 25.38
Anthony Middleton	5-29	2-4	0-10	1-5	0-0	2-8	0-0	0-0	0-2	17.2	+ 26.50
Jamie Snowden	5-23	1-7	2-5	2-6	0-1	0-1	0-1	0-0	0-2	21.7	+ 3.72
Bob Buckler	4-28	1-6	0-2	0-0	1-2	2-15	0-2	0-0	0-1	14.3	- 1.75
Milton Harris	4-18	0-1	3-9	0-4	0-0	1-2	0-1	0-0	0-1	22.2	+ 17.50

LEADING JUMP TRAINERS AT UTTOXETER (SINCE 2009)

	Total W-R	Nov Hdle	H'cap Hdle	Other Hdle	Nov Chase	H'cap Chase	Other Chase	Hunter Chase	N.H. Flat	Per cent	£1 Level stake
Donald McCain	45-227	13-51	6-39	15-69	0-9	1-19	5-12	0-1	5-27	19.8	- 5.68
Jonjo O'Neill	32-234	4-33	12-71	5-33	1-9	6-67	1-9	1-1	2-11	13.7	- 79.25
Nigel Twiston-Davies	24-129	5-18	4-28	7-18	3-8	3-40	0-3	0-0	2-14	18.6	- 12.40
Tim Vaughan	24-138	6-32	2-31	11-35	1-4	2-20	1-8	0-0	1-8	17.4	+ 15.81
David Pipe	22-115	2-12	5-39	4-25	1-4	7-26	2-3	0-0	1-6	19.1	+ 22.58
Kim Bailey	19-120	4-22	3-28	3-20	0-7	6-27	0-3	0-0	3-13	15.8	+ 8.09
Dr Richard Newland	17-50	3-7	6-21	3-8	1-1	3-10	1-2	0-0	0-1	34.0	+ 34.67
Peter Bowen	15-109	1-14	5-35	3-18	2-6	3-21	0-0	0-0	1-15	13.8	- 28.69
Nicky Henderson	10-43	2-10	1-10	4-11	0-3	0-0	1-1	0-0	2-8	23.3	- 5.89
Neil King	10-63	1-15	3-17	0-9	2-3	4-14	0-0	0-0	0-5	15.9	+ 18.20
Tony Carroll	10-90	2-23	5-46	2-7	0-4	1-6	0-0	0-0	0-4	11.1	+ 10.91
Jennie Candlish	10-74	0-14	4-29	0-11	2-3	3-8	0-2	0-0	1-7	13.5	- 9.12
Emma Lavelle	9-48	3-11	0-8	0-1	2-4	3-10	1-6	0-0	0-8	18.8	+ 8.74
Alan King	9-78	2-22	2-9	1-11	2-7	0-7	0-4	0-0	2-18	11.5	- 39.18
Charlie Longsdon	9-60	2-11	2-21	2-12	0-1	1-5	1-2	0-0	1-8	15.0	- 20.82
Philip Hobbs	8-56	1-6	1-11	4-14	1-2	0-11	0-3	0-0	1-9	14.3	- 27.60
Renee Robeson	8-34	2-6	1-8	1-5	1-2	2-7	0-1	0-0	1-5	23.5	+ 68.28
Rebecca Curtis	8-20	2-5	0-3	3-4	1-1	0-2	1-1	0-0	1-4	40.0	+ 3.06
Sue Smith	7-73	1-12	1-15	0-10	1-2	3-24	0-0	0-0	1-10	9.6	+ 4.50
Victor Dartnall	7-38	0-4	2-9	1-5	1-2	1-9	0-1	0-0	2-8	18.4	- 2.30
Colin Tizzard	7-29	0-1	1-4	0-0	0-3	4-17	2-3	0-0	0-1	24.1	+ 5.00
Evan Williams	7-100	1-18	2-17	0-24	1-9	3-24	0-5	0-0	0-3	7.0	- 43.13
Milton Harris	6-49	0-7	3-19	0-8	1-3	1-5	0-3	0-0	1-4	12.2	- 5.00
Charlie Mann	6-27	1-5	1-8	1-4	0-1	2-5	1-3	0-0	0-1	22.2	- 1.72
Venetia Williams	6-75	1-12	2-17	1-9	0-6	2-21	0-3	0-0	0-7	8.0	- 52.94
Caroline Bailey	6-50	0-8	1-7	1-10	0-1	3-15	1-4	0-0	0-5	12.0	+ 8.37
Ian Williams	6-67	3-20	1-23	0-12	0-1	2-7	0-0	0-0	0-4	9.0	- 37.63
Lawney Hill	5-47	0-5	1-16	1-10	1-3	2-12	0-1	0-0	0-0	10.6	- 24.63
Tom George	5-47	2-12	2-5	0-6	0-3	1-15	0-2	0-0	0-4	10.6	- 23.06
Nigel Hawke	5-25	0-1	0-6	0-1	1-2	3-11	1-1	0-0	0-3	20.0	+ 12.38
John Flint	5-26	0-1	4-13	1-7	0-0	0-2	0-0	0-0	0-3	19.2	+ 5.50

LEADING JUMP TRAINERS AT WARWICK (SINCE 2009)

	Total W-R	Nov Hdle	H'cap Hdle	Other Hdle	Nov Chase	H'cap Chase	Other Chase	Hunter Chase	N.H. Flat	Per cent	£1 Level stake
Alan King	19-102	5-19	0-12	5-20	2-13	4-13	0-2	0-0	3-23	18.6	- 28.03
Nigel Twiston-Davies	15-110	3-20	1-19	1-10	2-8	3-37	0-0	1-1	4-15	13.6	+ 20.23
Nicky Henderson	14-45	3-10	1-3	3-9	4-8	1-2	0-3	0-0	2-10	31.1	- 8.80
David Pipe	13-52	1-6	3-18	2-5	0-2	3-13	2-2	0-0	2-6	25.0	+ 15.53
Jonjo O'Neill	11-93	0-11	5-25	1-13	2-5	2-23	0-5	1-3	0-8	11.8	- 20.33
Venetia Williams	9-70	2-15	1-12	2-12	1-3	3-20	0-4	0-0	0-4	12.9	- 19.48
Charlie Longsdon	8-42	0-5	2-9	1-4	1-3	0-10	1-2	0-0	3-9	19.0	+ 38.25
Philip Hobbs	7-59	3-12	0-12	0-9	3-5	1-13	0-1	0-0	0-7	11.9	- 27.76
Charlie Mann	7-30	2-6	1-6	1-4	2-6	1-8	0-0	0-0	0-0	23.3	+ 1.42
Colin Tizzard	7-33	1-4	0-3	0-1	0-5	5-13	0-0	0-0	1-7	21.2	+ 45.50
Henry Daly	7-56	1-14	0-7	1-7	0-3	3-15	1-2	0-0	1-8	12.5	+ 13.75
Paul Nicholls	6-28	1-5	0-0	1-4	3-11	0-2	0-2	1-1	0-3	21.4	- 7.52
Neil King	6-34	0-1	2-8	0-7	1-1	2-15	0-0	0-0	1-2	17.6	- 6.68
Tony Carroll	5-54	1-13	4-23	0-7	0-2	0-2	0-0	0-0	0-7	9.3	- 17.25
Ian Williams	5-42	1-10	1-9	1-7	0-0	1-6	0-0	0-0	1-10	11.9	- 12.50
Brendan Powell	5-17	0-2	1-3	1-4	0-0	2-4	1-1	0-0	0-3	29.4	+ 23.25
Richard Lee	4-25	1-5	1-4	0-1	0-0	1-12	0-0	0-0	1-3	16.0	+ 7.25
Robin Dickin	4-44	1-10	2-15	0-5	0-0	1-7	0-0	0-0	0-7	9.1	+ 19.08
Richard Phillips	4-44	1-12	1-13	0-5	2-3	0-7	0-0	0-0	0-4	9.1	- 13.50
Tom George	4-22	0-3	0-5	0-2	2-3	2-5	0-2	0-1	0-1	18.2	- 3.00
Nick Williams	4-14	0-1	0-2	0-1	1-3	1-4	1-2	0-0	1-1	28.6	+ 8.88
Dr Richard Newland	4-14	0-1	2-3	0-2	0-0	2-8	0-0	0-0	0-0	28.6	+ 22.75
Tim Vaughan	4-18	0-3	2-4	2-6	0-1	0-2	0-0	0-0	0-2	22.2	+ 15.75
Kim Bailey	3-30	1-5	0-7	1-6	0-3	0-4	0-1	0-0	1-4	10.0	- 6.67
Anabel K Murphy	3-17	0-1	3-9	0-2	0-1	0-0	0-0	0-1	0-3	17.6	+ 17.00
Paul Webber	3-32	0-8	1-5	2-5	0-4	0-2	0-0	0-0	0-8	9.4	- 0.00
Pam Sly	2-14	2-7	0-5	0-0	0-0	0-0	0-0	0-0	0-2	14.3	- 10.18
Peter Pritchard	2-23	0-2	0-5	0-3	1-1	1-10	0-0	0-0	0-2	8.7	- 14.50
Dai Burchell	2-13	0-0	1-8	0-3	0-0	1-1	0-0	0-0	0-1	15.4	+ 31.00
David Arbuthnot	2-7	0-0	0-0	0-0	0-1	1-3	0-0	0-0	1-3	28.6	+ 3.50
Julian Smith	2-4	0-1	0-1	0-0	0-0	2-2	0-0	0-0	0-0	50.0	+ 10.00

LEADING JUMP TRAINERS AT WETHERBY (SINCE 2009)

	Total W-R	Nov Hdle	H'cap Hdle	Other Hdle	Nov Chase	H'cap Chase	Other Chase	Hunter Chase	N.H. Flat	Per cent	£1 Level stake
Donald McCain	23-106	7-17	1-23	4-22	1-13	4-16	3-7	0-0	3-8	21.7	- 16.54
Howard Johnson	22-107	1-20	4-22	6-24	3-12	3-15	2-4	0-1	3-9	20.6	+ 46.59
Sue Smith	16-148	2-22	5-32	1-15	2-12	6-59	0-1	0-0	0-7	10.8	- 57.52
Brian Ellison	15-66	1-4	3-23	6-20	3-5	2-10	0-1	0-0	0-3	22.7	- 3.98
Jonjo O'Neill	13-51	2-6	4-13	1-3	1-3	1-16	2-2	1-4	1-4	25.5	+ 1.76
Chris Grant	12-90	2-15	3-26	3-21	2-9	2-16	0-0	0-0	0-3	13.3	- 25.33
Tim Easterby	11-78	2-9	1-13	0-17	0-6	7-27	1-2	0-0	0-4	14.1	+ 19.00
Malcolm Jefferson	10-64	0-9	1-8	1-11	2-6	5-18	1-2	0-0	0-10	15.6	+ 22.30
Micky Hammond	10-142	1-19	1-52	1-16	1-5	5-38	1-2	0-0	0-10	7.0	- 76.55
Tim Vaughan	10-50	1-10	2-14	2-10	2-7	1-5	1-2	0-0	1-2	20.0	- 19.04
John Wade	8-76	0-11	1-13	0-3	2-8	5-33	0-3	0-2	0-3	10.5	- 40.88
Michael Easterby	7-45	1-8	4-11	1-11	0-1	0-6	0-0	0-0	1-8	15.6	+ 9.50
Ferdy Murphy	7-78	0-10	1-15	1-5	0-5	5-40	0-1	0-0	0-2	9.0	- 36.50
Evan Williams	7-30	0-3	0-7	4-6	0-4	0-6	3-4	0-0	0-0	23.3	- 6.83
Alan King	7-42	0-7	2-8	3-15	0-2	1-6	0-0	0-0	1-4	16.7	- 6.54
Nigel Twiston-Davies	6-33	1-4	0-2	1-6	1-3	1-11	0-2	1-1	1-4	18.2	- 3.38
Caroline Bailey	6-20	1-1	0-2	0-1	1-2	4-13	0-0	0-0	0-1	30.0	+ 33.13
Ian Williams	6-20	0-1	4-10	0-1	2-3	0-3	0-1	0-0	0-1	30.0	+ 10.58
Charlie Longsdon	6-26	0-3	1-3	1-7	0-0	2-8	0-1	0-0	2-4	23.1	- 1.62
George Moore	5-62	1-15	3-14	0-14	0-4	0-5	0-4	0-0	1-6	8.1	- 28.50
Tom George	5-28	2-4	0-2	1-3	1-3	0-9	1-5	0-0	0-2	17.9	+ 1.16
John Quinn	5-38	1-8	1-10	1-14	1-1	0-3	0-0	0-0	1-2	13.2	- 6.00
Paul Webber	5-21	3-7	0-2	1-5	0-1	0-2	0-2	0-0	1-2	23.8	+ 10.74
Martin Todhunter	5-43	0-4	1-12	0-7	0-1	4-17	0-2	0-0	0-0	11.6	- 14.17
David Pipe	5-25	1-3	0-4	0-4	2-2	1-5	1-4	0-0	0-3	20.0	- 11.66
Maurice Barnes	4-56	1-12	1-29	1-6	0-3	1-3	0-0	0-0	0-3	7.1	- 22.00
Alan Swinbank	4-33	1-5	0-7	0-5	0-2	1-3	0-2	0-0	2-9	12.1	- 11.88
Paul Nicholls	4-10	0-0	0-1	2-4	0-1	1-1	1-3	0-0	0-0	40.0	+ 2.60
J J Lambe	4-10	1-1	2-4	0-4	1-1	0-0	0-0	0-0	0-0	40.0	+ 3.25
Martin Keighley	4-21	1-1	1-4	0-6	1-2	1-6	0-0	0-0	0-2	19.0	+ 6.68
James Ewart	4-24	0-2	1-4	0-2	0-5	3-8	0-0	0-1	0-2	16.7	- 6.92

LEADING JUMP TRAINERS AT WINCANTON (SINCE 2009)

	Total W-R	Nov Hdle	H'cap Hdle	Other Hdle	Nov Chase	H'cap Chase	Other Chase	Hunter Chase	N.H. Flat	Per cent	£1 Level stake
Paul Nicholls	54-209	22-61	11-41	5-21	6-22	7-41	1-2	0-1	2-20	25.8	- 19.43
David Pipe	28-178	7-39	10-67	1-14	1-6	8-44	0-0	0-0	1-8	15.7	- 36.39
Colin Tizzard	26-181	3-41	3-29	2-8	2-15	12-69	0-2	0-1	4-16	14.4	- 17.73
Philip Hobbs	23-141	5-28	8-39	3-13	4-13	0-31	1-2	0-1	2-14	16.3	- 40.20
Alan King	16-112	2-32	6-28	5-11	2-9	0-18	1-3	0-1	0-10	14.3	- 42.43
Tom George	11-46	0-4	1-5	1-3	2-8	7-23	0-1	0-0	0-2	23.9	+ 6.82
Tim Vaughan	11-49	5-10	2-21	0-2	1-6	1-5	0-0	1-2	1-3	22.4	+ 7.59
Andy Turnell	10-56	3-18	5-20	0-5	1-4	0-7	0-0	0-0	1-2	17.9	- 1.40
Jeremy Scott	9-59	3-18	3-13	1-5	1-3	1-10	0-3	0-0	0-7	15.3	- 9.38
Emma Lavelle	9-50	2-11	0-11	1-4	0-2	2-11	1-2	0-0	3-9	18.0	+ 1.08
Charlie Mann	8-51	2-14	1-10	0-4	1-2	3-19	1-1	0-1	0-0	15.7	- 15.55
Victor Dartnall	8-61	1-10	3-22	0-1	1-4	3-17	0-0	0-1	0-6	13.1	- 6.00
Venetia Williams	8-91	0-11	2-29	0-7	3-12	3-28	0-2	0-0	0-2	8.8	- 51.08
Brendan Powell	8-48	1-7	3-18	0-1	1-4	2-15	0-0	0-0	1-3	16.7	+ 50.08
Nicky Henderson	7-46	3-12	1-12	2-9	0-4	0-4	1-1	0-0	0-4	15.2	- 32.52
Chris Down	7-59	2-16	3-26	0-4	0-1	2-5	0-0	0-0	0-7	11.9	+ 63.50
Seamus Mullins	7-91	2-23	1-26	1-6	1-10	1-19	0-0	0-0	1-7	7.7	+ 1.83
Gary Moore	7-49	2-9	2-24	2-4	1-3	0-7	0-0	0-0	0-2	14.3	- 1.95
Neil Mulholland	7-113	3-45	0-24	0-10	0-6	4-23	0-0	0-0	0-5	6.2	- 81.17
Jonjo O'Neill	6-37	0-6	3-16	2-9	1-1	0-4	0-0	0-1	0-0	16.2	+ 5.45
Bob Buckler	6-53	0-9	0-1	0-1	2-4	3-27	0-0	0-1	1-10	11.3	- 16.29
David Arbuthnot	5-19	0-4	1-2	0-3	1-2	2-6	0-1	0-0	1-1	26.3	+ 0.60
Susan Gardner	5-31	0-5	3-14	0-3	0-1	2-5	0-0	0-0	0-3	16.1	+ 12.00
Nick Williams	5-33	2-8	0-7	0-1	1-2	1-11	0-0	0-0	1-4	15.2	+ 0.42
Rebecca Curtis	5-20	1-3	1-9	1-3	1-1	0-2	0-0	0-0	1-2	25.0	+ 3.30
Nigel Twiston-Davies	4-37	0-5	2-9	0-0	0-4	2-16	0-0	0-0	0-3	10.8	+ 2.75
Ben De Haan	4-21	2-8	0-4	1-4	1-3	0-1	0-0	0-0	0-1	19.0	- 2.07
Evan Williams	4-48	1-15	1-16	0-1	2-6	0-10	0-0	0-0	0-0	8.3	- 26.25
Michael Blake	4-31	1-7	2-13	0-3	0-3	1-4	0-0	0-0	0-1	12.9	- 4.87
Paul Henderson	4-72	1-9	1-23	0-3	0-7	1-23	0-0	0-0	1-7	5.6	- 3.50
Jamie Snowden	4-35	0-6	1-7	0-5	1-5	2-10	0-0	0-0	0-2	11.4	- 2.6

LEADING JUMP TRAINERS AT WORCESTER (SINCE 2009)

	Total W-R	Nov Hdle	H'cap Hdle	Other Hdle	Nov Chase	H'cap Chase	Other Chase	Hunter Chase	N.H. Flat	Per cent	£1 Level stake
Jonjo O'Neill	37-193	7-23	14-48	2-36	3-17	4-43	3-6	1-1	3-19	19.2	- 3.67
Tim Vaughan	23-136	3-25	4-34	5-29	4-10	3-25	2-4	0-0	2-9	16.9	- 25.31
Evan Williams	17-118	5-15	2-21	4-31	1-13	4-32	1-6	0-0	0-0	14.4	- 13.84
Paul Nicholls	16-63	2-4	1-7	5-13	3-10	3-9	1-12	0-0	1-8	25.4	- 10.15
David Pipe	15-116	0-11	5-45	3-16	1-8	3-21	2-6	0-0	1-9	12.9	- 55.81
Charlie Longsdon	11-53	0-8	0-7	0-5	2-5	4-15	1-2	0-0	4-11	20.8	+ 4.61
Philip Hobbs	10-70	0-4	2-15	2-17	1-6	1-16	3-5	0-0	1-7	14.3	- 13.27
Nigel Twiston-Davies	10-104	4-19	0-25	3-15	1-6	2-29	0-1	0-0	0-9	9.6	- 51.00
Lawney Hill	10-45	2-11	1-11	2-4	0-3	3-8	0-1	0-0	2-7	22.2	+ 91.50
Rebecca Curtis	10-35	1-4	1-5	2-8	3-4	0-5	1-2	0-0	2-7	28.6	+ 6.75
Nicky Henderson	9-39	4-8	1-12	1-9	0-1	1-2	0-0	0-0	2-7	23.1	- 8.45
Peter Bowen	8-84	1-18	2-17	1-13	0-6	2-18	0-3	0-0	2-9	9.5	- 35.00
Ian Williams	8-40	4-6	0-12	1-12	0-3	2-3	1-2	0-0	0-2	20.0	- 5.92
Shaun Lycett	8-61	1-9	4-27	2-15	0-2	0-2	0-0	0-0	1-6	13.1	- 1.55
Brendan Powell	7-62	1-11	1-19	0-12	1-2	3-13	0-2	0-0	1-3	11.3	- 10.50
Donald McCain	7-55	0-8	4-6	1-18	0-3	2-10	0-1	0-0	0-9	12.7	+ 0.41
Anthony Honeyball	7-27	0-5	3-8	0-1	1-1	0-1	1-1	0-0	2-10	25.9	+ 33.50
Paul Webber	6-53	0-6	0-4	1-13	0-7	3-14	0-2	0-0	2-7	11.3	- 21.33
Richard Lee	5-46	0-3	1-8	1-6	0-2	3-24	0-1	0-0	0-2	10.9	- 7.25
Jeremy Scott	5-15	1-4	2-6	0-0	1-1	1-2	0-0	0-0	0-2	33.3	+ 17.00
Andy Turnell	5-27	1-2	1-5	1-2	0-3	1-8	1-3	0-0	0-4	18.5	+ 27.62
Brian Ellison	5-10	1-2	1-1	1-3	0-1	2-3	0-0	0-0	0-0	50.0	+ 5.48
Richard Phillips	5-40	0-9	4-17	1-3	0-0	0-6	0-1	0-0	0-4	12.5	+ 4.50
James Evans	5-36	0-9	2-6	0-5	0-3	2-10	0-0	0-0	1-3	13.9	- 1.00
Tony Carroll	5-36	0-1	5-23	0-4	0-2	0-4	0-0	0-0	0-2	13.9	+ 18.50
Keith Goldsworthy	5-41	2-10	0-4	0-9	0-1	0-4	0-0	0-0	3-13	12.2	- 20.01
Rachel Hobbs	5-61	1-13	1-21	2-12	0-2	1-5	0-1	0-1	0-6	8.2	- 2.50
Oliver Sherwood	4-21	1-1	1-6	1-6	0-2	0-1	0-2	0-0	1-3	19.0	+ 3.50
Bill Turner	4-12	1-3	0-1	0-3	1-1	1-1	0-1	0-0	1-2	33.3	+ 24.50
David Evans	4-24	1-2	0-6	1-6	1-1	0-3	0-0	0-0	1-6	16.7	- 5.30
Venetia Williams	4-15	0-0	2-5	0-4	1-1	0-3	0-0	0-0	1-2	26.7	+ 2.63

SEASON STATISTICS TRAINERS – BRITISH JUMPS 2012-2013

NAME	WINS	RUNS	2nd	3rd	4th	WIN PRIZE	TOTAL PRIZE	£1 STAKE
Nicky Henderson	125-509	25%	79	56	33	£2,220,033	£2,924,917	-52.16
Paul Nicholls	131-565	23%	107	72	53	£1,553,145	£2,375,585	-102.66
David Pipe	104-624	17%	72	64	76	£702,610	£1,142,418	-182.28
Alan King	60-419	14%	68	68	54	£565,939	£1,066,685	-53.47
Nigel Twiston-Davies	74-542	14%	69	69	64	£575,290	£1,026,314	-154.24
Donald McCain	141-734	19%	117	96	68	£617,742	£992,458	-219.80
Venetia Williams	90-533	17%	77	65	46	£639,355	£967,579	-40.56
Philip Hobbs	68-504	13%	75	59	52	£449,682	£902,487	-84.28
Sue Smith	31-276	11%	30	34	26	£699,165	£822,156	-3.70
Colin Tizzard	43-311	14%	29	44	31	£577,391	£812,834	-6.94
Evan Williams	57-506	11%	63	64	63	£307,858	£703,297	-161.33
Jonjo O'Neill	90-705	13%	59	67	70	£462,834	£692,664	-205.36
W P Mullins	6-51	12%	4	5	3	£444,746	£688,531	-5.90
Rebecca Curtis	49-210	23%	33	28	15	£342,483	£562,663	-18.22
Tom George	39-243	16%	39	30	32	£307,847	£478,434	-49.75
Tim Vaughan	85-646	13%	104	93	83	£262,561	£477,422	-208.48
Lucinda Russell	59-478	12%	68	64	60	£239,804	£408,617	-185.57
Gary Moore	33-282	12%	36	24	31	£284,514	£397,607	-0.65
Peter Bowen	48-365	13%	53	42	33	£242,273	£378,662	-94.09
Charlie Longsdon	54-404	13%	46	45	37	£225,528	£343,229	-110.30
Brian Ellison	40-274	15%	43	29	34	£224,723	£342,301	-11.99
Nick Williams	20-120	17%	13	17	12	£184,931	£327,699	-18.52
Harry Fry	20-72	28%	11	9	5	£155,350	£277,102	+52.02
Gordon Elliott	17-91	19%	19	5	10	£199,151	£263,623	+19.29
Malcolm Jefferson	23-151	15%	22	18	18	£167,950	£251,069	+15.35
C Byrnes	3-11	27%	2	0	1	£234,722	£245,603	+5.50
John Quinn	20-69	29%	8	9	6	£163,958	£236,480	+27.27
Dr Richard Newland	35-146	24%	26	18	15	£151,567	£228,255	-7.47
Henry Daly	20-174	11%	18	22	20	£178,668	£227,659	-51.68
Emma Lavelle	12-175	7%	26	26	13	£105,278	£223,829	-98.50
M F Morris	1-6	17%	3	1	0	£84,478	£216,994	-1.50
Martin Keighley	30-200	15%	25	23	24	£132,379	£215,179	-33.19
Jeremy Scott	30-213	14%	33	34	28	£122,263	£198,591	-59.28
Kim Bailey	27-244	11%	32	38	20	£119,133	£189,938	-61.24
Oliver Sherwood	26-168	15%	30	15	14	£112,085	£186,567	-51.57
Keith Reveley	34-153	22%	21	17	14	£130,870	£184,166	+31.25
D T Hughes	2-21	10%	3	4	0	£78,350	£179,895	+5.00
John Ferguson	23-124	19%	17	17	20	£89,084	£166,917	-46.26
David Bridgwater	16-101	16%	20	13	11	£73,623	£165,217	-22.28
Fergal O'Brien	28-231	12%	36	25	24	£92,046	£162,637	-33.22
Nick Gifford	10-105	10%	10	14	13	£121,067	£162,029	-14.26
Steve Gollings	16-71	23%	10	5	10	£116,695	£158,454	+4.88
Nicky Richards	25-156	16%	19	18	18	£86,707	£157,963	-8.87
Tim Easterby	16-97	16%	10	12	11	£111,248	£151,710	-2.22
Richard Lee	21-161	13%	17	20	22	£95,959	£151,509	-33.19
Paul Webber	22-209	11%	22	19	29	£90,311	£149,120	-55.61
Henry De Bromhead	1-8	13%	1	1	0	£62,190	£145,938	+21.00
Chris Grant	20-213	9%	30	30	23	£75,688	£134,291	-59.38
John Wade	24-226	11%	20	26	34	£86,952	£133,790	-102.84
N W Alexander	28-184	15%	21	16	15	£91,157	£131,807	+6.40